Organizations and Social Networking: Utilizing Social Media to Engage Consumers

Eldon Y. Li
*National Chengchi University, Taiwan & California Polytechnic
State University, USA*

Stanley Loh
Lutheran University of Brazil (ULBRA), Brazil & Faculty of Technolofgy Senac, Brazil

Cain Evans
Birmingham City University, UK

Fabiana Lorenzi
Lutheran University of Brazil (ULBRA), Brazil

A volume in the Advances in Marketing,
Customer Relationship Management, and
E-Services (AMCRMES) Book Series

Managing Director:	Lindsay Johnston
Editorial Director:	Joel Gamon
Book Production Manager:	Jennifer Yoder
Publishing Systems Analyst:	Adrienne Freeland
Development Editor:	Austin DeMarco
Assistant Acquisitions Editor:	Kayla Wolfe
Typesetter:	Alyson Zerbe
Cover Design:	Jason Mull

Published in the United States of America by
  Business Science Reference (an imprint of IGI Global)
  701 E. Chocolate Avenue
  Hershey PA 17033
  Tel: 717-533-8845
  Fax: 717-533-8661
  E-mail: cust@igi-global.com
  Web site: http://www.igi-global.com

Library of Congress Cataloging-in-Publication Data

Organizations and social networking : utilizing social media to engage consumers / Eldon Y. Li, Stanley Loh, Cain Evans and Fabiana Lorenzi, editors.
    pages cm.
  Includes bibliographical references and index.
  Summary: "This book provides a broad investigation into the use of social technologies in business practices through theoretical research and practical applications, exploring the opportunities and challenges brought about by the advent of various 21st century online business web tools and platforms"--Provided by publisher.
  ISBN 978-1-4666-4026-9 (hardcover) -- ISBN 978-1-4666-4027-6 (ebook) -- ISBN 978-1-4666-4028-3 (print & perpetual access) 1. Internet marketing--Social aspects. 2. Social media--Economic aspects. 3. Consumer behavior. 4. Electronic commerce--Social aspects. 5. Management--Social aspects. I. Li, Eldon Yu-zen, 1952-

  HF5415.1265.O74 2013
  658.8'72--dc23

                              2013001745

This book is published in the IGI Global book series Advances in Marketing, Customer Relationship Management, and E-Services (AMCRMES) Book Series (ISSN: Pending; eISSN: Pending)

British Cataloguing in Publication Data
A Cataloguing in Publication record for this book is available from the British Library.

All work contributed to this book is new, previously-unpublished material. The views expressed in this book are those of the authors, but not necessarily of the publisher.

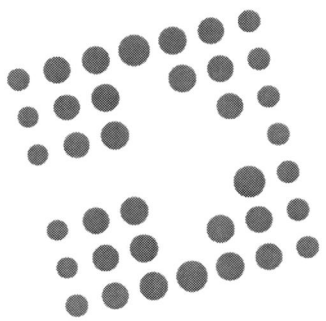

Advances in Marketing, Customer Relationship Management, and E-Services (AMCRMES) Book Series

Eldon Y. Li
*National Chengchi University, Taiwan &
California Polytechnic State University, USA*

ISSN: Pending
EISSN: Pending

MISSION

Business processes, services, and communications are important factors in the management of good customer relationship, which is the foundation of any well organized business. Technology continues to play a vital role in the organization and automation of business processes for marketing, sales, and customer service. These features aid in the attraction of new clients and maintaining existing relationships.

The Advances in Marketing, Customer Relationship Management, and E-Services (AMCRMES) Book Series addresses success factors for customer relationship management, marketing, and electronic services and its performance outcomes. This collection of reference source covers aspects of consumer behavior and marketing business strategies aiming towards researchers, scholars, and practitioners in the fields of marketing management.

COVERAGE

- B2B Marketing
- CRM and Customer Trust
- CRM in Financial Services
- CRM Strategies
- Customer Relationship Management
- Data Mining and Marketing
- E-Service Innovation
- Ethical Considerations in E-Marketing
- Legal Considerations in E-Marketing
- Online Community Management and Behavior
- Relationship Marketing
- Social Networking and Marketing
- Web Mining and Marketing

IGI Global is currently accepting manuscripts for publication within this series. To submit a proposal for a volume in this series, please contact our Acquisition Editors at Acquisitions@igi-global.com or visit: http://www.igi-global.com/publish/.

Titles in this Series

For a list of additional titles in this series, please visit: www.igi-global.com

Organizations and Social Networking Utilizing Social Media to Engage Consumers
Eldon Y. Li (National Chengchi University, Taiwan & California Polytechnic State University, USA) Stanley Loh (Lutheran University of Brasil (ULBRA), Brazil & Technology Faculty Senac Pelotas, Brazil) Cain Evans (University of Central England in Birmingham, UK) and Fabiana Lorenzi (Lutheran University of Brasil (ULBRA), Brazil)
Business Science Reference • copyright 2013 • 329pp • H/C (ISBN: 9781466640269) • US $185.00 (our price)

Consumer Information Systems and Relationship Management Design, Implementation, and Use
Angela Lin (University of Sheffield, UK) and Jonathan Foster (University of Sheffield, UK)
Business Science Reference • copyright 2013 • 313pp • H/C (ISBN: 9781466640825) • US $165.00 (our price)

Marketing Decision Making and the Management of Pricing Successful Business Tools
Dr. Rajagopal (EGADE Business School, Tecnologico de Monterrey (ITESM), Mexico)
Business Science Reference • copyright 2013 • 358pp • H/C (ISBN: 9781466640948) • US $185.00 (our price)

Online Advertising and Promotion Modern Technologies for Marketing
Payam Hanafizadeh (Allameh Tabataba'i University) and Mehdi Behboudi (Islamic Azad University, Iran)
Business Science Reference • copyright 2012 • 248pp • H/C (ISBN: 9781466608856) • US $185.00 (our price)

Branding and Sustainable Competitive Advantage Building Virtual Presence
Avinash Kapoor (Management Development Institute (MDI), India) and Chinmaya Kulshrestha (Management Development Institute (MDI), India)
Business Science Reference • copyright 2012 • 294pp • H/C (ISBN: 9781613501719) • US $185.00 (our price)

Advanced Technologies Management for Retailing Frameworks and Cases
Eleonora Pantano (University of Calabria, Italy) and Harry Timmermans (Eindhoven University of Technology, The Netherlands)
Business Science Reference • copyright 2011 • 408pp • H/C (ISBN: 9781609607388) • US $195.00 (our price)

Mobilized Marketing and the Consumer Technological Developments and Challenges
Gonca Telli Yamamoto (Okan University, Turkey)
Business Science Reference • copyright 2010 • 292pp • H/C (ISBN: 9781605669168) • US $180.00 (our price)

DISSEMINATOR OF KNOWLEDGE

www.igi-global.com

701 E. Chocolate Ave., Hershey, PA 17033
Order online at www.igi-global.com or call 717-533-8845 x100
To place a standing order for titles released in this series, contact: cust@igi-global.com
Mon-Fri 8:00 am - 5:00 pm (est) or fax 24 hours a day 717-533-8661

Editorial Advisory Board

Table of Contents

Section 3
Social Networking with Social Media

Section 4
Social Marketing

Section 5
Customer Relationship Management with Social Media

Section 6
Organizations and Social Technologies

Detailed Table of Contents

Section 1
Overview

Consumers are increasingly consuming, participating, contributing, and sharing different types of online content. This is influencing the marketing activities traditionally controlled and performed by companies. The aim of this chapter is to conceptualise the activities consumers perform in social media. Social media denote content created by individual consumers such as online ratings or verbal reviews, online message boards/forums, photos/video sites, blogs, tags, and social networking sites. A conceptual framework for consumers' social media activities is developed and qualitatively substantiated. Social media activities are based on the motives for the activities, including information, social connection, and entertainment. The chapter contributes to research on social media and online communities by describing user behaviour and motivations related to the user-created services. Managerially, the study deepens the understanding of different challenges related to users' activities on social media and the motivations associated with those activities.

This chapter analyzes the use of social media in health risk prevention campaigns. According to the Positive Community Norms (PCN) framework, prevention is defined as the process of proactively cultivating positive cultures through transformational leadership, communications, and an integrated portfolio of strategies. This chapter focuses on social media strategies. We review two extant prevention models (Everett Rogers's framework and the PCN framework), examine underlying theoretical explanations for consumer behaviors related to prevention and the use of social media, provide three brief case studies of prevention campaigns at various stages of maturity and success, and offer caveats for campaign managers who might be considering using social media to reach out to audiences. We intend this material to prove beneficial for researchers, public policymakers, and managers of prevention campaigns.

Section 2
User Behaviors in Social Media

Research on digital media has mostly paid attention to users' demographics, motivations, and efficacy, but with increasingly popular web tools like social media, it is important to study more stable psychological characteristics such as users' personality traits, as they may significantly affect how people use the Web to communicate and socialize. Relying on the "Big Five Framework" as a theoretical approach, this chapter explores such relationships. Survey data from a national sample of U.S. adults shows that more extraverted people are more likely to use social networking sites, instant messaging, and video chats, while those more open to new experiences tend to use social networking sites more frequently. Also, emotional stability is a negative predictor of social networking site use. That is, individuals who are more anxious and unstable tend to rely on these sites. When looking at a specific use of social media–to create political content—emotional stability was a negative predictor, whereas extraversion had a positive impact. These findings confirm the usefulness of combining explorations of personality and digital media usage.

Available research indicates that consumers are more likely to accept social media advertising when such content appeals to their motivations for joining the site. However, this research generally assumes that the forces driving a user's initial motivations for social media acceptance and usage remain constant through time. Given the fact this assumption may, indeed, be a faulty one, this chapter is specifically concerned with exploring the idea that user motivations may exist as evolving factors with the potential to impact the efficacy of e-business initiatives on social media sites. In support of this goal, in this chapter we: (1) define and contextually discuss social media; (2) review extant literature as it relates to motivations for media use; (3) discuss the idea of temporal motivations; (4) present the results of a pilot study that provides empirical evidence for the evolving nature of motivations; and (5) discuss the theoretical and practical implications of our results.

Chapter 5

Andreas M. Kaplan, ESCP Europe, France
Michael Haenlein, ESCP Europe, France

Although the hype around virtual worlds has slowed down in recent months, chances are high that this type of social media will increase in importance over years to come. Many companies which pioneered in entering virtual worlds have left these environments after their first steps. One of the reasons for these initial failures is likely the lack of understanding of in-world consumers and their expectations toward virtual commerce. The purpose of the authors' chapter is therefore to investigate consumer purchase behavior within the virtual social world Second Life. Specifically, the authors analyze the types of purchase behavior consumers show within such an environment (planned purchases vs. impulse buying) and the factors that influence the decision to buy virtual products and services in exchange for real life money. For this, the authors' study is based on a combination of a qualitative pre-study consisting of 29 in-depth interviews and a quantitative analysis based on responses obtained from a representative sample of 580 Second Life residents. The authors' analysis results in the following three findings: First, the authors show that Second Life residents engage in two different types of purchase behavior: planned purchases and impulse buying. Second, the authors show that traditional consumer behavior theories and concepts can be transferred to similar behavior in a virtual world, although with different degrees of importance for different variables. And finally, the authors show that a Second Life resident's usage intensity and consumption experience have a significant moderating influence on planned purchase behavior but not on impulse buying. From a managerial perspective, the authors' results imply that Real Life companies that maintain Second Life flagship stores may consider communicating about their virtual products and services within real life. Additionally, Second Life stores should try to make the purchasing process as simple and convenient as possible (in order to increase planned purchases) and to create an overall exciting and pleasant shopping environment to elicit positive emotions among their potential customers (in order to maximize the probability of impulse buying). Finally, since purchasing behavior within Second Life appears to be more individualistic than what can be observed in real life, firms can consider offering virtual products and services in Second Life that are highly extravagant and may never be purchased in Real Life due to fear of other people's opinions--which is likely to be of particular importance for fashion goods.

Section 3
Social Networking with Social Media

Chapter 6

Eric Shiu, The University of Birmingham, UK

One key impact of consumer generated media on today's firms is that it has become an increasingly important source of information for consumers in their decision making process. Firms that are able to gather positive messages about themselves and their products or services on consumer generated media can be instrumental to the survival and success of their business. The quality and growth of consumer generated media depend on contributions from the consumer public, and some people are more likely to post their own messages, written or otherwise, on consumer generated media than others. Understanding some typical characteristics of these people, termed active contributors to consumer generated media in this chapter, is beneficial for firms, as they can be more ready to identify them and could do something to turn them in their flavour. Based on literature review, this study has identified a number of hypothetical variables that may influence whether a person is an active contributor to consumer generated media. A questionnaire survey on 430 respondents has shown that global innovativeness, electronic innovativeness and consumer involvement significantly affect contributions to consumer generated media. Active contributors to this new medium are also more likely to be male and of a younger age.

Chapter 7

Soyean (Julia) Kim, Boston University, USA
Barbara A. Bickart, Boston University, USA
Frédéric F. Brunel, Boston University, USA
Seema Pai, Boston University, USA

In this chapter, we develop a theoretical framework that explains how blogs can be categorized based on audiences' perceptions and how bloggers use different strategies to shape or shift their audiences' perceptions and increase the persuasiveness of their messages. We posit that bloggers use two distinguishable communication strategies: (a) developing and sustaining an illusion of relationship between the blogger and the reader in order to individualize the communication, and (b) maintaining a level of ambiguity in their commercial interests in order to conceal the commercial nature of some blogs. We describe the tactics underlying the use of these strategies as well as the efficacy and ethics of these practices.

Chapter 8

Eldon Y. Li, National Chengchi University, Taiwan & California Polytechnic State University, USA
Shu-Hsun Chang, National Chengchi University, Taiwan

As the advance of Internet technology continues, various applications, services, and business models are emerging in the market. The online video sharing website is the hottest application nowadays; thus it is important to understand the key factors influencing user's behavior on these websites. In this chapter, the authors propose a conceptual model which is based on the integrated model of user satisfaction and technology acceptance developed by Wixom and Todd (2005). To comprehend the user's behavior intention toward using the website, the authors also add the potential factors about community which influence user's behavior on video sharing websites. The results indicate that community satisfaction, content satisfaction, and system satisfaction all have significant positive impact on usefulness and ease of use, and that community satisfaction has a much higher impact than the other two types of satisfaction. This finding reveals an important attribute of video sharing websites, namely, the users of the website care most about the entire website community. Indeed, reliable system operations and useful, interactive content are two factors influencing the community satisfaction. For designers who want to set up a video sharing website, this research provides more comprehensive information on how to invest the limited resources on the critical variables in order to maximize the service value.

Section 4
Social Marketing

Chapter 9

Erkan Akar, Afyon Kocatepe University, Turkey
Mete Karayel, Afyon Kocatepe University, Turkey

This study aims to evaluate and compare the Web 2.0 applications as marketing tools. In this context, blogs, micro-blogs, collaborative projects (wikis and social bookmarking), content communities, social networking sites, and virtual worlds have been examined. Eventually, it can be expected that blogs will provide more transparent feedback; micro-blogs will provide instant feedback; wikis will make the cooperative efforts of product development easier; social bookmarking will enable search-engine marketing; content communities will enable easy product training; social networking sites will create brand communities; and virtual worlds will provide new places to interact more effectively. All of these tools can come into prominence in the context of marketing.

Chapter 10

Xiaojing Lu, Shanghai Jiao Tong University, China
Ronald E. Goldsmith, Florida State University, USA
Margherita Pagani, Bocconi University, Italy

This chapter introduces the concept of "two-sided" markets and shows how they comprise a unique type of social media that facilitates the development of social networks oriented toward specific product domains (e.g., restaurants), specific brands (e.g., Starbucks), or common consumer concerns (e.g., Yelp.com). Not only do two-sided-markets constitute a unique type of Website, they can be integrated with or linked to other social media, thereby enriching the value of both the two-sided market and its partner(s). Because a two-sided market increases in value for all three parties that constitute it (consumers, the platform, and vendors) as the number of both vendors and consumer participants grows, platform managers are eager to use incentive strategies to encourage consumers to increase their active use of the site. Among these incentive strategies are various reward programs that stimulate use by rewarding consumers who add content, post reviews, comment on others' reviews, and more. Part of this chapter describes two online experiments that demonstrate that two types of common reward programs, monetary and social rewards (Heyman & Ariely, 2004), are effective in stimulating consumer intent to use the site more actively than without a reward. Finally, we make several suggestions for integrating two-sided markets into other social media, and we propose several avenues for future research into this topic that should increase our understanding of how consumers behave in two-sided markets and how platform managers can both enhance active use and use the information derived from this use.

Chapter 11

María-del-Carmen Alarcón-del-Amo, Universitat Autònoma de Barcelona, Spain
Carlota Lorenzo-Romero, University of Castilla-La Mancha, Spain
Efthymios Constantinides, University of Twente, The Netherlands

The chapter explores the factors influencing the adoption process and the degree of engagement of the social media as part of the online marketing strategy by Spanish retailers. A retail industry survey identifies four different segments of retailers depending on the level of implementation of social media marketing strategies. The study examines the antecedents of the social media tools' adoption process across the dimensions of a Technology Adoption Model (TAM) and assesses various other factors likely to affect the degree of the adoption. One essential conclusion is that the company size is not important but that the level of adoption social media marketing is related to the organizational maturity in the areas of management attitudes, employee empowerment, access to Internet technologies, and technological infrastructure. The study proposes a future research agenda including cross-cultural studies for better understanding the global business attitudes in this area and underlines the need for development of benchmarks and metrics necessary for better assessing the value of social media marketing.

Section 5
Customer Relationship Management with Social Media

Chapter 12

Huliane Medeiros da Silva, Universidade Federal do Rio Grande do Norte, Brazil
Gilson Gomes da Silva, Universidade Federal do Rio Grande do Norte, Brazil
Flavius da Luz e Gorgônio, Universidade Federal do Rio Grande do Norte, Brazil

For a great deal of people, social media is the gateway to the Internet and it would not be feasible use of the network if it was not through them. Social media revolutionized not only the Internet but also the way people communicate and, consequently, the way consumers and businesses interact. Therefore, companies need to know and master the use of social media for competitive advantage. The current forms of interaction between businesses and consumers still leave much to be desired and it is not rare to find companies that make mistakes in the process of communication with their consumers through social media. This chapter aims to evaluate the communication channels based on social media used by businesses and consumers, showing successful and non-successful cases in the communication process and suggesting trends of usage of these channels more efficiently.

Chapter 13

Goetz Greve, HSBA Hamburg School of Business Administration, Germany

Social network data can be used to identify key influencers within a company's customer database. Key influencers are consumers that are equipped with a large and strong network of connected neighbors. Within such a strong network, marketing messages can be passed on easily via the key influencers. The purpose of the chapter is to elaborate on the social effects of customer networks and the possibility to use data from these networks for Social CRM. First, the foundations of social contagion in networks and the relationship between social effects and Social CRM performance measures are explained. Second, possible ways of data acquisition and data integration are discussed and an overview of analytical software solutions is given. Fourth, the implementation process and its challenges are elaborated. The chapter closes with an outline of further research directions.

This chapter presents a study of integration of traditional CRM systems with new social networking technologies available on the Web, such as Twitter, blogs, and communities, showing a set of the best practices on the use of these technologies to improve business relationships with customers. The authors present a set of best practices with guidance on how social networking technologies can help companies squeeze and improve the relationship with their customers.

Section 6
Organizations and Social Technologies

E-business has changed the external face of many organizations widening and extending access to products and services. This has required large scale changes to be made to business processes to accommodate new ways of working. Social media technologies have introduced a new wave of change through organizational trading networks. Further business transformation is needed to embrace the opportunities and challenges of social media technologies. This chapter presents a framework to help morphing organizations plan the business transformation needed to embed social media technologies within their e-business service provision. Business and technological maturity models are analysed and a set of maturity measures for e-business is proposed. The business transformation needed to embed e-business technology in organizational systems is discussed in two UK manufacturers. Dimensions of business transformation and critical success factors for adopting social media technologies are proposed from these cases.

Globalization and the resultant transition to virtual work are changing the dynamics of critical business relationships today. The organizational fabric is undergoing a transformation. The new knowledge economy, coupled with the modern customer based relationship approach has transformed the shape of business, catalyzed further by the internet revolution. Shrinking distance barriers and the emergence of new ways of building and delivering products and services online, is enabling the rapid globalization of markets. This chapter traces how the new knowledge economy, along with the modern customer based relationship approach, impacts the organizational fabric. The collaborative Web along with the e-enterprise, has brought into vogue the use of emergent social software platforms within companies, or between companies and their partners or customers. This, along with organizational willingness to take risks, has created new opportunities for companies in the domain of innovation, Internet based collaboration and co-creation.

Chapter 17

Nosheen Riaz, Government College University, Pakistan

Moez Rehman, Government College University, Pakistan

Electronic negotiation is one of many applications that software agents can perform to facilitate electronic business. Negotiations between software agents and humans (hybrid negotiation), can make electronic business efficient and intelligent. It can save time, effort and other valueable resources by replacing the human in electronic business activities and many other domains. However, to enable hybrid negotiation, a software agent needs clear machine interpretable semantics to understand and generate natural language content. Although it is not simple to make natural language content understandable by software agents as a whole, it can be achieved in different domains--in this case electronic business. For this purpose, an example of hybrid negotiation is presented, in which a software agent and a human agent negotiate for a business contract. Problems involved in this negotiation process are partially resolved through ontologies (the main Semantic Web technology), NSS (negotiation support system) and hand written rules.

Chapter 18

Anna Farmery, University of Bradford, UK

Over the last decade, digital technology in general and social media in particular, has changed the way people interact and communicate. Current day marketers have embraced the technological tools to socialise with the customer but those tools are now spreading across e-business and breaking down the traditional business walls. It is argued in this chapter that social media is now transforming into a wider ``social business' concept with marketing being just one element of the potential social relationship between business and consumer. Using the emergence of 3D printing as an example, this chapter highlight how the consumer is not only gaining the power of voice, but also the power of production. It discusses the potential effects on future commercial revenue streams and what business needs to do today to protect their economic value and business model of tomorrow. It argues that this transformative technology should not be seen as a threat to business but an opportunity to create a revolutionary social business model with the customer.

Preface

INTRODUCTION

Internet. World Wide Web. Social Media. These terms have become synonymous with the rapid growth of online user generated content and consumer generated content in recent years. This paradigm shift from corporate content generation could have only been possible with the congruence of technological change and accessibility of social networking Websites. Around the world today there is a growing demand for business practices to change, transform, and adapt enabling online consumers to become part of the business, not only seen as external to the business but become part of the fabric. This existential change is needed and is driven by the growth of social media as a currency of trade. Radical paradigm shifts in business models have driven IT-enabled organizations to think differently about its products, services, and its markets. Businesses are spending an enormous amount of capital to invest in new technologies that support online presence through social media, online communities, and online commerce.

Developing new channels of distribution is seen by marketers as a way to increase brand awareness, consumer focused services, and a method to understand consumers. Noticeable is the use of social media to market premium brands, but what is more interesting is that online consumers are willing to pay a premium for brands that deliver great service through social media. Social CRM has become an integral part of business today and it is a service that every business needs to get right.

This book intends to stimulate discussion and understanding by presenting theoretical and empirical research on social CRM and interactive social networking Websites. Research results and future perspectives are presented for the development and sustainable deployment of social CRM and interactive social networking websites supporting an online presence both in a virtual and real-world environment.

There are 18 chapters in this book, which is organized into five sections: the first section provides an overview of social media and its use by consumers; the second section examines the user behaviors in social media; the third section highlights the characteristics of social networking with social media; the fourth section explores how social media can be used as a marketing tool; the fifth section presents applications of social media to customer relationship management; finally, the sixth section centers on how organizations can use social media and Internet-based technologies to transform their businesses. By and large, this book intends to provide a reference guide for social marketing and social networking using the new media technologies.

BOOK ORGANIZATION

Section 1: Overview

Chapter 1 (*Social Media Activities: Understanding What Consumers Do in Social Media*) addresses the activities of online consumers in social media. A conceptual framework is outlined based on user motivations and user generated content. The authors suggest that there are several implications for managers using social media as a tool. Emphasizing both conceptual and empirical issues, this chapter highlights the importance of companies understanding their roles in this emerging media dominated by users. The proposed conceptual framework of consumer social media activities contributes to the management of social media.

Chapter 2 (*Using Social Media to Cultivate Positive Community Norms*) examines underlying theoretical explanations for consumer behaviors related to prevention and the use of social media. The authors identify that by limiting access to only approved audiences runs the risk that the organization will be perceived by the public as being insincere about wanting to interact with them through social media.

Section 2: User Behaviors in Social Media

Chapter 3 (*Personality and Social Media Use*) presents research on digital media and suggests that this has mostly paid attention to users' demographics, motivations, and efficacy. With increasingly popular Web tools like social media, it is important to study more stable psychological characteristics such as users' personality traits, as they may significantly affect how people use the Web to communicate and socialize. The authors identify that more extraverted people tend to take advantage of the user-generated Web that provide venues for communication and socialization.

Chapter 4 (*How Motivations for Social Media Usage Can Change and What It Means for E-Businesses*) explores the idea that user motivations may exist as evolving factors with the potential to impact the efficacy of e-business initiatives on social media sites. The author finds that individuals who joined social media Websites such as Facebook found new reasons for usage such as self-expression, replacing older media, and professional aspects, among others.

Chapter 5 (*Understanding Purchasing Behavior within Virtual Worlds: Planned Purchases and Impulse Buying*) addresses a central concern with planned and impulse purchases using virtual worlds (Second Life). The authors identify that Second Life users are more likely to be technologically more advanced than those using high-street department stores.

Section 3: Social Networking with Social Media

Chapter 6 (*Typical Innovative and Involvement Characteristics of Contributors to Consumer Generated Media*) presents a view of different forms of digital communications whereby consumers openly share their opinions and experiences, often about their reactions to products and services. The author explores various forms of blogs, podcasts, Internet forums, online communities, and online social networks using questionnaires to ascertain data.

Chapter 7 (*Can Your Business Have One Million Friends? Understanding and Using Blogs as One-to-One Mass Media*) examines a theoretical framework that explains how blogs can be categorized based on audiences' perceptions and how bloggers use different strategies to shape or shift their audiences' perceptions and increase the persuasiveness of their messages. The authors find that social media marketing is not a black box, but also not a magic bullet. The chapter provides insights that can help practitioners leverage the power of blogs as a form of marketing communication.

Chapter 8 (*User Intention of Sharing Video Clips on Web 2.0 Social Networking Websites*) looks at the use of video sharing community Websites, which has increased dramatically in recent years and the growth has changed the way that Web users view internet content. Sharing video content requires bandwidth and most countries have increased their network backbone technologies due to the demand in P2P. The authors identify and analyze community sharing of video clips, quality of the content, user behavior, and satisfaction of users of community shared video content.

Section 4: Social Marketing

Chapter 9 (*Comparing Web 2.0 Applications as Marketing Tools*) discusses Web 2.0 applications as marketing tools. In this context, blogs, micro-blogs, collaborative projects (wikis and social bookmarking), content communities, social networking sites, and virtual worlds are reviewed. The authors explain that collaborative projects are strong marketing tools for facilitating search engine marketing and search engine optimization. However, the difficulty of selecting the correct keywords, as well as producing attractive content, is their weak side. They are very suitable for generating new product ideas.

Chapter 10 (*Two-Sided Markets and Social Media*) examines simple reward programs to enhance user active participation on a Website, thus improving its satisfaction for users and increasing the value of the Website for the vendors. The authors introduce the concept of "two-sided" markets and show how these comprise a unique type of social media that facilitate the development of social networks oriented toward specific product domains (e.g., restaurants), specific brands (e.g., Starbucks), or common consumer concerns (e.g., Yelp.com).

Chapter 11 (*Application of Social Media Tools by Retailers*) explores the factors influencing the adoption process and the degree of engagement of the social media as part of the online marketing strategy by Spanish retailers. The authors find that retailers learning about social media tools and understanding their usefulness will lead to positive attitudes and wider adoption of social media as a way to better engage with their customers and extract strategic value from these tools.

Section 5: Customer Relationship Management with Social Media

Chapter 12 (*Interaction between Consumers and Businesses through Social Media: Trends and Future*) evaluates the communication channels based on social media used by businesses and consumers, showing successful and non-successful cases in the communication process and suggesting trends of usage of these channels more efficiently. The author identifies that the costs of using social media are much lower than traditional media, especially when trying to reach a large volume of consumers, which attracts the attention of advertisers and marketers for their use.

Chapter 13 (*Using Social Network Data to Identify Key Influencers for Social CRM Activities*) identifies key influencers within a company's customer database and consumers that are equipped with a large and strong network of connected neighbors. The authors identify that key influencers within a company's customer database can lead to substantial improvements in facilitating CRM.

Chapter 14 (*Best Practices for Social CRM*) presents a study of integration of traditional CRM systems with new social networking technologies available on the Web, such as Twitter, blogs, and communities, showing a set of best practices on the use of these technologies to improve business relationships with customers. The authors present a set of best practices with guidance on how social networking technologies can help companies to squeeze and improve the relationship with their customers.

Section 6: Organizations and Social Technologies

Chapter 15 (*E-Business Planning in Morphing Organizations: Maturity Models of Business Transformation*) explores maturity models and social media and how social media technology provides organizations with the means to extend their reach with multimedia rich content. The author introduces a new framework that has been recommended which enables the planning of social media technologies to be directly aligned with organizational objectives and ensures that the potential impact on business processes is identified at an early stage.

Chapter 16 (*The New Age E-Enterprise: Internet-Based Collaboration, Innovation and Co-Creation*) explores how the enterprise has changed in recent years and transformed itself into one that utilizes virtual work practices. This transformation has helped enterprises to shape how new products and services are developed, impacting the way the enterprise functions in the world of social collaboration. The authors review various technologies that underpin the Internet-based collaboration platforms and suggest that globalization provides a rich source of collaboration.

Chapter 17 (*Negotiation by Software Agents in Electronic Business: An Example of Hybrid Negotiation*) identifies electronic negotiation as one of many applications that software agents can perform to facilitate electronic business. Negotiations between a software agent and human (hybrid negotiation) could make electronic business efficient and intelligent. The authors present a framework representing communication between a human agent and intelligent software agents.

Chapter 18 (*The Transformative Effect of Social Media: Revolutionizing Business Models of Mass Production to Individual Production by the Masses*) illustrates how digital technology in general and social media in particular, has changed the way people interact and communicate. The author suggests that business is now on the verge of being transformed, with the customer not just an invited guest but as a potentially fully paid up part of the business.

Eldon Y. Li
National Chengchi University, Taiwan & California Polytechnic State University, USA

Stanley Loh
Lutheran University of Brazil (ULBRA), Brazil

Cain Evans
Birmingham City University, UK

Fabiana Lorenzi
Lutheran University of Brazil (ULBRA), Brazil

Section 1
Overview

Chapter 1
Social Media Activities:
Understanding What Consumers Do in Social Media

Kristina Heinonen
Hanken School of Economics, Finland

ABSTRACT

Consumers are increasingly consuming, participating, contributing, and sharing different types of online content. This is influencing the marketing activities traditionally controlled and performed by companies. The aim of this chapter is to conceptualize the activities consumers perform in social media. Social media denote content created by individual consumers such as online ratings or verbal reviews, online message boards/forums, photos/video sites, blogs, tags, and social networking sites. A conceptual framework for consumers' social media activities is developed and qualitatively substantiated. Social media activities are based on the motives for the activities, including information, social connection, and entertainment. The chapter contributes to research on social media and online communities by describing user behavior and motivations related to the user-created services. Managerially, the study deepens the understanding of different challenges related to users' activities on social media and the motivations associated with those activities.

INTRODUCTION

Consumers are increasingly active online. They are consuming, participating, contributing, and sharing different types of online content. Where individuals have traditionally been seen as passive consumers of different marketing content, they are gradually influencing the marketing activities traditionally controlled and performed

by companies. Although the use of social media is growing and user-generated content (UGC) is exploding in sites like YouTube, MySpace, Facebook, and Wikipedia, few academic studies have been conducted concerning individuals' use of social media, and many studies are conceptually oriented. Many emerging studies are currently focusing on the use of social media in different service sectors, including museums, libraries,

DOI: 10.4018/978-1-4666-4026-9.ch001

sports and entertainment venues (Kidd, 2011; Hall, 2011; Rotschild, 2011). But what citizens and active consumers are doing in social media needs more attention. Studies have shown that consumers' activity influences the value that is created in the use of a service (Heinonen, 2009; Heinonen & Strandvik, 2009). More studies of social media are needed to respond to consumers' enormous interests in and activity related to social media.

Current social media research emphasizes individuals' motivations for creating content or the role of personality on social media use. The majority of recent studies are exploring individuals' reasons to use social media (Park, Kee & Valenzuela, 2009; Raacke & Bonds-Raacke, 2008; Baker & White, 2011; Shao, 2009). Many studies are also emphasizing social networking sites (Ross et al., 2009; Boyd & Ellison, 2008; Utz, 2010), leaving other types of social media unexplored. Some research positioned in the service science field has used activity theory to describe social media services (Multisilta, 2009). However, what is lacking is a deeper understanding of what individuals do and the influence of these activities on individuals' perceptions and behavior. More importantly, little is known about individuals' interest in activity and willingness to collaborate in this type of peer-created and-dominated service.

The aim of this chapter is to conceptualize the activities consumers perform in social media. Social media denote the content created by individual consumers such as online ratings or verbal reviews, online discussions/conversations, photos/video sites, blogs, tags, and social networking sites. A conceptual framework for consumer activities and perceptions of user-created content is developed and qualitatively substantiated. The following research questions are addressed: What activities regarding social media are consumers involved in? What motivates consumers' activities in social media?

The chapter contributes to research on social media and online communities by describing consumer behavior and motivations related to the user-created services. Managerially, the study deepens the understanding of different strategies related to consumers' activities in social media and the motivations associated with those activities.

The chapter is structured in the following way. First is a general overview of the perspective and approach on social media and user-generated content taken in this chapter. Secondly follows a review of previous research on consumers' motivations to use social media as well as a review of research on consumers' activities on social media. Next, a conceptual framework for consumers' activities social media is proposed. Thereafter the empirical study is presented, and the findings are used to develop and substantiate the conceptual framework. The findings are then discussed on a more general level and managerial strategies based on social media activities are presented. The final conclusions include implications and recommendations for researchers and managers. Based on issues not covered in the current study agendas for future research are also identified.

SOCIAL MEDIA AND USER-GENERATED CONTENT

Social media is a rather new phenomenon, the use of social networking sites and user-generated services intensified from 2003 onward (Boyd & Ellison 2008). The social media research has been approached from different perspectives, using various concepts including social networking sites (Boyd & Ellison 2008, Utz 2010), user-generated content (Muñiz & Schau, 2011; Shao, 2009), and social media (Mangold & Faulds, 2009). Essentially, user-generated content are used to describe the phenomenon where consumers are creating, designing, consuming, or editing content created by others (Krishnamurthy & Dou 2008). Social media in turn are connected platforms for the public exchange of information between consumers (Boyd & Ellison 2008) in a democratic manner

(Drury, 2008). Although there are implied differences between the many concepts of these media, the concepts social media and user-generated content have been used semi-interchangeably (Kaplan & Haenlein, 2010). In this chapter, social media are defined as user-created content (i.e., user-generated content (UGC) and social media are seen to represent the same thing).

Social media have been classified in many ways, depending on the type and characteristics (Boyd & Ellison, 2008; Krishnamurthy & Dou, 2008). Kaplan and Haenlein (2010) included six types of social media (i.e., collaborative projects, blogs, content communities, social networking sites, virtual game worlds, and virtual social worlds). Collaborative projects are websites allowing multiple users to collectively edit or contribute to the content. Blogs are often seen as online diaries by individual users who want to express their views and opinions to be open publicly. Content communities, such as YouTube, Flickr, and Dopplr are websites that allow users to share content with each other. Social networking sites, such as Facebook or LinkedIn, connect users to each other or to a particular community. The last two social media types, virtual game worlds and social worlds, connect gamers to each other in virtual worlds, such as Second Life or World of Warcraft. The motives to use these six social media types are different, where some are more entertainment-oriented and other more network-oriented. Consequently, the activities consumers engage in are also different.

Motivators to Activity

Exploring consumer motivations to engage in social media enables an understanding of consumers' activities. Studies focusing on consumers' motivation are emerging rapidly. The classic uses and gratification approach (Blumler & Katz, 1974) has been the starting point for many studies on internet usage in general (Ko, Cho & Roberts, 2005) and

social media and user-generated content in particular (Shao 2009; Stafford, Stafford & Schkade, 2004). This approach explores the relationships between users' motives for a specific medium and the consequences of those motives. Research on internet uses and gratifications indicate that consumers' motives have processual elements, content elements, and social elements (Stafford, Stafford & Schkade, 2004). The motives consist of information, convenience, entertainment, and social interaction (Ko, Cho, & Roberts, 2005). In line with these findings, recent research on user-generated media found similar motives including information, entertainment, social interaction and community development, and self-actualization and self-expression (Shao 2009, Courtois et al., 2009). Similar motives have been linked to social networking sites including socializing, entertainment, self-status seeking, and information (Park, Kee, & Valenzuela, 2009). The motives have been linked to consumers' activities on social media (Shao, 2009).

Consumer Social Media Activities

Previous research on social media activity has emphasized how actively (or passively) consumers behave online. The starting point is frequently consumers' communication behavior that ranges between different levels of consumption or production of social media content. The poster-lurker dichotomy (i.e., portraying consumers as either posting or reading content), is a key approach to consumer activity (Schlosser, 2005; Shang, Chen, & Liao, 2006). Based on the poster-lurker communication behavior (de Valck, van Bruggen, & Wierenga, 2009) consumers can be either active contributors to the community in terms of retrieving, supplying, or discussing the information, or more passive consumers of the content. Consumption can take various forms where community users discuss information, retrieve and supply information, or maintain and update personal information. Whereas this poster-lurker categorization is focused on communication behavior, other types of activities are not identified.

Shao (2009) explored consumers' social media behavior based on their motives and consumers were categorized in three groups based on their behavior. First, consumers consumed social media for information and entertainment, i.e. they mainly read the content posted by others. Second, participants used social media for social interaction and community development, and they frequently commented others' content. Third, producers of social media had self-expression and self-actualization motives for posting social media content. Although these activities–consuming, participating, and producing–were described as different activities, Shao (2009) argued that they are highly interconnected as users often fall into two or all three categories simultaneously. This broad categorization groups users based on their level of activity, but it does not further describe the different sub-activities performed by users. Moreover, it has been argued that consumers are in fact not very active online and that they are consuming rather than participating or contributing to the social media content (Jones, Ravid, & Rafaeli, 2004; Joyce & Kraut, 2006; Preece, Nonnecke, & Andrews, 2004). In other words, the categorization into the three main activities does not necessarily differentiate between what consumers do in social media.

CONCEPTUALIZING SOCIAL MEDIA ACTIVITIES BASED ON USER MOTIVES

In this chapter, we conceptualize consumers' social media activities based on consumer motivations. Three types of motives have been found to be related to consumers' use of media (Shao, 2009; Ko, Cho, & Robert, 2005; Park, Kee, & Valenzuela, 2009): (1) Social interaction, (2) Entertainment, and (3) Information.

These motives can thus be used for further exploring the different activities consumers perform in social media. Figure 1 presents a conceptual framework of consumers' activities in social media. The activities are based on motivation including information, social connection, and entertainment. The interconnectedness of the three dimensions is based on the different level of hedonic and utilitarian elements. This is illustrated with the circles of the dimensions passing over each other.

The elements of the framework have been discussed in previous research, but existing studies have not combined activities with motivation. In the empirical study different activities are identified and based on these three dimensions of social media activities.

Empirical Study

An empirical study was conducted in 2009 to explore the various activities related to social media. Young individuals were chosen as a target group because they represent the largest group of social media users (Correa 2010; Courtois et al., 2009; Park, Kee, & Valenzuela, 2009). Fifty-seven marketing students were asked to evaluate and report their use of five different user-created services, resulting in a total sample size of 285

Figure 1. Social media activities based on user motivations

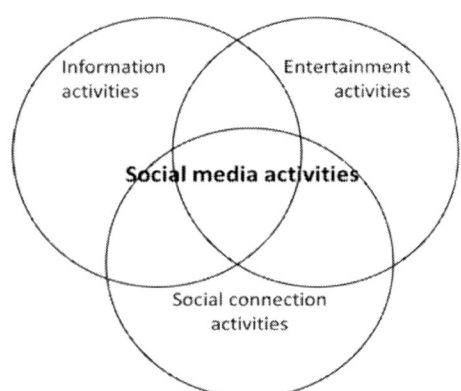

journal entries. Of the respondents, 34 were women and 23 were men.

An exploratory study design was chosen. The data was collected with a mixed method approach (Tashakkori & Teddlie, 1998) based on qualitative questions in a self-administered questionnaire. This approach is similar to the diary method that has been used to capture respondents' daily events and experiences in a natural and spontaneous setting (Bolger, Davis, & Rafaeli 2003). A diary was generated based on a qualitative questionnaire mapping respondents' activities and perceptions concerning their activities on social media sites. Respondents were asked to report their thoughts and emotions directly after using a particular user- created social media site. The resulting narratives are based on the respondent's own verbal depiction of using each site.

The diary was based on three parts. The first part provided an overview of the use of the particular social media site, including information such as name of the site, the type of user-generated content, as well as the date, time and length of visit. Additionally, the diary was based on structured thematic questions representing the main source for identifying the main activities proposed in the conceptual framework. For every social media site, the respondents answered the following questions:

1. Describe the content (e.g., opinions, experiences, advice, and commentary). What did you experience?
2. Describe the activities (consumption, participation, production). What did you do and why?
3. What effect did the social media site have on you? How did the social media site influence your activities and perceptions?
4. What did you learn from the social media site? What was the main insight? Please describe.
5. What was your motivation to use the social media site (e.g., knowledge sharing, advocacy, social connection, self-expression, or other--please specify)?

These questions were used to generate insight about what the respondents did on the social media site. Additionally, the respondents were asked rate on a seven-point Likert scale their likelihood of returning to the site, their level of engagement in the site, their perceived usefulness of the site, the level of perceived entertainment, and likelihood of recommending the site to a friend. The diary is outlined in its entirety in Appendix 1.

The data was analyzed in the following way. A variable-oriented approach (Miles & Huberman, 1994) was used to group and categorize the narratives based on the dimensions of the conceptual framework. The narratives were sorted based on data pertaining to (1) information activities, (2) entertainment activities, and (3) social connection activities. The dimensions cut across cases and the narratives were further analyzed to identify sub-categories to the identified dimensions. This was done by conceptualizing and abstracting the meaning of the words (Strauss & Corbin, 1998). Data pertaining to the three motivation types (information, social connection, and entertainment) were grouped into different categories. Each category included several sub-categories that emerged inductively.

Findings

The findings from the study are structured with the proposed conceptual framework of social media activities. The findings indicated that consumers are mostly consuming the content; only few respondents were contributors or producers of user-created services. Of the sample, 71% were related to consumption activities, the respondents typically did not participate by writing comments nor produce their own content on the sites. In some cases, consumption activities were linked with participation (15%), mainly on social networking sites such as Facebook. Twelve percent were related to a combination of consumption, participation, and production activities. For example, respondents reported leaving comments on discussion boards and writing reviews. Some respondents also reported production on websites other than social networking sites, such as posting and sharing own music and writing an informative blog. The rest was a small number of either consumption-production activities or participation activities. The data included only a few pure production activities.

The following social media sites were included most often: Facebook (18%), YouTube (19%), Wikipedia (11%), blogs (14%), or other social media sites, such as hobby-related sites or sites of opinion leaders and gurus (8%). Social connection activities were also often related to content creation and contribution, especially in comparison to the other two activity types. The rest were sites that were mentioned less frequently, such as Twitter (4%), MySpace (4%), or IMDb (4%), and other sites that were mentioned only a few times.

Social Media Activities

The conceptual framework based on information, entertainment, and social connection activities are used to further describe the different activities related to social media.

Information Processing

Two distinct information procession activities were the collection of factual information and application of knowledge. The information was gathered for solving a clear problem or task, and often the source was based on collaborative content, for example Wikipedia. Linked to collecting information, was the application of that knowledge. The collected information was used for different purposes, such as processing the content further for own benefit or exchanging products. Another key information processing activity involved searching for product information or content. This information retrieval was more entertainment-related, as it included other than factual information such as music or software.

Sharing information and accessing shared knowledge online represented a third form of information processing activity. This information had both collaborative and entertainment elements, as it included reviews, opinions, and experiences from other users. These user-generated perspectives and thoughts were perceived to be more reliable and value-adding. Similarly, news surveillance was an information processing activity that was linked with entertainment and social motives. Respondents noted a need to be updated concerning current activities and frequently visited different social media sites to acquire sufficient information. This type of activity can be compared to and sometimes even replaced reading newspapers and watching the news on TV.

Table 1 summarizes information processing activities with illustrative quotes from the journal entries. In the table, the first two activities are the only strictly information-related activity types, while the other activities involve either entertainment motives and/or social motives.

Entertainment Activities

Pure entertainment activities were related to distraction or relaxation, such as escaping the real world. Content sharing sites, such as YouTube, were used for escapist reasons, as the respondents wanted to detach themselves from the current context. Entertaining oneself was another activity, and it was mainly related to consumption of illegal postings of TV shows or music videos. A third type of entertainment activity was linked with information motives. Respondents reported that they wanted to get inspired or be happier by using social media. Social media provided content for encouragement and inspiration, such ideas regarding style or design. Self-expression was a fourth type of entertainment activity and it was related to social connection motives. It involved managing one's own image and getting awareness from others. This activity was less frequently

Table 1. Information processing activities

Dimension	Description	Illustrative Quote
Application of knowledge	Using knowledge for own benefits, such as processing content or exchanging products	*This time, the Internet Movie Database helped me choose between quite a few movies that I want to see. Although I'm not entirely sure which one I'll see yet, my choices were narrowed down significantly. AP* *Earn some money on selling items I don't use/need AR (online auction site)*
Collection of factual information	Gathering information from more formal user-generated sources, such as Wikipedia.	*I use Wikipedia to get information and I get what I am searching for, but the entertainment level is quite low.AI* *It's a good way to look up topics of interest. AR Wikipedia* *I used the site to collect information for my personal use. BC, MySpace*
Retrieval of product information or content	Obtaining product information or downloading content	*I was delighted to find out about the existence of SeriesYonkis because it allows me to watch my favorite series for free any time and any place most convenient for me. AK- (website for watching TV-shows)* *My motivation to use YouTube was to get information about a product i.e. to see how it works, how it looks like, what you can do with it and what the good vs. bad aspects of it are. BE*
News surveillance	Following current news from all over the world	*It is very interesting to read what people think about the contemporary occurrences. D (Online discussion forum of a daily magazine)* *It is interesting to see what happens in the fashion world. L, (a fashion blog)*
Sharing and accessing opinions, reviews and rating	Sharing information and accessing shared knowledge online, such as opinions and comments	*It feels like a reliable way to get opinions of products. The people who are writing at Afterdawn don't benefit anything from advertising a certain product which means they are going to tell the truth about what they think about some certain product. AA (technology forum Afterdawn.com)* *It changed my opinion of what hotel I should stay in. And will not visit the hotel the travel agency suggested. AC (Tripadvisor)*

mentioned compared to the other entertainment activities.

Table 2 summarizes the entertainment activities. Whereas the first two activities are purely entertainment activities, the other two activities have elements of information or social connection motives.

Social Connection

As social networking sites represented a large part of the social media sites included in the data, activities related to social connection were frequently mentioned by most respondents. This group included many activities, especially regarding the ability to connect to and interact with other users. One social connection activity is belonging and bonding with other users. Respondents noted they wanted to share their lives with each other, and typically posted personal information on so-

cial networking sites or commented other users' posts. Some respondents visited a UGC site in order to find out what other people were talking about and to enable bonding between members of their social context. The findings also indicated that although social connection occurs online, it can enable a sense of belonging and bonding to a certain offline community. This bonding and belonging blurs the boundaries between the online and offline worlds. For example, respondents described that they searched for interesting or entertaining content online and then they shared this content with their offline friends.

Another social connection activity was keeping up relationships and connecting with family and friends. This was naturally enabled by social networking sites, but it also involved content sharing sites such as Flickr or blogs that facilitated interaction between users. Creating and maintaining a social network was a third social connection

Table 2. Entertainment activities

Dimension	Description	Illustrative Quote
Escaping reality and relaxing	Episodic relaxation or escape	*I felt relaxed and amused and it offered a well deserved break from the work I was doing. AS (YouTube)* *When I opened the site I was pretty tired but after listening to a couple of good and energetic songs my mood changed. AT, YouTube*
Entertainment	Enjoying oneself online	*It's highly entertaining to watch people debate and express their opinions. The fact that you can do this anonymously makes it somewhat funnier when people say things more straight up. BC (Online student discussion forum)* *I use the site quite frequently for listening to music and watching other interesting videos. AB YouTube*
Becoming inspired, mood management	Looking for inspiration and encouragement	*I looked at the new pictures to get some inspiration to my own style. AD- Hel-Looks* *For a photography-interested person Flickr is a good tool for inspiration. I will most certainly visit the website again, as I always find new lovely pictures and spot new trends. S*
Self-expression	Self-articulation and self-promotion	*But also there is a kind of self-expression. This usually happens when I upload my playlists. My music tells who I am. A, YouTube*

activity. This can be considered as a main social connection activity, as the purpose with many social networking sites is to enable users to share their personal information with others.

A fourth social connection activity was being up-to-date and knowing what is happening in the own community. Social connection thus improved the respondents' awareness regarding current events or social gatherings. Social media sites seem to have changed the need to be up-to-date on current happenings, as sites such as Facebook and Twitter enable users to constantly share personal news with all friends.

Collaborative experiencing such as sharing experiences and content with other users represented a fifth social connection activity. In this way many respondents perceived that they were influenced by others' opinions on discussion forums or blogs. Many times this occurred after visiting and reading an online discussion board. The main goal with this activity was to share experiences with friends and family.

Social surveillance represents a sixth activity where respondents reported that they wanted to follow the doings of their network of friends and acquaintances. This activity involves learning about the people in the own circles and it differs from being up-to-date since the goal is to be en-

tertainment rather than getting factual information about happenings.

The findings on social connection activities are summarised in Table 3. The first two activities, belonging and staying in touch were pure social connection activities whereas the other activities involved either information or entertainment motives. Social networking and being up-to-date included elements of information motives, as respondents noted that they needed sufficient information about their social network. Collaborative experiencing in contrast included entertainment motives, as respondents noted that they wanted to amuse themselves and share content with their friends. Social surveillance has elements of all three motives, as this activity is linked with collective, entertaining, and informative reasons.

Overview of Social Media Activities

The activities are further categorized based on the proposed conceptual framework (Figure 2). The three motives for using social media were linked to several activities. The motives for consuming a social media site were fairly similar to participating in or producing content on the site. Whereas some activities were purely based on one motive, many activities were connected with two or even

Table 3. Social connection activities

Dimension	Description	Illustrative Quote
Belonging and bonding	Connecting with people	*I felt urged to comment on my friend's status AW (Facebook)* *I get a feeling of belonging when I can easily listen to the same music as my friends are listening and talking about.AD MySpace* *My motivation was that many friends had Facebook accounts and I wanted to be a part of that as well. E*
Staying in touch	Keeping relationships with own network	*The community is an important part of my social life. L, IRC-Galleria* *It is an easy and cheap way to keep in contact with friends whether they are in the same or different country. It's easy to follow how friends are doing by looking their account. AD Facebook*
Social networking	Creating and maintaining a social network of friends and acquaintants	*It is useful because it saves time. I have sort of collected all my friends at one place and it is an easy and fast way to share my life with them on Facebook. O*
Being up-to-date	Knowing what is happening in the own community	*My friends invite me to various events which I would have no idea about if it wasn't for Facebook. J* *I know for certain that I will go back to this site because I use it almost daily to check out if my friends have written something to me or if there is something going on. AU, Facebook* *It made me feel I was up to date with what some of my friends were doing. AS, Facebook*
Collaborative experiencing	Sharing and experiencing with others	*You occasionally talk about what you have been watching on YouTube or show them new videos or advice them to see something. AE YouTube* *I watched some funny clips together with family and friends. AZ, YouTube*
Social surveillance	Learning about friends and acquaintances	*Well, I found out stuff about my friends I would not know without Facebook. AE* *Certainly entertaining. Getting to know peoples' thoughts. In the future more entertaining when it gains wider popularity here and people you know are involved. AV, Twitter*

all three motives. The conceptual framework thus needs to incorporate this interconnection between the three dimensions of motivation. Figure 2 illustrates users' main activities related to social media.

Figure 2 also illustrates the connectedness of the activities and motivations, i.e. that some activities have dual motivations. Acquiring information is one of the main reasons why the respondents visited social media sites and this was mainly based on information motives. However, information activities were only partly linked with strictly information motives. Retrieving product information or content was combined with entertainment needs, as was seen by respondents searching for entertaining content. Similarly, entertainment activities were not related only to entertainment motives. Becoming inspired, mood management, and retrieving information and content were closely linked with information motives. In contrast, sharing and experiencing with others and self-expression also included social connection motives. Not surprisingly, social connection activities were mainly related with social relationships (i.e., staying in touch and belonging). However, they were also linked with information motives such as managing social networks on sites such as Facebook. Also, being informed of current events in the social network combined information and social connection motives. Some activities were related to all three motivations. Positioned at the intersection of all three dimensions are social surveillance, sharing and accessing opin-

Figure 2. An overview of social media activities

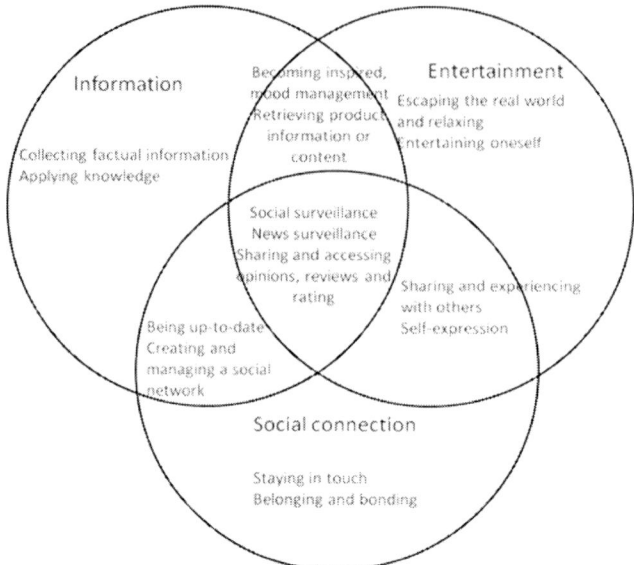

ions, reviews and rating, and news surveillance. These activities were the most complex.

SOLUTIONS AND RECOMMENDATIONS

The study extends existing research on consumers' use of social media by characterizing different consumer activities. By focusing on activities rather than only on motivations or gratifications it was possible to deepen the understanding of why consumers are interested in social media. In other words, this study extends the research on uses and gratifications (Stafford, Stafford & Schkade 2004; Park, Kee, & Valenzuela, 2009) by identifying several activities related to each gratification. Moreover, by linking activity and motivations it was possible to generate a deeper understanding of activities performed in relation to social media. The conceptual framework substantiated with empirical findings provides an in-depth description of the activities performed by consumers. Also, in contrast to the study by Shao (2009), with this conceptualization it is suggested

that the activities of consumption, participation, and production are not only related to certain motivations; rather that the activities are based on many motivations.

The study has several implications for managers. Emphasizing both conceptual and empirical issues, this paper highlights the importance of companies' understanding their role in this emerging media dominated by users. The proposed conceptual framework of consumer social media activities contributes to the management of social media. Service companies are challenged with the input of individuals traditionally seen as consumers or customers. The study suggests that the role of user-generated content in directing consumer behavior diminishes the influence of traditional marketing communication. Consumers can easily share information and opinions, and thus, as an alternative to commercial marketing, they can create collective and sometimes rather critical information about their experiences. Through social media this content is visible to a larger community of consumers compared to offline word-of-mouth communication. Typically, consumers tend to believe and appreciate reviews and opinions of their peers rather than commercial messages created by companies. Consequently, it is more difficult to get the consumers´ attention with traditional marketing campaigns. Marketers need to be more creative and aware of their customers' behavior. Rather than relying solely on marketing communication, companies must to a higher extent try to involve themselves in individuals' activities, in order to understand their brand image and also to facilitate interactions with potential customers. Moreover, instead of attempting to control the activity in social media, companies need to incorporate an open and transparent communication strategy. In other words, companies need to overtly and proactively link their communication flow with customers' interest areas. More importantly, considering that consumers are more active than before, those active consumers can be engaged as partners with the company to function as a bridge between the company and the target audience. In fact, the coexistence of companies, of consumers who actively produce social media content, and of large masses of consumers who mainly consume the social media content is one of the main challenges and opportunities in the modern social media environment.

FUTURE RESEARCH DIRECTIONS

The study takes an exploratory approach and many agendas for future research emerge. In the study we included different types of social media to generate various activities. However, in the analysis we did not specifically emphasize the differences between the types and the activities related to each type. An agenda for future research is to identify and describe the activities relevant for different social media environments. New content is emerging and a more structured understanding about the differences and similarities is needed.

Future research is also related to the design of the empirical studies and methods used to understand the use of social media. New types of research methods are needed for approaching and truly understanding behavior regarding user-created content. Here personal diaries designed with a multi-method approach were used to solicit both narratives and quantitative information about individuals' social media use. In the current empirical study the respondents' were asked to reflect upon their activities after the situation. New methods that are real-time and unobtrusive, but still with the benefits of deep ethnographical insight about user activities must be created. Also, future research also needs to use more quantitative information to be able to draw conclusions about the effect of the activities on for example brand image, customer satisfaction, and word-of-mouth intentions.

CONCLUSION

Social media behavior is increasing rapidly and this involves challenges for both academic research and industry practice. Academic research is faced with the need oto create conceptual ideas of social media behavior complemented with empirical findings from the user perspective. Emphasizing both conceptual and empirical issues, this chapter highlights the importance of companies understanding their role in this emerging media dominated by users. Instead of focusing on technology applications or push-marketing, social media strategies must take a customer dominant mindset starting (Heinonen et al, 2010) from the customers' perspective on activities and practices on social media. From a managerial perspective, the increasing use of social media by both consumers and marketers result in a need for critical outlook on the benefits of social media. Certainly, there are many possibilities in terms of intensified consumer interaction and more knowledge about customers. However, as this study has shown, consumers perform a multitude of activities in social media and companies need to understand how these activities can be managed and utilized to improve company performance.

REFERENCES

Baker, R. K., & White, K. M. (2011). In Their Own Words: Why Teenagers Don't Use Social Networking Sites. Cyberpsychology, Behavior, and Social Networking, 14(6), 395-398.

Blumler, J. G., & Katz, E. (1974). *The Uses of Mass Communication*. Newbury Park, CA: Sage.

Bolger, N., Davis, A., & Rafaeli, E. (2003). Diary methods: Capturing life as it is lived. *Annual Review of Psychology*, *54*(1), 579–616. doi:10.1146/annurev.psych.54.101601.145030 PMID:12499517.

Boyd, D. M., & Ellison, N. B. (2008). Social Network Sites: Definition, History, and Scholarship. *Journal of Computer-Mediated Communication*, *13*, 210–230. doi:10.1111/j.1083-6101.2007.00393.x.

Correa, T. (2010). The Participation Divide Among "Online Experts": Experience, Skills and Psychological Factors as Predictors of College Students' Web Content Creation. *Journal of Computer-Mediated Communication*, *16*, 71–92. doi:10.1111/j.1083-6101.2010.01532.x.

Courtois, C., Mechant, P., De Marez, L., & Verleye, G. (2009). Gratifications and Seeding Behavior of Online Adolescents. *Journal of Computer-Mediated Communication*, *15*, 109–137. doi:10.1111/j.1083-6101.2009.01496.x.

de Valck, K., van Bruggen, G., & Wierenga, B. (2009). Virtual communities: A marketing perspective. *Decision Support Systems*, *47*, 185–203. doi:10.1016/j.dss.2009.02.008.

Drury, G. (2008). Social media: Should marketers engage and how can it be done effectively? *Journal of Direct. Data and Digital Marketing Practice*, *9*(3), 274–277. doi:10.1057/palgrave.dddmp.4350096.

Hall, H. (2011). Relationship and role transformations in social media environments. *The Electronic Library*, *29*(4), 421–428. doi:10.1108/02640471111156704.

Heinonen, K. (2009). The Influence of Customer Activity on e-Service Value-in-use. *International Journal of Electronic Business*, *7*(2), 190–214. doi:10.1504/IJEB.2009.024627.

Heinonen, K., & Strandvik, T. (2009). Monitoring value-in-use of e-service. *Journal of Service Management*, *20*(1), 33–51. doi:10.1108/09564230910936841.

Heinonen, K., Strandvik, T., Mickelsson, K.-J., Edvardsson, B., Sundström, E., & Andersson, P. (2010). A Customer Dominant Logic of Service. *Journal of Service Management*, *21*(4), 531–548. doi:10.1108/09564231011066088.

Jones, Q., Ravid, G., & Rafaeli, S. (2004). Information overload and the message dynamics of online interaction spaces. *Information Systems Research*, *15*(2), 194–210. doi:10.1287/isre.1040.0023.

Joyce, E., & Kraut, R. E. (2006). Predicting Continued Participation in Newsgroups. *Journal of Computer-Mediated Communication*, *11*(3), 723–747. doi:10.1111/j.1083-6101.2006.00033.x.

Kaplan, A. M., & Haenlein, M. (2010). Users of the world, unite! The challenges and opportunities of Social Media. *Business Horizons*, *53*, 59–68. doi:10.1016/j.bushor.2009.09.003.

Kidd, J. (2011). Enacting engagement online: Framing social media use for the museum. *Information Technology & People*, *24*(1), 64–77. doi:10.1108/09593841111109422.

Ko, H., Cho, C.-H., & Roberts, M. S. (2005). Internet uses and gratifications: A structural equation model of interactive advertising. *Journal of Advertising*, *34*(2), 57–70. doi:10.1080/0091336 7.2005.10639191.

Krishnamurthy, S., & Dou, W. (2008). Advertising with User-Generated Content: A Framework and Research Agenda. *Journal of Interactive Advertising*, *8*(2), 1–7.

Mangold, G. W., & Faulds, D. J. (2009). Social media: The new hybrid element in the promotions mix. *Business Horizons*, *54*, 209–217.

Miles, M.B. & Huberman, M. (1994). *Qualitative data analysis: An expanded sourcebook.*

Multisilta, J. (2009). A service science perspective on the design of social media activities. *International Journal of Web Engineering and Technology*, *5*(3), 327–342. doi:10.1504/ IJWET.2009.031013.

Muñiz, A. C., & Schau, H. J. (2011). How to inspire value-laden collaborative consumer-generated content. *Business Horizons*, *54*, 209–217. doi:10.1016/j.bushor.2011.01.002.

Park, N., Kee, K. F., & Valenzuela, S. (2009). Being Immersed in Social Networking Environment: Facebook Groups, Uses and Gratifications, and Social Outcomes. *Cyberpsychology & Behavior*, *12*(6), 729–733. doi:10.1089/cpb.2009.0003 PMID:19619037.

Preece, J., Nonnecke, B., & Andrews, D. (2004). The top 5 reasons for lurking: Improving community experiences for everyone. *Computers in Human Behavior*, *20*(2), 201–223. doi:10.1016/j. chb.2003.10.015.

Raacke, J., & Bonds-Raacke, J. (2008). MySpace and Facebook: Applying the Uses and Gratifications Theory to Exploring Friend-Networking Sites. *Cyberpsychology & Behavior*, *11*(2), 169–174. doi:10.1089/cpb.2007.0056 PMID:18422409.

Ross, C., Orr, E. S., Sisic, M., Arseneault, J. M., Simmering, M. G., & Orr, R. R. (2009). Personality and motivations associated with Facebook use. *Computers in Human Behavior*, *25*, 578–586. doi:10.1016/j.chb.2008.12.024.

Rotschild, C. (2011). Social media use in sports and entertainment venues. *International Journal of Event and Festival Management*, *2*(2), 139–150. doi:10.1108/17582951111136568.

Schlosser, A. E. (2005). Posting versus lurking: Communicating in a multiple audience context. *The Journal of Consumer Research*, *32*(2), 260–265. doi:10.1086/432235.

Shang, R.-A., Chen, Y.-C., & Liao, H.-J. (2006). The value of participation in virtual consumer communities on brand loyalty. *Internet Research*, *16*(4), 398–418. doi:10.1108/10662240610690025.

Shao, G. (2009). Understanding the Appeal of User-Generated Media: A Uses and Gratification Perspective. *Internet Research*, *19*(1), 7–25. doi:10.1108/10662240910927795.

Stafford, T. F., Stafford, M., & Schkade, L. L. (2004). Determining Uses and Gratifications for the Internet. *Decision Sciences*, *35*(2), 259–288. doi:10.1111/j.00117315.2004.02524.x.

Strauss, A., & Corbin, J. (1998). *Basics of Qualitative Research: Techniques and Procedures for Developing Grounded Theory* (2nd ed.). Thousand Oaks, CA: Sage.

Tashakkori, A., & Teddlie, C. (1998). *Mixed Methodology: Combining Qualitative and Quantitative Approaches*. Thousand Oaks, CA: Sage Publications.

Utz, S. (2010). Show me your friends and I will tell you what type of person you are: How one's profile, number of friends, and type of friends influence impression formation on social network sites. *Journal of Computer-Mediated Communication*, *15*, 314–335. doi:10.1111/j.1083-6101.2010.01522.x.

ADDITIONAL READING

Cooke, M., & Buckley, N. (2008). Web 2.0, social networks and the future of market research. *International Journal of Market Research, 50*(2), 267–292.

Cova, B., & Cova, V. (2002). Tribal marketing: The tribalisation of society and its impact on the conduct of marketing. *European Journal of Marketing, 36*(5/6), 595–620. doi:10.1108/03090560210423023.

Grace-Farfaglia, P., Dekkers, A., & Sundararajan, B. (2006). Multinational web uses and gratifications: Measuring the social impact of online community participation across national boundaries. *Electronic Commerce Research, 6*(1), 75–101. doi:10.1007/s10660-006-5989-6.

Griffin, A., & Hauser, J. R. (1993). The voice of the customer. *Marketing Science, 12*(1), 1–27. doi:10.1287/mksc.12.1.1.

Heinonen, K. (2011). Conceptualising consumers' dynamic relationship engagement: The development of online community relationships. *Journal of Customer Behavior, 10*(1), 49–72. doi:10.1362/147539211X570519.

Huang, C.-Y., Shen, Y.-Z., & Chang, S.-S. (2007). Bloggers motivations and behaviors: A model. *Journal of Advertising Research*, (December): 472–484. doi:10.2501/S0021849907070493.

Leung, L. (2003). Impacts of Net-Generation Attributes, Seductive Properties of the Internet, and Gratifications-Obtained on Internet Use. *Telematics and Informatics, 20*, 107–129. doi:10.1016/S0736-5853(02)00019-9.

Walker Rettberg, J. (2009). Freshly Generated for You, and Barack Obama: How Social Media Represent Your Life. *European Journal of Communication, 24*(4), 451–466. doi:10.1177/0267323109345715.

Wheeler, L., & Reis, H. T. (1991). Self-Recording of Everyday Life Events: Origins, Types, and Uses. *Journal of Personality, 59*(3), 339–354. doi:10.1111/j.1467-6494.1991.tb00252.x.

Zeithaml, V. A., Parasuraman, A., & Malhotra, A. (2005). A multiple-item scale for assessing electronic service quality. *Journal of Service Research, 7*(3), 213–233. doi:10.1177/1094670504271156.

KEY TERMS AND DEFINITIONS

Consumer Activity: The activities users perform on social media sites, typically separated into consumption, participation, or production.

Social Media: Websites with content created by individual consumers such as online ratings or verbal reviews, online message boards/forums, photos/video sites, blogs, tags, and social networking sites.

Social Networking Site: A website that connect users to each other, such as Facebook, or Linkedin.

User-Generated Content (UGC): Online content created, designed, consumed, or edited by users, such as YouTube, MySpace, Facebook, Wikipedia.

APPENDIX: DIARY

Diary of user generated content

Your name: Journal entry no: _____

Name of site:

Site address:

Date of visit:

Time visit occurred:

Length of visit in minutes:

Type of UGC site: [ ] ratings, [ ] verbal reviews, [ ] discussions/conversations, [ ] photos,
                           [ ] blogs, [ ] videos, [ ] tags, [ ] social networking,
                           [ ] other, specify_____

Describe the content (e.g., opinions, experiences, advice and commentary). What did you experience?

Describe the activities (consumption, participation, production). What did you do and why?

What effect did the UGC have on you? How did the UGC influence your activities and perceptions?

How likely is it that you will go back to this site? Why?

Extremely						Extremely
unlikely						likely
1	2	3	4	5	6	7

Your level of engagement in the UGC. Explain why.

| Low | | | | | | High |
| 1 | 2 | 3 | 4 | 5 | 6 | 7 |

The relevance of the specific UGC for you. Explain why.

| Low | | | | | | High |
| 1 | 2 | 3 | 4 | 5 | 6 | 7 |

The usefulness of the UGC. Explain why.

| Low | | | | | | High |
| 1 | 2 | 3 | 4 | 5 | 6 | 7 |

The level of entertainment of the UGC. Explain why.

| Low | | | | | | High |
| 1 | 2 | 3 | 4 | 5 | 6 | 7 |

How likely is it that you will tell about this site to a friend? Explain why.

| Low | | | | | | High |
| 1 | 2 | 3 | 4 | 5 | 6 | 7 |

What did you learn from the UGC? What was the main insight? Describe.

What was your motivation to use the UGC? E.g. knowledge sharing, advocacy, social connection, self-expression, or other, specify.

Chapter 2
Using Social Media to Cultivate Positive Community Norms

Caroline Graham Austin
Montana State University, USA

Jeff Linkenbach
Montana State University, USA

Sarah N. Keller
Montana State University Billings, USA

Jay Otto
Montana State University, USA

ABSTRACT

This chapter analyzes the use of social media in health risk prevention campaigns. According to the Positive Community Norms (PCN) framework, prevention is defined as the process of proactively cultivating positive cultures through transformational leadership, communications, and an integrated portfolio of strategies. This chapter focuses on social media strategies. We review two extant prevention models (Everett Rogers's framework and the PCN framework), examine underlying theoretical explanations for consumer behaviors related to prevention and the use of social media, provide three brief case studies of prevention campaigns at various stages of maturity and success, and offer caveats for campaign managers who might be considering using social media to reach out to audiences. We intend this material to prove beneficial for researchers, public policymakers, and managers of prevention campaigns.

DOI: 10.4018/978-1-4666-4026-9.ch002

INTRODUCTION

Transformative Consumer Research (TCR) is defined as "investigations that are framed by a fundamental problem or opportunity, and that strive to respect, uphold, and improve life in relation to the myriad conditions, demands, potentialities, and effects of consumption" (Mick, 2006, p. 2). Prevention of health risk behavior is an area in which TCR can be applied on both academic and practical levels. Prevention has many definitions. According to the Positive Community Norms (PCN) framework, prevention is defined as the process of proactively cultivating positive cultures through transformational leadership, communications, and an integrated portfolio of health-promotion strategies (Linkenbach & Otto, 2009). For example, by correcting misperceptions of norms related to binge drinking, by promoting healthy body image, or by normalizing safe cell phone use/non-use while driving, norms can be impacted in a positive manner.

Social media provide a set of key tools that TCR strategists can use to achieve their goals, such as prevention of health and safety risks. In the era of Facebook, Twitter, YouTube, Blogger, and other social media platforms, people have the ability to cultivate positive cultures—teaching and learning, supporting and critiquing each other—irrespective of traditional boundaries, such as geography and sociocultural status. Word-of-mouth communication has exploded in the Internet era (Dellarocas, 2003), and has caused a paradigm shift in the way that people interact with each other, both as individuals, and as agents of larger entities (e.g., brands, clubs, schools, causes) that they feel a part of (Austin, Zinkhan, & Song, 2007). As such, social media are ideal platforms for nonprofit organizations, non-governmental organizations (NGOs), and community-based businesses to conduct TCR, and develop and distribute health risk prevention materials.

Successful prevention campaigns have been "investigator-driven, theory-based, focused on changing a target behavior, and replicated with fidelity over time" (Rotherham-Borus & Duan, 2003, p. 518). By emphasizing the relative advantages of engaging in desired behaviors, using up-to-date, factual messages that do not overstate their claims, and selecting social media outlets that enhance the message and the audience's preferences, prevention campaigns can see gradual changes in audience behaviors, though it often takes considerable time to see such results (Rogers, 2002).

This chapter takes an in-depth look at how social media can be used in prevention campaigns to help positively transform consumer behavior. We examine, in detail, a strategic framework for diffusing preventive innovations that Everett Rogers outlined in 2002. Rogers called for leveraging peer networks to change norms and perceptions about prevention innovations in order to achieve change (Rogers, 2002). Using data from existing prevention campaigns, we analyze how Rogers's recommendations have been applied over the past decade within the emerging social media paradigm.

Although we find it to be a powerful tool, Rogers's framework does not specifically address social ecology, which renders it less useful than it could otherwise be. Social ecology theory seeks to explain people's behavior in terms of an "ecology" of forces at the individual, social, political, cultural, and other levels, rather than simply at the individual level (Bronfenbrenner, 1979). Therefore, in this chapter, we supplement Rogers's recommendations with similar proposals from the PCN model of social transformation (MOST of Us, 2010), which strives to account for the myriad influences on individual and collective behaviors within populations. We also identify consumer behavior theories that underlie both Rogers's and the PCN model, in order to create a more comprehensive explanation/prediction of how social media can be used most effectively in prevention efforts.

In addition to a critical examination of Rogers's model, this chapter provides extended examinations of three successful social media prevention campaigns currently in progress: Weight Watchers, It Gets Better, and text4baby. We also provide prevention campaign managers with caveats for potential campaign pitfalls. We intend this material to prove beneficial for researchers, public policymakers, and managers of prevention campaigns, regardless of their organizational affiliations.

BACKGROUND

Social Media Defined

A 2010 *Business Horizons* article defines social media as "a group of Internet-based Web applications that build on the ideological and technological foundations of Web 2.0, and that allow the creation and exchange of User Generated Content" (Kaplan & Haenlein, 2010, p. 61). This broad-based definition allows for the growth and change of individual social media sites (e.g., Blogger, Facebook, YouTube) and tools (e.g., Weblogs, videos), while still capturing the essential interactive features that define social media.

Ease of use, interactivity, and user-generated content are the hallmarks of social media; all are necessary for social media to be successful. As Kozinets, Belz, and McDonagh said, "The media could not be social without the virtual messengers, and the online community could not communicate without the technological medium" (2012, p. 207).

Hayes and Papworth (2008) have created a social media model that is particularly useful because it outlines the major ways that people act within the social media environment. In the following list, we explain key attributes of consumer behavior with regards to social media:

1. **Involvement:** Interacting with others on a personal or quasi-personal level, for example, engaging on networking sites (e.g., Facebook, LinkedIn), microblogging (e.g., Twitter, Tumblr), and in the comments sections of a wide variety of Web pages (e.g., Amazon.com, online versions of newspapers, YouTube).
2. **Creation:** Generating and uploading video, music, text, photos, podcasts, wiki pages, etc.
3. **Discussion:** Conversation revolving around content available on and off the Web, such as news articles, blog posts, videos, movies, other people's content, etc.
4. **Promotion:** Linking sites together that have some relevance to a theme, a group of users, to create or synthesize knowledge, or merely because the linker likes them and thinks others will as well.
5. **Measurement:** Analyzing the massive amount of information available in consumer databases to help understand people's thoughts, feelings, and behaviors (e.g., Google Analytics, Zillow, Digg).

Social Media and the Communication of Ideas

Although social media are revolutionizing the *ways* that people interact with each other, their success relies on the fact that they leverage people's *fundamental desire* to interact with each other—intellectually and emotionally. Social media facilitate such connections without regard to conventional barriers, such as geographic distance. In other words, these media provide a new way to meet an age-old human need for social connection, and as such, they have significant potential to encourage engagement that enables people to transform their own lives, and their communities.

Social media foster opportunities for persuasion and change. Rogers ascertained that communications involving peer-to-peer (i.e., horizontal) exchanges, rather than top-down (i.e., vertical) diffusion of ideas were more likely to effectively induce behavioral change. Rogers wrote,

Mass media channels are more effective in creating initial knowledge of innovations, whereas interpersonal channels are more effective in forming and changing attitudes toward a new idea, and thus in influencing the decision to adopt or reject a new idea. Most individuals evaluate an innovation, not on the basis of scientific research by experts, but through the subjective evaluations of near-peers who have already adopted the innovation. Diffusion is essentially a social process through which people talking to people spread an innovation (2002).

It is a marketing truism that word-of-mouth communication and other forms of interpersonal interaction can successfully break through advertising clutter (Austin, Zinkhan, & Song, 2007). As such, many organizations have rushed to establish online identities in the social media milieu. However, those firms that wish to foster true communication with stakeholders in social media settings should do so only if/when they have a deep understanding of the people in the communities that they are hoping to connect with (Hayes & Papworth, 2008). After all, people who share values and interests trust each other's opinions and recommendations much more highly than those they receive from strangers or organizations that they suspect to be self-interested.

For instance, teenagers like to chat and hang out with each other; social media allow them to do so in their own houses at times of the day or night when they have historically been cut off from each other by parental curfews and physical separation (Brown & Bobkowski, 2011). As such, social media tools have been lauded for increasing people's sense of community and connectedness, but also lambasted for isolating people in front of

their computers, game consoles, and smart phones (Turkle, 2011). It is likely that both opinions have merit. However, recent investigations of social media reveal that, across both strong and weak ties between people, these new forms of communication and connection help users generate and sustain social capital (Hoffman, 2012; Mathwick, Wiertz, & de Ruyter, 2008).

Social Norms

Social norms, which are society's expectations of behavior for its members, are usually classified as either descriptive—how people generally act—or prescriptive—how people should act. Social norms depend on people's perceptions of what is normal behavior, regardless of whether this perception is correct or accurate (MOST of Us, 2012a).

Perceptions of social norms are people's *beliefs* about the norms of their peers. Perceptions of social norms play an extremely important role in shaping our individual behavior. Our perception of what is acceptable, majority behavior—how fast we think most people drive, whether we think most people wear seatbelts, how many drinks we think most people have before getting behind the wheel—play a large role in our own behavioral decisions. Unfortunately, we often misperceive the social norms of our peers, thinking that risky behavior occurs with far greater frequency and social acceptance than it actually does (Linkenbach, 2006).

If people believe that risky behaviors are typical, they are more likely to engage in those behaviors for several reasons: (a) People may be more likely to take part in a high-risk activity if they misperceive it as the norm; (b) those who regularly engage in high-risk activities will wrongly think that their behavior is accepted social practice; and (c) fear of social disapproval can make people reluctant to intervene to stop dangerous behaviors that they believe are socially sanctioned (Linkenbach, 2006).

The Positive Community Norms Framework

The PCN framework is a process that promotes both individual health behavior change, and transformation across the socio-ecological continuum, based on a synthesis of existing theories from health education, community psychology, social psychology, and education. The PCN process not only attempts to synthesize lessons learned from a wide range of theoretical approaches, but also offers potential solutions to some of the limitations of prior models. Specifically, the PCN approach aims to grow positive community norms across the social ecology by focusing on transformational leadership, communications, and an integrated portfolio of health-promotion strategies. Like many community and population-focused approaches, PCN combines techniques from health communications and social marketing in a variety of health risk promotion campaigns. The primary focus of PCN campaigns is to challenge people's commonly-held perceptions and misperceptions about their environment and the behavior of their peers, as well as their beliefs about how community-wide problems should be confronted (MOST of Us, 2010). These efforts are designed to shift the normative context and re-direct public conversations toward the desired health and safety aims.

Drawing from social ecology, the PCN framework argues that both internal and external transformational processes are critical—that individual and community transformation are inter-dependent (MOST of Us, 2010). Systems theory recognizes that focusing intervention efforts on only one component of a larger system will not result in sustained or significant change within the system as a whole. As with TCR, systems theorists remind community researchers to focus on individuals and cultures—and all points in between——to ensure that communities are receptive to intervention efforts (Watkins & Marsick, 1999).

PCN is based upon an ecological risk/protective model (Bronfenbrenner, 1979; Mills & Bogenschneider, 2001) which states that the most effective approach to supporting positive changes within communities is (a) to reduce risks that compromise healthy development, and (b) to enhance protective factors that mitigate risks and encourage health and well-being. Central to this ecological perspective is the notion that individuals develop within dynamic communities that act and interact to shape the environments where people live. Thus, the PCN framework encourages a holistic approach to assessing the multiple factors that contribute to individual and community health problems; it correspondingly offers a multifaceted approach to intervention programs.

Historically, prevention campaigns have tended to assign individual blame (and celebrate individual victories) in their messaging. Rather than focusing on individuals, PCN approaches involve individuals, small groups, organizations, community leaders, policy-makers, governments, and cultures. More specifically, PCN differs from other approaches insofar as it involves whole communities in the process of transformation and health improvement, and documents positive changes that occur along the way as part of the campaign.

USING SOCIAL MEDIA TO CULTIVATE POSITIVE COMMUNITY NORMS

Social Media and Health Related Behaviors

Health-related programs that leverage social engagement and interaction, such as Alcoholics Anonymous and Weight Watchers (Rotherham-Borus & Duan, 2003), existed prior to the development of social media. However, the engagement of interactive online communities makes these types of programs much easier to carry out from a logistical standpoint, and extends their reach to a far larger pool of potential participants/beneficiaries. As such, Weight Watchers and other prevention communities have extended their operations (and commensurate successes) since the advent of social media (Brown & Bobkowski, 2011; Jones, 2011).

To date, only a handful of small-scale new media interventions have been evaluated, however, early measures seem to indicate the success of public health interventions that effectively leverage new communication technologies (Honan, 2008; Levine et al., 2008). In 2006, the San Francisco Department of Public Health (SFDPH) collaborated with the Internet Sexuality Information Services, Inc. (ISIS-Inc.) to develop a sexual health text messaging service with the goal of decreasing sexually transmitted infection (STI) rates among adolescents in San Francisco. SEXINFO, which is targeted to urban African-American adolescents age 12 to 24, provides basic facts about sexual health and relationships, along with referrals to youth-oriented clinics and social services. A preliminary evaluation to determine the number of youth using the service and the most frequent requests revealed that more than 4,500 inquiries were sent in the first 25 weeks of the service, and 2,500 of those inquiries led to information and referrals (Levine et al., 2008).

The data show that using social media in prevention campaigns is a natural extension of previous public health efforts: Although the United States does not yet have universal Internet access for its population (it currently stands at 69% of the population [Chou et al., 2009]), 58% of American Internet users report seeking health-related information online (Atkinson, Saperstein, & Pleis, 2009) and 84% claim membership in at least one virtual group (Mathwick, Wiertz, & de Ruyter, 2008). Audiences for prevention messages have been shown to respond positively to settings in which they feel at home (Rotherham-Borus & Duan, 2003), which should be relatively easy in this domain, since social media have been adopted by virtually every Internet user, irrespective of race, education, or health care access (Chou et al., 2009).

This is not to ignore the presence of a digital divide between those who have Internet access and those who do not. Rather, we acknowledge that while this discrepancy is shrinking (Hoffman, 2012), access to and use of the Internet will never be 100%. However, social media (and the Internet in general) have the capacity to provide health care information to consumers who were previously unable to access it, and, in some cases, answers to health-related questions to users who lack access to those answers in any other way. Those consumers who do not participate in social media—either involuntarily or by choice—may find themselves increasingly disempowered in a world where most consumers are online. Consumer empowerment involves six characteristics: "(1) presence of choices, (2) ability to participate, (3) provision of adequate information, (4) inculcation of positive attitudes, (5) possession of relevant skills, and (6) development of knowledge" (Kozinets, Belz, & McDonagh, 2012, p. 217). We believe that from this point forward, most prevention efforts will include substantial social media components to assist in the process of empowering consumers and proactively generating positive cultures.

Social Media and the Rogers Model

In 2002—the eve of the social media revolution—Rogers outlined five strategies that could speed the diffusion of preventive innovations:

1. Change the perceived attributes of preventive innovations.
2. Utilize champions to promote preventive innovations.
3. Change the norms of the system regarding preventive innovations through peer support.
4. Use entertainment-education to promote preventive innovations.
5. Activate peer networks to diffuse preventive innovations (2002).

Rogers made these recommendations to an audience that was familiar with traditional (i.e., one-way) Websites, e-mail, chat rooms, and instant messaging (such as AOL Instant Messenger), all precursors to truly collaborative social media. However, the technological revolution that generated Web 2.0—Websites that embraced two-way communication—had not really emerged yet. Friendster, which kicked off the social media revolution, launched in 2002; MySpace appeared in 2003, and Facebook emerged at Harvard in 2004, and to the public at large in 2005 (Boyd & Ellison, 2007).

Thus, Rogers's list, especially the last three recommendations, is remarkably prescient. One idea that he does not explicitly name, but that is a resulting boon of social media's popularity, is that users benefit from the trust, community, and reciprocity that can emerge within their networks, regardless of whether they are active participants or lurkers who consume, but don't contribute to their evolution (Hoffman, 2012). We will now examine each of his recommendations in light of existing prevention programs, consumer behavior theories, and the PCN framework.

Change the Perceived Attributes of Preventive Innovations

Because the ill effects of negative health-related behaviors often don't show up for years, or even decades (e.g., cancers, cirrhosis, children's cognitive delays), prevention managers must find the best ways to persuade people to believe that their messages are true and relevant. As such, changing the perceived attributes of preventive innovations—in Rogers's terms, demonstrating their advantages relative to the audience's current behaviors—is likely the most difficult step for prevention campaign managers to accomplish, irrespective of the medium used to deliver the message (Rogers, 2002). For example, research demonstrates that the early versions of the DARE

program (Drug Awareness Resistance Education) has not been successful in preventing children from using drugs when they get older (Rogers, 2002; Rotherham-Borus & Duan 2003), because the negative consequences of using drugs are not usually immediate for young users, and may not occur at all.

Social media provide an advantage to managers of all types of organizations (not just prevention campaigns), by allowing information to be presented in myriad ways that are customizable by its managers/moderators and the intended audience, to best suit their needs. Kozinets, Belz, and McDonagh write:

The online community…provided a place where a complex social issue could be boiled down to its most important constituent elements and then "baked in" to the elements of a reasonable, and reasonably viable, lifestyle. Much of the advice seems targeted to answer this sort of modern plea for consumption advice: "Tell me three things I need to know about what I am buying and two relatively easy things I can do or buy or help" (2012, p. 217).

Further supporting the idea of social media as an agent for positive change in consumers' perceptions of prevention attributes, social identity theory (Tajfel & Turner, 1979) explains that "people are more likely to identify with an organization when they perceive its identity to be enduring, distinctive, and capable of enhancing their self-esteem" (Sen and Bhattacharya, 2001, p. 228). This is a recurring finding within marketing and TCR research—that people connect with, and respond best to, groups/organizations that they perceive to be authentic and like themselves (Austin, Zinkhan, & Song, 2007; Bandura, 1977; Tajfel & Turner, 1979; Zaichkowsky, 1985). Thus, prevention-oriented groups should select social media channels that resonate with their own and their intended audience's values and goals. If they do not, they run the risk of seeming fake or like they are trying too hard, and their message is likely to be lost in the medium itself.

Prevention campaigns also have to be careful of potential boomerang effects (Wolburg, 2006). Teens' exposure to television ads from the National Youth Anti-Drug Media Campaign has been alarmingly associated with stronger perceptions that their peers were using marijuana, lower intentions to not use marijuana, and higher initiation of use. Evidence suggests that the campaign generated a meta-message that marijuana use was widespread among adolescents, which, in turn, stimulated an increase in youths' marijuana use (Orwin, Francisco, & Bernichon, 2001).

In addition, audience members of prevention campaigns may respond with reactance (Brehm, 1966), by counter-arguing with the message and digging in their heels. For example, when presented with anti-smoking messages (e.g., those produced by the Truth campaign) many smokers' response is to strengthen their resolve to smoke—the opposite effect of what the campaign intends (Miller et al., 2006; Witte, Meyer, & Martell, 2001). Researchers have identified psychological reactance (defensiveness) as a key predictor of success for antismoking message among adolescents (Witte, Meyer, & Martell, 2001).

One source of reactance and boomerang effects is the tendency of health communicators to focus on the negative consequences of risky behavior (Cho & Salmon, 2007; Guttman & Salmon, 2004). The PCN framework's focus on the positive factors in a community stems from lessons learned from ill-fated fear campaigns (such as DARE). PCN campaigns work to refocus public vision on the relative advantages of positive, healthy, normative behavior among the communities where they are applied. Because social media are, by definition, most effective when they connect and engage communities of like-minded people, they are extremely useful tools to help audiences focus on common goals and support each other's efforts to effect positive changes.

Utilize Champions to Promote Preventive Innovations

A prevention campaign's champion does not have to be a celebrity spokesperson (e.g., Jennifer Hudson for Weight Watchers); rather, a champion simply needs to be someone whom the audience perceives as trustworthy and influential, and who believes strongly in the message that is being promoted. Social media offer many different opportunities to champion prevention messages. Bloggers are perhaps the most obvious champions that prevention campaign managers can cultivate, since blogs can provide audiences with expert information and informed opinions; incorporate text, photos, and videos; provide channels for readers to give feedback, ask questions, and interact with each other; and can direct users to other Websites for further reading (Chou et al., 2009). Similarly, online group members with extensive knowledge and expertise frequently emerge as champions, or mavens, within online communities (Chou et al., 2009; Kozinets, 2002). Prevention managers can, and should, where appropriate, cultivate both official (bloggers, site moderators) and unofficial (audience members) as champions of their messages.

Evidence shows that in certain circumstances, people may actually prefer the anonymity of the Internet when discussing sensitive issues (e.g., high-risk behaviors, sexual health) (Rhodes, 2004). A prevention campaign that frequently provides the audience with a knowledgeable champion (for instance, during a regularly scheduled live chat session [Rhodes, 2004]), allows users to engage in a dialogue about the topic at hand without fear that the information they are receiving is inaccurate or untrue (Chou et al., 2009). Furthermore, in other interactive formats (e.g., discussion boards officially hosted and moderated by prevention campaigns), audience members can ask follow-up questions and discuss the topic at length within the forum until their knowledge and social needs are satisfied (Rhodes, 2004).

An established online community generates a spirit of trust and credibility among its members as they collaborate to solve problems and answer questions together (Mathwick, Wiertz, & de Ruyter, 2008). Participants in social media fall along a spectrum from complete strangers to good friends or family members, and champions can emerge anywhere along the spectrum. Research demonstrates that, historically, people have felt more comfortable seeking help from friends than from strangers, but this might be a factor of the social costs associated with asking for help—embarrassment and loss of esteem (Shapiro, 1980). Social media lower these costs, and as such, there is newer evidence that demonstrates that even people with weak ties are happy to help each other when they are participating as members of an online group (Constant, Sproull, & Kiesler, 1996).

Bandura's Social Learning and Social Cognitive Theories have long called for the use of positive, credible role models (i.e., champions) in the marketing of health messages (Bandura, 1986). According to Bandura, people need to like and identify with the speaker in order to achieve learning through role modeling. Rogers' early involvement in international entertainment-education campaigns leaned heavily on Bandura's model to communicate health behavior changes to Third World countries via popular TV and radio soap operas (Singhal & Rogers, 1999). More recently, Planned Parenthood Federation of America has used prominent social media content creators as champions to engage Web visitors on topics such as pregnancy prevention, STD prevention, and other health messages (Planned Parenthood Federation of America, 2012).

In addition to answering questions and providing information, the PCN framework calls upon champions, such as community leaders and prevention specialists, to pursue environment-level advocacy throughout the course of any prevention campaign they undertake. The model also recommends training community members—who can likewise be seen as program champions—to document the shifts in public perceptions and norms throughout the intervention process, and the transformation in community members' use of language specific to the intervention (MOST of Us, 2010). Such introspection and critical discussion (from the individual to the community level) are the two key components of change in Mezirow's Transformational Learning Theory (Mezirow, 1995; 1998; 2000; 2003), as well as in TCR research (Kozinets, Belz, & McDonagh, 2012) and the PCN framework.

Change the Norms of the System Regarding Preventive Innovations through Peer Support

In terms of social media, a Weblog that draws a high volume of comments on its posts, a Twitter feed with a large number of followers, and a YouTube video with millions of views all help generate the perception that the messages therein are normal, and are therefore normative (Cialdini, Reno, & Kallgren, 1990).

Many prevention campaigns are designed to help change people's perceptions and misperceptions of social norms. Social media can be used to provide peer support to help change descriptive and prescriptive norms related to health and well-being, at the individual and societal levels. When PCN-based prevention messages achieve critical mass, the behaviors they promote gradually become the new normal, replacing previous standards (Most of Us, 2012b). Often, PCN messages run counter to prevailing descriptive norms/stereotypes in the media, such as behaviors related to alcohol use (while driving, while pregnant, in excessive amounts) and teen sex.

In some cases, when mere mass approval is not enough to encourage people to follow social norms, people might need to rely on specific feedback from community members, or situational cues, to help them exert self-control and conform to pro-social behaviors (e.g., not smoking), since the fear of being caught can be a good motivator for people to follow social norms that they otherwise might choose to break (DeBono, Shmueli, & Muraven, 2011). This is one of the reasons that there is a ritual weigh-in at every Weight Watchers meeting—those members who have lost weight are rewarded with praise from their peers, while those who have not stuck to their diets will be "discovered" (Rotherham-Borus & Duan, 2003) by their group leaders. Social media can also help in these types of situations, as in using an online support group, posting a tweet or status update that solicits encouragement from others (e.g., "Help—I'm really craving a cigarette right now!"), or receiving frequent electronic inspiration and praise from a mentor or friend (e.g., in the form of text messages) (text4baby, 2012a).

The PCN process incorporates elements of the social norms approach. The social norms approach to prevention has emerged as a way of explaining and shaping human behavior based upon the powerful roles of perception (Perkins & Berkowitz, 1986) and meta-perception (Laing, Phillipson, & Lee, 1966). PCN seeks to change behavior by shifting common misperceptions of the normative behavior of their peers. Social norms studies have repeatedly found that people think risk-taking behavior is more prevalent than it actually is (Perkins, 2003). PCN campaigns and extensive social norms research have shown that if public misperceptions are corrected to reflect the actual, less risky, more protective behaviors and attitudes that are the norm in their communities, people are more likely to behave in accordance with those positive standards (Cialdini, 2003; Perkins, 2003).

Use Entertainment-Education to Promote Preventive Innovations

When people are having fun, or are otherwise highly involved with a persuasive message they are more likely to adopt a positive view of the product or idea that the message represents (Hol-brook & Hirschman, 1982; Zaichkowsky, 1985). One example of entertainment-education in use is a MOST Of Us project that focused on reducing tobacco use among teenagers. Preliminary focus groups indicated that the project needed to develop materials that were particularly engaging for high school audiences. One way the campaign's managers addressed this recommendation was to use feedback they received about their television and radio ads to stimulate additional conversation about the campaign.

Many of the students who saw the anti-smoking ads, posters, and other campaign materials didn't believe the information contained therein (which were challenging misperceptions of norms), and the teens were not shy about expressing their disbelief. Instead of becoming defensive, the developers of the campaign actually encouraged such critical dialogue, and developed a mini campaign about making fun of the original campaign. The new, funny marketing materials helped frame the conversations that the students were having amongst themselves about smoking, and these peer conversations consequently removed some of the disbelief/reactance to the original materials. In addition, conversations and meta-conversations about the campaign were not limited to the teen-aged audience, but also reached other levels of the social ecology including teachers, younger students, parents, and community members (MOST of Us, 2010).

Social media are notable for how fun they can be and how sticky their Websites are—how much time users can spend creating and consuming their contents. Thus, prevention campaigns should include social media tools that motivate the audience's positive affect towards the message by leveraging sticky, persuasive entertainment-education in their messaging. Not all messages lend themselves to humor and play, and social media tools allow messengers to find the tone that's most appropriate, for example, if the message itself is sad or disturbing (which is often the case in prevention campaigns).

Prevention campaigns can readily avail themselves of social media tools by using videos, photos, creative writing, music, lectures, games, graphics, role-playing, calculators, and more to engage their audiences and get their educational and persuasive messages across. Some of these innovations are more interactive than others—for example, allowing consumers to calculate the size of their carbon footprints using an avatar-based simulation (Global Footprint Network, 2012), rather than simply posting a video, or publishing an essay, or reprinting statistics, about personal energy usage.

Activate Peer Networks to Diffuse Preventive Innovations

The essence of social media is that people are constantly interacting with one another: collaborating, debating, creating and discussing content, sharing jokes, evaluating their environments, and soliciting feedback on the substance and fluff of their lives. As discussed above, consumer activities in the social media sphere lend themselves to prevention efforts as though they were invented expressly to do so. People are likely to share—pass along and/or link to—prevention messages that are highly salient to themselves (Visser & Mirabile, 2004), because it is human nature, and the nature of social media communications.

Social media are revolutionary because they enable people to share ideas with each other with very little friction, or loss of the idea's fidelity. With traditional, literal word-of-mouth communication, there is always the possibility that something will be lost in translation—something misheard, misremembered, and/or misunderstood. With social media, all users have to do to share an idea or a message is to click a link (or maybe a few), and the contents are perfectly reproduced for a new audience member. Online files are easily passed from one user to another, and most Websites now encourage users to do just that, using tools that link out to social media sites such

as Facebook, Twitter, Delicious, Flicker, and Linkedin. The speed with which popular content can reach enormous numbers of people was first demonstrated in 2005, when Carlton Draught's very funny "Big Ad" received one million page hits within two weeks of being launched online, thanks to friends e-mailing friends about it (Lee, 2005; Lees, 2005).

PCN calls on prevention leaders to activate peer networks when they pursue community change:

We need resources that address all members in a group (i.e., universal strategies), those members who are at-risk for a certain behavior (i.e., selected strategies), and interventions for individuals who are exhibiting the behavior (i.e., indicated populations)....PCN moves beyond a comprehensive paradigm (which is by definition deficit-based and focused on reducing the problem) to a holistic process of community leadership development. A holistic approach occurs when the many activities and efforts work together as a system in a synergistic way (Linkenbach & Otto, 2009, p. 7).

The PCN framework calls for prevention leaders to embrace all sectors of a community to work together towards reconfiguring perceptions of social norms. Members of each sector can then activate their peer networks in pursuit of more accurate perceptions of prescriptive norms, and work towards positive change. By providing a virtual arena where interrelated people, institutions, and communities can interact with and influence each other, social media foster environments where PCN interventions can potentially thrive.

Examples of Successful Social Media Educational Campaigns: Three Case Studies

The following case studies demonstrate how the Rogers framework and the PCN framework can be effective in real-life prevention situations. As far as we know, none of the three examples below used either of these models in their design, but nonetheless illustrate how effective their precepts can be.

Weight Watchers

Weight Watchers is an example of an older prevention program that has successfully adapted—and is currently thriving—in the social media paradigm. This for-profit organization has been in existence for 45 years, and uses evidence-based strategies to help its members lose weight and stay slim. Although the program supports individual-level goals, one of its "four pillars" of healthy weight loss is for members to support each other as they move towards greater health (Weight Watchers, 2012a).

In the non-social media model, Weight Watchers members gather weekly with each other and a trained group leader (who has successfully lost weight using the Weight Watchers program) for a private weigh-in and a group conversation. At meetings, members discuss their goals, their personal victories and challenges, and their strategies for accomplishing their weight-loss objectives.

Weight Watchers' community-based model has been shown to be extremely effective for achieving a healthy weight over the long term. An international study published in *The Lancet* in

October 2011 demonstrated that Weight Watchers participants lost twice as much weight as a control group whose weight loss was monitored by their primary care physicians (Jebb et al., 2011). This article, and dozens of others about weight loss and fitness, is archived on the Weight Watchers Website for members to read, and the evidence contained therein comes from prestigious international health and medical journals (Weight Watchers, 2012b).

Weight Watchers claims that "People who attend Weight Watchers meetings and use Weight Watchers eTools lose 50% more weight than those who attend meetings alone!" (Weight Watchers, 2012c) These social media tools include food and activity calculators, menu planners, progress trackers, videos, and a very active online community. In the community area of the Weight Watchers Website, members carry on online conversations through a variety of blogs, bulletin boards, and groups. They applaud each other's successes via a "celebration wall," and share recipes. They can search for other people like themselves with the Weight Watchers friend finder, and pose (or accept) challenges that encourage healthy long-term behavioral changes (such as eating more vegetables, or taking an activity-oriented vacation). See Table 1.

Table 1. Weight Watchers

Rogers's Model	PCN Model	Weight Watchers
Change perceived attributes	Messages support positive behavior	Presents the message that weight loss can be accomplished through consistent, incremental changes in lifestyle
Use of champions	Role models who exhibit positive behavior are featured	Group leaders, group members, bloggers, online community members
Change norms via peer support	Environmental advocacy conducted to build cross-sectoral partnerships	Meetings, message boards, recipe swapping
Use entertainment-education	Message development, pilot testing, and communications strategy are carefully planned	"Success Stories," blogs, planning tools, videos, "Science Center"
Peer network diffusion	Perceptions of social norms are shifted to initiate a snowball effect	Internal Website encourages significant interaction among members, extremely easy to share info via social media tools (provided by Weight Watchers)

It Gets Better

Another outstanding example of how social media can be used to create an effective, highly interactive prevention campaign is the It Gets Better project (It Gets Better Project, 2012a). It Gets Better was started by advice columnist Dan Savage in September 2010, as a deeply felt personal response to a rash of suicides among gay teenagers. Savage, who is gay, created and posted a video of himself and his husband, Terry Miller, talking about how difficult life was for them growing up gay, and promising the audience that "it gets better" (It Gets Better Project, 2012b).

The project was an immediate success as a social media prevention effort: by the end of 2010, it had inspired 10,000 people to create and upload their own testimonies, which can be viewed on the project's Website and on YouTube. These videos include encouragement and wisdom from popular entertainers, religious leaders, and politicians (including Barack Obama), but the overwhelming majority are from average people who want to make a positive difference in teenagers' lives. These videos had been watched more than 30 million times within six months of the project's launch (It Gets Better Project, 2012c).

Also on the project's Website are a blog (which contains information related to the Project, and allows readers to comment), an event calendar (which allows users to find events and/or post their own), instructions on how audience members can make and post their own videos, share links to Facebook and Twitter, its own Twitter feed, information on where suicidal teens can get help, a merchandise order form (for t-shirts and the *It Gets Better* book, published in March, 2011), and a pledge form (where audience members submit their names, zip codes, and e-mail addresses— ostensibly to build a user database).

The cumulative effect of all these social media tools being marshaled in support of a single cause is truly revolutionary. The campaign manages to be simultaneously public, and intensely personal.

Audience members can use the site's resources as much as they need to, and disclose as little (or as much) as they want to the site's administrators. Users who upload videos are encouraged to include tags (e.g., "Christian," "lesbian," "Nebraska") so that teens searching for a closer feeling of connection can find messages from people who really understand their individual circumstances. Because it is so new in the marketplace of ideas, there are no data available regarding its effectiveness as a prevention tool. As a social media campaign, however, it is clearly a success, in terms of inspiring users to create and upload their own content, to interact with each other, and to feel like they are a part of a genuine community of spirit and intent. Furthermore, its messages of hope and tolerance are amplified throughout the social media environment because they are echoed by similar organizations, such as The Trevor Project (2012) and The We Got Your Back Project (2012). See Table 2.

text4baby

The text4baby program is an example of a mobile media-based prevention campaign that uses weekly text messaging to provide information and support to expectant and new mothers (text4baby, 2012a). Participants receive three text messages per week—either in English or Spanish—which are targeted specifically to the gestational/actual age of the child (up to 1 year). From the program's Website:

These messages focus on a variety of topics critical to your health and the health of your baby, including immunization (shots), nutrition, seasonal flu, prenatal care, emotional well-being, drugs and alcohol, labor and delivery, stopping smoking, breastfeeding, mental health, birth defects prevention, oral health, car seat safety, exercise and fitness, developmental milestones, safe sleep, family violence, and more (text4baby, 2012b).

Table 2. It Gets Better

Rogers's Model	PCN Model	It Gets Better Project
Change perceived attributes	Messages support positive behavior	Presents twinned messages: "Life gets better," and "You are not alone"
Use of champions	Role models who exhibit positive behavior are featured	Dan Savage, celebrities, *plus* each person who uploads a video of his/her own
Change norms via peer support	Environmental advocacy conducted to build cross-sectoral partnerships	Searchable tags allow users to find others like themselves, or who they'd like to emulate
Use entertainment-education	Message development, pilot testing, and communications strategy are carefully planned	Videos run the gamut: they're funny, moving, uplifting, thought-provoking – very sticky
Peer network diffusion	Perceptions of social norms are shifted to initiate a snowball effect	All information is online and extremely easy to share via social media tools

The program, which launched in February 2010 and signed up over 130,000 users in its first year (Centers for Disease Control and Prevention, 2012), is designed to improve prenatal and infant health outcomes in the United States, especially in reducing infant mortality rates. It is a partnership of the National Healthy Mothers, Healthy Babies Coalition (2012), The Wireless Foundation (2012), and hundreds of other organizations, including the White House Office of Science and Technology Policy, the U.S. Department of Health and Human Services, Johnson & Johnson, Pfizer, Blue Cross Blue Shield, and MTV (text4baby, 2012c). The content of the messages is provided by the Centers for Disease Control and Prevention, but the tone of the messages is friendly, rather than scientific, in order to increase audience members' receptivity (i.e., reduce reactance) to the advice that they are receiving (Bornstein, 2011).

The program's Website encourages text4baby users to join them on Facebook and Twitter, and to encourage other potential audience members to do the same.

The program now has a YouTube channel where both campaign partners and text4baby participating parents can upload videos. "Share your story with us!" the Website urges its visitors (text4baby, 2012d). For those audience members who might not have access to video equipment, text4baby has developed what it calls a Legacy Program that lends cameras and editing software for up to two weeks to participants (both individuals and groups) in order to achieve a more interesting and intimate social media presence through the use of first-person video testimonials (text4baby, 2012e).

Like the It Gets Better project, text4baby is so new that there is little data available to determine how successfully it has affected maternal and newborn health outcomes. However, there are currently six projects in progress that are evaluating the program, and initial indicators show that users are overwhelmingly satisfied with their participation—96% said that they would recommend the program to a pregnant friend or family member. As a result, the program announced in November 2010 that they had set a goal of reaching one million expectant and new mothers by 2012 (text4baby, 2012f). A preliminary study conducted by researchers at California State University, San Marcos reports, "high satisfaction with the service and an increase in users' health knowledge, improved interaction with healthcare providers, improved adherence to appointments and, immunizations and increased access to health resources" (Vaughan, 2011). See Table 3.

Table 3. text4baby

Rogers's Model	PCN Model	It Gets Better Project
Change perceived attributes	Messages supportive of positive behavior	Presents message – via quick tips – that prenatal and baby care are relatively easy and straightforward
Use of champions	Role models who exhibit positive behavior are featured	National and regional sponsors, plus users uploading video, and joining on Facebook and Twitter
Change norms via peer support	Environmental advocacy conducted to build cross-sectoral partnerships	Using subscribers to spread the message to others
Use entertainment-education	Message development, pilot testing, and communications strategy are carefully planned	Friendly tone, user-created videos, Facebook page
Peer network diffusion	Perceptions of social norms are shifted to enact a snowball effect	Information is online and extremely easy to share via social media tools, Outreach Partners

SOLUTIONS AND RECOMMENDATIONS

Managers of prevention campaigns must be careful when entering the social media fray, since there is a definite possibility that they could lose control of their message, thereby diminishing or entirely wiping out the positive effects they are trying to create. Audience members of a campaign can use a variety of commonly available social media tools to put their own twists on the message if they choose (Aubert-Gamet & Cova, 1997), resulting in a larger meta-message that has more impact than the original, intended idea does. These twists can be malicious, or humorous, or angry, and they can take on a life of their own.

Being top-down in a prevention message's design and delivery is particularly detrimental to achieving PCN goals. Messages produced by judgmental authors are inherently likely to alienate audiences, discourage hope, and re-enforce defensive reactions. As with adolescents reacting to parents, audiences who are judged harshly are likely to do the opposite of what they are told. The boomerang effect, a term coined by psychologists Hovland, Janis, and Kelly, refers to the reaction by an audience that is opposite to the intended response of persuasion messages (Hovland, Janis, & Kelly, 1953).

As such, prevention managers also need to carefully choose which tools and messages they will control, and which they should open up for their audiences to manipulate. While encouraging interactivity—which makes Websites much stickier, and therefore more effective in delivering their messages—campaign managers should be aware of the fact that it is possible for organizations (not just prevention-oriented ones) to lose control of the medium and/or the messages that they are trying to send. Therefore, these organizations need to carefully consider their choice of media, and the communication options that they choose to offer their audience members (e.g., message boards, consumer-generated content, etc.). Even a tool as basic and well established as the comments section on a blog, a Website, or YouTube, can leave the site's owners vulnerable to undesired responses and attention. Internet trolls are people who purposely stir up controversy for its own sake by posting inflammatory remarks on sites where they know they are likely to draw impassioned arguments from loyal community members.

Comments sections can also inspire readers to compete with each other to come up with the cleverest parodies of the original material. Creative consumers can generate quite a bit of buzz online by devising parody displays of popular messages. YouTube, Blogger, and other social media sites allow administrators the option of moderating comments, or turning them off completely, in order to prevent comments from becoming mean, personal, or off-topic. However, while controlling the medium is essential for any organization's online administrator, another pitfall that promotion campaign managers should avoid when using social media, is trying *too* hard to control consumer input to their sites.

Users' comments and parodies of an organization's messages (and image) are very useful feedback—an invaluable source of information about whether the messages are being heard, understood, and heeded, and if so, by whom. Engaging in an ongoing conversation with one's audience is much more likely to result in a positive outcome than will fighting with them, or shutting them down. However, sometimes audience members are not interested in arguing about an organization's message; they simply want to make fun of an easy target.

This problem is not limited to social media; in fact, making fun of prevention campaigns has been popular for decades, as evidenced by the poster in Figure 1—a parody of the Partnership for a Drug Free America's 1987 television spot (Amazon.com, 2012).

If the original message is not drowned out by the parody message (e.g., being shown to be silly, or out-of-touch, or insincere), parody can actually increase attention to an organization's message, ultimately drawing a larger audience and giving the idea greater impact than originally expected. Prevention organizations need to monitor—without suppressing—the buzz around their social media offerings and analyze what people are saying to see if any criticism is valid feedback that can be used to fine-tune the site's contents or the organization's image.

Figure 1. Drug prevention poster

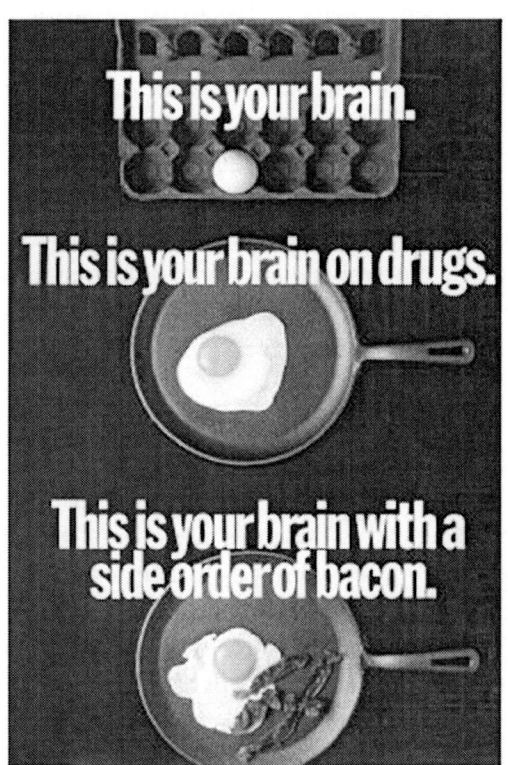

FUTURE RESEARCH DIRECTIONS

Despite the many promising aspects of PCN as a framework for organizing and implementing health behavior change through social media at the individual and community levels, there are certainly some limitations. Most prominent is the absence of empirical data on which to base PCN recommendations.

More research is needed to explore social media activities that attempt to change environments around risky health practices. Such research could capture or codify improvements to the environment in policies and regulations (i.e., laws). A holistic approach, modeled after PCN, would involve many different activities and efforts working throughout a community. More pilot studies and randomized control trials involving PCN-framed social media are needed to test the premises put forth in this article.

More data are needed to explain the role of environmental factors in health risk behavior, and the complexity of risk in society. More work is also needed to learn how to reduce the blame that is placed on risk populations and to move toward policies and actions that correct misperceptions and encourage positive health. Prevention campaigns that use social media approaches to address positive, cultural and environmental approaches must be created that are based on findings of the research described above.

CONCLUSION

It bears repeating that in terms of social ecology, it takes an entire community to diffuse and implement a prevention intervention in order for it to be effective. Due to its ecological nature, many of the factors that PCN proposes to address are hard to operationalize and measure. The broader an intervention is, the more difficult it becomes to monitor. For PCN, the broad scope is further complicated by an emphasis on transformative processes that may change the nature of what is being studied during the course of a study. Quite possibly, this framework does not lend itself to traditional evaluation paradigms; its interactive and circular nature does not easily fit into linear logic models. New evaluation methods may be needed to measure PCN social media interventions that borrow from ethnography, chaos theory, participatory action research, and other fields of study.

Multi-sectoral support is needed to employ a new paradigm such as PCN, and to overcome cultural resistance to transformational leadership, new definitions of interventions, and long-term models of change. This type of support could help overcome the political, cultural, and financial resistance mentioned above. Any intervention or model of change that looks at systemic causes of behavior and health will be difficult to achieve and will require courageous leadership.

Applying a systemic model of change to new media presents additional challenges. All users of social media, from individuals to multinational corporations, must figure out how much access to give to other users—a delicate balancing act for entities who are trying to achieve the simultaneous goals of reaching out, being inclusive, and retaining control of their messaging. Full access for everyone means there is greater risk that a message could be misinterpreted, misapplied, or parodied. Limiting access to only approved audiences runs the risk that the organization will be perceived by the public as being insincere about wanting to interact with them. Limiting access also means that the message will go unheard by unidentified segments of potential beneficiaries (i.e., those consumers whom the campaign's managers do not realize would benefit from being included), or by potential audience members who do not respond to traditional outreach methods, but could find the material if it were freely available when they sought it out on their own.

However, in spite of the above limitations, TCR holds tremendous potential when combined with a PCN framework in proactively cultivating positive cultures through social media use. In the era of Facebook, Twitter, YouTube, Blogger, and other social media platforms, people have the ability to cultivate positive cultures through teaching and learning, and supporting and critiquing each other. This hope for a healthier world deserves further exploration.

ACKNOWLEDGMENT

The authors wish to give special thanks to Rilla Esbjornson for copy editing this chapter.

REFERENCES

Amazon.com. (2012). *This is your brain on 80s.* Retrieved April 4, 2012, from http://www.amazon.com/Brain-Drugs-Bacon-Poster-Print/dp/B000R2LTTW

Atkinson, N. L., Saperstein, S. L., & Pleis, J. (2009). Using the Internet for health-related activities: Findings from a national probability sample. *Journal of Medical Internet Research, 11*(1), e4. doi:10.2196/jmir.1035 PMID:19275980.

Aubert-Gamet, V., & Cova, B. (1997, April). *Exit, voice, loyalty and twist: consumer research in search of the subject.* Paper presented at the European Institute for Advanced Studies in Management Workshop on Interpretive Consumer Research, Oxford, England.

Austin, C. G., Zinkhan, G. M., & Song, J. H. (2007). Peer-to-peer media opportunities. In Tellis, G. J., & Ambler, T. (Eds.), *The SAGE Handbook of Advertising* (pp. 349–365). London: Sage Publications Ltd. doi:10.4135/9781848607897.n22.

Bandura, A. (1977). Self-efficacy: Toward a unifying theory of behavioral change. *Psychological Review, 84*(2), 191–215. doi:10.1037/0033-295X.84.2.191 PMID:847061.

Bandura, A. (1986). *Social Foundations of Thought and Action.* Englewood Cliffs, NJ: Prentice-Hall.

Bornstein, D. (2011). Mothers-to-be are getting the message. *New York Times.* Retrieved February 7, 2011, from http://opinionator.blogs.nytimes.com/2011/02/07/pregnant-mothers-are-getting-the-message

Boyd, D. M., & Ellison, N. B. (2007). Social network sites: Definition, history, and scholarship. *Journal of Computer-Mediated Communication, 13*(1), 210–230. doi:10.1111/j.1083-6101.2007.00393.x.

Brehm, J. W. (1966). *A Theory of Psychological Reactance.* New York: Academic Press.

Bronfenbrenner, U. (1979). *The Ecology of Human Development: Experiments by Nature and Design.* Cambridge, MA: Harvard University Press.

Brown, J. D., & Bobkowski, P. S. (2011). Older and newer media: Patterns of use and effects on adolescents' health and well-being. *Journal of Research on Adolescence, 21*(1), 95–113. doi:10.1111/j.1532-7795.2010.00717.x.

Centers for Disease Control and Prevention. (2012). *Are you pregnant or a new mom?* Retrieved April 2, 2012, from http://www.cdc.gov/Features/Text4Baby

Cho, H., & Salmon, C. (2007). Unintended effects of health communication campaigns. *The Journal of Communication, 57*(2), 293–317. doi:10.1111/j.1460-2466.2007.00344.x.

Chou, W. S., Hunt, Y. M., Beckjord, E. B., Moser, R. P., & Hesse, B. W. (2009). Social media use in the United States: Implications for health communication. *Journal of Medical Internet Research, 11*(4), e48. doi:10.2196/jmir.1249 PMID:19945947.

Cialdini, R. B. (2003). Crafting normative messages to protect the environment. *Current Directions in Psychological Science, 12*(4), 105–109. doi:10.1111/1467-8721.01242.

Cialdini, R. B., Reno, R. R., & Kallgren, C. A. (1990). A focus theory of normative conduct: Recycling the concept of norms to reduce littering in public places. *Journal of Personality and Social Psychology, 58*(6), 1015–1026. doi:10.1037/0022-3514.58.6.1015.

Constant, D., Sproull, L., & Kiesler, S. (1996). The kindness of strangers: The usefulness of electronic weak ties for technical advice. *Organization Science, 7*(2), 119–135. doi:10.1287/orsc.7.2.119.

DeBono, A., Shmueli, D., & Muraven, M. (2011). Rude and inappropriate: The role of self-control in following social norms. *Personality and Social Psychology Bulletin, 37*(1), 136–146. doi:10.1177/0146167210391478 PMID:21177879.

Dellarocas, C. (2003). The digitization of word of mouth: Promises and challenges of online feedback mechanisms. *Management Science, 49*(10), 1407–1424. doi:10.1287/mnsc.49.10.1407.17308.

Global Footprint Network. (2012). *Personal footprint*. Retrieved April 2, 2012, from http://www.footprintnetwork.org/en/index.php/GFN/page/personal_footprint

Guttman, N., & Salmon, C. T. (2004). Guilt, fear, stigma and knowledge gaps: Ethical issues in public health communication interventions. *Bioethics, 18*(6), 531–553. doi:10.1111/j.1467-8519.2004.00415.x PMID:15580723.

Hayes, G., & Papworth, L. (2008). *The future of social media entertainment*. Paper presented at the Screen Producers Association of Australia Fringe. Sydney, Australia.

Hoffman, D. L. (2012). Internet indispensability, online social capital, and consumer well-being. In Mick, D. G., Pettigrew, S., Pechmann, C., & Ozanne, J. L. (Eds.), *Transformative Consumer Research for Personal and Collective Well-being* (pp. 193–204). New York: Routledge.

Holbrook, M. B., & Hirschman, E. C. (1982). The experiential aspects of consumption: Consumer fantasies, feelings, and fun. *The Journal of Consumer Research, 9*(2), 132–140. doi:10.1086/208906.

Honan, E. (2008). Web site allows anonymous warnings of STD infections. Retrieved February 14, 2008, from http://www.reuters.com/article/2008/02/14/us-syphilis-website-idUSN1419876020080214

Hovland, C. I., Janis, I. L., & Kelly, H. H. (1953). *Communication and Persuasion: Psychological Studies of Opinion Change*. New Haven, CT: Yale University Press.

http://www.text4baby.org/index.php/about/partners

It Gets Better Project. (2012a). *It Gets Better Project | Give hope to LGBT youth*. Retrieved April 2, 2012, from http://www.itgetsbetter.org/

It Gets Better Project. (2012b). *It Gets Better Project: Dan and Terry*. Retrieved September 18, 2012, from http://www.itgetsbetter.org/#7IcVyvg2Qlo

It Gets Better Project. (2012c). *What is the It Gets Better Project?* Retrieved September 18, 2012, from http://www.itgetsbetter.org/pages/about-it-gets-better-project/

Jebb, S. A., Ahern, A. L., Olson, A. D., Aston, L. M., Holzapfel, C., Stoll, J., & Caterson, I. D. (2011). Primary care referral to a commercial provider for weight loss treatment versus standard care: A randomised controlled trial. *Lancet, 378*(9801), 1485–1492. doi:10.1016/S0140-6736(11)61344-5 PMID:21906798.

Jones, K. (2011). Effect of social media intervention on chlamydia incidence when compared with no formalized Internet instruction. *Western Journal of Nursing Research, 33*(8), 1114–1115. doi:10.1177/0193945911413677.

Kaplan, A. M., & Haenlein, M. (2010). Users of the world, unite! The challenges and opportunities of social media. *Business Horizons, 53*, 59–68. doi:10.1016/j.bushor.2009.09.003.

Kozinets, R. V. (2002). The field behind the screen: Using netnography for marketing research in online communities. *JMR, Journal of Marketing Research, 39*(1), 61–72. doi:10.1509/jmkr.39.1.61.18935.

Kozinets, R. V., Belz, F. M., & McDonagh, P. (2012). Social media for social change: A transformative consumer research perspective. In Mick, D. G., Pettigrew, S., Pechmann, C., & Ozanne, J. L. (Eds.), *Transformative Consumer Research for Personal and Collective Well-being* (pp. 205–223). New York: Routledge.

Laing, R. D., Phillipson, H., & Lee, A. R. (1966). *Interpersonal Perception: A Theory and a Method of Research*. New York: Springer.

Lee, J. (2005). Very big ad shows why we still call Carlton a beer. *The Sydney Morning Herald*, Business, July 29, p. 28.

Lees, N. (2005). Big ad hits one millionth viewer. *AdNews*. Retrieved June 30, 2007, from http://www.AdNews.com.au

Levine, D., McCright, J., Dobkin, L., Woodruff, A., & Klausner, J. (2008). SexInfo: A sexual health text messaging service for San Francisco youth. *American Journal of Public Health*, 98(3), 393–395. doi:10.2105/AJPH.2007.110767 PMID:18235068.

Linkenbach, J., & Otto, J. (2009). *The Positive Community Norms Overview*. Bozeman, MT: The Montana Institute.

Linkenbach, J. W. (2006). *How to Use Social Norms Marketing to Prevent Driving After Drinking: A MOST Of US® Toolkit. MOST of Us® Institute*. MT: Bozeman.

Mathwick, C., Wiertz, C., & de Ruyter, K. (2008). Social capital production in a virtual P3 community. *The Journal of Consumer Research*, 34(6), 832–849. doi:10.1086/523291.

Mezirow, J. (1995). Transformation theory of adult learning. In Welton, M. R. (Ed.), *Defense of the Life-world* (pp. 39–70). Albany, NY: State University of New York Press.

Mezirow, J. (1998). On critical reflection. *Adult Education Quarterly*, 48(3), 185–191. doi:10.1177/074171369804800305.

Mezirow, J. (2000). Learning to think like an adult: Core concepts of transformation theory. In Mezirow, J. et al. (Eds.), *Learning as Transformation* (pp. 3–34). San Francisco, CA: Jossey-Bass.

Mezirow, J. (2003). Transformative learning as discourse. *Journal of Transformative Education*, 1(1), 58–63. doi:10.1177/1541344603252172.

Mick, D. G. (2006). Presidential address: Meaning and mattering through transformative consumer research. *Advances in Consumer Research. Association for Consumer Research (U. S.)*, 33, 1–4.

Miller, C. H., Burgoon, M., Grandpre, J. R., & Alvaro, E. M. (2006). Identifying principal risk factors for the initiation of adolescent smoking behaviors: The significance of psychological reactance. *Health Communication*, 19(3), 241–252. doi:10.1207/s15327027hc1903_6 PMID:16719727.

Mills, J., & Bogenschneider, K. (2001). Can communities assess support for preventing adolescent alcohol and other drug use? Reliability and validity of a community assessment inventory. *Family Relations*, 50(4), 355–375. doi:10.1111/j.1741-3729.2001.00355.x.

MOST of Us. (2010). *The Positive Community Norms Workbook*. Bozeman, MT: The Montana Institute.

MOST of Us. (2012a). *What is Social Norms Marketing?* Retrieved May 16, 2012, from http://www.mostofus.org/about-us/what-is-social-norms-marketing/

MOST of Us. (2012b). *What is the Positive Community Norms Model?* Retrieved September 18, 2012, from http://www.mostofus.org/about-us/what-is-the-positive-community-

National Healthy Mothers. Healthy Babies Coalition. (2012). You're pregnant! *National Healthy Mothers, Healthy Babies Coalition.* Retrieved April 2, 2012, from http://www.hmhb.org/pregnant.html

Orwin, R. G., Francisco, L., & Bernichon, T. (2001). *Effectiveness of Women's Substance Abuse Treatment Programs: A Meta-analysis,* (NEDS Contract No. 270–97–7016), Substance Abuse and Mental Health Services Administration (SAMHSA), Center for Substance Abuse Treatment, Arlington, VA.

Perkins, H. W. (Ed.). (2003). *The Social Norms Approach to Preventing School and College Age Substance Abuse: A Handbook For Educators, Counselors, and Clinicians.* San Francisco, CA: Jossey-Bass.

Perkins, H. W., & Berkowitz, A. D. (1986). Perceiving the community norms of alcohol use among students: some research implications for campus alcohol education programming. *Substance Use & Misuse, 21*(9-10), 961–976. doi:10.3109/10826088609077249 PMID:3793315.

Planned Parenthood Federation of America. (2012). Retrieved April 2, 2012, from http://www.ppfa.org

Project. Retrieved September 18, 2012, from http://www.thetrevorproject.org

Rhodes, S. D. (2004). Hookups or health promotion? An exploratory study of a chat room-based HIV prevention intervention for men who have sex with men. *AIDS Education and Prevention, 16*(4), 315–327. doi:10.1521/aeap.16.4.315.40399 PMID:15342334.

Rogers, E. M. (2002). Diffusion of preventive innovations. *Addictive Behaviors, 27*(6), 989–993. doi:10.1016/S0306-4603(02)00300-3 PMID:12369480.

Rotherham-Borus, M. J., & Duan, N. (2003). Next generation of preventive interventions. *Journal of the American Academy of Child and Adolescent Psychiatry, 42*(5), 518–526. doi:10.1097/01.CHI.0000046836.90931.E9 PMID:12707555.

Sen, S., & Bhattacharya, C. B. (2001). Does doing good always lead to doing better? Consumer reactions to corporate social responsibility. *JMR, Journal of Marketing Research, 38*(2), 225–243. doi:10.1509/jmkr.38.2.225.18838.

Shapiro, E. G. (1980). Is seeking help from a friend like seeking help from a stranger? *Social Psychology Quarterly, 43*(2), 259–263. doi:10.2307/3033629.

Singhal, A., & Rogers, E. M. (1999). *Entertainment-education: A Communication Strategy for Social Change.* Mahwah, NJ: Lawrence Erlbaum.

Tajfel, H., & Turner, J. C. (1979). An integrative theory of intergroup conflict. In Austin, W. G., & Worchel, S. (Eds.), *The Social Psychology of Intergroup Relations* (pp. 33–47). Monterey, CA: Brooks/Cole.

text4baby. (2012a). Retrieved May 15, 2012, from http://text4baby.org

text4baby. (2012b). *text4baby –FAQ.* Retrieved May 15, 2012, from http://www.text4baby.org/index.php/about/faq

text4baby. (2012c). *text4baby – Who Involved.* Retrieved May 15, 2012, from

text4baby. (2012d). *text4baby – Get Involved.* Retrieved May 15, 2012, from http://www.text4baby.org/index.php/get-involved-pg

text4baby. (2012e). *text4baby – Legacy Camera Program.* Retrieved May 15, 2012, from http://www.text4baby.org/index.php/get-involved-pg/2-uncategorised/165

text4baby. (2012f). *News – text4baby.* Retrieved March 19, 2011, from http://www.text4baby.org/news/t4b_comprehensive_platform.html

The Trevor Project. (2012). *Preventing Suicide Amond LGBTQ Youth | The Trevor*

The We Got Your Back Project. (2012). Retrieved May 15, 2012, from http://wegotyourbackproject. wordpress.com

The Wireless Foundation. (2012). *CTIA The Wireless Foundation*. Retrieved May 15, 2012, from http://wirelessfoundation.org/Home.aspx

Turkle, S. (2011). *Alone Together: Why We Expect More From Technology and Less From Each Other*. New York: Basic Books.

Vaughan, C. (2011). San Diego researchers first to report positive impact of Text4Baby program. Retrieved March 4, 2012, from http://www.text-4baby.org/index.php/news/180-sdpressrelease

Visser, P. S., & Mirabile, R. R. (2004). Attitudes in the social context: The impact of social network composition on individual-level attitude strength. *Journal of Personality and Social Psychology*, *87*(6), 779–795. doi:10.1037/0022-3514.87.6.779 PMID:15598106.

Watkins, K. E., & Marsick, V. J. (1999). Sculpting the learning community: New forms of working and organizing. *National Association of Secondary School Principals Bulletin*, *83*(604), 78–88.

Weight Watchers. (2012a). *The Four Pillars: Supportive Atmosphere*. Retrieved September 18, 2012, from http://www.weightwatchers.com/util/art/index_art.aspx?tabnum=4&art_id

Weight Watchers. (2012b). *Weightwatchers.com: Science Center*. Retrieved September 18, 2012, from http://www.weightwatchers.com/health/sciencecenter/index.aspx

Weight Watchers. (2012c). *Weightwatchers.com: Monthly Pass*. Retrieved September 18, 2012, from http://www.weightwatchers.com/monthlypass/index.aspx

Witte, K., Meyer, G., & Martell, D. (2001). *Effective Health Risk Messages: A Step-by-step Guide*. Thousand Oaks, CA: Sage Publications.

Wolburg, J. M. (2006). College students' responses to antismoking messages: Denial, defiance, and other boomerang effects. *The Journal of Consumer Affairs*, *40*(2), 294–323. doi:10.1111/j.1745-6606.2006.00059.x.

Zaichkowsky, J. L. (1985). Measuring the involvement construct. *The Journal of Consumer Research*, *12*(3), 341–352. doi:10.1086/208520.

ADDITIONAL READING

Anderson, R., & Braud, W. (2011). *Transforming Self and Others Through Research*. Albany, NY: State University of New York Press.

Bhattacharya, C. B., & Korschun, D. (2008). Stakeholder marketing: beyond the four Ps and the customer. *Journal of Public Policy & Marketing*, *27*(1), 113–116. doi:10.1509/jppm.27.1.113.

Block, P. (2003). *The Answer to How is Yes*. San Francisco, CA: Berrett-Koehler Publishers.

Block, P. (2009). *Community: The Structure of Belonging*. San Francisco, CA: Berrett-Koehler Publishers.

Carpenter, C., & Pechmann, C. (2011). Exposure to 'Above the Influence' anti-drug advertisements and youth marijuana use in the US, 2006-2008. *American Journal of Public Health*, *101*(5), 948–954. doi:10.2105/AJPH.2010.300040 PMID:21421952.

Feldman, S. R. (2009). *Compartments: How the Brightest, Best Trained, and Most Caring People Can Make Judgments that are Completely and Utterly Wrong*. Bloomington, IN: Xlibris Corporation.

Glassner, B. (2010). *The Culture Of Fear: Why Americans are Afraid of the Wrong Things: Crime, Drugs, Minorities, Teen Moms, Killer Kids, Mutant Microbes, Plane Crashes, Road Rage, & So Much More*. New York: Basic Books.

Hammond, S. A. (1998). *The Thin Book of Appreciative Inquiry*. Bend, OR: Thin Book Publishing Company.

Kotler, P., & Lee, N. R. (2008). *Social Marketing: Influencing Behaviors for Good*. Thousand Oaks, CA: Sage Publications, Inc..

Kretzmann, J. P., & McKnight, J. L. (1993). *Building Communities from the Inside Out*. Skokie, IL: ACTA Publications.

Mari, C. (2008). Doctoral education and transformative consumer research. *Journal of Marketing Education*, *30*(1), 5–11. doi:10.1177/0273475307312194.

McKnight, J. (1996). *The Careless Society: Community and its Counterfeits*. New York: Basic Books.

Ozanne, J. L., & Anderson, L. (2010). Community Action Research. *Journal of Public Policy & Marketing*, *29*(1), 123–137. doi:10.1509/jppm.29.1.123.

Ozanne, J. L., & Saatcioglu, B. (2008). Participatory Action Research. *The Journal of Consumer Research*, *35*(3), 423–439. doi:10.1086/586911.

Pechmann, C., Biglan, A., Grube, J. W., & Cody, C. (2012). Transformative consumer research for addressing tobacco and alcohol consumption. In Mick, D., Pettigrew, S., Pechmann, C., & Ozanne, J. (Eds.), *Transformative Consumer Research for Personal and Collective Well Being: Reviews and Frontiers* (pp. 353–389). New York: Routledge.

Pechmann, C., & Knight, S. J. (2002). An experimental investigation of the joint effects of advertising and peers on adolescents' beliefs and intentions about cigarette consumption. *The Journal of Consumer Research*, *29*(1), 5–19. doi:10.1086/339918.

Pechmann, C., & Wang, L. (2010). Effects of indirectly and directly competing reference group messages and persuasion knowledge: Implications for educational placements. *JMR, Journal of Marketing Research*, *47*(1), 134–145. doi:10.1509/jmkr.47.1.134.

Petkus, E. (2010). Incorporating transformative consumer research into the consumer behavior course experience. *Journal of Marketing Education*, *32*(3), 292–299. doi:10.1177/0273475310377784.

Scammon, D. L., Keller, P. A., Albinsson, P. A., Bahl, S., Catlin, J. R., & Schindler, R. M. (2011). Transforming consumer health. *Journal of Public Policy & Marketing*, *30*(1), 14–22. doi:10.1509/jppm.30.1.14.

KEY TERMS AND DEFINITIONS

Community: A group of people who are connected to each other in some significant way, and who hold some/all values in common.

Health Promotion: The institutionalized support of environments and communities that allow people to improve their own and others' physical and mental health.

Peer-to-Peer (or Word-Of Mouth) Communication: The transfer of information from one person to another.

Perception of Norms: People's beliefs about what behaviors are acceptable among the majority of members of their community. These beliefs are not always correct.

Positive Community Norms (PCN) Framework: A process that promotes both individual health behavior change, and transformation across the socio-ecological continuum, based on a synthesis of existing theories from health education, community psychology, social psychology, and education.

Prevention: The process of proactively cultivating positive cultures through transformational leadership, communications, and an integrated portfolio of strategies.

Social Ecology Theory: The understanding that individual people and a variety of internal and external contextual factors interact to create the physical and cultural community in which people live.

Social Media: Interactive Web-based applications that allow users to create and share electronic content.

Social Norms: A society's expectations of behavior for its members.

Section 2
User Behaviors in Social Media

Chapter 3
Personality and Social Media Use

Teresa Correa
Diego Portales University, Chile

Ingrid Bachmann
Pontificia Universidad Católica de Chile, Chile

Amber W. Hinsley
St. Louis University, USA

Homero Gil de Zúñiga
University of Texas at Austin, USA

ABSTRACT

Research on digital media has mostly paid attention to users' demographics, motivations, and efficacy, but with increasingly popular web tools like social media, it is important to study more stable psychological characteristics such as users' personality traits, as they may significantly affect how people use the Web to communicate and socialize. Relying on the "Big Five Framework" as a theoretical approach, this chapter explores such relationships. Survey data from a national sample of U.S. adults show that more extraverted people are more likely to use social networking sites, instant messaging, and video chats, while those more open to new experiences tend to use social networking sites more frequently. Also, emotional stability is a negative predictor of social networking site use. That is, individuals who are more anxious and unstable tend to rely on these sites. When looking at a specific use of social media–to create political content—emotional stability was a negative predictor, whereas extraversion had a positive impact. These findings confirm the usefulness of combining explorations of personality and digital media usage.

DOI: 10.4018/978-1-4666-4026-9.ch003

INTRODUCTION

The evolution of the Web increasingly opens more opportunities and spaces for people to interact, socialize, promote their work, create, and share material online. By early 2012, 48 hours of video were uploaded every minute to YouTube (YouTube, 2012). In 2011 the number of people in the U.S. using a social networking site had doubled from 2008; nearly half of adults and 59% of Internet users has used a social networking site like Facebook or LinkedIn at least once (Hampton, Sessions Goulet, Rainie, & Purcell, 2011).

In the early stages of the Internet, people went online seeking the anonymity it offered (McKenna & Bargh, 2000); now they use the Web to communicate, socialize with people they do know and expand their network (Jones & Fox, 2009). The tools that allow these connections are social media including social networking sites, microblogging, video-sharing sites, and blogs (Ellison, Steinfield, & Lampe, 2007; Jones & Fox, 2009; Lenhart, 2009; Raacke & Bonds-Raacke, 2008). The increasing interactivity and users' involvement in the Web necessitates exploring the types of people who are more likely to rely on these participatory tools and their psychological characteristics.

The literature on digital media has paid significant attention to the users' demographics and some of their psychological characteristics such as motivation, Internet self-efficacy, and life satisfaction. These psychological characteristics, however, may change over time. People may become more or less motivated, efficacious and satisfied with life. Thus, it is important to pay attention to the role of more stable psychological traits such as people's personalities. In other words, how dispositional and stable features rooted in biology may have a significant effect on the way people engage with digital media tools and social media in particular.

Uncovering the factors that prevent or facilitate the adoption of social media enables web content producers and policymakers interested in increasing media access to have a better understanding of how to make the Internet more approachable to different kinds of users. Also, marketing professionals are increasingly using social media to connect with audiences. Therefore, understanding the characteristics of people who are likely to engage in these types of online media more intensely may help marketers to understand—and reach–their audience.

One of these characteristics is people's personality. Personality refers to a stable psychological characteristic that predicts a wide range of attitudes and behaviors such as people's music tastes, clothing, speech, and more. In the past two decades, psychology scholars have reached a working consensus that most individual differences in personality can be categorized in five major domains: extraversion, emotional stability, openness to new experiences, agreeableness, and conscientiousness (McCrae & Costa, 1997; John & Srivastava, 1999).

Thanks to the development of this framework, labeled the "Big Five," research on digital media has devoted attention to the relationship between people's personality traits and digital media use. In the beginning, scholars investigated the links between personality and Internet usage in general (e.g., Amichai-Hamburger, Wainapel & Fox, 2002; Hamburger & Artzi, 2000). Currently, this line of research is focusing on specific uses of digital media, including social media applications (Amichai-Hamburger & Vinitzky, 2010; Correa, Hinsley, & de Zúñiga, 2010; Guadagno, Okdie, & Eno, 2008; Ross et al., 2009; Zywica & Danowski, 2008).

Although research on personality and digital media is looking more thoroughly at specific social media applications (e.g., Correa, 2010; Hargittai & Walejko, 2008; Kalmus, Pruulmann-Vengerfeldt, Runnel, & Siibak, 2009), it does not take into account that most people are driven by a purpose when they engage with social media. They may interact to do some business, meet people, express their culture or thoughts, or promote their work (Correa & Jeong, 2011). Thus, it is relevant to move the discussion forward by investigating more thoroughly the links between users' personality and purposeful forms of participation using social media (Bachmann, Correa, & Gil de Zúñiga, 2013).

Using a national sample of U.S. adults, in this chapter we explore the relationship between people's personality and social media use in general. In doing so, we look at the Big Five traits as well as specific social media applications and activities including social networking sites, instant messaging, and video chats. Finally, we investigate the link between personality and more purposeful social media use such as the utilization of these social tools to create political content.

PREDICTORS OF SOCIAL MEDIA USE: WHO INTERACTS ON THE WEB

The factors related to social media use have been investigated from sociological and psychological perspectives. From a sociological standpoint, research has mainly focused on structural factors such as users' socio-demographics and has found that social media usage is not equally distributed among groups. For instance, there are consistent differences by age, race, and gender. Among individuals who have access to the Internet, it has been consistently found that teens and young adults (18 to 30-years-old) are more likely than older generations to create content (Jones & Fox, 2009; Lenhart et al., 2004). Also, contrary to the trend in which ethnic minority groups lag behind in new technology usage, early studies on content creation found that among online users there was no difference among racial groups (Lenhart et al., 2004). Recent studies in the United States, however, have consistently found that Whites are less likely than minority groups—i.e., African Americans, Hispanics and Asians— to use social media and create content (Correa, Hinsley, & Gil de Zúñiga; Correa, 2010; Lenhart, 2009).

Regarding gender differences, girls tend to use blogs more often while boys are more likely to upload videos (Lenhart, Madden, McGill, & Smith, 2007). Also, Hargittai and Walejko (2008) found that female college students are less likely to share online content. Similarly, Correa (2010) found that among college students, men are somewhat more likely than women to participate in the Web by creating content.

From a psychological perspective, people tend to use these social tools if they are motivated (Correa, 2010), believe they have the skills to use them (Livingstone & Helsper, 2007), are happy with their lives (Valenzuela, Park, & Kee, 2009), or want to increase their personal contentment (Ellison, Steinfeld, & Lampe, 2007). Further, an experiment using physical and psychological measurements —including blood volume pulse, electroencephalogram, pupil dilation, and respiratory activity—found that social network sites use induces high arousal and elevates mood. In other words, social network sites induce positive emotional experiences (Mauri, Cipresso, Balgera, Villamira, & Riva, 2011). Finally, using two different studies, Pagani and colleagues (2011) found that people's innovativeness is related to active and passive usage of social network sites. They also found that individuals' expression of both self-identity and social identity is correlated with active usage of these sites.

In addition to these psychological findings, it is also relevant to pay attention to a stable psychological characteristic: people's personality.

Personality and the Big Five

Personality is a stable psychological feature that is related to a broad range of behaviors and attitudes. In the past two decades, the psychology field has developed a framework called the Big Five-Factor Model (Goldberg, 1990; McCrae & Costa, 1997; John & Srivastava, 1999), which structures most of the current studies of personality. This broad and hierarchical approach asserts that personality traits can be categorized and reliably measured in five domains: extraversion, emotional stability (also called neuroticism, its reverse), openness to new experiences, agreeableness, and conscientiousness. Each factor is bipolar (e.g., extraversion vs. introversion) and includes specific aspects (e.g., sociability), which in turn encompass more detailed traits (e.g., talkative, outgoing). Therefore, personality differences cannot be reduced to the Big Five traits. Rather, they represent personality at the broadest level of abstraction (John & Srivastava, 1999).

The literature suggests that these five traits are rooted in genetics (Bouchard, 1997; Van Gestel & Van Broeckhoven, 2003). This means that personality affects other variables rather than being influenced by social contexts. The Big Five dimensions come from self-rating responses in which people evaluate the extent to which they possess a series of attributes, and it has consistently shown high levels of validity and reliability across languages and cultures (John, Robins, & Pervin, 2008).

Because the literature has found extraversion, emotional stability, and openness to bew experience as consistently central to digital media use (Guadagno, Okdie, & Eno, 2008; Ross et al., 2009; Zywica & Danowski, 2008), this chapter will focus only on these three traits. Extraversion indicates the tendency to be active, sociable, lively, and assertive while introversion is associated with shyness and passivity. Emotional stability—also referred by its reverse, neuroticism—is linked to different levels of anxiety, instability, and excitability. Openness to experience is related to different degrees of open-mindedness, creativity, imagination, originality, curiosity, and complexity.

Linking Personality and Social Media Use

Early inquiries that investigated the link between people's personality and Internet use in general found extraversion and neuroticism were associated with online activities (i.e., Amichai-Hamburger, 2002; Amichai-Hamburger & Ben-Artzi, 2003; Amichai-Hamburger, Wainapel, & Fox, 2002). Specifically, people who had lower levels of extraversion and high degrees of neuroticism were more heavy Internet users than extraverted and less neurotic individuals (Amichai-Hamburger et al., 2002). In the early 2000s, scholars hypothesized that the anonymity provided by the Internet—at that time—attracted people who were less comfortable with themselves and who otherwise had trouble making connections with others. These people might have relied on the social services provided by the Web such as online chats and discussion groups to reduce their loneliness (Hamburger & Ben-Artzi, 2000).

Studies conducted more recently, however, have seen a reversal in the relationships between people's personality and some types of Internet uses, particularly social media applications. Social media use is defined as the consumption of digital media or Internet that is not related to the traditional informational uses. On the contrary, social media provide mechanisms to connect, communicate, and interact with each other through applications such as instant messaging, chatting, social networking sites, and microblogging.

Investigations are consistently finding that more extraverted people tend to be drawn to social media. This may occur in part because anonymity is not a characteristic in the most popular types of current online applications, such as social networking sites. Most people use these sites to interact with individuals they already know and do not tend to engage with strangers (Lampe, Ellison, & Steinfeld, 2006; Valenzuela, Park, &

Kee, 2009). Therefore, these sites may be more likely to appeal to extraverts. In a similar vein, while chat rooms allow group-like conversations between individuals who are largely unknown to each other, instant messaging is generally used for conversations between single users who are familiar with each other (Quan-Haase, 2007).

Studies that have examined the link between personality and social networking have found that three dimensions of personality are consistently related to social media use: extraversion, neuroticism, and openness to experience (Ross et al., 2009; Zywica & Danowski, 2008). Extraverted people were more connected with others through social networking sites and in the "real world" (Gosling, Augustine, Vazire, Holtzmann, & Gaddis, 2011; Zywica & Danowski, 2008). Ross and colleagues (2009) found extraversion was positively associated with belonging to Facebook groups, but it was not related to how they communicated on the site. At that time, they hypothesized the lack of instant messaging in Facebook users may not have fulfilled their need for immediate communication. Since Facebook introduced an instant messaging application, extraversion has been positively correlated with social networking site use (Amichai-Hamburger & Vinitzky, 2010; Gosling et al., 2011). A recent study conducted by Quercia and colleagues (forthcoming) found that extraversion is a positive predictor of both number of friends in the real world and number of Facebook contacts. Although they expected to find that sociable people would present themselves in likable ways on Facebook and would maintain superficial relationships, they did not find evidence supporting that hypothesis. In a similar study, this team of researchers also revealed that extraversion was positively related to Twitter usage (Quercia, Kosinski, Stillwell, & Crowcroft, 2011).

When looking at emotional stability (or neuroticism), the literature has found that more neurotic people prefer instant messaging use than face-to-face interactions (Ehrenberg et al., 2008).

The scholars hypothesize this preference occurs because instant messaging allows more time to contemplate responses. Thus, for people who are more emotionally instable it is easier to communicate with others. Other studies of adolescents and young adults show support for this finding and, for instance, among younger adolescents, those who were more likely to experience social anxiety used webcams less frequently (Peter et al., 2007). Similarly, in an experiment, college-aged women were more likely to experience feelings of shyness when they used webcams to converse with others (Brunet & Schmidt, 2007). This finding also suggests that whereas more neurotic people may prefer instant messaging, they may also avoid video chats.

Finally, evidence also suggests people who are open to new experiences are heavier users of social media (Guadagno et al., 2008; Ross et al., 2009). High openness to experience is reflected in curiosity and novelty-seeking; low levels are evident in preferences for adhering to convention and established patterns (John & Srivastava, 1999). Therefore, because social media are relatively new applications of Internet technology those who are more open to experiences are more likely to experiment with creating online profiles and chatting using instant messages and videos.

A very recent study conducted by Hughes and colleagues (2012) examined the relationship between the traditional five dimensions of people's personality (extraversion, neuroticism, openness to experience, conscientiousness, and agreeableness) as well as sociability and need for cognition and social and informational uses of both Facebook and Twitter. These researchers demonstrated that personality is related to both informational and social uses of these sites, although the relationships were not as strong as previous literature suggested. Results also showed that differences in personality were related to preferences for either Facebook or Twitter.

EXPLORING PERSONALITY AND SOCIAL MEDIA WITH A NATIONAL SAMPLE

In order to explore the relationship between personality traits and social media use, we used data from an online survey conducted in the United States a few weeks after the 2008 election. The Media Research Lab at the University of Texas at Austin collected the data, based on a panel of U.S. adults. As a means to favor an accurate representation of the national population, a sample of 10,000 randomly-drawn participants was matched to fit the distribution of two variables from the U.S. Census: age (18-34: 30%; 35-54: 39%; 55 and older: 31%) and gender (male: 50.2%; female 49.8%). Past research suggests that such a procedure can help overcome the generalizability limitations of Web-based surveys (Bennett & Iyengar, 2008; Vavreck, 2007).

On December 15, 2008, we sent an email invitation with the survey URL to the 10,000 selected panel members. In an effort to increase the response rate, we included information about a monetary incentive drawing for their participation and we also sent up to three reminders in the following weeks. The final message was sent January 5, 2009. Almost 1,500 email addresses turned out to be invalid and we ended up with 1,482 valid cases for a 17.3% response rate. For the analyses presented in this chapter, we rely on a subsample of 959 cases, the number of participants who consistently answered the questions relevant for study. In the end, the sample had a gender skew: 67% of respondents were females, and 33% were men. In addition, participants' ages went from 18 to 84 (M=46, SD=12.4). Regarding race/ethnicity, 84.4% of respondents were White/ Caucasian, 5% African American, 4.5% Hispanic, 3% Asian, and 1% accounted for Native American, Pacific Islander, and Other. On average, the highest level of education completed was 2-year college degree, and the average annual income ranged from $50,000 to $59,999.

We used several variables in our analyses. We wanted to tap into different online applications that allow for social interactions and thus we asked respondents' on a 10-point scale—ranging from never to all the time— how often they used social networking sites, instant messages and video chats. Eventually the latter variable was dichotomized, as more than 70% of respondents said they never used this kind of application.

Because the relationship between using social networking sites and instant messaging was strong and the literature suggests they relate to personality in a similar manner, we created a construct of social media use adding these two online applications (r=.41, p<.001, M=8.03, SD=5.79). First, we explored how personality is related to social media use as a construct. Then, we investigated how personality is associated with each application (social networking sites, instant messaging, and video chats) to have a more nuanced understanding of role of personality on social media use.

Finally, we explored a more purposive usage of social media. Thus, we investigated how personality is related to social media for political purposes. We created a construct of social media use for political purposes. It was an additive index of four items that asked participants how often they wrote or posted on their own blogs, posted comments on somebody else's blog, created and posted online their own videos about current events, and contributed their own news reports to a user-generated website. While the first three items had a 10-point scale, the last one used a seven-point scale. This index had a Cronbach's alpha of .76 (M=6.81, SD=5.81).

For the personality traits, we focused on the three dimensions that past research has singled out as important regarding digital media—namely, extraversion, emotional stability (a.k.a neuroticism), and openness to new experiences. We relied on the 10-Item Personality Inventory, a scale showing acceptable validity and reliability levels and thus can serve as a proxy for the longer Big-Five instruments (Gosling, Rentfrow, & Swann, 2003). Two items were used to measure each trait, with every item asking respondents to assess on a 10-point scale the extent to which respondents agreed that different pairs of characteristics described them well. They were told to rate these pairs even if they thought one the descriptors applied to them to a greater degree. Using this approach, we computed extraversion by adding the scores of the pairs reserved-quiet (reversed) and extraverted-enthusiastic (r=.43, p<.001, M=11.35; SD=4.56). The sum of anxious-easily upset (reversed) and calm-emotionally stable resulted in a skewed variable so we recoded the outliers (the scores below 5, representing 3.7% of the sample) to compute the emotional stability measure (r=.47, p<.001; M=13.73; SD=4.16). Similarly, openness to new experiences is the summation of the conventional-uncreative (reversed) and open to new experience-complex pairs, after recording the outliers, which accounted for 3.2% of the sample (r=.29, p<.001; M=14.28; SD=3.53).

Finally, as controls, we used the respondents' socio-demographic characteristics: age, education level, gender, annual household income and race/ethnicity (recoded as White =1 and non-Whites=0). We also used as control a measure for life satisfaction, as the literature shows that personal contentment levels are strongly correlated to the three personality traits under study here (Chen, 2008; Schimmack, Shigehiro, Furr, & Funder, 2008). In this study, we used three items from the Satisfaction with Life Scale (Diener, Emmons, Larson, & Griffin, 1985) to compute the variable as an additive scale. Accordingly, respondents had to rate their agreement on with three separate assertions: "In most ways my life is close to my ideal," "Things in my life are difficult," later reversed, and "I'm satisfied with my life." This scale reached a Cronbach's alpha of .83 (M=16.88, SD=7.01).

RESULTS ON PERSONALITY AND SOCIAL MEDIA

First, we analyzed the relationships between personality traits and social media use in general. Consistent with the literature, our survey revealed that the usage of social media is extensive. Of the total sample, almost three fourths (72.5%) of the respondents use social media (74.8% of women and 67.7% of men). On a scale from 1 to 10, where 1 means never/rarely and 10 means very often, people rated their average social media use at 8.03 (SD=5.79). This number suggests that, generally, Internet users rely on these social applications quite often.

When we look at simple correlations among personality traits and social media use, Table 1 shows that personality traits were positively related with each other, just as the literature suggests (Gosling et al., 2003). The strongest association was openness with extraversion (r=.35, p<.001). In other words, people with high levels of extraversion tend to be more emotionally stable and open to new experiences. Simple associations also suggest that personality traits are significantly associated with social media use; more extraverted people tend to use social media more often and people who are open to new experiences are also more likely to use social media. However, emotional stability is negatively related to social media use. This means that people who are more neurotic tend to rely on these social applications rather than those who have greater levels of emotional stability.

To see whether these relationships are maintained when controlling for life satisfaction, socio-demographic variables and the remaining personality traits, we conducted multiple regressions, where block 1 contains the control variables (i.e., socio-demographics and life satisfaction) and block 2 shows the prediction of the three personality traits on social media use (see Table 2). We found that three personality traits are still associated with social media use, even when taking into account the demographic characteristics of the

Table 1. Correlations among social media use, personality, demographics, and life satisfaction (N = 959)

Variables	1	2	3	4	5	6	7	8	9
1. Social media use									
2. Extraversion	.14***								
3. Emotional stability	-.12***	.09**							
4. Openness	.10**	.35***	.18***						
5. Life satisfaction	-.09**	.14***	.39***	.07					
6. Gender (male)	-.04	-.08	.09**	-.05	.04				
7. Race (white)	.06	-.07	-.00	-.03	-.02				
8. Education	.09**	.04	.12***	.06	.26***	.12***	-.04		
9. Income	-.04	.07	.15***	.06	.32***	.13***	.01	.45***	
10. Age	-.34***	-.05	.16***	.02	.04	.11**	.18**	.06	.02

**p <.01, *** p <.001

Note: This table was previously published by the authors in Correa, T., Willard Hinsley, A., Gil de Zúñiga, H. (2010). Who interacts on the Web? The intersection of users' personality and social media use. *Computers in Human Behavior, 26*(2), 247-253.

Table 2. Personality predicting social media use using multiple regression (N = 959)

	Beta	s.e.	*p* value
Control Variables			
Gender	.02	.38	.63
Race	-.10	.49	.001
Education	-.03	.14	.35
Income	-.01	.05	.87
Age	-.29	.02	.000
Life Satisfaction	-.06	.03	.11
Personality Traits			
Extraversion	.13	.04	.000
Emotional Stability	-.08	.05	.02
Openness	.08	.05	.01
R^2	15.7%		

Betas are standardized coefficients.

Note: A version of this table was previously published by the authors in Correa, T., Willard Hinsley, A., Gil de Zúñiga, H. (2010). Who interacts on the Web? The intersection of users' personality and social media use. *Computers in Human Behavior, 26*(2), 247-253.

sample and people's personal contentment. This means that people's personality matters independently of their gender, race, income, education, and level of satisfaction with their lives.

Specifically, more extraverted people tend to be heavier users of social media. Also, people who are more emotionally stable will use social media less frequently. In other words, anxious and worrisome individuals tend to use social media more frequently than those who are emotionally stable. Finally, people who are open to new experiences, innovative, and creative will use social media more frequently (see Table 2). It is also important to note that among the personality traits, extraversion was the strongest predictor of social media use. The block of the demographic variables and life satisfaction of the model explained 12.5% of the variance of social media use ($F_{(6,957)} = 22.59$, p<.001). The relationship between life satisfaction and social media use was negative and statistically significant (b=.06, p=.05). When personality traits were included in the model, they explained 3.2% of the variance of social media usage ($F_{(9,957)} = 19.61$, p<.001), and life satisfaction was no longer significant (b=.06, p=.11).

This result shows that although personality is definitely related to social media usage, the associations are not strong as the literature is increasingly suggesting (e.g., Hughes et al., 2012).

In the next section, we look in more detail the relationships between personality and three social media applications: social networking sites, instant messaging, and video chats.

LOOKING DEEPER: PERSONALITY AND SPECIFIC SOCIAL MEDIA APPLICATIONS

When investigating specific social media applications, the survey revealed respondents used instant messaging more frequently followed by social networking sites. Video chatting was the least frequent activity of them all. On a scale from 1 to 10, where 1 means never/rarely and 10 means often, respondents rated their average instant message use at 4.37 (SD=3.56), social networking site use at 3.66 (SD=3.34), and video chat use at 2.23 (SD=2.45). Of the total sample, 51.8% use social network sites, 99.9% use instant messages, and 29% use video chats.

To test whether there is a relationship between personality traits and use of social networking sites and instant messaging, controlling for demographic variables, life satisfaction, and the remaining personality traits, we conducted multiple regressions. To analyze the association among personality traits, life satisfaction and video-chat use, we performed a logistic regression because video chat use was dichotomized between use and no-use.

The analyses revealed that people who are more extraverted will use social networking sites, instant messaging, and video chats more frequently, even after controlling for respondents' socio-demographic characteristics and life satisfaction (see Table 3 for social networking sites and instant messaging and Table 4 for video chats). That is, people with higher levels of extraversion tend to be heavier users of different social media applications.

When analyzing the relationship between emotional stability and the three social media

Table 3. Looking in more detail- personality predicting social networking site use and instant messaging (N = 959)

	Social Networking Site Use			Instant Messaging		
	Beta	**s.e.**	***p* value**	**Beta**	**s.e.**	***p* value**
Control Variables						
Gender	.01	.21	.70	.01	.24	.63
Race	-.05	.28	.08	-.11	.31	.001
Education	.02	.07	.54	-.07	.08	.35
Income	-.02	.03	.60	.01	.03	.87
Life Satisfaction	-.06	.03	.23	-.05	.02	.15
Personality Traits						
Extraversion	.09	.04	.005	.13	.03	.000
Emotional Stability	-.11	.05	.001	-.02	.03	.48
Openness	.08	.05	.02	.06	.03	.08
R^2	17.1%			8.0%		

Betas are standardized coefficients

Table 4. Looking in more detail: personality predicting video chat use (N = 959)

	B	Wald	s.e.	*p* value
Control Variables				
Gender	.50	9.80	.16	.002
Race	-.14	.48	.20	.49
Education	.05	.94	.05	.33
Income	-.04	2.62	.02	.11
Age	-.04	32.50	.01	.000
Life Satisfaction	.004	.10	.01	.75
Personality Traits				
Extraversion	.06	11.91	.02	.001
Emotional Stability	.02	.72	.02	.40
Openness	-.01	.37	.02	.54
Nagelkerke R^2		8.5%		

applications, the results did not follow the same pattern. Specifically, people who are more anxious and worrisome use social networking sites more frequently than those who are more emotionally stable (see Table 3). The results showed that the relationships between emotional stability, instant messaging and video chatting were not significant (see Table 3 and Table 4).

Finally, people who are more open to new experiences use social networking sites more frequently. This means that people who use social networking sites more often tend to be more innovative and creative. However, being open was not associated with instant messaging and video chatting.

In the following section, we explore how people's personality is associated with a more purposive usage of social media, namely for political purposes.

SATISFYING MOTIVATIONS: PERSONALITY AND USE OF SOCIAL MEDIA FOR POLITICAL PURPOSES

A separate examination of the relationship between personality traits, demographics and social media use for political purposes sheds further light on the factors influencing individuals' behaviors in online settings —in this case, political life. Recent studies suggest that online conversations are as effective in influencing political activities as face-to-face discussions (Kerbel & Bloom, 2005; Shah et al., 2005). There is evidence that Internet users are increasingly embracing online technology to engage in public life (Gil de Zúñiga & Valenzuela, 2011; Jennings & Zeitner, 2003; Wellman et al., 2003; Williams & Tedesco, 2006). Some active online behaviors are related to participation (Rojas & Puig-i-Abril, 2009), and arguably social media use for political purposes may lead people to be engaged in political and civic spheres, as new user-generated technologies of the Web, such as blogs, citizen journalism sites, and video-sharing sites, should facilitate engaging in horizontal discussions where anyone can potentially participate in the public discourse. Recent investigations have found that active usage of the Web, such as messaging over the Internet, has positive effects on, for example, civic participation (Shah et al., 2005), The reason behind this finding is that online conversations often are text-based, purposive, and goal-oriented (Berger, 2009), thus they effectively mobilize people.

Much of the political research on the Big Five has focused on political ideology and attitudes (Alford & Hibbing 2007; Carney et al., 2008; Gerber et al., 2010). Now, scholars are moving toward political behavior such as political participation and civic engagement (e.g., Anderson, 2009; Mondak & Halperin, 2008; Mondak et al., 2010). Evidence suggests that extraversion and openness to experience are positively related to political participation (Gerber et al., 2011). The positive relationship between extraversion and political participation may be explained by the fact that social interaction is a key characteristic of extraverted people and, at the same time, a condition of many political participatory acts, including attending to a political rally, signing a petition, and involvement in a political discussion. The positive link between openness and political participation is also expected because people who are more open to experience are more likely to be interested in politics, attentive to the opportunities to be exposed to new ideas and experiences (Mondak & Halperin, 2008).

The results of the effects of emotional stability on political participation have been mixed. Some findings suggest the emotional stability is associated with, for example, lower turnout in voting and rallies (Anderson, 2009; Mondak et al., 2010), other studies found the opposite association (Gerber et al., 2011). There are explanations for both results. The cool "keep-to-themselves" feature of emotionally stable people make less likely that they engage in often-heated political interactions. At the same time, more anxious and worrisome individuals may tend to avoid political meetings or group-based political acts.

Within this context, for our study we integrated two lines of research: personality and politics and personality and social media usage. An analysis of simple correlations shows that younger people and those with lower income are more likely to use social media for political purposes, such as uploading a political video, posting on a blog about politics or submitting a news report to a user-generated website about politics or current affairs (see Table 5). Indeed, social media use for political purposes was negatively correlated with age and with income (see Table 5). The results showed no significant association between political social media use and gender, race, or education.

Furthermore, and in line with the results described above, the correlations also showed that two personality traits were significantly associated with political social media use: extraversion and emotional stability. In other words, those with higher levels of extraversion tend to be more frequent users of social media for political purposes. People who blog, post comments, submit

Table 5. Correlations among social media use for political purposes, personality, demographics, and life satisfaction

Variables	1	2	3	4	5	6	7	8	9	10
1.Social media use for politics	--									
2.Gender (male)	-.04	--								
3.Race (white)	-.04	-.02	--							
4.Education	-.05	.12***	-.05	--						
5.Income	-.10*	.13***	-.02	.42***	--					
6.Age	-.16***	.12**	.18***	.06*	-.03	--				
7.Extraversion	.10*	-.08*	.06#	.06#	.07*	-.06#	--			
8.Emotional stability	-.10**	.10**	-.10*	.13***	.15***	.16***	.10**	--		
9.Openness	.06#	-.05	-.01	.06#	-.01	.02	.35***	.18**	--	
10.Life satisfaction	-.10*	.04	-.02	.25**	.33***	.05	.14***	.40***	.10*	--

N = 959

# p <.10, * p <.05, ** p <.01 *** p <.001

Note: This table was previously published by the authors in Bachmann, I., Correa, T., & Gil de Zúñiga, H. (2012). Profiling political online content creators: Advancing the paths to democracy, *International Journal of E-Politics. 3*(4), 1-19 their own news reports and both create and post their own videos about current affairs also tend to be less stable. These characteristics could explain these users' draw to social media and political life online—arguably, these users are counteracting their discontent by creating content and expressing themselves. While positive, the correlation between the third trait, openness to new experiences, and social media use for political purposes only approaches significance.

Wanting to see if these results would hold with a more stringent multivariate test, we opted for a multiple regression analysis that used the socio-demographic variables and life satisfaction as controls. The results, however, offer mixed evidence for the relationship between political social media use and personality, as none of the personality traits stay as significant predictors in the regression (see Table 6). Extraversion was the only trait that approached significance, and did so in the expected positive direction. While both blocks in the regression model were significant, the only significant variable with a significant effect was age. In other words, younger people

Table 6. Personality predicting social media use for political purposes (N = 959)

	Beta	s.e.	p value
Control Variables			
Age	-.14	.15	.000
Education	-.01	.21	.742
Gender (male)	.01	.41	.933
Income	-.04	.07	.236
Race (white)	-.02	.53	.531
Life satisfaction	-.06	.03	.135
Personality Traits			
Extraversion	.07	.05	.058
Emotional stability	-.05	.05	.174
Openness to new experiences	.05	.06	.122
Total R²			4.3%

are more likely to write on blogs, upload videos about public affairs and submit news reports and thus use social media with political purposes.

CONCLUSION

This chapter advances the literature on the factors affecting uses of new technologies in society by exploring the relationship between people's personality and uses of the user-generated Web. In particular, it focuses on social media use, a concept that captures the ways in which Internet users connect, communicate and interact with each other through different applications including social networking sites, instant messaging, video chatting, and video-sharing. We wanted to see to what extent people's personality was related to social media use based on the psychological Big-Five framework (Amichai-Hamburger et al., 2002; John & Srivastava, 1999; Ross et al., 2009). Currently, this is the most accepted approach to measure individuals' personality characteristics because research has reached a consensus that most individual personality differences can be classified in a broad and hierarchical approach that categorizes personality in five domains: extraversion, emotional stability (or neuroticism), openness to new experiences, agreeableness, and conscientiousness. Because the literature has consistently found that three traits are related to Internet and social media use, we focused on extraversion, emotional stability, and openness to experience.

Overall, we found that characteristics rooted in genetics such as people's personality traits—extraversion, emotional stability and openness to experience—are related to the uses of interactive social media. These findings are in line with the investigations conducted in the early stages of the Internet diffusion by Amichai-Hamburger and Ben-Artzi (2000; 2002; 2003), who tested how personality played a role in Internet use. They are also consistent with studies that examined more current online applications that involved some level of social interaction such as blogs and Facebook (Amichai-Hamburger & Vinitzky, 2010; Guadagno et al., 2008; Ross et al., 2009).

Perhaps our most consistent finding was that extraversion was positively related to social media use. We not only found this when analyzing social media as construct but also when we analyzed three different social media applications such as social networking sites, instant messaging and video chatting. This finding is both interesting and quite relevant because it contradicts the results of the early studies that linked personality and Internet use in general.

Early studies that investigated the association between personality and different uses of the Internet revealed extraversion was negatively related to uses of social services such as chat rooms (Hamburger & Ben-Artzi, 2000). That is, more introverted people were more likely to rely on those tools. The explanation was that social interactions via those social services were different from offline interactions because physical appearance and physical proximity was not relevant (McKenna & Bargh, 2000). Therefore, people who tend to be more anxious, lonely, and introverted used the Internet to compensate their real-world isolation in these early studies of Internet use (Amichai-Hamburger & Ben-Artzi, 2003; Bargh, McKenna, & Fitzsimons, 2002).

Currently, the results of studies that involve social media tools including social networking sites, instant messaging, and video chatting differ from early investigations on social services because they do not necessarily provide anonymity. This fact may explain why extraverted, rather than introverted, individuals are more likely to rely in social media use (Correa, Willard Hinsley, & Gil de Zúñiga, 2010). This result is line with other investigations that have explored the link between personality traits and Facebook use (Ross et al., 2009; Hughes et al., 2012).

We also found emotional stability was negatively associated with social media use. That is, individuals with higher levels of neuroticism and negative affectivity are more likely to engage in these social activities. Interestingly, the relationship between lower levels of life satisfaction and greater social media use that we found when analyzing simple correlations disappeared when emotional stability was taken into account in the analysis (see regression in Table 2). This phenomenon suggests that greater degrees of anxiety, and not level of personal well-being, actually predict social media use. Our result supports previous investigations that have found higher levels of neuroticism were related to the uses of social services of the Internet such as chat rooms (Hamburger & Ben-Artzi, 2000) and instant messaging (Ehrenberg et al., 2008). Because neuroticism is associated with loneliness, one could argue that nervous and anxious individuals use these services to seek support and company. They also give more time for contemplation before acting compared to offline or face-to-face interactions (Ehrenberg et al., 2008; Ross et al., 2009).

It is important to note, however, that our more detailed analysis revealed that the negative relationship between emotional stability and social media use was evident only for social networking site usage than the other two applications analyzed in this chapter. In the case of instant messaging and video chats, the relationship was not significant. These results may suggest that, as the literature has demonstrated, people with greater levels of neuroticism or less emotional stability tend to be drawn to online social applications that allow some reflection before acting such as social networking sites but not to those applications that resemble face-to-face interactions where physical appearance and auditory cues become important such as video chats (McKenna & Bargh, 2000; Peter et al., 2007).

We found a positive association between openness to experiences and social media use, particularly social networking site use. This is expected because of the novel nature of these technologies, particularly at the time the data of our survey was collected—at thr end of 2008 and beginning of 2009. Although the first recognizable social networking site was launched in 1997 (Six-Degrees.com), the most widely used sites in the U.S.--MySpace and Facebook— were introduced much later. MySpace was launched in 2003 and Facebook in 2004 to Harvard students. Only in 2006 it became available to everyone. Twitter, an increasingly popular microblogging service, was launched in 2006.

Finally, it is important to move the discussion forward by including the purpose and content of the social media interaction. People use social media to promote something, to do some networking, to express themselves or their culture. In this case, we investigated the usage of social media for political purposes. We found an association between people's personality and political social media use. Consistent with the findings on personality and social media use in general as well as personality and politics, more extraverted people tend to post on blogs and upload videos with political content. Social interaction, a key feature of extraverted individuals, explains that people want to participate in politics even in the online arena. The literature on emotional stability and politics has been mixed but this study found that people who are less emotionally stable tend to use social media for political purposes, which is in line with the literature on personality and social media in general. These findings do not remain significant when including socio-demographics and life satisfaction in the analyses. It is possible that the relationship between personality and social media for politics is stronger for a demographic group. Future studies should explore the how these relationships work for different socio-demographic groups.

The consistency of the relationships between individual's personality traits and a wide range of social media applications, including purposive usage of certain tools, show that it is safe to conclude that, nowadays, more extraverted people tend to take advantage of the user-generated Web that provide venues for communication and socialization. It is also relatively safe to suggest that users of social media tend to have higher degrees of neuroticism and anxiety. Perhaps they use these social tools to assuage their anxiety by seeking company. Although the findings are less consistent than the other two traits, people who use social media also tend to be more open to new experience, innovative.

These findings suggest that given the influence of these social media on today's social interactions —more than half of America's adults use them (Hampton et al., 2011)—Internet designers should take into account users' characteristics and need. From a marketing standpoint, marketers are increasingly relying on these tools. Studies like this one help to disentangle the characteristics of the users and understand the audience. The results show that people who are more open to new experiences are more likely to rely on social media, which helps to identify a very useful segment for marketers. Also, the fact that more extraverted people use social media and that they connect with people they already know suggests that the boundaries between offline and online networks are blurring. Therefore, these social tools become very useful to transmit ideas, concepts, and brands.

This study has taken this line of research a step further in various ways. First, the survey was conducted among a national sample of U.S. adults and not only college students, which provide a broader and more reliable snapshot of social media users and their personality. In addition, the analyses have controlled for the effect of a set of socio-demographic variables (age, gender, race, education and income) and levels of life satisfaction to isolate the predicting relationships among our variables of interest. The inclusion of these factors as controls was relevant because previous evidence had identified some personality traits were related to demographic variables and personal well-being.

Although in this chapter we analyzed different applications of social media, including social media use for political purposes, future investigations should explore the link between personality and other motivations or purposes when using these social tools, such as networking, promotion of oneself or a brand, or self-expression. Our data was based on online participants' recruitment. Although we intended to assure the most accurate representation of U.S. national population, the final subsample yielded a larger proportion of women taking the survey than males, which should be noted as one limitation of this study.

We did not explore all possible dimensions of personality. We decided to include those traits that, according to the literature, were relevant for digital media use. We examined the Big-Five model with a brief index specially designed for studies that cannot test a large instrument because of time and space constraints. This instrument, however, has showed consistency. Future research, however, should also include other personality traits that might predict social media use such as conscientiousness and agreeableness. Overall, this chapter contributes to the understanding of how individual's personality features predict their social media use on the Internet. Scholars need to keep uncovering the psychological factors that lead people to engage in these participatory media. This line of research is relevant in an ever-increasing user-generated Web where people's engagement and participation may become key for advancing in social spheres

REFERENCES

Alford, J. R., & Hibbing, J. R. (2007). Personal, interpersonal, and political temperaments. *ANNALS of the American Academy of Political and Social Sciences, 614*, 696–212. doi:10.1177/0002716207305621.

Amichai-Hamburger, Y. (2002). Internet and personality. *Computers in Human Behavior, 18*(1), 1–10. doi:10.1016/S0747-5632(01)00034-6.

Amichai-Hamburger, Y., & Ben-Artzi, E. (2003). Loneliness and Internet use. *Computers in Human Behavior, 19*(1), 71–80. doi:10.1016/S0747-5632(02)00014-6.

Amichai-Hamburger, Y., & Vinitzky, G. (2010). Social network use and personality. *Computers in Human Behavior, 26*(6), 1289–1295. doi:10.1016/j.chb.2010.03.018.

Amichai-Hamburger, Y., Wainapel, G., & Fox, S. (2002). "On the Internet no one knows I'm an introvert": Extraversion, neuroticism, and Internet interaction. *Cyberpsychology & Behavior, 5*(2), 125–128. doi:10.1089/109493102753770507 PMID:12025878.

Anderson, M. R. (2009). Beyond membership: A sense of community and political behavior. *Political Behavior, 31*(4), 603–627. doi:10.1007/s11109-009-9089-x.

Bachmann, I., Correa, T., & Gil de Zúñiga, H. (2012). Profiling online political content creators: Advancing the paths to democracy. *International Journal of E-Politics. 3*(4), 1-19.

Bargh, J. A., McKenna, K. Y. A., & Fitzsimons, G. M. (2002). Can you see the real me? Activation and expression of the "true self" on the Internet. *The Journal of Social Issues, 58*(1), 33–48. doi:10.1111/1540-4560.00247.

Bennett, W. L., & Iyengar, S. (2008). A new era of minimal effects? The changing foundations of political communication. *The Journal of Communication*, *58*(4), 707–731. doi:10.1111/j.1460-2466.2008.00410.x.

Berger, C. R. (2009). Interpersonal communication. In Tacks, D. W., & Salwen, M. B. (Eds.), *An integrated approach to communication theory and research* (pp. 260–279). Mahwah, NJ: Lawrence Erlbaum Associates.

Bouchard, Y. J. J. (1997). The genetics of personality. In Blum, K., & Noble, E. P. (Eds.), *Handbook of Psychiatric Genetics* (pp. 273–296). Boca Raton, FL: CRC Press.

Brunet, P. M., & Schmidt, L. A. (2007). Is shyness context specific? Relation between shyness and online self-disclosure with and without a live webcam in young adults. *Journal of Research in Personality*, *41*(4), 938–945. doi:10.1016/j.jrp.2006.09.001.

Carney, D. R., Jost, J. T., Gosling, S. D., & Potter, J. (2008). The secret lives of liberals and conservatives: Personality profiles, interaction styles, and the things they leave behind. *Political Psychology*, *29*(6), 807–840. doi:10.1111/j.1467-9221.2008.00668.x.

Chen, L. S.-L. (2008). Subjective well-being: Evidence from the different personality traits of online game teenager players. *Cyberpsychology & Behavior*, *11*(5), 579–581. doi:10.1089/cpb.2007.0192 PMID:18771394.

Correa, T. (2010). The participation divide among "online experts": Experience, skills, and psychological factors as predictors of college students' web content creation. *Journal of Computer-Mediated Communication*, *16*(1), 71–92. doi:10.1111/j.1083-6101.2010.01532.x.

Correa, T., & Jeong, S.-H. (2011). Race and online content creation: Why minorities are actively participating in the Web. *Information Communication and Society*, *14*(5), 638–659. doi:10.1080/1369118X.2010.514355.

Correa, T., Willard Hinsley, A., & Gil de Zúñiga, H. (2010). Who interacts on the Web?: The intersection between users' personality and social media use. *Computers in Human Behavior*, *26*(2), 247–253. doi:10.1016/j.chb.2009.09.003.

Diener, E., Emmons, R., Larsen, R., & Griffin, S. (1985). The satisfaction with life scale. *Journal of Personality Assessment*, *49*(1), 71–75. doi:10.1207/s15327752jpa4901_13 PMID:16367493.

Ehrenberg, A., Juckes, S., White, K. M., & Walsh, S. P. (2008). Personality and self-esteem as predictors of young people's technology use. *Cyberpsychology & Behavior*, *11*(6), 739–741. doi:10.1089/cpb.2008.0030 PMID:18991531.

Ellison, N. B., Steinfield, C., & Lampe, C. (2007). The benefits of Facebook "friends": Social capital and college students' use of online social network sites. *Journal of Computer-Mediated Communication*, *12*(4), 1143–1168. doi:10.1111/j.1083-6101.2007.00367.x.

Gerber, A. S., Huber, G. A., Doherty, D., & Dowling, C. M. (2011). Big Five personality traits in the political arena. *Annual Review of Political Science*, *14*, 265–281. doi:10.1146/annurev-polisci-051010-111659.

Gerber, A. S., Huber, G. A., Doherty, D., Dowling, C. M., & Ha, S. E. (2010). Personality and political attitudes: Relationships across issue domains and political contexts. *The American Political Science Review*, *104*, 111–133. doi:10.1017/S0003055410000031.

Gil de Zúñiga, H., & Valenzuela, S. (2011). The mediating path to a stronger citizenship: Online and offline networks, weak ties and civic engagement. *Communication Research*, *38*(3), 397–421. doi:10.1177/0093650210384984.

Goldberg, L. R. (1990). An alternative "description of personality": The Big-Five Factor Structure. *Journal of Personality and Social Psychology*, *59*(6), 1216–1229. doi:10.1037/0022-3514.59.6.1216 PMID:2283588.

Gosling, S. D., Augustine, A. A., Vazire, S., Holtzman, N., & Gaddis, S. (2011). Manifestations of personality on online social networks: Self-reported Facebook-related behaviors and observable profile information. *Cyberpsychology, Behavior, and Social Networking*, *14*(9), 483–488. doi:10.1089/cyber.2010.0087 PMID:21254929.

Gosling, S. D., Rentfrow, P. J., & Swann, W. B. J. (2003). A very brief measure of the big five personality domains. *Journal of Research in Personality*, *37*(6), 504–528. doi:10.1016/S0092-6566(03)00046-1.

Guadagno, R. E., Okdie, B. M., & Eno, C. A. (2008). Who blogs? Personality predictors of blogging. *Computers in Human Behavior*, *24*, 1993–2004. doi:10.1016/j.chb.2007.09.001.

Hamburger, Y. A., & Ben-Artzi, E. (2000). The relationship between extraversion and neuroticism and the different uses of the Internet. *Computers in Human Behavior*, *16*(4), 441–449. doi:10.1016/S0747-5632(00)00017-0.

Hampton, K. N., Sessions Goulet, L., Rainie, L., & Purcell, K. (2011). *Social networking sites and our lives*. Washingston, D.C.: Pew Internet & American Life Project.

Hargittai, E., & Walejko, G. (2008). The participation divide: Content creation and sharing in the digital age. *Information Communication and Society*, *11*(2), 239–256. doi:10.1080/13691180801946150.

Hughes, D. J., Rowe, M., Batey, M., & Lee, A. (2012). A tale of two sites: Twitter vs. Facebook and the personality predictors of social media usage. *Computers in Human Behavior*, *28*(2), 561–569. doi:10.1016/j.chb.2011.11.001.

Jennings, M. K., & Zeitner, V. (2003). Internet use and civic engagement: A longitudinal analysis. *Public Opinion Quarterly*, *67*(3), 311–334. doi:10.1086/376947.

John, O. P., Robins, L. W., & Pervin, L. A. (2008). *Handbook of personality: Theory and research.* New York: Guilford.

John, O. P., & Srivastava, S. (1999). The Big Five trait taxonomy: History, measurement, and theoretical perspectives. In Pervin, L. A., & John, O. P. (Eds.), *Handbook of personality: Theory and research* (2nd ed., pp. 102–138). New York: Guilford.

Jones, S., & Fox, S. (2009). Generations online in 2009. Pew Internet and American Life Project. Retrieved March 19, 2009, from http://www.pewinternet.org/Reports/2009/Generations-Online-in-2009.aspx

Kalmus, V., Pruulmann-Vengerfeldt, P., Runnel, P., & Siibak, A. (2009). Mapping the terrain of generation C: Places and practices of online content creation among Estonian teenagers. *Journal of Computer-Mediated Communication*, *14*(4), 1257–1282. doi:10.1111/j.1083-6101.2009.01489.x.

Kerbel, M. R., & Bloom, J. D. (2005). Blog for America and civic involvement. *The Harvard International Journal of Press/Politics*, *10*(4), 3–27. doi:10.1177/1081180X05281395.

Lampe, C., Ellison, N., & Steinfeld, C. (2006). A face(book) in the crowd: Social searching vs. social browsing. In *Proceedings of the 2006 20th anniversary conference on computer-supported cooperative work (CSCW 2006)* (pp. 167–170). New York: ACM Press.

Lenhart, A. (2009). *Adults and social network Web sites*. Retrieved March 19, 2009, from http://www.pewinternet.org/Reports/2009/Adults-and-Social-Network-Websites.aspx

Lenhart, A., Horrigan, J., & Farrows, D. (2004). *Content creation online*. Retrieved March 19, 2009, from http://www.pewinternet.org/Reports/2004/Content-Creation-Online.aspx.

Lenhart, A., Madden, M., Macgill, A. R., & Smith, A. (2007). *Teens and social media*. Retrieved March 19, 2009, from http://www.pewinternet.org/Reports/2007/Teens-and-Social-Media.aspx

Livingstone, S., & Helsper, E. (2007). Gradations in digital inclusion: Children, young people and the digital divide. *New Media & Society*, *9*(4), 671–696. doi:10.1177/1461444807080335.

Mauri, M., Cipresso, P., Balgera, A., Villamira, M., & Riva, G. (2011). Why is Facebook so successful? Psychophysiological measures describe a core flow state while using Facebook. *Cyberpsychology, Behavior, and Social Networking*, *14*(12), 723–731. doi:10.1089/cyber.2010.0377 PMID:21879884.

McCrae, R. R., & Costa, P. T. (1997). Personality trait structure as a human universal. *The American Psychologist*, *52*(5), 509–516. doi:10.1037/0003-066X.52.5.509 PMID:9145021.

McKenna, K. Y. A., & Bargh, J. A. (2000). Plan 9 from cyberspace: The implications of the Internet for personality and social psychology. *Personality and Social Psychology Review*, *4*(1), 57–75. doi:10.1207/S15327957PSPR0401_6.

Mondak, J. J., & Halperin, K. (2008). A framework for the study of personality and political behaviour. *British Journal of Political Science*, *38*(2), 335–362. doi:10.1017/S0007123408000173.

Mondak, J. J., Hibbing, M. V., Canache, D., Selgson, M. A., & Anderson, M. R. (2010). Personality and civic engagement: An integrative framework for the study of trait effects on political behavior. *The American Political Science Review*, *104*, 85–110. doi:10.1017/S0003055409990359.

Pagani, M., Hofacker, C. F., & Goldsmith, R. E. (2011). The influence of personality on active and passive use of social networking sites. *Psychology and Marketing*, *28*(5), 441–456. doi:10.1002/mar.20395.

Peter, J., Valkenburg, P. M., & Schouten, A. P. (2007). Precursors of adolescents' use of visual and audio devices during online communication. *Computers in Human Behavior*, *23*(5), 2473–2487. doi:10.1016/j.chb.2006.04.002.

Quan-Haase, A. (2007). College students' local and distance communication: Blending online and offline media. *Information Communication and Society*, *10*(5), 671–693. doi:10.1080/13691180701658020.

Quercia, D., Kosinski, M., Stillwell, D., & Crowcroft, J. (2011). *Our Twitter profiles, our selves: Predicting personality with Twitter*. Paper presented at the 3rd IEEE Conference on Social Computing (SocialCom). Boston, MA.

Quercia, D., Lambiotte, R., Kosinski, M., Stillwell, D., & Crowcroft, J. (in press). The personality of popular Facebook users. *Proceedings of the Association of Computing Machinery Conference on Computer Supported Cooperative Work 2012*.

Raacke, J., & Bonds-Raacke, J. (2008). MySpace and Facebook: Applying the uses and gratifications theory to exploring friend-networking sites. *Cyberpsychology & Behavior*, *11*(2), 169–174. doi:10.1089/cpb.2007.0056 PMID:18422409.

Rojas, H., & Puig-i-Abril, E. (2009). Mobilizers mobilized: Information, expression, mobilization and participation in the digital age. *Journal of Computer-Mediated Communication*, *14*(4), 902–927. doi:10.1111/j.1083-6101.2009.01475.x.

Ross, C., Orr, E. S., Sisic, M., Arseneault, J. M., Simmering, M. G., & Orr, R. R. (2009). Personality and motivations associated with Facebook use. *Computers in Human Behavior*, *25*(2), 578–586. doi:10.1016/j.chb.2008.12.024.

Schimmack, U., Shigehiro, O., Furr, R. M., & Funder, D. C. (2008). Personality and life satisfaction: A facet-level analysis. *Personality and Social Psychology Bulletin*, *30*(8), 1065–1075. PMID:15257789.

Shah, D., Cho, J., Eveland, W. P. J., & Kwak, N. (2005). Information and expression in a digital age: Modeling internet effects on civic participation. *Communication Research*, *32*(5), 531–565. doi:10.1177/0093650205279209.

Valenzuela, S., Park, N., & Kee, K. F. (2009). Is there social capital in a social network site?: Facebook use and college students' life satisfaction, trust and participation. *Journal of Computer-Mediated Communication*, *14*(4), 875–901. doi:10.1111/j.1083-6101.2009.01474.x.

Van Gestel, S., & Van Broeckhoven, C. (2003). Genetics of personality: Are we making progress? *Molecular Psychiatry*, *8*, 840–852. doi:10.1038/sj.mp.4001367 PMID:14515135.

Vavreck, L. (2007). The exaggerated effects of advertising on turnout: The dangers of self-reports. *Quarterly Journal of Political Science*, *2*(4), 325–343. doi:10.1561/100.00006005.

Wellman, B., Quan-Haase, A., Boase, J., Chen, W., Hampton, K., Isla de Diaz, I., et al. (2003). The social affordances of the Internet for networked individualism. *Journal of Computer-Mediated Communication*, *8*(3). Retrieved January 10, 2009, from http://jcmc.indiana.edu/vol8/issue3/wellman.html

Williams, A. P., & Tedesco, J. C. (2006). *The Internet election: Perspectives on the Web in campaign 2004*. New York: Rowman & Littlefield.

YouTube. (2012). *Statistics*. Retrieved February 16, 2012, from http://www.youtube.com/t/press_statistics

Zywica, J., & Danowski, J. (2008). The faces of Facebookers: Investigating social enhancement and social compensation hypotheses. *Journal of Computer-Mediated Communication*, *14*(1), 1–34. doi:10.1111/j.1083-6101.2008.01429.x.

ADDITIONAL READING

Bouchard, T., & McGue, M. (2003). Genetic and environmental influences on human psychological differences. *Journal of Neurobiology*, *54*(1), 4–45. doi:10.1002/neu.10160 PMID:12486697.

Boyd, D. M., & Ellison, N. B. (2007). Social network sites: Definition, history, and scholarship. *Journal of Computer-Mediated Communication*, *13*(1). Retrieved from http://jcmc.indiana.edu/vol13/issue1/ boyd.ellison.html doi:10.1111/j.1083-6101.2007.00393.x.

Gerber, A. S., Huber, G. A., Doherty, D., & Dowling, C. M. (2009). Reassessing the effects of personality on political attitudes and behaviors: Aggregate relationships and subgroup differences. SSRN working paper. Retrieved March 15, 2010, from http://ssrn.com/abstract=1412839

Gil de Zúñiga, H., & Valenzuela, S. (2010). Disentangling facebookers: A snapshot of social network site users in the United States. In Wittkower, D. (Ed.), *Facebook and philosophy* (pp. xxxi–xxxvii). Chicago, IL: Open Court Publishing.

Gil de Zúñiga, H., Veenstra, A., Vraga, E., & Shah, D. (2010). Digital democracy: Re-imagining pathways to political participation. *Journal of Information Technology & Politics*, *7*(1), 36–51. doi:10.1080/19331680903316742.

Goldberg, L. R., & Rosolack, T. K. (1994). The Big Five factor structure as an integrative framework: An empirical comparison with Eysenck's P-E-N model. In Halverson, C. F., Kohnstamm, G. A., & Martin, R. P. (Eds.), *The developing structure of temperament and personality from infancy to adulthood* (pp. 7–36). England: Lawrence Erlbaum Associates.

Gosling, S., & Vazire, S. (2007). Personality impressions based on Facebook profiles. Paper presented at the International Conference on Weblogs and Social Media (ICWSM). Boulder, CO.

Heimpel, S. A., Elliot, A. J., & Wood, J. V. (2006). Basic personality dispositions, self-esteem, and personal goals: An approach-avoidance analysis. *Journal of Personality*, *74*(5), 1293–1320. doi:10.1111/j.1467-6494.2006.00410.x PMID:16958703.

Ito, M., Horst, H., & Bittani, M. boyd, D., Herr-Stephenson, B., Lange, P. G., et al. (2008). Living and learning with new media: Summary of findings from the digital youth project. Cambridge: The MIT Press.

Kent, M. (2010). Directions in social media for professionals and scholars. In Heath, R. (Ed.), *Handbook of Public Relations* (2nd ed., pp. 643–656). Thousand Oaks, CA: Sage.

Landers, R. N., & Lounsbury, J. W. (2006). An investigation of Big Five and narrow personality traits in relation to Internet usage. *Computers in Human Behavior*, *22*(2), 283–293. doi:10.1016/j.chb.2004.06.001.

Livingstone, S. (2004). Media literacy and the challenge of new information and communication technologies. *Communication Review*, *7*(1), 3–14. doi:10.1080/10714420490280152.

Livingstone, S., Bober, M., & Helsper, E. J. (2005). Active participation or just more information? Young people's take-up of opportunities to act and interact on the internet. *Information Communication and Society*, *8*(3), 287–314. doi:10.1080/13691180500259103.

McCrae, R. R. (1992). The five-factor model: Issues and applications. *Journal of Personality*, *60*(2). doi:10.1111/j.1467-6494.1992.tb00970.x.

Odekerken-Schroder, G., Wulf, K. D., & Schumacher, P. (2003). Strengthening outcomes of retailer-consumer relationships: The dual impact of relationship marketing tactics and consumer personality. *Journal of Business Research*, *56*(3), 177–190. doi:10.1016/S0148-2963(01)00219-3.

Papacharissi, Z. (2011). *A networked self: Identity, community, and culture on social network sites.* Taylor & Francis.

Park, N., Kee, K. F., & Valenzuela, S. (2009). Being immersed in social networking environment: Facebook groups, uses and gratifications, and social outcomes. *Cyberpsychology & Behavior*, *12*(6), 729–733. doi:10.1089/cpb.2009.0003 PMID:19619037.

Pavot, W. G., Diener, E., Colvin, C. R., & Sandvik, E. (1991). Further validation of the satisfaction with life scale: Evidence for the cross-method convergence of well-being measures. *Journal of Personality Assessment*, *57*, 149–161. doi:10.1207/s15327752jpa5701_17 PMID:1920028.

Rosen, P., & Kluemper, D. (2008). The impact of the Big Five personality traits on the acceptance of social networking website. *Information Systems Journal*. Retrieved from http://aisel.aisnet.org/cgi/viewcontent.cgi?article=1276&context=amcis2008

Smith, A., Lehmann Scholzman, K., Verba, S., & Brady, H. (2009). *The Internet and civic engagement.* Washington, DC: Pew Internet & American Life Project.

Swickert, R. J., Hittner, J. B., Harris, J. L., & Herring, J. A. (2002). Relationships among Internet use, personality, and social support. *Computers in Human Behavior*, *18*(4), 437–451. doi:10.1016/S0747-5632(01)00054-1.

Tong, S. T., Heide, B. V. D., Langwell, L., & Walther, J. B. (2008). Too much of a good thing? The relationship between number of friends and interpersonal impressions on Facebook. *Journal of Computer-Mediated Communication*, *13*(3), 531–549. doi:10.1111/j.1083-6101.2008.00409.x.

Verhulst, B., Hatemi, P. K., & Martin, N. G. (2010). The nature of the relationship between personality traits and political attitudes. *Personality and Individual Differences*, *49*(4), 306–316. doi:10.1016/j.paid.2009.11.013.

Watkins, C. (2009). *The young and the digital: What the migration to social network sites, games, and anytime anywhere media means for our future*. Boston, MA: Beacon.

Winter, D. G. (2003). Personality and political behavior. In Sears, D. O., Huddy, L., & Jervis, R. (Eds.), *Oxford Handbook of Political Psychology* (pp. 110–145). New York: Oxford University Press.

Wolfradt, U., & Doll, J. (2001). Motives of adolescents to use the Internet as a function of personality traits, personal and social factors. *Journal of Educational Computing Research*, *24*(1), 13–27. doi:10.2190/ANPM-LN97-AUT2-D2EJ.

KEY TERMS AND DEFINITIONS

Big Five: A broad model that uses five domains to categorize and reliably measure individual's personality traits—extraversion, emotional stability, openness to new experiences, agreeableness, and conscientiousness.

Emotional Stability: Personality trait related to different levels of anxiety, instability, and excitability. Its reverse is called neuroticism.

Extraversion: Personality trait that indicates one's tendency to be active, sociable, lively, and assertive. Its reverse is introversion, which is associated with shyness and passivity.

Openness to New Experiences: Personality trait linked to different degrees of open-mindedness, creativity, imagination, originality, curiosity, and complexity.

Personality: Stable psychological feature related to a wide range of an individual's attitudes and behaviors.

Social Media Use: Consumption of digital media or Internet related to communication and interaction purposes, rather than informational uses. This includes services such as chatting, instant messaging, microblogging and social networking sites.

Chapter 4
How Motivations for Social Media Usage Can Change and What It Means for E-Businesses

Tobias Hopp
University of Oregon, USA

Harsha Gangadharbatla
University of Oregon, USA

Kim Sheehan
University of Oregon, USA

ABSTRACT

Available research indicates that consumers are more likely to accept social media advertising when such content appeals to their motivations for joining the site. However, this research generally assumes that the forces driving a user's initial motivations for social media acceptance and usage remain constant through time. Given the fact this assumption may, indeed, be a faulty one, this chapter is specifically concerned with exploring the idea that user motivations may exist as evolving factors with the potential to impact the efficacy of e-business initiatives on social media sites. In support of this goal, in this chapter we: (1) define and contextually discuss social media; (2) review extant literature as it relates to motivations for media use; (3) discuss the idea of temporal motivations; (4) present the results of a pilot study that provides empirical evidence for the evolving nature of motivations; and (5) discuss the theoretical and practical implications of our results.

DOI: 10.4018/978-1-4666-4026-9.ch004

INTRODUCTION

With feverish irreverence, social networking sites (SNS) have rapidly come to occupy a significant space in the corporate world's mediated consciousness. Marketers fret over consumer-generated content and its impact on their brand's equity. Advertisers worry about reaching their audiences who now also assume the role of content creators. Public relations professionals have to deal with SNS and the rapid pace with which information spreads through these networks. Businesses work diligently to design, create, and implement effective viral campaigns and seek positive response in the form of reviews, likes, fan following, increase in website traffic, and ultimately, sales. In short, social media are transforming businesses, particularly e-businesses, in ways previously unimaginable.

Exploring the role of social media in e-business has proven to be a complex endeavor, especially for practitioners charged with making sense of the mercurial world of social media. Nonetheless, it is quite apparent that acquiring an understanding of social media is crucial to both the present and the future of e-business. Several practitioners, such as Edelman CEO, Richard Edelman, have called for present-day corporations to think beyond the paid and traditional media and embrace emerging media such as social networking sites (Van Grove, 2010). This comes in the light of increasing membership of social networking sites with over 70% of young adults in the US logging into one or more such sites and almost 50% of all adults using them regularly (Lenhart, 2009). Globally, 22% of all time spent online is spent on an SNS (Nielson, 2010). Of the popular social media destinations, Facebook outranks others with almost 750 million global users (Facebook Facts, 2011). Twitter, a micro-blogging website that limits each post to 140 characters or less, is also quite popular, featuring over 175 million users worldwide (Twitter, 2011).

Many businesses and prominent personalities have already adopted social media as a powerful means of connecting with audiences. The amount of money spent by U.S. advertisers and marketers in 2010 was approximately $1.7 billion (USD). Worldwide, this number is almost double the amount ($3.3 billion USD) and is estimated to be growing rapidly (eMarketer, 2010). Advertising expenditures on Facebook have grown at an exponential rate for the last three years with the largest spenders on Facebook increasing their annual expenditures by nearly 900% (Womack, 2010). Many analysts, such as eMarketer's Debra Williamson, claim that Facebook will soon become a dominant force not just for SNS advertising but also for all of online advertising (Brown, 2011). Despite these numbers and optimistic predictions, very little is known about the effectiveness of social media advertising. As more and more users flock to social networking sites, it becomes imperative for corporations interested in reaching these consumers with their marketing and promotional messages to develop a better understanding of how these new media vehicles function.

Very little research in the area of social media advertising has been done to date. Both academics and practitioners are only beginning to scratch of surface of understanding how to target SNS users with any real measure of effectiveness (Clemons, 2009; Zubcsek and Sarvary, 2011). Initial research seems to indicate that social media advertising may not be producing the desirable effects that e-businesses are hoping for (Johnson, 2010; Taylor, Lewin, & Strutton, 2011). In a 2010 study conducted by the online research firm Dynamic Logic, researchers found that only 22% of SNS users had a positive opinion of advertising on social network platforms and, further, that nearly 10% of SNS participants had abandoned online social networking because they perceived advertising content to be excessive. Similarly, researchers at the Internet Data Corporation (IDC) found that less than one-fourth of SNS users found on-site advertising helpful or relevant to their lives (Weide & Dangson, 2008).

In order to better understand the factors influencing the effectiveness of social media advertising, it is important to examine user motivations for social media adoption and usage. Research indicates that marketing efforts on social media can be effective if done right. For instance, in Taylor, Lewin, and Strutton's (2011) study on SNS advertising, the authors found SNS users were significantly more likely to accept advertising content if that content appealed to their motivations for joining the site. Specifically, the authors drew upon extant theory in social psychology, marketing, and advertising in order to assert that "when SNA delivers content that is consistent with the motivations originally expressed in media uses and gratification theory, consumers were more likely to ascribe positive attitudes toward advertising conveyed to them through an SNS medium" (p. 269). If, indeed, it is the case that social media users will accept advertising when such advertising corresponds to their motivations for use, there exists a strong impetus to further understand and evaluate motivations for social media adoption and usage. A few researchers have begun investigating the motivations for social media usage (e.g., Gangadharbatla, 2008) but to date there have not been any studies that explore usage motivations within a temporal continuum, meaning, in a dynamic state. In other words, researchers have conceived user motivations as static in nature assuming that the forces driving a user's initial motivations for social media usage remain the same as those forces that motivate his or her ongoing use of the platform. There is a need to examine user motivations as evolving, dynamic forces that contribute indirectly to the success or failure of marketing campaigns on social media.

To this end, the current chapter investigates user motivations for social media usage, their changing nature, and their potential impact(s) on marketing campaigns. More precisely, we begin with a background on social media and their role in e-business. Second, we review literature to list various motivations for social media adoption and usage. Third, we introduce and discuss the idea of temporal motivations, or the concept that user motivations for SNS use can and do evolve over time. Fourth, we briefly present the results of a pilot study that provides empirical evidence for the evolving nature of motivations. Fifth, we present both the theoretical and practical implications of evolving social media usage motivations in direct relation to marketing and e-business for academics, marketers, advertisers, and other e-business professionals. Finally, we end by listing some areas that we think are ripe for future inquiry and understanding of the role of social media in e-business transformation.

BACKGROUND

Social media are often referred to as social networking sites, Web 2.0 technologies, user-generated content, consumer-generated content, and a host of other names. Whatever the name, the common, underlying aspects of such websites are fourfold: (a) users of social media can create a public or semi-public profile, (b) share their list of friends or connections with other users, (c) view the list of connections of their friends or followers (Boyd & Ellison, 2007), and (d) create most of all of the content on these systems (Gangadharbatla, 2012). These online networks are different from offline networks because they allow users to make their connections publicly available to everyone and, in so doing, enable users to construct and manage a virtual persona on these systems (Boyd & Ellison, 2007). Social media (at least in theory) allow users to present themselves on their own terms, communicate with whomever they choose, and develop networks of friends and associates based around shared interests or other commonalities. According to Choi, Watt, Dekkers, and Park (2004), SNS sites are inherently defined by their capability to stretch users' personal networks across both space and class. Most recently, Solis defined social media as "the democratization of information, transforming people from content readers into publishers. It is the shift from a broadcast mechanism, one-to-many, to a many-to-one model, rooted in conversations between authors, people, and peers" (2010, p. 37).

Of all the distinguishing features of social media, the most remarkable one—as Solis points out in his definition of social media—is that most or all of the content on social media websites is created and shared by the users of these sites. It truly is a many-to-many model of communication. Content on social media can appear in a variety of places (walls, newsfeed, private messages, IM chat, etc.) and formats (text, photos, audio, and video). The wall and newsfeed features are included in many social media websites such as Facebook, Google+, Twitter, Mixi, Orkut, and Linkedin. While the wall serves as a primary means of interpersonal communication that more often than not happens in the public sphere, newsfeeds function as content aggregators that display information published by the users for their friends' benefit. Additionally, social media allow users to create and/or join fan pages and groups based around shared interests. Examples of popular, interest-based groups on Facebook include groups dedicated to Lady Gaga (over 43 million members), Starbucks (over 24 million members), the Manchester United football club (over 18 million fans), and Victoria's Secret (over 15 million members). Once a member, or a "fan," of these groups, content posted by the group administrator(s) appears in the user's newsfeed. Moreover, social media users can post content on the group's wall and discuss various topics of interest with fellow members.

As social media gain in popularity, the race to become the go-to platform for all individual needs and activities on the Internet is also heating up. For instance, Facebook has incorporated (or has plans to incorporate) photo/image-sharing, music, gaming, voice and video chat, marketplace and e-business activities, and even a currency of their own to encourage its users to spend more and more time on their system. This would not only facilitate the collection of more information and data from its users but also increase the advertising revenues generated every year. Competitors of Facebook—Google+, for example—have introduced similar features to their networks that make the "hangout" aspect of communities of social media users cheaper, faster, and easier (Google, 2011). An implication of such a fast-paced, ever-changing, ever-evolving environment is that today's leaders are tomorrow's losers. As an example, in 2006, MySpace, fresh off the heels of a $900 million (USD) advertising deal with Google, was the market leader with almost 200 million registered users. According to a report by comScore it was the most popular site on the Internet that year (Sorice, 2006). However, it did not take long for the leader to lose its market share due to its failure to act fast and upgrade its features, improve its design, and/or reach new demographics (Adams, 2011). Today, less than 60 million active users inhabit what has come to be known as the slum of social media websites and almost half of its corporate staff was recently laid off (Arrington, 2011). Facebook, on the other hand, constantly adds new features and functionality to its website, frequently changes its design, and amends its privacy options. Perhaps, these constant and frequent changes to Facebook relate to its users' motivations for usage that are also constantly and frequently evolving.

Regardless of the reasons for rapid changes to the social media landscape, the constant change in demographic and technological character of these websites has resulted in a significant knowledge gap relating to user motivations for usage and its impact on e-business for both practitioners and academics. One of the challenges to understanding the role of social media in e-business relates to our ability to understand cognitive usage motivations and how that translates to effective business strategies. For example, as discussed earlier, the Taylor,

Lewin, and Strutton's (2011) study of effectiveness of advertising on social media websites confirms that users were more likely to accept advertising content on SNS when that content appealed to their original motivations for joining the SNS site. The authors further noted that a crucially important (and perhaps quite obvious) ingredient to any successful SNS advertising strategy is to "create messages that provide some sort of explicit value to SNS users" (p. 269).

Based on the discussion above, we continue with a brief review of research on media use motivations derived from a uses and gratifications theory perspective and relate that to current literature that identifies social-psychological motivations for social media usage.

MOTIVATIONS FOR SNS USAGE

In order to understand the specific motivations for social media usage, it is important to first acquire a general understanding of motivation, especially as it relates to media usage. Human motivation is the process by which goal-related activity is "instigated and sustained" (Kao, Wu, and Tsai, 2011, p. 406). Motivations, themselves, can be broken into two general categories: intrinsic motives and extrinsic motivations. People are intrinsically motivated to undertake a task because they see the "task itself as interesting, appealing, and satisfying" (Prat-Sala & Redford, 2010, p. 284). On the other hand, people are extrinsically motivated to engage with a task in order to attain some form of separable, tangible outcomes (Ryan & Deci, 2000). Media usage can be influenced by both intrinsic and extrinsic motivations.

There are numerous mass media-oriented theories that attempt to explain media attendance. Some of these theories, such as need for cognition (e.g., Petty & Cacioppo, 1986), posit that individuals use media in order to experience feelings of engagement and cognitive stimulation. Other perspectives, inclusive of the social identity

theory (e.g., Tajfel, 1981), argue that media use is innervated by social and group considerations. Still other theoretical bodies assert that engagement is spurred by attitudinal concerns. For example, Katz's (1960) functional theory maintains that four primary functional sources of attitude, or motivations, form the foundation for subsequent attitude formation. For its part, the uses and gratifications approach (Katz, Blumler, & Gurevitch, 1974; Rubin, 1984) stresses an active audience that uses media to gratify an array of psychological needs. While each theoretical perspective certainly has its own applications and limitations, generally speaking, they homogenously propose that audiences are selective in nature and consume, construct, and create media in order to achieve a variety of social or psychological goals. In addition, most current theoretical perspectives assert that motivation, as an individual-level variable, is context dependent (Prat-Sala & Redford, 2010).

Current research on user motivations for social media adoption comes from socio-psychological research on Internet usage in general. Applying the motivations for Internet use, several communication researchers have explained topics such as uses of instant messages and email, discussion forums and virtual communities, blog creation and readership, and user-generated content (Daughetry, Eastin, & Bright, 2008; Huffaker & Calvert, 2005; Kaye, 2005; Ramirez, Dimmick, Feaster, & Shu-Fang, 2008; Wei, 2004). The most commonly explored motivations for social media usage include social motivations (Barker, 2009; Choi et al., 2004; Farquhar & Meeds, 2007; Ginossar, 2005; Nambisan & Watt, 2004); knowledge acquisition (Chung & Kim, 2007; Sweetser & Kaid, 2008; Tustin, 2010; Wei, 2009); enjoyment (Hwang, 2005; LaRose & Eastin, 2002; Lee, 2004; Leung, 2009); cognitive stimulation (Gangadharbatla, 2008); value expression (Daughtry, Eastin, & Bright, 2008); and self expression (Li, 2007; Trammell, 2005; Trammell et al., 2006).

Within the spectrum of media and communication research, the most commonly utilized theoretical perspective is undoubtedly the uses and gratifications perspective. The uses and gratifications approach to media usage assumes that individuals use media to gratify their needs and wants (Katz, Blumler, & Gurevitch, 1973; Rubin, 1984). It asserts that individuals are not stationary targets of the mass media but, instead, active participants who make media consumption choices based upon a desire to achieve, or *gratify*, certain needs and/or desires (Daugherty, Eastin, & Bright, 2008; Papacharissi & Rubin, 2000; Sheehan, 2002). Unlike many motivational theories in the cognitive sciences, the uses and gratifications approach can be used in an inductive manner and is hence well-suited for use in areas of research still in their iterative phases, such as the current exploration of social media usage motivations in relation to e-business. As discussed by Katz, Blumler, and Gurevitch (1974), uses and gratifications research focuses on "(1) the social and psychological origins of (2) needs, which generate (3) expectations of (4) the mass media…which lead to (5) differential patterns of media exposure… resulting in (6) need gratifications and (7) other consequences" (p. 20). Current uses and gratifications literature has identified a number of pursued needs, including information acquisition, affective needs related to emotion, pleasure and feeling, ego-defense needs associated with credibility, status, and projection of personal, moral values, social needs associated with communicating with loved ones and friends, and needs associated with diversion, passing time, and escape. According to the uses and gratification perspective, individuals actively chose media based on the media's ability to gratify five different categories of needs: (1) cognitive needs associated with acquiring information, knowledge and understanding; (2) affective needs associated emotion, pleasure, and feelings; (3) personal integrative needs associated with credibility, stability, and status; (4) social integrative needs associated with communicating with family and friends; and (5) tension release needs, or those needs associated with escape and

diversion (e.g., Blumler & Katz, 1974; Katz, Blumler, & Gurevitch, 1973; Palmgreen, Wenner, & Rosengren, 1985; Rubin, 1984).

Although the uses and gratifications perspective was originally developed to explain engagement with traditional media such as newspapers and radio, it has hence been well applied to a variety of media including the Internet and social media. In terms of Internet usage, researchers have identified the same general categories of needs. For example, in their multivariate analysis of Internet use, Korgaonkar and Wolin (1999) identified seven factors that influence the use of Internet: escapism, transactional security and privacy, surveillance, interactive control, socialization, non-transactional privacy, and economic motivation. Within this set of seven influence variables, the authors further discerned that information seeking and socialization/escapism were the two primary factors that most influenced Internet usage. Similarly, a study of adolescents and young adults, Papacharissi and Rubin (2000) identified five motives for use of the Internet: interpersonal utility, passing time, convenience, information seeking, and entertainment.

With the emergence of social media, several researchers, including a co-author of this chapter, began employing uses and gratifications perspective to social media usage. Using a focus group methodology, Gangadharbatla (2009) identified five broad motivations for social media adoption and usage: entertainment, need to belong, information-seeking, commercial uses, and identity or self-expression. These five broad motivations for social media usage that emerged from the focus groups include and extend the uses and gratifications perspective to social media usage.

Having identified the main motivations for social media usage from a review of literature in this area, we turn our attention to the transient nature of motivations by posing the question: can motivations for social media usage change over time?

Can Motivations Change Over Time?

Despite the fact that motivations for media usage have been relatively well explored by empirical researchers from a wide array of scholarly traditions, very little is known about the temporality or the dynamic nature of motivations. In fact, we did not find even a single study in our review of available literature in the marketing, advertising, psychology, or communication that directly examined the dynamic nature of motivations for social media usage. Given this gap, we collected some primary data in the form of open-ended surveys to investigate whether or not motivations for social media usage changed over time. Our approach was exploratory in nature with the goal of understanding more in depth the changing nature of motivations more so than generalizing our results across populations and situations.

Data were collected online using open-ended questionnaires hosted on the online feedback management tool, Qualtrics. We asked respondents to (a) list the reasons why they chose to join a popular social media website, Facebook, originally and (b) to list how these reasons changed over time identifying any new reasons that may have emerged after using it for a while. Given that our objective was not to generalize but to explore in depth the motivations for social media usage and how they change over time, we used a "snowball" sampling technique to collect our data. Data collection started with researchers posting a link to the survey on their Facebook and Twitter pages and asking the participants to do the same

after taking part in our study. A total of 66 people responded to our open-ended survey. Respondent ages ranged from 18 to 65. Most respondents had been on Facebook for at least one year; however, several participants indicated that they had been Facebook users since the site's inception in 2004.

Two of the researchers evaluated the responses by working independently. Five broad reasons for originally joining the social media website emerged in both cases. These categories, summarized in the table below, were mostly consistent with the ones identified in our literature review above, particularly with the ones identified by Gangadharbatla (2009). The judges charged with evaluating the responses agreed on over 95% of the cases. See Table 1.

Of these five broad motivations, four were exactly the same as Gangadharbatla (2009). These motivations included need to belong, communication, entertainment, and information seeking. Two of these were more frequently mentioned than the rest: communication and need to belong. Interestingly, quite a number of the respondents indicated that they joined the site in order to connect to a specific individual. Accordingly, while a manifest desire to satisfy general social needs was observed, these motivations were very much tempered by a desire to interact with a specified, sharply defined individual or group of individuals. As it related to the motivations representing entertainment and information seeking behavior, respondents were very specific in identifying and mentioning them. For instance, entertainment included playing online games, viewing photos,

Table 1. Original motivations for joining the social media website

Motivation	Examples	No. of Respondents
Need to belong	"I like the idea of reconnecting with people I hadn't seen for many years."	19
Communication	"...to keep in contact with cousins and friends."	12
Entertainment	"...to play online games with friends and family [e.g., Farmville]"	3
Information	"...to get insight into undergraduate life..."	8
Bandwagon Effect	"...my friends were on it and pestered me."	24

and listening to music their friends were interested in, and in the information category, respondents mentioned looking for specific individuals, events, topics, and groups. Finally, and perhaps surprisingly, we uncovered a motivation that represented a novelty, or "bandwagon" effect. Reasons under this category included the newness associated with Facebook, its potential over other social media websites, friends and family recommending it, etc. These motivations seem to stem from expectations that others in their offline network seem to place on the individuals. Users who joined in this fashion mentioned no particular reason or gratification sought from it. They were doing it simply because everyone else seemed to be doing it.

In order to examine whether there were any changes in motivations after joining, we analyzed the responses to the second open-ended question in a similar fashion. The agreement here was also over 95%. The results are presented in Table 2.

As noted earlier, the second research question dealt with exploring a change in user motivations over time. As seen in Table 2, a manifest shift of motivations for use was observed. The change occurred in two ways: one, the number of respondents citing a particular motivation either increased or decreased, and two, at least three new motivations emerged from our analysis that were cited as new motivations for continued usage of the

social media website. While we cannot generalize with confidence intervals and statistical significance—as our objective is more along the lines of establishing a directionality and gaining an in depth understanding through exploratory open-ended methodology—we found differences in the number of respondents mentioning a particular motivation for joining and for continued usage. For instance, the number of respondents citing a reason that fell under need to belong increased from 19 to 28, similarly the number increased from 12 to 19 for communication, 3 to 10 for entertainment, and 8 to 11 for information. The only decrease occurred for the motivation originally described as bandwagon effect. This is interesting as it seems to suggest that once an individual joins a social media website for reasons falling under bandwagon effect, those reasons do not seem to play any role in its continued usage.

The other important changes to motivations occurred in the form of new reasons that respondents cited for usage after joining, namely: self-expression, replacing older media, and professional reasons. It can be safely said that users were discovering new motivations once they joined Facebook and started using it regularly. For instance, users discovered that they "can [now] control what and how people think of [them]." They found that social media could replace older media and be used to meet needs formerly met by

Table 2. Changes in motivations after joining the social media website

Category	Examples	No. of Respondents
Need to belong	"It feels like a way to stay connected in a busy world even if there isn't time to have an actual conversation."	28
Communication	"I use it today to keep in touch with friends I see on a regular basis, as well as long-distance or older friends."	19
Entertainment	"To check my farm on Farmville."	10
Information	"I use it to share info about events, my work, my opinions, etc."	11
Self-expression	"I can control what/how people think of me."	2
Replacing older media	"I use it in place of email."	5
Professional contacts	"There are professional dimensions now."	6

older media. Finally, respondents also discovered the professional aspect of social media and its use in enhancing their professional networks, finding jobs, and connecting with others in the industry.

What Do Changing User SNS Motivations Mean E-Businesses? Four Recommendations

Based on our review of literature and findings from our exploratory study, we can make numerous recommendations for both practitioners and academics interested in the future of e-businesses. With social media playing an increasingly important role in today's e-businesses, it becomes imperative that e-business professionals and managers be aware of the ways in which the motivations for social media usage can impact the communication and marketing strategies of e-businesses. As noted in our introduction, e-businesses are increasingly using social media as advertising and marketing vehicles. And knowing that advertisements on social networking sites that appeal to users' motivations for joining the site tend to be more effective than others (Taylor, Lewin, & Strutton, 2011), e-business practitioners are advised to pay particular attention to user motivations for using a particular technology before deciding to invest in advertising on that medium.

Second, the idea that motivations for social media site usage change over time requires that e-business practitioners remain vigilant in assessing their applied social media strategies. The online social world is evolving at a rapid pace. As with all technologies, social media website adoption and use goes through stages of diffusion of innovations. The motivations to use social media also seem to vary with the stages of the diffusion. In our study, we found that the initial motivation of bandwagon effect was almost not reported at all once users started using Facebook. This means that depending on what stage of adoption a particular social media website is in, owners of that site can devise strategies to increase membership

based on the motivations that correspond to that stage. Along the same lines, if a social media website is in its early stages of adoption, devising promotional material or ads to be placed on that site that appeal to a bandwagon effect may be more effective than other strategies. For instance, Facebook is in its early stages of adoption in some countries so using an appeal to the "bandwagon effect" in ads for users of that country might yield favorable results. However, it should be noted that nothing can be said about the percentage of users that actually join a social media website because of something like the bandwagon effect. Future research needs to address this issue through a more quantitative approach.

Third, the discovery of self-expression as a new motivation for social media usage has several implications for both social media websites and e-businesses. Self-expression and personal brand management is becoming important, and in some ways, easier on social media. Social media websites are run almost entirely by user-generated content. Users can create and maintain a certain personal brand by picking and choosing what content about them is visible to their friends and public. For instance, an individual can position him or herself as an expert in a certain area by regularly posting links to news and articles in that area, by creating and regularly updating a blog in that area, or by "liking" topics and activities on a website that establish a certain level of credibility. Gillin (2007) calls such an expert the "new influencer." E-businesses can start by identifying such "influencers" in online networks as these individuals act as key links between marketers and the public in general. Orienting marketing activities around these influencers can potentially yield greater ROI than targeting the public at large. Personal brand management is not a new concept; people have been managing their personal brands knowingly or unknowingly over the years. However, the advent of social media has brought the issue to forefront, so much so that universities such as Syracuse and Emory have started offering classes and workshops in personal brand management particularly via social media. As the general public becomes more aware of tools to manage their individual brands and the importance of doing so, they are more likely to demand e-businesses be more responsible with their database and privacy policies. In the future, consumers, well versed in personal brand management, may demand that e-businesses provide them with complete access to read, edit and delete all data collected about them.

Fourth, along the lines of personal brand management is our finding that social media users are using such websites as tools to enhance and build professional networks. What this means for e-businesses is that social media need to be well incorporated into not just their marketing and communications plans but also into HR and hiring plans. This finding and implication is underscored by the fact that recently the main social networking site for professionals, LinkedIn, went public and generated a market value of $9 billion USD, the highest for any Internet company since Google (Liedtke, 2011). Social media websites such as LinkedIn provide e-businesses opportunities to find and hire employees based exactly on their needs. The online profiles—personal brands—and the wealth of content created by social media users provides e-businesses all the necessary information that is needed in their hiring process. In that sense, social media are set to entirely transform the way businesses hire, retain and fire employees in the future. From an academic perspective, the motivation to use social media, or any media for that matter, for professional goals has completely been overlooked. From a traditional media vantage (i.e., newspapers, radio, and televisions) the professional aspects are limited to classified ads and job postings in those media. With regard to social media, however, entire professional networks are being built and used at every step of the hiring process.

Finally, our finding that users are discovering some motivations for social media usage that displace the needs formerly met by older media has implications for e-businesses as well. As social media become more and more prevalent, not only will they replace the communicative functions of older media, they will also replace the information, entertainment, and socialization functions of older media (newspapers, radio and television). This bodes well for e-businesses vested in bringing older media functions to the social media realm. For instance, it would make sense for Facebook to integrate with either a music streaming or video streaming company (Spotify or Hulu.com) and add the traditional functions of radio and television to their site. This would ensure that users spend more time watching content or listening to music on their site bringing in additional advertising dollars with them.

FUTURE RESEARCH DIRECTIONS

In terms of future research, there are a number of areas that deal with motivations for media usage and social media that should be explored in future research endeavors. This chapter, by design, is only the first exploratory step in that direction. As a starting point for future research, the ideas expressed in this chapter could be tested via quantitative surveys and real-time data with a representative sample so that generalizations could be made. E-businesses would also benefit from rigorous, quantitatively-oriented longitudinal study of the topics discussed here. Specifically, researchers could design a series of experiments that measure motivations for use as social media engagement "matures." Simple t-tests or ANOVA tests of variables that measure motivations should give us more insight into the dynamic (or changing) nature of motivations. Such efforts would add substantive validity to the results presented in this chapter.

The study of motivations in a social media context is somewhat under-researched and e-businesses could benefit from an exploration of the types of motivations that impact social media usage. For example, we identified somewhat broadly defined communication-based motivations for social media usage. By refining these motivations through empirical testing, i.e., developing and testing motivation scales in a social media context, researchers will eventually be able to explore usage motivations in a more robust, deductive manner.

Next, the idea that social media can be used to network with future employers and other professionals, to promote personal brands, and to replace older media is somewhat unexplored and certainly requires more investigation. How does a heightened sense of personal brand impact e-businesses? What new and improved privacy measures do e-businesses need to adopt given that more and more individuals are now concerned about controlling and protecting their personal brands online. Finally, future research should spend time investigating and comparing individual sites within the realm of social media. For instance, there may be differences in motivations for usage of Facebook and motivations for usage of Twitter. The idea that not all social media are the same is something that needs further exploration.

CONCLUSION

The current chapter examined motivations for joining social media websites and the changing/ dynamic nature of these motivations for continued usage. The main motivations for joining a social media website are a need to belong, communication, entertainment, information, and because it seems to be what everyone else is doing. In our research, we found that these reasons are transient and changed with usage. Users discovered new motivations and uses with increased usage and this was reflected in their responses. For instance, if respondents initially joined Facebook to keep in touch with a specific individual or a group of individuals, they indicated that with increased usage it became a part of their day-to-day routine

and they began to use the site as a medium for communication. In some cases, it entirely replaced e-mail as a means of communication. In other cases, its uses extended from staying in touch to forming new relationships and enhancing their professional networks. The overarching conclusion from our review of literature and open-ended exploratory research is that individuals' motivations for social media usage change over time. More specifically, individuals who joined social media websites such as Facebook found news reasons for usage such as self-expression, replacing older media, and professional aspects. In addition, the bandwagon effect of joining Facebook because everyone else seems to be doing so did not seem to play a significant role once they started using the site. This is expected as once users make it a part of their daily routine the novelty should wear off a bit.

Given the fact that social networking use and online commerce are significantly and intimately intertwined, e-businesses should remain cognizant that user motivations for social networking engagement change over time. In this chapter, we suggest four primary recommendations based upon our findings. First, advertising and marketing content on social networking sites should be flexibly calibrated to match user motivations for social networking use. As these motivations change over time, so too should marketing and advertising content. Second, marketing and advertising strategies should be linked to the diffusion stage of the social networking platform itself. As pointed out in this chapter, networking platforms such as Facebook are, geographically speaking, in different stages of user-acceptance. To that end, a "one-size fits all" approach is likely to be ineffective. Emergent markets--in terms of the social networking platform's social penetration--must be treated differently than mature markets in terms of advertising content. Moreover, we note that it is likely than Facebook will not retain its dominant status forever. If, for instance, an emergent social networking platform begins to achieve significant levels of user adoption, it is unlikely that simply "copying and pasting" strategic marketing and advertising elements from more mature social networking sites will prove to be either an effective or efficient use of resources. Third, we suggest in this chapter that brand management strategies should incorporate factors related to SNS users' desire for self-expression. People believe that they have something worth saying. Brands that can successfully listen to these consumers are likely to see significant return on their investment. Fourth, and finally, we suggest that e-businesses incorporate "personal brand" factors into their HR planning. As shown in this chapter, people are increasingly using social networking sites as a means of managing and promoting their professional selves. E-business firms should utilize such motivations as a way of informing their human resources and employee management activities.

Considered, perhaps, in its broadest possible sense, this chapter underscores the idea that the simple act of establishing a social networking presence will not yield tangible benefits for e-businesses. If firms are interested in maximizing the potential of social network sites, they should, on a continuous basis, seek to align their SNS advertising and marketing efforts with the temporally dynamic motivations that drive social network use.

REFERENCES

Adams, R. (2011). MySpace cuts 47% of workforce. *The Wall Street Journal*. Retrieved May 20, 2011, from http://online.wsj.com/article/SB10001424052748703791904576075892399066126.html

Arrington, M. (2011). Amazingly, Myspace's decline is accelerating. *TechCrunch*. Retrieved August 10, 2011, from http://techcrunch.com/2011/03/23/amazingly-myspaces-decline-is-accelerating/

Barker, V. (2009). Older adolescents' motivations for social network site use: The influence of gender, group identity, and collective self-esteem. *CyberPyschology and Behavior, 12*, 209–213. doi:10.1089/cpb.2008.0228 PMID:19250021.

Blumler, J., & Katz, E. (1974). *The uses of mass communication research: Current perspectives on gratifications research*. Beverly Hills, CA: Sage Publications.

Boyd, D. M., & Ellison, N. B. (2007). Social network sites: Definition, history, and scholarship. *Journal of Computer-Mediated Communication, 13*.

Brown, S. (2011). Social networks will receive 11% of online ad spending in 2011. *WealthVest Marketing*. Retrieved August 20, 2011, from http://www.wealthvest.com/blog/2011/01/20/statistics-social-networks-will-recieve-11-of-online-ad-spending-in-2011/

Choi, J., Watt, J., Dekkers, A., & Park, S. (2004). *Motives of Internet uses: Crosscultural perspective - the US, the Netherlands, and S. Korea*. Paper presented at annual meeting of the International Communication Association. New Orleans, LA.

Chung, D., & Kim, S. (2007). *Blog use among cancer patients and their companions: Uses, gratifications, and predictors of outcomes*. Paper presented at annual meeting of the International Communication Association. San Francisco, CA.

Clemons, E. (2009). The complex problem of monetizing virtual electronic social networks. *Decision Support Systems, 48*, 46–56. doi:10.1016/j.dss.2009.05.003.

Daugherty, T., Eastin, M. S., & Bright, L. (2008). Exploring consumer motivations for creating user-generated content. *Journal of Interactive Advertising, 8*, 16–25.

eMarketer (2010). *Social network ad spending to approach $1.7 billion this year*. Retrieved May 10, 2011, from http://www.mcvaynewmedia.com/social-network-ad-spending-to-approach-17-billion-this-year/

Farquhar, L., & Meeds, R. (2007). Types of fantasy sports users and their motivations. *Journal of Computer-Mediated Communication, 12*, 1208–1228. doi:10.1111/j.1083-6101.2007.00370.x.

Gangadharbatla, H. (2008). Facebook me: Collective self-esteem, need to belong, and Internet self-efficacy as predictors of the iGeneration's attitudes toward social networking sites. *Journal of Interactive Advertising, 8*, 5–15.

Gangadharbatla, H. (2009). Exploring Gen Y's motivations to join social networking sites. *Media Asia, 36*, 240–248.

Gangadharbatla, H. (2012). Social media and advertising theory. In Rodgers, S., & Thorson, E. (Eds.), *Advertising Theory* (pp. 402–416). New York: Routledge.

Gillin, P. (2007). *The new influencers: A marketer's guide to the new social media*. Sanger, CA: Quill Driver.

Ginossar, T. (2005). *Exploring participation in cancer-related virtual communities*. Paper presented at annual meeting of the International Communication Association. New York.

Google. (2011). Introducing the Google+ project: Real-life sharing, rethought for the web. *Google Blog*. Retrieved Aug 15, 2011, from http://google-blog.blogspot.com/2011/06/introducing-google-project-real-life.html

Huffaker, D. A., & Calvert, S. L. (2005). Gender, identity, and language use in teenage blogs. *Journal of Computer-Mediated Communication, 10*, 30–56.

Hwang, H. (2005). *Predictors of instant messaging: Gratifications sought, gratifications obtained, and social presence*. Paper presented at annual meeting of the International Communication Association. New York.

Johnson, B. (2010). Turmoil at Myspace blamed on News Corporation. *The Guardian*. Retrieved May 21, 2011, from http://www.guardian.co.uk/technology/2010/feb/14/myspace-news-corporation-owen-van-natta.

Kao, C., Wu, Y., & Tsai, C. (2011). Elementary school teachers' motivation toward web-based professional development, and the relationship with Internet self-efficacy and belief about web-based learning. *Teaching and Teacher Education, 27*, 406–415. doi:10.1016/j.tate.2010.09.010.

Kargaonkar, P. K., & Wolin, L. D. (1999). A multivariate analysis of web usage. *Journal of Advertising Research, 39*, 53–68.

Katz, D. (1960). The functional approach to the study of attitudes. *Public Opinion Quarterly, 24*, 27–46. doi:10.1086/266945.

Katz, E., Blumler, J., & Gurevitch, M. (1973). Uses and gratifications research. *Public Opinion Quarterly, 37*, 509–523. doi:10.1086/268109.

Katz, E., Blumler, J., & Gurevitch, M. (1974). Utilization of mass communication by the individual. In Blumler, J. G., & Katz, E. (Eds.), *The uses of mass communications: Current perspectives on gratifications research*. Beverly Hills, CA: Sage Publications.

Kaye, B. (2005). It's a blog, blog, blog world: Users and uses of weblogs. *Atlantic Journal of Communication, 13*, 73–95. doi:10.1207/s15456889ajc1302_2.

LaRose, R., & Eastin, M. S. (2002). *A social cognitive explanation of Internet uses and gratifications: Toward a new theory of media attendance*. Paper presented at annual meeting of the International Communication Association. Seoul, Korea.

Lee, S. (2004). *The uses and gratifications approach in the Internet age.* Paper presented at annual meeting of the International Communication Association. New Orleans, LA.

Lenhart, A. (2009). Adults and social network websites. *Pew Internet & American Life Project.* Retrieved February 20, 2011, from http://www. pewinternet.org/Reports/2009/Adults-and-Social-Network-Websites.aspx

Leung, L. (2009). User-generated content on the Internet: An examination of gratifications, civic engagement and psychological empowerment. *New Media & Society, 11,* 1327–1347. doi:10.1177/1461444809341264.

Li, D. (2007). *Why do you blog: A uses-and-gratifications inquiry into bloggers' motivations.* Paper presented at annual meeting of the International Communication Association. San Francisco, CA.

Liedtke, M. (2011). LinkedIn market value now $9 billion. *The Sun News.* Retrieved August 10, 2011, from http://www.thesunnews. com/2011/05/20/2169130/linkedin-market-value-now-9-billion.html

Nambisan, P., & Watt, J. (2004). *The impact of online community participation: Insights from the uses and gratifications' perspective.* Paper presented at annual meeting of the International Communication Association. New Orleans, LA.

Nielson. (2010). Social networks/blogs now account for one in every four and a half minutes online. *Nielsen Wire.* Retrieved June 10, 2011, from http://blog.nielsen.com/nielsenwire/ online_mobile/social-media-accounts-for-22-percent-of-time-online/

Palmgreen, P., Wenner, L. A., & Rosengren, K. E. (1985). Uses and gratifications research: The past ten years. In Rosengren, K. E., Wenner, L. A., & Palmgreen, P. C. (Eds.), *Uses and gratifications research: Current perspectives.* Beverly Hills, CA: Sage Publications.

Papacharissi, Z., & Rubin, A. M. (2000). Predictors of Internet use. *Journal of Broadcasting & Electronic Media, 44,* 175–196. doi:10.1207/ s15506878jobem4402_2.

Petty, R. E., & Cacioppo, J. T. (1986). *Communication and persuasion: Central and peripheral routes to attitude change.* New York: Springer-Verlag.

Prat-Sala, M., & Redford, P. (2010). The interplay between motivation, self-efficacy, and approaches to studying. *The British Journal of Psychology, 80,* 283–305. PMID:20021729.

Ramirez, J., Dimmick, J., Feaster, J., & Shu-Fang, L. (2008). Revisiting interpersonal media competition: The gratification niches of instant messaging, e-mail, and the telephone. *Communication Research, 35,* 529–547. doi:10.1177/0093650208315979.

Rubin, A. M. (1984). Ritualized and instrumental television viewing. *The Journal of Communication, 34,* 67–81. doi:10.1111/j.1460-2466.1984. tb02174.x.

Ryan, R. M., & Deci, E. L. (2000). Self-determination theory and the facilitation of intrinsic motivation, social development, and well-being. *The American Psychologist, 55,* 68–78. doi:10.1037/0003-066X.55.1.68 PMID:11392867.

Solis, B. (2010). *Engage!: The Complete Guide for Brands and Businesses to Build, Cultivate, and Measure Success in the New Web.* Hoboken, NJ: Wiley.

Sorice, C. (2006). It's official(sih): Myspace is the biggest site on the Internet. *TechCrunch.* Retrieved May 15, 2011, from http://techcrunch. com/2006/12/12/its-officialish-myspace-is-biggest-site-on-internet/

Sweetser, K., & Kaid, L. (2008). Stealth soapboxes: Political information efficacy, cynicism and uses of celebrity weblogs among readers. *New Media & Society*, *10*, 67–91. doi:10.1177/1461444807085322.

Tajfel, H. (1981). *Human groups and social categories*. Cambridge, MA: Cambridge University Press.

Taylor, D., Lewin, J., & Strutton, D. (2011). Friends, fans, and followers: Do ads work on social networks? How gender and age shape receptivity. *Journal of Advertising Research*, *51*, 258–275. doi:10.2501/JAR-51-1-258-275.

Trammell, K. (2005*). Looking at the pieces to understand the whole: An analysis of blog posts, comments, and trackbacks*. Paper presented at annual meeting of the International Communication Association. New York.

Trammell, K., Tarkowski, A., Hofmokl, J., & Sapp, A. (2006). Rzeczpospolita blogów [Republic of Blog]: Examining Polish bloggers through content analysis. *Journal of Computer-Mediated Communication*, *11*, 702–722. doi:10.1111/j.1083-6101.2006.00032.x.

Tustin, N. (2010). The role of patient satisfaction in online health information seeking. *Journal of Health Communication*, *15*, 3–17. doi:10.1080/10810730903465491 PMID:20390974.

Twitter. (2011). *About*. Retrieved August 15, 2011, from http://twitter.com/abou

Van Grove, J. (2010). How CEOs will use social media in the future. *Gist*. Retrieved May 30, 2011, from http://mashable.com/2010/08/30/ceo-social-media-future/

Wei, C. (2004). Formation of norms in a blog community. In L. Gurak, S. Antonijevic, L. Johnson, C. Ratliff, & J. Reyman (Eds.), *Into the blogosphere: Rhetoric, community, and the culture of weblogs*. Retrieved May 15, 2011, from http://blog.lib.umn.edu/blogosphere/formation_of_norms.html

Wei, F. (2009). Birthdays then and now: Applying uses and gratifications theory to analyze the media progression cycle. *Communication Teacher*, *23*, 23–27. doi:10.1080/17404620802592940.

Weide, K., & Dangson, C. (2008). *U.S. consumer online attitudes survey results, part III: Social networking*. Framingham, MA: Internet Data Corporation.

Womack, B. (2010). Facebook advertisers boost spending 10-fold, COO says. *Bloomberg Businessweek*. Retrieved May 10, 2011, from http://www.businessweek.com/news/2010-08-04/facebook-advertisers-boost-spending-10-fold-coo-says.html

Zubcsek, P., & Sarvary, M. (2011). Advertising to a social network. *Quantitative Marketing and Economics*, *19*, 71–107. doi:10.1007/s11129-010-9093-9.

ADDITIONAL READING

Barker, V. (2009). Older adolescents' motivations for social network site use: The influence of gender, group identity, and collective self-esteem. *CyberPyschology and Behavior*, *12*, 209–213. doi:10.1089/cpb.2008.0228 PMID:19250021.

Bonds-Raacke, J., & Raacke, J. (2010). Myspace and Facebook: Identifying dimensions of uses and gratifications for friend networking sites. *Individual Differences Research*, *8*, 27–33.

Boyd, D. M., & Ellison, N. B. (2007). Social network sites: Definition, history, and scholarship. *Journal of Computer-Mediated Communication, 13.*

Chen, G. (2011). Tweet this: A uses and gratifications perspective on how active twitter use gratifies a need to connect with others. *Computers in Human Behavior, 27,* 755–762. doi:10.1016/j.chb.2010.10.023.

Cheung, C., Chiu, P., & Lee, M. (2011). Online social networks: Why do students use Facebook? *Computers in Human Behavior, 27,* 1337–1343. doi:10.1016/j.chb.2010.07.028.

creating user-generated content. *Journal of Interactive Advertising, 8,* 16–25.

Daugherty, T., Eastin, M. S., & Bright, L. (2008). Exploring consumer motivations for

Gangadharbatla, H. (2008). Facebook me: Collective self-esteem, need to belong, and Internet self-efficacy as predictors of the iGeneration's attitudes toward social networking sites. *Journal of Interactive Advertising, 8,* 5–15.

Gillin, P. (2007). *The New Influencers: A Marketer's Guide to the New Social Media.* Sanger, CA: Quill Driver.

Haas, S., Trump, T., Gerhards, M., & Klingler, W. (2007). Web 2.0: Usage and usage types. An analysis on the basis of quantitative and qualitative examinations. *Media Perspektiven, 4,* 215–222.

Harrison, T., & Barthel, B. (2009). Wielding new media in Web 2.0: Exploring the history of engagement with the collaborative construction of media products. *New Media & Society, 11,* 155–178. doi:10.1177/1461444808099580.

Kim, J., & Rubin, A. M. (1997). The variable influence of audience activity on media effects. *Communication Research, 24,* 107–135. doi:10.1177/009365097024002001.

Ko, H., Cho, C., & Roberts, M. (2005). Internet uses and gratifications: A structural equation model of interactive advertising. *Journal of Advertising, 34,* 57–70. doi:10.1080/00913367.2005.10639191.

Madupu, V., & Cooley, D. (2010). Antecedents and consequences of online brand community participation: A conceptual framework. *Journal of Internet Commerce, 9,* 127–147. doi:10.1080/15332861.2010.503850.

Park, N., Kee, K., & Valenzuela, S. (2009). Being immersed in social networking environment: Facebook groups, uses and gratifications, and social outcomes. *Cyberpsychology & Behavior, 12,* 729–733. doi:10.1089/cpb.2009.0003 PMID:19619037.

Petrescu, M., & Korgaonkar, P. (2011). Viral advertising: Definitional review and synthesis. *Journal of Internet Commerce, 10,* 208–226. doi:10.1080/15332861.2011.596007.

Quan-Haase, A., & Young, A. (2010). Uses and gratifications of social media: A comparison of Facebook and instant messaging. *Bulletin of Science, Technology & Society, 30,* 350–361. doi:10.1177/0270467610380009.

Ritson, M., & Elliott, R. (1999). The social uses of advertising: An ethnographic study of adolescent advertising audiences. *The Journal of Consumer Research, 26,* 260–277. doi:10.1086/209562.

Ruggiero, T. (2000). Uses and Gratifications Theory in the 21st Century. *Mass Communication & Society, 3,* 3–37. doi:10.1207/S15327825MCS0301_02.

Schroeder, J., & Hertel, G. (2009). Voluntary engagement in an open web-based encyclopedia: Wikipedians and why they do it. *Media Psychology, 12,* 96–120. doi:10.1080/15213260802669466.

Sheehan, K. B. (2002). Of surfing, searching, and newshounds: A typology of Internet users' online sessions. *Journal of Advertising Research*, *42*, 62–71.

Tuten, T. (2008). *Advertising 2.0: Social media marketing in a Web 2.0 world*. Westport, CT: Praeger.

KEY TERMS AND DEFINITIONS

Bandwagon Effect: The act of joining a social networking site because "everyone else is doing it."

Extrinsic Motivation: The drive to engage in activities on the basis of their ability to result in the attainment of some form of separable, tangible outcome.

Human Motivation: The process by which goal-seeking behavior is initiated and sustained over time.

Intrinsic Motivation: The drive to engage in activities that one finds inherently enjoyable, satisfying, or otherwise interesting.

Personal Brand Management: An individual's attempt to position his or herself as a subject matter expert through the use of social media.

Social Networking Site (SNS): A broad classification of online networks that allow users to create public/semi-public profiles for the purposes of sharing news, information, and other content with a selected group of individuals who also own/possess profiles on the site. Common examples of social networking sites include Facebook, MySpace, and LinkedIn.

Uses and Gratifications Approach: A theoretical perspective for understanding media selection and use. Under the uses and gratifications approach, it is assumed that media audiences actively choose/select media products that gratify specified psychological needs.

Chapter 5
Understanding Purchasing Behavior within Virtual Worlds:
Planned Purchases and Impulse Buying

Andreas M. Kaplan
ESCP Europe, France

Michael Haenlein
ESCP Europe, France

ABSTRACT

Although the hype around virtual worlds has slowed down in recent months, chances are high that this type of social media will increase in importance over years to come. Many companies which pioneered in entering virtual worlds have left these environments after their first steps. One of the reasons for these initial failures is likely the lack of understanding of in-world consumers and their expectations toward virtual commerce. The purpose of the authors' chapter is therefore to investigate consumer purchase behavior within the virtual social world Second Life. Specifically, the authors analyze the types of purchase behavior consumers show within such an environment (planned purchases vs. impulse buying) and the factors that influence the decision to buy virtual products and services in exchange for real life money. For this, the authors' study is based on a combination of a qualitative pre-study consisting of 29 in-depth interviews and a quantitative analysis based on responses obtained from a representative sample of 580 Second Life residents. The authors' analysis results in the following three findings: First, the authors show that Second Life residents engage in two different types of purchase behavior: planned purchases and impulse buying. Second, the authors show that traditional consumer behavior theories and concepts can be transferred to similar behavior in a virtual world, although with different degrees of importance for different variables. And finally, the authors show that a Second Life resident's usage intensity and consumption experience have a significant moderating influence on planned purchase behavior but not on impulse buying. From a managerial perspective, the authors' results imply that Real Life companies that maintain Second Life flagship stores may consider communicating about their virtual products and services within real life. Additionally, Second Life stores should try to make the

DOI: 10.4018/978-1-4666-4026-9.ch005

purchasing process as simple and convenient as possible (in order to increase planned purchases) and to create an overall exciting and pleasant shopping environment to elicit positive emotions among their potential customers (in order to maximize the probability of impulse buying). Finally, since purchasing behavior within Second Life appears to be more individualistic than what can be observed in real life, firms can consider offering virtual products and services in Second Life that are highly extravagant and may never be purchased in Real Life due to fear of other people's opinions--which is likely to be of particular importance for fashion goods.

INTRODUCTION

Although the hype around virtual worlds has slowed down in recent years, chances are high that this type of social media[1] will increase in importance over years to come (Gartner Inc., 2008). Many of the pioneers who first entered this domain have failed miserably and abandoned their activities in the meantime (Rowan, 2009). Nevertheless it appears clear that virtual worlds, together with other types of social media, such as collaborative projects, content communities, social networking sites, and micro-blogging services (Kaplan & Haenlein 2011a) will be a central part of the Internet in future for a variety of business applications reaching from distribution to viral marketing (Kaplan & Haenlein 2011b; 2012). This evolution will even be amplified with the advent of the so-called mobile social media[2] such as Four-square or MyTown. One of the most prominent applications in the large area of virtual worlds is probably Second Life, a three-dimensional virtual social world that opened to the public in 2003 and is maintained by the U.S.-based Linden Research, Inc. By entering it via a downloadable client program, users (who are called 'residents') can interact based on personalized avatars (Holz-warth et al., 2006, for a more detailed discussion of avatars), meet and speak with each other or buy a wide variety of virtual products, ranging from shoes to cars and houses. The currency in Second Life is the Linden dollar, which can either be earned in-world or exchanged via the Second Life Exchange at a floating exchange rate that is approximately stable at 250 Linden dollars to the U.S. dollar. More interestingly, Linden dollars can also be re-exchanged into US dollars, making it possible to earn real life money by selling virtual products and services within Second Life.

The high popularity of Second Life has moti-vated several real life companies such as BMW, Dell, or Wells Fargo, to start activities within this environment and to set up virtual flagship brand stores, called 'islands.' These stores were subsequently used as hubs for brand communi-ties and the distribution of virtual products and services, such as virtual bikes, fashion items, or furniture for the avatars' virtual houses. But also real-life products could be purchased on Second Life. Dell, for example, offered virtual PCs (being customized through Second Life residents) which were able to perform simple tasks, such as alert-ing a resident when one of his/her friends were nearby. These virtual PCs could furthermore be purchased in their real world form via a link from Second life to the Dell website. Another example is Starfruit, a Swiss based company, which offered a gift service within Second Life that allowed users to send flowers, chocolates and jewelry as real gifts to friends in the real world. However, most of these first initiatives in the area of virtual commerce have been stopped in the meantime. It is likely that this has occurred for the following three reasons: First, many companies entered the virtual world without a clear objective other than getting some free public relations in the real world. Second, companies frequently had unre-alistic expectations about the potential of virtual worlds and were disappointed when they noticed that virtual worlds are just not yet mature enough for a broad corporate use. Third, firms often did not well understand the consumer in Second Life and his in-world purchasing behavior. The latter reason is the motivation for this study.

Next to this managerial interest, virtual worlds have also received substantial interest within the academic community. Previous studies have, among others, focused on how the geographic characteristics of such environments influence social relations (Schroeder et al., 2001), how virtual worlds can be used to simulate and predict the spread of diseases (Lofgren & Fefferman, 2007) and how virtual product interaction and object interactivity translate into mental images, product attitudes and purchase intent (Schlosser, 2003; Schlosser, 2006). With respect to Second Life in particular, several studies have investigated how and for what reasons companies and consumers decide to interact in such environments. With respect to consumer use, research (Haenlein & Kaplan, 2009; Kaplan & Haenlein 2009a; 2009b) has shown that usage can be extensive (on average 4 hours a day) and is driven by four use gratifications: the search for diversion, the desire to build personal relationships, the need to learn and the wish to earn (real life) money. Regarding the business potential of such environments, Shen and Eder (2009) analyze how the perceived usefulness and ease of use of virtual worlds relate to the intention to use them for business and Kaplan and Haenlein (2009c) provide examples of how firms already rely on virtual worlds for advertising/ communication, virtual product sales, marketing research, human resources and internal process management. Furthermore, Kaplan and Haenlein display the potential of virtual worlds within the IT industry (Kaplan & Haenlein, 2010a), for the special case of business schools (Kaplan, 2009) as well as the concept of mass customization (Kaplan, 2010; Kaplan & Haenlein, 2006). Only a few studies have, however, looked at the interface between consumer use and business potential, specifically purchase behavior within Second

Life. This is surprising as the ability to develop virtual products and exchange them for Real Life money is a unique characteristic of Second Life.

A notable exception in this context is the work of Arakji and Lang (2008), which investigates the business value of maintaining retail outlets within virtual worlds. The authors develop a theoretical framework as well as a decision tool for evaluating and managing value creation in virtual worlds. They furthermore propose to monitor both tangible traffic metrics and intangible factors that play a role in determining the success of in-world virtual retail outlets. One success story is the going virtual of Gossip Girl, an American television teen drama. The Second Life Gossip Girl world looks like the set of the television show, with the same streets, the same hot spots, and even the same characters. Fans of the show can build and customize their own avatar, have a dance party with other fans and friends of the show, play Gossip Girl games, watch clips, or even full episodes of the show. Thus fans have the opportunity to spend time with their favorite show 24/7 on this virtual world community and not only during the short period when the actual show is aired on TV. According to Metaverse Mod Squad, virtual Gossip Girl attracted approximately 38,000 unique visitors per month with 21,000 of them coming back later resulting in a monthly average of over 100,000 visits.

While Arakji and Lang's (2008) work is mainly conceptual in nature, the purpose of our manuscript is to provide an empirical insight within this area. Based on a survey conducted among a representative panel of 580 Second Life users, we investigate the types of purchase behavior, consumers show within Second Life and the factors that influence the decision to buy virtual products and services in exchange for real life money. In the next part, we will develop our research framework as well as hypotheses. In part three of this chapter, we will explain our methodology as well as describe the study's results. Finally, we will conclude with the discussion part highlighting theoretical and managerial implications, limitations as well as ideas for future research in this area.

RESEARCH FRAMEWORK AND HYPOTHESES

Our research framework builds on the key assumption that similar to what can be observed in traditional retail environments, purchase behavior within Second Life can be split into two different categories: planned purchases and impulse buying (Cobb & Hoyer, 1986). We hence assume that, despite what one might belief at first glance, some purchases within Second Life are conducted in a planned and considered way. We will now develop two different sets of hypotheses, one for planned

purchases and one for impulse buying, which are summarized in the conceptual models visualized in Figures 1 and 2.

Planned Purchases

To analyze a resident's decision to conduct planned purchases within Second Life we rely on the Theory of Planned Behavior (Ajzen, 1991). The Theory of Planned Behavior is similar to the Theory of Reasoned Action (Ajzen & Fishbein, 1980; Sheppard et al., 1988) in the sense that it assumes that the behavioral intention to perform a certain behavior is influenced by two factors: the individual's positive or negative evaluation of performing the behavior (attitude towards the behavior) and the individual's perception of social pressures put on him/her to perform or not

Figure 1. Conceptual framework and hypotheses – planned purchases

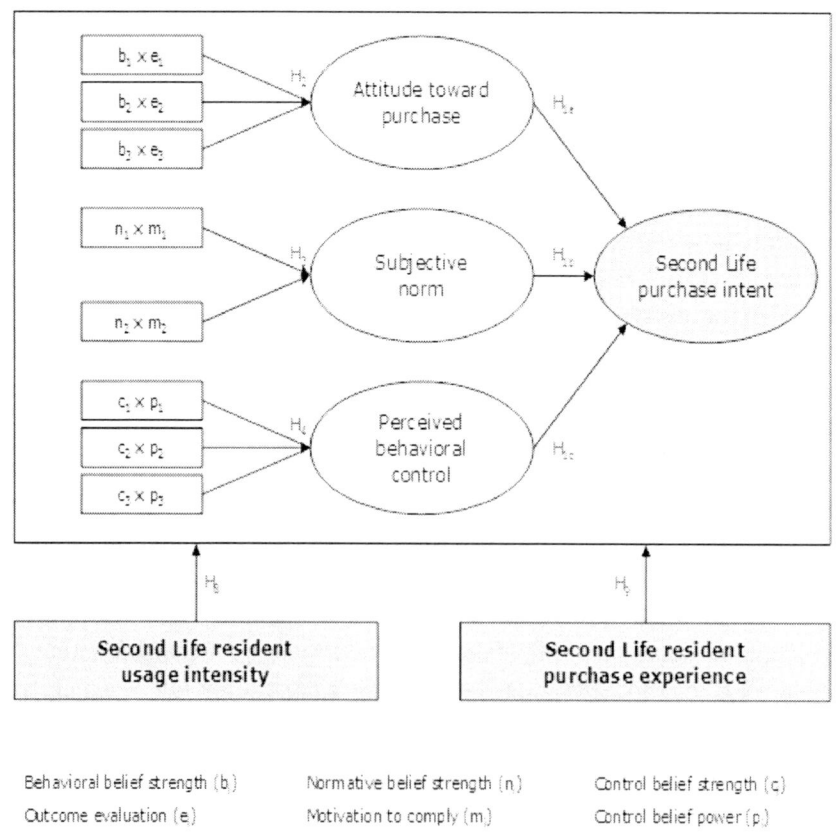

Figure 2. Conceptual framework and hypotheses – impulse buying

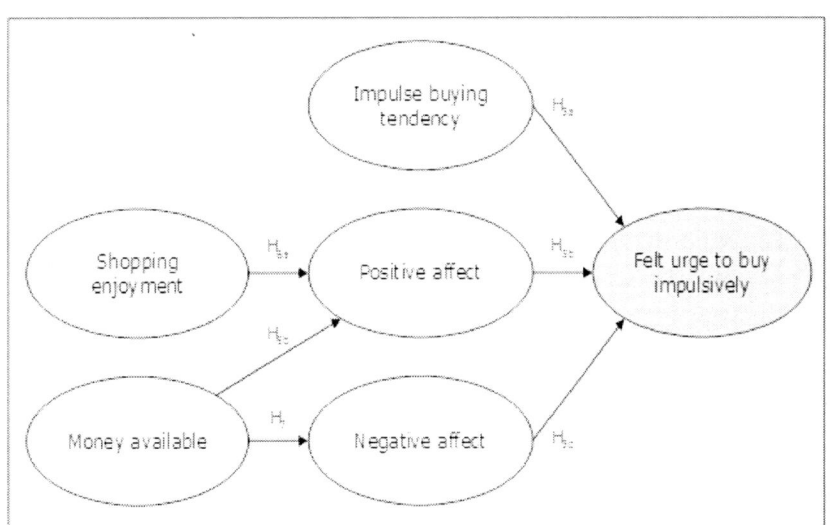

to perform the behavior (subjective norm). Yet, in addition to these two constructs, the Theory of Planned Behavior also takes account of the fact that the resources and opportunities available to an individual influence to some extent the likelihood of behavioral achievement. This is reflected by the variable 'perceived behavioral control', which refers to the individual's perception of the ease or difficulty of performing the behavior of interest. The Theory of Planned Behavior can therefore be considered as an adaptation of the Theory of Reasoned Action for situations where individuals have only incomplete volitional control over their behavior. The Theory of Planned Behavior is one of the most well-known theories to explain human behavior. It has been used widely in the Marketing discipline to explain phenomena such as new product adoption (Taylor & Todd, 1995), online purchases (Lim & Dubinsky, 2005), and participation in brand communities (Bagozzi & Dholakia, 2006; Bagozzi & Dholakia, 2002).

Within the Theory of Planned Behavior each of these three intention antecedents is assumed to depend on a small set of behavioral beliefs. The attitude towards the behavior is driven by the individual's behavioral beliefs (i.e., the ex-

pected consequences of performing the behavior), weighted by their outcome evaluation (i.e., the perceived importance of each potential consequence). The subjective norm is driven by the individual's normative beliefs (i.e. the expected reaction of social reference groups), weighted by their motivation to comply (i.e., the perceived importance of each social reference group). Finally, the perceived behavioral control is driven by the individual's control beliefs (i.e. the perceived skills and resources of the individual), weighted by the control power (i.e., the perceived importance of these skills and resources for the behavior under investigation). As we will highlight below, for the specific case of Second Life purchase behavior, behavioral beliefs represent the desire to improve avatar appearance, the wish to have an exciting Second Life experience and the support of relationships with Second Life friends; normative beliefs represent the reactions of friends in Real Life and Second Life; and control beliefs represent the availability of a sufficient amount of Linden Dollars as well as potential problems regarding the complexity of the purchasing process and technical reliability. Combined, this leads to the following set of hypotheses:

H$_1$: A resident's Second Life purchase intent is influenced by the resident's (a) attitude towards the purchase, (b) subjective norm, and (c) perceived behavioral control.

H$_2$: A resident's attitude towards the purchase is influenced by the resident's behavioral belief strength and outcome evaluation.

H$_3$: A resident's subjective norm is influenced by the resident's normative belief strength and motivation to comply.

H$_4$: A resident's perceived behavioral control is influenced by the resident's control belief strength and control belief power.

Impulse Buying

Besides planned purchases, we also expect impulse buying to play an important role within Second Life. Impulse buying is a major facet of consumption behavior and has been considered as such for over forty years (Kollat & Willett, 1967; Stern, 1962). According to Rook (1987) it is said to occur 'when a consumer experiences a sudden, often powerful and persistent urge to buy something immediately.' Impulse buying has a hedonic component (Hausman, 2000; Rook, 1987) and often occurs with diminished regard for its consequences. In the context of our research, we expect impulse buying to play an important role within virtual social worlds in general and Second Life in particular, for the following two reasons: First, such platforms fulfill most of the factors Stern (1962) describes as drivers of this type of behavior: Items sold are digital, which removes any potential transportation and storage cost, and relatively cheap (e.g., the cost of buying a virtual car in Second Life is about L\$250.00 or US\$1.00). Furthermore, distribution is self-service based and, due to the absence of physical space and distances, access to a point-of-sales is nearly instantaneous. Second, according to Dittmar and Drury (2000), impulse purchasing behavior is more prevalent in retail environments when there is an increase in disposable income, which is likely to be the case in Second Life where users need to exchange Real Life currency into Linden Dollars which may be perceived as 'play money' which the resident is 'allowed' to spend during his/ her Second Life usage.

In one of the first studies systematically comparing planned purchases and impulse buying behavior, Cobb and Hoyer (1986) highlight that 'impulse purchasers' buy products without having had the intent to purchase the specific brand or even the product category before entering the store, which makes this group different from 'partial planners' who enter the store with the intention to buy a product category but postpone the actual brand choice decision to the time where the actual purchase takes place. The relationship between buying impulsiveness and actual impulse buying behavior is moderated by the consumer's normative evaluations (i.e., judgments about the appropriateness of engaging in impulse buying behavior), as shown by Rook and Fisher (1995). In order to explain the conditions under which consumers are likely to conduct impulse purchases within Second Life, we build on the work of Beatty and Ferrell (1998). These authors show that in traditional settings the likelihood of making an impulse purchase is influenced by situational variables (e.g., the availability of money) and consumer characteristics (shopping enjoyment, i.e., the pleasure one obtains in the shopping process, and impulse buying tendency). These variables impact a set of endogenous variables (positive/ negative affect and the felt urge to buy impulsively), which together result in a felt urge to buy impulsively. This felt urge to buy impulsively can be considered as the analogous construct to the purchase intent in the context of planned purchases. Combined, this results in the following three hypotheses:

H$_5$: A resident's felt urge to buy impulsively within Second Life is influenced by the resident's (a) impulse buying tendency, (b) positive affect, and (c) negative affect.

H$_6$: A resident's positive affect is influenced by the resident's (a) shopping enjoyment and (b) money available.

H$_7$: A resident's negative affect is influenced by the resident's money available.

Moderating Role of Usage Intensity and Purchase Experience

Within this general framework, we assume that for the case of planned purchases the relative importance of different variables is not the same for different types of Second Life residents. Specifically, we hypothesize a moderating role of a Second Life resident's usage intensity and purchase experience on planned purchases but not on impulse buying behavior. Generally, it has been shown that repeated exposure to an activity leads to different types of behavior due to mechanisms such as conditioning (Wofford & Goodwin, 1990) or the use of scripts as a basis for decision taking. Exemplary studies that support such thinking in an online context include Gefen et al. (2003) for e-Commerce, Kang et al. (2006) for the use of e-coupons, Qiu and Papatla (2008) for the acquisition of free online content, and Lemmens and Bushman (2006) for the emotional consequences of violent video game consumption.

For planned purchases we expect that behavioral, normative and control beliefs which are important at low levels of usage intensity/ purchase experience are not necessarily the same as those that play a role at higher levels. This viewpoint is consistent with the belief-adjustment model proposed by Hogarth and Einhorn (1992), which postulates that current beliefs are continuously updated in light of additional information in order to form revised beliefs. The belief-adjustment model has received consistent empirical support in

a variety of settings. Bolton (1998), for example, showed that customers update their beliefs about the future value of a relationship with a continuous service provider (cellular telephone provider) over time, and Mittal et al. (1999) provide an indication that in the context of automobile purchases the relative importance of different attributes with respect to satisfaction shifts over time. Consistent with these findings we assume that beliefs that are salient at low levels of usage intensity and purchase experience are updated with increasing experience and replaced by other beliefs that become more salient over time.

For impulse buying it has been highlighted that the 'often powerful and persistent urge to buy something immediately ... with diminished regard for its consequences' (Rook, 1987), which defines this type of behavior, is particularly likely to occur when consumers are low on self-regulatory resources, for example because they have experienced situations requiring a high degree of self-control and willpower prior to entering the shopping environment (Vohs & Faber, 2007). This implies that a user's tendency to conduct impulse purchases within Second Life is likely to depend on the amount of self-regulatory resources available when entering the virtual world and, ultimately, on situations experienced prior to using Second Life. Given that there is no reason to assume that with increasing usage intensity and/ or consumption frequency, users are more likely to experience situations that require high self-control within their Real Life, we expect a user's tendency to conduct impulse purchases to be independent from his/ her usage intensity and/ or consumption frequency. This leads to the following two hypotheses:

H$_8$: A resident's usage intensity of Second Life will have a moderating influence on his/ her planned purchase behavior.

H$_9$: A resident's purchase experience within Second Life will have a moderating influence on his/ her planned purchase behavior.

Methodology and Results

Study 1: Qualitative Pre-Study

Research design: We decided to conduct a qualitative pre-study (Kaplan & Haenlein, 2009a) prior to our quantitative analysis for the following two reasons: First, as highlighted above, empirical research about purchasing behavior within virtual social worlds is still scarce. It is therefore advisable to first test the overall validity of our research framework using a series of in-depth interviews prior to performing a full quantitative analysis. Second, as recommended by Ajzen (2006), the belief structure underlying the attitude towards purchase, subjective norm and perceived behavioral control within the Theory of Planned Behavior can best be identified by a qualitative (vs. quantitative) approach. In total, we conducted 29 in-depth interviews with Second Life residents, with an average duration of 50 minutes each. To select our interview partners, we entered Second Life at different moments of the day and teleported to popular locations. Within each location, potential interview partners were randomly approached and asked whether they would be willing to participate in an academic research project. Once respondents agreed to participate, interviews were conducted using a semi-structured interview guide which focused, among others, on the Second Life exchange relationship, specifically the type of purchase behavior shown, as well as the reasons for conducting purchases, the influence of social reference groups and the potential barriers for buying items in Second Life.

Our 29 interview partners were largely male (72%), on average 35 years old, and originating from 11 different countries, with the top four being the United States, Germany, France, and the United Kingdom. These values correspond closely to the characteristics of the general Second Life population (65% male, on average 33.5 years old, stemming from 99 different countries with the same top four countries as above), which leads to

the assumption that our sample can be considered as representative of the Second Life user base. These 29 interviews resulted in a total of 150 pages of interview transcripts (i.e., roughly 5 pages per interview), which we analyzed as recommended by Spiggle (1994) and LeCompte (2000): Interviews were first printed out and then catalogued, labeled, and reviewed according to our interview guide. Subsequently, we categorized them on the individual level to identify passages or themes that described the same general phenomenon. Finally, we grouped these empirically observed categories into more general conceptual classes, which we compared across different interviews. This process was iterated until no further modifications within our framework were necessary.

Main findings: With respect to the type of Second Life purchase behavior, some of our respondents stated that they made most of their purchases in an impulsive manner ('I buy whenever I see something I like', Guillaume, male, age unknown, France). However, the majority of our informants told us they conduct at least some part of their purchases in a planned and considered way. Elizabeth (female, 23 years, country unknown), for example, said 'I usually plan ahead when buying furniture items and know what I'm looking for', and Samantha (female, 40–60 years, U.S.) mentioned 'Although I do impulse buying occasionally, most of the time it's planned purchasing.' This can be seen as first empirical support for our key assumption that purchasing behavior within Second Life summarizes planned purchases as well as impulse buying.

Regarding the reasons which our respondents provide for purchasing virtual products and services within Second Life, most claim to buy items to improve the appearance of their Second Life avatar (e.g., 'I like to look and act like I dream of', Jack, male, 36 years, UK). Others report purchasing for fun, excitement or to be able to perform sexual activities ('I recently bought an Xcite X2 Starter Pack. Very convenient for having sex', Thomas, male, 19 years, UK). Interestingly, some respondents also mention spending money and buying items to support their friends or to perform group activities. Nicolas (male, 51 years, US) for example, said 'I have some friends who are dancers and I tip them to be polite' and Chloé (female, 37 years, France) told us 'Last week me and my friends wanted to go for a bike tour and so I had to purchase a bike'. Based on these comments, we identify three main behavioral beliefs that influence the attitude towards purchasing in Second Life: the desire to improve avatar appearance, the wish to have an exciting Second Life experience and the support of relationships with Second Life friends.

Looking on the social influences that impact purchase behavior within Second Life, we find that the main social reference group for Second Life residents are their virtual friends, who play an essential part in their Second Life experience. As Daniel (male, 55 years, U.S.) puts it: 'The Second Life experience is communal. Although you can experience so much alone or as an individual, you need support, conversations, attention and affection to LIVE.' Real life friends are often claimed to be largely unaware of the Second Life usage. Elizabeth (female, 23 years, country unknown) said 'Not many people actually know I even play Second Life' and Marie (female, 37 years, Germany) mentioned that Second Life 'has never been a subject of discussion', not even with her closest family. This results in two main social reference groups that we expect to impact the subjective norm of a Second Life user, namely his/her Second Life and Real Life friends.

Finally, when being asked about factors that encumber purchasing within Second Life, several users mentioned the need to exchange Real Life currency into Linden Dollars. Yet, the underlying issue does not seem to be the technical process associated with such an exchange but the wish to control in-world spending, as highlighted by Alejandro (male, 33 years, Spain): 'I try to avoid exchanging Real Life money into Linden Dollars. I think, if I do it once, I'll do it most of the time–and I need to pay some bills in real life, too!' Another point highlighted is technical issues such as the difficult navigation (Hannah, female, 37 years, U.S.) as well as the overhead of rendering and slowness (Jacob, male, 46 years, U.S.). We therefore included the following three control beliefs into our model: a lack of Linden Dollars, as well as the issue regarding the complexity of the purchasing process and technical reliability.

Conclusion: Summarizing, our qualitative interviews provide a clear indication that Second Life residents engage in two different types of purchase behavior: considered purchases and impulse buying. Hence, users spend time, at least occasionally, outside Second Life to plan purchases for their next visit and therefore engage in activities that span beyond the single usage occasion. This makes Second Life different from, for example, video games, where involvement is usually limited to the time spent on the game. Furthermore, our respondents indicate a certain influence of social processes in the purchasing process leading, in the extreme case, to purchases that are only conducted to support or engage with others. This is surprising, as one would expect social factors to be less important in Second Life than in Real Life, due to the lack of face-to-face contact and anonymity inherent in such a medium.

Study 2: Quantitative Analysis

Research design - measurement scales: To follow-up on the results of our qualitative pre-study and to perform a formal test of our conceptual framework, we subsequently conducted a quantitative analysis. For the planned purchase model, behavioral, normative and control belief strength were measured as suggested by Hrubes et al. (2001), building on the results of our qualitative pre-study. The operationalization of outcome evaluations, motivations to comply, and control belief power followed Ajzen (2006). Attitudes towards purchasing on Second Life, subjective norm and perceived behavioral control were measured as suggested by Beck and

Ajzen (1991), and Second Life purchase intent by applying a scale previously used by Schifter and Ajzen (1985). For impulse buying, we followed Beatty and Ferrell (1998) for the measurement of shopping enjoyment, money availability and felt urge to buy impulsively. Impulse buying tendency was operationalized as suggested by Weun et al. (1998).[3] For the measurement of positive/ negative affect we relied on the PANAS scales (1988), which has previously been applied in the marketing discipline (Lee & Shavitt, 2009), and used the four items that proved to have highest loadings on positive and negative affect respectively. Following the recommendations of Cox (1980), all items were measured on 7-point Likert scales with the majority of response cues being strongly disagree (-3) and strongly agree (+3). Different anchors were used for the attitude towards purchasing on Second Life and positive/ negative affect where we applied semantic differential scales. When necessary, wording of items was mildly adapted to fit the context of our study. Finally, the resident's usage intensity of Second Life and purchase experience were measured by two questions each, covering usage duration/ weekly usage and shopping/ purchase frequency (see appendix for a summary of all scales).

Research design – data collection: Since the nature of Second Life makes it difficult to obtain a sufficiently large sample of potential survey participants, we collaborated with a market research firm (Repères) that maintains a representative panel of 10,000 Second Life residents. For our study, we contacted a subset of this panel with an e-Mail including an embedded URL linking to our online questionnaire. Respondents were first asked about their planned purchase behavior within Second Life. Subsequently, we asked them whether they had ever purchased products within Second Life in exchange for Linden Dollars. In case they did, they were invited to describe their last purchase occasion and to answer the impulse buying questions based on this purchase experience. At the end, respondents provided information on their Second Life usage intensity and purchase experience as well as on a series of demographic questions, before they received a compensation to remunerate them for their effort.

Data collection resulted in a total of 717 responses out of which we deleted 65 records due to multiple submissions of the same respondents and 42 records due to drop-out before survey completion. In the remaining set of 610 respondents we deleted 30 records that showed particularly high or low survey response times to minimize any potential distortions in our dataset due to careless answers. This resulted in a final sample of 580 respondents, out of which all completed the planned purchase section and 476 the impulse buying section.[4] Survey participants are approximately equally split between men (55.5%) and women (44.5%). The majority (28.8%) are between 25 and 34 years old, with roughly 80% lying in the 18–44 year age bracket.[5] Comparing these characteristics with general Second Life user statistics based on total hours and avatar count shows that respondents are similar to the overall Second Life population average.

Main findings – analysis approach: To test the theoretical relationships reflected within our research framework, we estimated the structural equation models visualized in Figures 1 and 2 using the Mplus software tool (means, intercepts and thresholds not included in the analysis model; information matrix estimated using second-order derivatives), Version 5 (Muthén & Muthén, 1998-2007). To control for common method bias we relied on an approach suggested by Podsakoff et al. (2003) and allowed all items to load on their theoretical constructs as well as on a latent common methods variance factor, uncorrelated to all other model constructs. To take account of the multiplicative nature of the belief structure inherent in the Theory of Planned Behavior, we used a MIMC (multiple indicators, multiple causes) specification (Jöreskog & Goldberger, 1975) for the planned purchase model. We first multiplied the behavioral, normative and control belief strength with their corresponding outcome evaluation, motivation to comply and control belief power (bi ei, ni mi, ci pi). The resulting product terms were then used as formative indicators of attitude towards purchase, subjective norm and perceived behavioral control in combination with the set of reflective indicators specified in the appendix.

To test for a potential moderating impact of usage intensity and purchase experience we followed a two-step approach recommended by MacKenzie and Spreng (1992): We first estimated group-specific models (covariances, variances and residual variances assumed to be equal across groups) and compared the change in model chi-square between a model in which parameters were allowed to vary freely across groups and one where they were constrained to equality. If the constraint model proved to fit the data significantly worse than the free model, we considered this as an omnibus indication of moderation. In case moderation was indicated on an overall level, we subsequently identified specific moderating effects by constraining individual paths to be equal across groups (while letting all other paths vary freely) and compared the change in model chi-square to a fully unconstrained model.

Main findings – hypothesis testing: Table 1 shows the estimation results for the planned purchase model. A comparison of the overall model fit indices (CFI, TLI, RMSEA, SRMR) with the thresholds recommended in the literature (Bentler, 1990; Hu and Bentler, 1999) indicates acceptable model fit, especially when taking the complex

Table 1. Model estimation results – planned purchases

		Baseline Model				Overview of Moderating Effects (p-value)			
		Parameter Estimates				Usage Duration	Weekly Usage	Shopping Frequency	Purchase Frequency
		Est.	SE	Est./SE	p-value				
		Omnibus test of moderation				0.0027	0.0474	0.0000	0.0025
Improved appearance	→ Purchase attitude	0.092	0.011	8.364	**0.0000**	**0.0047**	0.3151	**0.0004**	**0.0079**
Exciting experience	→ Purchase attitude	0.078	0.011	7.091	**0.0000**	0.0638	0.3640	0.0983	0.5220
Social relationships	→ Purchase attitude	-0.001	0.008	-0.125	0.9005	0.4705	0.6145	0.1947	0.3668
Second Life friends	→ Subjective norm	0.042	0.019	2.211	**0.0271**	**0.0048**	0.0738	0.0894	**0.0227**
Real Life friends	→ Subjective norm	-0.008	0.018	-0.444	0.6567	**0.0011**	**0.0003**	0.2099	0.4251
Availability of L$	→ Behavioral control	-0.033	0.011	-3.000	**0.0027**	0.3942	0.2162	0.1185	0.3420
Complexity	→ Behavioral control	0.110	0.014	7.857	**0.0000**	0.2723	0.1602	0.0690	0.9975
Technical reliability	→ Behavioral control	0.059	0.015	3.933	**0.0001**	0.3570	0.4812	0.0779	0.8847
Purchase attitude	→ SL purchase intent	0.552	0.057	9.684	**0.0000**	0.4475	0.9076	0.1948	**0.0149**
Subjective norm	→ SL purchase intent	-0.014	0.038	-0.368	0.7126	0.7906	0.5174	**0.0337**	0.7664
Behavioral control	→ SL purchase intent	0.369	0.052	7.096	**0.0000**	0.1470	0.6182	**0.0022**	0.1604
Tests of model fit (Baseline model)		CFI	0.933	RMSEA	0.060				
		TLI	0.916	SRMR	0.087				

MIMC specification into account.[6] We observe that Second Life purchase intent is significantly influenced by a resident's attitude towards the purchase and perceived behavioral control but not by subjective norm (p-value: 0.7126). This results in support for H1(a) and H1(c) and rejection of H1(b). With respect to the underlying belief structure, attitude towards the purchase has a significant relationship to the desire to improve avatar appearance and to the wish to have an exciting Second Life experience, but not to the support of relationships with Second Life friends (p-value: 0.9005), which provides partial support for H2. Subjective norm is driven by the attitude of Second Life, but not of Real Life, friends (p-value: 0.6567), which provides partial support for H3. Finally, perceived behavioral control has a significant relationship to all three underlying beliefs, that is, a lack of Linden Dollars as well as issues regarding the complexity of the purchasing process and technical reliability, which results in full support for H4.

Table 2 mirrors Table 1 for the impulse buying model. Model fit as indicated by CFI, TLI, RMSEA and SRMR can be considered as excellent.

We observe that a resident's felt urge to buy impulsively is significantly influenced by the resident's impulse buying tendency and positive effect, but not by negative effect (p-value: 0.3409), leading to support for H5(a) and H5(b) and rejection of H5(c). Positive effect is significantly related to shopping enjoyment, but not to the availability of virtual money (p-value: 0.9276), which supports H6(a) and rejects H6(b). Finally, we do not observe a significant relationship between money availability and negative effect in contradiction to H7

To test for a potential moderating impact of usage intensity and purchase experience on these relationships, we proceeded as outlined above and performed an omnibus test of moderation for each construct. For the planned purchase model we find indication for a moderating impact of all four variables (usage intensity, weekly usage, shopping/purchase frequency), while for the impulse buying model all moderating effects are insignificant (p-values of 0.1637 and above). Combined, this results in support for H8 and H9.

Table 2. Model estimation results – impulse buying

		Baseline Model				Overview of Moderating Effects (p-value)			
		Parameter Estimates				Usage Duration	Weekly Usage	Shopping Frequency	Purchase Frequency
		Est.	SE	Est./SE	p-value				
		Omnibus test of moderation				0.3751	0.1637	0.1740	0.2667
Money available	→ Negative affect	-0.037	0.038	-0.974	0.3302				
Money available	→ Positive affect	0.003	0.033	0.091	0.9276				
Shopping enjoyment	→ Positive affect	-0.256	0.063	-4.063	**0.0000**				
Negative affect	→ Felt urge to buy	-0.140	0.147	-0.952	0.3409				
Positive affect	→ Felt urge to buy	0.358	0.066	5.424	**0.0000**				
Impulse buying ten.	→ Felt urge to buy	-0.578	0.065	-8.892	**0.0000**				
Tests of model fit		CFI	0.970	RMSEA	0.042				
		TLI	0.959	SRMR	0.046				

DISCUSSION

Theoretical Implications

From a theoretical perspective, our analysis results in the following three findings: First, both our qualitative and quantitative study provide a clear indication that Second Life residents engage in two different types of purchase behavior: planned purchases and impulse buying. This finding is somewhat surprising as one would expect at first glance that purchases within virtual social worlds are uniquely conducted on a whim as, at the end, paying real money (although previously exchanged into virtual money) to buy something to wear, eat or drink for an avatar who cannot feel cold, hunger or thirst results in only limited actual product value. Yet, we find clear indication that a substantial part of Second Life purchases are conducted in a planned and considered way which gives room for the speculation that, for its users, Second Life is more than a mere computer game, and rather an extension of their real life (Kaplan 2011).

Second, with respect to purchase antecedents, we show that, on an overall level, planned purchases within Second Life are only influenced by a user's attitude towards the purchase and perceived behavioral control. Buying behavior is therefore more individualistic than can be expected based on the Theory of Planned Behavior. Regarding impulse buying, we observe that the felt urge to buy impulsively is largely influenced by individual consumer characteristics (impulse buying tendency and shopping enjoyment mediated by positive effect). Specifically, situational factors, such as the availability of a sufficient amount of virtual money, do not seem to have the same effect as what has been observed in traditional impulse buying situations (Beatty & Ferrell, 1998).

Third, we show that a Second Life resident's usage intensity and consumption experience have a significant moderating influence on planned purchase behavior but not on impulse buying.

A more detailed analysis of group-specific path coefficients, for example, reveals that the opinions of real life friends have a significant influence on subjective norm for high levels of usage duration (longer than 6 months). Combined, this implies that the key differences that we observe in the baseline model when comparing our results to our theoretical expectations start to disappear and that, over time, consumer behavior within Second Life starts to more closely mirror what can be observed in real life settings.

Managerial Implications

From a managerial viewpoint, our results have the following four implications: First, the fact that consumers, among others, engage in planned purchase behavior within Second Life implies that real life companies that maintain Second Life flagship stores may consider communicating about their virtual products and services within real life. Fashion companies could, for example, offer a voucher for their digital products in Second Life to all consumers who purchase an item in real life. Since our results indicate that Second Life residents spent at least some time off-world to think about their next purchase, this could serve as a tool to strengthen brand awareness and brand exposure in both Second Life and real life. Second, since our analysis shows that in addition to the attitude towards the purchase only perceived behavioral control influences Second Life purchase intent, firms who offer products in Second Life should try to make the purchasing process as simple and convenient as possible. Among others, this implies designing stores that are technically reliable and do not take an excessive time to render on screen. It could, however, also mean that firms sell items on credit to customers who do not happen to have a sufficient amount of Linden Dollars available to finance their purchase. Third, since purchasing behavior within Second Life appears to be more individualistic than what can be observed in Real Life, indicated by the fact that subjective norm does not have a significant impact on Second Life purchase intent, firms can consider offering virtual products and services in Second Life that are highly extravagant and may never be purchased in Real Life due to fear of other people's opinion–which is likely to be of particular importance for fashion goods. Finally, for impulse buying our results show that positive (but not negative) effect has a significant influence on the felt urge to buy impulsively. Firms should therefore try to create an overall exciting and pleasant shopping environment within their Second Life stores to elicit positive emotions among their potential customers in order to maximize the probability of impulse buying.

Limitations

As with any empirical piece of work, our analysis also contains some limitations that future studies could address in order to further strengthen our findings: First, within our measurement model we assumed that shopping enjoyment and impulse buying tendency are identical within Second Life and real life. It is, however, conceivable that an individual might be more impulsive in Second Life due to the smaller cost involved in the purchase (compared to traditional retail settings) and that Second Life residents enjoy shopping in Second Life more or less than in real life. Future studies should test the robustness of our findings by measuring shopping enjoyment and impulse buying tendency separately for Second Life and real life. Second, our one-time survey approach does not allow us to formally test whether users evolve with increasing usage intensity and purchase experience. Although we observe a moderating impact of these two variables, a formal test would require a longitudinal design in which the same Second Life users are surveyed at regular intervals. Future studies could address this weakness in order to truly show that Second Life users evolve during their usage. Finally, it is possible that our sample, although representative of the Second Life population based on its basic characteristics, contains Second Life users with above-average involvement and interest in Second Life. It is widely known from panel analysis that mere membership in a panel might introduce a (panel) bias into any type of analysis. Future studies could therefore consider replicating our analysis using a sample of Second Life users recruited by other means.

Areas of Future Research

Our analysis can only be seen as a first step to better understand the consumer use and business potential of virtual hyper-realities in general and Second Life in particular. On the one hand, future studies could build on our results to obtain a more complete understanding of purchase behavior within virtual worlds. It would, for example, be interesting to investigate whether product category or retail outlet characteristics influence the relative frequency of planned purchases vs. impulse buying. Even within virtual worlds it is conceivable that consumers differentiate between hedonic and utilitarian goods and engage in different purchase behavior for virtual fashion items than for virtual household appliances (Dhar & Wertenbroch, 2000). Alternatively, it would be interesting to test whether models that have been used to explain online shopping behavior (Gefen et al., 2003; Kuk & Yeung, 2002; Lim & Dubinsky, 2005) can also be applied to virtual words and whether factors such as trust and interactivity are equally important in both settings. Finally, future studies could rely on a longitudinal design to obtain a better understanding of how consumers evolve with increasing Second Life usage intensity and consumption frequency.

On the other hand, it might also be interesting to take a company vs. consumer-perspective and analyze benefits that real life companies may be able to achieve by setting up flagship brand stores within virtual social worlds, especially in the area of advertising. The relatively high prices for real estate within Second Life combined with the cost of setting up a virtual flagship store make it unlikely that companies will be able to achieve a positive return-on-investment from the sale of virtual products and services alone. It is therefore necessary to investigate additional uses of virtual flagship stores in order to justify an investment within virtual worlds, such as the advertising function of such flagship stores and the impact of virtual store exposure on real life brand attitudes and purchase intent.

CONCLUSION

Our analysis provides an indication that Second Life residents engage in two different types of purchase behavior: planned purchases and impulse buying. Although these two types of behavior are familiar from traditional settings, their joint occurrence within virtual worlds is surprising as it indicates that even in an environment where no actual value can be gained from the product itself, consumers take time to make a planned and considered decision – at least occasionally. Regarding the factors that influence the intention to buy, we observe that traditional consumer behavior theories and concepts can be transferred to similar behavior in a virtual world, although with different degrees of importance for different variables. Additionally, we see that a Second Life resident's usage intensity and consumption frequency have a moderating impact on planned purchase behavior, which provides an indication that Second Life residents evolve during their Second Life usage. From a managerial perspective, our results imply that real life companies that maintain Second Life flagship stores may consider communicating about their virtual products and services within real life. Additionally, Second Life stores should try to make the purchasing process as simple and convenient as possible (in order to increase planned purchases) and to create an overall exciting and pleasant shopping environment

to elicit positive emotions among their potential customers (in order to maximize the probability of impulse buying). Finally, since purchasing behavior within Second Life appears to be more individualistic than what can be observed in real life, firms can consider offering virtual products and services in Second Life that are highly extravagant and may never be purchased in real life due to fear of other people's opinions–which is likely to be of particular importance for fashion goods. Although virtual worlds have become less prominent in business press at the moment, it is certainly a wise strategy to be prepared for their increasing importance in the future. This implies building sufficient expertise in the organization today to be ready for tomorrow. In the worst case, virtual social worlds are just another form of channel that firms can use to reach a segment of highly creative and technologically advanced consumers. But they may also be the beginning of a whole new area of retailing and selling products.

REFERENCES

Ajzen, I. (1991). The theory of planned behavior. *Organizational Behavior and Human Decision Processes*, *50*(2), 179–211. doi:10.1016/0749-5978(91)90020-T.

Ajzen, I. (2006). *Constructing a TpB questionnaire: Conceptual and methodological considerations*: Retrieved from http://www.people.umass.edu/aizen/tpb.html

Ajzen, I., & Fishbein, M. (1980). *Understanding attitudes and predicting social behavior*. Upper Saddle River, NJ: Prentice Hall.

Arakji, R. Y. & Lang, K. R. (2008). "Avatar business value analysis: A method for the evaluation of business value creation in virtual commerce. *Journal of Electronic Commerce Research, 9*(3)3, 207-218.

Bagozzi, R. P., & Dholakia, U. M. (2002). Intentional social action in virtual communities. *Journal of Interactive Marketing*, *16*(2), 2–21. doi:10.1002/dir.10006.

Bagozzi, R. P., & Dholakia, U. M. (2006). Antecedents and purchase consequences of customer participation in small group brand communities. *International Journal of Research in Marketing*, *23*(1), 45–61. doi:10.1016/j.ijresmar.2006.01.005.

Beatty, S. E., & Ferrell, M. E. (1998). Impulse buying: Modeling its precursors. *Journal of Retailing*, *74*(2), 169–191. doi:10.1016/S0022-4359(99)80092-X.

Beck, L., & Ajzen, I. (1991). Predicting dishonest actions using the theory of planned behavior. *Journal of Research in Personality*, *25*(3), 285–301. doi:10.1016/0092-6566(91)90021-H.

Bentler, P. M. (1990). Comparative fit indexes in structural models. *Psychological Bulletin*, *107*(2), 238–246. doi:10.1037/0033-2909.107.2.238 PMID:2320703.

Bolton, R. N. (1998). A dynamic model of the duration of the customer's relationship with a continuous service provider: The role of satisfaction. *Marketing Science*, *17*(1), 45–65. doi:10.1287/mksc.17.1.45.

Cobb, C. J., & Hoyer, W. D. (1986). Planned versus impulse purchase behavior. *Journal of Retailing*, *62*(4), 384–409.

Cox, E. P. I. (1980). The optimal number of response alternatives for a scale: A review. *JMR, Journal of Marketing Research*, *17*(4), 407–422. doi:10.2307/3150495.

Dhar, R., & Wertenbroch, K. (2000). Consumer choice between hedonic and utilitarian goods. *JMR, Journal of Marketing Research*, *37*(1), 60–71. doi:10.1509/jmkr.37.1.60.18718.

Dittmar, H., & Drury, J. (2000). Self-image – is it in the bag? A qualitative comparison between "ordinary" and "excessive" consumers. *Journal of Economic Psychology*, *21*(2), 109–142. doi:10.1016/S0167-4870(99)00039-2.

Gartner Inc. (2008). *Gartner says 90 per cent of corporate virtual world projects fail within 18 months*. Retrieved from http://www.gartner.com/it/page.jsp?id=670507

Gefen, D., Karahanna, E., & Straub, D. W. (2003). Trust and TAM in online shopping: An integrated model. *Management Information Systems Quarterly*, *27*(1), 51–90.

Haenlein, M., & Kaplan, A. M. (2009). Flagship brand stores within virtual worlds: The impact of virtual store exposure on real life band attitudes and purchase intent. *Recherche et Applications en Marketing*, *24*(3), 57–80. doi:10.1177/076737010902400304.

Hausman, A. (2000). A multi-method investigation of consumer motivations in impulse buying behavior. *Journal of Consumer Marketing*, *17*(5), 403–426. doi:10.1108/07363760010341045.

Hogarth, R. M., & Einhorn, H. J. (1992). Order effects in belief updating: The belief-adjustment model. *Cognitive Psychology*, *24*(1), 1–55. doi:10.1016/0010-0285(92)90002-J.

Holzwarth, M., Janiszewski, C., & Neumann, M. M. (2006). The influence of avatars on online consumer shopping behavior. *Journal of Marketing*, *70*(4), 19–36. doi:10.1509/jmkg.70.4.19.

Hrubes, D., Ajzen, I., & Daigle, J. (2001). Predicting hunting intentions and behavior: An application of the theory of planned behavior. *Leisure Sciences*, *23*(3), 165–178. doi:10.1080/014904001316896855.

Hu, L.-T., & Bentler, P. M. (1999). Cutoff criteria for fit indexes in covariance structure analysis: Conventional criteria versus new alternatives. *Structural Equation Modeling*, *6*(1), 1–55. doi:10.1080/10705519909540118.

Jöreskog, K. G., & Goldberger, A. S. (1975). Estimation of a model with multiple indicators and multiple causes of a single latent variable. *Journal of the American Statistical Association*, *70*(351), 631–639. doi:10.2307/2285946.

Kang, H., Hahn, M., Fortin, D. R., Hyun, Y. J., & Eom, Y. (2006). Effects of perceived behavioral control on the consumer usage intention of e-coupons. *Psychology and Marketing*, *23*(10), 841–864. doi:10.1002/mar.20136.

Kaplan, A. M. (2009), Virtual worlds and business schools: The case of INSEAD. In C. Wankel, J. Kingsley, Higher education in virtual worlds: Teaching and learning in second life. Bingley, UK: Emerald Group Publishing.

Kaplan, A. M. & Haenlein, M. (2009a). Consumer use and business potential of virtual worlds: The case of Second Life. The International Journal on Media Management, 11(¾), 93-101.

Kaplan, A. M. (2010). User participation within virtual worlds. In Fogliatto, F. S., & Da Silveira, G. J. C. (Eds.), *Mass customization – Engineering and managing global operations* (pp. 333–351). Springer.

Kaplan, A. M. (2011). Social media between the real and the virtual: How Facebook, YouTube & Co. can become an extension of the real life of their users - And sometimes even more. *Prospective Stratégique*, *38*(March), 8–13.

Kaplan, A. M. (2012). If you love something, let it go mobile: Mobile marketing and mobile social media 4x4. *Business Horizons*, 55.

Kaplan, A. M., & Haenlein, M. (2006). Toward a parsimonious definition of traditional and electronic mass customization. *Journal of Product Innovation Management*, *23*(2), 168–182. doi:10.1111/j.1540-5885.2006.00190.x.

Kaplan, A. M., & Haenlein, M. (2009b). Consumers, companies and virtual social worlds: A qualitative analysis of Second Life. *Advances in Consumer Research. Association for Consumer Research (U. S.)*, *36*(1), 873–874.

Kaplan, A. M., & Haenlein, M. (2009c). The fairyland of Second Life: About virtual social worlds and how to use them. *Business Horizons*, *52*(6), 563–572. doi:10.1016/j.bushor.2009.07.002.

Kaplan, A. M., & Haenlein, M. (2010a). From Real to Virtual and Back Again: The Use and Potential of Virtual Social Worlds within the IT Industry. In Papadopoulou, P., Kanellis, P., & Martakos, D. (Eds.), *Social Computing Theory And Practice: Interdisciplinary Approaches* (pp. 285–300). Hershey, PA: IGI Global. doi:10.4018/978-1-61692-904-6.ch014.

Kaplan, A. M., & Haenlein, M. (2010b). Users of the world, unite! The challenges and opportunities of social media. *Business Horizons*, *53*(1), 59–68. doi:10.1016/j.bushor.2009.09.003.

Kaplan, A. M., & Haenlein, M. (2011a). The early bird catches the news: Nine things you should know about micro-blogging. *Business Horizons*, *54*(2), 105–113. doi:10.1016/j.bushor.2010.09.004.

Kaplan, A. M., & Haenlein, M. (2011b). Two hearts in 3/4 time: How to waltz the Social Media – Viral Marketing dance. *Business Horizons*, *54*(3), 253–263. doi:10.1016/j.bushor.2011.01.006.

Kaplan, A. M., & Haenlein, M. (2012). The Britney Spears universe: Social media and viral marketing at its best. *Business Horizons*, 55.

Kollat, D. T., & Willett, R. P. (1967). Customer impulse purchasing behavior. *JMR, Journal of Marketing Research, 4*(1), 21–31. doi:10.2307/3150160.

Kuk, G., & Yeung, F. T. (2002). Interactivity in e-Commerce. *Quarterly Journal of Electronic Commerce, 3*(3), 223–234.

LeCompte, M. D. (2000). Analyzing qualitative data. *Theory into Practice, 39*(3), 146–154. doi:10.1207/s15430421tip3903_5.

Lee, K., & Shavitt, S. (2009). Can McDonald's food ever be considered healthful? Metacognitive experiences affect the perceived understanding of a brand. *JMR, Journal of Marketing Research, 46*(2), 222–233. doi:10.1509/jmkr.46.2.222.

Lemmens, J. S., & Bushman, B. J. (2006). The appeal of violent video games to lower educated aggressive adolescent boys from two countries. *Cyberpsychology & Behavior, 9*(5), 638–641. doi:10.1089/cpb.2006.9.638 PMID:17034335.

Lim, H., & Dubinsky, A. J. (2005). The theory of planned behavior in e-Commerce: Making a case for interdependencies between salient beliefs. *Psychology and Marketing, 22*(10), 833–855. doi:10.1002/mar.20086.

Lofgren, E. T., & Fefferman, N. H. (2007). The untapped potential of virtual game worlds to shed light on real world epidemics. *The Lancet Infectious Diseases, 7*(9), 625–629. doi:10.1016/S1473-3099(07)70212-8 PMID:17714675.

MacKenzie, S. B., & Spreng, R. A. (1992). How does motivation moderate the impact of central and peripheral processing on brand attitudes and intentions? *The Journal of Consumer Research, 18*(4), 519–529. doi:10.1086/209278.

Mittal, V., Kumar, P., & Tsiros, M. (1999). Attribute-level performance, satisfaction and behavioral intentions over time: A consumption-system approach. *Journal of Marketing, 63*(2), 88–101. doi:10.2307/1251947.

Muthén, L. K., & Muthén, B. O. (1998-2007). *Mplus User's Guide* (5th ed.). Los Angeles, CA: Muthen & Muthen.

Podsakoff, P. M., MacKenzie, S. B., Lee, J.-Y., & Podsakoff, N. P. (2003). Common method bias in behavioral research: A critical review of the literature and recommended remedies. *The Journal of Applied Psychology, 88*(5), 879–903. doi:10.1037/0021-9010.88.5.879 PMID:14516251.

Qiu, G., & Papatla, P. (2008). An empirical analysis of inter-acquisition time of free online content. *Journal of Interactive Marketing, 22*(2), 19–27. doi:10.1002/dir.20111.

Rook, D. W. (1987). The buying impulse. *The Journal of Consumer Research, 14*(2), 189–199. doi:10.1086/209105.

Rook, D. W., & Fisher, R. J. (1995). Normative influences on impulsive buying behavior. *The Journal of Consumer Research, 22*(3), 305–313. doi:10.1086/209452.

Rowan, D. (2009). The suits come to Second Life. *Times (London, England)*.

Schifter, D. E., & Ajzen, I. (1985). Intention, perceived control, and weight loss: An application of the theory of planned behavior. *Journal of Personality and Social Psychology, 49*(3), 843–851. doi:10.1037/0022-3514.49.3.843 PMID:4045706.

Schlosser, A. E. (2003). Experiencing products in the virtual world: The role of goal and imagery in influencing attitudes versus purchase intentions. *The Journal of Consumer Research, 30*(2), 184–198. doi:10.1086/376807.

Schlosser, A. E. (2006). Learning through virtual product experience: The role of imagery on true versus false memories. *The Journal of Consumer Research, 33*(3), 377–383. doi:10.1086/508522.

Schroeder, R., Huxor, A., & Smith, A. (2001). Activeworlds: Geography and social interaction in virtual reality. *Futures*, *33*(7), 569–587. doi:10.1016/S0016-3287(01)00002-7.

Shen, J., & Eder, L. B. (2009). Exploring intentions to use virtual worlds for business. *Journal of Electronic Commerce Research*, *10*(2), 94–103.

Sheppard, B. H., Hartwick, J., & Warshaw, P. R. (1988). The theory of reasoned action: A meta-analysis of past research with recommendations for modifications and future research. *The Journal of Consumer Research*, *15*(3), 325–343. doi:10.1086/209170.

Spiggle, S. (1994). Analysis and interpretation of qualitative data in consumer research. *The Journal of Consumer Research*, *21*(3), 491–503. doi:10.1086/209413.

Stern, H. (1962). The significance of impulse buying today. *Journal of Marketing*, *26*(2), 59–62. doi:10.2307/1248439.

Taylor, S., & Todd, P. (1995). Decomposition and crossover effects in the theory of planned behavior: A study of consumer adoption intentions. *International Journal of Research in Marketing*, *12*(2), 137–155. doi:10.1016/0167-8116(94)00019-K.

Vohs, K. D., & Faber, R. J. (2007). Spent resources: Self-regulatory resource availability affects impulse buying. *The Journal of Consumer Research*, *33*(4), 537–547. doi:10.1086/510228.

Watson, D., Clark, L. A., & Tellegen, A. (1988). Development and validation of brief measures of positive and negative affect: The PANAS scales. *Journal of Personality and Social Psychology*, *54*(6), 1063–1070. doi:10.1037/0022-3514.54.6.1063 PMID:3397865.

Weun, S., Jones, M. A., & Beatty, S. E. (1998). Development and validation of the impulse buying tendency scale. *Psychological Reports*, *82*(4), 1123–1133. PMID:9709520.

Wofford, J. C., & Goodwin, V. L. (1990). Effects of feedback on cognitive processing and choice of decision style. *The Journal of Applied Psychology*, *75*(6), 603–612. doi:10.1037/0021-9010.75.6.603.

KEY TERMS AND DEFINITIONS

Second Life: Three-dimensional virtual social world that opened to the public in 2003 and is maintained by the US-based Linden Research, Inc.

Social Media: "Group of Internet-based applications that build on the ideological and technological foundations of Web 2.0, and that allow the creation and exchange of User Generated Content" (Kaplan and Haenlein 2010b, p. 61).

Virtual Game World: Subgroup of virtual worlds that require their users to behave according to strict rules in the context of a massively multiplayer online role-playing game (MMORPG); e.g. World of Warcraft.

Virtual Social World: Subgroup of virtual worlds that allow residents to choose their behavior in a rather free manner and to, essentially, live a virtual life similar to their real life; e.g. Second Life.

Virtual World: Social media applications which take the form of computer-based simulated environments and through which users can interact with one another and use and create objects.

ENDNOTES

[1] Social media are "a group of Internet-based applications that build on the ideological and technological foundations of Web 2.0, which allows the creation and exchange of user-generated content" (Kaplan & Haenlein 2010b, p.61).

[2] Mobile social media are "a group of mobile marketing applications that allow the

creation and exchange of user generated content" (Kaplan, 2012).

[3] For the purpose of our study we consider shopping enjoyment and impulse buying tendency as general character traits that are identical for purchases in Real Life and Second Life. We therefore relied on a general wording for these two constructs and did not adapt the scale items to Second Life in particular.

[4] The remaining 104 participants indicated that they had never purchased products within Second Life in exchange for Linden Dollars.

[5] Very few respondents (4) indicated they were between 13 and 17 years old. This is surprising as Second Life requires a minimum age of 18. However, deleting these 4 respondents does not lead to any substantial changes in our results.

[6] The thresholds recommended in literature are: CFI/ TLI > 0.95; RMSEA < 0.06, SRMR < 0.08. The fit indices for a model excluding beliefs are as follows: CFI: 0.993, TLI: 0.989, RMSEA: 0.032, SRMR: 0.024.

APPENDIX: MEASUREMENT SCALES

All measures employ 7-point scales with 'strongly disagree/ agree' as anchors, except where noted otherwise.

Planned Purchases

Behavioral belief strength (Ajzen, 2006)

b_1: Purchasing goods on Second Life helps me to improve my avatar's appearance.

b_2: Purchasing goods on Second Life makes my Second Life experience more exciting.

b_3: Purchasing goods on Second Life helps me to maintain relationships with my friends within Second Life.

Outcome evaluation (Hrubes et al., 2001)

e_1: Improving my avatar's appearance is important to me.

e_2: Having an exciting experience in Second Life is important to me.

e_3: Maintaining relationships with my friends within Second Life is important to me.

Normative belief strength (Ajzen, 2006)

n_1: My Second Life friends would encourage me to purchase goods on Second Life.

n_2: My Real Life friends would encourage me to purchase goods on Second Life.

Motivation to comply (Hrubes et al., 2001)

m_1: When it comes to purchasing goods on Second Life, I want to do what my Second Life friends think I should do.

m_2: When it comes to purchasing goods on Second Life, I want to do what my Real Life friends think I should do.

Control belief strength (Ajzen, 2006)

c_1: I usually do not have many Linden Dollars available when I am on Second Life.

c_2: Purchasing goods on Second Life is complicated.

c_3: Purchasing goods on Second Life is technically unreliable.

Control belief power (Beck and Ajzen, 1991, AVE: 0.550)

p_1: Without a sufficient amount of Linden Dollars available, it would be more difficult for me to purchase goods on Second Life.

p_2: The complexity of Second Life makes it more difficult for me to purchase goods on Second Life.

p_3: The low technical reliability of Second Life makes it more difficult for me to purchase goods on Second Life.

Attitude towards purchase (Beck and Ajzen, 1991, AVE: 0.565)

- Purchasing goods on Second Life is
  - Bad/good
  - Unpleasant/pleasant
  - Foolish/wise
  - Unattractive/attractive

Subjective norm (Beck and Ajzen, 1991, AVE: 0.529)

- Most of the people who are important to me would disapprove of me purchasing goods on Second Life.
- No one who is important to me thinks it is OK to purchase goods on Second Life.
- Most people who are important to me would look down on me if I purchased goods on Second Life.

Perceived behavioral control (Schifter and Ajzen, 1985, AVE: 0.673)

- It is easy for me to purchase goods on Second Life.
- If I want to, I can purchase goods on Second Life.

Second Life purchase intent (Beatty and Ferrell, 1998, AVE: 0.513)

- I intend to purchase goods on Second Life over the next month.
- I will try to purchase goods on Second Life over the next month.
- I have decided to purchase goods on Second Life over the next month.
- I am determined to purchase goods on Second Life over the next month.

Impulse Buying

Shopping enjoyment (Weun et al., 1998, AVE: 0.439)

- Shopping is a waste of time.
- Shopping is not a way I like to spend my leisure time.
- Shopping is not entertaining to me.
- Shopping is not one of my favorite activities.

Impulse buying tendency (Beatty and Ferrell, 1998, AVE: 1.668)

- When I go shopping, I rarely buy things that I had not intended to purchase.
- I am a person who rarely makes unplanned purchases.
- I avoid buying things that are not on my shopping list.

Positive/Negative affect (Watson et al., 1988, AVE: 0.547/0.253)

- Indicate to what extent you have felt this way during your last shopping occasion (1: not at all, 7: extremely).
  - Enthusiastic - Scared
  - Interested - Afraid
  - Determined - Upset
  - Excited

Money available (Beatty and Ferrell, 1998, AVE: 0.523)
- I did not feel I could afford to make any unplanned purchase on my last shopping occasion.
- I was on a tight budget during my last shopping occasion.

Felt urge to buy impulsively
- On my last shopping occasion, I experienced a number of sudden urges to buy things I had not planned to purchase on that trip.
- On my last shopping occasion, I saw a number of things I wanted to buy even though they were not on my shopping list.
- I experienced no strong urges to make unplanned purchases on my last shopping occasion (reverse coded).
- On my last shopping occasion, I felt a sudden urge to buy something.

Moderating Variables

Usage Intensity of Second Life
- **Usage Duration:** When did you start using Second Life?
  - 0–6 months ago
  - 6–12 months ago
  - 12+ months ago
- **Weekly Usage:** How many hours do you spend per week on Second Life?
  - 0–14 hours
  - 15–24 hours
  - 25+ hours

Purchase Experience
- **Shopping Frequency:** How often do you go shopping on Second Life?
  - Never/less than once a week
  - Once a week
  - Several times a week or more often
- **Purchase Frequency:** How often do you make a purchase on Second Life?
  - Never/less than once a week
  - Once a week
  - Several times a week or more often

Section 3
Social Networking with Social Media

Chapter 6
Typical Innovative and Involvement Characteristics of Contributors to Consumer Generated Media

Eric Shiu
The University of Birmingham, UK

ABSTRACT

One key impact of consumer generated media on today's firms is that it has become an increasingly important source of information for consumers in their decision making process. Firms that are able to gather positive messages about themselves and their products or services on consumer generated media can be instrumental to the survival and success of their business. The quality and growth of consumer generated media depend on contributions from the consumer public, and some people are more likely to post their own messages, written or otherwise, on consumer generated media than others. Understanding some typical characteristics of these people, termed active contributors to consumer generated media in this chapter, is beneficial for firms, as they can be more ready to identify them and could do something to turn them in their flavour. Based on literature review, this study has identified a number of hypothetical variables that may influence whether a person is an active contributor to consumer generated media. A questionnaire survey on 430 respondents has shown that global innovativeness, electronic innovativeness and consumer involvement significantly affect contributions to consumer generated media. Active contributors to this new medium are also more likely to be male and of a younger age.

DOI: 10.4018/978-1-4666-4026-9.ch006

This importance of peer recommendations and consumer opinions online justifies the attention marketers continue to pay to the use of social and consume generated media. -from Nielsen Global Online Consumer Survey Report (2009)

INTRODUCTION

Consumer generated media is a collective name applied to different forms of digital communications whereby consumers openly share their opinions and experiences, often about their reactions to products and services (Shiu et al., 2009). It can take the form of blogs, podcasts, Internet forums, online community, and online social network (Table 1). It reflects the availability of new ways for authoring content that can be easily disseminated through the Internet (Dwyer, 2007). Consumer generated media should be treated differently from traditional media and its significance to businesses is likely to be greater than traditional media, because on this media platform consumers can consume, interact with, control, create, and distribute the media content.

Historically, consumer generated media or user-generated media as some other researchers may call, can be traced back to the bulletin boards on portal websites such as Yahoo and AOL in the 1990s. Over time, the number of 'appearances' of consumer generated media has been increasing.

Some of the appearances, such as Wikipedia, function as a collective gathering of information. Some others such as MySpace and YouTube are about personal sites. Others like Flickr are the result of a combination of collective and personal sites (Lanchester, 2006). Daugherty, Eastin and Bright (2008) categorised consumer generated media into eight major types and studied differences in popularity between these types, among consumer generated media contributors and users respectively (Table 2). Their results show that 46.5% of the respondents have participated in a discussion forum, while 44% of the

Table 2. Types of consumer generated media that contributors and users go for

Type	Contributors	Users
Discussion forums	46.5	20.6
Pictures	44.0	51.1
Personal websites	42.3	25.5
Blogs	40.8	23.4
Videos	21.1	48.9
Other	11.3	8.3
Audios	9.9	19.1
Drawings	7.0	6.8
Wikied	4.2	11.7

The figures are expressed in percentage. Each one represents the percentage of the respondents to Daugherty, Eastin and Bright's (2008) survey who go for the respective type of consumer generated media for their contribution or usage purpose.

Table 1. Some major forms of consumer generated media

Form	Meaning
Blog	A user-generated website where entries, which contain commentary or news on a particular subject, are made in journal style and displayed in a reverse chronological order.
Podcast	An audio (or occasionally video) recording available on an Internet source (website, blog, etc) for real-time listening or downloading.
Internet forum	A web application for holding discussions and posting user generated content.
Online community	A group of people that primarily interact via a computer network.
Online social network	A collection of various web-based ways for users to interact, such as chat, messaging, email, video, voice chat, file sharing, blogging, and discussion groups.

Source: Shiu et al. (2009)

respondents have contributed pictures to the consumer generated media community. These have been followed by 42.3% of the respondents who have created their own websites, and 41% of the respondents who have creased a blog. One can therefore see that texts and pictures are the most popular means through which people contribute to consumer generated media, while audios and drawings are comparatively less popular.

The situation is very difficult if consumer generated media is accessed merely for the purpose of using the content it provides. In this purpose situation, people are most likely to choose pictures and videos. The next popular grounds for consumer generated media users are personal websites, blogs and discussion forums. Therefore contributors and users of consumer generated media are different not only in their personal backgrounds, but also in their preferences towards consumer generated media.

In recent years there has been a drastic increase in the amount of information on the consumer generated media. In addition more and more

consumers are relying on this information for making consumption and purchase decisions. A global online consumer survey study in 2009 by Nielsen shows that 'recommendations from people I know' is the leading source of product and brand information that consumers trust completely, while 'consumers opinions posted online' is the joint second most trusted source, which far exceeds other traditional advertising sources such as advertisements on television, in newspapers, in magazines, or on radio (Figure 1). Therefore it is fair to say the consumer generated media has generated a powerful online word of mouth effect, which modern businesses can't afford to ignore.

There have been an army of consumers who are contributors to consumer generated media. They are more likely than other consumers to proactively post their consumer opinions online. Much research has been done on understanding the characteristics of consumers, termed innovators, who are the most likely to try new products than all other consumers. These innovators have been found to possess certain characteristics, such

Figure 1. Global consumer trust in different sources of product and brand information

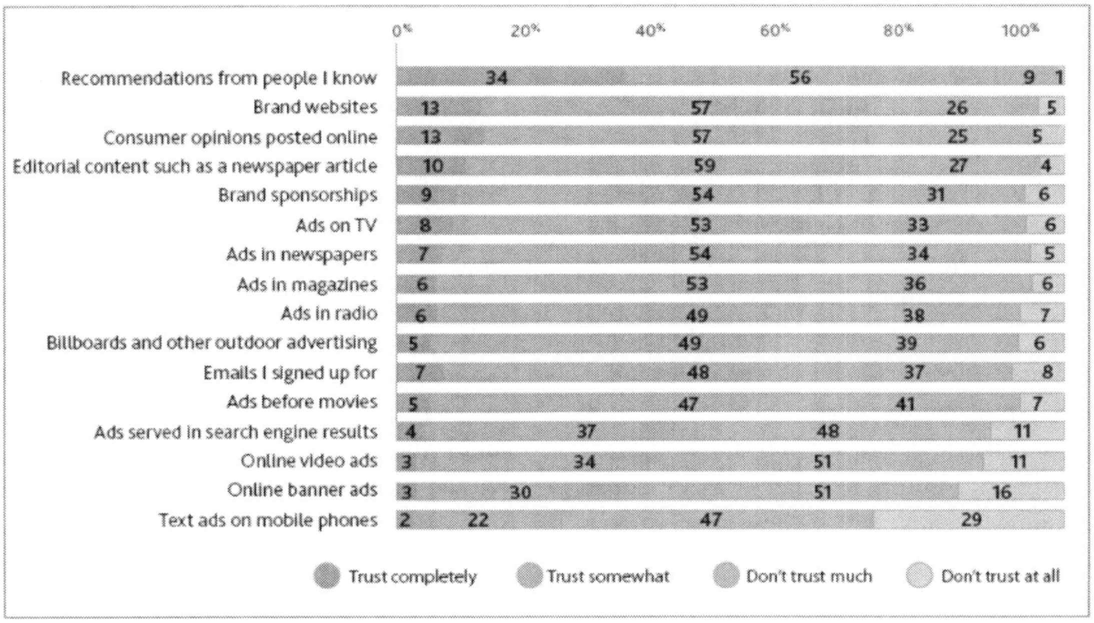

Source: Nielsen Global Online Consumer Survey--Trust, Value and Engagement in Advertising, July 2009, p.3

as higher income, lower age, higher education, and heavier social participation (Dickerson & Gentry 1983; Robertson &Gatignon, 1991; Rogers, 2005; Steenkamp et al., 1999). Consumer generated media can be viewed as a new type of media, and it is logical to hypothesize that certain types of people are more likely than other people to generate information (i.e., their own consumer opinions) on consumer generated media. Understanding the characteristics of these people is beneficial to modern businesses. These people, through the online word of mouth effect that they create, exert a potentially potent influence on the fortune of a business. If the business possesses more knowledge of who these people are, it can target at them more specifically, and tries to turn around their consumer opinions in the business' flavour.

In spite of the obvious benefits arising from a better understanding of contributors to consumer generated media, so far there have been only a few studies specifically on them. One such study is Daugherty, Eastin and Bright (2008), who explored the impacts of motivational factors on contributions to consumer-generated media (they used the term "user generated content" which is analogous in its meaning to our term "consumer generated media." Another is Yoo and Gretzel (2011), focusing on the personality factors. Additionally, although Shao's (2009) paper is purely conceptual and strictly speaking does not add to our understanding of consumer generated media contributors, he has provided an insightful framework illustrating the interdependence among the three behaviours towards consumer generated media (i.e., consuming, participating, and producing). This chapter addresses the research gap of the relative lack of research on background characteristics of consumer generated media contributors in general, and focuses on the innovativeness and involvement aspects of the contributors, which hitherto have not been studied, in particular.

REVIEW OF PREVIOUS RESEARCH

As noted above, the only major research done on factors contributing to consumer generated media content generation is the 2008 article by Daugherty, Eastin and Bright. The key theory they relied on in their paper is the functional theory (Katz, 1960). This theory is hailed as essential for our understanding the complexity of motivational underpinnings and functions in formulating one's attitude towards a particular object, including content creation in consumer generated media. Functional theory says that, subject to the purpose, a particular attitude can serve a variety of motivations, such that one's behaviour is a function of his/her attitude towards that behaviour (O'Keefe, 2002).

Overall consumer researchers widely accept Katz's (1960) functional theory as a robust framework for further studying diverse motivational forces in consumers. The theory posits that any given attitude serves one or more of four distinct personality functions: utilitarian, knowledge, ego-defensive, and value expressive.

The utilitarian function insists that consumers are motivated to gain rewards and avoid punishment, implying an attitude based on self-interest. In consumer generated media, consumers make contribution primarily for their own personal incentives.

The knowledge function acknowledges the need of people at large to gain information in order to organise and understand their environment. Contributors to consumer generated media would produce contents because doing so would make them feel a sense of intrinsic wisdom. This can help them to organise and understand their environment, a specific topic of research interest, and/or themselves.

The value-expressive function is related to attitudes that let people express or relate their self-concepts and values. This can improve one's image in the eyes of the world through matching moral beliefs. Therefore, in consumer generated media, contributors can feel inherently gratified with a sense of self-esteem because they have generated content and become members of an online community that shares the principles regarded as important by the community.

The ego-defensive function is about motivations that can protect people from internal insecurities or external challenges, through which one's internal function of defending his/her self-image can be served. In the case of consumer generated media, people contribute in order to minimise their self-doubts, feel a good sense of belonging to the community, and even reduce a guilty feeling about inaction.

Besides the above four functions that come from functional theory, follow-up research has added other new functions. One important added function is from Smith (1973), who proposed an extension of the value-expressive function and took close note of social adjustment. The resulting new function, called social function, acknowledges that people do things that are agreeable to others. This social function makes people seek opportunities to interact with friends or participate in activities perceived favourably by others (Clay et al., 1998). Applying this function to consumer generated media, the relevance can be seen through the concepts of sharing and interacting in this new media.

Results from Daugherty, Eastin and Bright's study show that the ego-defensive and social functions exert significant impacts on consumer attitudes that lead to contributions to consumer generated media. The ego-defensive function urges people to protect themselves from internal insecurities and external challenges. By contributing to consumer generated media, the contributor can help their self-doubts minimised or reduced, and has a greater chance to feel a sense of community. On the other hand, the social function helps contributors in their seeking out activities that are perceived as favourable by other people.

Yoo and Gretzel (2011) is another of a few recent studies on identifying the background characteristics of consumer generated media con-

tributors. Although they referred to travel-related consumer generated media in their study, there is no obvious rationale for suggesting that their results cannot be applicable to other consumer generated media situations. They have found out that extraversion can increase the likelihood to have CGM creation experience. Another personality factor, openness, has also been found to bring an increase in the likelihood of travellers writing travel blogs for a known audience. Yoo and Gretzel (2011) have also found that some personality characteristics exert an impact on the choice of the types of consumer generated media to create online contents. More specifically neuroticism decreases the likelihood to contribute to a travel-related discussion board/forum. Furthermore, extraverts are more likely to respond to other people's blogs with comments, while people high in the scores for openness, agreeableness and conscientiousness show a high motivation to post travel views.

Shao (2009) is another recent addition to the study of consumer generated media. This study is purely conceptual and therefore does not offer any empirical backup. Nevertheless it is still worth introducing Shao (2009) in this chapter because the author has put forward a conceptual model demonstrating the interdependence of people's consuming, participating, and producing on consumer-generated media (Shao used the term user-generated media in his study), providing us with a complete picture of the three different types of users or uses of consumer generated media.

The first type is 'consuming for information and entertainment' (Shao, 2009). People can surf on consumer-generated media websites to consume contents in the form of video clips, blogs, pictures, and music. The questions posed by Shao (2009) are about why people choose to consume contents offered by consumer-generated media and what gratifications they expect to receive from such consumption. Typically people consume these contents to serve their two motives for media consumption, namely information seeking and entertainment (Graber 1993; Katz et al., 1974;

Korgaonkar & Wolin, 1999; McQuail, 1983; McQuail, 2000; Zillmann & Bryant, 1985). And like consuming traditional media such as television and magazines, people consume contents in consumer generated media for escaping from problems, relaxing, getting aesthetical enjoyment, filling time, seeking emotional release and sexual arousal (Katz et al., 1973; McQuail, 1983). In addition, in the course of being entertained in consumer generated media, people could be able to alter their prevailing mood states, which are theorised in mood management theory (Bryant & Davies, 2006; Bryant & Zillmann, 1984; Zillmann, 1988).

The second type is 'participating for social interaction and community development' (Shao, 2009). People participate in consumer generated media through interacting with its content and with other users. More specifically, users are interacting with the content on consumer generated media when they are rating the content, saving it as their favourites, sharing it with others, post comments about the content, etc. On the other hand, users are interacting with other users when they interact each other through email, instant message, chat room, message boards or other online venues. Chan (2006) categorised the user-to-content interaction as indirect, and the user-to-user interaction as direct way for users to satisfy their needs for social interaction.

Indeed the Internet has become an important place for social interaction ever since its inception (McKenna et al., 2002). But an on-going debate is about whether consumer generated media can really help users satisfy their social interaction needs. The 'negative side' camp said no mainly because the Internet is inherently antithetical to the nature of human life, and although it has been technologically improved continuously, it is still too limited (compared to traditional personal interaction) to foster meaningful relationships (Beniger, 1988; Stoll, 1995). On the contrary, the 'positive side' camp said otherwise and claimed that participation through the Internet such as in the form of consumer generated media can lead to increased self-acceptance, greater liking and acceptance by others, widened social circles, decreased loneliness, decreased estrangement and isolation, and decreased depression (Cole, 2000; McKenna & Bargh, 1999; McKenna & Bargh, 2000; McKenna et al., 2002; Walther, 1997).

The third type is 'producing for self-expression and self-actualisation.' People make use of consumer generated media sites to produce and publish their own content there. The content can be in the form of videos, pictures, blogs, and personal home pages. Although consumers can also produce their own content in many old and new media, consumer generated media by its nature grows out of and are specifically designed for incorporating people's producing behaviour. Indeed without the contents produced by users, consumer generated media will die out. A related question addressed in Shao's (2009) study is about what have made people voluntarily willing to produce on consumer-generated media. Based on the assumption that human beings are generally self-interested, Shao (2009) put forward self-expression and self-actualisation as important factors driving people to voluntarily produce on consumer generated media.

Self-expression is concerned with the expression of one's own identity, in particular one's individuality. In general people have a desire to present their true or inner self to other people, and to have other people know them as they know themselves (Goffman, 1959; Swann, 1983). This common desire can be fulfilled through blogging, video casting and other self-presentation activities available on consumer generated media websites. Self-expression can be explicit, such as through direct self-disclosure; it can also be implicit, perhaps through choices of specific topics, words, illustrations and styles (VanLear et al., 2005). This self-expression desire on consumer generated media may be particularly strong for those people who feel highly constrained by the roles at work or in society as a whole that they need to adhere to (McKenna & Bargh 1999).

Self-actualisation can be broadly defined as "working on one's own identity and reflecting on one's own personality" (Trepte, 2005). According to Mook (1996), the motive of self-actualisation is predominantly unconscious. Even so, it is widely treated as a psychological motive that attempts to achieve specific personal goals such as seeking recognition, fame, or personal efficacy (Bughin, 2007; Kollock, 1999; Rheingold, 1993). For example, when people post their own information on consumer generated media, they may feel that they have contributed something valid to the world, and this feeling could support their own self-image as an efficacious person (Bandura, 1995; Kollock,1999). On the other hand, Bughin (2007) posited that desire for fame is an important motivation for people publishing their own information on YouTube and MySpace.

According to Shao (2009), although the above three types of users or uses of consumer generated media are analytically separate, they are interdependent in a number of aspects. Some people may undergo a path of gradual involvement with consumer generated media, from being a consumer, to being a participant, and then to being a producer. They visit consumer generated media websites and consume the contents there in order to look for information or entertainment. At this stage they are yet to participate or contribute. After being more accustomed to and interested in those websites on whose contents they consume, they would be more involved by participating in them through interacting with the content and other users. This kind of interaction is extremely important in helping them establish and expand their social connection and virtual communities. They would then move to the next stage as producers, or what this chapter calls contributors, of the contents of consumer generated media. This three-stage path of gradual involvement is followed by some people but not others. Some other people may not have gone through the participation stage before producing their own information on consumer generated media websites. Some other people

may always and only be consumers, and would not move to the participation or production stage throughout their life in future. According to Shao (2009) most people are consumer generated media consumers only. Indeed, the 80/20 rule could apply to production of contents on consumer generated media, in that a minority of people involved in consumer generated media contribute to the majority of its contents. They are the lifeblood of consumer generated media. It is important that we conduct enough research in order to have an adequate understanding of this group of people.

Shao's (2009) also put forward the two concepts of "easy to use" and "let users control", which he regarded as the two key usability aspects of consumer generated media. "Easy to use" allows consumers to input relatively very little, but the output may be a lot. This "easy to use" concept is consistent with the utility theory, which suggests that people desire those things that can maximise their pleasure (higher output to input ratio). "Let users control" covers interpersonal control, content-based control, and interface-based control. According to Shao (2009) all these controls appeal to people in both technical and psychological manners.

Both of the aforesaid concepts, in the consumer generated media environment, enable consumers to consume, participate or produce in consumer generated media in a more efficient and controlled manner, and this will help them to derive greater gratification during the process (Shao, 2009).

Recently Correa, Hinsley and de Zuniga (2010) focused on the personality factors and examine their likely impact on the usage of consumer generated media. Using a national sample of U.S. adults, which is much more representative than college-aged samples used in many academic papers, their results reveal that extraversion and openness to experiences are positively related to the use of this new type of media. On the other hand, emotional stability is a negative predictor of the use. Although Correa, Hinsley and de Zuniga (2010) looked into the usage or consumption of consumer generated media, rather than production of or contribution to consumer generated media that this chapter focuses on, they put forward a probable scenario that some personality traits may also exert an influence on the contribution to consumer generated media.

Consumer Innovativeness

Consumer innovativeness is a key contributor to the behaviour of a consumer. As Hirschman (1980) noted, "Innovativeness is one of the few concepts that are so important to the consumer behaviour. The consumer's tendency to adopt new products, ideas, goods or services, plays an important role of the theories concerning brand loyalty, decision making, preferences and communication. From the personal point of view, each consumer is, generally speaking, an innovator, each of us adopting some goods or ideas regarded as new by us through our lives." It is no wonder that research has been conducted on the relationship between consumer innovativeness and different aspects of consumer behaviour, such as new product adoption, dogmatism, novelty seeking, the need for knowledge and the need for change (Midgley & Dowling, 1978; Wood & Swait, 2002). Yet the potential relationship between consumer innovativeness and consumer behaviour in consumer generated media has not yet been explored.

The consumer generated media is regarded as a relatively new form of social and informational communities, and therefore is likely to be more heavily adopted by innovative consumers. Previous research has confirmed a significant relationship between consumer innovativeness and certain innovative behaviours such as adoption of new products or new ideas, looking for novelty and creativity, and the need for change (Hirschman, 1980; Midgley & Dowling, 1978; Wood & Swait, 2002).

One popular concept of consumer innovativeness that has been widely adopted is Midgley and Dowling's (1978) notion of three levels of con-

sumer innovativeness, i.e. global innovativeness, domain-specific innovativeness, and concrete innovativeness. Global innovativeness is described as a broad, abstract personality trait that Midgley and Dowling (1978) defined as 'the degree to which an individual makes innovation decisions independently of the communicated experience of others'. Domain-specific innovativeness is referred to as consumer innovativeness in a specific domain such as in electronic products. This level of innovativeness exists because a consumer can have a high innovativeness in one domain such as electronic products but a low innovativeness in another domain such as fashion products. Concrete innovativeness measures innovative purchasing behaviours on an individual product basis. In other words, it measures whether a consumer actually purchases an innovative product concerned. This study will include global innovativeness and domain-specific innovativeness in attempting to examine their possible relationship to contributions to consumer generated media. As consumer generated media requires a computer and its associated accessories as well as the Internet, this study uses the electronic products as the domain for identifying items measuring domain-specific innovativeness. Concrete innovativeness, which is concerned with actual purchase of respective innovative products, is excluded from this study because previous research (Midgley & Dowling, 1978) has shown that if a person is high in domain-specific innovativeness, he/she is expected to be also high in concrete innovativeness. Including domain-specific innovativeness without including concrete innovativeness can help to simplify the regression modelling process run in this study.

Consumer Involvement

Zaichkowsky (1985) defined involvement as 'a person's perceived relevance of the object based on inherent needs, values, and interests', and developed a 20-item scale known as Personal Involvement Inventory to measure an individual's involvement with a product, advertisement, or purchase decision. Zzichkowsky (1985) found that consumer involvement is positively correlated with an interest in reading more about the product, a process of detailed product comparison before purchase, and the eventual purchase of a product.

Dwyer (2007) drew on Zaichkowsky's (1985) work on consumer involvement and expanded it to relate to post-purchase evaluation and sharing in an online community. He noted that the resources of an online community can be used by prospective buyers to not only help with their information gathering but also connect with a community of users that can enhance their enjoyment after purchasing and using the product. He proposed online community participation is directly correlated to consumer involvement. As Vickery and Wunsch-Vincent,(2007) noted, online community encourages sharing and joint production of information, ideas, opinions and knowledge, and it is logical to deduce that people who are actively participating in an online community can be seen as someone who demonstrates high involvement. Indeed as early as 1977, Holmes and Lett discovered a positive correlation between consumer involvement and traditional word-of-mouth behaviour. It thus sounds logical to extend Holmes and Lett's (1977) findings to today's consumer generated media and hypothesise a positive relationship between consumer involvement and electronic word-of-mouth behaviour. This study follows Holmes and Lett (1977) and Wunsch-Vincent and Vickery's (2007) by attempting to identify whether there is a significant relationship between consumer involvement and contributions to consume generated media.

A blog is a common manifestation of consumer generated media. A study in the U.S. has revealed that 76% of bloggers who do blogs because they want to document their personal experiences or share these experiences with others. Sharing practical knowledge or skills with others is also another common reason for engaging in the blogging behaviour, as agreed by 64% of bloggers being

studied (Table 3). Therefore we can deduce that a common motivating factor of active participation in consumer generated media is sharing, which can be seen as an involvement.

What do people usually put in consumer generated media? According to Lenhart (2006) who investigated into the content of blogs, a major form of consumer generated media, he found that the primary topic is "my life and experiences", which can be anything to do with the product, brand and/or company they know or use. Altogether 37% of bloggers cite this as their primary topic. "Politics and government" was the next most popular topic, but it is already far behind "my life and experiences" as only 11% of bloggers cited issues of public life as the main subject of their blogs. These two most common topics are then followed by sports (6%), general news and current events (5%), business (5%), technology (4%), religion, spirituality or faith (2%), a specific hobby or a health problem or illness (each

Table 3. Reasons for blogging

	Major Reason	Minor Reason	Not a Reason
To express yourself creatively	52	25	23
To document your personal experiences or share them with others	50	26	24
To stay in touch with friends and family	37	22	40
To share practical knowledge or skills with others	34	30	35
To motivate other people to action	29	32	38
To entertain people	28	33	39
To store resources or information that is important to you	28	21	52
To influence the way other people think	27	24	49
To network or to meet new people	16	34	50
To make money	7	8	85

Source: Lenhart 2006

comprising 1%). Other topics mentioned by bloggers in Lenhart's (2006) study include opinions, volunteering, education, photography, and organisations.

Consumer generated media, such as blogs, can be seen not only as a place where people can share things with other people and thus get involved, it can also be seen as a new network phenomenon in which people get involved through electronic words of month. Indeed Dwyer (2007) depicted the virtual community in which consumer generated media was created, spread and shared as a dual network, which is facilitated by electronic word-of-mouth behaviours of the network participants. As can be seen in Figure 2, the dual network consists of the information network and the social network. The information network is the one where people create ties to other people with the exchange of units of messages, and on the basis of this information network, people who participate create a social network among themselves. The person-to-person connections in this dual network are made possible through people's electronic word-of-mouth behaviours.

A detailed study of the nature of consumer involvement by Houston and Rothschild (1978) showed that consumer involvement can be categorised into enduring involvement and situational involvement. Houston and Rothschild (1978) claimed that external stimuli (for example, a new washing machine was sought because the old one was out of order) causes situational involvement, while internal factors such as a high linkage between product use and personal happiness causes enduring involvement. It has been found that, between these two types of involvement, enduring involvement is the major reason for online community participation (Wang and Fesenmaier 2003). Therefore we can reasonably deduce that consumers contributing to consumer generated media do so partly because they can derive personal happiness from being at a state of enduring involvement through for example sharing their experiences with other bloggers.

Personal Characteristics

If consumer generated media is seen as a new product which exists as a form of new media, people who most likely to contribute to consumer generated media can be treated as what the diffusion theory (Rogers, 2005) categorised as innovators. Innovators are the first group of people in a society who try a new product, and they have been found to possess certain personal characteristics. They tend to have graduated from

Figure 2. Virtual consumer generated media community as a dual network

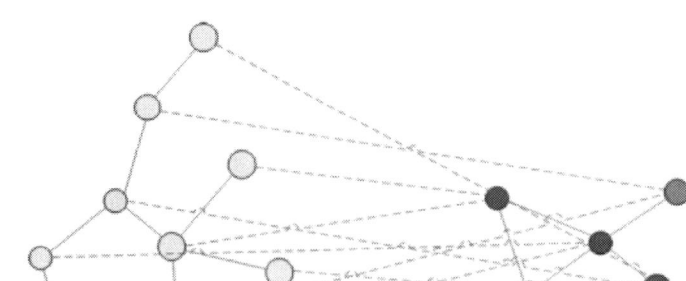

university, have a good job, enjoy a higher living standard, and earn higher income (Robertson, 1971; LaBay & Kinnear, 1981; Plummer, 1981). Higher education allows an individual to better understand performances of an innovation and figure out any complex part of the innovation, thereby explaining its close relationship to the likelihood of an individual being a consumer innovator. Better job, higher living standard and higher income can reduce the perceived financial risk involved in purchasing an innovative product, which all contribute to an individual to become a consumer innovator. More recently, Dorbe et al., (2009) found that innovators are likely to be young people and cosmopolitans.

As there has been clear evidence of the relationship between consumer innovators and certain personal characteristics, and if we treat people who most actively contribute to consumer generated media as innovators in this new media, we can conjecture that they may possess certain personal characteristics that make them distinct from other people in the society. Therefore, this study attempts to identify whether there is a significant relationship between contributions to consumer generated media and specific personal characteristics.

Personal characteristics can be of demographic, lifestyle or other natures. Previous studies (Summer, 1971; Ostlund, 1974; Labay & Kinnear, 1981; Dickerson & Gentry,1983; Martinex et al., 1998; Midgley & Dowling, 1993) overwhelmingly chose demographic variables to identify and depict people who buy a particular new product. This demonstrates that demographic variables have been consistently perceived as reliable predictors of people's innovative behaviours. Additionally, it is usually easier to develop demographic questions than questions of other personal characteristics for the questionnaire.

In deciding which demographic variables should be chosen, this research referred to Lenhart (2006), which attempted to describe bloggers by gender and age. These descriptions are to be compared to those for Internet users, and some interesting results have been found. As can be seen in Table 4, an Internet user has a nearly equal chance to be male or female, but a blogger is more likely to be a male. There is no clear upward or downward age trend in a person being an Internet user. In contrast, bloggers are more likely to be younger. One can conclude that gender and age have a clear say in whether a person is a blogger or not, and therefore this research used gender and age to represent respondents' personal characteristics. Other personal characteristics, such as personality traits, are left out because consumer innovativeness and involvement, rather than any personal characteristics, have been determined to be the main factors of interest in this chapter.

METHODOLOGY

A causal research design was developed in order to test whether consumer innovativeness and consumer involvement play a significant role in moulding a person to become a contributor to consumer generated media. Logistic regression would be used for the test. Additionally chi-square tests would be conducted to ascertain whether contributors to consumer generated media possess certain personal characteristics. Two personal

Table 4. Gender and age characteristics of bloggers vs. internet users

Demographic Variables	Bloggers	Internet Users
Gender		
Male	54	49
Female	46	51
Age		
18-29	54	24
30-49	30	45
50-64	14	24
65+	2	7

Source: Lenhart (2006)

characteristics used in this study are gender and age. A questionnaire was developed to collect the necessary data as input to the logistic regression analysis and chi-square tests.

The questionnaire was divided into four parts. The first part aimed at collecting respondents' usage of consumer generated media. As consumer generated media consists of several forms, this study focused only on two forms–blogs and online forums. The key reason is that these two forms are the most promising and convenient for businesses to implement their marketing strategies such as establishing an official blog or posting promotion information on online forums.

The second part was about measuring the two levels of consumer innovativeness (i.e., global innovativeness and domain-specific innovativeness). Eight items were used to measure global innovativeness.

Item 1: I would rather stick to a brand I usually buy than try something I am not very sure of.

Item 2: I enjoy taking chances in buying unfamiliar brands just to get some variety in my purchase.

Item 3: When I see a new brand on the shelf, I am not afraid of giving it a try.

Item 4: I am reluctant about adopting new ways of doing things until I see them working for people around me.

Item 5: I am generally cautious about accepting new ideas.

Item 6: I must see other people using new innovations before I will consider them.

Item 7: I rarely trust new ideas until I can see whether the vast majority of people around me accept them.

Item 8: I tend to feel that the old way of living and doing things is the best way.

As this study was focused on consumer generated media which is made possible with the presence of a computer and its associated accessories as well as the Internet, electronic innovativeness was used to represent domain-specific innovativeness. Goldsmith and Hofacker's (1991) work on electronic innovativeness was consulted and as a result six items in their work were used to measure electronic innovativeness. The validity and reliability of this six-item domain-specific innovativeness construct were confirmed in Goldsmith and Flynn (1992) and Flynn and Goldsmith (1993). These six items are:

Item 1: Compared to my friends, I own very little electronic entertainment equipment.

Item 2: In general, I am the last in my circle of friends to know the latest new electronic entertainment equipment.

Item 3: In general, I am among the first in my circle of friends to buy new electronic entertainment equipment when it appears.

Item 4: If I heard that a new electronic entertainment equipment was available in the store, I would be interested enough to buy it.

Item 5: I will buy a new item of electronic entertainment equipment, even if I have little experience with it.

Item 6: I know the names of new electronic entertainment equipment before other people do.

The third part contains five items that were adapted from Zaichkowsky's inventory of consumer involvement items. Each of these items measures the degree of involvement of a consumer in the product concerned in different ways. These five adapted items are:

Item 1: I would be interested in reading information about how the product is made.

Item 2: I have compared product characteristics among brands.

Item 3: I have a most-preferred brand of a specific product.

Item 4: I think there is a great deal of differences among brands.

Item 5: I would be interested in reading the article about the product.

The fourth part collected the gender and age information from respondents. The age question is categorical and respondents were asked to choose the category that includes their actual age. Compared to asking respondents their actual age, this age categories approach was expected to reduce non-response to this question as some respondents might find it difficult to disclose their actual age to the interviewer who is in essence a stranger to them. There are six age categories in the questionnaire, including 'under 18', '18-24', '25-30', '31-40', '41-50', and '50 and above.'

The questionnaire survey was conducted in Taiwan, which has witnessed an increasingly popular consumer generated media phenomenon in recent years especially among the younger population. Respondents were requested to go to a specific website (Youthwant Survey System) to fill in the questionnaire. Web survey was adopted because it entails speedy data collection, as evidenced by the fact that 460 completed questionnaires were collected for this study in a week's time. In addition, as this study investigated the use of consumer generated media which is conditional on Internet access, adopting the Web to conduct the survey ensures that all the respondents have access to the Internet.

RESULTS

At the end of the questionnaire survey fieldwork, 460 questionnaires were obtained. However, a careful check on these questionnaires revealed that 30 of them were substantially incomplete or answered illogically, and therefore should be discarded. As a result 430 questionnaires were retained and used for data analysis.

The respondents in this study were generally young, with nearly 80% aged below 30. This may be a clear indication that younger people are more likely to be involved in consumer generated media. Most of the respondents were well-educated, as 57.7% held an undergraduate degree while 37.2%

were master degree graduates. Females, occupying 54.4% of the sample, were slightly overrepresented in the sample. In the sample, high income respondents were unusual as only 3.3% earned a monthly income of over NT$80,000.

This study uses a number of constructs, including global innovativeness, domain-specific innovativeness, and consumer involvement. All these constructs are borrowed from previous studies that have demonstrated the quality of these constructs. However, as they are being used in another country and social context, it is essential to check their reliability in order to ascertain they are of good quality. Reliability tests show that the Cronbach's alpha is 0.767 for the global innovativeness construct, 0.75 for the domain-specific construct, and 0.70 for the consumer involvement construct. Therefore, the reliabilities of all these constructs are satisfactory, and therefore they were allowed to be included in further data analysis.

The questionnaire contains a statement question exploring how influential consumer generated media is in consumer purchase decision making. This question is not related to the main stream analysis of this research, which is concerned with identifying typical characteristics of contributors to consumer generated media, but is worth being included in the survey because consumers' responses to this question can shed light on the degree of importance of contributors to consumer generated media. The more the consumer public follows what is said in consumer generated media, the more important the contributors are to the companies concerned, and the more valuable it will be to learn more about the characteristics of these contributors.

Results show that the majority of the respondents' purchase decision making was influenced by what they read in consumer generated media. Only 8.6% of the respondents said that they don't think consumer generated media influences their purchase decision making (Table 5).

The next analysis is concerned with respondents' usage of consumer generated media, which

Table 5. Responses to the statement "consumer generated media influences your purchase decision making"

Level of Agreement/ Disagreement	% of Respondents	Cumulative % of Respondents
Strongly agree	9.5	9.5
Agree	25.3	34.8
Slightly agree	24.1	58.9
Neutral	32.5	91.4
Slightly disagree	6.7	98.1
Disagree	1.4	99.5
Strongly disagree	0.5	100.0
Total	100.0	

can be categorised into three different types. First is that the respondent has posted own articles and also surfed other people's articles, and 53.4% of the sample were of this type. Second is that the respondent has posted own articles but hasn't yet surfed other people's articles, with only 0.6% of the sample belonging to this type. Last is that the respondent has surfed other people's articles but hasn't yet posted his/her own article. 46% of the sample belonged to the last type. Respondents having posted their own articles on consumer generated media are considered active contributors, while those who have only surfed other people's articles are regarded as passive users.

Therefore, in Taiwan, among the Internet users (as the survey for this research was conducted online and therefore non-Internet users wouldn't be part of the sample for the survey), a slight majority (54%) of them are active contributors to consumer generated media. If we compare this figure to corresponding figures in the US (Table 6), apparently the percentage of Internet users who have created contents in consumer generated media is higher in Taiwan than in the US. Although the comparison is not like for like (focus on blogging only in the US, whilst the online content creations are not limited to those in blogs in Taiwan), the relative popularity of posting something in consumer generated media in Taiwan is beyond doubt, and this further supports the choice of Taiwan for this research.

A chi-square test has been conducted to check any relationship between gender and involvement in consumer generated media. Results show that a whopping 60.7% of the male respondents are active contributors, with the remaining 39.3% as passive users. This result is statistically significant at $p=0.05$.

Another chi-square test to identify any possible relationship between age and involvement in consumer generated media concludes that the younger a person is, the more likely this person is an active contributor to consumer generated media. This result is significant at $p=0.05$.

Table 6. User created content in consumer generated media in the US

	Internet Users in General	Home Broadband Internet Users	Home and/or Office Internet Users (in millions)	Non-Home or Non-Office Internet Users (in millions)
Create or work on your own online journal or blog	8%	11%	9	2
Create or work on your own webpage	14%	17%	18	2
Create or work on web pages or blogs for others including friends, groups your belong to, or work	13%	16%	16	2
Share something online that you created yourself, such as your own artwork, photos, stories or videos	26%	32%	32	4
Percentage who have done at least one of the above 'content' activities	35%	42%	43	5

Next the logistic regression technique has been deployed to find out whether consumer innovativeness and consumer involvement have any significant bearing on whether a person is an active contributor to consumer generated media. Results show that both levels of consumer innovativeness (global innovativeness and domain-specific (electronic products) innovativeness, as well as consumer involvement, have exerted a significant impact on whether a person is an active contributor to consumer generated media. As shown in Table 7, all these three variables are significant at p=0.05. A more detailed look at the same table reveals that the beta coefficient of global innovativeness is 0.302, the beta coefficient of electronic innovativeness is 0.080, and the beta coefficient of consumer involvement is 0.068.

Overall these results have confirmed the conjectured relationships as described in the earlier part of this chapter that an active contributor to consumer generated media is more likely to be a consumer innovator. This active contributor is also more likely to demonstrate a greater sense of consumer involvement in consumer generated media. Besides a confirmation of these conjectured relationships, Table 7 additionally provides the relative strengths of each of these different variables in influencing consumers' usage consumer generated media. In short, as global innovativeness records the highest beta coefficient compared to

Table 7. Logistic regression of the variables influencing whether a person becomes an active contributor to consumer generated media

Variables	Standardised Beta Coefficient	t	Sig.
Constant		5.699	0.000
Global innovativeness	0.308	6.533	0.000
Electronic innovativeness	0.080	2.044	0.042
Consumer involvement	0.068	1.660	0.049

electronic innovativeness and consumer involvement, it demonstrates the greatest relative impact on a person's involvement in consumer generated media. This is followed by electronic innovativeness, meaning that a consumer who is innovative in the electronic products domain is likely to become an active contributor to consumer generated media. Consumer involvement comes last, albeit it is still regarded as another significant variable affecting how a person uses consumer generated media.

CONCLUSION

In retrospect, in spite of all the efforts on conducting this research, a number of limitations were envisaged. First, in the item "I would be interested in reading information about how the product is made," the word "product" could mean different products to different respondents, and therefore was ambiguous. This item should be worded as "I would be interested in reading information about how the electronic entertainment product is made."

In addition, at the end of a questionnaire survey, one respondent commented that the item "I will buy a new item of electronic entertainment equipment, even if I have little experience in it" did not sound logical. According to this respondent, since the product was a new one to the respondent concerned, he/she should not have an experience in it. This respondent suggested that the item can be changed to "I will buy a new item of electronic entertainment equipment, even if I have little experience in related products." This is a useful feedback and the author of this research and other innovation researchers should refer to this feedback when identifying items to capture the totality of meaning of domain-specific consumer innovativeness.

The sample used in this study is a convenience one and therefore we cannot claim the generalizability of the results of this study to a wider population. Nevertheless, as the principal aim of this study was to explore the potential relationships between different hypothetical factors and contributions to consumer generated media, rather than to generalise findings to a wider population, using a less representative sample would be acceptable (Calder, Phillips & Tybout, 1981).

This study has a number of other limitations. First, the variable determining whether a person is an active contributor to consumer generated media can be defined in a more refined manner, i.e. this variable can be treated as containing more levels than the two levels used in this study, which can then lead to more refined results. Second, an additional follow up qualitative research can be conducted in order to explain the relative sizes of the impact of different variables on a person's involvement in consumer generated media. Third, the study was conducted in Taiwan and it would be useful to replicate the same study in other country contexts in order to check the cross-cultural applicability of this study's results.

In spite of the fact that there are quite many limitations as described above, none of them is too critical to damage the contributions of this study. The study adds to the knowledge of consumer generated media by having a better understanding of some typical characteristics of active contributors to consumer generated media. The three types of characteristics or variables tested in this chapter are all drawn from literature review and therefore possess a conceptual foundation. A number of statistical tests have been conducted and results generally have confirmed the conjectured relationships that active contributors to consumer generated media are more likely to possess high global innovativeness, high electronic innovativeness and high consumer involvement. Between these three variables, the global innovativeness trait is the most influential. Active contributors to consumer generated media are also more likely to be male and younger people.

Active contributors to consumer generated media can potentially influence a firm's fortune because they are more likely to post their own articles on consumer generated media discussing or criticising the firm or its products or services. This kind of consumer opinions posted online, as found by a global online consumer survey conducted by Nielsen in 2009, are a leading trusted source of information for the consumer public to use and follow. Firms can't afford to ignore what these active contributors are going to write and post on consumer generated media. By developing a better understanding of the typical characteristics of these active contributors, firms know more who they are and where to find them. By proactively getting in touch with these active contributors and inviting them to try another new, good quality product or service offered by the firm, the firm stands a better chance to have a good image on consumer generated media and benefits from this good message.

This study is partly a response to Shao's (2009) call for studies on individual differences in socio-economic and personality characteristics in effecting people's use (including consumption, participation and production [or contribution]) of consumer generated media. Future research along this topic can add more variables in order to develop an even better understanding of the identity of active contributors to consumer generated media. One interesting and potentially important variable is consumer creativity. It is likely that these active contributors are more creative as a consumer, contributing to their possibly seeing something about the firm and its products and services that other consumers don't see as much, as well as contributing to their taking the initiative to write articles expressing their opinions.

Additionally, consumer generated media are a broad category, and people's contributions in different sub-categories as well as the backgrounds of the people most likely to contribute to each of the different sub-categories could be significantly different from each other. Future research can explore such potential differences.

Methodologically, quantitative survey is often an appropriate way to collect large amount of data from consumers and then use this date to identify heavier contributors and key characteristics of these heavier contributors. However, at times it is also worth considering using qualitative content analysis of posted videos, blogs, home pages, comments and other documents available on consumer social media in order to complement results from the quantitative survey as well as to provide additional insights that cannot be obtained from the quantitative approach. Apart from the qualitative approach, researchers can also consider adopting experimental design for studying contribution to and use of consumer social media. Two possible areas that Shao (2009) suggested and that can be suitable for exploration in experimental design environment are the applicability of the mood management theory and utility theory to the consumer generated media environment.

REFERENCES

Bandura, A. (Ed.). (1995). *Self-efficacy in Changing Societies*. Cambridge, MA: Cambridge University Press. doi:10.1017/CBO9780511527692.

Beniger, J. (1988). 'The personalization of mass media and the growth of pseudo-community. *Communication Research*, *14*(3), 352–371. doi:10.1177/009365087014003005.

Bryant, J., & Davies, L. (2006). Selective exposure processes. In Bryant, J., & Vorderer, P. (Eds.), *Psychology of Entertainment* (pp. 19–33). Mahwah, NJ: Lawrence Erlbaum Associates.

Bryant, J., & Zillmann, D. (1984). 'Using television to alleviate boredom and stress: Selective exposure as a function of induced excitational states. *Journal of Broadcasting*, *28*(1), 1–20. doi:10.1080/08838158409386511.

Bughin, J. (2007). How companies can make the most of user-generated content. Retrieved from http://www.mckinseyquarterly.com/article_abstract_visitor.aspx?ar=2041&12=16&13=16

Calder, B. J., Phillips, L. W., & Tybout, A. M. (1981). Designing research for application. *The Journal of Consumer Research*, *8*(September), 197–207. doi:10.1086/208856.

Chan, A. (2006). Social interaction design case study: MySpace'. Retrieved from http://www.gravity7.com/G7_SID_case_myspace_v2.pdf

Clay, E. G., Snyder, M., Ridge, R., Copeland, J., Stukas, A., Haugen, J., & Miene, P. (1998). Understanding and assessing the motivations of volunteers: A functional approach. *Journal of Personality and Social Psychology*, *74*(6), 1516–1530. doi:10.1037/0022-3514.74.6.1516 PMID:9654757.

Cole, J. (2000). *Surveying the Digital Future*. Los Angeles: UCLA Center for Communication Policy.

Correa, T., Hinsley, A. W., & de Zuniga, H. G. (2010). Who interacts on the Web?: The intersection of users' personality and social media use. *Computers in Human Behavior*, *26*, 247–253. doi:10.1016/j.chb.2009.09.003.

Daugherty, T., Eastin, M. S., & Bright, L. (2008). Exploring consumer motivations for creating user-generated content. *Journal of Interactive Advertising*, *8*(2), 16–25.

Dickerson, M. D., & Gentry, J. W. (1983). Characteristics of Adopters and Non-Adopters of Home Computers. *The Journal of Consumer Research*, *10*(September), 225–235. doi:10.1086/208961.

Dorbe, C., Dragomir, A., & Preda, G. (2009). Consumer Innovativeness: A Marketing Approach. *Journal of Management & Marketing*, *4*(2), 19–34.

Dwyer, P. (2007). Measuring the Value of Electronic word of Mouth and Its Impact in Consumer Communities. *Journal of Interactive Marketing*, *21*(2), 63–79. doi:10.1002/dir.20078.

Flynn, L. R., & Goldsmith, R. (1993). A validation of the Goldsmith and Hofacker innovativeness scale. *Educational and Psychological Measurement, 53*(4), 1105–1116. doi:10.1177/00131644 93053004023.

Goffman, E. (1959). *The Presentation of Self in Everyday Life*. New York: Doubleday.

Goldsmith, R., & Flynn, L. R. (1992). Identifying innovators in consumer product markets. *European Journal of Marketing, 26*(2), 42–55. doi:10.1108/03090569210022498.

Goldsmith, R. E., & Hofacker, C. F. (1991). Measuriing Consumer Innovativeness. *Journal of the Academy of Marketing Science, 19*, 209–221. doi:10.1007/BF02726497.

Grabber, D. A. (1993). *Mass Media and American Politics* (4th ed.). Washington, DC: Congressional Quarterly.

Hirschman, E. C. (1980). Innnovativeness, Novelty Seeking and Consumer Creativity. *The Journal of Consumer Research, 7*, 283–295. doi:10.1086/208816.

Holmes, J. H., & Letts, J. D. (1977). Product sampling and word of mouth. *Journal of Advertising Research, 17*(5), 35–40.

Houston, M.J., & Rothschild, M.L. (1978). Conceptual and methodological perspectives on involvement. *Research Frontiers in Marketing: Dialogues and Directions*,184-187.

Katz, D. (1960). The functional approach to the study of attitudes. *Public Opinion Quarterly, 24*, 27–46. doi:10.1086/266945.

Katz, E., Blumler, J., & Gurevitch, M. (1974). Utilization of mass communication by the individual. In J. Blumler., & E. Katz (Eds.), The Uses of Mass Communications: Current Perspectives on Gratifications Research. Beverly Hills, CA: Sage.

Katz, E., Gurevitch, M., & Haas, H. (1973). On the use of the mass media for important things. *American Sociological Review, 38*(April), 164–181. doi:10.2307/2094393.

Kollock, P. (1999). The economics of online cooperation: Gifts and public goods in cyberspace. In Smith, M., & Kollock, P. (Eds.), *Communities in Cyberspace* (pp. 220–242). London: Routledge.

Korgaonkar, P., & Wolin, L. (1999). 'A multivariate analysis of web usage. *Journal of Advertising Research, 39*(2), 53–68.

Kyung-Hyan, Y., & Gretzel, U. (2011). Influence of personality on travel-related consumer-generated media creation. *Computers in Human Behavior, 27*(2), 609–621. doi:10.1016/j.chb.2010.05.002.

Lanchester, J. (2006). *A bigger bang*. Retrieved from www.guardian.co.uk/weekend/story/0,1937496,00.html

Lenhart, A., & Fox, S. (2006). Bloggers: A portrait of the internet's new story tellers. *Pew Internet and American Life Project*. Retrieved on August 4, 2009, from www.pewinternet.org

Martinex, E., Yolanda, P., & Carlos, F. (1998). The Acceptance and Diffusion of New Consumer Durables: Difference between First and Last Adopter. *Journal of Consumer Marketing, 15*(4), 323–342. doi:10.1108/07363769810225975.

McKenna, K., & Bargh, J. (1999). Causes and consequences of social interaction on the Internet: A conceptual framework. *Media Psychology, 1*(3), 249–269. doi:10.1207/s1532785xmep0103_4.

McKenna, K., & Bargh, J. (2000). 'Plan 9 from cyberspace: The implications of the Internet for personality and social psychology. *Personality and Social Psychology Review, 4*(1), 57–75. doi:10.1207/S15327957PSPR0401_6.

McKenna, K., Green, A., & Gleason, M. (2002). Relationship formation on the Internet: What's the big attraction? *The Journal of Social Issues, 58*(1), 9–31. doi:10.1111/1540-4560.00246.

McQuail, D. (1983). Mass Communication Theory (1st ed.). London: Sage.

McQuail, D. (2000). *McQuail's Mass Communication Theory* (4th ed.). London: Sage.

Midgley, D. F., & Dowling, G. R. (1993). A longitudinal study of product form innovation: The interaction between predispositions and social messages. *The Journal of Consumer Research, 19*, 611–625. doi:10.1086/209326.

Midgley, E. D., & Grahame, R. D. (1978). Innovativeness: The Concept and Its Measurement. *The Journal of Consumer Research, 4*(March), 229–242. doi:10.1086/208701.

Mook, D. G. (1996). *Motivation* (2nd ed.). New York: Norton.

Ostlund, L. E. (1974). Perceived Innovation Attributes as Predictors of Innovativeness. *The Journal of Consumer Research, 1*(September), 23–29. doi:10.1086/208587.

Plummer, J. T. (1981). Life style patterns and commercial bank credit card usage. *Journal of Marketing, 35*(April), 35–41.

Robertson, T. S. (1971). *Innovative Behavior and Communication*. New York: Holt, Rinehart and Winston Publishing.

Robertson, T. S., & Gatignon, H. (1991). How innovators thwart new entrants into their market. *Strategy and Leadership, 19*(5), 4–11. doi:10.1108/eb054333.

Rogers, E. M. (2005). Diffusion of Innovations (4th ed.). New York: The Free PressRheingold, H. (1993). The Virtual Community: Homesteading on the Electronic Frontier. Reading, MA: Addison-Wesley.

Shiu, E., Hair, J., Bush, R., & Ortinau, D. (2009). *Marketing Research*. McGraw-Hill Higher Education.

Smith, M. B. (1973). Political attitudes. In Knutson, J. (Ed.), *Handbook of Political Psychology*. San Francisco, CA: Jossey-Bass.

Steenkamp, Jan-Benedict, E.M., Frenkel ter H., & Michael, W. (1999). A Cross-National Investigation into the Individual and National Cultural Antecedents of Consumer Innovativeness. *Journal of Marketing, 63*(April), 55–69. doi:10.2307/1251945.

Stoll, C. (1995). *Silicon Snake Oil: Second Thoughts on the Information Highway*. New York: Doubleday.

Summers, J. O. (1971). 'Generalized Change Agents and Innovativeness. *JMR, Journal of Marketing Research, 8*(August), 313–316. doi:10.2307/3149568.

Swann, W. B. (1983). Self-verification: Bringing social reality into harmony with the self. In Suls, J., & Greenwald, A. G. (Eds.), *Social Psychological Perspectives on the Self*. Hillsdale, NJ: Erlbaum.

The Nielsen Company. (2009). *Nielsen Global Online Consumer Survey: Trust, Value, and Engagement in Advertising*. Retrieved on August 1, 2009, from www.nielsen.comShao, G. (2009). Understanding the appeal of user-generated media: A uses and gratification perspective. *Internet Research, 19*(1), 7-25.

Trepte, S. (2005). Daily talk as self-actualisation: An empirical study on participation in daily talk shows. *Media Psychology, 7*(2), 165–189. doi:10.1207/S1532785XMEP0702_3.

VanLear, C., Sheehan, M., Withers, L., & Walker, R. (2005). AA online: The enactment of supportive computer mediated communication. *Western Journal of Communication, 69*(1), 5–26. doi:10.1080/10570310500033941.

Vickery, G., & Wunsch-Vincent, S. (2007). *Participative web and user-created content: Web 2.0 Wikis and social networking*. Paris, France: OECD.

Walther, J. (1997). Group and interpersonal effects in international computer-mediated communication. *Human Communication Research*, *23*(3), 342–369. doi:10.1111/j.1468-2958.1997.tb00400.x.

Wang, Y., & Fesenmaier, D. R. (2003). Assessing Motivation of Contribution in Online Communities: An Empirical Investigation of an Online Travel Community. *Electronic Markets*, *13*(1), 33–45. doi:10.1080/1019678032000052934.

Wood, S. L., & Swait, J. Psychological indicators of innovation adoption: cross-classification based need for cognition and need for change. *Journal of Consumer Psychology*, *12*(1), 1–13. doi:10.1207/S15327663JCP1201_01.

Zaichkowsky, J. (1985). Measuring the Involvement Construct. *The Journal of Consumer Research*, *12*(December), 341–352. doi:10.1086/208520.

Zillmann, D. (1988). Mood management: Using entertainment to full advantage. In Donohew, L., Sypher, H., & Higgins, E. (Eds.), *Communication, Social Cognition and Affect*. Hillsdale, NJ: Lawrence Erlbaum Associates.

Zillmann, D., & Bryant, J. (Eds.). (1985). *Selective Exposure to Communication*. Hillsdale, NJ: Lawrence Erlbaum Associates.

ADDITIONAL READING

Brady, M. (2005). Blogging, personal participation in public knowledge-building on the web. Chimera Working Paper 2005-02. Colchester: University of Essex, UK. Retrieved on August 4, 2009, from www.essex.ac.uk/chimera/

Cassar, K. (2008). The On-line and In-Store Crossover Conundrum: Pinpointing the Value of Multi-channel Behaviour, Industry Insight. *The Nielsen Company, 10*. Retrieved on July 3, 2009, from http://www.nielsen.com/consumer_insight/ci_story1.html

Cheung, F. M., Leung, K., Zhang, J. X., Sun, H. F., Gan, Y. Q., & Song, W. Z. et al. (2001). Indigenous Chinese Personality Constructs: Is the Five-Factor Model Complete? *Journal of Cross-Cultural Psychology*, (32): 407. doi:10.1177/0022022101032004003.

Dorbe, C., & Man, C. (2003). Opinions on the Use of Cultural and Social Values in Romanian Advertising., *Strategijski Manadzement. Casopis za Strategijski Medadzment I sisteme podrske strategijskom medadzmentu, 4*.

Dwyer, S., Mesak, H., & Hsu, M. (1999). An Exploratory Examination of the Influence of National Culture on Cross- National Product Diffusion. *Journal of International Marketing*, *13*(7).

Foxall, G. R. (1988). Consumer Innovativeness: Novelty-Seeking, Creativity, and Cognitive Style. *Research in Consumer Behaviour*, *3*, 79–113.

Foxall, G. R. (1995). Cognitive Styles of Consumer Initiators. *Technovation*, *15*(5), 269–288. doi:10.1016/0166-4972(95)96600-X.

Goldsmith, R. E. (1984). Personality Characteristics Associated with Adaption-Innovation. *The Journal of Psychology*, *117*, 159–165. doi:10.1080/00223980.1984.9923672.

Goldsmith, R. E. (1986). Convergent Validity of Four Innovativeness Scales'. *Educational and Psychological Measurement*, *46*, 81–87. doi:10.1177/0013164486461007.

Goldsmith, R. E., D' Hauteville, F., & Flynn, L. R. (1998). Theory and Measurement of Consumer Innovativeness: A Transnational Evaluation. *European Journal of Marketing, 32,* 340–353. doi:10.1108/03090569810204634.

Goldsmith, R. E., Freiden, J. B., & Eastman, J. K. (1995). The Generality/ Specificity Issue in Consumer Innovativeness Research. *Technovation, 15*(10), 601–612. doi:10.1016/0166-4972(95)99328-D.

Gruhl, D., Guha, R., Kumar, R., Novak, J., & Tomkins, A. (2005). *The Predictive Power of Online Chatter.* Chicago, IL: Research Track Paper.

Hirschman, E. C. (1983). Consumer Intelligence, Creativity, and Consciousness: Implication for Consumer protection and Education. *Journal of Public Policy & Marketing, 2*(1), 153–170.

Holak, S. L., & Donald, R. L. (1990). Intention and the Dimensions of Innovation: An Exploratory Model. *Journal of Product Innovation Management, 7,* 59–73. doi:10.1016/0737-6782(90)90032-A.

Houston, M. J., & Michael, L. R. (1978). Conceptual and Methodological Perspectives in Involvement. In Jain, S. (Ed.), *Research Frontiers in Marketing: Dialogues and Directions* (pp. 184–187). Chicago, IL: American Marketing Association.

Hurt, H. T., Katherine, J., & Chester, D. C. (1977). Scale for the Measurement of Innovativeness? *Human Communication Research, 4*(Fall), 58–65. doi:10.1111/j.1468-2958.1977.tb00597.x.

Im, S., Bayus, B. L., & Mason, C. H. (2003). An Empirical Study of Innate Consumer Innovativeness, Personal Characteristics, and New-Product Adoption Behaviour. *Journal of the Academy of Marketing Science, 31*(1), 61–73. doi:10.1177/0092070302238602.

Kirton, M. J. (1976). Adaptors and Innovators: A Description and Measure. *The Journal of Applied Psychology, 61*(5), 622–629. doi:10.1037/0021-9010.61.5.622.

Kohn, C. A., & Jacob, J. (1973). Operationally Defining the Consumer Innovator. In *Proceedings of the American Psychological Association* (pp 837-838). Washington, DC: American Psychological Association.

Labay, D. G., & Thomas, C. K. (1981). Exploring the Consumer Decision Process in the Adoption of Solar Energy Systems. *The Journal of Consumer Research, 8*(December), 271–278. doi:10.1086/208865.

Midgley, D. F., & Dowling, G. R. (1998). Innovativeness: The Concept and Its Measurement. *European Journal of Marketing, 32,* 340–353.

Mudd, S. (1990). The Place of Innovativeness in Models of the Adoption Process: An Integrative Review. *Technovation, 10*(2), 119–134. doi:10.1016/0166-4972(90)90032-F.

O'Keefe, D. J. (2002). *Persuasion: Theory and Research* (2nd ed.). Thousand Oaks, CA: Sage Publications.

Paunonen, S. V., & Ashton, M. C. (2001). Big Five Factors and the Prediction of Behaviour. *Journal of Personality and Social Psychology, 81*(3), 524–539. doi:10.1037/0022-3514.81.3.524 PMID:11554651.

Prescott, L. A., & Hanchard, S. (2006). *Hitwise US Consumer Generated Media Report.* New York: Hitwise.

Reinecke, F. L., & Goldsmith, R. E. (1993). Identifying Innovators in Consumer Marketers. *The Service Industries Journal, 13*(3), 97–109. doi:10.1080/02642069300000052.

Richins, M. L., Bloch, P. H., & McQuarrie, E. F. (1992). How Enduring and Situational Involvement Combine to Create Involvement Responses. *Journal of Consumer Psychology*, *1*(2), 143–153. doi:10.1016/S1057-7408(08)80054-X.

Ringmar, E. (2007). *A blogger's Manifesto: Free Speech and Censorship in the Age of the Internet.* London: Anthem Press. Retrieved on July 3, 2009, from http://www.nielsen.com/consumer_insight/ci_story1.html

KEY TERMS AND DEFINITIONS

Consumer Generated Media (CGM): A collective name applied to different forms of digital communications whereby consumers openly share their opinions and experiences, often about their reactions to products and services.

Consumer Innovativeness: The consumer's tendency to adopt new products, ideas, goods or service.

Consumer Involvement: A person's perceived relevance of the object based on inherent needs, values, and interests.

Domain-Specific Innovativeness: Consumer innovativeness in a specific domain.

Electronic Innovativeness: Consumer innovativeness in the electronic products domain.

Global Innovativeness: The degree to which an individual makes innovation decisions independently of the communicated experience of others.

Innovativeness: The tendency to adopt new products, ideas, goods or services; it can be referred to consumer innovativeness, product innovativeness, or firm innovativeness.

Involvement: Can be consumer involvement or involvement of other entities, but is referred to as consumer involvement in this chapter.

Chapter 7

Can Your Business Have One Million Friends?
Understanding and Using Blogs as One–to–One Mass Media

Soyean (Julia) Kim
Boston University, USA & Kyung Hee University, Korea

Barbara A. Bickart
Boston University, USA

Frédéric F. Brunel
Boston University, USA

Seema Pai
Boston University, USA

ABSTRACT

In this chapter, we develop a theoretical framework that explains how blogs can be categorized based on audiences' perceptions and how bloggers use different strategies to shape or shift their audiences' perceptions and increase the persuasiveness of their messages. We posit that bloggers use two distinguishable communication strategies: (a) developing and sustaining an illusion of relationship between the blogger and the reader in order to individualize the communication, and (b) maintaining a level of ambiguity in their commercial interests in order to conceal the commercial nature of some blogs. We describe the tactics underlying the use of these strategies as well as the efficacy and ethics of these practices.

DOI: 10.4018/978-1-4666-4026-9.ch007

INTRODUCTION

Rumi: It's a day of errands for me... wearing vintage collar, Ralph Lauren blazer, Zara skirt, Céline bag and sunglasses, and Rag & Bone boots.

Comment: I remember that blazer! It's super old, right? It's neat to see how it still fits into your style now, like 5 years later haha. This is why I can never do a decent closet cleanse--I feel like I'll want to wear it again later.

Comment: You always look great when things get hectic. And I've told you before how well you wear Céline.

Comment: My day started as an errand day and ended up being a shopping spree day! Hope yours was great too!

This posting by famous fashion blogger Rumi (fashiontoast.com), along with three of the many comments that she received on that day, illustrate how Rumi has successfully created a communication environment where brands are discussed and celebrated but also where friendships and intimate relationships might prevail. Although it is unlikely that Rumi has a meaningful relationship with each of her 133,672 readers, it is clear that many of them believe they have a close friendship with her. They relate to and connect with her at an interpersonal level, sharing slice of life stories, remembering past events, and engaging in brand level discussions. This level of closeness is rather counterintuitive especially if we consider that blogs are, by definition, a form of broadcast media in which a blogger shares his or her views with a large audience. It is therefore worthwhile understanding how bloggers develop different communication strategies that allow them to achieve specific communication objectives.

Although by their inherent nature, blogs are a form of one-to-many mass media, we propose that not all blogs adhere to the principles of traditional mass communication models. On one hand, we acknowledge that some blogs may follow a broadcast model where the bloggers serve as the focal sources or messengers of information and where their readers are the target recipients of that information. These types of blogs adhere to communication and persuasion principles similar to those that govern other forms of mass media communication (e.g., broadcast advertising or print ads). In other blogs, however, readers may feel that they play an integral role in the communication exchange. In these instances, readers perceive the blogs to be interpersonal and conversational spaces. In other words, blogs can be a unique form of a one-to-many broadcast medium that functions like a one-to-one communication model. Indeed, as shown in our introductory example, some bloggers like Rumi are able to relate very personally to, and ultimately influence, a large audience by developing an intimate communication style. In these cases, readers feel as if they are having one-to-one conversations with the blogger. Unlike advertising and other broadcast media, the overall effectiveness of these one-to-one blogs appears to stem from the personal and intimate relationship that bloggers are able to form with their many readers. The goal of this chapter is to describe how specific persuasion elements actually operate in blogs and in particular what kinds of communication strategies bloggers should use in order to increase the effectiveness and persuasiveness of their messages.

Specifically, in this chapter, by drawing from theory on persuasion in both one-to-one and one-to-many communication media as well as observing a series of blogs, we develop a theoretical framework that explains how blogs can be categorized based on audiences' perceptions and how bloggers use different strategies to shape or shift their audiences' perceptions and increase the persuasiveness of their messages. As we develop this framework, we also recognize that some blogs might have direct commercial interests (e.g., a company blog) while others might not have immediate commercial interests linked with the content of the blogs (e.g., a product review blog by an independent news organization). This distinction is important as we believe that readers will resist or yield to persuasion attempts differently based on their perceptions of the existence of bloggers' commercial interests. Furthermore, we suggest that third party bloggers (those not directly affiliated with a company or product) often try to maintain an appearance of commercial independence even if they have commercial interests of their own. We will discuss the efficacy and ethics of these practices.

BACKGROUND

Although blogs are a form of one-to-many mass media, the interaction between bloggers and readers on many blogs resembles one-to-one communications between friends. In this chapter we pay close attention to these instances and describe the communication strategies that bloggers use to be more persuasive and to achieve the efficiency of one-to-many communication with the effectiveness of one-to-one communication. In particular, we posit that bloggers may use two distinguishable communication strategies: (a) developing and sustaining an *illusion of relationship* between the blogger and the reader in order to individualize the communication and (b) maintaining a level of *ambiguity in their commercial interests* in order to conceal the commercial nature of some blogs.

First, many bloggers seek to escape the distant, impersonal and one-size-fits-all nature of most one-to-many communication models. However, that goal has to be reconciled with the recognition that these bloggers can't have meaningful and personalized relationships with each of their readers. Thus, in order to balance these countervailing forces, bloggers create *illusions of relationships*. They achieve the perception of relationship intimacy by disclosing personal information and explicitly discussing their life events and concerns (Collins & Miller, 1994; Fletcher & Kerr, 2010; Murray, Holmes, & Griffin, 1996). Although

they lack a real, lived, and one-to-one relationship where trust is built over time through direct interactions, these intimacy-creating mechanisms allow audience members to feel connected to the bloggers and to feel they have relationships with the bloggers. As a result, the readers are likely to trust the bloggers and might be more prone to following their recommendations (Chai & Kim, 2010; Giffin, 1967; Winster & Swamynathan, 2010).

While building an illusion of relationship is a frequently implemented strategy on blogs, some bloggers also use a second strategy, that is, *ambiguity in their commercial interests*. Bloggers' own commercial interests are often difficult to identify, vague and potentially contradictory (Nardi et al., 2004) and consequently, readers don't always comprehend if the basis of communication is a friendship, a pure commercial relationship, or a commercial friendship (e.g., Price & Arnould, 1999). Although it is an ethically questionable practice, bloggers might attempt to conceal their commercial interests in order to increase their perceived credibility and persuasion effectiveness. Because online content is often consumer-generated, bloggers might want to cultivate the impression that they are part of this consumer-centered ethos and appear to be independent of marketers' influence, thereby increasing trust in the information and its potential persuasive impact (Bickart & Schindler, 2001). Even though ambiguous or hidden commercial motives might decrease readers' skepticism and increase bloggers persuasion effectiveness, the practice raises public policy concerns as consumers are more likely to accept information as objective and therefore potentially be misled by deceptive information they consider emanating from consumers like them (Balasubramanian, 1994; Darke & Ritchie, 2007; Petty & Andrew, 2008).

This chapter provides insights into social media strategies through the development of a categorization framework based on how blogs' communication strategies are perceived by their readers. In the first section, we first discuss how blogs function, especially if we consider them according to a strict categorization as one-to-many (mass-media) forums. However, we also relax this definitional perspective and allow for a more nuanced categorization based on how readers perceive blogs. This allows us to develop a framework organized around two strategic communication dimensions: (a) *the perceived target audience (mass versus one-to-one); and* (b) *the perceived level of the blogger's commercial interest (explicit commercial interests versus no explicit commercial interests).* The two dimensions allow us to identify four different types of blogs. In the second section, we elaborate on two communication strategies that bloggers use to create these perceptions, namely: (a) *illusion of relationship* and (b) *ambiguity in commercial interests.* In particular, we examine how bloggers use these strategies (either independently or in combination) to refashion the rules of one-to-one communication to accommodate a mass audience. By selectively using these strategies, bloggers can shift and/or maintain the position of their blogs within the typology identified in the first section. Finally, in the third section, we discuss the practical implications of this framework for bloggers, including specific approaches for increasing the persuasive impact of blogs as well as ethical issues associated with the use of these strategies.

HOW DO READERS PERCEIVE BLOGS?

In this section, we develop a categorization scheme by first considering how blogs actually function as a one-to-many communication medium. Then, we describe how this categorization scheme changes when we consider how blogs are perceived by their audiences. Our analysis results in a categorization of blogs based on two dimensions: (a) the perceived target audience (mass versus one-to-one); and (b) the blogger's communication interest (explicit commercial interests versus no explicit commercial interests).

Blogs as One-to-Many Mass Media

Blogs are "frequently updated web pages with a series of archived posts, typically in reverse-chronological order" (Nardi et al., 2004, p.1). Blog content can be provided by an individual writer or can be curated from a variety of sources (Blood, 2002; Herring et al., 2005). In either case, blogs function as a mass communication medium in which content provided by a particular source is distributed to a large audience (Hoffman & Novak, 1996). Because of their mass target audiences, we would expect blogs to function similarly to other mass media (McQuail, 1987).

Indeed, the defining characteristic of traditional one-to-many media is their capacity for mass production and dissemination of messages. Blogs can be seen as a modern manifestation of older forms of technology enabled mass media, allowing for communication with a large and largely anonymous audience (Schramm, 1954). Similar to mass media where messages flow widely from a small set of sources to a large target population (Katz & Lazarsfeld, 1955), messages on blogs also flow from the blogger through a network of blog followers. Thus, blogs can be seen as a reinvented form of a well understood communication process: a one-to-many communication that transfers messages on a massive scale.

Although, by definition, all blogs function as mass media, the blogger's intentions can be either commercial or non-commercial. This distinction is illustrated in Figure 1. In order to offer bases of comparison and contextualize the different types of blogs, Figure 1 also includes some examples of other forms of marketing communications (the white circles in the figure). We refer to blogs that have an explicit commercial interest and that target a mass audience as *Commercial Blogs* (see upper left quadrant in Figure 1). Commercial blogs include corporate blogs as well as blogs focused on specific brands. The authors of these blogs

Figure 1. Basic blog types and selected other communication forms

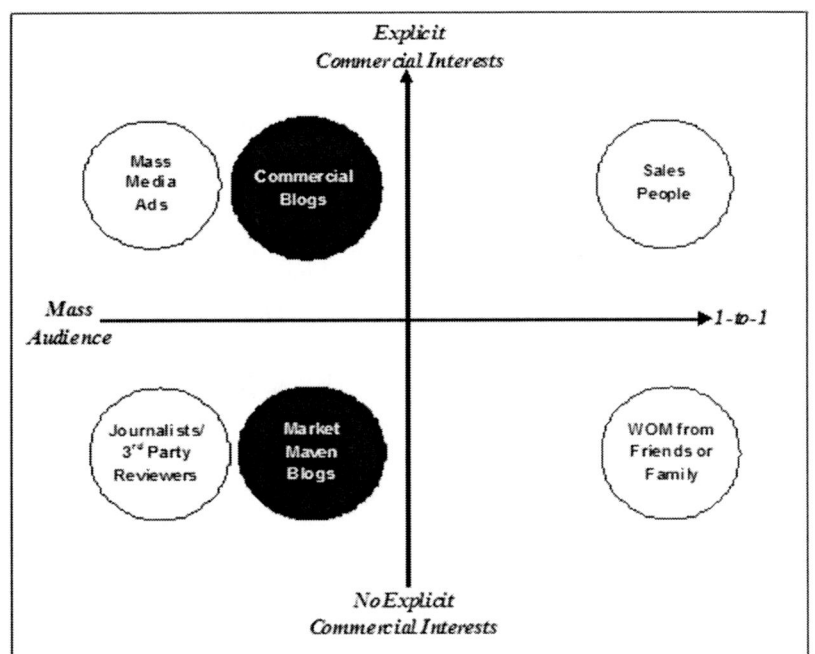

(whether it is an individual or a corporation) generate income through their blogs (e.g., via ads or affiliate programs run through the blog site) or through the sales of their own products or services as a result of the blogging activity. For example, the corporate blog of Sephora (blog. sephora.com) provides descriptions of giveaways and products sold by Sephora and thus builds the Sephora brand and leads to product sales through the Sephora website or its numerous brick and mortar retail outlets.

Commercial blogs are not necessarily sponsored by corporations. For example, the mommy blog "5 Minutes for Mom" (www.5minutesformom. com) has an explicit commercial interest. Over 90 percent of the posts on this blog are product recommendations, most of which are sponsored reviews. Indeed, Susan and Janice, the bloggers behind "5 Minutes for Mom" actively seek marketing opportunities and explicitly state that:

5 Minutes for Mom.com is the perfect website for promoting products of interest to mothers. We are a family friendly site, committed to maintaining an atmosphere of respect and positivity. Since our website is a combination of shopping and parenting related topics, our readers expect and want us to inform them about quality products. We specialize in creating exciting, unique campaigns that get your message to our readers.

At the other end of the continuum is what we refer to as *Market Maven Blogs* (see lower left quadrant in Figure 1). These blogs have no explicit commercial intent, and in fact, the bloggers go out of their way to avoid appearing biased by possible commercial conflicts. These blogs are typically focused on providing information on a specific topic to a mass audience. They are similar to the independent journalistic reviews that one might encounter in a newspaper or magazine. For example, the popular tech review blog by Walter Mossberg, Mossblog, (allthingsd.com) falls into this category as he provides reviews for tech gadgets without accepting any money, free products, or anything else of value, from advertising agencies or companies whose products he features. He provides a very clear and detailed ethics statement to assure the reader of his lack of a commercial interest:

Here is a statement of my ethics and coverage policies. It is more than most of you want to know, but, in the age of suspicion of the media, I am laying it all out. I am not an objective news reporter, and am not responsible for business coverage of technology companies. I am a subjective opinion columnist, a reviewer of consumer technology products and a commentator on technology issues. I don't accept any money, free products, or anything else of value, from the companies whose products I cover, or from their public relations or advertising agencies. I also don't accept trips, speaking fees, or product discounts from companies whose products I cover, or from their public relations or advertising agencies. I don't serve as a consultant to any companies, or serve on any corporate boards or advisory boards. The products I review are typically lent to me by their manufacturers for a few weeks or months. I return any products I am lent for review, except for items of minor value that companies typically don't want back, such as computer mice or inexpensive software. In the case of these items, I either discard them or give them away to charity.

As shown in Figure 1, Commercial and Market Maven blogs target mass audiences but have different commercial interests. It should be noted, however, that this categorization is based on readers' perceptions based on the overall actions and communications of the bloggers rather than the actual motives of the bloggers. Usually, blogs' readers have access to limited information regarding bloggers' real motives, blogs' intended target audience and audience size, and in particular the real underlying commercial incentives/interests

that bloggers might have. The important distinction between commercial and non-commercial interests is thus perceived rather than actual. For example, when professional golfer Michelle Wie writes about her thoughts and experiences on her blog (ablackflamingo.blogspot.com), her commercial interests and intended audience may be unclear to readers. She has no advertisements on her blog and does not sell anything directly, so there are no overtly explicit commercial interests. Wie wrote the following about her attendance at the Evian Masters Junior Cup:

Wie: Gave out the trophies to the winners of the Evian Masters Junior cup! Congratulations France! Evian is AWESOME...but...I miss my puppppy!!!

Because she writes solely about her personal experiences and displays no advertising, readers are likely to perceive Wie's blog as having no explicit commercial interest. Her blog, however, is likely to increase awareness of golf events such as the Evian Masters Junior cup (events for which she might get an appearance fee), and more generally increase Wie's brand equity and marketability as a sports celebrity and corporate endorser. Thus, it is arguable that she has underlying commercial interests linked to her blogging. Further, when Wie says she misses her puppy, it sounds more like a message directed at a friendly acquaintance rather than a promotional message targeted at a mass audience. In conclusion, although her blog is a sport celebrity blog directed at her numerous fans, a mass commercial audience, the content of the blog seems designed to avoid the perception of explicit commercial interests and encourage the perception of a one-to-one relationship with her readers.

We can see from this example that both the bloggers' interests (explicit commercial interests versus no explicit commercial interests) and intended target audience (mass versus on-to-one) may not be fully apparent based on a surface reading of the content. Further, readers' perceptions could be influenced by specific cues on the website. For example, significant advertising on the blog might suggest commercial interests, while personal photographs might suggest a lack of commercial interest. We will discuss these differences further in the next section. By providing a better understanding of the characteristics that drive audiences' categorization of blogs, we can provide specific input to bloggers on how to better manage their intended positioning.

Blogs as One-to-One Media

As discussed above, blogs are inherently mass communication media with varying degrees of explicit commercial interests. However, as suggested by our last example, readers might also distinguish amongst blogs based on perceptions of the audience as either a mass audience or an individual reader. Because some blogs allow for extensive and personal interaction between the blogger and the reader, audiences may perceive these blogs as one-to-one communication media. Thus, audiences can develop an illusion that they have a close, intimate relationship with a blogger.

For example, food blogger, Katie (katieatthekitchendoor.com) wrote about her inner thoughts, feelings, and experiences when introducing a new recipe:

Katie: When you picture yourself happy, what do you see? And I don't mean this in a melodramatic, how-do-you-really-want-to-live-your-life way. And I don't mean to imply that I am unhappy and thinking about the "if onlys" all the time. What I mean is, when you're having a crappy day at work, or you miss the bus and get stuck walking home and it's sleeting, or you're feeling uninspired and bored, what is the image that pops into your mind? The very first one, before you actively construct a daydream? When I picture myself happy, I am usually alone. Is that weird? Alone, but not

lonely...... No matter, whether you're an introvert or an extrovert, you're cooking for a crowd or just for yourself on a random weeknight, this [recipe] is sure to please....

As shown below, Katie's audience responded as if they were having a one-to-one conversation in a private setting:

Comment: I am very much like you....I enjoy the company of others, but truly enjoy my downtime. I am not sure if I would call myself an introvert, but an extrovert I am not. Maybe just a mid-vert. A boring weekend to most is refreshing to me. I like to busy myself, by myself. I would have to say that my happy place is either in a grove of trees or somewhere wide and open. I find I get the same comfort from a wide open prairie or the ocean... wide open spaces please my soul. Glad I am not the only one:)

As shown in Figure 2, in addition to variation in the extent to which commercial interests are explicit versus non-explicit, blogs can vary in the degree to which the perceived audience is mass versus one-to-one. Thus, we expand the typology from Figure 1 and identify two additional types of blogs, for a total of four types. In addition to *Commercial Blogs* (upper left quadrant; blogs with explicit commercial interests and a perceived mass target audience) and *Market Maven Blogs* (lower left quadrant; blogs with no explicit commercial interests and a perceived mass target audience), we identify two types of blogs that are perceived to be targeting an individual: *Commercial Friendship Blogs* (upper right quadrant; blogs with explicit commercial interests and a perceived one-to-one target audience) and *Community-Based Friendship Blogs* (lower right quadrant; blogs with no explicit commercial interests and a perceived one-to-one target audience).

As illustrated, Katie's blog (katieatthekitchendoor.com) falls into the Community-Based

Figure 2. Perceived blog types and selected other communication forms

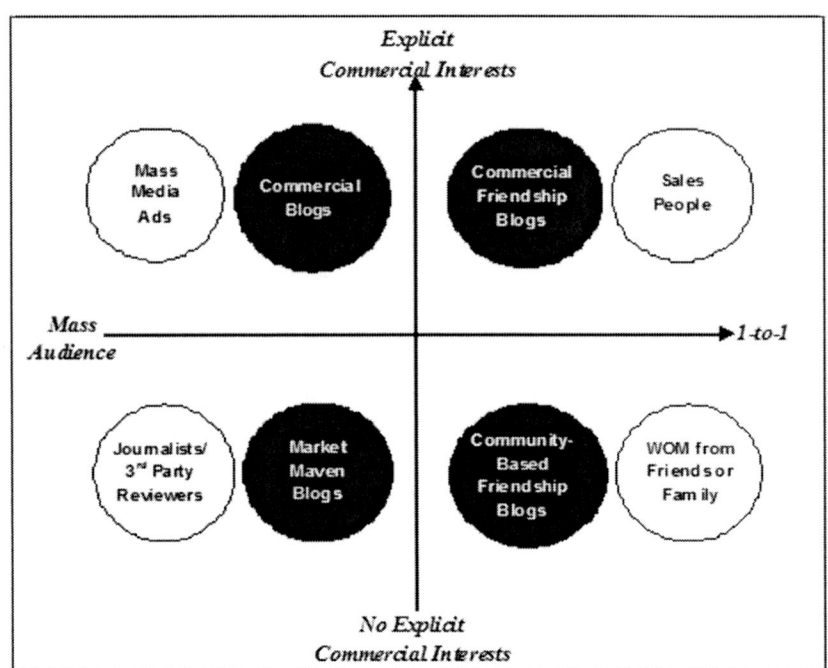

Friendship category. Community-Based Friendship blogs do not have explicit commercial interests and readers perceive that the blogger is talking directly to them on a one-to-one basis. These bloggers' posts are driven mostly by their excitement or knowledge about a specific topic and connecting with others who share these interests. For example, Katie's blog focuses on sharing information about cooking and recipes. Yet, contrary to market maven blogs, these blogs are not limited to communication about the focal topic of interest (e.g. cooking in Katie's case) but also include communications exchanges about intimate issues such as emotions, personal stories and life concerns. Commercial Friendships blogs also include similar personal communications. In these blogs, however, bloggers also communicate their explicit commercial interests and leverage the perceived one-to-one connections they have with each audience member as a mechanism for increasing revenue. For example, Jill's blog

(Glamamom.com) includes many sponsored reviews and her commercial intent is clear. As the example below illustrates, however, Jill also creates a feeling of intimacy by including personal details within the sponsored post:

Jill: Thanks to Kohl's, a lucky group of Glam Media's personal style bloggers and I received glamorous, Rock & Republic makeovers last month at Beaver Studio in Lower Manhattan. I'd been working on the launch of Rock & Republic for Kohl's all winter, so it was a blast to finally try on all the clothes and accessories I'd seen on the runway and been drooling over. Pasternak led us in a short but demanding workout of drills that rotated between walking squats and shuffling, arm curls with his own "Harley Bar," planking, jumping, and jogging, to a soundtrack of his A-list clients including: Lady Gaga, Katy Perry, and Kesha. I was definitely huffing and puffing and mega-sore the next couple of days but today

I feel great and am super inspired by Pasternak's recommendations.

We took home two of his books: The 5-Factor Diet and the newly released The 5-Factor World Diet, which outline Pasternak's 5-Factor principles–five meals a day, five core ingredients, and five-minute prep-times. They also include great recipes and pantry-stocking tips. I love trying new workouts and it's always a treat to gain insight into how celebs maintain those rock hard bodies. Thanks to Lady Foot Locker, New Balance, and Harley Pasternak for having us, and to Warrior Fitness Boot Camp for hosting.

Jill's readers do not appear to be bothered by this sponsored post, as illustrated by the following responses:

Comment 1: *You look good even when you work out?! I ... I still like you.*
Comment 2: *Omg you're gorgeous, work out gear and all...*

In sum, we suggest that there is a discrepancy between how blogs should be expected to function based on their mass media nature and how they actually work based on the four ways in which readers may perceive them. The multifaceted nature of blogs is influenced mainly by the communication strategies used by bloggers. Specifically, readers perceive blogs differently depending on cues such as the blog's layout, its communication content (including the mix of personal anecdotes, product reviews, sponsored posts, contests, disclosures, and other types of information), the number of advertisements, and the number of responses to comments. These kinds of cues are central to the execution of a blogger's communication strategy. We propose that by strategically managing these cues, bloggers can effectively position themselves in one of the quadrants in Figure 2. In the second section, we provide some specific strategies that

bloggers may use to shift or maintain the audience's perception of a blog.

WHAT KINDS OF COMMUNICATION STRATEGIES DO BLOGGERS USE TO INCREASE THE EFFECTIVENESS AND PERSUASIVENESS OF THEIR MESSAGES?

In the first section, we suggested that there is a discrepancy between how blogs should function if we think of them as a type of traditional mass media versus the four different ways in which audiences may perceive blogs. In particular, the reader's impression of a blog appears to reflect a mixture of "reality" and "illusion", both in regards to the intended target audience and the explicitness of the commercial interest of the blogger. We now describe how the perception of blogs can shift or be maintained through the use of two communication strategies: (a) *illusion of relationship* and (b) *ambiguity in commercial interests*.

How Do Bloggers Create an Illusion of Relationship?

The illusion of relationship strategy seeks to build intimacy and perception of a close interpersonal relationship between the blogger and the reader. It is akin to the seduction strategy that has been described in marketing and rhetoric (Deighton & Grayson, 1995; Simon, 1996) where the communicator uses charm and support to enhance trust and thus be more persuasive. To better understand how the illusion of a relationship is created and maintained in blogs, we draw from the relationships literature. We focus on social penetration theory (Altman & Taylor, 1973), the literature on tie strength (Granovetter, 1973), and the similarity-attraction hypothesis (Berscheid & Walster, 1978; Byrne, 1971). Understanding how bloggers create an intimate feel is important because when a relationship is strong and intimate, a receiver perceives the communicator as credible and trustworthy and thus is more likely to follow her recommendation (Bansal & Voyer, 2000; Goldenberg, Libai, & Muller, 2001). In order to leverage the benefits of the illusion of relationship strategy, bloggers intentionally create an intimate communication environment by using the following tactics: (a) increasing the depth (quality) as well as the breadth (quantity) of self-disclosures (Cozby, 1973; Derlega & Berg, 1987; Altman & Taylor, 1973), (b) increasing the frequency and the duration of interactions (Granovetter, 1973; Marsden & Campbell, 1984), and (c) increasing the perception of shared common interests (Berscheid & Walster, 1978; Byrne, 1971; Morry, 2005; Rose, 1985; Weiss & Lowenthal, 1975) outside the focal topic area. These efforts, in turn, increase the reader's trust in the blog. Figure 3 illustrates how the use of the illusion of relationship strategy can

shift readers' perceptions of the blog away from a mass audience toward a one-to-one audience. In addition, implementation of this strategy can help bloggers maintain the perception of being a one-to-one medium once they have created Commercial Friendship blogs or Community-Based Friendship blogs. In this section we explore in greater depth the three specific tactics that bloggers use to create this sense of intimacy.

Increasing the Depth and Breadth of Self-Disclosures

One tactic used by bloggers to create a sense of intimacy is to disclose personal thoughts, feelings, and behaviors. Social penetration theory (Altman & Taylor, 1973) posits that "self-disclosures" allow individuals to develop relational "closeness" as information exchange moves from superficial to intimate levels. Self-disclosure is broadly defined

Figure 3. Illusion of relationship strategy

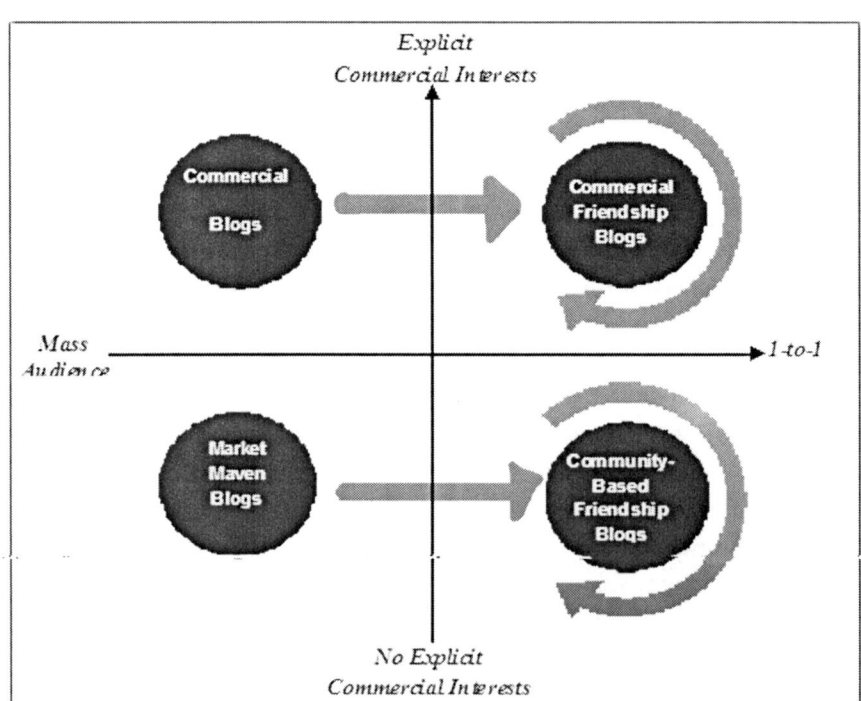

Note: Straight arrows indicate the use of the illusion of relationship strategy in order to reposition a blog away from mass media. The circular arrows indicate the use of the illusion of relationship strategy in order to maintain the perception of 1-to-1 relationship.

as providing others with personal information about oneself (Cozby, 1973; Derlega & Berg, 1987; Jourard, 1971). More specifically, self-disclosure is communication that "includes any information exchange that refers to the self, including personal states, dispositions, events in the past, and plans for the future" (Derlega & Grzelak, 1979, p. 152).

Self-disclosure is frequently used by bloggers. For example, Michael Sheehan, a technology blogger (www.hightechdad.com) begins a posting about consumer clouds with the following self-disclosure:

Michael: I have multiple personalities. No, I'm not schizophrenic but I do have alter egos. During the day, I live and breathe cloud computing with my job as Technology Evangelist at GoGrid, a cloud infrastructure provider. And then the rest of my hours when I'm awake, I'm a dad, husband and technologist, trying to figure out how it all fits together without busting at the seams.

In this post, Michael tells the reader that he is a father and husband. In addition, he describes his job. These self-disclosures help the reader identify with Michael and provide perspective on the information discussed in his blog postings. Michael's self-disclosures are relatively fact-based (although he does admit to some anxiety with his multiple roles). Some bloggers, however, provide deeper and more revealing self-disclosures. For example, blogger Tracey, on Just Another Mommy Blog (tracey-justanothermommyblog.blogspot.com) posted the following description of being at home alone with her newborn son:

Tracey: I was utterly alone in my new motherhood. Well, not utterly. I had plenty of family who loved me. I had friends who adored my son. But there wasn't a single, solitary soul who was home during the day to talk to. There wasn't anyone who was marching through the infancy stage with me. Justin was rapidly nearing his sixth week and I was rapidly approaching my return to the office.

Torn by the overwhelming desire for human contact and the primal need to stay with my baby, I was a gigantic mess of hormones and mood swings. I am so grateful for the Internet. What I wouldn't have done for its instant connection to similar people and similar issues. I love you, Internet. You beautiful, shiny, brilliant creature. Muwah.

In this post, Tracey discloses some very personal and emotional life concerns: the deep loneliness she felt being home alone with her first child, and her relief in finding similar people on the Internet. Her readers respond by reaffirming the anxiety that Tracey feels and disclosing their own feelings of loneliness at this point in their lives:

Comment 1: I feel the same way now. I live in a neighborhood where everyone works all day long. So I am all alone M-F. I know poor me but it is lonely. It is really hard to find good friends. Especially friends that you would be friends with even if you didn't have kids.:)
Comment 2: I am so sorry sweets. I know what that's like. We were the first couple in our social circle to have a child. It was hard to relate to them and even worse...I had no one to talk to during the day. When I reached out to my OB after "losing my marbles" he made me sign up for a mom and babies group. I had no idea it even existed. Those women saved me more times than I can count. The internet is an amazing supportive place, but sometimes you just need that physical presence.
Comment 3: oh my gosh! This breaks my heart! You are SO not alone--we have all been in those depths of despair--e-mail/comment any time for commiseration from a fellow mom-who-is-there. In the meantime, thanks for your honesty!:)

Tracey's emotional self-disclosures evoke reciprocal revelations from her readers, as well as offers of support. These comments reflect how disclosing deeply personal information can induce genuine intimate exchange, resulting in a relationship that is more meaningful and enduring. In this specific case, it is clear that Tracey's blog is not a mass audience medium but rather a communication space where readers perceive they have a one-to-one relationship with the blogger.

The types of self-disclosure illustrated in the previous two examples are consistent with social penetration theory, which suggests that self-disclosure proceeds in "layers" that represent levels of self-identity. Disclosure of factual information (e.g., Michael's post above) presents a "public" self. In contrast, disclosure of values and deep emotions (such as Tracey's) reflect the inner self or one's core identity. Relational closeness is determined by the degree to which individuals disclose personal, sometimes vulnerable information about the self. Individuals, indeed, are much less likely to disclose information closer to their inner core because of this increased perception of vulnerability. Readers, however, clearly appreciate a blogger's exposed vulnerability and interpret this as a manifestation of trust; trust that they in turn reciprocate toward the blogger. For example, notice how the reader in comment 3 thanks Tracey for her honesty in describing her loneliness. Likewise, we see this in the nature of the responses to photography blogger Amanda's (www.amandakern. com) post about her miscarriage.

Amanda: The last few weeks I've been keeping a pretty big secret from everyone in hopes to have shared great news today that our family was expecting our third child. However, after going to the doctor for the fourth time in just over two weeks it was confirmed today that the baby that I've been carrying for nearly seven weeks does not have a heartbeat. It's extremely tough to accept, but for the third time in just over ten years I have miscarried another baby. During these tough times I am reminded that our loss is heaven's gain.

Comment 1: Amanda, I knew you would express your feelings with writing and photography. It is a gift and talent God gave you and as you can tell, we all appreciate you letting us in that way.

I can only say that I love you all and will be there in any way that you need me. I am so proud of you and Jason. You are beautiful parents. And Hope is such a great big sister. I don't know why this would happen to you again, but I know that only God could love that baby more. It's as you said, "Our loss is Heaven's gain". I told Hope the baby was a tiny little angel that will be flickering around, watching over you all now. Keep your hearts open. You are surrounded by love.
Comment 2: I am in tears right now as I reply to you…I can't begin to write even half of what you have put together in … wow a wonderful self-expression of feelings. I can say I have been where you are now, but without the courage to tell anyone.

Again, sharing with her readers such an intimate personal family tragedy results in eliciting reciprocal self-disclosures and enhancing trust in the blogger.

In addition to revealing feelings, depth of self-disclosure can be enhanced by providing concrete details about the experience. Concrete information is more memorable, interesting, and easier to understand (see, for example, Rubin, 1997; Sadoski, Goetz & Rodriguez, 2000). One way to achieve depth in this way is through the posting of photos and videos. For example, mommy blogger Jamie (blondemomblog.com) visited Disney World with her family, and shared both a day-by-day description and photographs of the trip on her site. Readers respond by telling Jamie how much they enjoyed the photos. The photos provide readers with a deeper sense of Jamie's Disneyland experience. For example:

Comment 1: Great photos! Thanks for giving me some ideas on what to expect inside Disneyland. I hope HK Disneyland is the same since I'll be closer to it.
Comment 2: Never been to Disney World. Thanks for sharing the pics. Would love to go one day!

Intimacy, and consequently trust, can also be increased by enhancing the breadth of self-disclosures, or how much information is exchanged through interaction (Altman & Taylor, 1973). Bloggers who successfully implement the illusion of relationship strategy are likely to provide self-disclosures that are not only deep and concrete (the examples above) but also broad. For example, Rachel, of Fit Mom's Blog (fitnessformommies.net) posts primarily about fitness-related topics, yet here she provides some breadth by describing her excitement and feelings about getting a hair-cut. Note that she also provides a link to photos and an earlier haircut story, increasing the depth of the post:

Rachel: Women, how many of you love getting your hair done? Honestly, I do. It's so rare that I get to look like a girl (when my hairdresser does it) that I am excited to come home with a new "do". Remember this? {photos here} Also, I love the girl time in the chair where I have 1.5 hours to chat with a girl on things that I don't normally have time or energy to talk about. Being a mommy doesn't allow for lots of uninterrupted chat time. Except, husband and boys don't seem to appreciate my new hairdo and leave me with comments like "that color makes you look like a teenager", or "your bangs look very bangggggggy...", or mom, did you get your hair done, "yes", it looks "flippy" and he makes the motion of a fish. Husband (yes, I love you) is famous for his particular type of com-ment, such as _____ (says nothing and walks out the door)!

We also see bloggers provide detailed accounts of many aspects of their life. For example, posts on Finslippy (www.finslippy.com) cover a diverse set of topics about blogger Alice Bradley, includ-ing her overweight cat, her scratched cornea, working at home with her husband, and stories of her life as a middle school student. Because the self-disclosures are so comprehensive (and deep), readers feel that they are friends with Alice, as shown by the comments below in response to a post about a hat she received for Christmas:

Comment 1: well, it's a good thing you know me, because while I don't have book smarts, life smart AND hat smarts I DO have. (god has truly blessed me, i know this.) And because I have hat smart, let me just say, you MUST wear that hat every day. It's simply amazing on you.
Comment 2: Tricky Mubbles? Hat smarts? Oh, how I love you.
Comment 3: I really think I might love you. I am as straight as the graphics in a geometry textbook, but still. Alice! I love you! Marry me in a totally non-gay way.

To summarize, bloggers often open up about their lives and themselves by revealing their feelings, beliefs, attitudes, values, and deep emotions through their posts and photos in their blogs. Increasing both the depth and breadth of self-disclosures can strengthen the illusion of a relationship. Furthermore, sharing concrete details and artifacts enhances the power of these self-disclosures. Popular bloggers use this strategy to build an intimate feeling, enhancing trust and loyalty among their readers.

Increasing the Frequency and Duration of Interactions

The second tactic bloggers can use to create an illusion of one-to-one relationship is to interact frequently with their audience and to encourage interaction over a longer period of time. Frequency of interaction, indeed, has long been studied as an important aspect of intimate relationships (Altman & Taylor, 1973; Delia & O'Keefe, 1979; Little, 1972; Werner, 1957). Similarly, sociologists have examined the frequency of interaction as a foundation for strong ties, resulting in close relationships (Granovetter, 1973; Marsden & Campbell, 1984; Weimann, 1991). There is substantial evidence that increased frequency of interaction leads to closer relationships and associated outcomes. For example, frequency of interaction is positively correlated with marital happiness (Kirchler, 1988). Likewise, routine casual conversation can allow relationship partners to predict each other's mood and behavior and reduce the probability of conflict (Metts, 1997). Couples who talk at the end of the workday on a regular basis have higher levels of satisfaction than those who do not (Vangelisti & Banski, 1993). Further, everyday casual interaction provides a safe context within which more intimate conversations can take place and partners can learn about one another (Duck, 1991). In sum, researchers conclude that everyday casual interaction plays a significant role in the development of intimate relationships (Duck, 1991; Duck, Rutt, Hurst, & Strejc, 1991; Stafford, Kline & Rankin, 2004).

Bloggers who post regularly are able to develop a loyal, committed readership. A great example of this is blogger Heather B. Armstrong (dooce. com), who started her blog in February 2001 and as of March 2012 has 1.5 million followers on Twitter. Her blog includes both a "daily photo" (usually of her children) and a "daily chuck" (a photo of her dog). She also writes almost every day about some aspect of her life. This frequent posting encourages readers to check back in daily. Readers keep up with changes in Armstrong's life and relate them to their own. For example, a post that included a story about her dog Chuck elicited the following response from a reader:

Comment: I started reading your blog as a single apartment-dweller who never was allowed a dog in her life by cat-loving parents and dog-hating landlords. I lived vicariously through you and Chuck, and always dreamed of having my own dog who would don eyeliner and retreat to the basement to listen to the Cure. (As I recall you describing him once.) An aging 80s former goth-

girl myself, that sounded like the dog I've always wanted. Fast-forward to 2009, I am married with a house and yard that begs for a dog's playfulness, and my husband (not an animal lover at all) consents to my adoption of a gorgeous male pit bull rescue we named Giles. My dream came true - he is loving and smart, but also a brooder of the highest regard. Everything about him was perfect.

As the comment above illustrates, duration of interaction is also important for building an intimate relationship. Duration refers to either the amount of time an individual spends for a single interaction/conversation with their partner or the total amount of time they spend to develop and maintain a particular relationship. Indeed, the amount of time couples spend participating in leisure activities together, conversations, or sharing tasks, is positively associated with their relational satisfaction (Reissman, Aron, & Bergen, 1993; Richmond, 1995) and strength of ties (Granovetter, 1973; Marsden & Campbell, 1984).

Another way that bloggers can increase the frequency and duration of interaction is by giving readers a reason to return to the blog each day. For example, Alice on Finslippy had a series of posts in which she described each of her school years. The posts were accompanied by Alice's school photo for that year. By slowly revealing aspects of her life in this format, Alice encourages readers to return to the blog each day. Readers were excited about these posts and seemed to enjoy watching Alice's development through school and comparing it to their own, as shown in the following comments:

Comment 1: Alice-- your 12th grade photo so painfully reminds me of my own senior year in H.S. Why did I think it was a good idea to wear my mom's old work clothes from The Limited's "Outback Red" line to school?
Comment 2: Man. You are really good at blending eye shadow. And, as others have noted, great teeth! I am sad this series has come to its end, yet I am so

happy those teachers helped put you on the path to become the writer you are. I've been reading your blog since 2004 and laughing with you in the shallow end the whole time. Thanks for that!

By revealing her ups and downs during her school years, Alice is telling a story, which is an effective mechanism for increasing the frequency and duration of interaction with a blog. There is evidence that the use of narrative increases engagement and persuasion (Green & Brock, 2000). When readers are engaged in a story, they don't simply visualize the narrative, but they actually mentally simulate the experience (Zwaan & Radvansky, 1998). This mental simulation process results in a number of outcomes, including increased perceptions of credibility, understanding and an increased likelihood to take action (Deighton, Romer, & McQueen, 1989; Escalas, 2004).

For example, Gluten Free Girl (www.glutenfreegirl.com) is primarily a food blog featuring gluten-free recipes for people with celiac's disease. Yet since beginning blogging in 2005, writer Shauna often discloses details of her life that are unrelated to recipes. Readers have been following stories about her relationship with her now-husband and their struggles with getting pregnant. Below is a reader's response to Shauna's announcement that she is pregnant:

Comment: O, felicitations to you both! I am so happy to read this! You have written so much about both of you wanting children and I would always read and feel a wish for you, you know, I mean, you said it, the odds at 41 … because you both seem so wonderful and authentic and open and will make such incredible parents. The way you both embrace the journey of life, and man, KIDS. You will see and I am glad for it.

From this post, the reader views this announcement as the happy ending to a story that has unfolded on the blog. The reader's post suggests that she has empathized with Shauna's story

and has developed the perception of a personal relationship with Shauna as a result.

To summarize, bloggers use several approaches to encourage readers to return to their blogs regularly and to continue to do so over a long period of time in an attempt to give readers the impression that they share a one-to-one relationship with the blogger.

Increasing the Perception of Shared Common Interests

The last tactic used by bloggers to create an illusion of one-to-one relationship is by discussing non-focal interests they share with their readers. Although these shared interests are outside the focal blog topics, readers feel more connected to the bloggers as a result of these shared interests (e.g., fashion, music or sports). This tactic is somewhat different, but related to the tactic of increasing the breadth of self-disclosures. By increasing the breadth of self-disclosures, the blogger reveals more aspects of her personality and life to the readers, thereby giving readers the illusion of knowing her personally and intimately. On the other hand, by discussing non-focal interests, the blogger increases the chances of readers finding *shared* tastes/preferences with the blogger. In other words, this tactic allows readers to feel more similar to the blogger. Indeed, the similarity-attraction hypothesis posits that individuals are attracted to others who share similar characteristics (Byrne, 1971). Specifically, the more similar two individuals think they are, the higher the attraction between them (Byrne & Nelson, 1965). Likewise, lay theories for new friendships and maintaining ongoing friendships posit that friendships typically involve common or similar beliefs, shared interests, and activities (Morry, 2005; Rose, 1985; Weiss & Lowenthal, 1975). The literature on romantic relationships also suggests that shared interest is an important quality in a spouse and for a successful marriage (Harding, Phillips & Fogarty, 1986). These similarity perceptions can be based on simple categories such as demographic characteristics, academic interests, leisure activities, personalities, and values (Fehr, 2000).

Similar logic applies to blogger-audience relationships. Shared interests are likely to create a connection and the illusion of relationship can be further developed by these shared interests outside the focal topic area. For example, if audiences read blog content that highlights similarity in interests (e.g., having a dog, loving the color pink) outside a focal topic, they may feel very close to a blogger and therefore relate more deeply with the blogger. For example, Donald, on Running and Rambling (www.runningandrambling.com) posts regularly about his runs and running-related products. Occasionally, however, he posts about other topics, including this post about the musician Natalie Merchant:

Donald: My girlfriend got me into this band when we were dating, and they became one of the first "bands with a conscience" that I fell really hard for back in the late 80s and early 90s. Combine that with the fact that the girlfriend became my wife, and there will always be a soft spot in my heart for Natalie Merchant and company.

Donald then includes a video clip of Merchant's band (10,000 Maniacs) singing "Like the Weather". A reader commented on the shared interest in the music:

Comment: My heart does a skip when I hear that song too, though it has nothing to do with falling in love. I used to hum it when I was training for my first marathon in rain....

To summarize, bloggers can use several tactics to implement the illusion of relationship strategy. First, they can disclose details of their life that reveal emotions and feelings and make them vulnerable to their audience in some way. Depth of disclosure can be increased via the use of photographs, as well as additional details.

Broader disclosure should also enhance the illusion of relationship. Second, by posting frequently, responding to readers' comments, and by telling a story over time, bloggers can increase engagement with the blog and hence the frequency and duration of interaction with their audience, both of which increase the illusion of relationship. Finally, bloggers can connect with their readers by identifying shared interests beyond the blog topic, increasing perceptions of similarity. Together, these tactics should enhance the illusion of relationship and from the audiences' perspective, move the blog from a one-to-many medium to a one-to-one medium.

How Do Bloggers Increase Ambiguity in Commercial Interests?

Some bloggers are agents or principals in commercial enterprises and thus have direct commercial interests linked to their blogging activities. However, the presence of commercial interests extends beyond just this group as many other bloggers also derive financial rewards from their blogging (e.g., through ads on their blogs, various types of affiliate programs, free goods sent to them, etc.). Thus, although many bloggers have a commercial interest in blogging (they want to make money), they may not want their audience to be aware of this motive.

Audiences are more likely to resist persuasion attempts when they believe that the message source has an ulterior motive (Friestad & Wright, 1994). In particular, in traditional one-to-many communication modes the audience is typically aware of the source's commercial interests and consequently approaches the source with suspicion (Boush, Friestad, & Rose, 1994; Campbell & Kirmani, 2000; Ford, Smith, & Swasy, 1990; Friestad & Wright, 1994). For example, in mass media advertising, consumers are generally aware that the advertiser has a commercial interest in selling products or services. Based on this "persuasion knowledge", consumers develop strategies to cope with marketers' influence attempts (Friestad & Wright, 1994) and may become broadly suspicious about the validity of advertising messages. Consumers use their knowledge of persuasion motives to identify, evaluate, and respond to these persuasion attempts, and the use of persuasion knowledge increases when the accessibility of ulterior motives, such as motive to persuade or make money, increases (Campbell & Kirmani, 2000). For these reasons, bloggers may want to avoid such resistance, and thus may try to hide or obfuscate their commercial interests.

In the following section, we identify several tactics that bloggers can use as part of a strategy aimed at creating or maintaining ambiguity in their commercial interests. These tactics include (a) hiding commercial interests, (b) stressing communal/benevolent interests while acknowledging the existence of commercial interests, and (c) mixing content topics. Bloggers implement these

tactics to reduce the tension created by their attempts to fulfill both, seemingly contradicting goals of making money and serving the needs of their audience through blogging. This tension increases as bloggers participate in word-of-mouth marketing campaigns (Kozinets et al., 2010) more frequently or when they display more of affiliate links in their posts and therefore, the need for the implementation of ambiguity in commercial interests strategy also increases.

As shown in Figure 4, the ambiguity in commercial interests strategy and its associated tactics can be used to either shift perceptions of the blog from Commercial to Market Maven or from Commercial Friendship to Community-Based Friendship. In addition, this strategy (and tactics) can help bloggers in the lower half of Figure 4 maintain perceptions that they do not have commercial interests.

Figure 4. Ambiguity in commercial interests strategy

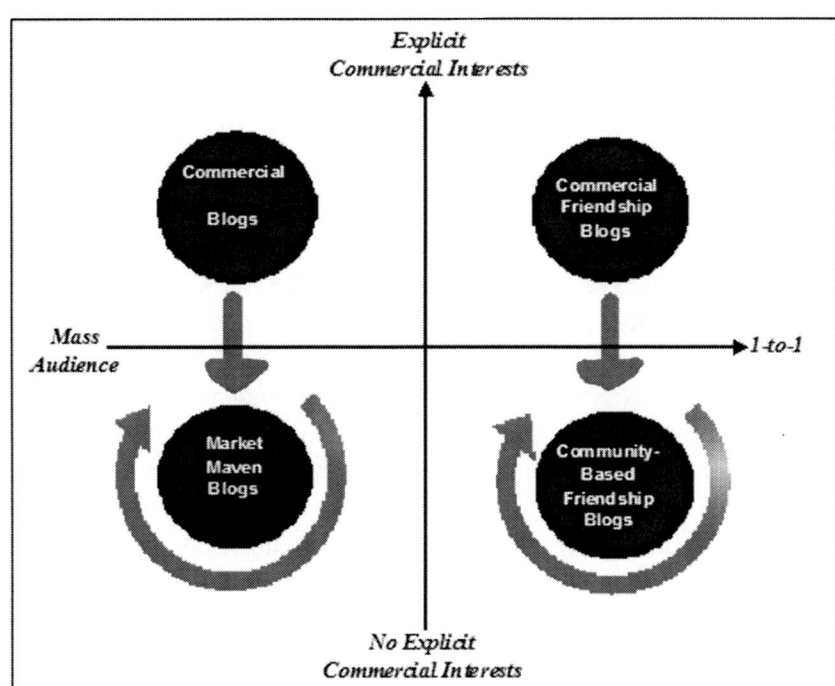

Note: Straight arrows indicate the use of the ambiguity in commercial interests strategy in order to reduce the perceptions of explicit commercial interests in a blog. The circular arrows indicate the use of the ambiguity in commercial interests strategy in order to maintain the perception of no explicit commercial interests.

Hiding Commercial Interests

One approach taken by bloggers is to attempt to hide their commercial interests. This hiding commercial interests tactic is similar to the "lying by omission" psychological manipulative tactic described in the psychology literature (Simon, 1996). According to Simon (1996), this is a very subtle form of lying, in which a fair amount of the truth is concealed from the audience. Some bloggers, indeed, withhold the truth regarding their commercial interests. For example, they may not explicitly reveal commercial interests in their word-of-mouth posts and their site may not include a conflict of interest disclosure policy statement. Thus, these bloggers operate as though they do not have commercial interests when they actually have such interests. For example, in a study of bloggers who had been seeded with a word-of-mouth marketing campaign about a cell phone, Kozinets et al. (2010) found that a subset of the bloggers hid the existence of the sponsor in their posts about the phone. To conceal their commercial interests in the phone, these bloggers tended to focus more on describing the phone's features.

In the U.S. this tactic is counter to the Federal Trade Commission guidelines for Use of Endorsements and Testimonials in Advertising (16 C.F.R. §§ 255.0-255.5), which mandates bloggers to disclose all forms of compensation they receive from the sponsor of a product or service. In practice, it appears that many bloggers in the U.S. are not fully compliant with the FTC rules. Even if there were no regulatory framework governing these practices, hiding one's commercial interests is arguably deceptive and unethical.

There are various ways in which bloggers hide their commercial interests. First, they may simply not reveal participation in affiliate programs or other conflicts. For example, Legacy Learning and Smith, a company that sells a series of guitar-lesson DVDs was charged by the FTC with a failure to disclose that affiliates providing endorsements of the program via blogs and other social media received payment for sales generated (FTC press release, March 15 2011). Legacy paid the FTC $250,000 to settle these charges.

In addition, some bloggers obfuscate their commercial interests by making the sponsorship or affiliate disclosure policy very difficult to find on their blog. While some blogs have a clearly identified tab for "disclosures" on the top of the main page, others seem to walk a fine line by providing a disclosure statement but "burying" the link to it --often in a small font size and dull color-- at the bottom of a long webpage where much scrolling is needed to find the link and where it seems that only a very motivated reader purposely hunting for it would actually encounter it. For example, Gabrielle of DesignMom blog (www.designmom.com) has her disclosure policy statement within the frequently asked questions (FAQ) section, rather than a separate tab. Within the FAQ, the policy statement is located at the bottom and requires a long scroll. Gabrielle's FAQ section starts with answers to questions about a unique sink, her work/life balance, and whether she plans to have more kids. She describes her sources of revenue and affiliate links at the very end of the FAQ. Though Gabrielle often discloses sponsorship or affiliate programs in a specific post, more general information about her policy is difficult to find.

Further, the practice of having one "umbrella" affiliate or conflict disclosure versus including "post-specific" disclosures varies across sites, possibly creating additional ambiguity. While some sites have a site-wide disclosure policy, others such as The Blonde Mom Blog (blondemomblog.com) include disclosures with each specific give-away or offer. For example, in a post about a Vicks vaporizer give-away, the blogger Jamie provides the following disclosure:

Jamie: I am being compensated for my work this winter with Vicks but, as always, the words and stories I share with you are all my own.

Although Jamie discloses her commercial interest, she seems to be aware of the potential loss of credibility and thus makes sure to stress that she is speaking her own words, with the implication that readers should still trust her. In a later post, she discloses her affiliation with Vicks in a less formal way, embedding it in a self-disclosure about her husband's allergies, the romance in her bedroom, and their need for sleep, probably in an effort to distance her opinions from her commercial interests linked with the brand:

Jamie: Every winter we fire up our Vicks humidifier. In fact, it's been a hot and sexy bedside master bedroom item for a couple of years. (Ha, ha.) My husband has allergy issues and it helps keep the air hydrated and us feeling more restful in the morning which is pretty much the only selling point us parental types need, right? Sleep. It is like gold. Yo. Since I'm working with Vicks this winter I want to share the humidifier love with you! One lucky reader will not only win a Vicks Warm Mist GermFree" Humidifier (germaphobes rejoice as it kills 99.999% of germs, mold, and bacteria before the steam even hits the air) but some other goodies mentioned below.

As shown in this example, bloggers can obscure the tension between their commercial interests and the interests of their audience by connecting the sponsorship disclosure to a personal story. This way, the potential conflict may appear less salient to readers. In addition, Jamie does not reveal what she receives from Vicks, thus concealing part of the truth from the audience. As a result, the nature of her relationship with Vicks (and hence, her commercial interest) is ambiguous and readers may be less suspicious of ulterior motives.

Likewise, Bryanboy (www.bryanboy.com), a famous fashion blogger, showed photographs of a personalized iPad case he received from Valentino, along with a personalized note from the designer with an invitation to his show. Through this photograph, Bryanboy subtly discloses his relationship with the designer—namely, the designer gave Bryanboy an iPad case as an incentive to attend (and presumably promote) the Valentino show. Possibly because Bryanboy's disclosure is so subtle, readers' comments showed no trace of suspicion. Rather, they envied Bryanboy and went even further to provide some styling tips for that sponsored product. For example, one reader said;

Comment: Ohh, it's beautiful!!! Now you need a white Pad to go with your new case and your future white Givenchy bag ;-) xx Emily

To summarize, bloggers can hide their commercial interests in several ways. First, they can simply fail to disclose their relationship with the sponsor. They can also make it difficult for readers to locate a site-wide conflict disclosure statement. Finally, they can obfuscate when providing the conflict disclosure by embedding it in a personal story or by leaving out concrete details. In all cases, it becomes difficult for consumers to understand the nature of the relationship between the blogger and the sponsor, thus hiding commercial intent.

Stressing Benevolent Communal Interests

A second tactic used in creating ambiguity with regards to commercial interests is to explicitly acknowledge the existence of commercial interests, but to also stress communal and benevolent motives. This tactic is similar to the rhetorical strategy of "playing the servant role" (Simon, 1996). Playing the servant role allows communicators to hide their self-serving agenda by claiming instead that they are acting in service of the greater good of the community. Bloggers using this tactic downplay their commercial interests by suggesting they are motivated to help their audience obtain important product information, get a good deal, or participate in a give-away. For example, Kristen, who blogged at the Beauty Addict (www.beautyaddict.blogspot.com, no longer active) states explicitly in her disclosure policy that she received beauty products to review. Kristen also states that she cares about her readers' welfare and that the informational value of her reviews serves *their* benefit. Kristen's assurance regarding her devotion to her audience and community helps her stay persuasive while still disclosing her commercial interests. Because readers expect the editorial content of communal blogs to be benevolent and written based on personal experience with the products or services, they will often downplay the role of sponsors even when an explicit disclosure is made (Kozinets et al., 2010).

Thus, by stressing her benevolent commitment to the community and by presenting information that is relevant and useful, framed within her own experiences and personal life stories, Kristen could remain persuasive. Even when she discloses her commercial interests, her readers refrain from resisting these types of persuasion attempts. In fact, her readers do not seem to care much about how she acquires the products she reviews or any potential conflict of interest, as illustrated by the comments below on a review of Victoria's Secret Beach Sexy Tan Moisturizer:

Comment 1: Always looking for a good self tanner without the bad smell! So many of them smell after you leave them on for awhile. I am looking forward to trying this one!

Comment 2: Does this product come in SPF 30? I was also wondering, does it protect against UVA and UVB rays? It would be nice to see these things in a self-tanner.

Comment 3: This appears to have everything in it! I would love it if there was a purely zinc oxide sunscreen that had a 'natural' tanner too. Come on chemists, start inventing!

Mixing Topics and Content Type

Finally, bloggers can minimize perceptions of commercial interests by introducing a mix of loosely related topics and varying the type of content in their blogs. This tactic is similar to the "diversion" rhetorical tactic (Simon, 1996), which is about introducing several diverse topics in an attempt to direct audience attention away from the persuasion goal. Specifically, discussing a variety of topics on a blog makes it difficult or impossible for the reader to identify whether the blogger has an underlying commercial interest. For example, over a two-week period, technology blogger Matt Cutts (www.mattcutts.com/blog/) posted about his 30 day challenges over the past year (going vegan, growing a mustache, running a marathon, etc.), his wife's foot surgery, online privacy legislation, Google search games, and a book review. Given the diverse set of topics covered, readers may have difficulty discerning if Matt is pursuing some specific self-serving commercial interest with his blog. Likewise, a popular mommy blog, The Pioneer Woman (http://thepioneerwoman.com/), includes a mix of recipes, contests, decorating tips, photographs, and stories. Again, this diversity in content type makes it more difficult for the reader to identify the clear presence of a specific commercial interest for the blogger. As such, the default assumption is likely to be that there is no commercial interest.

These strategies have a lasting effect because once readers make an inference about the presence or absence of commercial intent of a blog, they are likely to categorize it as such. Early on, readers may look for cues that indicate the blogger has commercial intent and thus cannot be trusted. These cues are harder to locate and isolate when faced with blogs that feature a diverse set of topics and content types.

FUTURE RESEARCH DIRECTIONS

Social media channels have changed not only the way in which consumers exchange and gather information but also the way researchers study persuasion. While most persuasion theory has been developed independently either for one-to-many broadcast medium or for one-to-one communication, the unique nature of blogs calls for additional understanding on how these two streams of persuasion research can be further integrated. Until now, extant studies on social media communication have been fragmented. Social network analysis connects micro level communication dyads to inform macro level flow of messages and provides a structural level analysis of information transmission. However, this method does not explain how and why persuasion among strangers is achieved in social media and what the persuasion bases are in these contexts. This integration of these two perspectives on persuasion is an exciting area with the potential to make significant contributions to both theory and practice.

An additional step for a deeper understanding of persuasion in blogs would involve studying how the various types of blogs differ in their persuasion bases (e.g., authority, relevance, individuation, fandom, etc.), as well as the relative effectiveness of these bases. Understanding the persuasion bases of each type of blog is important because it can help managers identify the most effective strategies given their commercial interests and target audience. Further, it is important to understand how different bases of persuasion can be best used depending on the blogs' stage of development. For example, for new bloggers trying to attract an audience, are the best persuasion bases relevance and authority? As bloggers' objectives switch from attracting an audience to maintaining an audience, what is the best basis for persuasion? Examining how persuasion bases evolve over the life cycle of the blog is an important topic for future research.

CONCLUSION

With the proliferation of social media outlets, consumers' use of social media as a primary information source has increased. Fifty percent of participants in a recent eMarketer trend survey said that they were influenced by information shared on social media when making a purchase decision (eMarketer, March 2011). Similarly, Facebook, Twitter, blogs, and consumer review sites were listed as very effective venues for consumers to gain access to new product information (Etailing Survey, September 2009). Thus, there is no doubt that social media is and will be a powerful marketing communication tool and that business practitioners should consider developing social media strategies when they introduce a new product to the market, design marketing promotions/deals, and position their brands. However, the "how to" of social media marketing is still relatively unknown and remains mostly a black box. Practitioners have just started learning about social media by experimenting with numerous tactics (e.g., seeded word-of-mouth marketing, sponsoring influential bloggers) that would make their communication more effective and persuasive. By providing a typology of blogs and identifying key strategies used by bloggers to persuade their readers, our chapter is an attempt at demystifying this process. We identify tactics that bloggers use to influence readers and also shed some light on how these tactics shape readers' perceptions vis-à-vis the blogger. These insights should help marketers better tailor their social media strategies depending on their goals and the intended audience.

In this chapter, we propose a categorization scheme for blogs based on *the perceived target audience (mass versus one-to-one)* and *the perceived level of the blogger's commercial interest (explicit commercial interests versus no explicit commercial interests)*. Our proposed scheme provides insights to marketers looking to leverage social media marketing strategies as well as to bloggers attempting to maximize the persuasiveness and reach of their communication. Using this scheme, we categorized blogs into four types: *Commercial, Market Maven, Commercial Friendship*, and *Community-Based Friendship*.

We discuss how bloggers can intentionally implement two key communication strategies, *illusion of relationship* and *ambiguity in commercial interests* to shift their audiences' perceptions and thus make their messages more effective and persuasive.

For instance, by using the *illusion of relationship* strategy, bloggers can shift their audiences' perception of their blogs from *Commercial* to *Commercial Friendship* and *Market Maven* to *Community-Based Friendship*. This perceptual shift from mass to one-to-one may create a feeling of intimacy, increase the level of trust, and enhance the quality of the blogger-audience relationship. Such a shift can be achieved through increases in: (a) the depth and breadth of self-disclosures, (b) the frequency and duration of interactions, and (c) the perception of shared common interests. These tactics for achieving perceptual shifts from mass to one-to-one may help marketers build long-term, stable relationships with their target audience.

The use of the *ambiguity in communication interests* strategy can shift audiences' perceptions of blogs from *Commercial* to *Market Maven* and *Commercial Friendship* to *Community-Based Friendship*. This perceptual shift from commercial blogs to non-commercial creates a feeling of benevolence and care, increases audiences' trust towards the blogger, and strengthens the persuasive impact of the bloggers' messages. Such a shift can be attained through: (a) hiding commercial interests, (b) stressing benevolent communal interests, and (c) mixing diverse topics and content types. These practices for stimulating perceptual shifts from commercial to non-commercial can help business practitioners increase the persuasiveness of their marketing messages.

We should also note the ethical and potential legal implications of using these strategies, in particular the *ambiguity in commercial interests* strategy. This strategy should only be used properly within the applicable ethical and legal framework (e.g. in the U.S., this is governed by the Federal Trade Commission guideline 16 C.F.R. §§ 255.0-255.5). If misused, it may raise consumer welfare concerns as people are more likely to be misled by deceptive information from peer sources (Balasubramanian, 1994; Darke & Ritchie, 2007; Petty & Andrew, 2008). For example, consider the case of Salwa Mbarouk, a 22-year-old London designer and digital artist, who bought an e-book after reading a glowing blog review and then later realized that she was one of many consumers who had been misled by a company-sponsored review that posed as a third-party blog (Wall Street Journal, 2009). This example represents the downside of "misused" blog marketing communication. Although, bloggers may benefit from not explicitly stating their commercial interests, they have a legal and ethical responsibility to not misuse this form of marketing communication. They have a responsibility to be explicit about their affiliation with as well as any compensation received from advertisers and sponsors.

As evidenced from the various examples in this chapter, social media marketing is not a black box, but also not a magic bullet. Even though this chapter provides insights that can help practitioners leverage the power of blogs as a form of marketing communication, we need to further understand how blogs and social media are best integrated with other marketing strategies. This integration is even more complex if we consider that blogs are often only loosely affiliated with the company and thus not under its direct control. Thus, there is a need for future research in this area.

REFERENCES

Altman, I., & Taylor, D. A. (1973). *Social penetration: The development of interpersonal relationships*. Oxford, UK: Holt, Rinehart & Winston.

Balasubramanian, S. K. (1994). Beyond advertising and publicity: Hybrid messages and public policy issues. *Journal of Advertising, 23*(4), 29–46.

Bansal, H. S., & Voyer, P. A. (2000). Word-of-mouth processes within a services purchase decision context. *Journal of Service Research, 3*(2), 166–177. doi:10.1177/109467050032005.

Berscheid, E., & Walster, E. H. (1978). *Interpersonal attraction*. Reading, MA: Addison-Wesley.

Bickart, B., & Schindler, R. M. (2001). Internet forums as influential sources of consumer information. *Journal of Interactive Marketing, 15*(3), 31–40. doi:10.1002/dir.1014.

Blood, R. (2002). *The weblog handbook: Practical advice on creating and maintaining your blog*. Cambridge, MA: Perseus Publishing.

Boush, D. M., Friestad, M., & Rose, G. M. (1994). Adolescent skepticism toward TV advertising and knowledge of advertiser tactics. *The Journal of Consumer Research, 21*(1), 165–175. doi:10.1086/209390.

Bustillo, M., & Zimmerman, A. (2009, April 23). Paid to pitch: Product reviews by bloggers draw scrutiny. *The Wall Street Journal*, p. B9.

Byrne, D., & Nelson, D. (1965). Attraction as a linear function of proportion of positive reinforcements. *Journal of Personality and Social Psychology, 1*(6), 659. doi:10.1037/h0022073 PMID:14300244.

Byrne, D. E. (1971). *The attraction paradigm*. New York, NY: Academic Press.

Campbell, M. C., & Kirmani, A. (2000). Consumers' use of persuasion knowledge: The effects of accessibility and cognitive capacity on perceptions of an influence agent. *The Journal of Consumer Research, 27*(1), 69–83. doi:10.1086/314309.

Chai, S., & Kim, M. (2010). What makes bloggers share knowledge? An investigation on the role of trust. *International Journal of Information Management, 30*(5), 408–415. doi:10.1016/j.ijinfomgt.2010.02.005.

Collins, N. L., & Miller, L. C. (1994). Self-disclosure and liking: A meta-analytic review. *Psychological Bulletin, 116*(3), 457–475. doi:10.1037/0033-2909.116.3.457 PMID:7809308.

Cozby, P. C. (1973). Self-disclosure: A literature review. *Psychological Bulletin, 79*(2), 73. doi:10.1037/h0033950 PMID:4567729.

Darke, P. R., & Ritchie, R. J. B. (2007). The defensive consumer: Advertising deception, defensive processing, and distrust. *JMR, Journal of Marketing Research, 44*(1), 114–127. doi:10.1509/jmkr.44.1.114.

Deighton, J., & Grayson, K. (1995). Marketing and seduction: Building exchange relationships by managing social consensus. *The Journal of Consumer Research, 36*(1), 660–676. doi:10.1086/209426.

Deighton, J., Romer, D., & McQueen, J. (1989). Using drama to persuade. *The Journal of Consumer Research, 16*(3), 335–343. doi:10.1086/209219.

Delia, J. G., & O'Keefe, B. J. (1979). Constructivism: The development of communication in children. In Wartella, E. (Ed.), *Children communicating: Media and development of thought, speech, understanding* (pp. 157–185). Beverly Hills, CA: Sage.

Derlega, V. J., & Berg, J. H. (1987). *Self-disclosure: Theory, research, and therapy*. Newbury Park, CA: Sage.

Derlega, V. J., & Grzelak, J. (1979). Appropriateness of self-disclosure. In Chelune, G. J. (Ed.), *Self-disclosure: Origins, Patterns, and Implications of Openness in Interpersonal Relationships* (pp. 151–176). San Francisco, CA: Jossey-Bass.

Duck, S. (1991). *Understanding relationships.* New York: The Guilford Press.

Duck, S., Rutt, D. J., Hoy, M., & Strejc, H. H. (1991). Some evident truths about conversations in everyday relationships all communications are not created equal. *Human Communication Research*, *18*(2), 228–267. doi:10.1111/j.1468-2958.1991.tb00545.x.

E-tailing Group. (2009). *The E-tailing group/Power Reviews 1ˢᵗ annual community and social media survey.* Retrieved August 1, 2011, from http://www.e-tailing.com/content/?p=120

Escalas, J. E. (2004). Imagine yourself in the product: Mental simulation, narrative transportation, and persuasion. *Journal of Advertising*, *33*(2), 37–48. doi:10.1080/00913367.2004.10639163.

Fehr, B. (2000). The life cycle of friendship. In Hendrick, C., & Hendrick, S. S. (Eds.), *Close relationships: A sourcebook* (pp. 71–82). Thousand Oaks, CA: Sage. doi:10.4135/9781452220437.n6.

Fletcher, G. J. O., & Kerr, P. S. G. (2010). Through the eyes of love: Reality and illusion in intimate relationships. *Psychological Bulletin*, *136*(4), 627–658. doi:10.1037/a0019792 PMID:20565171.

Ford, G. T., Smith, D. B., & Swasy, J. L. (1990). Consumer skepticism of advertising claims: Testing hypotheses from economics of information. *The Journal of Consumer Research*, *16*(4), 433–441. doi:10.1086/209228.

Friestad, M., & Wright, P. (1994). The persuasion knowledge model: How people cope with persuasion attempts. *The Journal of Consumer Research*, *21*(1), 1–31. doi:10.1086/209380.

FTC. (2009). Guides concerning the use of endorsements and testimonials in advertising. Retrieved August 1, 2011 from http://www.ftc.gov/os/2009/10/091005 revisedendorsementguides.pdf

Giffin, K. (1967). The contribution of studies of source credibility to a theory of interpersonal trust in the communication process. *Psychological Bulletin*, *68*(2), 104–120. doi:10.1037/h0024833 PMID:6065581.

Goldenberg, J., Libai, B., & Muller, E. (2001). Talk of the network: A complex systems look at the underlying process of word-of-mouth. *Marketing Letters*, *12*(3), 211–223. doi:10.1023/A:1011122126881.

Granovetter, M. S. (1973). The strength of weak ties. *American Journal of Sociology*, *78*(6), 1360–1380. doi:10.1086/225469.

Green, M. C., & Brock, T. C. (2000). The role of transportation in the persuasiveness of public narratives. *Journal of Personality and Social Psychology*, *79*(5), 701. doi:10.1037/0022-3514.79.5.701 PMID:11079236.

Harding, S., Phillips, D., & Fogarty, M. P. (1986). *Contrasting values in Western Europe: Unity, diversity and change.* London: Macmillan.

Herring, S. C., Scheidt, L. A., Wright, E., & Bonus, S. (2005). Weblogs as a bridging genre. *Information Technology & People*, *18*(2), 142–171. doi:10.1108/09593840510601513.

Hoffman, D. L., & Novak, T. P. (1996). Marketing in hypermedia computer-mediated environments: Conceptual foundations. *Journal of Marketing*, *60*(3), 50–68. doi:10.2307/1251841.

Jourard, S. M. (1971). *Self-disclosure: An experimental analysis of the transparent self.* New York: Wiley-Interscience.

Katz, E., & Lazarsfeld, P. F. (1955). *Personal influence: The part played by people in the flow of mass communications*. New York: Free Press.

Kirchler, E. (1988). Diary reports on daily economic decisions of happy versus unhappy couples. *Journal of Economic Psychology*, *9*(3), 327–357. doi:10.1016/0167-4870(88)90039-6.

Kozinets, R. V., De Valck, K., Wojnicki, A. C., & Wilner, S. J. S. (2010). Networked narratives: Understanding word-of-mouth marketing in online communities. *Journal of Marketing*, *74*(2), 71–89. doi:10.1509/jmkg.74.2.71.

Little, B. R. (1972). Psychological man as scientist, humanist and specialist. *Journal of Experimental Research in Personality*, *6*(2), 95–118.

Marsden, P. V., & Campbell, K. E. (1984). Measuring tie strength. *Social Forces*, *63*(2), 482–501.

McQuail, D. (1987). *Mass communication theory: An introduction*. Thousand Oaks, CA: Sage.

Metts, S. (1997). Face and facework: Implications for the study of personal relationships. In Duck, S. (Ed.), *Handbook of personal relationships* (pp. 373–390). Hillsdale, NJ: Lawrence Erlbaum Associates.

Morry, M. M. (2005). Relationship satisfaction as a predictor of similarity ratings: A test of the attraction-similarity hypothesis. *Journal of Social and Personal Relationships*, *22*(4), 561–584. doi:10.1177/0265407505054524.

Murray, S. L., Holmes, J. G., & Griffin, D. W. (1996). The self-fulfilling nature of positive illusions in romantic relationships: Love is not blind, but prescient. *Journal of Personality and Social Psychology*, *71*(6), 1155–1180. doi:10.1037/0022-3514.71.6.1155 PMID:8979384.

Nardi, B. A., Schiano, D. J., Gumbrecht, M., & Swartz, L. (2004). Why we blog. *Communications of the ACM*, *47*(12), 41–46. doi:10.1145/1035134.1035163.

Petty, R. D., & Andrews, J. C. (2008). Covert marketing unmasked: A legal and regulatory guide for practices that mask marketing messages. *Journal of Public Policy & Marketing*, *27*(1), 7–18. doi:10.1509/jppm.27.1.7.

Price, L. L., & Arnould, E. J. (1999). Commercial friendships: Service provider-client relationships in context. *Journal of Marketing*, *63*(4), 38–56. doi:10.2307/1251973.

Reissman, C., Aron, A., & Bergen, M. R. (1993). Shared activities and marital satisfaction: Causal direction and self-expansion versus boredom. *Journal of Social and Personal Relationships*, *10*(2), 243–254. doi:10.1177/026540759301000205.

Richmond, V. P. (1995). Amount of communication in marital dyads as a function of dyad and individual marital satisfaction. *Communication Research Reports*, *12*(2), 152–159. doi:10.1080/08824099509362051.

Rose, S. M. (1985). Same-and cross-sex friendships and the psychology of homosociality. *Sex Roles*, *12*(1), 63–74. doi:10.1007/BF00288037.

Rubin, D. C. (1997). *Memory in oral traditions: The cognitive psychology of epic, ballads, and counting-out rhymes*. New York: Oxford University Press.

Sadoski, M., Goetz, E. T., & Rodriguez, M. (2000). Engaging texts: Effects of concreteness on comprehensibility, interest, and recall in four text types. *Journal of Educational Psychology*, *92*(1), 85–95. doi:10.1037/0022-0663.92.1.85.

Schramm, W. (1954). *The process and effects of mass communication*. Urbana, IL: University of Illinois Press.

Simon, G. K. (1996). *In sheep's clothing: Understanding and dealing with manipulative people*. Little Rock, AR: A. J. Christopher & Co..

Stafford, L., Kline, S. L., & Rankin, C. T. (2004). Married individuals, cohabiters, and cohabiters who marry: A longitudinal study of relational and individual well-being. *Journal of Social and Personal Relationships, 21*(2), 231–248. doi:10.1177/0265407504041385.

Vangelisti, A. L., & Banski, M. A. (1993). Couples' debriefing conversations: The impact of gender, occupation, and demographic characteristics. *Family Relations, 42*(2), 149–157. doi:10.2307/585448.

Weimann, G. (1991). The influentials: back to the concept of opinion leaders? *Public Opinion Quarterly, 55*(2), 267–279. doi:10.1086/269257.

Weiss, L., & Lowenthal, M. F. (1975). Life-course perspectives on friendship. In Lowenthal, M. F., Thurnher, M., & Chiriboga, D. (Eds.), *Four stages of life: A comparative study of women and men facing transitions* (pp. 48–61). San Francisco, CA: Jossey-Bass.

Werner, H. (1957). The concept of development from a comparative and organismic point of view. In Harris, D. (Ed.), *The Concept of Development*. Minneapolis, MN: University of Minnesota Press.

Williams, D. A. (2011). U.S. social network usage: 2011 demographic and behavioral trends. Retrieved August 1, 2011, from http://www.emarketer.com/docs/eMarketer_US_Social_Network_Usage-2011_Demographic_and_Behavioral_Trends.pdf

Winster, S. G., & Swamynathan, S. (2010). Blog Trust Model for Blog Readers. In *Proceedings of International Conference on Recent Trends in Information Telecommunication and Computing* (pp. 314-317). Kerala, India: ACEEE.

Zwaan, R. A., & Radvansky, G. A. (1998). Situation models in language comprehension and memory. *Psychological Bulletin, 123*(2), 162–185. doi:10.1037/0033-2909.123.2.162 PMID:9522683.

ADDITIONAL READING

Allen, M. (1998). Comparing the persuasive effectiveness one- and two-sided message. In Allen, M., & Preiss, R. W. (Eds.), *Persuasion: Advances through Meta-Analysis* (pp. 87–89). Cresskill, NJ: Hampton Press.

Berscheid, E. (1966). Opinion change and communicator-communicatee similarity and dissimilarity. *Journal of Personality and Social Psychology, 4*(6), 670–680. doi:10.1037/h0021193.

Burgoon, M. (1989). Messages and persuasive effects. In Bradac, J. J. (Ed.), *Message Effects in Communication Science* (pp. 129–164). Newbury Park, CA: Sage.

Chaiken, S., Wood, W., & Eagly, A. H. (1996). Principles of persuasion. In Higgins, E. T., & Kruglanski, A. W. (Eds.), *Social psychology: Handbook of basic principles* (pp. 702–742). New York: Guliford Press.

Cialdini, R. B. (2001). *Influence: Science and practice*. Boston, MA: Allyn & Bacon.

Conger, J. A. (1988). The necessary art of persuasion. *Harvard Business Review, 76*, 84–95. PMID:10179656.

Derlega, V. J., & Chaikin, A. L. (1975). *Sharing intimacy: Why we reveal to others and why*. Englewood Cliffs, NJ: Prentice-Hall.

Feick, L. F., & Price, L. L. (1987). The market maven: A diffuser of marketplace information. *Journal of Marketing, 51*(1), 83–97. doi:10.2307/1251146.

Gladwell, M. (2002). *The tipping point: How little things can make a big difference*. Boston, MA: Back Bay Books.

Goffman, E. (1959). *The presentation of self in everyday life*. New York: Doubleday Anchor Books.

Heath, C., & Heath, D. (2007). *Made to stick: Why some ideas survive and others die*. New York: Random House.

Herr, P. M., Kardes, F. R., & Kim, J. (1991). Effects of word-of-mouth and product attribute information on persuasion: An accessibility-diagnosticity perspective. *The Journal of Consumer Research*, *17*(4), 454–462. doi:10.1086/208570.

Hovland, C. I., Janis, I. L., & Kelley, H. H. (1953). *Communication and persuasion: Psychological studies of opinion change*. New Haven, CT: Yale University Press.

Kaplan, A. M., & Haenlein, M. (2010). Users of the world, unite! The challenges and opportunities of social media. *Business Horizons*, *53*(1), 59–68. doi:10.1016/j.bushor.2009.09.003.

Kazoleas, D. C. (1993). A comparison of the persuasive effectiveness of qualitative versus quantitative evidence: A test of explanatory hypotheses. *Communication Quarterly*, *41*(1), 40–50. doi:10.1080/01463379309369866.

Kelman, H. C., & Hamilton, V. L. (1989). *Crime of obedience: Toward a social psychology of authority and responsibility*. New Haven, CT: Yale University Press.

Kim, M.-S., & Hunter, J. E. (1993). Attitude-behavior relations: A meta-analysis of attitudinal relevance and topic. *The Journal of Communication*, *43*(1), 101–142. doi:10.1111/j.1460-2466.1993.tb01251.x.

Kline, S. L., & Stafford, L. (2004). A comparison of interaction rules and interaction frequency in relationship to marital quality. *Communication Reports*, *17*(1), 11–26. doi:10.1080/08934210409389370.

Kozinets, R. V. (2002). The field behind the screen: Using netnography for marketing research in online communities. *JMR, Journal of Marketing Research*, *39*(1), 61–72. doi:10.1509/jmkr.39.1.61.18935.

Littlejohn, S. W. (1990). *Theories of human communication*. Belmont, CA: Wadsworth.

McBane, D. A. (1995). Empathy and the salesperson: A multidimensional perspective. *Psychology and Marketing*, *12*(4), 349–369. doi:10.1002/mar.4220120409.

McCombs, M., & Reynolds, A. (2001). News influence on our pictures of the world. In Bryant, J., & Zillmann, D. (Eds.), *Media effects: Advances in Theory and Research* (pp. 1–18). Mahwah, NJ: Lawrence Erlbaum Associates.

McCraken, G. (1989). Who is the celebrity endorser?: Cultural foundations of the endorsement process. *The Journal of Consumer Research*, *16*(3), 310–321. doi:10.1086/209217.

McGuire, W. J. (1969). The nature of attitudes and attitude change. In Lindzey, G., & Aronson, E. (Eds.), *Handbook of Social Psychology* (pp. 136–314). Reading, MA: Addison-Wesley.

McKenna, K. Y. A., Green, A. S., & Gleason, M. E. J. (2002). Relationship formation on the Internet: What's the big attraction? *The Journal of Social Issues*, *58*(1), 9–31. doi:10.1111/1540-4560.00246.

Muniz, A. M., & O'Guinn, T. C. (2001). Brand community. *The Journal of Consumer Research*, *27*(4), 412–432. doi:10.1086/319618.

O'Keefe, D. J. (1990). *Persuasion: Theory and research*. Newbury Park, CA: Sage.

Perloff, R. M. (2003). *The dynamics of persuasion: Communication and attitudes in the 21st century*. Mahwah, NJ: Lawrence Erlbaum Associates.

Petty, R. E., & Cacioppo, J. T. (1986). The effects of involvement on responses to argument quantity and quality: Central and peripheral routes to persuasion. *Journal of Personality and Social Psychology*, *46*(1), 69–81. doi:10.1037/0022-3514.46.1.69.

Powell, G. R., Groves, S. W., & Dimos, J. (2011). *ROI of social media: How to improve the return on your social marketing investment*. New York: John Wiley & Sons.

Rinchins, M. L. (1991). Social comparison and the idealized images of advertising. *The Journal of Consumer Research*, *18*(1), 71–83. doi:10.1086/209242.

Stern, B. (1994). A revised model for advertising: Multiple dimensions of the source, the message, and the recipient. *Journal of Advertising*, *23*(2), 5–16.

Wimmer, R. D., & Dominick, J. R. (2010). *Mass media research: An introduction*. Belmont, CA: Wadsworth Publishing.

KEY TERMS AND DEFINITIONS

Ambiguity in Commercial Interests: A strategy that bloggers use to deemphasize the presence of commercial interests. It disguises or hides the bloggers' commercial motives behind the communication.

Commercial Blogs: Blogs that are perceived as communicating with a mass audience and have explicit commercial interests behind their communication.

Commercial Friendship Blogs: Blogs that are perceived as communicating on a one-to-one basis with their target audience and have explicit commercial interests.

Community-Based Friendship Blogs: Blogs that are perceived as communicating on a one-to-one basis with their target audience and have no explicit commercial interests.

Illusion of Relationship: A strategy that bloggers use to shift readers' perceptions of the blog away from a mass audience toward a one-to-one audience. The strategy creates a feeling of intimacy and personalized relationship between bloggers and their audience.

Market Maven Blogs: Blogs that are perceived as communicating with a mass audience and have no explicit commercial interests behind their communication.

Chapter 8
User Intention of Sharing Video Clips on Web 2.0 Social Network Websites

Eldon Y. Li
National Chengchi University, Taiwan & California Polytechnic State University, USA

Shu-Hsun Chang
National Chengchi University, Taiwan

ABSTRACT

As the advance of Internet technology continues, various applications, services, and business models are emerging in the market. The online video sharing website is the hottest application nowadays; thus it is important to understand the key factors influencing user's behavior on these websites. In this chapter, the authors propose a conceptual model which is based on the integrated model of user satisfaction and technology acceptance developed by Wixom and Todd (2005). To comprehend the user's behavior intention toward using the website, the authors also add the potential factors about community which influence user's behavior on video sharing websites. The results indicate that community satisfaction, content satisfaction, and system satisfaction all have significant positive impact on usefulness and ease of use, and that community satisfaction has a much higher impact than the other two types of satisfaction. This finding reveals an important attribute of video sharing websites, namely, the users of the website care most about the entire website community. Indeed, reliable system operations and useful, interactive content are two factors influencing the community satisfaction. For designers who want to set up a video sharing website, this research provides more comprehensive information on how to invest the limited resources on the critical variables in order to maximize the service value.

DOI: 10.4018/978-1-4666-4026-9.ch008

INTRODUCTION

Since the advent of Internet technology, various applications, services, and business models have been introduced. Tim O'Reilly (2004) and Paul Graham (2005) introduced the concept of Web 2.0 to describe this kind of phenomenon, showing that Internet service has entered a new era. Among different services related to Web 2.0, video sharing is the most important application nowadays. According to YouTube.com (2012), there are 72 hours of video uploaded to YouTube every minute and over 3 billion hours of video are watched each month on its website. The company website boasts over 800 million unique users visiting YouTube each month and there were more than 1 trillion views in 2011.

Despite the intensive competition across different websites, web-based video sharing is still emerging and developing. There are no fixed rules in terms of website design, video content and marketing methods. Given that, this research attempts to understand Web 2.0 online video sharing websites and the behavioral intentions of users to discover the principles for designing Web 2.0 websites as well as factors affecting user behaviors. Based on the above motives, there are two research objectives of this study:

1. To identify the key factors that might influence the quality of Web 2.0 video sharing websites. Each website, with its different market share in the Web 2.0 video sharing market, provides particular services and value to its users. However, there are also some common factors for these websites such as system stability and content richness. This study attempts to find out key factors that influence the quality of various video sharing websites.
2. To understand the user attitude and intention to use Web 2.0 video sharing websites. Each of the numerous users of Web 2.0 websites has his or her individual attitude and reasons

to accept the video sharing websites. There are likely some common factors affecting the user's acceptance and intentions toward video sharing websites. This study expects to find out the factors that influence users' attitudes and behavioral intentions regarding using Web 2.0 video sharing websites.

Different from the website environment of Web 1.0, the user environment of Web 2.0 enhances the user intention to browse websites according to its key features. Therefore, this study adopts the Technology Acceptance Model (TAM) and proposes a holistic integrated model combining the original TAM with website quality and satisfaction. Also, related concepts of Web 2.0 were added to the research model to further understand behavioral intention of Web 2.0 users. Furthermore, for video sharing website owners, this study provides the principles for investing limited resources on critical variables to maximize service value.

LITERATURE REVIEW

Features of Web 2.0

The concept of Web 2.0 began in a brainstorming session between Dale Dougherty, web pioneer and VP of O'Reilly, and Craig Cline of Media Live International in the 2004 O'Reilly Media Conference. Back then, they explained this term in several instances but failed to define it clearly. Web 2.0 is defined by John Musser and Tim O'Reilly (2006) as follows:

Web 2.0 is a set of economic, social, and technology trends that collectively form the basis for the next generation of the Internet—a more mature, distinctive medium characterized by user participation, openness, and network effects.

Such a web-oriented application enables users to play the roles of commentators and/or content providers. The former refers to participants in the group/community discussion board who usually give individual opinions on some issues in the websites. The latter refers to users who provide their photo, blogs, and video/audio clips sharing in their personal profile in the websites. For example, thousands of videos are uploaded to YouTube every day, exerting a new web-based phenomenon.

A web-based community refers to a platform by which users can provide useful advice to solve other's issues by sharing their knowledge and expertise (Constant et al., 1996; Galegher et al., 1998; Lakhani & von Hippel, 2003). In other words, users can conduct a series of community-based interactions addressing the issue brought about by a user message. According to a report from Institute for Information Industry (2006) in Taiwan, Web 2.0 services are characterized by 4Cs: Content, Community, Consumer experience, and Cross-service integration. See Table 1.

Among the 4Cs, content and community have been used to assess the quality of the video sharing platform whereas the applications of the other two elements are lacking so far. Thus, both content and community were applied to the conceptual model of this research.

Information System Success Model

DeLone and McLean (1992) proposed an information systems (IS) success model as a framework for conceptualizing and operationalizing IS success. They described two quality factors in their framework, namely, information quality and system quality. An additional factor, service quality, was included in the updated model (DeLone & McLean, 2003). This was because the changing nature of IS function in which service quality has becoming ever important when evaluating information system success. Another modification was replacing individual impact and organization impact with an aggregate measure of impacts, called "net benefit." Therefore, the updated model can assess the benefit at any level of analysis. In the updated model, they suggest that a high-quality system will result in higher degree of satisfaction, system use, and net benefit. They further suggest that the updated model can be adapted to measure the success of the new Internet websites.

Since DeLone and McLean proposed the IS success model, it has been applied to various IS researches (Seddon & Kiew, 1994; Goodhue & Thompson, 1995; Igbaria & Tan, 1997; Rai et al., 2002). Based on the model, this study adapted service quality and information quality with community quality and content quality for the context of online video sharing systems. The

Table 1. The 4C of Web 2.0

Dimension	Characteristics
Content	Since Web 2.0 stresses user-participation and user-contributed value, users are both content readers and providers; that is, services values are enhanced via user-generated contents.
Community	Community in the Web 2.0 website expands its social network through resources shared by users. Users strengthen the stickiness to websites through interpersonal connections and resource sharing via the Internet in terms of their respective attributes (e.g., jobs, ages, and interests).
Consumer Experience	A well-designed user interface brings a positive user experience; good user experience would lead to continuous intention of using the websites.
Cross-Service Integration	Application programming interfaces are available via Web 2.0 environment; users can use this interface to create mashup or remade new services as well as embed service effortlessly.

Source: Institute for Information Industry, Taiwan (2006)

concept of community is an essential function in online video sharing websites, representing a kind of service application. Furthermore, content quality transcends information quality as a quality factor; it reflects the media richness of online video sharing websites.

Measuring the Quality of Video Sharing Websites

This study attempts to assess the quality of video sharing websites by using the community quality, content quality, and system quality factors. The review of these factors follows.

Community Quality

A review of the related literature suggests that the quality of community be assessed from 4 dimensions: mass size, community diversification, service diversification, and interactivity.

1. **Mass Size:** A considerable number of members is a basic element to a community. According to the theory of critical mass by Oliver and Marwell (2001), the mass would not perform a social tendency unless the number of community members exceeds the threshold. From the innovation diffusion theory by Rogers and Allbritton (1995), the critical mass refers to the minimum number of users required for innovation to diffuse via interaction. Consequently, prolific user interactions demand a certain number of community members as a fundamental requirement; then users can be satisfied during the process of interaction with others. In other words, a user cannot share anything when he is essentially alone in a virtual community with few acquaintances with whom to share.

2. **Diversification of Community:** Community diversification refers to communities consisting of website users in terms of specific attributes and categories. Generally, such communities are classified pursuant to geographic features, interests and occupations. According to Lin (2001), social, informative, trading and experience are four common values that virtual community members expect to obtain/exchange through participating in such a community. Regarding websites, communities with different attributes and categories represent personalized optimal value portfolios. As a result, a website with diversification to some extent might fulfill personalized optimal value portfolios, leading to high community satisfaction.

3. **Diversification of Service Type:** Diversification of service type refers to the service categories available to community members in many ways. Generally, diversified information and values are exchanged via distinct services such as message boards, blogs, albums, videos, votes, labels and private letters. Given that, diversified service might stimulate community users to interact with each other according to their preferences, leading to higher user satisfaction toward the community.

4. **Interactivity:** Reid (1995) identified a virtual community as a cyberspace where a user communicates with others via imagination and creativity. Indeed, users also can be delighted with positive feelings during their social interactivities, hereby obtaining satisfaction toward the community. Thus, the higher interactivity across community members might lead to the greater user satisfaction.

Content Quality

Based on the related literature, there are 5 dimensions of content quality to consider, including resolution, entertainment, education, quantity, and diversification. These dimensions are discussed as follows:

- **Resolution:** The quality of format has been regarded as a essential factor to assess content quality of a system (Seddon & Kiew, 1994). In the context of our study, there are different formats used to record the video, such as audio video interleaved (avi) and moving picture experts group (mpeg). Each type of video has its respective resolution. High resolution video can show greater detail and improve the presentation. Therefore, in this study, resolution is regarded as an important factor.

- **Entertainment:** According to Kao (2007), the top two categories for most-viewed films are entertainment and fun videos, indicating that entertainment is important on its own and should be an essential factor.

- **Education:** In addition to entertainment, many users search the videos mainly for watching the demonstration or instructional movies on subjects such as cooking, dancing, and make-up, etc. Chen (2008) indicated that education affects the user's attitude regarding Web 2.0 video sharing websites since many viewers expect to learn useful skills like dancing, cooking and music via watching video clips.

- **Quantity:** The main purpose of a Web 2.0 viewer is to watch video clips on the website, so the quantity of available clips to viewers becomes a determinant to both initial visit and continuous usage. In other words, users may step back if they cannot find their desired films on the website. Lee et al. (2002) showed that a proper quantity of information is an important factor to assess content quality.

- **Diversification:** Liu and Arnett (2000) identified flexible and customized information presentation and product/service differentiation as key factors to assess content quality. In the context of video sharing websites, users usually demand diverse types of video clips according to different

purposes, interests, contexts, and communities. Greater content diversification could attract and satisfy a wide variety of users.

System Quality

According to the literature, we adapted five related factors to the video sharing websites context and developed the factors to form system quality, namely download/upload speed, search accuracy, human-computer interface design, privacy, and upload space.

1. **Download/Upload Speed:** Download/upload time means the speed with which content is transferred up or down from the Internet. Normally, users may be turned off if they need to wait for a long time to download or upload videos, leading to user dissatisfaction.

2. **Search Accuracy:** A good search mechanism can rapidly and accurately respond to user requirements and make the surfing experience more fulfilling (Koufaris, 2002), especially when there are voluminous videos provided by the website. Correctly offering what users want is an essential factor of system quality.

3. **Human-Computer Interface Design:** Human-computer interface design is adapted from the user-based design construct of Zviran et al. (2006). When users access websites, they expect to effectively and easily navigate the sites and accomplish their tasks. A good human- computer interface design renders improved ease of use and coordination between user and computer, leading to higher system satisfaction.

4. **Privacy:** Generally, a community-based video sharing website will make individual videos available to users with different access authorization. Users may request that some personal videos be accessible only by authorized users, rather than general public.

Failure to ensure privacy and authorization control could cause a legal litigation and result in system dissatisfaction.

5. **Upload Space:** The size of storage a user may store their uploaded video files is usually limited. Some video file may be too large to store, high-definition video in particular. Many websites limit the size of a single file or the total storage for a single user uploading videos. Small storage capacity for uploaded files would cause an upload to fail, influencing the perception of system quality.

Technology Acceptance Model (TAM)

Technology acceptance model (TAM) proposed by Davis (1989) is based on the theory of reasoned action (TRA) (Fishbein & Ajzen, 1975). In TRA, there are 4 stages of process: belief, attitude, intention, and behavior. The theory prescribes 2 general constructs influencing behavioral intention (BI): behavioral attitude (BA) and subjective norm (SN). A person's behavioral intention depends on the person's attitude toward the behavior and subjective norm (BI = BA + SN).

To improve the TRA, Ajzen (1991) developed the theory of planned behavior (TPB) by adding the construct of perceived behavior control (PBC). They postulated the factor of PBC being affected by perceived facilitation and perceived control beliefs. The former refers to the resources available to performance a behavior and the latter refer to an individual's subjective determination thereto (Bandura, 1982). Because of low influential power, theoretical uncertainty, and challenges for psychological measurement, Davis et al. (1989) abandoned the use of subjective norm and proposed technology acceptance model (TAM). The model contains two constructs, namely usefulness and ease of use, that affect the attitude to use technology and further determine behavioral intention. Behavioral intention, in turn, affects usage behavior.

Since its introduction, the TAM has been applied to integrate different theories for the explanation and exploration of various phenomena in the IS field. For example, Wixom and Todd (2005) developed an integrated model by integrating satisfaction theory with TAM; this model is also used to predict the IS usage. According to their research model, IS quality (content and system quality) represented object-based beliefs and user satisfaction referred to object-based attitude determined by IS quality. Increased user satisfaction leads to greater behavioral beliefs and behavioral attitude, where the behavioral beliefs correspond to the TAM's concepts of usefulness and ease of use.

An integrated model of satisfaction and TAM illustrates how user attitude impacts behavioral intention. It also shows how usefulness and ease of use influence user attitudes toward the IS. Furthermore, quality constructs such as reliability, flexibility, integration, accessibility, timeliness, among others, act as the antecedents which affect user satisfaction.

In accordance with Benbasat and Barki (2007), the TAM-related studies shall focus on antecedents and consequences of usefulness; thereupon, we employ an expanded TAM by integrating the theoretical model of Wixom and Todd (2005) in association with satisfaction to explain user behavior of using Web 2.0 video sharing websites. The research model of measuring satisfaction corresponds to the purpose of this research, that is, to find out key factors affecting user behavioral intention. Our methodology is in the following chapter.

Research Model and Constructs

We aim to identify the factors affecting user intention towards Web 2.0 video sharing websites. Based on the literature review in the previous section, the key factors concerned are community, content and system quality. Meanwhile, the integrated model consisting of user satisfaction and TAM proposed by Wixom and Todd (2005) serves as the conceptual model for this study (see Figure 1).

Object-based beliefs covering community, content and system quality refer to user beliefs regarding video sharing websites. Object-based attitude includes community, content and system satisfaction, and refers to user attitudes toward video sharing websites. Behavioral beliefs are comprised of usefulness and ease of use, and refer to user post-use beliefs. Behavioral attitude refers to user post-use attitudes. The operationalization of each construct is defined in Table 2.

Hypothesis Development

In this research, we follow Wixom and Todd's (2005) model and regard three quality-related constructs (community quality, content quality, and system quality) as antecedents of satisfaction. The justification is presented as follows.

Figure 1. Research model

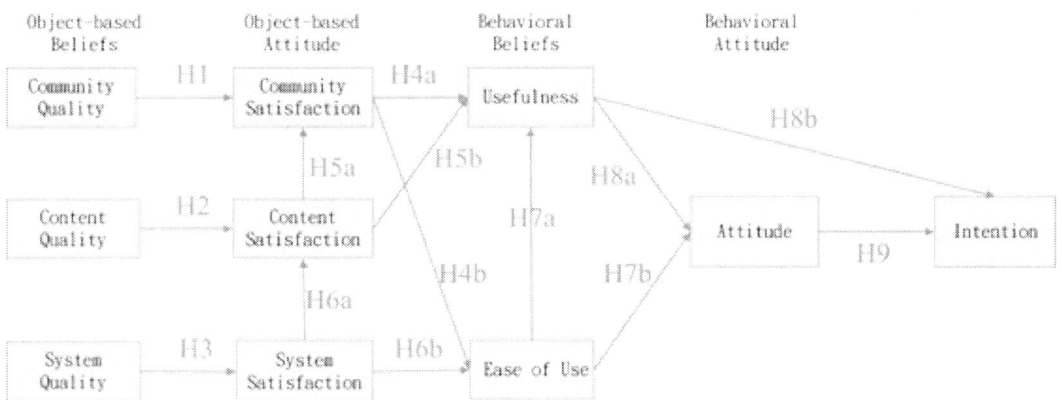

Table 2. Operational definitions of variables

Construct	Definition
Community quality	Community quality is concerned with such issues as mass number, community diversification, diversification of service type, and interactivity among users in the video sharing websites.
Content quality	Content quality is concerned with such issues as resolution, entertainment, education, quantity, and diversification content accessible from the video sharing websites.
System quality	System quality is concerned with downloading and uploading speed, accurate search, human machine interface design, privacy and upload space provided by websites.
Community satisfaction	Community satisfaction is defined as a subjective judgment of the community setting up in the video sharing websites which meets user social needs.
Content satisfaction	Content satisfaction is defined as a subjective judgment of the content provided by the video sharing websites.
System satisfaction	System quality is defined as a subjective judgment of the operational functions provided by website system.
Usefulness	The degree to which the user believes that using the video sharing websites has improved his or her productivity of watching videos.
Ease of use	The degree to which the user believes that using the video sharing websites is easy and definite.
Attitude	Attitude is defined as the feelings of favorableness towards using the video sharing websites.
Intention	Intention is defined as the intent of using or recommending to others about the video sharing websites in the future.

Community Quality

Service providers should not only furnish the services that fulfill demands of customers but also satisfy the needs of spiritual support and social interactions. These services also can effectively promote customer participation in the meantime. In a community of Web 2.0 website, participants can have opportunities for social interactions. They can attend the social activities in the communities. When users have higher levels of interaction with others in the community, they realize their commitment to the community and have the intent to share their opinions and resources with other participants. Furthermore, the greater level of socialization among participants, the more they understand the prescribed roles they play in the community; the congruence between the expected and actual roles lead to more satisfaction (Parasuraman et al., 1988).

A web-based community is an excellent medium to fulfill the demand of socialization. Service providers can set up a variety of communities to spark interests in participation of users. In other words, users can be enticed to surf the communities in the website and interact with others to satisfy their need for social interaction and spiritual communication. A good community with sound services available to users would lead to positive community satisfaction; that is, the higher the community service quality, the greater user satisfaction toward web-based communities. Hence, the postulation follows.

H1: Community quality has a positive effect on community satisfaction in video sharing websites.

Content Quality

Content quality adapted from the DeLone and McLean's IS success model (1992; 2003) was used to measure the quality of information content. Here, we applied it to evaluate the content quality of Web 2.0 video sharing websites. Normally, users can view various films with they want and obtain content satisfaction. For example, users may intend to view a specific video from a website and watch the related clips as well. A site with good content quality may have abundant videos, fulfilling user requirements and expectations, thus, leading to user satisfaction. Related studies also indicated similar evidence (Rai et al., 2002; Wang, 2008; Cheung & Lee, 2008; Petter & McLean, 2009). Hence, we propose that higher content quality may lead to greater content satisfaction for the user. Hence is the hypothesis:

H2: Content quality has a positive effect on content satisfaction in video sharing websites.

System Quality

System quality is also a key attribute in the model of DeLone and McLean (1992; 2003). System quality is related to download speed or the search mechanism. For example, a fast download speed allows users to watch on line videos expeditiously. A satisfying search mechanism can accurately find the content corresponding to user requirements. A high level of system quality can supply users with more convenient and faster responses. Several studies have shown that good system quality can result in greater user satisfaction (Rai et al., 2002; Wang, 2008; Cheung & Lee, 2008; Petter & McLean, 2009). Hence is the hypothesis:

H3: System quality has a positive effect on system satisfaction in video sharing websites.

User Satisfaction and Behavioral Beliefs

According to Wixom and Todd (2005), object-based attitudes will affect behavioral beliefs. Thus, in our research model, the community, content, and system satisfaction are regarded as the external variables shaping behavioral beliefs (usefulness and ease of use) respectively. That is, the degree of satisfaction would serve as the determinant of beliefs about the outcome of using the systems (Ajzen & Fishbein, 1980). The related hypotheses are postulated as follows.

A web-based community offers its users a useful medium for social interaction. Most users of video sharing websites expect to interact with others and find desirable video clips. A high degree of community satisfaction indicates the users have positive interactions with others or the diverse services provided by the community have fulfilled the demands of the users, leading to an increase in the perception of usefulness. Thus, we propose the following hypothesis:

H4a: Community satisfaction has a positive effect on usefulness in video sharing websites.

Community satisfaction is an overall consequence of user's interaction with the community members through the website. For example, one may find a group of members who have the same interest by using the community-based functions of the website. A user may effectively communicate with others via sharing video clips online at a lower cost in time and money as compared to other means (e.g., e-mail the video file to others). Hence, we postulate that high community satisfaction results in increasing the perception of ease of use.

H4b: Community satisfaction has a positive effect on ease of use in video sharing websites.

According to our research model, the degree of content satisfaction is likely to affect the degree of community satisfaction. Users with high content satisfaction might be the result of the diversification of video clips or abundant comments from other viewers. It is very likely that content satisfaction will stimulate members to share their own opinions, leading to more social interactions and higher community satisfaction.

Thus, users who have higher content satisfaction tend to have higher community satisfaction. Hence is the hypothesis:

H5a: Content satisfaction has a positive effect on community satisfaction in video sharing websites.

According to Wixom and Todd (2005), improved content quality via increasingly informative contents may result in greater content satisfaction. This outcome may further help users realize the perception of usefulness. A user's usefulness of a video sharing website may increase because the content fulfills the personal demands. For example, one user may be eager to obtain knowledge for specific issues by viewing particular videos, while another may acquire pleasures by viewing funny videos if he or she just wants to relax after work. Hence is the hypothesis:

H5b: Content satisfaction has a positive effect on usefulness in video sharing websites.

In general, high system quality might be attributed to improved human-machine interface design or search precision. Well-designed human-machine interfaces enable informative content to be presented in a simple and clear manner, promoting content satisfaction. Likewise, a user could find needed information in a rapid and accurate way via the search mechanism provided by the system, leading to high content satisfaction. Thus, the degree of system satisfaction is likely to influence the degree of content satisfaction. Hence is the hypothesis.

H6a: System satisfaction has a positive effect on content satisfaction in video sharing websites.

System satisfaction reflects the degree of which the user likes and interacts with the system (Wixom & Todd, 2005). High system satisfaction may indicate that the user likes the system and is willing to interact more with the system. For example, high system satisfaction might result from excellent human-machine interface design that enables a user to use the website in a simple and effortless manner. Also, ease of use might be ascertained via the rapid download speed which allows the user to save time and effort. By using such a system, a user is likely to discover that the system is easy to use. Thus, we posited the following hypothesis:

H6b: System satisfaction has a positive effect on ease of use in video sharing websites.

Original Hypotheses in TAM

According to TAM (Davis, 1989), ease of use and usefulness might impact user attitudes toward using the system. It reflects that users have perceptions of favorableness towards using the system since they received the useful information and positive experience in using video sharing websites. Further, other relationships were illustrated from Davis et al. (1989). They concluded that attitude toward usage and usefulness impact behavioral intention, and ease of use impacts usefulness. Since the related hypotheses in this model have been widely tested by previous technology acceptance behavioral studies in various contexts (Venkatech & Bala, 2008; Taylor & Todd, 1995; Ahn et al., 2007; Moon & Kim, 2001), we postulate the same hypotheses below.

H7a: Ease of use has a positive effect on usefulness in video sharing websites.
H7b: Ease of use has a positive effect on attitude in video sharing websites.
H8a: Usefulness has a positive effect on attitude in video sharing websites.
H8b: Usefulness has a positive effect on intention in video sharing websites.
H9: Attitude has a positive effect on intention in video sharing websites.

METHOD AND RESULTS

Demographics

This study conducted a web-based survey on experienced users from video sharing website. Compared to a traditional mail-based questionnaire, the online version has several advantages: (1) the sample is not restricted to a single geographical area, (2) lower cost, and (3) shorter time frame (Tan & Teo, 2000). The questionnaire included three parts. In the first part, respondents were asked to answer the questions regarding personal profile, including gender, education, age, and experience of Web usage. The questions in the second part are about the habits of using the video sharing websites (e.g., the number of times they used video sharing websites per week, the length of time they used the site per week, etc.). The last part of the questionnaire was related to the measurement of our research constructs.

To avoid invalid responses, the online system checked to make sure all items in the questionnaire are filled out by each respondent before the responses are stored into the database. Moreover, in order to promote the response rate, the opening instructions informed the respondent that five gift certificates would be awarded to respondents randomly chosen from the complete questionnaires.

The invitation messages were sent to 1,000 members randomly chosen from several video sharing websites in Taiwan. After three weeks, 280 members replied to our questionnaire and 220 of the responses were validated. According to the validated sample, the proportions of male and female were 39.5% and 60.5%, respectively. When it comes to the experience with the Web, 92.1% of respondents had more than five years and 6.8% had 3.5 years. Regarding the experience with video sharing website usage, 36.3% of respondents were using such websites more than 20 minutes per day, 48.6% used the websites for 40 to 60 minutes, and 15.0% exceeded one hour. The majority of users were female within the ages of 18-25; this is consistent with the structure of a survey sample reported in a behavioral survey on online video entertainment population conducted by the Institute for Information Industry (2006).

Assessment of Measurement Model

According to Hair et al. (2000), the value of the composite reliability (CR) of a construct should exceed 0.7, representing the acceptable level of the overall reliability in a heterogeneous data collection. Table 3 shows that the values of all reflective constructs in our model exceeded 0.7, ranged from 0.86 to 0.97.

As for validity of each construct, a confirmatory factor analysis (CFA) was applied. The convergent validity is tested by examining the value of factor loading. In accordance with Fornell and Bookstein (1982), the value of factor loading should exceed 0.5 for good convergent validity. The discriminant validity might be tested by the square root of an average variance extracted (AVE) exceeding the coefficient between two constructs (Fornell & Larcker, 1981) as shown in Table 4.

With regard to formative constructs, the weight of each item in a construct surpassed the recommended level suggested by Chin et al. (2003). Tables 3, 4 and 5 showed that both formative and

Table 3. Assessment of reliability and convergent validity of reflective constructs

Construct	Items	Loading	CR	AVE	SE	t
CMS	The functions provided from video sharing website satisfied my social needs.	0.87	0.86	0.76	0.021	41.94
	Overall, I am satisfied with the functions about communities from the video sharing website.	0.87			0.020	44.20
COS	The information I got from video sharing website satisfied my needs.	0.93	0.93	0.88	0.011	82.43
	Overall, I am satisfied with the video clips provided from the video sharing website.	0.94			0.011	82.94
SYS	The design of video sharing website satisfied my needs.	0.95	0.95	0.91	0.009	108.2
	Overall, I am satisfied with the design of the video sharing website.	0.95			0.008	122.9
USF	The content provided from video sharing website is what I want	0.90	0.90	0.82	0.020	45.60
	Overall, I think the video sharing website is useful to me.	0.91			0.013	68.15
EOU	It is easy to use the video sharing website.	0.97	0.97	0.95	0.006	151.1
	The website is simple to use	0.97			0.006	173.3
ATT	Overall, I like to use the video sharing website.	0.59	0.95	0.90	0.008	118.8
	I would get the positive feeling about this video sharing website.	0.90			0.010	94.39
INT	I will keep use this video sharing website in the future.	0.59			0.009	94.88
	Despite other similar websites, I will use this video sharing website rather than others.	0.59	0.92	0.79	0.015	60.31
	I will recommend others to use this video sharing website.	0.90			0.016	55.53

CMS = community satisfaction; COS = content satisfaction; SYS = system satisfaction; USF = usefulness; EOU = ease of use; ATT = attitude; INT = intention

Table 4. Assessment of discriminate validity

Construct	CMS	COS	SYS	USF	EOU	ATT	INT
CMS	**0.87**						
COS	0.70	**0.94**					
SYS	0.41	0.49	**0.95**				
USF	0.63	0.62	0.52	**0.91**			
EOU	0.64	0.55	0.42	0.77	**0.97**		
ATT	0.69	0.56	0.48	0.73	0.73	**0.95**	
INT	0.78	0.57	0.44	0.73	0.72	0.83	**0.89**

CMS = community satisfaction, COS = content satisfaction, SYS = system satisfaction, USF = usefulness, EOU = ease of use, ATT = attitude, INT = intention

reflective constructs were robust related to convergent and discriminate validity of the instruments in our study.

The square root of an AVE serves as a diagonal entry where a correlation coefficient is beneath it.

Assessment of Structural Model

This study conducted a partial least square (PLS) to test the structural model. A linear structural relation model (LISREL) demands a large sampling size, whereas a partial least square (PLS) analysis is free of the limitation of variable patterns and sampling sizes but requires a good ability to predict and explain (Anderson & Gerbing, 1988), so the latter is adopted for a total of 10 constructs with 44 items. Also, through the Kolmogorov-Smirnov test which demonstrated the non-normal distribution (p<0.001) of our data, PLS is adequate to this study (Chin et al., 2003).

After ascertaining the validity, we conducted the structural assessment using PLS (Figure 2) in which outcomes were shown by path coefficients and R-squared values; the former represents the affected levels of respective constructs and the latter indicates the variance of dependent variables explained by the independent ones.

Table 6 shows the analysis results supporting all hypotheses from H1 to H9. As for quality-related constructs (H1-H3), system quality has the highest impact on satisfaction, followed by content quality and community quality. However, satisfaction-related constructs are in reversed order affecting ease of use and usefulness constructs. Usually, a video sharing website is comprised of content generated by users and/or communities instead of by webmasters. As a result, a video sharing website having rich content and reliable system but few users and passive communities would not be sustainable, causing low community satisfaction. Thus, community satisfaction having the most significant impact on ease of use and usefulness conforms to expectation.

To sum up, the explanatory power based on R-square value of the three satisfactions was 56% on construct of usefulness, but only 51% on ease of use. In addition, the R-squared value of use intention reached 0.72 showing a considerable explanatory power from attitude and usefulness and conforming to previous studies (Davis, 1989; Davis et al., 1992). This evidences that the model developed in this study can properly explain the intention of using video sharing websites.

Finally, we considered direct and indirect effects of respective antecedents on intention in terms of standardized path coefficients as shown in Table 7. To behavioral intention, the direct effect is from only two constructs: attitude (0.63) and usefulness (0.27). All constructs, except attitude,

Table 5. Assessment of formative constructs

Item	Contents	Weight	SE	t
Community Quality (CMQ)				
Mass number	There are mass members in the video sharing website.	0.25	0.027	9.36**
	There are mass users in the video sharing website.	0.21	0.012	17.73**
Diversification of community	The video sharing website provided completed types of virtual communities.	0.11	0.021	5.18**
	The video sharing website provided a variety of virtual communities.	0.20	0.017	11.66**
Diversification of service type	The video sharing website provided full of community functions	0.21	0.012	17.73**
	The video sharing website provided various community services	0.10	0.028	3.55**
Interactivity	You can interact with others in the video sharing website.	0.31	0.030	10.19**
	You can build friendship with others in the video sharing website.	0.13	0.037	3.42**
Content Quality (COQ)				
Resolution	The resolution of video ships is satisfied.	0.11	0.021	5.14**
	The video sharing website provided high quality of videos.	0.09	0.015	5.64**
Entertainment	Funny films are available in the video sharing website.	0.17	0.015	11.42**
	I am pleased by viewing films in the video sharing website.	0.18	0.012	14.98**
Education	Films provided from the video sharing website are educational	0.14	0.024	5.74**
	Films provided from the video sharing website fulfills my demands for learning	0.08	0.029	2.68**
Quantity	There are a great number of videos in the video sharing website.	0.22	0.016	13.42**
	The video number is unsatisfactory. (reverse)	0.13	0.028	4.54**
Diversification	The video categories are abundant in the video sharing website.	0.23	0.022	10.47**
	The video categories are complete in the video sharing website.	0.24	0.024	10.06**
System Quality (SYQ)				
Download/ upload speed	It is not need to take lots of time to download the videos.	0.13	0.020	6.46**
	There were delay or lag problems when watching the films.	0.05	0.020	2.57**
Accurate search	It is easy to find what I want by using the searching functions.	0.17	0.017	10.24**
	Tags the categories in the video sharing website help me to find videos in need.	0.12	0.018	7.11**
Computer-user interface design	The video sharing website displays visually pleasing design.	0.16	0.034	4.85**
	Overall, the video sharing website provided good user-interface design.	0.19	0.012	15.57**
Privacy	The video sharing website can protect personal profile from leaking out.	0.11	0.02	5.46**
	The video sharing website provided the authority control for private clips.	0.12	0.020	6.01**
	I feel safe to use the video sharing website.	0.18	0.017	10.48**
Upload space	The video sharing website provided sufficient capacity for single clip upload	0.15	0.031	4.91**
	The video sharing website provided sufficient capacity for upload all of my clips	0.21	0.023	9.36**

** P<0.01

have indirect effects ranging from 0.1 to 0.55. The constructs having most total effects in sequence are attitude (0.63), ease of use (0.55), usefulness (0.52), and community satisfaction (0.45). The total effects of the other constructs are insignificant, ranging from 0.10 to 0.31.

Figure 2. Results of PLS analysis

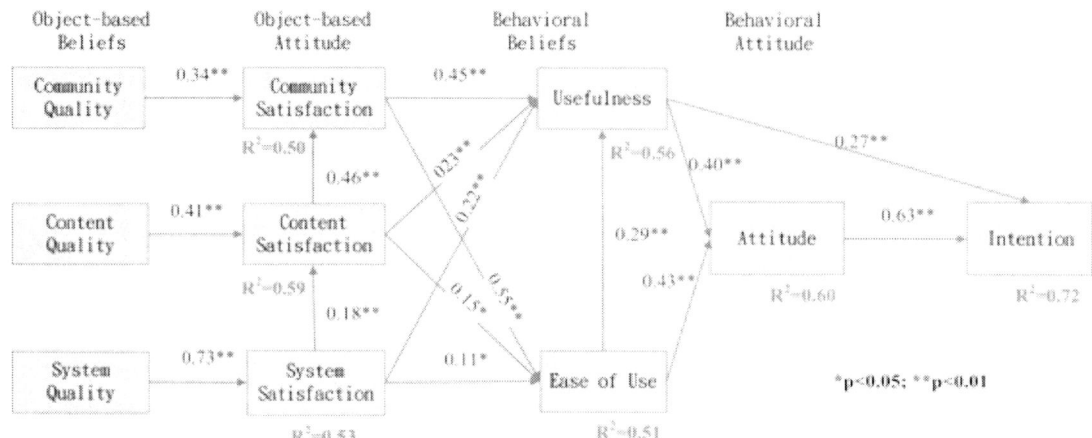

Table 6. Results of hypothesis testing

Hypothesis	Content	β	Significant
H1	Community quality has a positive effect on community satisfaction in video sharing websites.	β=0.34 p<0.01)	YES
H2	Content quality has a positive effect on content satisfaction in video sharing websites.	β=0.41 (<0.01)	YES
H3	System quality has a positive effect on system satisfaction in video sharing websites.	β=0.73 p<0.01)	YES
H4a	Community satisfaction has a positive effect on usefulness in video sharing websites.	β=0.19 (p<0.05)	YES
H4b	Community satisfaction has a positive effect on ease of use in video sharing websites.	β=0.63 (p<0.01)	YES
H5a	Content satisfaction has a positive effect on community satisfaction in video sharing websites.	β=0.46 (p<0.01)	YES
H5b	Content satisfaction has a positive effect on usefulness in video sharing websites.	β=0.20 (p<0.05)	YES
H6a	System satisfaction has a positive effect on content satisfaction in video sharing websites.	β=0.18 (p<0.05)	YES
H6b	System satisfaction has a positive effect on ease of use in video sharing websites.	β=0.14 (p<0.05)	YES
H7a	Ease of use has a positive effect on usefulness in video sharing websites.	β=0.54 (p<0.01)	YES
H7b	Ease of use has a positive effect on attitude in video sharing websites.	β=0.42 (p<0.01)	YES
H8a	Usefulness has a positive effect on attitude in video sharing websites.	β=0.40 (p<0.01)	YES
H8b	Usefulness has a positive effect on intention in video sharing websites.	β=0.27 (p<0.01)	YES
H9	Attitude has a positive effect on intention in video sharing websites.	β=0.63 (p<0.01)	YES

Table 7. The effects of research constructs on intention

Research Construct	Direct Effect	Indirect Effect	Total Effect
Community quality	NA	0.15	0.15
Content quality	NA	0.21	0.21
System quality	NA	0.10	0.10
Community satisfaction	NA	0.45	0.45
Content satisfaction	NA	0.31	0.31
System satisfaction	NA	0.13	0.13
Usefulness	0.27	0.25	0.52
Ease of use	NA	0.55	0.55
Attitude	0.63	NA	0.63

Note: NA = No assertion of any effect of such construct on intention

MANAGERIAL IMPLICATIONS

Based on the research results, this study provides the following implications for practitioners and webmasters when designing and operating video sharing websites.

Video sharing websites often are regarded as the websites hosting large databases to store lots of video clips. The webmasters used to overlook the community quality with a mentality of "sharing first, socializing second." However, with the maturity of Web 2.0 development, they start to realize the value of socialization among community members on the websites, and thus consider that community plays a key factor to future development in the market. For instance, YouTube and Yahoo have been dedicated to developing community-based services. Consequently, we identify four community-related constructs (i.e., mass size, diversification of community, diversification of service type, and interactivity) for the webmasters to design, build, and measure community-based services on video sharing websites. For example, supplying some functions for users to interact with each other might improve the

intra-community interactivity and fulfill the user's spiritual satisfaction via community-generated interaction.

In addition, webmasters must not only encourage users to upload video clips, but also control content quality such as resolution, entertainment, education and diversification, so that user may be able to find what they need rather than a plethora of rough information.

Next, system quality is of high importance to a website where content and community rely on system operations. The main concerns of system quality include download/upload speed, search accuracy, user interface design, safety, and upload space, which assure good system quality and in term enhance user experience with content and community.

Finally, webmasters should pay timely attention to user satisfaction. Satisfaction is the important factor that determines how a user views a website and further affects user intention to reuse it. With the rapid change of web technology and user habits, satisfying the users in the ever-changing Internet is not easy. Webmasters must make feedback channels available to users, such as message boards and blogs for both parties, to maintain real-time responsiveness so the website can give timely adjustments of services to fulfill user demands. This practice will significantly heighten the value of the website.

CONCLUSION

Since Internet bandwidth and storage technology are advancing rapidly, more and more entrepreneurs are entering the industry of video sharing websites. Through a model combining user satisfaction and TAM by Wixom and Todd (2005), we aim to build a behavioral model by identifying the key factors affecting user intentions toward video sharing websites. The research results allow us to draw the following conclusions.

1. The research model proposed in the study has high explanatory power. All postulated relationship between the constructs in the model are significant at p<0.05 level.

2. The three quality constructs (community, content, and system qualities) respectively affect the satisfaction toward community, content, and system. Among the three, community satisfaction is the most critical satisfaction construct as system satisfaction affects content satisfaction, and content satisfaction subsequently affects community satisfaction. Moreover, it yields the highest effects on usefulness and ease of use constructs as evidence by the β coefficients in Figure 2.

   Both usefulness and ease of use have significant and positive influence on attitude. This results in community satisfaction having the highest indirect effects on attitude among the three kinds of satisfaction constructs. It demonstrates that community satisfaction is the key factor affecting the user attitude toward the video sharing websites.

3. Usefulness and attitude have positive impact on user intention of using video sharing websites. This evidence corresponded with the research result from Davis (1989). Therefore, improving the user satisfaction about the community, the content, and the website system would influence usefulness and ease of use and further impact user attitude and use intention.

4. The two phases of user behavioral process we adapted from Wixom and Todd are valid and sound for video sharing behavior. First of all, the gap between expectation and confirmation lead to user satisfaction, representing a kind of object-based attitude toward the video sharing websites. Then, this object-based attitude transforms into the behavioral beliefs and attitudes regarding the use of video sharing websites. This illustrates that having a good experience using the video

sharing websites plays a key role and probably leads the user to revisit and reuse the websites.

REFERENCES

Ahn, T. R., Ryu, S., & Han, I. (2007). The impact of Web quality and playfulness on user acceptance of online retailing. *Information & Management*, *44*(3), 263–275. doi:10.1016/j.im.2006.12.008.

Ajzen, I. (1991). The theory of planned behavior. *Organizational Behavior and Human Decision Processes*, *50*(2), 179–211. doi:10.1016/0749-5978(91)90020-T.

Ajzen, I., & Fishbein, M. (1980). *Understanding Attitude and Predicting Social Behavior*. NJ: Prentice-Hall.

Anderson, J. C., & Gerbing, D. W. (1988). Structural Equation modeling in Practice: A Review and Recommended two-step Approach. *Psychological Bulletin*, *13*(3), 411–423. doi:10.1037/0033-2909.103.3.411.

Bandura, A. (1982). Self-efficacy mechanism in human agency. *The American Psychologist*, *37*(2), 122–147. doi:10.1037/0003-066X.37.2.122.

Benbasat, I., & Barki, H. (2007). Quo Vadis TAM? *Journal of the Association for Information Systems*, *8*(4), 211–218.

Chen, Y. F. (2008). *A Study for the Effect of the experience Characteristics of the Web 2.0 based Video Blog on the User's Intention. Unpublished Master's theses*. Taiwan: Chung Yuan Christian University.

Cheung, C. M. K., & Lee, M. K. O. (2008). The structure of Web-based information systems satisfaction: Testing of competing models. *Journal of the American Society for Information Science and Technology*, *59*(10), 1617–1630. doi:10.1002/asi.20881.

Chin, W. W., Marcolin, B. L., & Newsted, P. R. (2003). A partial least squares latent variable modeling approach for measuring interaction effects: Results form a Monte Carlo simulation study and an electronic-mail emotion adoption study. *Information Systems Research, 14*(2), 189–217. doi:10.1287/isre.14.2.189.16018.

Constant, D., Sproull, L., & Kiesler, S. (1996). The kindness of strangers: The usefulness of electronic weak ties for technical advice. *Organization Science, 7*(2), 119–135. doi:10.1287/orsc.7.2.119.

Davis, F. D. (1989). Perceived usefulness, perceived ease of use, and user acceptance of information technology. *Management Information Systems Quarterly, 13*(3), 319–340. doi:10.2307/249008.

Davis, F. D., Bagozzi, R. P., & Warshaw, P. R. (1989). User acceptance of computer technology: A comparison of two theoretical models. *Management Science, 35*(8), 982–1003. doi:10.1287/mnsc.35.8.982.

Davis, F. D., Bagozzi, R. P., & Warshaw, P. R. (1992). Extrinsic and intrinsic motivation to use computers in the workplace. *Journal of Applied Social Psychology, 22*(14), 1111–1132. doi:10.1111/j.1559-1816.1992.tb00945.x.

DeLone, W. H., & McLean, E. R. (1992). Information systems success: The quest for the dependent variable. *Information Systems Research, 3*(1), 60–95. doi:10.1287/isre.3.1.60.

DeLone, W. H., & McLean, E. R. (2003). The DeLone and McLean Model of Information System success: A ten-year update. *Journal of Management Information Systems, 19*(4), 9–30.

Fishbein, M., & Ajzen, I. (1975). *Belief, attitude, intentions and behavior: An introduction to theory and research.* Boston, MA: Addison-Wesley.

Fornell, C., & Larcker, D. F. (1981). Structural equation models with unobservable variables and measurement error: Algebra and statistics. *JMR, Journal of Marketing Research, 18*(3), 382–388. doi:10.2307/3150980.

Fornell, C. R., & Bookstein, F. L. (1982). Two structural equation model: LISREL and PLS Applied to Consumer Exit-Voice Theory. *JMR, Journal of Marketing Research, 19*(4), 440–452. doi:10.2307/3151718.

Galegher, J., Sproull, L., & Kiesler, S. (1998). Legitimacy, authority, and community in electronic support groups. *Written Communication, 15*(4), 493–530. doi:10.1177/0741088398015004003.

Goodhue, D. L., & Thompson, R. L. (1995). Task-technology fit and individual performance. *Management Information Systems Quarterly, 19*(2), 213–236. doi:10.2307/249689.

Graham, P. (2005). *Web 2.0.* Retrieved October 11, 2006, from http://www.paulgraham.com/web20.html

Hair, J. F. Jr, Anderson, R. E., Tatham, R. L., & Black, W. C. (2000). *Multivariate data analysis with reading.* New York: MacMillan.

Igbaria, M., & Tan, M. (1997). The consequences of the information technology acceptance on subsequent individual performance. *Information & Management, 32*(3), 113–121. doi:10.1016/S0378-7206(97)00006-2.

Institute for Information Industry. (2006). *Applications for Web2.0 innovations cases.* Taipei, Taiwan. Institute for Information Industry. ISBN/ISSN: 9789575813475.

Kao, N.-Y. (2007). *Uses and Gratifications Theory On Web 2.0 Application-A Case of Online Video Sharing Websites. Unpublished master theses.* Taiwan: National Taiwan University of Science and Technology.

Koufaris, M. (2002). Applying the Technology Acceptance Model and Flow Theory to Online Consumer Behavior. *Information Systems Research, 13*(2), 205–223. doi:10.1287/isre.13.2.205.83.

Lakhani, K. R., & von Hippel, E. (2003). How open source software works: Free user-to-user assistance. *Research Policy, 32*(6), 923–943. doi:10.1016/S0048-7333(02)00095-1.

Lee, Y. W., Strong, D. M., Kahn, B. K., & Wang, R. Y. (2002). AIMQ: A methodology for information quality assessment. *Information & Management, 42*(2), 133–146. doi:10.1016/S0378-7206(02)00043-5.

Lin, K. (2001). *An Exploratory Study for Commercial Application of Virtual Community. Unpublished Master's theses*. Taiwan: Soochow University.

Liu, C., & Arnett, K. P. (2000). Exploring the factors associated with Web site success in the context of electronic commerce. *Information & Management, 38*(1), 23–34. doi:10.1016/S0378-7206(00)00049-5.

Moon, J.-W., & Kim, Y.-G. (2001). Extending the TAM for a World-Wide-Web context. *Information and Management, 38*(4), 217.230.

O'Reilly, T. (2004). *What Is Web 2.0*. Retrieved September 30, 2005, from http://www.oreillynet.com/pub/a/oreilly/tim/news/2005/09/30/what-is-web-20.html

O'Reilly, T. (2006). *Web 2.0 Principles and Best Practice*s. Retrieved May 29, 2009, from http://oreilly.com/catalog/web2report/chapter/web20_report_excerpt.pdf

Oliver, P. E., & Marwell, G. (2001). Whatever happened to critical mass theory? A retrospective and assessment. *Sociological Theory, 19*(3), 292–311. doi:10.1111/0735-2751.00142.

Parasuraman, A., Zeithaml, V. A., & Berry, L. L. (1988). SERVQUAL: A Multiple-Item Scale for Measuring Consumer Perceptions of Service Quality. *Journal of Retailing, 64*(1), 12–40.

Petter, S., & McLean, E. R. (2009). A meta-analytic assessment of the DeLone and McLean IS success model: An examination of IS success at the individual level. *Information & Management, 46*(3), 159–166. doi:10.1016/j.im.2008.12.006.

Rai, A., Lang, S. S., & Welker, R. B. (2002). Assessing the validity of IS success models: An empirical test and theoretical analysis. *Information Systems Research, 13*(1), 50–69. doi:10.1287/isre.13.1.50.96.

Reid, E. (1995). Virtual worlds: Culture and imagination. In Jones, S. G. (Ed.), *CyberSociety: Computer-mediated communication and community* (pp. 164–183). Thousand Oaks, CA: Sage.

Rogers, E. M., & Allbritton, M. M. (1995). Interactive communication technologies in business organizations. *Journal of Business Communication, 32*(2), 175–195. doi:10.1177/002194369503200206.

Seddon, P. B., & Kiew, M. Y. (1994). A partial test and development of DeLone and McLean's model of IS success. In J.I. DeGross, S.L. Huff, & M.C. Munro (Eds.), *Proceedings of the International Conference on Information Systems* (pp. 99-110). Atlanta, GA: Association for Information Systems.

Tan, M., & Teo, T. (2000). Factors influencing the adoption of Internet banking. *Journal of the Association for Information Systems, 1*(5), 1–44.

Taylor, S., & Todd, P. A. (1995). Assessing IT Usage: The role of prior experience. *Management Information Systems Quarterly, 19*(4), 561–570. doi:10.2307/249633.

Venkatesh, V., & Bala, H. (2008). Technology Acceptance Model 3 and a Research Agenda on Interventions. *Decision Sciences, 39*(2), 273–315. doi:10.1111/j.1540-5915.2008.00192.x.

Wang, Y.-S. (2008). Assessing e-commerce systems success: A respecification and validation of the DeLone and McLean model of IS success. *Information Systems Journal, 18*(5), 529–557. doi:10.1111/j.1365-2575.2007.00268.x.

Wixom, B. H., & Todd, P. A. (2005). A Theoretical Integration of User Satisfaction and Technology Acceptance. *Information Systems Research, 16*(1), 85–102. doi:10.1287/isre.1050.0042.

YouTube. (2012). *Statistics*. Retrieved June 30, 2012, from http://www.youtube.com/t/press_statistics?hl=en Zviran, M., Glezer, C., & Avni, I. (2006). User satisfaction from commercial web sites: The effect of design and use. *Information and Management, 43*(2), 157-178.

KEY TERMS AND DEFINITIONS

Attitude: Beliefs about favorableness towards using the websites.

Community Quality: Community quality is concerned with the measurements of attributes about community within the website, such as mass size, community diversification, diversification of service type, and interactivity among users in the video sharing websites.

Content Quality: Content quality is concerned with the measurements of website output, such as resolution, entertainment, education, quantity, and accessibility to diversified content.

Community Satisfaction: An affective state that is the emotional reaction to the community setting up in the video sharing websites.

Content Satisfaction: An affective state that is the emotional reaction to the information provided by the video sharing websites.

Ease of Use: The degree to which a user believes that using the websites is free of effort.

Intention: A state of mind in which a person has the intent to use the website or recommend it to others in the future.

System Quality: System quality is concerned with the measurements of the processing system itself, such as downloading and uploading speed, search accuracy, human-machine interface design, privacy, and upload space.

System Satisfaction: An affective state that is the emotional reaction to the operational functions provided by website system.

Usefulness: The degree to which a user believes that using the websites has improved the performance of watching videos.

Webmaster: The person who oversees and maintains the community, the system, and the content qualities of a website.

APPENDIX

This section includes the descriptions of questionnaire items. Respondents were asked to answer to each item by a 5-point Likert scale in which "1" is "strongly disagree" and "5" is "strongly agree."

Community Quality

1. There are mass members in the video sharing website. (Mass size)
2. There are many users online on the video sharing website. (Mass size)
3. The video sharing website provides completed types of virtual communities. (Diversification of community)
4. The video sharing website provides a variety of virtual communities for me to join. (Diversification of community)
5. The video sharing website is full of community functions. (Diversification of service type)
6. The video sharing website provides various community services. (Diversification of service type)
7. You can interact with others in the video sharing website. (Interactivity)
8. You can build up friendship with others in the video sharing website. (Interactivity)

Content Quality

1. The resolution of video clips is satisfactory. (Resolution)
2. The video sharing website provides high quality of videos. (Resolution)
3. Funny films are available in the video sharing website. (Entertainment)
4. I am pleased by viewing films in the video sharing website. (Entertainment)
5. Films provided from the video sharing website are educational. (Education)
6. Films provided from the video sharing website fulfill my demands for learning. (Education)
7. There are a great number of videos in the video sharing website. (Quantity)
8. The number of available video clips is unsatisfactory. (reverse) (Quantity)
9. The video categories are abundant in the video sharing website. (Diversification)
10. The video categories are complete in the video sharing website. (Diversification)

System Quality

1. I can quickly download the videos from the website. (Download/upload speed)
2. There are delay or lag problems when watching the films. (reverse) (Download/upload speed)
3. It is easy to find what I want by using the searching functions. (Search accuracy)
4. Tagging the categories in the video sharing website helps me to find videos in need. (Search accuracy)
5. The video sharing website displays visually pleasing design. (Computer-user interface design)
6. Overall, the video sharing website provides good user-interface design. (Computer-user interface design)
7. The video sharing website can protect personal profile from leaking out. (Privacy)
8. The video sharing website provides the authorization control for private clips. (Privacy)

9. I feel safe to use the video sharing website. (Privacy)
10. The video sharing website provides sufficient capacity for me to upload a large video clip (Upload space)
11. The video sharing website provides sufficient capacity for me to upload all of my video clips (Upload space)

Community Satisfaction

1. The functions provided by the video sharing website satisfy my social needs.
2. Overall, I am satisfied with the functions provided by the communities on the video sharing website.
3. Content Satisfaction:
4. The information I got from the video sharing website satisfies my needs.
5. Overall, I am satisfied with the video clips provided from the video sharing website.

System Satisfaction

1. The design of the video sharing website satisfies my needs.
2. Overall, I am satisfied with the design of the video sharing website.

Usefulness

1. The content provided by the video sharing website is what I want.
2. Overall, I think the video sharing website is useful to me.

Ease of Use

1. It is easy to use the video sharing website.
2. The website is simple to use

Attitude

1. Overall, I like to use the video sharing website.
2. When using the video sharing website, I can get positive feeling about it.

Intention

1. I will keep using this video sharing website in the future.
2. Despite other similar websites, I will use this video sharing website rather than the others.
3. I will recommend others to use this video sharing website.

Section 4
Social Marketing

Chapter 9
Comparing Web 2.0 Applications as Marketing Tools[1]

Erkan Akar
Afyon Kocatepe University, Turkey

Mete Karayel
Afyon Kocatepe University, Turkey

ABSTRACT

This study aims to evaluate and compare the Web 2.0 applications as marketing tools. In this context, blogs, micro-blogs, collaborative projects (wikis and social bookmarking), content communities, social networking sites, and virtual worlds have been examined. Eventually, it can be expected that blogs will provide more transparent feedback; micro-blogs will provide instant feedback; wikis will make the co-operative efforts of product development easier; social bookmarking will enable search-engine marketing; content communities will enable easy product training; social networking sites will create brand communities; and virtual worlds will provide new places to interact more effectively. All of these tools can come into prominence in the context of marketing.

INTRODUCTION

A decade ago, the Web was thought to be the future of the new digital era. The phenomenon of the Internet was to establish Web pages, publishing popular content for people to surf. Nowadays, the Internet, which helps people meet their needs and where users can create their own virtual communities to share common interests, has become the main communication platform. With the help of Web technology, the personal-focus has transformed to community-focus, which means a shift from Web 1.0 to Web 2.0 in terms of fundamental concept (Lee & Lan, 2007).

While Web 1.0, also originally called Websites, included only one-way communication through static Web pages with publishers communicating with users as if lecturing, today's Web 2.0 includes sharing, linking, collaborating, and user-generated content. Thus, Internet users participate collec-

DOI: 10.4018/978-1-4666-4026-9.ch009

tively in conversations, which lead to collective intelligence. Thanks to Web 2.0 applications, users can both produce and distribute the information (Thackeray et al., 2008); while Web 1.0 has a wide "read-only" base, Web 2.0 has "read-write-participate" base (Hardey, 2008).

The term Web 2.0 stands for an updated and improved version of the Web and has been widely used since 2004. The term has become popular and attempts to generate variations have arisen, such as Marketing 2.0, PR 2.0, etc. (Hardey, 2008).

Constantinides and Fountain (2008) mentioned that, Web 2.0 is a new step in the marketing environment as well as in the development process of the Internet. These authors have expressed that, as a new marketing environment, Web 2.0 makes the traditional purchasing process more complex.

The stimuli-response model, expressed by Kotler and Keller (2006) as the starting point in understanding customer behavior, refers to customer behavior in traditional terms (decision-making process in purchasing and purchasing behavior). According to them, in this model, marketing stimuli and environmental stimuli find their way into the customer's consciousness. A set of psychological processes combine with specific customer characteristics that result in the decision-making process and purchasing process. Constantinides (2004) has added Web experience as online controllable marketing factors to this model. In this way, Constantinides presents the Web as a new input that affects the behavior of the customer. Besides this, next to Web experience in the framework of today's digital focused marketing, Constantinides and Fountain (2008) have added a new input, Web 2.0 experience, to this model as an online, uncontrollable marketing factor. They define online uncontrollable marketing factors as applications such as blogs, wikis, social networks, tagging, forums, and others.

Each of the online, uncontrollable marketing factors that contain Web 2.0 applications can be considered as a marketing environment and/or a tool having different features. It then becomes necessary for the marketers to use these Web 2.0 applications more effectively, which makes the decision-making process and purchasing behavior of the customer more complex. Because of this, it is useful to compare Web 2.0 applications as marketing tools. This study contributes to the literature with this dimension. Additionally, it is thought that this study will be beneficial for the marketers in choosing the right Web 2.0 applications and/or using the chosen Web 2.0 applications more effectively.

While many businesses are trying to integrate various types of social media applications into their marketing strategies, very few academic studies have explored the appropriateness and importance of these applications as a strategic marketing tool (Constantinides et al., 2008).

Tredinnick (2006, p. 229) did note "the application of Web 2.0 technologies to business intranets, and their potential use in managing and developing business information and knowledge assets." Anderson (2007) acknowledged the "well-known and commonly used Web 2.0 services/applications with a view to providing a common grounding for educational and institutional issues." Kaplan and Haenlein (2010, p. 59) provided "a classification of Social Media which groups applications currently subsumed under the generalized term into more specific categories by characteristic: collaborative projects, blogs, content communities, social networking sites, virtual game worlds, and virtual social worlds." Constantinides et al. (2008, p. 1) also explained "what the new face of the Internet, widely referred to as Web 2.0 or Social Media, is, identifying its importance as a strategic marketing tool and proposing a number of alternative strategies for retailers."

In this study, the importance and use of Web 2.0 applications as marketing tools are highlighted, as well as their strengths and weaknesses as such tools.

LITERATURE REVIEW

What is Web 2.0?

The term Web 2.0, first coined by Tim O'Reilly (Petrassi, 2008), contains Web-based tools that have recently appeared and that have been increasing gradually in usage (Akar, 2009). According to O'Reilly (2005), Web 2.0, strategically, is the Web as platform on which users can control their own data, and core competencies, such as services rather than packaged software, architecture of participation, cost-effective scalability, remixable data sources and data transformations, software above the level of a single device, and harnessing collective intelligence, are included.

Web 2.0 refers to the second generation of the WWW, the focus of which is the ability of people to cooperate and share information online (Cronin, 2009). The discourse surrounding the WWW and networked information applications have been dominated by Web 2.0, which provides a more powerful, more engaging, and more interactive user experience (Tredinnick, 2006).

Web 2.0 is typically used in two contexts. The first is its technical aspect of building Web-based applications that include enhanced user experience via technologies and standards such as AJAX, and protocols such as RSS. The second is its functional aspect, which refers to the interactive opportunities provided to users. That is, it is based on user-generated content, which means enabling people to collectively aggregate and structure large amounts of information; in other words, the concept of "folksonomy" and "social software" (Krämer, 2006).

Constantinides et al. (2008) stated that Web 2.0 has three dimensions:

- **Application Types:** Applications can be classified in five categories. These are blogs, social networks, (content) communities, forums/bulletin boards, and content aggregators.

- **Social Effects:** The key advantage of Web 2.0 applications is enabling seamless generation of information and easy access to it. Social effects include empowerment, participation, openness, networking, conversation, community and democratization/user control.

- **Enabling Technologies:** Most technologies in the Web 2.0 domain are not new. There is a basic difference between Web 2.0 and the previous generation of Internet applications. Many Web 2.0 applications are based on open source software; thus, they are the results of collaborative development and continuous, real-time improvement. The most important enabling technologies and development tools are open source, RSS, wikis, widgets, mash-ups, and AJAX. However, the aim of this study is not to examine this aspect.

This study focuses on the functional aspect of Web 2.0 rather than its technical aspect. This functional aspect of Web 2.0 can broadly be termed "social media."

In some studies, Web 2.0 and social media have been deemed to mean the same thing (Fox, 2009; Borges, 2009), whereas in others they have used in different ways (Postman, 2009; Bruns & Bahnich, 2009; Akar, 2010). Thereby, in looking at the technical and functional differences of Web 2.0, it can be stated that the functional aspect is what makes social media come into prominence.

Web 2.0 can be thought of as social programming for everyone rather than as a specific set of technologies. Creating a blog or writing a comment about a book purchased from Amazon.com can be easy and intuitive with the help of this "social software." By using Web 2.0, users have become "co-developers" utilizing a "collective intelligence" that promotes the development of a "participatory culture" (Hardey, 2008).

The Rise of Web 2.0 as a Marketing Platform

Relative to just a few years ago, people now shop and learn in a brand-new way--they shop and gather information via search engines, blogs and social media sites, such as Twitter, Facebook, Digg, YouTube, and others. Therefore, today's marketers need to adapt to this new way or risk extinction (Halligan & Shah, 2010).

The Internet is in an evolutionary process and in this process Web 2.0 is a new step as a marketing environment (Constantinides & Fountain, 2008). The Web 2.0 approach put forward a dominant logic in marketing: "Value is defined by collaborating and co-creation with and learning from customers" (Parise & Guinan, 2008). The New Media Emergence in DM & Brand report stated that Web 2.0 is making direct and brand marketing easy, enabling real-time dialog with customers and creation of content with collaboration. This increases sales and improves brand awareness and perception (Marketing Charts, 2008).

D'Angelo (2010) indicated that Web 2.0 is a phenomenon that attracts the attention of many business owners as a suitable form of marketing. Messages about a specific product or service are spread with the aid of social media tools and viral marketing techniques on the Internet. Because social networking sites like Friendster, Facebook, and LinkedIn are being used by all ages and consumers generally have more confidence in the opinion of their peers, many businesses have become involved with this new media platform for marketing purposes (D'Angelo, 2010).

The second annual PR*Week*/MS&L Group Social Media Survey (2010) revealed that, 71% of 262 marketers use social media tools in marketing activities. Among the respondents of this survey, 48 % of them are using social networks, 34% are using blogs, 32% are using digital video and audio tools, 26% are using micro-blogs such as Twitter, 25% are using discussion forums, 15% are using social bookmarking sites, and 13% are using mobile-based services. The same survey showed that the primary business uses of social media are managing/monitoring customer feedback (39%) and creating communities (26%). Also it is reported in the survey by the respondents that social media tools are used for media relations (25%), market research (25%), understanding competitive landscape (24%), reaching key influencers (21%), lead generation (18%), product launches (17%), monitoring conversations (14%), and product reviews (12%) (PR*Week*, 2010).

According to the 2011 Social Media Marketing Industry Report, 90% of marketers (over 3,300) indicate that social media is vital for their business. 58% have used social media for 6 hours or more each week, and 34% have invested 11 or more hours weekly. The top four social media tools used by marketers are Facebook, Twitter, LinkedIn, and blogs. Facebook has surpassed Twitter and takes the top position since the 2010 study (Stelzner, 2011).

WEB 2.0 APPLICATIONS/ SOCIAL MEDIA SITES AS MARKETING TOOLS

Web 2.0 applications/Social media sites are classified in different ways in various studies. Some of these classifications are shown in Table 1.

Kaplan and Haenlein have updated their previous classification which was published by Business Horizons in 2010, namely "Users of the world, unite! The challenges and opportunities of social media" and added micro-blogs to social media classification (Kaplan & Haenlein, 2011).

In this study, Kaplan and Haenlein's social media classification, which also includes micro-blogs, is used, and in this context, the Web 2.0 applications to be evaluated as marketing tools are blogs, micro-blogs, collaborative projects (wikis and social bookmarking), content communities, social networking sites, and virtual worlds (virtual game worlds and virtual social worlds).

Table 1. Some classifications of Web 2.0 applications/social media sites

Rhodus et al. (2007)	**Web 2.0 Technology** • Podcasting (Podcast Maker, ProfCast, Odeo) • Collaborative authoring (MediaWiki) • Photo and image management (Flickr, Slide, Zoto) • Social tagging (Delicious, Blinklist, Stumbleupon) • Peer production news (Digg, Newsvine, Gabbr) • Video collections (YouTube, MetaCafe) • Blogging (Blogger, WordPress) • Content management systems (CMS) (Joomla, Drupal) • Social networking (Facebook, MySpace) • Collaborative writing (GoogleDocs, Rallypoint) • Customized search engines (Google, Yahoo Answers, IMDB) • Mapping (Wayfaring, Frappr, HousingMaps)

Mangold & Faulds (2009)	**Examples of Social Media**
	• Social networking sites (Facebook, MySpace)
	• Creativity works sharing sites:
	  o Video sharing sites (YouTube)
	  o Photo sharing sites (Flickr)
	  o Music sharing sites (Jamendo.com)
	  o Content sharing combined with assistance (Piczo.com)
	  o General intellectual property sharing sites (Creative Commons)
	• User-sponsored blogs (The Unofficial Apple Weblog, Cnet.com)
	• Company-sponsored Websites/blogs (Apple.com, P&G's Vocalpoint)
	• Company-sponsored cause/help sites (Dove's Campaign for Real Beauty, click2quit.com)
	• Invitation-only social networks (ASmallWorld.net)
	• Business networking sites (LinkedIn)
	• Collaborative websites (Wikipedia)
	• Virtual worlds (Second Life)
	• Commerce communities (eBay, Amazon.com, Craig's List, iStockphoto, Threadless.com)
	• Podcasts ("For Immediate Release: The Hobson and Holtz Report")
	• News delivery sites (Current TV)
	• Educational materials sharing (MIT OpenCourseWare, MERLOT)
	• Open Source Software communities (Mozilla's spreadfirefox.com, Linux.org)
	• Social bookmarking sites allowing users to recommend online news stories, music, videos, etc. (Digg, del.icio.us, Newsvine, Mixx it, Reddit)

Lincoln (2009)	**Key Social Media Tools** • Blogging • Microblogging • RSS • Widgets • Social networking • Chat rooms • Message boards • Podcasts • Video sharing • Photo sharing
Zarrella (2010)	**Social Media Forms** • Blogs • Micro-blogs (Twitter) • Social networks (Facebook, LinkedIn) • Media-sharing sites (YouTube, Flickr) • Social bookmarking and voting sites (Digg, Reddit) • Review sites (Yelp) • Forums • Virtual worlds (Second Life)
Kaplan & Haenlein (2010)	**Classification of Social Media** • Blogs • Collaborative projects (Wikipedia, Delicious) • Social networking sites (Facebook) • Content communities (YouTube) • Virtual social worlds (Second Life) • Virtual game wolds (World of Warcraft)

Blogs in Marketing

Blogs, short for Weblogs, are often described as online diaries (Wibbels, 2006). They are interactive and written in a conversational voice (Harris & Rae, 2011). Blogs contain a series of dated postings in reverse chronological order (Thelwall, 2008) and are frequently updated (Harris & Rae, 2011; Dacko, 2008). A blog can work as a standalone marketing tool (Harris & Rae, 2011) and also be used by individuals or organizations for marketing purposes (Dacko, 2008).

Past marketing efforts were one-way communications aimed at transmitting messages from companies to a wide group of audiences, such as advertisements. However, with blogs, companies have a chance to engage with their customers. Blogs help create a different kind of experience between the company and its customers. They enable legal conversation, which was no possible before blogging. Blogging means that companies no longer have to depend on expensive focus groups, feedback forms, e-mail, and other time wasting and boring methods of getting feedback (Wright, 2006). Thus, two-way communication via blogs can be gained.

Companies can use blogs to talk with their customers receiving feedback about their products, services and brands. Blogging means "living the brand" for Jonathan Schwartz, CEO of Sun Microsystems which is one of the most successful example of corporate blogging, and it creates an authentic voice for the organization (Lincoln, 2009).

Since blogs provide opportunities for people to voice their opinions, they also enable companies to see their organizations from customers' viewpoint. Companies letting their customers to directly communicate with them can have a more in-depth understanding of their customers' likes, dislikes, interests and concerns. In this way, marketers can find a chance to respond customers' comments. At the same time, the companies can develop more customized products and services which can meet customers' expectations (Singh et al., 2008).

Different aspects of corporate functioning in which the power of online conversation via blogging has been proved, are marketing, sales, reputation and brand management, public relations (PR), customer relationship management (CRM), human resources management (HRM) and crisis management (Pal & Kapur, 2010).

Blogs provide the following benefits for marketers, among others (Seda, 2007):

- Instantly publishing timely information.
- Creating a controllable community and conversations with readers/consumers.
- Turning negative publicity into positive publicity.
- Building your status as an expert.
- Improving your organic search rankings.
- Getting media coverage and attracting new customers.

Micro-Blogs in Marketing

Micro-blogs are a relatively new form of communication (Zhao & Rosson, 2009; Jansen et al., 2009). Microblogging is used for broadcasting information and has become popular quite quickly (Zhao & Rosson, 2009). Micro-blogs comprise of short comments or posts and these are delivered by instant messages (IM), mobile phones, e-mail or the Web (Jansen et al., 2009). Microblogging is also known as micro-sharing, micro-updating or Twittering (Jansen et al., 2009), because Twitter is now the most popular microblogging service (Jansen et al., 2009; Barnes & Böhringer, 2009).

Micro-blogs unite the characteristics of social networking and mobility, and they are smaller forms of blogs (Barnes & Böhringer, 2009). Microblogging is a compact version of blogging. There is no limitation for blogging, but microblogging is generally restricted to a specific number of characters (Beaumont, 2008). Most of the microblogging services limit the posts to 140 characters or similar (Barnes & Böhringer, 2009).

A standard micro-blog post is almost the length of a typical newspaper headline and subhead (Jansen et al., 2009). Because of this, micro-blog posts are easier to produce and consume (Jansen et al., 2009; Li & Li, 2011).

Microblogging shortens the time requirements and allotted time for thinking for content generation (Yazdanifard et al., 2011). Consequently, huge amounts of information can be generated by this way (Zhang et al., 2010).

With rapidly growing popularity, micro-blogs have become a big source of consumer ideas (Li & Li, 2011). Micro-blogs allow marketers to track trends and mine data related to the success of products, performance, or services. At the same time, micro-blogs, such as Twitter, build relationship with customers, partners and the people who are dealing with your business (Yazdanifard et al., 2011).

Dell, Carnival Cruise Lines, and JetBlue Airways are some of the corporate marketers which use Twitter. Carnival Cruise Lines uses Twitter to give company news and updates. In this context, a company responds with direct messages to all messages from followers and @CarnivalCruise messages from other users as "must answer" messages. Dell Outlet offers promotions that can only be found via Twitter (Kim, 2007).

Companies such as Cisco, Jet Blue and Whole Foods have used Twitter to communicate with employees, vendors, and customers. Companies such as Cisco, Whole Foods Market, Dell, Zappos.com and ComCast use Twitter to provide updates to customers. Companies have begun using Twitter as a free marketing research service and to get instant feedback on products and services (Safko & Brake, 2009).

Collaborative Projects in Marketing

Collaborative projects allow many different end users to create the content in a joint and simultaneous way. Collaborative projects include wikis and social bookmarking applications (Kaplan &

Haenlein, 2010). These are explained below in detail.

Wikis in Marketing

A wiki can be defined as a collection of interlinked Web pages created by collaborative effort. While wiki pages are accessed asynchronously from any Web browser, content management systems and other collaborative alternatives usually require dedicated software. Among Web 2.0 technologies, readers may be more familiar with blogs than wikis (Cronin, 2009). Indeed, wikis are very different from blogs.

Wikis are edited by as many people as possible (Quiggin, 2006), whereas blogs are owned by one person (Cronin, 2009). The documents in wikis can be written collectively, which is referred to as co-authoring. A wiki is a collection of pages consisting of hyperlinks and has a very simple relational database (Quiggin, 2006). In this context, collaborative editing and hyperlinking are two defining features of wikis (Cronin, 2009). In addition, other characteristics of wikis are history (basically saves all previous versions or modifications of any single page), recent changes (either provides a current overview of a certain number of recent changes to wiki pages or all changes within a predefined time period), sandbox (usually offers instructions and introductions on the homepage, which serves to facilitate working with the system), and search functions (offering a classic full-text or title search for the wiki pages) (Ebersbach et al., 2008). The most popular example of a wiki is *Wikipedia* (http://www.wikipedia.org/), an online encyclopedia (Quiggin, 2006).

A wiki has a wide variety of specific uses that makes it different from an encyclopedia. These uses are as follows (Mader, 2008):

- Building a peer directory.
- Creating agendas, declaring meetings and projects as a whole.
- Managing projects.

- Building a database or support sites.
- Event planning.
- Using as an intranet or extranet.
- Blogging.
- Providing external communication.
- Using as public Website.
- Using for product development.

When wikis are used in marketing, product development gains importance among these uses. A wiki is ideal for a business to manage product development to its production, marketing, and support. Product designers and engineers can use wikis to cooperate about a product's technical features, design, and basic features (Mader, 2008). Finally, wikis are one of the Web 2.0 technologies that increasingly being used within companies and organizations to make the creation and dissemination of information easy. Additionally, they facilitate effective communication with customers, partners, and the public. Wikis are also useful for providing information and gathering feedback; for example, Microsoft uses wikis to gather customer input and ideas (The Gilbane Report, 2005).

Social Bookmarking Applications in Marketing

Social bookmarking sites or services allow people to share bookmarks for Internet pages (Warr, 2008), and collect and annotate (tag[1]) their favorite Web links in an online, open environment. Social bookmarking is a perfect resource discovery tool. With social bookmarking, users can see the collective list of resources from all others, and they are the ones who share a common research interest. In this way, it helps develop communities of interest and expertise. Thanks to social bookmarking, useful connections with online resources and contacts can be created (Boulos & Wheeler, 2007).

From a corporate viewpoint, companies must be aware that social bookmarking applications are becoming the main source of information for many consumers, like wikis. Therefore, for example, "American computer software company

Adobe Systems maintains a list of bookmarks to company-related Websites and conversations on Delicious" (Kaplan & Haenlein, 2010, p. 62-63).

Marketers can use social bookmarking applications in many ways. These are as follows (Zimmerman & Sahlin, 2010):

- Improved search engine ranking.
- Inbound links.
- Increased brand visibility and traffic.
- Increased readership and membership.
- Increased earnings.
- Triggering the influential.

When social bookmarking sites are evaluated as marketing tools, content comes into prominence. It should be known that every site has its own special audience. For example, Digg, one of the popular social bookmarking sites like Del.icio.us, is popular among game and technology lovers. For successful marketing, which type of content is liked should be observed, and contents not liked should be compared (Grappone & Couzin, 2008). Marketing efforts should be planned according to this.

Content Communities in Marketing

The principal aim of content communities is the sharing of media content between users. Content communities include different media types such as text (e.g., BookCrossing), photos (e.g., Flickr), videos (e.g., YouTube), and PowerPoint presentations (e.g., Slideshare) (Kaplan & Haenlein, 2010). In our study photo and video sharing sites are emphasized.

Photo sharing Websites allow people to easy upload photographs to share with others (Hulbert, 2008), and allow them to comment and vote on other people's photos (Roberts, 2008). There are several photo-sharing services, such as Flickr and Snapfish. As one of the most popular photo-sharing sites, Flickr (OECD, 2007) hosted 6 billion photos in August 2011 (Flickr Blog, 2011).

Flickr (www.flickr.com) is described as "a poster child for Web 2.0 offering users a way to share photos easily" (Teece, 2010, p. 178). Anyone can create a profile and upload photos for sharing using Flickr. It is well trafficked and sometimes displays standard search results. Flickr can be used as a participation and engagement style of marketing. It shouldn't be thought of as a technique of aggressive selling (Grappone & Couzin, 2008). "The Nikon Digital Learning Center on Flickr is a great example of perfect alignment between a brand, its audience, and the social media platform. Here Nikon connects on the world's biggest photo-sharing service with the world's passionate photographers. Its primary purpose is not to sell cameras, but to share information, build a user community, and promote image sharing around the emerging art and science of digital photography" Funk, 2011, p. 96). From a corporate perspective, having an account on Flickr enables ranking of images for specific image-related searches on Google (Funk, 2011).

Video sharing is a similar concept to photo-sharing (Hulbert, 2008). Today, it has become more and more popular among businesses that produce their own videos to post them on the Web (Roberts, 2008).

With the launch of video sharing sites, especially YouTube, Web 2.0 marketing has changed in a big way. From a corporate viewpoint, YouTube facilitates the presentation of product advertisements easily and economically. In addition, by posting audiovisual tutorials, YouTube makes it possible to train people about product use. People can watch both commercial videos and entertaining ones using YouTube. Marketing with YouTube and other media sharing Websites have resulted in reduced advertising costs and increased product exposure worldwide. When a good video about your product is uploaded to YouTube, it rapidly generates a high page rate, which fosters traffic on the site. Besides bringing a very effective solution to a viewer's problem, a good video message will always affect viewers, which then has a positive impact on sales efforts. Watching a good video that generates people's interest will create a positive state of mind, and this will have a positive effect on Website traffic (eUKhost.com, 2008). YouTube can be used for brand awareness, product advertising, retail promotion, direct sales, product support, internal training, employee communications, and recruiting (Miller, 2011).

Social Networking Sites in Marketing

Social networking sites, one of the latest online communication tools, allow users to create a public or semi-public profile, create, and view their own as well as other users' online social networks, and interact with people in their networks. The most popular examples of social networking sites are Facebook (Subrahmanyam et al., 2008) (most visited in the world), Friendster (popular in Asia), Orkut (popular in Brazil) and Vkon-takte.ru (popular in Russia) (Semertzidis et al., 2010). Social networking sites have attracted millions of users worldwide (Ploderer et al., 2008), and many of them have integrated these sites into their daily habits (Boyd & Ellison, 2008).

Social networking sites usually offer the same basic functions: network of friends' listings, person surfing, private messaging, discussion forums or communities, event management, blogging, commenting, and media uploading (Breslin & Decker, 2007). The focus in social networking sites is on the user and the network friends of the user (Gangadharbatla, 2009). In this context, social networking sites are important for two main reasons (Schmugar, 2008, p. 28):

- Social networking sites are "the epitome of Web 2.0, in which the network of users is the platform and the community drives the content."
- Social networking sites "combine elements of communication channels—such as email, message boards, instant messaging, and chat—with media vehicles—such as audio, video, and print."

Social networking is a growing trend, and social networking sites provide user-generated content, greater interactivity between customers and businesses, and increased transparency in customer relations (Processor, 2008). In addition, social networking sites are very important in affecting public opinion on nearly every aspect of commerce. Since they reinforce word-of-mouth marketing, they are becoming increasingly important in consumer purchasing decisions. It will be useful for marketers to learn how to use these sites effectively (Red Bridge Marketing, 2008).

In fact, it is risky to market in social networking sites, because the people building online communities in these sites don't like openly commercial messages (Scott, 2007). For this reason, if social networking sites are used in the context of marketing, it is better to join the communication that occurs on these sites or to lead a community rather than to interfere in these communications.

Virtual Worlds in Marketing

Virtual worlds, such as World of Warcraft, Second Life, and so on, are three-dimensional, online environments in which many people can simultaneously interact with each other. They can dramatically change the interaction among people, their navigation of Websites, and their conduct of business (Messinger et al., 2009; Mennecke et al., 2008). World of Warcraft is an example of virtual game worlds, while Second Life is an example of virtual social worlds (Kaplan & Haenlein, 2010).

Users are graphically represented by avatars in a virtual world, which is a computer-based, simulated environment where they can inhabit space and interact. A computer-simulated virtual world is similar to the real world, especially in certain areas; for example, gravity, topography, movement, real-time actions, and communication can all be simulated. Nevertheless, the virtual world does not need to parallel the real world. Technology and the designer's imagination are the only limits of virtual worlds (Wei & Williams,

2007). Virtual worlds can be used in many ways for entertainment and business. In recent years, these 3-D spaces have a growing use in these areas (Kock, 2008).

A unique combination of characteristics has been offered by virtual worlds such as Second Life, e.g. gaming, community, and user-generated content. With the help of all these characteristics, virtual worlds offer users nearly limitless opportunities for expression, exploration, association, collaboration, and social interaction (Kelly & Rhind, 2007). Many people think that virtual worlds are only games. Nonetheless, a society where social and economic interactions are the main drivers has evolved virtual worlds beyond their entertainment and game-play features (Serbmongkolchai & Chen, 2008). Virtual worlds are now a reality, and everyone can create a digital character representing themselves and interact with other computer-generated individuals, landscapes, and even virtually-run global businesses in real-time within virtual worlds such as Second Life and Entropia Universe (Bray & Konsynski, 2007). Effective business uses of Second Life are meetings and conferences, recruiting and interviewing, prototyping and testing, marketing, training and simulations, and market research (Rufer-bach, 2009). In Second Life, marketers allow customers to become involved in their brand, interact with their products, and become engaged with helpful salespeople in a totally new and interesting way (Mahar & Mahar, 2009). On the other hand, in-game advertising can be given as an example for business use of 'World of Warcraft', like product placement in movies (Kaplan & Haenlein, 2010).

Companies are allowed to use virtual worlds to connect successfully with their users, customers, and business partners by the level of immersion and the possibility of establishing deep relationships. Virtual worlds can be used for sales and marketing (promotional virtual events can also be organized or sponsored within virtual worlds), external relations (to provide support, encourage better relationships, and build communities), and recruiting (to connect with potential employees, and conduct virtual job interviews or collect curriculum vitae to select the most promising candidates) (Artesia, 2008).

APPROPRIATE WEB 2.0 APPLICATIONS FOR THE PURPOSE OF MARKETING

Gillin (2009) suggested a number of social media tools that were appropriate for an organization to carry out its business goals. These were blogs, podcasts, videos, social networking, private communities, customer review engines, and virtual worlds. This is shown in Table 2.

Since only Kaplan and Haenlein's social media classification, which also includes microblogs, are handled in this study; podcasting, private communities, and customer review engines are not mentioned further, however, video sharing

sites are considered under the wider concept of content communities. In this context, it is appropriate to add collaborative projects and microblogs to these social media tools, in addition to the ones suggested by Gillin.

When defining Web 2.0 applications as marketing tools, Constantinides et al. (2008) divided marketing objectives into passive (listening in) and active (public relations and direct marketing, reaching the new influencers, customer as co-producer, and customer advertising concepts and product reviews). This is shown in Table 3.

In this study, the business goals suggested by Gillin (2009) are classified according to the active marketing objectives stated by Constantinides et al. (2008). Marketing research is also included in addition to those objectives stated by Constantinides et al. (2008).

While Constantinides et al. (2008) divide Web 2.0 applications into five categories; they add wikis and social bookmarking under content com-

Table 2. Gillin's (2009) suggestion for appropriate social media tools

Business Goal	Social Media Tools						
	Blog	Podcasting	Video	Social Network	Private Community	Customer Review Engine	Virtual World
Build customer community	●		●	●	●	●	●
Counter negative publicity	●	●	●			●	
Crisis management	●	●	●	●		●	●
Customer conversation	●			●	●		●
Expose employee talent	●	●	●		●		●
Generate Website traffic	●		●			●	
Humanize the company	●	●	●		●		●
Market research/focus group testing	●			●	●	●	●
Media relations	●	●	●			●	●
Generate new product ideas	●		●	●	●		●
Product promotion	●	●	●	●		●	●
Product support/customer service	●	●	●		●		
Product/service feedback	●			●	●		
Recuit brand advocates	●		●	●	●		●
Sales leads	●	●	●	●		●	●

Source: Gillin, 2009.

munities together with photo and video sharing sites. In our study, photo and video sharing sites are handled under content communities, whereas wikis and social bookmarking sites are handled under collaborative projects.

Appropriate Web 2.0 applications for implementing marketing objectives are shown in Table 4.

Blogs are very suitable for public relations and direct marketing, marketing research and reaching the new influencers, while micro-blogs are very suitable for public relations and direct marketing, reaching the new influencers and customer advertising concepts and product reviews. Social networking sites are very suitable for marketing research and customer as co-producer while collaborative projects are very suitable for customer as co-producer. Content communities are very suitable for marketing research and customer advertising concepts and product reviews, while virtual worlds are only very suitable for customer as co-producer.

Each of the Web 2.0 applications evaluated as marketing tools is shown in Table 5.

CONCLUSION AND RECOMMENDATIONS FOR FURTHER RESEARCH

In the evolution of the Internet, Web 2.0 applications seem to be the new stage. These applications are suitable for using new forms of interactive, one-to-one marketing (Constantinides & Fountain, 2008). Web 2.0 applications are new, complementary marketing channels, but will likely not completely replace traditional marketing, such as TV advertisements (Bryant, 2008).

Web 2.0 applications provide a more participative, collaborative, and sharing marketing environment. All Web 2.0 applications, from blogs to micro-blogs, collaborative projects to content communities, social networking sites to virtual worlds, can be used for more targeted and effective marketing, so it will be useful to integrate them with traditional marketing. In developing marketing strategies, it is important to take into consideration Web 2.0 applications.

Blogs are strong marketing tools in terms of receiving transparent feedback from customers. They are one of the most suitable Web 2.0 applications for countering negative publicity, crisis management, and generating Website traffic. Micro-blogs are one of the most suitable marketing

Table 3. Suggestion of Constantinides and his colleagues (2008) for Web 2.0 applications as marketing tools

Marketing Objective	Application Type				
	Weblogs	(Content) Communities	Social Networks	Forums/Bulletin Boards	Content Aggregators
Passive					
Listening In	XXX	XX	X	XXX	
Active					
Public relations and direct marketing	XXX	X	XX	X	XX
Reaching the new influencers	XXX			X	XXX
Customer advertising concepts and product reviews	XX	XXX	X	XX	
Customer as co-producer	X	XXX	XX	XXX	

Source: Constantinides et al. 2008

Note: XXX: very suitable; XX: suitable; X: suitable sometimes.

Table 4. Appropriate Web 2.0 applications for marketing objectives

Marketing Objectives	Appropriate Web 2.0 Applications					
	Blog	Micro-blogs	Collaborative Projects	Social Networking Sites	Content Communities	Virtual World
Public Relations and Direct Marketing	XXX	XXX	X	XX	XX	XX
Media relations	●				●	●
Product promotion	●	●	●	●	●	●
Counter negative publicity	●				●	
Crisis management	●	●		●	●	●
Customer conversation	●	●		●		●
Expose employee talent	●		●		●	●
Humanize the company	●	●			●	●
Sales leads	●	●		●	●	●
Product support/customer service	●	●	●		●	
Marketing Research	XXX	XX	XX	XXX	XXX	XX
Generate Website traffic	●	●	●	●	●	
Market research/focus group testing	●	●		●		●
Reaching the New Influencers	XXX	XXX		X	X	X
Recruit brand advocates	●	●		●	●	●
Customer Advertising Concepts and Product Reviews	X	XXX	X	X	XXX	
Product/service feedback	●	●	●	●	●	
Customer as Co-Producer	X	XX	XXX	XXX	XX	XXX
Build customer community	●	●		●	●	●
Generate new product ideas	●	●	●	●	●	●

Source: Adapted from Gillin, 2009; Constantinides et al. 2008.
Note: XXX: very suitable; XX: suitable; X: suitable sometimes.

tools for getting the information and spreading it, and at the same time, they are the strongest Web 2.0 application for getting instant feedback about products, services and brand. While it is quite easy to use micro-blogs, the difficulty of expression is their weak side. The most important reason for this is the fact that the posts are limited to 140 characters.

Collaborative projects are strong marketing tools for facilitating search engine marketing and search engine optimization. However, the difficulty of selecting the correct keywords, as well as producing attractive content, is their weak side. They are very suitable for generating new product ideas. While social networking sites are very suitable Web 2.0 applications in terms of market research/focus group testing and building customer community, controlling the communication that takes place is the most difficult aspect of them. Content communities are very effective in generating Website traffic, as well as educating customers about products. Virtual worlds are very useful new places to improve interaction, building customer community and generating new product ideas.

Table 5. Evaluation of Web 2.0 applications as marketing tools

Web 2.0 Applications	Main Uses	Strengths	Weaknesses
Blogs	Informing of current events Informing of new products and services	Transparent feedback from customers	Require time and constant updating
Micro-blogs	Informing of company news and updates Informing of current and new products and services Promoting your products and services, special deals, discounts etc. Free marketing research service	Getting instant feedback on products and services Ease of spreading and getting the information about company and brand	Difficulty of expression
Collaborative Projects	Product development Informing of new products Developing communities of interest and expertise	Collaborative efforts Facilitating search engine marketing and search engine optimization	Difficulty of providing attractive content Difficulty of finding correct keywords as well as attractive content
Content Communities	Maintaining customer relationships Brand building	Training customers about product	Difficulty of providing audio and image of good quality
Social Networking Sites	Content sharing Creating and maintaining relationships	Building communities (especially brand communities) Market research about product, brand, and company focusing on a specific group Revealing new products	Control over communication is the most difficult
Virtual Worlds	Providing support about products and services Revealing new products Encouraging customer relationships Building communities	Building brand loyalty Providing new places for more effective interaction Building a conversation with customers	Meeting expectations is very difficult

Source: Adapted from Lehtimäki et al., 2009.

Companies should make considerable effort in using social media and being social. As Kaplan and Haenlein (2010) state:

- Be careful when choosing social media applications. Choosing the right application ensures that the message reach the right consumers.
- The most appropriate social media applications should be chosen or developed. For example, a social network for creating a private community could be established.
- Align all social media applications.
- Maintain integration of traditional media and social media.

- Ensure that all employees have access to social media applications.
- Be active. The content should be fresh, encouraging businesses to engage in discussions with customers.
- Be interesting. It will be impossible to connect with customers if you don't keep their interest.
- Be polite. Don't make others using social media feel that you know more than they do.
- Engage users by establishing common ground.
- Be honest. Avoid giving incorrect or inaccurate information. Always be truthful.

If Web 2.0 applications are to be used as effective marketing tools, the following suggestions can be useful:

- Use influencers.
- Listen to your audience. Let them know you value their opinions and ideas.
- Manage content effectively.
- Choose effective keywords.
- Be consistent and transparent.

It would be useful for future studies to evaluate the marketing dimension of Web 2.0 applications using empirical methods, to measure to what extent these applications support the literature presented here. It will be beneficial to quantify the effect of each Web 2.0 application, used as marketing tools, on the purchasing decisions of consumers. In the meantime, studies measuring the attitudes of consumers towards marketing activities via these Web 2.0 applications can be conducted. Consumer behaviors using the most effective or popular Web 2.0 applications users could also be researched.

REFERENCES

Akar, E. (2009). Web 2.0'la Değişen Pazarlama ve Yeni Kuralları. *Pazarlama ve İletişim Kültürü Dergisi. Bahar*, *02*, 50–55.

Akar, E. (2010). *Sosyal Medya Pazarlaması*. Ankara, Turkey: Efil Yayınevi.

Anderson, P. (2007). What is Web 2.0? Ideas, technologies and implications for education. *JISC Technology and Standards Watch*. Retrieved January 15, 2011, from http://www.jisc.ac.uk/media/documents/techwatch/tsw0701b.pdf

Artesia (2008). *Introduction to Virtual Worlds*. Retrieved January 15, 2011, from http://www.scribd.com/doc/5570819/Introduction-to-virtual-worlds

Barnes, S. J., & Böhringer, M. (2009). Continuance Usage Intention in Microblogging services: The Case of Twitter. In *Proceedings of the 17th European Conference on Information Systems (ECIS)*. Verona, Italy: ECIS. Retrieved July 18, 2010, from http://www.ecis2009.it/papers/ecis2009-0164.pdf

Beaumont, C. (2008). Tweet, tweet, here comes Twitter. *The Telegraph*. Retrieved February 11, 2012, from http://www.telegraph.co.uk/technology/3357007/Tweet-tweet-here-comes-Twitter.html

Borges, B. (2009). *Marketing 2.0 Bridging the Gap between Seller and Buyer through Social Media Marketing*. Tucson, AZ: Wheatmark.

Boulos, M. N. K., & Wheeler, S. (2007). The emerging Web 2.0 social software: An enabling suite of sociable technologies in health and health care education. *Health Information and Libraries Journal*, *24*, 2–23. doi:10.1111/j.1471-1842.2007.00701.x PMID:17331140.

Boyd, D. M., & Ellison, N. B. (2008). Social Network Sites: Definition, History, and Scholarship. *Journal of Computer-Mediated Communication*, *13*, 210–230. doi:10.1111/j.1083-6101.2007.00393.x.

Bray, D. A., & Konsynski, B. R. (2007). Virtual Worlds: Opportunities for Multi-Disciplinary Research. Draft Version: Final Version to appear in The Data Base for Advances in Information Systems, *SIGMIS Database. Special Issue on Virtual Worlds*, *38*(4), 17–25.

Breslin, J., & Decker, S. (2007). The Future of Social Networks on the Internet The Need for Semantics. *IEEE Internet Computing*, (November-December): 86–90. doi:10.1109/MIC.2007.138.

Bruns, A., & Bahnisch, M. (2009). Social Media: Tools for User-Generated Content Social Drivers behind Growing Consumer Participation in User-Led Content Generation. *State of the Art*. Retrieved May 18, 2011, from http://www.smartservicescrc. com.au/PDF/Social_Media_State_of_the%20 Art_March2009.pdf

Bryant, S. C. (2008). A Strategic Framework for Integrating Web 2.0 into the Marketing Mix. In Deans, P. C. (Ed.), *Social Software and Web 2.0 Technology Trends* (pp. 29–43). New York: Information Science Reference. doi:10.4018/978-1-60566-122-3.ch003.

Constantinides, E. (2004). Influencing the online consumer's behavior: The Web experience. *Internet Research*, *14*(2), 111–126. doi:10.1108/10662240410530835.

Constantinides, E., & Fountain, S. J. (2008). Web 2.0: Conceptual foundations and marketing issues. *Journal of Direct, Data and Digital Marketing Practice. Special Issue Papers*, *9*(3), 231–244.

Constantinides, E., Romero, C. L., & Boria, M. A. G. (2008). Social Media: A New Frontier for Retailers? *European Retail Research*, *22*, 1–28.

Cronin, J. J. (2009). Upgrading to Web 2.0: An Experiential Project to Build a Marketing Wiki. *Journal of Marketing Education*, *31*(1), 66–75. doi:10.1177/0273475308329250.

D'Angelo, J. M. (2010). *Spa Business Strategies: A Plan for Success* (2nd ed.). Milady.

Dacko, S. G. (2008). *Advanced Dictionary of Marketing: Putting Theory to Use*. Oxford, UK: Oxford University Press.

Ebersbach, A., Glaser, M., Heigl, R., & Warta, A. (2008). *Wiki Web Collaboration (2nded.)*. Berlin, Germany: Springer Verlag.

eUKhost.com. (2008). *What does YouTube Videos Mean To Internet Marketers?* Retrieved January 15, 2011, from http://blog.eukhost.com/web-hosting/what-does-youtube-mean-to-internet-marketers/

Flickr Blog. (2011, August 4). *6,000,000,000*. Retrieved February 25, 2012, from http://blog. flickr.net/en/2011/08/04/6000000000/

Fox, S. (2009). *e-Riches 2.0: Next-Generation Marketing Strategies for Making Millions Online*. New York: Amacom.

Funk, T. (2011). *Social Media Playbook for Business: Reaching Your Online Community with Twitter, Facebook, LinkedIn, and More*. Santa Barbara, CA: Praeger.

Gangadharbatla, H. (2009). Individual Differences in Social Networking Site Adoption. In Romm-Livermore, C., & Setzekorn, K. (Eds.), *Social Networking Communities and E-Dating Services: Concepts and Implications* (pp. 1–17). Hershey, PA: IGI Global. doi:10.4018/978-1-60566-984-7.ch101.

Gillin, P. (2009). *Secrets of Social Media Marketing*. Fresno, CA: Quill Driver Books.

Grappone, J., & Couzin, G. (2008). *Search Engine Optimization: An Hour A Day* (2nd ed.). Hoboken, NJ: Wiley Publishing.

Halligan, B., & Shah, D. (2010). *Inbound Marketing*. Hoboken, NJ: Wiley Publishing.

Hardey, M. (2008). Public health and Web 2.0. *The Journal of the Royal Society for the Promotion of Health*, *128*(4), 181–189. doi:10.1177/1466424008092228 PMID:18678114.

Harris, L., & Rae, A. (2011). Building a personal brand through social networking. *The Journal of Business Strategy*, *32*(5), 14–21. doi:10.1108/02756661111165435.

Hulbert, J. M. (2008). *Defining Relevancy: Managing the New Academic Library*. Oxford, UK: Harcourt Education.

Jansen, B. J., Zhang, M., Sobel, K., & Chowdury, A. (2009). Twitter Power: Tweets as Electronic Word of Mouth. *Journal of the American Society for Information Science and Technology*, *60*(11), 2169–2188. doi:10.1002/asi.21149.

Kaplan, A. M., & Haenlein, M. (2010). Users of the world, unite! The challenges and opportunities of Social Media. *Business Horizons*, *53*, 59–68. doi:10.1016/j.bushor.2009.09.003.

Kaplan, A. M., & Haenlein, M. (2011). The early bird catches the news: Nine things you should know about micro-blogging. *Business Horizons*, *54*, 105–113. doi:10.1016/j.bushor.2010.09.004.

Kelly, T. S., & Rhind, A. (2007). Marketing in Second Life and Other Virtual Worlds. *Media Contacts-Havas Digital*, October. Retrieved January 15, 2011, from http://www.mediacontacts.com/images/common/mc-insight/mc_insight_outubro.pdf

Kim, P. (2007, October 16). Microblogging For Marketers. *Forrester*. Retrieved July 18, 2010, from http://captivatingconnections.typepad.com/captivating_connections/files/051104355000.pdf

Kock, N. (2008). E-Collaboration and E-Commerce In Virtual Worlds: The Potential of Second Life and World of Warcraft. *International Journal of e-Collaboration*, *4*(3), 1–13. doi:10.4018/jec.2008070101.

Kotler, P., & Keller, K. L. (2006). *Marketing Management* (12th ed.) Ed. Upper Saddle River, NJ: Prentice Hall.

Krämer, K. (2006). Web 2.0 for the Enterprise. *YMC*. Retrieved January 15, 2011, from www.ymc.ch/content/download/487693/3301925/file/web20_for_the_enterprise_2008.pdf

Lee, M. R., & Lan, Y.-C. (2007). From Web 2.0 to Conversational Knowledge Management: Towards Collaborative Intelligence. *Journal of Entrepreneurship Research*, *2*(2), 47–62.

Lehtimäki, T., Salo, J., Hiltula, H., & Lankinen, M. (2009). Harnessing Web 2.0 for Business to Business Marketing - Literature Review and an Empirical Perspective from Finland. Working paper, Faculty of Economics and Business Administration, University of Oulu, Finland.

Li, Y.-M., & Li, T.-Y. (2011). Deriving Marketing Intelligence over Microblogs. In *Proceedings of the 44th Hawaii International Conference on System Sciences*. Koloa, HI: IEEE. Retrieved February 13, 2012, from http://www.lancs.ac.uk/ug/wilkina4/__files/Deriving%20Marketing%20Intelligence%20over%20Microblogs.pdf

Lincoln, S. R. (2009). *Mastering Web 2.0, Transform your business using key website and social media tools*. London: Kogan Page.

Mader, S. (2008). *Wikipatterns*. Indianapolis, IN: Wiley Publishing.

Mahar, S. M., & Mahar, J. (2009). *The Unofficial Guide to Building Your Business in the Second Life Virtual World*. New York: Amacom.

Mangold, W. G., & Faulds, D. J. (2009). Social media: The new hybrid element of the promotion mix. *Business Horizons*, *52*, 357–365. doi:10.1016/j.bushor.2009.03.002.

Marketing Charts. (2008). *Study: Web 2.0 Awesome for Integrating Brand and Direct Marketing*. Retrieved May 15, 2011, from http://www.marketingcharts.com/direct/study-web-20-awesome-for-integrating-brand-and-direct-marketing-4429/

Mennecke, B. E., McNeill, D., Ganis, M., Roche, E. M., Bray, D. A., Konsynski, B., et al. (2008). Second Life and Other Virtual Worlds: A Roadmap for Research. *Communications of the Association for Information Systems (CAIS), Article 20, 22*, 371-388. Retrieved January 15, 2011, from http://www.bus.iastate.edu/mennecke/CAIS-Vol22-Article20.pdf

Messinger, P. R., Stroulia, E., Lyons, K., Bone, M., Niu, R. H., Smirnov, K., & Perelgut, S. (2009). Virtual worlds -past, present, and future: New directions in social computing. *Decision Support Systems*, *47*(3), 204–228. doi:10.1016/j.dss.2009.02.014.

Miller, M. (2011). *YouTube for Business* (2nd ed.). Upper Saddle River, NJ: Que Publishing.

O'Reilly, T. (2005). What Is Web 2.0 Design Patterns and Business Models for the Next Generation of Software. *O'Reilly Network*. Retrieved January 15, 2011, from http://facweb.cti.depaul.edu/jnowotarski/se425/What%20Is%20Web%202%20point%200.pdf

OECD. (2007). *Participative Web and User-created Content Web 2.0, Wikis And Social Networking*. Paris, France: OECD Publications.

Pal, S. K., & Kapur, V. (2010). Blog Marketing Strategies for Mature and Emerging Markets. *International Journal of Innovation. Management and Technology*, *1*(4), 411–418.

Parise, S., & Guinan, P. J. (2008). Marketing Using Web 2.0. In *Proceedings of the 41st Hawaii International Conference on System Sciences*. Waikoloa, HI: IEEE.

Petrassi, J. (2008). Web 2.0 – Potential Impact On Business. *CSC Global Business Solutions, CSC Papers*. Retrieved January 15, 2011, from http://assets1.csc.com/lef/downloads/Web_Potential.pdf

Ploderer, B., Howard, S., & Thomas, P. (2008). Being Online, Living Offline: The Influence of Social Ties over the Appropriation of Social Network Sites. In *Proceedings of CSCW 2008*. Retrieved January 15, 2011, from http://disweb.dis.unimelb.edu.au/student/rhd/berndp/research/CSCW2008Ploderer.pdf

Postman, J. (2009). *SocialCorp: Social Media Goes Corporate*. Upper Saddle River, NJ: New Riders.

PR. *Week*. (2010). *Social Media Survey: The Social Connection*. Retrieved May 18, 2011, from http://www.mslworldwide.com/library/SocialMediaSurvey.pdf

Processor (2008). Social Networking Sites Pose New Opportunities. General Information. *Processor, 30*(48). Retrieved January 15, 2011, from http://s3.amazonaws.com/lyro-production/bf161e8907f9a079e0270230df68d594%2FSocial-Networking-Sites-Pose-New-Opportunities.pdf

Quiggin, J. (2006). Blogs, wikis and creative innovation. *International Journal of Cultural Studies*, *9*(4), 481–496. doi:10.1177/1367877906069897.

Red Bridge Marketing. (2008). *Social Network Marketing: The Basics*. Retrieved January 15, 2011, from http://www.redbridgemarketing.com/social_networking_the_basics.pdf

Rhodus, T., Buchem, V. V., & Witney, B. (2007). Web 2.0: Building Online Communities Using Social Networking Technologies. *The Buckeye*. Retrieved January 15, 2011, from http://webgarden.osu.edu/buckeye2007.pdf

Roberts, R. R. (2008). *Walk Like a Giant, Sell Like a Madman*. Hoboken, NJ: WileyPublishing.

Rufer-bach, K. (2009). *The Second Life Grid The Official Guide to Communication, Collaboration, and Community Engagement*. Indianapolis, IN: Wiley Publishing.

Safko, L., & Brake, D. K. (2009). *The Social Media Bible*. Hoboken, NJ: Wiley Publishing.

Schmugar, C. (2008). The Future of Social Networking Sites. *McAfee Security Journal*, Fall, 28-30.

Scott, D. M. (2007). *The New Rules of Marketing and PR: How to Use News Releases, Blogs, Podcasting, Viral Marketing and Online Media to Reach Buyers Directly*. Hoboken, NJ: Wiley Publishing.

Seda, C. (2007). *How to Win Sales & Influence Spiders: Boosting Your Business & Buzz on the Web (Voices That Matter)* (1st ed.). Berkeley, CA: New Riders Press.

Semertzidis, T., Daras, P., & Ballesteros, I. L. (2010). Social Networks Overview: Current Trends and Research Challenges. *European Commission, Information Society and Media*. Retrieved February 25, 2012, from http://cordis. europa.eu/fp7/ict/netmedia/docs/publications/ social-networks.pdf

Serbmongkolchai, V., & Chen, X. (2008). *v-Business model in virtual world Second Life case study*. Master's Thesis, Lund University, Sweden. Retrieved January 15, 2011, from http:// biblioteket.ehl.lu.se/olle/papers/0003119.pdf

Singh, T., Veron-Jackson, L., & Cullinane, J. (2008). Blogging: A new play in your marketing game plan. *Business Horizons*, *51*, 281–292. doi:10.1016/j.bushor.2008.02.002.

Smith, G. (2008). *Tagging People-Powered Metadata for the Social Web*. Berkeley, CA: New Riders.

Stelzner, A. M. (2011). 2011 Social Media Marketing Industry Report. *Social Media Examiner*, April. Retrieved May 18, 2011, from http://www. socialmediaexaminer.com/SocialMediaMarketingReport2011.pdf

Subrahmanyam, K., Reich, S. M., Waechter, N., & Espinoza, G. (2008). Online and offline social networks: Use of social networking sites by emerging adults. *Journal of Applied Developmental Psychology*, *29*, 420–433. doi:10.1016/j. appdev.2008.07.003.

Teece, D. J. (2010). Business Models, Business Strategy and Innovation. *Long Range Planning*, *43*, 172–194. doi:10.1016/j.lrp.2009.07.003.

Thackeray, R., Neiger, B. L., Hanson, C. L., & McKenzie, J. F. (2008). Enhancing Promotional Strategies Within Social Marketing Programs: Use of Web 2.0 Social Media. *Health Promotion Practice*, *9*(4), 338–343. doi:10.1177/1524839908325335 PMID:18936268.

The Gilbane Report. (2005). Blogs & Wikis: Technologies For Enterprise Applications? *12*(10). Retrieved January 15, 2011, from http://gilbane. com/artpdf/GR12.10.pdf

Thelwall, M. (2008). No place for news in social network web sites? *Online Information Review*, *32*(6), 726–744. doi:10.1108/14684520810923908.

Tredinnick, L. (2006). Web 2.0 and Business: A pointer to the intranets of the future? *Business Information Review*, *23*(4), 228–234. doi:10.1177/0266382106072239.

Warr, W. A. (2008). Social software: fun and games, or business tools? *Journal of Information Science*, *34*(4), 591–604. doi:10.1177/0165551508092259.

Wei, L., & Williams, M.-A. (2007). Strategies For Business In Virtual Worlds: Case Studies In Second Life. Retrieved January 15, 2011, from http://www.pacis-net.org/file/2008/PACIS2008_ Camera-Ready_Paper_198.pdf

Wibbels, A. (2006). *Blog Wild A Guide For Small Business Blogging*. New York: Penguin Group Inc..

Wright, J. (2006). *Blog Marketing*. New York: McGraw-Hill.

Yazdanifard, R., Obeidy, W. K., Yusoff, W. F. W., & Babaei, H. R. (2011). Social Networks and Microblogging: The Emerging Marketing Trends & Tools of the Twenty-first Century. In *Proceedings of International Conference on Computer Communication and Management.*Singapore:IACSIT Press, Singapore.

Zarrella, D. (2010). *The Social Media Marketing Book*. Sebastopol, Canada: O'Reilly Media, Inc..

Zhang, J., Qu, Y., Cody, J., & Wu, Y. (2010). A Case Study of Micro-blogging in the Enterprise: Use, Value, and Related Issues. Retrieved July 18, 2010, from http://networkcrowds.files.wordpress.com/2010/03/pap1633-zhang.pdf

Zhao, D., & Rosson, M. B. (2009). How and Why People Twitter: The Role that Microblogging Plays in Informal Communication at Work. In *Proceedings of GROUP 2009*. Sanibel Island, FL: ACM. Retrieved February 11, 2012, from http://www.personal.psu.edu/duz108/blogs/publications/group09%20microblogging.pdf

Zimmerman, J., & Sahlin, D. (2010). *Social Media Marketing All-In-One For Dummies*. Indianapolis, IN: Wiley Publishing. doi:10.1002/9781118257661.

ADDITIONAL READING

Boulaire, C., Hervet, G., & Graf, R. (2010). Creativity chains and playing in the crossfire on the video-sharing site YouTube. *Journal of Research in Interactive Marketing*, *4*(2), 111–141. doi:10.1108/17505931011051669.

Brown, J., Broderick, A. J., & Lee, N. (2007). Word of mouth communication within online communities: Conceptualizing the online social network. *Journal of Interactive Marketing*, *21*(3), 2–20. doi:10.1002/dir.20082.

Carter, S. (2009). *The New Language of Marketing 2.0: How to Use ANGELS to Energize Your Market*. New York: IBM Press.

Chen, Y., Fay, S., & Wang, Q. (2011). The Role of Marketing in Social Media: How Online Consumer Reviews Evolve. *Journal of Interactive Marketing*, *25*, 85–94. doi:10.1016/j.intmar.2011.01.003.

Clemons, E. K. (2009). The complex problem of monetizing virtual electronic social networks. *Decision Support Systems*, *48*, 46–56. doi:10.1016/j.dss.2009.05.003.

Funk, T. (2009). *Web 2.0 and Beyond: Understanding the New Online Business Models, Trends, and Technologies*. London: Praeger.

Gajendra, S., Sun, W., & Ye, Q. (2010). Second Life: A Strong Communication Tool in Social Networking and Business. *Information Technology Journal*, *9*, 524–534. doi:10.3923/itj.2010.524.534.

Gillin, P. (2007). *The New Influencers, A Marketer's Guide To The New Social Media*. Chicago, IL: Linden Publishing.

Harden, L., & Heyman, B. (2009). *Digital Engagement*. New York: Amacom.

Hargittai, E. (2007). Whose Space? Differences Among Users and Non-Users of Social Network Site. *Journal of Computer-Mediated Communication*, *13*(1), 276–297. doi:10.1111/j.1083-6101.2007.00396.x.

Heinone, K. (2011). Consumer activity in social media: Managerial approaches to consumers' social media behavior. *Journal of Consumer Behaviour*, *10*, 356–364. doi:10.1002/cb.376.

Herring, S., Scheidt, L., Bonus, S., & Wright, E. (2004). *Bridging the gap: A genre analysis of weblogs*. Paper Presented at the 37th Annual HICSS Conference. Big Island, Hawaii.

Hsu, C. L., & Lin, J. C. C. (2008). Acceptance of blog usage: The roles of technology acceptance, social influence and knowledge sharing motivation. *Information & Management, 45*(1), 65–74. doi:10.1016/j.im.2007.11.001.

Jain, A. (2007). *The 4Ps of Blog Marketing.* Retrieved January 15, 2011, from http://www.livemint.com/2007/10/20005256/the-4ps-of-blog-marketing.html

Kim, W., Jeong, O.-R., & Lee, S.-W. (2010). On Social Websites. *Information Systems, 35,* 215–236. doi:10.1016/j.is.2009.08.003.

Kwon, O., & Wen, Y. (2010). An empirical study of the factors affecting social network service use. *Computers in Human Behavior, 26*(2), 254–264. doi:10.1016/j.chb.2009.04.011.

McKinsey. (2007). How business are using Web 2.0: A McKinsey Global Survey. *The McKinsey Quarterly.*

Newman, A., & Thomas, J. (2009). *Enterprise 2.0 Implementation: Integrate Web 2.0 Services into Your Enterprise.* New York: McGraw Hill.

Pace, S. (2008). YouTube: An opportunity for consumer narrative analysis? *Qualitative Market Research: An International Journal, 11*(2), 213–226. doi:10.1108/13522750810864459.

Pinho, J. C. M. R., & Soares, A. M. (2011). Examining the technology acceptance model in the adoption of social networks. *Journal of Research in Interactive Marketing, 5*(2/3), 116–129. doi:10.1108/17505931111187767.

Reyneke, M., Pitt, L., & Berthon, P. R. (2011). Luxury wine brand visibility in social media: An exploratory study. *International Journal of Wine Business Research, 23*(1), 21–35. doi:10.1108/17511061111121380.

Royo-Vela, M., & Casamassima, P. (2011). The influence of belonging to virtual brand communities on consumers' affective commitment, satisfaction and word-of-mouth advertising The ZARA case. *Online Information Review, 35*(4), 517–542. doi:10.1108/14684521111161918.

Shi, N., Lee, M., Cheung, C., & Chen, H. (2010). The Continuance of Online Social Networks. In *Proceedings of the 43rd Hawaii International Conference on System Sciences.* Koloa, HI: IEEE.

Shields, L., Victor, S., Isobe, G., Hyung, K. J., & Wakeford, I. (2009). What Managers Need to Know About Web 2.0 (and a little 3). *Information Systems McGill MBA, Japan.* Retrieved January 15, 2011, from http://www.scribd.com/doc/8120640/What-Managers-Need-to-Know-About-Web-20-and-a-little-3

Shuen, A. (2008). *Web 2.0: A Strategy Guide: Business thinking and strategies behind successful Web 2.0 implementations* (1st ed.). Sebastopol, CA: O'Reilly.

Singh, T., Veron-Jackson, L. & Joe Cullinane, J. (2008). Blogging: A new play in your marketing game plan, *Business Horizons,* 51, 281-292.

Smith, P. R., & Zook, Z. (2011). *Marketing Communications Integrating offline and online with social media* (5th ed.). London: Kogan Page.

Tuten, T. L. (2008). *Advertising 2.0: Social Media Marketing in A Web 2.0 World.* London: Praeger.

Valck, K. D., Bruggen, G. H. V., & Wierenga, B. (2009). Virtual communities: A marketing perspective. *Decision Support Systems, 47,* 185–203. doi:10.1016/j.dss.2009.02.008.

VanRysdam, P., & Goldfarb, B. (2010). *Marketing in a Web 2.0 World: Using Social Media, Webinars, Blogs, and More to Boost Your Small Business on a Budget.* Ocala, FL: Atlantic Publishing Group.

Weinberg, T. (2009). *The New Community Rules: Marketing on the Social Web*. Sebastopol, CA: O'Reilly.

Wong, W. W., & Gupta, S. C. (2011). Plastic Surgery Marketing in a Generation of Tweeting. *Aesthetic Surgery Journal*, *31*(8), 972–976. doi:10.1177/1090820X11423764 PMID:22065887.

Wyld, D. C. (2010). A Second Life for organizations?: Managing in the new, virtual world. *Management Research Review*, *33*(6), 529–562. doi:10.1108/01409171011050181.

Xiang, Z., & Gretzel, U. (2010). Role of social media in online travel information search. *Tourism Management*, *31*, 179–188. doi:10.1016/j.tourman.2009.02.016.

KEY TERMS AND DEFINITIONS

Blog: Short for Weblog, it is an advanced genre of Website which involves short and regular entries in reverse chronological order. It supports embedded links and readers can comment on it.

Micro-Blog: A kind of blog which allows more frequent updates and sharing more abstract entries, for example 140-characters-long posts. One can also share short messages, images, videos, etc.

Podcast: Audio or video files which are downloaded to computers or mobile devices or iPods from the Internet for listening or viewing them later.

Really Simple Syndication, or Rich Site Summary (RSS): A Web feed format which presents all updates in a systematic way.

Social Bookmarking: Social bookmarking is an online version of Web browser bookmarking. Users can store, share, and categorize links of favorite Web pages on the internet using tags.

Social Media: The social or functional aspect of Web 2.0, which allows creation and sharing of user-generated content (video, audio, text, etc.) through social interactions.

Social Networking Site: A site that allows people to create and develop social relationships and social networks. Through these online networking sites, users can share information, photos, videos, audio, etc. Users create their own profile pages containing details about themselves, and this serves as a link for interacting with others.

Tag: A 'tag' is a keyword attached to a piece of information. The tag enables others to quickly identify the photo, video, etc.

Web 2.0: Web-based technologies and applications which facilitate user participation, experience and cooperation, and allow collective sharing of information.

Wiki: A collaborative Website in which participants can create and edit content. It is used collaboratively by multiple users.

ENDNOTES

[1] This study is improved version of the original, which was presented by Asst. Prof. Dr. Erkan AKAR with Mete KARAYEL at the 2nd International Conference on Social Sciences (ICSS) 2009 held in İzmir, Turkey

[2]. A tag is a keyword added to a digital object, such as a Website, photo, video clip, among others, in order to describe it (Anderson, 2007). Tagging, as it is known today, provides easy to access to data and services and extends existing technology with a social component (Smith, 2008).

Chapter 10
Two–Sided Markets and Social Media

Xiaojing Lu
Shanghai Jiao Tong University, China

Ronald E. Goldsmith
Florida State University, USA

Margherita Pagani
Bocconi University, Italy

ABSTRACT

This chapter introduces the concept of "two-sided" markets and shows how they comprise a unique type of social media that facilitates the development of social networks oriented toward specific product domains (e.g., restaurants), specific brands (e.g., Starbucks), or common consumer concerns (e.g., Yelp.com). Not only do two-sided-markets constitute a unique type of Website, they can be integrated with or linked to other social media, thereby enriching the value of both the two-sided market and its partner(s). Because a two-sided market increases in value for all three parties that constitute it (consumers, the platform, and vendors) as the number of both vendors and consumer participants grows, platform managers are eager to use incentive strategies to encourage consumers to increase their active use of the site. Among these incentive strategies are various reward programs that stimulate use by rewarding consumers who add content, post reviews, comment on others' reviews, and more. Part of this chapter describes two online experiments that demonstrate that two types of common reward programs, monetary and social rewards (Heyman & Ariely, 2004), are effective in stimulating consumer intent to use the site more actively than without a reward. Finally, we make several suggestions for integrating two-sided markets into other social media, and we propose several avenues for future research into this topic that should increase our understanding of how consumers behave in two-sided markets and how platform managers can both enhance active use and use the information derived from this use.

DOI: 10.4018/978-1-4666-4026-9.ch010

INTRODUCTION

The purpose of this chapter is to present the concept of "two-sided" markets and to show how they can be integrated into the larger e-business framework formed by social media and social networks. Briefly, two-sided markets are online-platforms or websites that link sellers with buyers by enabling the former to promote their products (stores, services, etc.) to buyers who are enabled and encouraged to review, comment, and discuss these vendors on the site in the form of blogs or discussion groups. Thus, a two-sided market benefits all three partners (consumers, platform, and vendors) and can be seen as a type of social medium. We discuss how such websites can be integrated into existing social networks and how they can be managed as such. Moreover, we propose that websites created as two-sided markets can encourage consumers to become actively engaged in the exchanges by contributing to the site that form the core value of the website, by rewarding them to do so, and we present experimental evidence that such tactics would work.

The following sections of this chapter will achieve this purpose by first describing many of the prevalent types of social media and the social networks that they make possible. Two-sided markets are a type of social media, but since this concept ultimately is derived from the field of economics (Rochet & Tirole, 2003), social media are usually not described in this way. Next, we describe two-sided markets in more detail, explaining how they form a type of social network of users and vendors. This understanding lays the foundation for our subsequent discussion. Because the value and utility of two-sided markets are derived largely from the number of users and vendors who participate in them, we focus on ways in which managers of the platforms that are integral to the two-sided markets can entice active use of them. Then, we present evidence from two experimental studies showing that simple reward programs might be able to enhance user active participation in the web site, thus improving its satisfaction for users and increasing the value of the website for the vendors. We conclude with some ideas for integrating two-sided market into existing social media and some suggestions for future research into this important topic. We feel that two-sided markets are an important type of social medium that deserves to be studied.

SOCIAL MEDIA AND SOCIAL NETWORKS

Social Media: Classification and Main Features

Social media can be defined as a group of Internet-based applications that allow the creation and exchange of user-generated content (Kaplan & Haenlein, 2010). As described in Table 1 we can classify six different types of social media according to their self-presentation/self disclosure and social presence/media richness levels: (1) collaborative projects; (2) blogs and micro-blogs; (3) content communities; (4) social networking sites; (5) virtual games worlds; (6) virtual social worlds.

Table 1. Classification of social media by self-presentation/self disclosure and social presence/media richness

Self-Presentation/ Self-Disclosure	Social Presence/Media Richness		
	Low	Medium	High
High	Blogs and Micro-Blogs	Social Networks	Virtual Social Worlds
Low	Collaborative Projects	Content Communities	Virtual Game Worlds

Source: Kaplan and Haenlein, 2010

Collaborative Projects

Collaborative projects, such as Wikipedia, allow end-users to jointly and simultaneously create content for the web site. They probably are the most democratic manifestation of user generated content (UGC) and can be differentiated between wikis–which are related to text-based content– and social bookmarking–which refers to group-collecting and group-rating of links and media contents. The basis of collaborative projects is that the joint effort of many users leads to a better outcome than individual efforts of the same users.

Blogs and Micro-Blogs

Blogs are websites that show date-stamped entries in reverse chronological order (OECD, 2007). They can be described as the social media version of personal web pages and can assume many different forms. They are generally related to a specific content area and managed by one user only, but others can interact by adding comments.

Recently, a new form within this category has been created: micro-blogging. It allows broadcasting a short sentence (i.e., Twitter), with a limited number of characters (SMS or Short Message Service), and, in some cases, other kinds of media such as an image or a video link (MMS or Multimedia Messaging Service). MMS social networking has spread greatly since its introduction so that currently Twitter has millions of users and transmits many millions of short messages every day.

Content Communities

This kind of social media allows users to use MMS to share various kinds of media content such as text, photos, videos (i.e., YouTube). The level of self-disclosure is, in general, very low and it is not required to create a personal profile. Many people, however, are eager to create content and actively share it on the Web with these sites.

Social Networking Websites

Social networking websites are Web-based services where members can create personal profiles, connect with other members, share personal connections, and establish or maintain relationships with others. In general, on these sites, users show their preferences by editing their personal profiles (Katona, Zubcsek, & Sarvary, 2011). Users can post any type of information, photos, videos, audio files, and links, in order to express their conscious or unconscious wish to present themselves in Cyberspace (Schau & Gilly, 2003). Social networks can be classified according to their access modality: it is possible to distinguish between open social networks (i.e., Facebook, MySpace, or Google+) and invitation-only social networks (i.e., ASmallWorld). While in the first case there are no entry restrictions, in the second case the target is a selected audience, in order to create a niche community that requires the existence of real-life connections.

Other categories can be classified according to the purpose of connections. LinkedIn was created in 2003 in order to allow users to establish professional connections. Foursquare has become the most popular location-based social networking application. The unique feature of Foursquare is that it uses the GPS feature on smartphones to share the location of an individual with others.

Virtual Game Worlds and Virtual Social Worlds

Virtual worlds, of all applications discussed thus far, provide the highest level of social presence and media richness. We can define them as virtual "platforms that replicate a three-dimensional environment in which users can appear in the form of personalized avatars and interact with each other as they would in real life" (Kaplan & Haenlein, 2010, p. 64).

These platforms can be divided between virtual game worlds and virtual social world. The first category implies a massively multiplayer online role-playing game (MMORPG), in which users are required to behave according to strict rules (i.e., World of Warcraft). The second group, virtual social worlds (i.e., Second Life), allow inhabitants to live a virtual life that is similar to reality. The range of strategies and interactions is almost unlimited, since users can freely decide how to behave (Kaplan & Haenlein, 2010).

Some of these social media already function as two-sided markets when they enable ordinary users to post their opinions of products, stores, and brands for others to read. As we examine two-sided-markets in more detail, we can argue that two-sided markets can be seen as a unique type of social medium most akin to the blogs and micro-blogs above in that they are high in self-presentation and self-disclosure but low in media richness.

TWO-SIDED MARKETS

Definition, Classification, and Main Features of Two-Sided Markets

Two-sided markets are generally defined as markets in which one or several platforms enable interactions between end-users and try to get the two sides "on board" by appropriately charging each side (Rochet & Tirole, 2003). Specifically, in a two-sided market, the platform first tries to attract all kind of users and benefits from their participation. Platforms are connected with two types of end-users and provide them with different goods or services. The supply and demand relation between a platform and each type of its end-users constitutes a market that is not independent and that leads to one side of the platform. That means each type of end-user constitutes one side to a platform, which was also the origin of the terminology "Two-Sided Market." Different types of end-users make deals and exchanges (of goods, services, information, etc.) on platforms.

The existence of platforms improves the efficiency of the deals or exchanges between different types of end-users.

Generally speaking, two-sided markets have the following several features: (1) a structure of two or more sides, a platform providing goods or services, and through the platform two or more types of end-users exchanging or interacting with each other; (2) significant across network externalities between different types of end-users who are brought together for platform services; (3) the pricing strategy adoption of a platform is not neutral. The pricing structure will also affect the business scale of the platform apart from the exact prices of the markets of both sides.

Baxter (1983) studied a two-sided business mode of payment based on bank cards in the first place, and his research became one of the earliest literature about two-sided markets. Rochet and Tirole (1999) analyzed the pricing strategies of exchange fees of monopoly bank card organizations, which was based on the research of Baxter. Xu and Chen (2006) investigated the Chinese band card industry and carried out some related research about pricing theory of bank cards. Rochet and Tirole (2003) deduced a pricing formula of usage fee charged by a monopoly platform in two-sided markets, which assumed that the logarithm of the revenue function was concave. The deduced formula was similar with Lerner Index. It was also concluded that one side of users of the platform with a relatively high price elasticity need to pay more than users of the other side, which was different with the outcome of traditional one-sided market. Armstrong (2002) discussed the usage of the two forms of price instruments—access fee and usage fee—and their effect to the equilibrium. Nocke, Peitz, & Stahl (2004) only considered access fees in their study of shopping mall. Rochet and Tirole (2003) mainly considered the situation in which a platform only adopted a usage fee. Chakravorti and Roson (2004) researched the difference of users on both sides with a hotelling model. Gabszewicz and Wauthy (2004) studied how users in two-sided markets choose a platform with a competitive model. Armstrong and Wright (2004) analyzed the effect of platform competition on the participating and using decision of users in two-sided markets.

Traditional examples of two-sided markets that have been deeply researched include videogame platforms (such as Nintendo, Sega, and Sony Play Station), TV networks and newspapers, credit card systems, etc. In all these cases, the success of the two-sided market depends on all three partners participating actively. Videogame platforms need to attract gamers in order to convince game developers to design and release games for the platforms, and meanwhile they also need games in order to induce gamers to buy and use their videogame console. TV networks and newspapers compete for advertisers and users or readers. Payment card systems need to attract both merchants and cardholders. Computer operation systems are also platforms that link users and software developers. In addition, recently there have appeared newer types of two-sided markets that exist primarily as locations for venders to promote their products and consumers to post their reviews and comments. Table 2 presents a breakdown of several types of two-sided markets and their characteristics.

With the fast and huge development of internet technologies, a great number of social media have appeared including social networks such as Facebook and eWOM (electronic word-of-mouth)

virtual communities like Yelp.com and Dianping.com. In addition to being social media, they are all two-sided markets. As for Facebook, this social network platform brought people who want to contact with friends together and made them a side. After that side was created, different advertisers joined the platform and became the other side of the market, which made Facebook become a two-sided market. As for Yelp.com and Dianping.com, they bring consumers and vendors together on the same platform. The more existing consumers there are on a platform, the more new consumers join the platform. Thus, more vendors are attracted, yielding a positive feedback situation.

Conceptually, the theory of two-sided markets is related to the theories of *network externalities*, which mean consumers (end-users) gain benefits from additional other consumers of the same type joining the platform. In other words, the more consumers in the market, the more utility every consumer can enjoy (e.g., mobile phone industries, virtual communities like Facebook.) In addition, the *across network externality* is another main feature of two-sided markets, which means the utility acquired by users of one side of the platform is affected by the scale of the other side. Actually it sometimes happens that a two-sided market has both network externalities and across network externalities. An eWOM virtual community is exactly the case. The different intensities of the across-network externalities are the main factor to

Table 2. Different types of two-sided platforms

Platforms	Users of Both Sides	Pricing Instruments	Characteristics
eWOM websites (Yelp.com, Dianping.com)	Users (Consumers)/Restaurants	Commissions, Advertising Fee	Network Externality of one side; Across Network Externalities between both sides
Credit/Debit Card System	Cardholders/Merchants	Transfer fee	Across Network Externalities between both sides
Shopping Mall	Consumers/Merchants	Rents, Free Parking	Across Network Externalities between both sides
Newspapers	Readers/Advertisers	Advertising fee	Across Network Externalities between both sides
Computer Operation Systems	Application Developers/Computer Users	Copyright usage fee developing instruments	Across Network Externalities between both sides
Dating Clubs	Men/Women	Entrance fees	Across Network Externalities between both sides

consider when deciding the pricing structure. Such differences probably make the across-network externality bigger generated by the augment of users from one side than the other side. From the perspective of platforms, they need to set different prices and adopt different strategies to attract users from both sides and make them interact with each other. In addition, they benefit from using other types of incentives (loyalty programs, contests) to attract users (Veith, 2011). In addition, reward programs might also serve to encourage active use by consumers.

eWOM Virtual Communities

With the development of the Internet, electronic word-of-mouth virtual communities (VCs) have appeared and developed very quickly in recent years and their proliferation has been gradually changing people's consuming habits. Consumers are relying more and more on eWOM VCs rather than traditional word-of-mouth (WOM) communication to gather information about goods and services.

eWOM VCs mainly focus on daily consumption, which almost covers all areas of people's daily life, such as restaurants, shopping, travelling, electronic products, automobiles, books, music, and movies. For example, Dianping.com in China is a eWOM VC mainly for restaurants, IMDB. com is for movies, and Yelp.com is a type of comprehensive two-sided market where a variety of vendors are reviewed.

Consumers search and browse the information and comments of goods and services in eWOM VCs before making purchasing decisions, which can decrease the negative utilities brought by information asymmetry. In this way, consumers can probably make better consumption decisions. Meanwhile, consumers can also make comments about goods and services after their consumption. In addition, the comments made by previous consumers can be conveyed to subsequent ones

through VCs. On the sellers' side, they can promote and advertise their goods and services through VCs. Such eWOM VCs function as platforms that link consumers and sellers of goods and services. Next we will take a brief look at Dianping.com as an example to show how an eWOM VC works.

On Dianping.com, every restaurant has a web-page of its own that has some basic information and customer reviews about the restaurant. The users of the website can read and post comments there. The comments can include everything about the restaurant, such as taste, environment, services, consumption per person, recommended food, parking services, and more. Many people who love great food gather together on Dianping. com. What they mostly do is to browse the reviews before going to a restaurant and express their consumption feelings and comments in the eWOM VC, which means that the users themselves are where the comments come from. The content of the website is not only received but also generated by users. The VC platform is only responsible for organizing, editing, classifying, and communicating the reviews. The operating cost will be decreased in this way and the information will be more authentic.

The communication and sharing of restaurants' information are the most important functions of Dianping.com to users. Other eWOM VCs are basically the same except for different goods and services. First, let's assume a consumer "A" wanted to go to a restaurant "R", but before going, A decided to check other users' comments about R. If A was unsatisfied, he or she would probably not go to R. If A was satisfied with the comments, he or she would go to R as originally planned. After consumption, A maybe would post new comments for R about its taste, services, and so on. These comments might consist of further comments on the reviews A had read. Then a subsequent consumer B would see the new comment made by A and other earlier comments as well. The consumption decision of B would also be affected by those comments about R. Such actions of reading and posting comments keep moving in circles, which constitute the fundamental consumer behaviors of Dianping.com. As more consumers post reviews and comments, the value of this information increases for subsequent consumers, so two-sided platform managers seek to motivate as many people as possible to use the site, both actively and passively. This is especially important for the passive users as they are likely to be less informed and experienced with the topic than are the active users.

The interaction and sharing process in circle would generate huge amounts of reviews information, which are actually the key factor for VCs to attract users. Assuming Dianping.com had very few reviews or even zero reviews, consumer A above would never probably access the community, not even mention the communication and sharing of information. Thus, the community would not last, and very likely, there would be no community at all. The more comments the community has, the bigger reference value would be for consumers when making consuming decisions, and the more willing are the consumers to join the community. Therefore, those accumulated comments are actually very important assets for VCs and what the competitors cannot easily imitate.

However, in reality not every consumer who had been to a restaurant would make a comment in the VC, which actually makes sense. Most of the user generated content on Websites comes from a minority of the users (Yoo & Gretzel, 2011). If assuming A was a rational consumer, nothing good would accrue to A for making comments, but they would still incur the cost of time. So according to an economic principle, rational people would do nothing. However, as we mentioned before, user comments are very important (van der Merwe & van Heerden, 2009), so Dianping.com has adopted some motivation methods to encourage people to comment. The first is psychological/social reward. Steinfield et al. (2008) show how much

influence such social rewards have in motivating online behavior. Every member of Dianping.com has a user level that depends on the quantity of the comments the user has made. The more comments a user has made, the higher his/her user level will be. Moreover, a high user level would probably bring the user sense of achievement and satisfaction. That's why we call it psychological/social reward. In addition, the VCs may also have monetary reward. Users might earn virtual money that a user could spend inside the VC. In the case of Dianping.com, D currency (the name of the virtual money on Dianping.com) can be paid for using some functions of the website, such as downloading restaurants' information to the cell phones (for instance, a piece of information about a restaurant's address and phone number costs 1 D currency). Moreover, there are often some free trials of new restaurants on Dianping.com, and these opportunities are usually sold by auctions bidden only with D currencies. To sum up, Dianping.com motivates users through two aspects--psychological and monetary.

However, these motivations do not always work. In other words, different users have different responses towards the motivations, which means they have different sensitiveness. Those who are relatively sensitive would probably increase their amounts of comments, that is, become more active users, and those who are not that sensitive might not act quite differently. Such motivation methods of eWOM VC platforms and users' responsive reactions have impacts on the operation and equilibrium of the market. Figure 1 depicts the consumer behavior on Dianping.com, including reading and posting comments, users being motivated, and more. This model can guide both management of the platform as well as research intended to understand how all three parties to the two-sided market behave. The model also leads to the key question, "How do the managers of two-sided markets profit from their investment?"

Figure 1. Consumer behavior in eWOM virtual communities

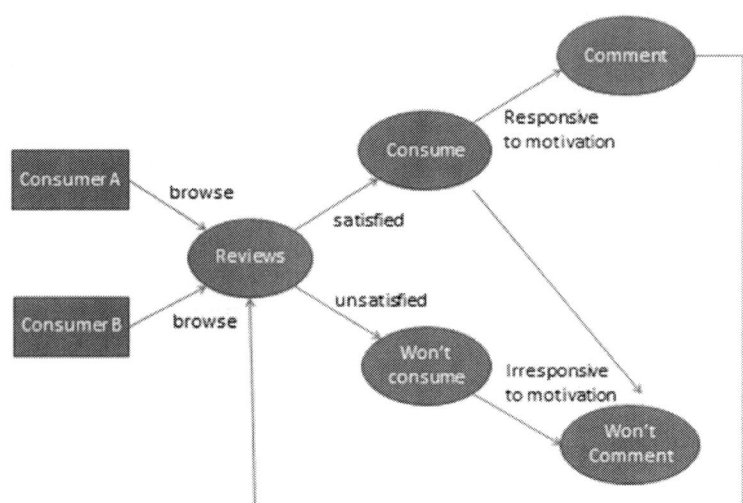

How Does the Platform Make Profits?

Most eWOM VCs like Dianping.com generate profit mainly through commissions and advertising fees charged to sellers or merchants who have access to the platforms. The commission mode is usually realized by membership cards, which also establish a linkage between VC users and merchants. Users of Dianping.com can get membership cards for free. Dianping.com makes contracts with some restaurants that any consumer who has a Dianping.com membership card will get a discount or earn credits (usually the credits can be accumulated and converted to more discount and gifts). Then the restaurants need to pay the commissions according to the specific amount of consumption. The commissions less the credits equals to income of the community. The commission rate of Dianping.com was estimated to 2%-5% around the year 2008. The restaurants can also place advertisements on Dianping.com. After inputting some key words about cuisine, location area, consumption per person, etc., a series of matched restaurants will be listed, and the users' comments will show up as well. The sequence of display is dependent on whether a restaurant has bought the advertisement and what the type of the advertisement is. The restaurants can also put electronic coupons on Dianping.com for promotion, which is also a kind of advertisement. Almost no eWOM VC charges users, who are the consumers. On the contrary, Dianping.com even subsidizes users with credits and discounts.

eWOM Virtual Communities and Two-Sided Markets

According to the features of two-sided markets, an eWOM virtual community is a two-sided platform that links consumers and vendors. As for Dianping.com, it links consumers and restaurants and provides different goods or services to the two sides. On the one hand, Dianping.com provides consumers with information and WOM about restaurants together with some discounts and coupons. After browsing all the contents about restaurants, consumers would make buying decisions that they thought most beneficial. And sometimes they also could use the coupons from Dianping.com to get more benefits. After returning from the restaurants, consumers could post reviews on Dianping.com. On the other hand, Dianping. com provides services of promotions and advertisements to the vendors, which could enhance their visibility and top-of-the-mind awareness and may enlarge the market for them. The restaurants would pay commission and fees to Dianping.com in return. The existence of Dianping.com makes the exchange between consumers and restaurants more efficient.

Across network externalities, which are a characteristic of two-sided markets, also appear in eWOM VCs. Firstly, the more consumers there are in a community, the more effective the promotions and advertisements of the vendors are. Thus, the scale of the consumers in a community has a positive across externality to the vendors. Secondly, as more vendors join the community, the more options and WOM information about the vendors become available to the consumers. Therefore, the number of the vendors also has a positive across externality to the consumers. The reason that we could see some restaurants with bad WOM on Dianping.com is mainly because of the positive across externality of the scale of the consumers to the restaurants. A restaurant would choose to access into the platform when the benefit of the positive across externality could make up for the loss of utility brought by negative WOM.

Moreover, the consumers' side of a eWOM VC has self network externality to some extent. Such kind of self network externality mainly derives from the eWOM communications between consumers. Hence we could surmise that part of consumers' utility is related to the number of people who write reviews in the community, which means the more consumers there are who express comments, the more benefits every consumer in the community will gain. Generally, a larger number of consumers in a community will generate more people who make comments. This is important to all parties because the accumulated evidence of many studies shows that consumers rely heavily on the recorded experiences of other consumers when making their online and offline purchase decisions (Zanker et al., 2010).

REWARD PROGRAMS: TWO EXPERIMENTS

We ran two online experiments to test whether two-different types of reward programs could raise consumer intentions to contribute to a two-sided market. The two reward programs we tested were a "monetary" reward versus a "social" reward, derived from similar studies of motivation in other areas (Heyman & Ariely, 2004; Steinfield et al., 2008).

Experiment One

In the first experiment, we created an online questionnaire describing a fictitious website patterned after Yelp.com, a successful review site. The survey ran from December 2011 to January 2012. A snowball sampling method was utilized that relies on referrals from initial subjects to generate additional subjects (Goldenberg, Han, Lehmann, & Hong, 2009). Initial subjects were generated from 1,000 contacts of a Web company based in northern Italy. These 1,000 people received an e-mail inviting them to fill in the questionnaire. To enlarge the potential sample the links to the questionnaires were posted on the social networking sites Facebook, Twitter, LinkedIn, Google+ and on online groups related to social marketing, digital marketing, social networking, and technologies. A Facebook advertising campaign was also used to approach other respondents. In order to reach a higher number of respondents and to increase the level of completion, two iTunes Cards were offered, for a prize draw, to motivate users who correctly fulfilled the survey.

We obtained completed questionnaires from 480 online users. The majority (360 or 75%) were Italian residents, with 52 (10.8%) coming from the U.S. The remainder came from a variety of countries in Europe, South America, Asia, and the Middle East. The questionnaire asked them to report which social networks they followed:

Facebook (95.8%), Twitter (44.2%), Google + (28.7%), and LinkedIn (52.3%). When totaled to create an overall measure of social media use, 146 (30.4%) followed only one social network, (34%) followed two social networks, (19.8%) followed three social networks, and (15.8%) followed all four social networks.

When they responded to the invitation and clicked to view the website, the participants saw a description of a fictitious web site:

Recommend.com is a leading review website that connects people with local businesses. It's a place where consumers share their experiences about their businesses consumption. It's word-of-mouth, but online. Recommend.com was founded in 2004 to help people find great local businesses like restaurants, dentists, hair stylists and mechanics. Users can access Recommend.com via iPhone, Android, BlackBerry, and more.

Recommend.com has an automated filter that suppresses a small portion of reviews - it targets those suspicious ones you see on other sites. The automated system applies the same objective criteria to all reviews regardless of a business's advertiser status. Recommend.com helps amplify and improve the reputation the businesses have earned offline. But sometimes some illegitimate content can't get caught. This is an unfortunate reality in an environment where some folks are determined to try to game the system, but it is also the reality offline.

All the participants were then asked the following question: "Please imagine that you became a member of Recommend.com so you could read and post reviews of the local businesses you patronize. How likely would you be to participate by posting reviews?" A five-point response format was provided where 1 = I definitely would not, 2 = somewhat likely, 3 = likely, 4 = very likely, 5 = I definitely would. Approximately one-third of the sample (n = 166), termed the control group,

responded to this question and then moved on to answer additional questions not related to this study.

In contrast, a second portion of the sample (n= 159) read a description of a proposed monetary reward program designed to encourage participation on Recommend.com by posting reviews: "Now, please imagine that Recommend.com began offering a reward program for users to encourage them to post more and better reviews. The reward would be in the form of virtual currency for each review. As a user collects more currency, he or she has the opportunity to spend this virtual currency on merchandise offered by the companies participating in the web site. Users with more currency can redeem it for larger reward than users with less currency. If the web site began offering this reward program, how likely would you be to participate by posting reviews?" The same five-point response format was provided so they could report their intended active participation. We termed this group of participants the "monetary reward" group.

The remaining third of the sample (n = 155), termed the "social reward" groups, viewed instead another description of a reward program intended to encourage active use of the site. "The reward would be in the form of stars for each review. As a user collects more stars, he or she gains status and prestige in the community as a trusted source of information about the topic of the web site. Users with higher status have more influence on other users owing to their exalted ranking." Then they were asked how likely they would be to participate using the five-point response format.

To analyze the data, we first compared the responses of all three groups to the initial description of the website. The control group reported a mean "intent to use" score of 2.72 (SD = 1.01), the monetary reward group's intent score was 2.68 (SD = 1.02), and the social reward group's mean was 2.68 (SD = 1.07). An ANOVA showed that there was no statistically significant difference between any of these three mean scores, indicating moderate levels of interest in actively using the review site.

However, after being told of the reward programs, the monetary reward group reported a mean intent to use score of 3.39 (SD = 1.04) and the social reward group reported a mean intent to use score of 3.19 (SD = 1.2). We used paired sample t-tests to compare the before with the after intent to use scores for both reward programs and found statistically significantly differences for both programs. The results for the monetary reward program were $t_{(157)} = 8.6$, $p < .0005$, and the results for the social reward were $t_{(154)} = 6.6$, $p<.0005$). Thus, we concluded that implementing a reward program would increase active use of the website. There was, however, no difference in effectiveness between the two reward programs in how effective they were in increasing active use, so we can conclude that the decision to use either a monetary or social reward program would best be made on some other criteria than effectiveness, such as its cost or difficulty in management.

Experiment Two

We wanted to replicate the results of the first experiment as well as modify the nature of the monetary and social reward programs to increase confidence in the findings, so we conducted a second experiment similar to the first. The survey ran from January 2012 to February 2012. A snowball sampling method was utilized that relies on referrals from initial subjects to generate additional subjects (Goldenberg, Han, Lehmann, & Hong, 2009). Initial subjects were generated from 1,000 contacts who received an e-mail inviting them to fill in the questionnaire. To enlarge the potential sample the links to the questionnaires were posted, as in the first experiment, on the Social Networking sites Facebook, Twitter, LinkedIn, Google+ and on online groups related to social marketing, digital marketing, social networking, and technologies. We obtained completed questionnaires from 324 online users.

The second experiment simply described two reward plans similar to those used in the first experiment. To begin, both treatment groups read a description of a prototypical two-sided market Website:

A review website is a place where consumers share their experiences with local businesses. A review website can help people find great local businesses like restaurants, dentists, hair stylists and mechanics, etc. Before making a purchase decision, consumers can search and read reviews and opinions about the goods and services they want from a review website. And after consumption, consumers can also share their consumption experiences on the website. It's online word-of-mouth.

They were then asked if they used such web sites and if so, how often. Next, they were asked to imagine how likely they would be to use such a web site as described with three different questions. These were a 7-point probability scale where 1 = I definitely would not and 7 = I definitely would; a probability estimating scale with 7 response options ranging from 0% probability to 100% probability in 20% increments; and a 10-point bi-polar scale asking them to pick the number representing what they would do where 0 = definitely will not use and 9 = definitely will use. Then the participants were randomly assigned to one of two treatments: monetary and social reward. The monetary (n = 150) reward stimulus read by the participants was worded:

Now, please imagine that this review website began offering virtual money to those who post reviews. The more reviews a user posts on the website, the more virtual money he or she could get. The virtual money could be used to purchase some functions of the website, such as downloading restaurants' information to cell phones. Moreover, there could often be some free trials of new restaurants on the website, and these opportunities would be sold by auction bidding only with the virtual money. The virtual money could be also exchanged for some real gifts on the website, such as books, phone cards, toys, and more. If the Website began offering this reward program, how likely would you be to participate by posting reviews?

A single 7-point probability response format was provided identical to the first probability scale described above where $1 = $ I definitely would not and $7 = $ I definitely would. The questionnaire closed with simple demographic questions. The social reward treatment ($n = 174$) was worded:

Now, please imagine that this review Website began offering a reward program for users who post reviews. Every user of the website had a user level which depended on the quantity of the comments the user had made. The more comments a user had made, the higher his/her user level would be. As a user gets higher level, he or she gains status and prestige on the website. Users with higher status have more influence on other users owing to their exalted ranking. If the web site began offering this reward program, how likely would you be to participate by posting reviews? The participants responded using the 7-point probability scale as above.

The sample consisted of 324 participants, 129 (40%) men and 195 (60%) women. Their ages ranged from 18 to 50+, with the majority (65%) in the 18 to 28 years range. The majority 205 (63%) resided in the U.S., 72 (22%) in Italy, and the remainder (15%) came from 24 other countries.

The data analysis using independent samples and a paired sample t-tests, showed that before the reward plan was described, both groups of consumers expressed moderate intentions to use the review website, but there were no statistically significant differences in their intention to use it as measured by any of the three intent-to-use scales; nor was there a statistically significant ($t_{(322)}=1.6$, $p=.104$) difference between the two reward groups in their intent-to-use scores after viewing the proposed reward program. However, the difference between intent to use the site scores before reading the reward program (M = 3.08, SD=1.2) and after reading a reward description (M = 3.7, SD = 1.5) was significant ($t_{(323)} = 8.7$, $p <.0005$).

Thus, the results of two online experiments consistently showed that, while there was no significant difference in the effectiveness of a monetary versus a social reward program in encouraging intent-to-use a two-sided market platform to post reviews, both reward programs were effective in enhancing intent-to-use the site compared with no reward program at all. Despite the shortcomings in these studies stemming from their limited samples and the absence of real behavioral data, the findings do suggest that rewarding consumers for actively contributing to a review site would encourage more active use by some of the users. We feel that they provide enough "proof of concept" to encourage additional study of the topic. The results of this research could provide managers with useful guidelines for developing strategies for promoting active use of their two-sided markets, which would benefit all three participants.

INTEGRATING TWO-SIDED MARKETS INTO OTHER SOCIAL MEDIA

Part of our interest in describing two-sided markets lies in the ways we feel that Website managers can integrate them into other social media to the benefit of both parties. Social media permit unprecedented interactions among potentially vast numbers of people. These interactions, as described above, vary widely in types and complexity. Two-sided markets also permit and encourage interactions among people and between consumers and vendors. Two-sided markets allow people to review vendors and describe their experiences for others to read and comment on, thus encouraging dialogs and debates. These interactions work to the benefit of both consumers and vendors. Consumers can use them to gather valuable information prior to making purchases, and vendors can glean from them valuable intelligence about their market offerings.

Integrating a two-sided market that permitted users to post and read reviews of vendors into an existing social media website that lacks such a feature would bring added interest to the website and permit users and additional means to interact. Focusing the two-sided market on a specific category of vendor, say restaurants, would create a synergy between this portion of the site and the remaining portions, giving users an additional motive to use the web site benefits all parties. In addition, managers of two-sided markets could increase their utility to users by borrowing a technique used by many other types of websites, the recommender system. "Recommender systems are intelligent applications that assist users in a decision-making process when they do not have sufficient personal experience to choose one item from an overwhelming set of alternative products or services" (Ricci & Werthner, 2006, p. 5). Recommender systems employ sophisticated algorithms, the "intelligent applications," that take users inputs in the form of their reviews and discussions, processes these inputs, and then directs them to appropriate recipients to use in their decision-making. Recommender systems take the user generated content of active users and makes it available to other users, often in the form of a ranked list. These recommendations perhaps are especially important to the passive users who read but don't comment.

On the other hand, platform managers could focus attention on the users who generate the most and the most influential content. These individuals are likely acting as important online opinion leaders. Research shows that opinion leaders play an especially important role in creating the social relationships that make up the core of the social network; and they are especially important to the

managers because they exert a disproportional influence on other users (van der Merwe & van Heerden, 2009; Momtaz et al., 2011). If these users can be identified, they can become the focus of special marketing strategies that harness their influence to the benefit of the platform.

Collaborative projects, such as Wikipedia, can also be integrated with the feature of two-sided markets. The platform of Wikipedia connects readers and creators (sometimes they can be the same); these are the users of the content. The more creators there are on the platforms, the more and better content will be generated. And that will attract more readers to access into the website. So collaborative projects need to attract enough creators and that way more people will use the platforms, which will create big room for revenues. Blogs and Micro-blogs can also be regarded as two-sided markets. Twitter links different users including those famous people, brands, public media, and more. A bigger scale of users will attract more users. Such a kind of platform needs to attract some icon or core users to generate a magnitude of people who use the platform. And if people around us were all using a social platform, we are more easy to be attracted to use it too, which would be concluded to the network externality of a two-sided market.

There are many other social media which can be integrated with two-sided markets. Social networking Websites such as Facebook connect different users and advertisers. Virtual game worlds link different players and display a main feature of two-sided markets--network externality. Spotify, which is a popular online music player, brings music fans, music records (or records companies) and advertisers into one platform. The more music there is on Spotify, the more people will choose to use the platform, and more advertisers will be attracted. We could find many advertisements on Spotify nowadays.

FUTURE RESEARCH DIRECTIONS

We feel that the concept of two-sided markets presents social science researchers with a fertile set of research topics that should both enhance our understanding of how people use social media and aid vendors in using social media to promote their products. For instance, the two experimental studies described above represent just a bare beginning of the types of studies that researchers could conduct to develop means by which managers of two-sided markets could encourage active use of their sites. We chose the topic of reward mechanisms because we felt these would be relatively easy for mangers to implement and offered real promise as effective encouragement mechanisms. The evidence we present suggests that our surmise was correct. Both types of reward, monetary and social, appear successful in encouraging users to increase their active use of two-sided markets. The fact that both programs seem to work equally well is encouraging in that this finding suggests that, should a manager chose to use a reward mechanism of this type, the decision of which one to use remains open. Thus, mangers can made these decisions on some basis other than mere effectiveness. These criteria might include cost of implementing and running the reward program, how appealing the program might be for the intended audience for the site, or the "fit" between the program and the type or types of vendors that participate. Experimentally competing reward programs against other types of motivation strategies to compare their relative effectiveness could extend this stream of research. In addition, although we strove for culturally diverse samples of users in our experiments, these studies would likely have to be done across different cultures to determine if cultural differences influenced the effectiveness of motivational strategies.

Another line of research could focus means other than reward programs to encourage active use. Research reported by Pagani et al. (2011) suggests that active website users have distinctive personality characteristics that predispose them to contribute valuable content in various ways to the website. Managers can use this information to help them design both the websites and the promotions for the websites to encourage active users to participate. An extension of this stream of research could investigate more specifically user motives for using two-sided markets both actively and passively. The presumption is that passive users, the vast bulk of those who visit such sites, do so merely for the utilitarian value of the information they get there from reading others reviews, but in an addition verifying this presumption empirically, researcher should study the motivating role played by the interactions users have with other users. Personality might play an important role in motivating use of social networks (e.g., Amichai-Hamburger, 2007; Amichai-Hamburger & Vinitzky, 2010).

A third research focus could investigate the best ways for managers to use the information contained in the two-sided market to the advantage of vendors. Google has pioneered such activities in their Google Analytics programs that collect click stream data from website visitors, process it searching for insights, and then making these available to marketers who can then use this information to improve aspects of their websites. In addition, Google's AdWords program can review online advertising campaigns and provide valuable data to marketers to help them improve their online ads. We can recommend one temptation to avoid, however. Given that the managers of the two-sided market reputation website make money from vendor advertising and participation, they should not extort higher fees from vendors by threatening to highlight or otherwise overemphasize negative reviews of their products (Burrows & Galante, 2008). Not only does this seem to be unethical, but two-sided platforms leave themselves open to potential lawsuits from unhappy vendors as well.

Vendors also can use the information contained in the reviews to improve their service if negative comments appear, or build on positive comments where those occur. Research can be done to examine the best ways for vendors to use this information to develop new products, improve service delivery, and perhaps reward and motivate employees. For example, could restaurant diners report a "like" to the Facebook account of a waiter? Researchers should investigate the feasibility and effectiveness of such uses of the content generated by users on two-sided markets. When and how vendors should react to the reviews of their products is also a fruitful topic for further study. Does a genuine dialogue between the vendor and the customer enhance the value of the platform, or at some point would consumers begin to feel that they were being taken advantage of by the other party.

Research could be done to document the value of two-sided markets to both users and vendors to explicate how and how much each side benefits from their participation. This type of research could be used to encourage vendors to sign on or to increase their participation if they already belong.

Some studies have already examined how important the eWOM posted by active users is to other consumers (Goldenburg et al., 2009; Horowitz & Goldsmith, 2006; Momtaz et al., 2011; Steinfield et al. 2008). The consensus seems to be that this type of social information outweighs the impact on consumer behavior of other marketing-dominated sources of information such as advertising and other promotions.

CONCLUSION

Although they are not often described as such, popular social media such as Twitter and Facebook are examples of two-sided markets. Conversely, we propose that other web sites, "pure" two-sided markets devoted more specifically to reading and posting reviews and exchanging opinions about specific brands or collections of businesses, should be thought of as examples of social media; and that the consumers and businesses that comprise

them should be thought of as examples of social networks. We also propose that two-sided markets might benefit from being managed as more-familiar social media are. Strategies that work for Facebook should also work for two-sided markets. In addition, we argue and present evidence that using simple reward programs could raise active use of two-sided markets, thereby increasing their value for all three parties, vendors, consumers, and managers.

Studies show that most of the online content is generated by a relatively small number of users and that most users just consume this information (Yoo & Gretzel, 2011). Encouraging participation in online communities is one of the greatest challenges for any online community provider (Bishop, 2007). Two-sided markets increase in value as the number of consumers and vendors grows. A word of warning is needed, however. The managers of a recommendation website, a two-sided market such as Dianping.com, should not give in to the temptation to manipulate the results of the users' comments to intimidate vendors and compel them the pay in order to keep negative comments off the site. Such behavior could result in a lawsuit (Burrows & Galante, 2008). Consequently, we propose that the search for means through which managers can attract increasingly large numbers of consumer users to their websites is an important managerial and empirical topic. We hope that we have contributed some small measure to this effort with our experiments and hope that other researchers will build on to the benefit of manages and this field of study as well.

REFERENCES

Amichai-Hamburger, Y. (2007). Personality, individual differences and internet use. In Joinson, A. N., McKenna, K. Y. A., Postmes, T., & Reips, U. (Eds.), *The Oxford Handbook of Internet Psychology* (pp. 187–204). Oxford, UK: Oxford University Press.

Amichai-Hamburger, Y., & Vinitzky, G. (2010). Social network use and personality. *Computers in Human Behavior, 26*(6), 1289–1295. doi:10.1016/j.chb.2010.03.018.

Armstrong, M. (2002). The theory of access pricing and interconnection. In Cave, M. et al. (Eds.), *Handbook of Telecommunications Economics* (*Vol. 1*, pp. 297–381). Amsterdam, The Netherlands: Elsevier.

Armstrong, M., & Wright, J. (2004). *Demand Estimation for Italian Newspapers: The Impact of Weekly Supplements*. Working Paper.

Baxter, W. F. (1983). Bank interchange of transactional paper: Legal and economic perspectives. *The Journal of Law & Economics, 26*, 541–588. doi:10.1086/467049.

Bishop, J. (2007). Increasing participation in online communities: A framework for human–computer interaction. *Computers in Human Behavior, 23*(4), 1881–1893. doi:10.1016/j.chb.2005.11.004.

Burrows, P., & Galante, J. (2008). Yelp: Advertise or else? *Bloomberg Businessweek*, March 15, 2010, p. 27.

Chakrovorti, S., & Roson, R. (2004). Platform competition in two-sided markets: The case of payment networks. *Federal Reserve Bank of Chicago Emerging Payments Occasional Paper Series*.

Gabszewicz, J. J., & Wauthy, X. Y. (2004). *Two-sided markets and price competition with multi-homing, Mimeo CORE*. Louvain-la-Neuve University.

Goldenberg, J., Han, S., Lehmann, D. R., & Hong, J. W. (2009). The role of hubs in the adoption process. *Journal of Marketing, 72*(March), 1–12. doi:10.1509/jmkg.73.2.1.

Heyman, J., & Ariely, D. (2004). Effort for payment: A tale of two markets. *Psychological Science, 15*(11), 787–793. doi:10.1111/j.0956-7976.2004.00757.x PMID:15482452.

Horowitz, D., & Goldsmith, R. E. (2006). Measuring motivations for online opinion seeking. *Journal of Interactive Advertising, 6*(2).

Kaplan, A. M., & Haenlein, M. (2010). Users of the world, unite! The challenges and opportunities of Social Media. *Business Horizons, 53*(1), 59–68. doi:10.1016/j.bushor.2009.09.003.

Katona, Z., Zubcsek, P., & Sarvary, M. (2011). Network effects and Personal Influences. *Marketing Science, 30*(1), 42–60.

Momtaz, N. J., Aghaie, A., & Alizadeh, S. (2011). Identifying opinion leaders for marketing by analyzing online social networks. *International Journal of Virtual Communities and Social Networking, 3*(1), 43–59. doi:10.4018/jvcsn.2011010105.

Nocke, V., Peitz, M., & Stahl, C. (2004). *Platform Ownership in Two-Sided Markets*. Mimeo.

OECD. (2007). *Participative web and user-created content: Web 2.0, wikis, and social networking*. Paris, France: Organisation for Economic Co-operation and Development.

Pagani, M., C., Hofacker, H., & Goldsmith, R.E.R. E. (2011). The influence of personality on active and passive use of social networking sites. *Psychology and Marketing, 28*(5), 441–456. doi:10.1002/mar.20395.

Ricci, F., & Werthner, H. (2006). Introduction to the special issue: Recommender systems. *International Journal of Electronic Commerce, 11*(2), 5–9. doi:10.2753/JEC1086-4415110200.

Rochet, J-C, & Tirole, J. (1999). *Cooperation among competitors: The economics of credit card associations*. C.E.P.R. Discussion Papers, No. 2101.

Rochet, J.-C., & Tirole, J. (2003). Platform competition in two-sided markets. *Journal of the European Economic Association, 1*(4), 990–1029. doi:10.1162/154247603322493212.

Schau, H. J., & Gilly, M. C. (2003). We are what we post? The presentation of self in personal websites. *The Journal of Consumer Research*, *30*(4), 384–404.

Steinfield, C., Ellison, N. B., & Lampe, C. (2008). Social capital, self-esteem, and use of online social network sites: A longitudinal analysis. *Journal of Applied Developmental Psychology*, *29*(6), 434–445. doi:10.1016/j.appdev.2008.07.002.

van der Merwe, R., & van Heerden, G. (2009). Finding and utilizing opinion leaders: Social networks and the power of relationships. *South African Journal of Business Management*, *40*(3), 65–76.

Veith, L. (2011). Insightful incentives. *Marketing News*, *45*(14), 8–8.

Xu, L., & Chen, H. M. (2006). The new development of pricing theory of bank cards. *China Industrial Economics*, *6*, 22–29.

Yoo, K.-H., & Gretzel, U. (2011). Influence of personality on travel-related consumer-generated media creation. *Computers in Human Behavior*, *27*(2), 609–621. doi:10.1016/j.chb.2010.05.002.

Zanker, M., Ricci, F. F., Jannach, D., & Terveen, L. (2010). Measuring the impact of personalization and recommendation on user behavior. *International Journal of Human-Computer Studies*, *68*, 469–471. doi:10.1016/j.ijhcs.2010.04.002.

ADDITIONAL READING

Xu, L., & Chen, H. M. (2007). *Two-sided markets: new vision of the competition environment of enterprises*. Shanghai: People's Press.

KEY TERMS AND DEFINITIONS

Active Use: When individuals click on a social media website, they have the option of providing content to the site in the form of written comments, videos, audio recordings, or other forms of user generated content. Active use is this activity, and varies by user.

Network Externalities: The effect that one user of a good or service has on the value of that product to other people. When network effect is present, the value of a product or service is dependent on the number of others using it.

Passive Use: Another option for social media participants is to "lurk" or passively consume the content on the site generated by the active users.

Recommender Systems: Intelligent computer programs that take as input the comments and reviews contributed to a website by active users and transforms them into buying recommendations for all users of the site, often in the form of a ranked list.

Reward Program: A type of customer relationship management strategy in which customers earn rewards by some activity such as purchasing, visiting, or posting, thereby boosting their active participation with the sponsor.

Social Media: A group of Internet-based applications that build on the ideological and technological foundations of Web 2.0, and that allow the creation and exchange of user-generated content. Social media is media for social interaction as a super-set beyond social communication.

Social Network: A group of people who have one-to-one relationships with each other; for our purposes, these are online communities of users who maintain contact with each other by posting and viewing content.

Two-Sided Markets: Websites consisting of a "platform" or common meeting ground where vendors can advertise their products and consumers can upload comments and reviews, and discuss their opinions of these vendors.

Chapter 11
Application of Social Media Tools by Retailers

María-del-Carmen Alarcón-del-Amo
Universitat Autònoma de Barcelona, Spain

Carlota Lorenzo-Romero
University of Castilla-La Mancha, Spain

Efthymios Constantinides
University of Twente, The Netherlands

ABSTRACT

The chapter explores the factors influencing the adoption process and the degree of engagement of the social media as part of the online marketing strategy by Spanish retailers. A retail industry survey identifies four different segments of retailers depending on the level of implementation of social media marketing strategies. The study examines the antecedents of the social media tools' adoption process across the dimensions of a Technology Adoption Model (TAM) and assesses various other factors likely to affect the degree of the adoption. One essential conclusion is that the company size is not important but that the level of adoption social media marketing is related to the organizational maturity in the areas of management attitudes, employee empowerment, access to Internet technologies, and technological infrastructure. The study proposes a future research agenda including cross-cultural studies for better understanding the global business attitudes in this area and underlines the need for development of benchmarks and metrics necessary for better assessing the value of social media marketing.

INTRODUCTION

The advances in the area of Information and Communication Technologies (ICT) have brought sweeping changes to peoples' lives and to the marketing practice. The Internet and increasingly the mobile telephone are the technologies with the greater impact on the commercial landscape (Biswas & Krishnan, 2004; Sharma & Sheth, 2004). With over 1.5 billion users, the Internet has become a mainstream phenomenon and an important marketing platform. The Web is already

DOI: 10.4018/978-1-4666-4026-9.ch011

the second most important retailing channel in the USA and the European Union (Eurostat, 2010)[1] and several other countries. There are strong indications that the Web has already become the primary customer information source about products or services for many of its users. As a result, the online marketing is claiming an ever increasing portion of the marketers' attention and corporate budget. According to a recent report of eMarketer (2010),[2] spending on print advertising in the U.S. was for the first time in history lower than spending in online advertising in 2010 and the difference is expected to increase in the future.

The most profound effect of the Internet on the marketing practice was the migration of market power from the corporation to the customer (Rogers et al., 1997; Wind & Mahajan, 2001; Varandarajan & Yadav, 2002, Rha et al., 2002; Urban, 2005; Constantinides et al., 2008). This is a continuous process that started in the beginning of the 1990s with the commercialization of the Internet, the development of the World Wide Web, the emergence of the first Web browsers and, of course, the advance of the adoption of personal computing. These developments brought about the first wave of customer empowerment: by accessing the Internet, customers obtained new tools and access to businesses on a global scale, giving them access to almost unlimited information about products and services while allowing them to virtually walk in a global high street.

Around the middle of the first decade of the 21st Century, a new development in the Internet domain became the source of a second wave of customer empowerment. This development is widely known as Web 2.0 or social media. The evolution of the Internet to the Web 2.0 era took place with the arrival of a new generation of interactive technologies and online applications allowing the easy publication, editing, and dissemination of content and also the creation of personal online networks and communities; these developments resulted in new forms of one-to-one

communication and one-to-many broadcasting of user generated content.

The Web 2.0 era dramatically increased the available information volume over products, services, and commercial outlets accessible to consumers but also radically affected the very nature and dissemination modes of marketing information. While traditionally marketing information was generated by corporations and channeled to markets through one way mass media or traditional direct media channels (like direct mail and tele-marketing) the social media-based product, brand and company information is user generated and transmitted through personal social networks, blogs, online communities, customer forums, and more. These channels are for all intents and purposes created outside the traditional marketing communication domain and therefore beyond the control of marketers a lot of the information exchanged refers to customer experiences from using products or services and user comments in the form of product reviews, recommendations to other customers, remarks about improvements and often even advices for use. There is evidence that customer generated information plays an increasingly important role in the decision making process (Constantinides et al., 2008), since this information is often perceived more reliable and unbiased. A recent report of the Opinion Research Corporation[3] found that 84% of Americans are influenced in their purchases by online customer generated product reviews while according to a Bizrate survey 59% of users consider customer reviews to be more reliable than those from experts.

The parallel information stream disseminated through peer-to-peer channels has therefore further empowered customers providing them with plenty and unbiased information allowing them to make better buying decisions. The result of customer decision making processes is today less dependent on corporate information and this has led to the decline of the effectiveness of the traditional marketing communication approaches. Many businesses are already trying to cope with the situation by, integrating social media strategies into their marketing programs. This new trend in consumer marketing is gaining momentum but there is limited academic research as to the exact factors underpinning the adoption of social media as marketing tools, the extent of these strategies and importantly the actual use and effectiveness of the social media as marketing tools.

This chapter presents the findings of a study aiming at mapping the use of social media as marketing tools by retailers in Spain. The study identifies the antecedents of the adoption of such applications by retailers, the motives and degree of adoption, and also maps the experiences of businesses from their social media marketing strategies.

BACKGROUND

Internet use has grown almost exponentially in recent years. Indeed, according to statistics provided by Internet World Stats[4], there are 2,095,006,005 Internet users in March 2011, more than a quarter of the world. Internet use in the world grew by 480% in the period 2000–2011.

In 1992, Tim Berners-Lee created the World Wide Web, which is currently known as Web 1.0. Pages in this Web were characterised by being static, with their administrators, or webmasters, having absolute control of all the information controlled therein. These pages were designed to be read, with essentially no interaction between users (O'Really, 2005). The role of the Internet user during this developmental phase of the Web was therefore as a mere information consumer.

The term Web 2.0, or Social Web, has been used more and more often recently to refer to a new trend in the design and use of web pages whereby the user is both the centre of the information and content generator. This concept has been conceived as a philosophy, an attitude, a new way of doing

things that has arisen due to the evolution of the technology itself, which has allowed Internet users to move on from being simply consumers to become producers and creators as well.

The birth of Web 2.0 was marked by the appearance of specific communication tools for Internet users, such as blogs, chats, newsgroups and SNSs, which promote a greater degree of participation. Indeed, as discussed by Riegner (2007), as well as providing benefits for consumers, this interaction has major commercial implications as the consumers themselves now have an increasing influence on products and the strategies used to sell them.

The difference between traditional web pages and Web 2.0 therefore lies in the fact that in the former individuals or organisation only provided information about themselves (Arroyo, 2007), whereas the communication channels in Web 2.0 are two-way: Top-down and bottom-up. As discussed by O'Reilly (2005), a true Web 2.0 application is one which improves the more people use it. The key to such applications therefore lies in finding a balance between personal and social interests.

This term Web 2.0 was introduced by O'Reilly (2005) as the new stage in the Internet evolution referring to a collection of online applications sharing a number of common characteristics: "The Web as a platform, Harnessing of the Collective Intelligence, Data is the Next Intel Inside, End of the Software Release Cycle, Lightweight Programming Models, Rich User Experiences." The Web 2.0 has been defined in the literature in different ways (Anderson, 2007; Birdsall, 2007; Coyle, 2007; Craig, 2007; Needleman, 2007; Swisher, 2007) but still no definition seems to have been gained universal approval. Moreover there is a steady decline of the use of the term Web 2.0 while the term social media is gaining popularity[5]. Some researchers use this terms interchangeably but there is in fact a difference between them. Constantinides and Fountain (2008) defined the Web 2.0 and described it as an online interactive platform consisting of three components:

Application Types, Social Effects and Enabling Technologies. These three elements are depicted in Figure 1.

The application types (Blogs, Social Networks, Content Online Communities, Forums/Bulletin Boards and Content Aggregators) are in fact the categories of interactive and customer c\generated content platforms used by customers for communication and creation, editing and dissemination of content; in this study the term social media refers to these five application types but alternatively the term "Web 2.0 applications" can be used also.

Regarding the social effects factors in the model, these include the customer empowerment, the democratization of technology and the social networking as the most important ones. The social effects have been an important factor in shaping the consumer of the 21st Century. Enabling seamless generation of information and easy access to it is the key advantage of Web 2.0 applications. Copying, sharing, editing, syndicating, reproducing and re-mixing information are common practices in the Web 2.0 domain. The creation, sharing and dissemination of information results to democratization of knowledge and allows the active participation of users as contributors, reviewers and editors. Users can easily create communities of special interests and further share their experience and knowledge but also engage in a transparent conversation with the industry or politicians. The result is as explained earlier a unique form of customer empowerment allowing customers to affect as never before the market power structures and more importantly the shape of the future marketing (Constantinides et al., 2008).

The third dimension of the model, the Enabling Technologies, includes the equipment and software necessary to create the interactive social media and realize the connectivity, creation, editing, and dissemination of the user generated content. For example, RSS (Really Simple Syndication) is a way to syndicate and customize online content, wikis are applications allowing collaborative publishing, widgets is a generic term for the part of a Graphical User Interface that displays information and allows users to interface with the application and operating system in different ways, mashups are aggregators of content from different online sources to create a new service, AJAX is short for Asynchronous JavaScript, XML is a web development technique used for creating interactive web applications, or RIA (Rich Internet Applications) are Web applications that have the features and functionality of traditional desktop applications.

Figure 1. Web 2.0 dimensions

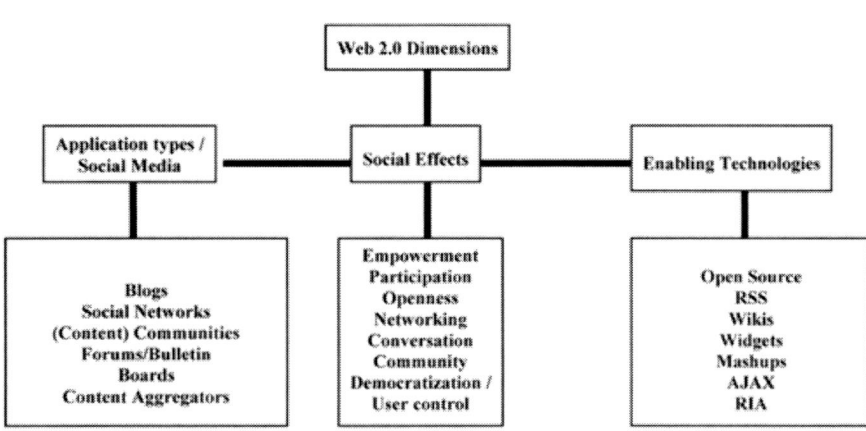

Source: Constantinides and Fountain (2008)

On the other hand, Cobo and Pardo (2007) propose a taxonomy of Web 2.0 applications and tools identifying four main application categories: Social Networking Sites, User Generated Content (UGC), intelligent information organization, and mashups.

- **Social Networking Sites:** Tools and applications for designing and creating websites to facilitate and promote social interchange spaces and communities (e.g., Facebook, LinkedIn).

- **User-Generated Content:** Applications that allow users to generate information in virtual environments using tools for upload and download contents and for writing, disseminating and bartering information. As tools for content generation, some examples could be: (a) weblogs software (blogware) that include content management software designed to create and administrate blogs (e.g., www.blogger.com), (b) blogging tools to improve blogs management such as readers, organizers, tagging tools, search tools, indexation tools (e.g., www.bloglines.com); (c) CMS, or Content Management Systems that can create and manage web sites in an easy manner (e.g., joomla, www.joomla.org); (d) wikis, as tools that allow users to upload and share contents and information generated by different users (e.g., Wikipedia, www.wikipedia.org); (e) online word processors (e.g., http://docs.google.com); online spreadsheets (e.g., http://spreadsheets.google.com); (f) Websites that allow the storage, publication, sharing and editing digital pictures (e.g. www.flickr.com); (g) tools and Websites that allow the access, editing and organizations of multimedia files (e.g., www.youtube.com); (h) virtual agendas and calendars that allow scheduling and shared planning (e.g., http://calendar.google.com); (i) tools for generating, publishing and sharing presentations (e.g., www.slide.com).

- **Intelligent Information Organization:** Tools, applications and resources that facilitate the arrangement, labeling, organization and arrangement of the information (e.g., http://del.icio.us). The contents syndication is a way to distribute and share information from a website. Then, other websites or users can easily access to these information. Most popular are RSS, Atom, RDF and OPML. The labeling or tagging allows Internet users to classify contents by assigning keywords called labels or tags. The folksonomies is a collective classification system that allows the information organization in a collective way, based on people that cooperate by arranging contents using tags.

- **Mashups:** Applications that allow the combination of resources and applications from different websites to offer an added value service (e.g., Panoramio uses Google Maps to locate pictures uploaded by the users).

The difference between traditional web sites and Web 2.0 sites lies in the fact that in the former individuals or organizations can merely present information about themselves and their activities in an one-way, downwards communication pattern (Arroyo, 2007) while in the interactive Web 2.0 the communication becomes two-way: downwards and upwards. O'Reilly (2005) states that network effects are obvious in this environment since a true Web 2.0 application becomes more valuable the more people use it. The key is the size of the users group and the search for balance between personal interests and public assets. Rheingold (2005) suggests that technology convergence has profound social repercussions; this because people use tools allowing them to adopt new forms of interaction, coordination and cooperation. These new forms facilitate the exchange of collective knowledge and the accumulation of a social capital, generated when social networking, trust, reciprocity, standards and values are shared encouraging people to collaborate and cooperate (Rheingold, 2005). O'Reilly (2005) defines this as the "architecture of participation" which underlines the need for Web 2.0 web sites allowing user participation, so that the architecture of participation is built around individuals, not around the technology.

The importance and popularity of the Social Media as marketing tools and communication channels have been steadily growing during the last six years (Deighton & Kornfeld, 2009) and research suggests that social media have become an important influencer of consumer behavior (Constantinides & Fountain, 2008). According to a Forrester Research Report (2008), the social media domain has become an important tool of Interactive Marketing and commercial budgets on Social Media marketing are growing at the cost of other forms of interactive and traditional marketing.

Most marketing practitioners already recognize the impact of the Social Media as a social and commercial phenomenon placing the customer rather than the marketer in control. In this line a key interest of marketers is how to minimize the negative effects of customer empowerment and utilize the Social Media to their advantage so that they can extract the maximum possible value from social media-based marketing approaches (Regus Report, 2010). In this sense we observe the last years an explosion in the number of social media applications adopted by businesses and particularly by retailers. Some of the methods proposed in the literature include getting real-time feedback on existing products or new product ideas/concepts, build "community" among consumers around their goods, services or brand, leverage customer self-service, and have consumers collaborating on developing future product strategies (Constantinides & Fountain, 2008; Parise & Guinan, 2008).

According to Bernoff and Li (2008), companies can deploy social applications in different departments to accomplish a variety of objectives (see Table 1).

MAIN FOCUS OF THE CHAPTER

The effects of the social media on people and businesses have been the focus of attention by practitioners and academics. Grewal, Iyer & Levy (2004) observed that "… no other innovation has received as much attention from retailers, manufacturers, consumers and the general public as has been accorded to Internet retailing or e-tailing. Indeed, no other form of intertype competition threatens to upset traditional retailing more than Internet retailing."

Academic research is mainly focused on the impact of the social media on corporate processes (Yakel, 2006; Craig, 2007), on the importance of online communities for corporations (Du & Wagner, 2006; Kolbitsch & Maurer, 2007; Swaine, 2007) or on issues regarding the effects of these new technologies on business (Karger & Quan, 2005; Biever, 2006; Deshpande & Jadad, 2006; Boll, 2007). Non-academic research also provides plenty of evidence as to how corporations integrate the Web 2.0 applications into their operations (DeFelice, 2006; McKinsey, 2007). An increasing number of studies suggest that corporate interest on the social media domain keeps growing and more and more firms are introducing different forms of social media into their daily business routines as well as into their marketing strategies (Cymfony, 2006).

Internet retailing has not escaped from these technology trends and e-tailing as a retail format has moved quickly through a cycle of fast technology change. Rightly Grewal *et al.* (2004) point to the fact that observations and contents regarding the actual state of internet retailing may be debatable or obsolete in a very short term.

Table 1. Deployment of social applications

Manager's role or department	Typical groundswell objective	Appropriate social applications	Success metrics
Research and Development	Listening: gaining insights from customers and using that input in the innovation process	• Brand monitoring • Research communities • Innovation communities	• Insights gained • Usable product ideas • Increased speed of development
Marketing	Talking: Using conversations with customers to promote products or services	• Blogs • Communities • Video on user-generated sites	• Better market awareness • Online "buzz" • Time spent on sites • Increased sales
Sales	Energizing: Identifying enthusiastic customers and using them to influence others	• Social networking sites • Brand ambassador programs • Communities • Embeddable "widgets"	• Community membership • Online "buzz" • Increased sales
Customer Support	Supporting: Enabling customers to help one another solve problems	• Support forums • Wikis	• Number of members participating • Volume of questions answered online • Decreased volume of support calls
Operations	Managing: Providing employees with tools so that they can assist one another in finding more effective ways of doing business	• Internal social networks • Wikis	• Number of members participating • Increased operational efficiency • Decreased volume of e-mail

Source: Bernoff and Li (2007, p. 41)

Issues, Controversies, Problems

As mentioned earlier the emergence and the mushrooming growth of Web 2.0 and in particular of the Social Media applications brought about a revolution in the marketing practice. Next to the customer empowerment Social Media-related additional trends and challenges for online retailers are the collaborative merchandising and the (mobile) comparison shopping (Forrester Research, 2008),

These challenges could be transformed though to opportunities; the Web 2.0 could give a new impulse to online retailing and in some cases alleviate some of the negative dimensions of the social media revolution. The effects of Web 2.0 in retailing can be broken down in three dimensions (Jain & Ganesh, 2007): content parameters, collaboration parameters and commerce parameters (see Table 2).

Content parameters are related to tools and techniques allowing a better and richer information environment. For example, RIAs (Rich Internet Applications) like FLEX allow a higher quality presentation format with an easier and more user-friendly interface that enhances the customer experience. The same happens with RSS feeds, podcasts, videocasts or mashups.

Collaboration parameters refer to applications that allow consumers-retailer interaction and participation of consumers and other agents on product or services productions (see the example of SAP or AMD at the beginning of the chapter).

Finally, commerce parameters are related to functionalities that can support consumer choices and/or give a higher value to the chosen option.

Table 2. The effects of Web 2.0 in retailing

Content parameters	Collaboration parameters	Commerce parameters
• Unique user experiences (RIA driven). • Dynamic user help (Peer-to-peer or central). • Data Feeds (RSS, ATOM, XML, JS). • Podcasts/Vodcasts. • Search (Semantic) • Aggregation mechanisms (Mashups)	• Customer peer-to peer network, Collective Intelligence (Blogs, Wikis, Discussion Forums, User Reviews, Tagging, etc.). • Collaborative product customizations	• End user product customizations. • Contextual shopping help (Live agent chat). • Voice based chopping help (VoIP) • Comparison shopping (across brands, end user recommendations)

Source: Jain and Ganesh (2007)

For example, offering some kind of shopping assistant or a complementary support service through voice or chatting tools.

The above classification highlights the fact that there are multiple factors and effects from implementing Web 2.0 applications/Social Media in retailing. The study attempts to provide a better understanding of the effects, experiences and potential of retailers by engaging social media as part of their marketing strategy. Next to these objectives the study also provides a picture of the businesses using these technologies by segmenting the market according to the intensity of use of social media strategies.

In summary the chapter will provide an answer to the following research questions:

- What are the different segments of retailing businesses in Spain based on the degree of engagement of Social Media Marketing tools?
- What are the characteristics of the retailing segments involved in social media marketing?
- What are the priorities of retailers in adopting social media as marketing tools?
- What internal, external and technological factors influencing the adoption of social media marketing by the various categories of retailers?
- Is the size of the business affecting the degree of the adoption process?

RESEARCH METHODOLOGY, SAMPLE, AND DATA PROCESSING

In order to evaluate the impact and potential effects of Web 2.0 concepts and tools an online questionnaire for data collection was developed. The sample was drawn from three categories of retailers: Large (more than 250 employees, more than 50 million euro of sales), Medium (between 50 and 250 employees, between 10 and 50 million euro of sales), and Small (less than 50 employees, less than 10 million euro of sales) companies from the Spanish retail sector (NACE2, 47). To identify and select the companies that meet these requirements the AMADEUS database edited by Bureau Van Dijk was used; this database contains financial information on over 10 million public and private companies in 41 countries. The potential participants were contacted by telephone in order to invite the right person (marketing manager) to participate in the study. Finally a representative sample of 90 companies was obtained.

The questionnaire was based on a combination of closed-ended, dichotomous and multichotomous questions, with single and multiple responses. The main objective was to acquire information about the Spanish companies' experience, use and opinion of the Social Media tools.

The latent segmentation methodology was used in order to define segments and to profile the companies. This method allows the assignment of companies to segments based on their probability of belonging to the clusters, breaking with the restrictions of deterministic assignment inherent to the non-hierarchical cluster analysis (Dillon & Kumar, 1994). Another advantage of latent class models is that they allow the inclusion of variables with different measurement scales (continual, ordinal or nominal) (Vermunt & Magidson, 2005).

The indicators for the latent segmentation were based on the different constructs of the Technology Acceptance Model (TAM) proposed by Davis, Bagozzi and Warshaw (1989) on a five-point Likert scale: Attitudes towards social media applications (Figure 1), perceived ease of use and usefulness of these tools, intention to use or continue using the social media, and actual use of these tools. Moreover, we have added more constructs to segment the companies, the perceived strategic value of these tools to their organization, based on Grandon and Pearson's research (2003) (see Table 3). Based on these variables, different grouping patterns that fulfill the principles of maximum internal coherence and maximum external differentiation were obtained; the Latent Gold 4.5. statistical software was used.

In order to use these constructs in the cluster segmentation, the content, convergent and discriminant validity and reliability of the constructs were verified first by means of the Partial Least Square (PLS) path model, using the SmartPLS software. Then, the resulting factor scores of the measurement model were used as measure of these indicators, so these variables are continuous defined in the real intervals (Brown, Pope & Voges, 2003; Allred, Smith & Swinyard, 2006; Mäenpää, 2006).

In order to refine the resulting segments, we have analyzed different variables that could have an influence on the degree of use of social media: Number of employees in the company, number of information and communication technologies (ICT) professionals working in the company, presence or not of formal policy guidelines on the use of Social Media, possession of broadband connection and Intranet site, possession of adequate software and hardware tools for social media–related activities, number of employees who can send e-mails internally, externally and visit Internet sites without restrictions. Finally, various social media applications that are not used or applications that companies were not planning to use in the future were identified as well as the applications actually used. For applications used businesses had to identify how these are actually used. Three options were possible here: for internal purposes, for customer–related purposes and for working with external partners/suppliers).

Table 3. Definitions of constructs

Construct	Definition
Attitude	"An individual's positive or negative feelings (evaluative affect) about performing the target behavior" (Fishbein and Ajzen, 1975, p. 216).
Perceived Ease of Use	"The degree to which a person believes that using a particular system would be free of effort" (Davis, 1989, p. 320).
Perceived Usefulness	"The degree to which a person believes that using a particular system would enhance his or her job performance" (Davis, 1989, p. 320).
Intention to Use	The company's intention to use the Web 2.0 tools (Davis, 1989).
Use	The degree of current usage of the Web 2.0 tools (Davis, 1989).
Perceived Strategic Value	"The summation of perceived benefits from (Web 2.0 tools) minus the summation of perceived cost over a period of time" (Kwun, Nickels, Alijani and Omar, 2010)

A TYPOLOGY OF COMPANIES ACCORDING TO SOCIAL MEDIA USE

In applying the latent segmentation approach, the first step consists of selecting the optimum number of segments. The model used estimated from one (no heterogeneity existed) up to eight (i.e. eight segments or heterogeneity existed). Table 4 shows the estimation process summary and the fit indexes for each of the eight models.

The model fit was evaluated according to the Bayesian Information Criterion (BIC) that allows the identification of the model with the least number of classes that best fits to the data. The lowest BIC value was considered as the best model indicator (Vermunt & Magidson, 2002; 2005). In this case, the best alternative was represented by four different user groups, as the BIC is minimized in this case. The statistic values

included in Table 4 indicate that the model has a good fit.

The Wald statistic was analyzed in order to evaluate the statistical significance within a group of estimated parameters (see Table 5). For all the indicators a significant p-value associated with the Wald statistics was obtained, confirming that each indicator discriminates between the clusters in a significant way (Vermunt & Magidson, 2005).

Table 5 also contains the profiles of the obtained clusters. In the upper part the size and name assigned to the four groups is shown: the cluster called "Passive" includes 20.49% of companies surveyed, the "Potential" 42.15%, the "Initiated" cluster 18.32% and "Expert" cluster 19.03%.

In addition, in the Table 5 we observe the average score that takes each segment in each of the indicators (note that these can take values between 0 and 5, since items that composed each

Table 4. Estimates and fit indexes

Number of conglomerates	LL	BIC(LL)	Npar	Class.Err.	E_s	R^2
1-Cluster	-803.9808	1661.1314	12	0.0000	1	1
2-Cluster	-668.2734	1447.3172	25	0.0133	0.9428	0.9558
3-Cluster	-592.4378	1353.2467	38	0.0317	0.9295	0.9317
4-Cluster	**-540.3367**	**1306.6450**	**51**	**0.0196**	**0.9529**	**0.9558**
5-Cluster	-512.4392	1308.4507	64	0.0135	0.9658	0.9670
6-Cluster	-474.1386	1289.4501	77	0.0167	0.9725	0.9673
7-Cluster	-478.9200	1356.6135	90	0.0121	0.9794	0.9772
8-Cluster	-457.1400	1370.6541	103	0.0265	0.9604	0.9503

LL=log likelihood; BIC=Bayesian information criterion; Npar=number of parameters; Class.Err.=classification error; E_s=entropy statistic (*entropy R-squared*); R^2=Standard R-squared

Table 5. Profiles of clusters

	PASSIVE	POTENTIAL	INITIATED	EXPERT	Wald	p-value	R^2
Cluster Size	20.49%	42.15%	18.32%	19.03%			
Indicators							
Attitude	2.2462	3.8415	3.5597	4.7548	111.1753	6.1e-24	0.5210
Perceived Ease of Use	2.3534	3.6777	3.2014	3.9302	24.0722	2.4e-5	0.2718
Intention to Use	1.8081	3.8550	3.6036	4.9858	627.9091	9.0e-136	0.7107
Perceived Usefulness	1.7480	2.9116	3.2434	4.3656	219.7572	2.3e-47	0.5949
Use	0.0000	0.0000	3.3170	3.8714	142.9491	8.7e-31	0.7514
Perceived Strategic Value	1.9313	3.1529	3.4147	3.9668	101.9836	5.8e-22	0.5180

scale were measured with five-point likert scales). We note that the clusters are ordered from lowest to highest use of social media tools. Thus the "Passive" and "Potential" clusters do not use any social media. However, the future intention to use of "Potential" cluster is greater than the intention to use of "Passive" cluster. In addition, "Potential" cluster has a more positive attitude towards Social Media tools and they perceived them as easier to use, more useful and are considered as providing greater strategic value to the company.

On the other hand, the companies included in the "Initiated" and "Expert" cluster are currently using social media. The use of Social Media by the "Expert" cluster is greater than the use of "Initiated" cluster. Furthermore, the intention to continue using these tools is higher in the "Expert" cluster. Moreover businesses belonging to the "Expert" cluster have the most positive attitudes towards these tools. In addition, they perceived them as easier to use, more useful and have greater strategic value to their business.

Completing the composition of the four segments the profile of the resulting groups according to the information from other variables was analyzed. Table 6 shows the groups' composition based on a number of descriptive criteria included in the analysis. Independence tests associated with

Table 6. Summary statistics of descriptive criteria

DESCRIPTIVE CRITERIA	CATEGORIES	Passive	Potential	Initiated	Expert	χ^2	p-value
Number of employees	Less than 25	**29.4%**	**38.9%**	13.3%	22.2%	22.605	0.365
	Between 25 and 50	17.6%	19.4%	**33.3%**	5.6%		
	Between 51 and 100	23.5%	8.3%	0.0%	22.2%		
	Between 101 and 250	5.9%	13.9%	6.7%	11.1%		
	Between 251 and 500	0.0%	8.3%	20.0%	16.7%		
	Between 501 and 1000	17.6%	8.3%	13.3%	5.6%		
	Between 1001 and 5000	0.0%	2.8%	6.7%	5.6%		
	More than 5000	5.9%	0.0%	6.7%	11.1%		
Number of ICT professionals working in the company	No one	47.1%	56.8%	20.0%	16.7%	28.158	0.021
	Between 1 and 2	35.3%	18.9%	**26.7%**	**27.8%**		
	Between 3 and 5	0.0%	10.8%	13.3%	16.7%		
	Between 6 and 10	0.0%	13.5%	20.0%	11.1%		
	Between 11 and 20	17.6%	0.0%	6.7%	22.2%		
	More than 20	0.0%	0.0%	13.3%	5.6%		
Formal policy guidelines on the use of Social Media	Yes	0.0%	5.4%	40.0%	**66.7%**	32.817	0.000
	No	**100.0%**	**94.6%**	60.0%	33.3%		
Broadband connection	Yes	**94.1%**	**91.9%**	**100.0%**	**100.0%**	3.316	0.768
	No	5.9%	5.4%	0.0%	0.0%		
	No Internet connection	0.0%	2.7%	0.0%	0.0%		
Intranet site	Yes	**52.9%**	43.2%	**80.0%**	**94.1%**	15.560	0.001
	No	47.1%	**56.8%**	20.0%	5.9%		
Adequate software/ hardware for Social Media – related activities	Yes	31.3%	**62.2%**	**86.7%**	**94.4%**	18.516	0.000
	No	**68.8%**	37.8%	13.3%	5.6%		
Amount of employees who can send internal emails	No one	11.8%	8.1%	0.0%	0.0%	17.688	0.039
	A few	**41.2%**	21.6%	20.0%	0.0%		
	The majority	17.6%	**40.5%**	26.7%	33.3%		
	Everyone	29.4%	29.7%	**53.3%**	**66.7%**		
Amount of employees who can send external emails	No one	11.8%	8.1%	0.0%	0.0%	11.713	0.230
	A few	29.4%	29.7%	26.7%	11.1%		
	The majority	23.5%	**43.2%**	33.3%	33.3%		
	Everyone	**35.3%**	18.9%	40.0%	**55.6%**		
Amount of employees who can visit Internet sites without restrictions	No one	5.9%	8.1%	0.0%	0.0%	15.877	0.069
	A few	**47.1%**	35.1%	26.7%	5.6%		
	The majority	17.6%	**37.8%**	**46.7%**	38.9%		
	Everyone	29.4%	18.9%	26.7%	**55.6%**		

statistic χ^2 conclude that significant differences exist between the segments regarding the number of ICT professionals working in the company, the presence of formal policy guidelines on the use of Social Media, the possession of adequate software and hardware tools for introducing social media–related activities, and the number of employees who can send email internally. So there is independence between different clusters regarding the number of company employees, the presence of broadband connection and Intranet, the number of employees who can send emails externally, and the number of employees who are able to visit Internet sites without restrictions.

With regard to the number of employees, the largest percentage of companies that belong to "Passive" and "Potential" cluster have fewer than 25 workers (29.4% and 38.9%, respectively), the largest percentage of those belonging to "Initiated" cluster have between 25 and 50 employees (33.3%) and with respect to the companies belonging to "Expert" cluster, there is an equal percentage with less than 25 and between 51 and 100 employees (22.2% each). It is worth noting the high percentage of companies belonging to "Expert" cluster, compared with the rest, with more than 5000 employees.

Moreover, related to employee, the highest percentage of companies belonging to "Potential" and "Passive" cluster do not have any ICT professionals working for them (41.1% and 56.8%, respectively). However, the highest proportion of companies belonging to "Initiated" and "Expert" cluster has between 1 and 2 ICT professionals (26.7% and 27.8%, respectively), in addition, the percentage of companies with more than 2 ICT professionals is also high.

An effective use of social media as marketing tools requires that the personnel is empowered to use them – privately or professionally - but the problem of responsible and prudent use is a realistic and serious one. It is therefore important for businesses to establish formal policy guidelines on the use of Social Media by employees.

The analysis indicates that only the majority of companies belonging to "Initiated" cluster, that is to say companies who in principle make relatively intensive use of social media tools, have such policy guidelines drafted. It seems that the intensive use of social media tools has triggered the need to implement these policy guidelines (or conversely, the development of these policies has led to a greater use of these tools).

In our segmentation there is a higher percentage of companies in the most social media active segments with broadband connection, intranet, adequate hardware/software infrastructure for implementing social media-related activities; this category has also the largest number of employees who can send emails internally, externally and can access the Internet without restrictions. So, we can conclude that the technology adoption, and more specifically the adoption of social media tools by companies, mainly depends on the technological context of the company.

In Table 7 are depicted various social media instruments and the use of these by companies per cluster. Companies that do not use any social media tools were asked whether they plan to use these in the future. Companies using social media tools were asked to identify the main purpose of their use: For internal purposes (for example, communicate, share information among employees), for customer-related purposes (communication with the customers) or for cooperating with external partners or suppliers.

Interestingly most companies from the "Passive" and "Potential" clusters do not use the Social Media tools mentioned and they do not plan to use them; this percentage is lower in companies from the Potential" cluster something also evident in Table 5 where the future intention to use was analyzed. With respect to additional tools they plan to use, companies from "Passive" cluster showed primarily Social Networking Sites (17.6%), customer reviews (11.8%), "listening" to the voice of the customer in the social space (11.8%), blogs (11.8%) and product suggestion box (11.8%).

Table 7. Summary statistics of social media instruments

		Passive	Potential	Initiated	Expert	χ^2	p-value
Social Networking Sits	Do not plan to use	**82.4%**	**78.4%**	20.0%	22.2%	51.072	0.000
	Plan to use	17.6%	21.6%	13.3%	16.7%		
	Used for internal purposes	0.0%	0.0%	20.0%	11.1%		
	Used for customer-related purposes	0.0%	0.0%	20.0%	**33.3%**		
	Used for working with suppliers	0.0%	0.0%	13.3%	11.1%		
	Do not know	0.0%	0.0%	13.3%	5.6%		
Customer reviews	Do not plan to use	**88.2%**	**73.0%**	13.3%	5.6%	55.697	0.000
	Plan to use	11.8%	10.8%	**33.3%**	11.1%		
	Used for internal purposes	0.0%	5.4%	6.7%	22.2%		
	Used for customer-related purposes	0.0%	5.4%	13.3%	**38.9%**		
	Used for working with suppliers	0.0%	0.0%	6.7%	11.1%		
	Do not know	0.0%	5.4%	26.7%	11.1%		
Blogs	Do not plan to use	**82.4%**	**78.4%**	**33.3%**	**27.8%**	38.275	0.001
	Plan to use	11.8%	16.2%	20.0%	22.2%		
	Used for internal purposes	0.0%	0.0%	6.7%	16.7%		
	Used for customer-related purposes	0.0%	0.0%	20.0%	**27.8%**		
	Used for working with suppliers	0.0%	0.0%	13.3%	5.6%		
	Do not know	5.9%	5.4%	6.7%	0.0%		
Youtube or other videos	Do not plan to use	**94.1%**	**83.8%**	13.3%	**33.3%**	55.175	0.000
	Plan to use	0.0%	8.1%	13.3%	11.1%		
	Used for internal purposes	0.0%	2.7%	20.0%	22.2%		
	Used for customer-related purposes	0.0%	0.0%	6.7%	22.2%		
	Used for working with suppliers	0.0%	0.0%	20.0%	0.0%		
	Do not know	5.9%	5.4%	**26.7%**	11.1%		
Social bookmarking sites/ tagging	Do not plan to use	**94.1%**	**75.7%**	**33.3%**	**27.8%**	36.759	0.001
	Plan to use	0.0%	5.4%	13.3%	11.1%		
	Used for internal purposes	0.0%	2.7%	0.0%	11.1%		
	Used for customer-related purposes	0.0%	0.0%	0.0%	11.1%		
	Used for working with suppliers	0.0%	0.0%	6.7%	0.0%		
	Do not know	5.9%	16.2%	**46.7%**	**38.9%**		
"Listening" to the voice of the customer in the social space	Do not plan to use	**76.5%**	**73.0%**	20.0%	11.1%	45.793	0.000
	Plan to use	11.8%	10.8%	20.0%	11.1%		
	Used for internal purposes	0.0%	2.7%	6.7%	**33.3%**		
	Used for customer-related purposes	5.9%	2.7%	20.0%	**33.3%**		
	Used for working with suppliers	0.0%	2.7%	6.7%	5.6%		
	Do not know	5.9%	8.1%	**26.7%**	5.6%		
Questions and answers	Do not plan to use	**88.2%**	**64.9%**	13.3%	5.6%	57.638	0.000
	Plan to use	5.9%	13.5%	13.3%	11.1%		
	Used for internal purposes	0.0%	8.1%	6.7%	27.8%		
	Used for customer-related purposes	0.0%	2.7%	**26.7%**	**50.0%**		
	Used for working with suppliers	0.0%	2.7%	13.3%	5.6%		
	Do not know	5.9%	8.1%	**26.7%**	0.0%		
Community forums	Do not plan to use	**88.2%**	**78.4%**	13.3%	11.1%	62.240	0.000
	Plan to use	5.9%	13.5%	20.0%	**27.8%**		
	Used for internal purposes	0.0%	0.0%	6.7%	**27.8%**		
	Used for customer-related purposes	0.0%	2.7%	20.0%	22.2%		
	Used for working with suppliers	0.0%	2.7%	6.7%	11.1%		
	Do not know	5.9%	2.7%	**33.3%**	0.0%		
Product suggestion box	Do not plan to use	**76.5%**	**59.5%**	0.0%	11.1%	42.478	0.000
	Plan to use	11.8%	16.2%	26.7%	11.1%		
	Used for internal purposes	0.0%	10.8%	13.3%	**33.3%**		
	Used for customer-related purposes	5.9%	10.8%	**33.3%**	**33.3%**		
	Used for working with suppliers	5.9%	0.0%	6.7%	5.6%		
	Do not know	0.0%	2.7%	20.0%	5.6%		

continued on following page

Table 7. Continued

Real Simple Syndication (RSS)	Do not plan to use	**94.1%**	**75.7%**	26.7%	22.2%	35.303	0.000
	Plan to use	0.0%	5.4%	13.3%	11.1%		
	Used for internal purposes	0.0%	0.0%	0.0%	0.0%		
	Used for customer-related purposes	0.0%	0.0%	13.3%	27.8%		
	Used for working with suppliers	0.0%	0.0%	0.0%	0.0%		
	Do not know	5.9%	18.9%	**46.7%**	38.9%		
Wikis	Do not plan to use	**94.1%**	**86.5%**	40.0%	55.6%	37.713	0.000
	Plan to use	0.0%	2.7%	0.0%	11.1%		
	Used for internal purposes	0.0%	0.0%	0.0%	16.7%		
	Used for customer-related purposes	0.0%	0.0%	13.3%	5.6%		
	Used for working with suppliers	0.0%	0.0%	0.0%	0.0%		
	Do not know	5.9%	10.8%	**46.7%**	11.1%		
Podcasts	Do not plan to use	**94.1%**	**81.1%**	46.7%	50.0%	21.297	0.046
	Plan to use	0.0%	2.7%	13.3%	5.6%		
	Used for internal purposes	0.0%	0.0%	0.0%	5.6%		
	Used for customer-related purposes	0.0%	0.0%	0.0%	5.6%		
	Used for working with suppliers	0.0%	0.0%	0.0%	0.0%		
	Do not know	5.9%	16.2%	40.0%	33.3%		
Product Reviews and Product Ratings	Do not plan to use	**94.1%**	**83.8%**	26.7%	22.2%	49.209	0.000
	Plan to use	0.0%	2.7%	**40.0%**	27.8%		
	Used for internal purposes	0.0%	2.7%	6.7%	11.1%		
	Used for customer-related purposes	0.0%	2.7%	6.7%	27.8%		
	Used for working with suppliers	0.0%	0.0%	0.0%	5.6%		
	Do not know	5.9%	8.1%	20.0%	5.6%		
Peer to peer (P2P) Networking	Do not plan to use	**94.1%**	**83.8%**	40.0%	66.7%	20.080	0.001
	Plan to use	0.0%	0.0%	0.0%	5.6%		
	Used for internal purposes	0.0%	0.0%	0.0%	11.1%		
	Used for customer-related purposes	0.0%	0.0%	0.0%	0.0%		
	Used for working with suppliers	0.0%	0.0%	0.0%	0.0%		
	Do not know	5.9%	16.2%	**60.0%**	16.7%		
Microblogging	Do not plan to use	**94.1%**	**83.8%**	33.3%	38.9%	43.945	0.000
	Plan to use	0.0%	0.0%	20.0%	16.7%		
	Used for internal purposes	0.0%	0.0%	6.7%	16.7%		
	Used for customer-related purposes	0.0%	0.0%	0.0%	16.7%		
	Used for working with suppliers	0.0%	0.0%	0.0%	0.0%		
	Do not know	5.9%	16.2%	**40.0%**	11.1%		
Mash-ups	Do not plan to use	**94.1%**	**67.6%**	13.3%	27.8%	41.404	0.000
	Plan to use	0.0%	10.8%	20.0%	11.1%		
	Used for internal purposes	0.0%	8.1%	6.7%	11.1%		
	Used for customer-related purposes	0.0%	2.7%	20.0%	**33.3%**		
	Used for working with suppliers	0.0%	2.7%	0.0%	5.6%		
	Do not know	5.9%	8.1%	**40.0%**	11.1%		
Real-time feed agregator	Do not plan to use	**94.1%**	**75.7%**	**46.7%**	38.9%	20.281	0.016
	Plan to use	0.0%	2.7%	13.3%	5.6%		
	Used for internal purposes	0.0%	0.0%	0.0%	5.6%		
	Used for customer-related purposes	0.0%	0.0%	0.0%	0.0%		
	Used for working with suppliers	0.0%	0.0%	0.0%	0.0%		
	Do not know	5.9%	21.6%	40.0%	**50.0%**		
Customization of products	Do not plan to use	**94.1%**	**81.1%**	26.7%	55.6%	26.510	0.009
	Plan to use	0.0%	2.7%	6.7%	11.1%		
	Used for internal purposes	0.0%	2.7%	13.3%	5.6%		
	Used for customer-related purposes	0.0%	0.0%	20.0%	11.1%		
	Used for working with suppliers	0.0%	0.0%	0.0%	0.0%		
	Do not know	5.9%	13.5%	**33.3%**	16.7%		

On the other hand, companies belonging to the "Potential" cluster saw interest in the same tools as above plus the creation of a Questions and Answers (Q&A) section (13.5%), forums (13.5%) and mash-ups (10.8%).

With regard to "Initiated" cluster, there are an equal percentage of companies using Social Networking Sites for internal purposes and for customer-related purposes (20% each). The highest percentage of companies uses a section on their web site with a product suggestion box (33.3%) and questions and answers (26.7%) for customer-related purposes. In addition, there is a high percentage of companies with own blog (20%), that use YouTube or other videos (20%), mash-ups (20%) and offer the possibility of customization of products (20%), all of these tools for customer-related purposes. However, there is not a high proportion of companies in this cluster that use the Web 2.0 tools for internal purposes or for cooperating with external partners or suppliers. The highest percentage of companies in "Initiated" cluster states that they plan to use in the future customer reviews (33.3%) and product reviews and ratings[6] (40%).

With regard to "Initiated" cluster, there are an equal percentage of companies using Social Networking Sites for internal purposes and for customer-related purposes (20% each). The highest percentage of companies uses a section on their web site with a product suggestion box (33.3%) and questions and answers (26.7%) for customer-related purposes. In addition, there is a high percentage of companies with own blog (20%), that use YouTube or other videos (20%), mash-ups (20%) and offer the possibility of customization of products (20%), all of these tools for customer-related purposes. However, there is not a high proportion of companies in this cluster that use the Web 2.0 tools for internal purposes or for cooperating with external partners or suppliers. The highest percentage of companies in "Initiated" cluster states that they plan to use in

the future customer reviews (33.3%) and product reviews and ratings[7] (40%).

In the "Expert" cluster the highest proportion of companies provides for a section on its website for questions and answers (50%) and consumer reviews (38.9%). 33.3% uses social networking, mash-ups (33.3%), blogs (27.8%) and product reviews and ratings (27.8%), all of this tools for customer-related purposes. The highest percentage of companies uses the forums for internal purposes (27.8%) and an equal percentage plan to use them for the same reason. Interestingly an equal percentage of companies use certain tools for internal and for customer-related purposes: "Listening" to the voice of the customer in the social space (33.3% for each purpose), providing a product suggestion box (33.3% for each purpose) and YouTube or other video exchange channels (22.2% for each purpose). On the other hand more than one quarter of the businesses in this cluster use Real Simple Syndication (RSS[8]) for customer-related purposes (27.8%).

The social media tools which companies use less and are not interest to use in the future are also visible In Table 7. These are tagging, social bookmarking (e.g., Del.icio.us, Digg, StumbleUpon), wikis (e.g., Wikipedia), podcasts, peer to peer networking (P2P[9]), micro-blogging (e.g., Twitter, Plurk, Jaiku) and real-time feed aggregators (e.g., Friendfeed[10]).

Solutions and Recommendations

Retailers perceiving the social media as easy to use, useful for the company and understand their strategic value are likely to develop a positive attitude as to the adoption of social media for current and future use. The availability, ease of use and variety of such applications increases by the day thanks to field initiatives and the open character of these applications allowing their constant improvement due to collaboration among individuals. It must not escape of our attention that applications like the Facebook, Twitter, LinkedIn and other have gained in very short tome hundreds of millions of followers. This gives to businesses a very strong signal but it seems that this is not always received by marketers. The findings of the study underline the fact a certain level of connection with the market and digital fluency is important; in that respect proactive attitudes of the management and the technology literacy of management and personnel are important conditions for understanding the benefits offered by these tools for the business.

In addition the company technological infrastructure and personnel access to technology is also related to the current use of Web 2.0 applications. Fundamentally, companies with higher proportion of adequate software/hardware for social media-related activities, employees who can send internal and external emails, visit Internet without restrictions, and have Intranet, are those who make more use of Social Media. An interesting issue for future research is to exactly measure and model the relationship between company technological context and adoption of Web 2.0 applications.

As a recommendation we suggest that corporations should introduce the position of an Online Community Manager, that is someone dedicated to maintain and improve the company's online presence not only as an web site but also as participant in the social Web; implementing various social media strategies for capturing the online customer voice and engage with customers (Constantinides et al., 2008). This can add high value to the company marketing program and generate the bidirectional communication typical of the social Web (company-consumer, consumer-company).

The focus on the social media marketing does not mean that businesses have to neglect their traditional online presence, the web site. As mentioned earlier the Website remains the number one information source for the vast majority of consumers. In this sense it is also necessary that the Online Community Manager places attention on search engine optimization (SEO) and search engine marketing (SEM), which are necessary an effective ways to reach the online consumers and engage with them.

FUTURE RESEARCH DIRECTIONS

The Internet marketing has become a mainstream commercial activity and the second generation of Internet applications–the Web 2.0 applications or social media–are becoming rapidly commonplace as marketing tools in the retailing sector. One should expect that after a period of experimentation and trial and error approaches the use of social media as part of the marketing strategy will enter a mature stage. Retailers and other businesses realize already that the adoption of these tools is the only way to achieve a balance against an empowered customer by engaging with customers and bringing the initiative of the social online activity to their own quarters.

Mapping the retail domain as to the adoption of the social media marketing, it can be argued that understanding the motives and barriers for adoption is the first step to the direction of developing better models and theory around this new marketing domain. This study provides a methodology to facilitate this process and offers a basis for follow-up studies focused on areas like segmentation, adoption criteria and processes, motives for adoption and effectiveness of social media marketing in the retail sector. However the study is limited to one European country: the global character of the Internet marketing requires that comparable research is conducted to more markets and geographical areas.

Another important line of future research is the assessment of performance of social media marketing efforts. This requires the development of industry benchmarks and performance metrics that will help marketers to follow up the progress and appraise the effectiveness of their strategies and improve them. Such metrics will also provide early warnings on changes in the social and technology domains that can affect the effectiveness of the social media strategies. Considering the fast technological change of the Internet domain this last element is of utmost importance.

Therefore the main lines of future research must be focused on similar studies in cross-cultural situations, the refinement of conclusions by focusing on specific research areas and the development of conceptual frameworks, benchmarks and measurement tools.

Considering the fact that Internet marketing and in particular the social media marketing is by all means a fact that will define the future of retailing and business in general this chapter provides a detailed view on the engagement of the Social media by retailers in Spain at this moment.

CONCLUSION

The Internet and its latest stage, the social media, have contributed to a radical transformation of the marketing practice, the customer behavior and the e-business. Deighton and Konrfeld (2009) argue that considering the fact that the social media enabled the substantial increase of customer power, engaging the social media as marketing is a logical business choice. There are indications that the impact of the social Web is indeed very significant in several business activity areas and particularly the areas of marketing communication and product innovation (Piller & Walcher, 2006; Kim & Bae, 2008). For retailers already in the forefront of e-business, the social media developments can have substantial impact on their online strategies and markets. Many retailers are already active in social media marketing and many more are planning activities in this domain. This explorative study examines the antecedents of the adoption of the social media by Spanish retailers and the way they engage them as part of their online marketing strategy.

The article defines the social media and explains their potential functionalities and benefits when applied to the retail sector. The retailing environment becomes increasingly competitive and the future survival and success will greatly depend on the degree retailers will understand and approach the empowered and highly sophisticated future consumer.

The latent segmentation statistical technique was used to classify and profile companies with regard to their use of social media for marketing. Latent class models can incorporate variables with different scales, both metric and non metric and the differentiation between indicators to generate clusters allows a better framework to define, profile and explain the differences between segments. After the application of this methodology four different segments have been obtained on the basis of retailers' attitudes and maturity towards the social media; these segments were labeled as "Passives", "Potentials", "Initiators" and "Experts."

Companies in the "Passive" segment (20.49%) are not currently using the social media and have no intention of using them. These retailers are skeptics as to online technologies, considering such tools difficult to use, useless and not adding strategic value to the company. Also the Passives are characterized by low use of online communication tools within the company.

Companies in the "Potential" segment (42.15%) do not use the social media but unlike the "Passive" retailers their intention is to use at least some of them in the future, primarily for customer-related purposes.

Companies in the "Initiator" segment (18.32%) already use some of the social media with a medium frequency, primarily for customer-related purposes. Moreover they indicate a high degree of intention to continue using these tools and even increase their use in the future.

Finally, businesses belonging to the "Expert" segment (19.03%) form a group that uses most often the different social media. The intention of these retailers to continue using these tools and using new ones is also very high. Notably, this group of companies has a very positive attitude towards the social media, they perceive them as very easy to use, very useful and that provide a great strategic value for the company.

The retailers engaged in social media marketing in Spain are at the moment in the minority. A possible explanation for this is ignorance or lack of information. The attitude, the perceived usefulness and the perceived strategic value of the social media tools by marketers, are some of the main factors which affect to the adoption of these tools. This means that learning about them and understanding their usefulness will lead to positive attitudes and wider adoption of the social media as a way to better engage with their customers and extract strategic value from these tools.

Finally, the study suggests that important factors affecting the degree of adoption of social media by Spanish retailers are the number of ICT professionals working in the company, the presence of formal policy guidelines on the use of social media, the possession of adequate software and hardware tools for introducing social media–related activities and the number of employees who can e-mail internally. In that respect it is interesting that the technological context is more important for the adoption of social Web tools, than the size of the business. Two other important factors are the management mindset and the prior experience with the ICT.

ACKNOWLEDGMENT

This study is framed within Research Project reference number ECO2009-08708 (Ministry of Science and Innovation, Government of Spain, 2010-2013).

REFERENCES

Allred, C. R., Smith, S. M., & Swinyard, W. R. (2006). E-shopping lovers and fearful conservatives: A market segmentation analysis. *International Journal of Retail & Distribution Management, 34*(4/5), 308–333. doi:10.1108/09590550610660251.

Anderson, P. (2007). What is Web 2.0? Ideas, technologies and implications for education. *JISC Technology and Standards Watch*, February, 1-64. Retrieved December 15, 2010, from http://www. educause.edu/ir/library/pdf/ERM0621.pdf

Arroyo, N. (2007). ¿Web 2.0? ¿web social? ¿qué es eso? [Web 2.0?, Social Web? What it is?]. *Educación y biblioteca, 161*, 69-74.

Bernoff, J., & Li, C. (2008). Harnessing the Power of the Oh-So-Social Web. *MIT Sloan Management Review, 49*(3), 36-42. Retrieved January 15, 2012, from http://www.inforesearching.com/downloads/oh-so-social-web.pdf

Biever, C. (2006). Web 2.0 is all about the feel-good factor. *New Scientist, 192*(December), 30. doi:10.1016/S0262-4079(06)61451-6.

Birdsall, W. F. (2007). Web 2.0 as a social movement. *Webology, 4*(2). Retrieves January 18, 2011, from http://www.webology.ir/2007/v4n2/a40.html

Biswas, A., & Krishnan, R. (2004). The Internet's impact on marketing. *Journal of Business Research, 57*(7), 681–684. doi:10.1016/S0148-2963(02)00346-6.

Boll, S. (2007). MultiTube—Where Web 2.0 and Multimedia Could Meet. *IEEE MultiMedia, 14*(1), 9–13. doi:10.1109/MMUL.2007.17.

Brown, M. R., Pope, N., & Voges, K. E. (2003). Buying or browsing? An exploration of shopping orientations and online purchase intentions. *European Journal of Marketing, 37*(11/12), 1666–1684. doi:10.1108/03090560310495401.

Cobo, C., & Pardo, H. (2007). *Planeta web 2.0. Inteligencia colectiva o medios fast food [Web 2.0 planet. Collective intelligence or fast food media].* Barcelona / México DF: Grup de Recerca d'Interaccions Digitals, Universitat de Vic. Flacso México.

Constantinides, E., & Fountain, S. (2008). Web 2.0: Conceptual foundations and marketing Issues. *Journal of Direct. Data and Digital Marketing Practice, 9*(3), 231–244. doi:10.1057/palgrave. dddmp.4350098.

Constantinides, E., Lorenzo, C., & Gómez, M. A. (2008). Social Media: A New Frontier for Retailers? *European Retail Research, 22*(1), 1–28.

Coyle, K. (2007). The Library Catalog in a 2.0 World. *Journal of Academic Librarianship, 33*(2), 289–291. doi:10.1016/j.acalib.2007.02.003.

Craig, E. (2007). Changing paradigms: Managed learning environments and Web 2.0. *Campus-Wide Information Systems, 24*(3), 151–161. doi:10.1108/10650740710762185.

Cymfony. (2006). Making the case for a social media strategy. Retrieved October 8, 2010, from http://www.nedma.com/pdfs/making%20the%20 case%20for%20social%20media%202007.pdf

Davis, F. D. (1989). Perceived usefulness, perceived ease of use and user acceptance of Information Technology. *Management Information Systems Quarterly, 13*(3), 319–340. doi:10.2307/249008.

DeFelice, A. (2006). A new Marketing Medium. *CRM Magazine, 10*(1), 32–35.

Deighton, J., & Kornfeld, L. (2009). Interactivity's unanticipated consequences for marketers and Marketing. *Journal of Interactive Marketing, 23*, 4–10. doi:10.1016/j.intmar.2008.10.001.

Deshpande, A., & Jadad, A. (2006). Web 2.0: Could it help move the health system into the 21st century? *Journal of Men's Health & Gender, 3*(4), 332–336. doi:10.1016/j.jmhg.2006.09.004.

Dillon, W. R., & Kumar, A. (1994). Latent Structure and Other Mixture Models in Marketing: An Integrative Survey and Overview. In Bagozzi, R. P. (Ed.), *Advanced Methods of Marketing Research* (pp. 259–351). Cambridge, MA: Blackwell Business.

Du, H., & Wagner, C. (2006). Weblog success: Exploring the role of Technology. *International Journal of Human-Computer Studies, 64*, 789–798. doi:10.1016/j.ijhcs.2006.04.002.

Forrester Research. (2008). Trends 2008: European eCommerce and Online Retail. Retrieved September 23, 2010, from http://www.forrester. com/Trends+2008+European+eCommerce+An d+Online+Retail/fulltext/-/E-RES44528

Grandon, E., & Pearson, J. (2003). Strategic Value and Adoption of Electronic Commerce: An Empirical Study of Chilean Small and Medium Businesses. *Journal of Global Information Technology Management, 6*(3), 22–43.

Grewal, D., Iyer, G. R., & Levy, M. (2004). Internet retailing: Enablers, limiters and market consequences. *Journal of Business Research, 57*(7), 703–713. doi:10.1016/S0148-2963(02)00348-X.

Jain, A., & Ganesh, J. (2007). *Harnessing the Power of Web 2.0 in Online Retail. Part II: An Implementation Roadmap for Retailers.* Retrieved June 1, 2010, from http://www.infosys.com/of-ferings/industries/retail/white-papers/documents/ harnessing-power-2.pdf

Karger, D., & Quan, D. (2005). What would it mean to blog on the semantic web? *Web Semantics: Science. Services and Agents on the World Wide Web, 3*(2/3), 147–157. doi:10.1016/j.web-sem.2005.06.002.

Kim, J., & Bae, Z. (2008). The role of online brand community in New Product Development. *International Journal of Innovation Management, 12*(3), 357–376. doi:10.1142/S1363919608002011.

Kolbitsch, J., & Mauer, H. (2007). *The growing importance of e-communities on the Web.*

Mäenpää, K. (2006). Clustering the consumers on the basis of their perceptions of the Internet banking. *Internet Research, 16*(3), 304–322. doi:10.1108/10662240610673718.

McKinsey. (2007). How companies are marketing online. *The McKinsey Quarterly*, September. Retrieved October 15, 2010, from www.mckinseyquarterly.com/Marketing/Digital_Marketing

Needleman, M. (2007). Web 2.0/Lib 2.0—What Is It? (If It's Anything at All). *Serials Review, 33*(3), 202–203. doi:10.1016/j.serrev.2007.05.001.

O'Reilly, T. (2005). What is Web 2.0. Design patterns and business models for the next generation of software. Retrieved February 15, 2010, from http://www.oreillynet.com/pub/a/oreilly/tim/news/2005/09/30/what-is-web-20.html

Parise, S., & Guinan, P. J. (2008). Marketing using Web 2.0. In *Proceedings of the 41st Annual Hawaii International Conference on System Sciences*. Waikoloa, HI: IEEE.

Piller, F., & Walcher, D. (2006). Toolkits for idea competitions: a novel method to integrate users in new product development. *R & D Management, 36*(3), 307–318. doi:10.1111/j.1467-9310.2006.00432.x.

Regus Report. (2010). A global survey of business social networking. Retrieved February 1, 2010, from https://www.regus.presscentre.com/imagelibrary/downloadMedia.ashx?MediaDetailsID=463

Rha, J.-Y., Widdows, R., Hooker, N. H., & Montalto, C. P. (2002). E-consumerism as a tool for empowerment. *Journal of Consumer Education, 19*(20), 61–69.

Rheingold, H. (2005). Mobile Phones, Ritual Interaction and Social Capital. *The Feature*. Retrieved February 15, 2010, from http://www.thefeaturearchives.com/topic/Culture/Mobile_Phones__ Ritual_Interaction_and_Social_Capital.html

Riegner, C. (2007). Word of Mouth on the Web: The Impact of Web 2.0 on Consumer Purchase Decisions. *Journal of Advertising Research, 47*(4), 436–447. doi:10.2501/S0021849907070456.

Rogers, E. S., Chamberlin, J., Ellison, M. L., & Crean, T. (1997). A consumer-constructed scale to measure empowerment among users of mental health services. *Psychiatric Services (Washington, D.C.), 48*(8), 1041–1047. PMID:9255837.

Sharma, A., & Sheth, J. N. (2004). Web-based marketing: The coming revolution in marketing thought and strategy. *Journal of Business Research, 57*(7), 696–702. doi:10.1016/S0148-2963(02)00350-8.

Swaine, M. (2007). Web 2.0 and the engineering of trust. *Dr. Dobb's Journal, 32*(1), 16–18.

Swisher, P. S. (2007). The managed web: A look at the impact of Web 2.0 on media asset management for the enterprise. *Journal of Digital Asset Management, 3*, 32–42. doi:10.1057/palgrave.dam.3650061.

Urban, G. (2005). *Don't Just Relate - Advocate!: A Blueprint for Profit in the Era of Customer Power*. Wharton School Publishing.

Varadarajan, R., & Yadav, M. (2002). Marketing Strategy and the Internet: An Organizing Framework. *Journal of the Academy of Marketing Science, 30*(4), 296–312. doi:10.1177/009207002236907.

Vermunt, J. K., & Magidson, J. (2002). Latent class cluster analysis. In Hagenaars, J., & McCutcheon, A. (Eds.), *Applied Latent Class Models* (pp. 89–106). New York: Cambridge University Press. doi:10.1017/CBO9780511499531.004.

Vermunt, J. K., & Magidson, J. (2005). *Latent GOLD 4.0 User's Guide*. Washington, DC: IEEE.

Wind, J., & Mahajan, V. (2001). The Challenge of Digital Marketing. In Wind, J., & Mahajan, V. (Eds.), *Digital Marketing: Global Strategies from the world's leading experts* (pp. 3–25). New York: Wiley Publishing.

Yakel, E. (2006). Inviting the user into the virtual archives. *OCLC Systems & Services*, *22*(3), 159–163. doi:10.1108/10650750610686207.

ADDITIONAL READING

Adriole, S. J. (2010). Business impact of Web 2.0 technologies. *Communications of the ACM*, *53*(12), 67–79. doi:10.1145/1859204.1859225.

Filipe, J. Cordeiro, & Pedrosa, V. (Eds.), Web Informations Systems and Technologies (pp. 19-37). Verlag Berlin, Germany: Springer.

Fishbein, M., & Ajzen, I. (Eds.). (1975). *Belief, Attitude, Intention, and Behavior: An Introduction to Theory and Research*. Reading, MA: Addison-Wesley.

Kwun, O., Nickels, D., Alijani, G.S., & Omar, A. (2010). The perceived strategic value of e-commerce in the face of natural disaster: E-commerce adoption by small businesses in post-Katrina New Orleans. *International Journal of Entrepreneurship, 14.*

Rinner, C., Kebler, C., & Andrulis, S. (2008). The use of Web 2.0 concepts to support deliberation in spatial decision-making. *Computers, Environment and Urban Systems*, *32*(5), 386–395. doi:10.1016/j.compenvurbsys.2008.08.004.

Sankar, K., & Bouchard, S. A. (2009). *Enterprise Web 2.0 Fundamentals*. Indianapolis, IN: Cisco Press.

KEY TERMS AND DEFINITIONS

Latent Segmentation: Part of a more general class of statistical models called finite mixture models or unmixing models. This method allows the assignment of companies to segments based on their probability of belonging to the clusters, breaking with the restrictions of deterministic assignment inherent to the non-hierarchical cluster analysis. Basically, it assumes that the data contain several homogeneous segments that have been mixed together in unknown proportions. Therefore, we must unmix the data to reveal their true number and definition.

Mashups: Applications that allow the combination of resources and applications from different websites to offer an added value service.

Partial Least Square (PLS) Path Modeling: A method of modeling a causal network of latent variables. This technique is a form of structural equation modeling, distinguished from the classical method by being component-based rather than covariance-based.

Perceived Strategic Value: The summation of perceived benefits from the technology minus the summation of perceived cost over a period of time.

Social Networking Site: Tools and applications for designing and creating websites to facilitate and promote social interchange spaces and communities (e.g., Facebook, LinkedIn).

Technology Acceptance Model (TAM): An information systems theory that explains how users come to accept and use a technology. This model explains perceived usefulness and usage intentions in terms of social influence and cognitive instrumental processes.

User-Generated Content: Applications that allow users to generate information in virtual environments using tools for upload and download contents and for writing, disseminating and bartering information.

Web 2.0: New trend in the design and use of web pages whereby the user is both the centre of the information and the content generator. The Web 2.0 allows the direct connectivity and interaction between individuals and the easy publication and editing of content.

ENDNOTES

1   http://europa.eu/rapid/pressReleasesAction. do?reference=STAT/10/12&type=HTML

2   http://www.emarketer.com/Article. aspx?R=1008126

3   http://www.bizreport.com/2009/04/84_ of_americans_influenced_by_online_cus- tomer_reviews.html

4   http:///www.internetworldstats.com/

5   http://www.google.com/insights/ search/#q=Web%202.0%2CSocial%20 Media&cmpt=q

6   A rating is the evaluation or assessment of something (products, services, persons, etc.), sometimes a classification according to order or grade.

7   A rating is the evaluation or assessment of something (products, services, persons, etc.), sometimes a classification according to order or grade.

8   RSS is a family o f web feed formats used to publish frequently updated works (such as blog entries, news headlines, audio, and video) in standardized format.

9   A P2P distributed network architecture is composed of participants that make a por- tion of their resources (such as processing power, disk storage or network bandwidth) directly available to other network partici- pants, without the need for central coordina- tion instances. Peers are both suppliers and consumers of resources (for example, peer communication systems using technology similar to Skype, BiTorrent, and eMule).

10   FriendFeed is a real-time feed aggregator that consolidates the updates from social media and social networking websites, social book- marking websites, blogs and micro-blogging updates, as well as any other type of RSS/ Atom feed. It is useful to create groups and share social networking services.

Section 5
Customer Relationship Management with Social Media

Chapter 12
Interaction between Consumers and Businesses through Social Media:
Trends and Future

Huliane Medeiros da Silva
Universidade Federal do Rio Grande do Norte, Brazil

Gilson Gomes da Silva
Universidade Federal do Rio Grande do Norte, Brazil

Flavius da Luz e Gorgônio
Universidade Federal do Rio Grande do Norte, Brazil

ABSTRACT

For a great deal of people, social media is the gateway to the Internet and it would not be feasible use of the network if it was not through them. Social media revolutionized not only the Internet but also the way people communicate and, consequently, the way consumers and businesses interact. Therefore, companies need to know and master the use of social media for competitive advantage. The current forms of interaction between businesses and consumers still leave much to be desired and it is not rare to find companies that make mistakes in the process of communication with their consumers through social media. This chapter aims to evaluate the communication channels based on social media used by businesses and consumers, showing successful and non-successful cases in the communication process and suggesting trends of usage of these channels more efficiently.

DOI: 10.4018/978-1-4666-4026-9.ch012

INTRODUCTION

Social media is defined as a group of Internet-based applications, built on the ideological and technological basis and Web 2.0, and which enable the creation and exchange of user-generated content (Kling, 2007; Kaplan & Haenlein, 2010). Thus, it is possible to be considered as social media, any technologies or interactive practices, over the Internet, that enable sharing of content, opinions, ideas, experiences and media, making possible the exchange of information about a particular subject (Costa, 2005). The concept of social media can be defined more generally as a set of mechanisms and communication technologies that enables social interaction among its users (Diani & McAdam, 2003).

In recent years, social media have become the main form of Internet access. For most users, particularly for the younger users, the Internet is synonymous with social media and vice versa. If the popularization of the Internet represents a revolution in communication among people, the emergence of social media further potentiated this revolution. Messages previously sent via e-mail and mailing lists have been gradually replaced by postings on social networking and updates on microbloggings, which, quickly replicated, achieves a far superior range It is the dissemination of information in all directions and at the speed of thought.

As the popularity of these communication channels grows exponentially, the interest of companies towards its usage increases, in order to strengthen its relationships with its customers and identify future business opportunities, which makes interaction between companies and customers more profitable. So social media have become the focus of several studies in this area and attracted the attention of managers, publicists and marketers.

However, a problem that arises is that a significant portion of business managers as well as marketing and advertising professionals is still dealing with social media as they do with traditional media. But however, unlike a magazine or television, where consumers can not directly interact with the transmission means to select the desired content, social media have interactivity and some given content can be ignored whenever the user wants, by simply deleting a message or ignoring a post. This feature allows consumers to filter the content submitted, selecting only what they want and eliminating unwanted advertisement, commonly known as spam.

Moreover, as the company cannot control the content flowing through the network, social media are, somehow, like a mechanism for advertising, which can act positively or negatively in the construction of the image of a company. Therefore, the use of social media as a communication tool between businesses and consumers should be strategically planned in order to facilitate a healthy and sustainable relationship, where topics of interest to both parties are constantly discussed (Haythornthwaite, 2005; Greco & White, 2009). The main interest in the use of these channels is not the advertising itself, but the image that the company cultivates with its customers.

According to Owyang et al. (2009), most companies today still use social media combining the publication of news of general interest to the promotion of products and services offered. However, this kind of static content is not enough to create interaction between users, which is the main "fuel" for Web 2.0. The use of social media requires more dynamic postings, such as the transmission of news to disseminate humanitarian actions undertaken by the company, its involvement in social causes or the position of the company on controversial issues (Owyang et al., 2009).

Publications with this type of content provoke the consumer and urge him to share the content seen with other consumers. After all, it is easier for a client to resend a post about a high-impact social action performed by a particular company than a discount offer of a product or service. Moreover, the spread of news and discussion of the subject by several other consumers have greater strength than mere propaganda (Bacon, 2012; Barefoot & Szabo, 2009).

This chapter examines the use of social media by technology companies and proposes a set of trends to be considered by companies which intend to use social media in a satisfactory manner. After all, social media are not just another channel of communication, but an important and dynamic vehicle that, when properly used, can be a great advantage of making simple consumers skilled influencers (Barefoot & Szabo, 2009).

SOCIAL MEDIA BACKGROUND

According to Torres (2009), social media are Internet sites that enable the creation and sharing of information and content by people and for people in which each individual is both producer and consumer of information. They are so called because they are media (i.e., they are a mechanism for transmission of information and content), and because they are social (i.e., they are free and open to its collaboration and interaction of members).

Initially, before presenting the different types of social media, it is necessary to distinguish between two concepts often confused: social media and social networks. Social media is a broader concept, including the set of all types and forms of collaborative media on which Web 2.0 is based, being fit in this classification the sites of multimedia content storage, wiki tools, blogs and microblogging, collaborative websites and relationship websites, also known as social networks.

Therefore, social networks are a specific type of social media containing features that enable interaction and exchange of information among people who participate in that network, usually from the consent of both parties. Thus, users of social networks produce multimedia content to be viewed, consumed and shared among its peers over the Internet (Torres, 2009; Telles, 2010)

The number of social media available over the Internet increases every day, and although this phenomenon is no news to anyone, it is still causing many changes in society. A good example of this are the constant changes in the manner people relate to each other nowadays, or the way they interact with companies and organizations, such relationships have changed completely in all aspects.

The way that communication takes place today remarkably differs from earlier times, even when dealing with relatively recent times. These changes include not only aspects related to the pace with which information circulates on the planet, but also regarding to the volume of information produced and its range. The emergence of mass media outlets such as newspaper, radio and television drove people to seek information about the events that were happening in their region and country.

Today, with the advent of the Internet and social media, the changes in this scenario are even more intensified. Individuals live almost all the time connected to the media, being able to follow the news both in real time, and thereafter, at the moment they want to. Moreover, once that the Internet has not only local, rather global reach, unlike traditional vehicles, their access allows the user to keep abreast not only of what is happening in his/her area, but anywhere on the planet, or even space. Finally, mankind lives in the digital age, where access to information is guaranteed and facilitated, therefore, social media gain more space in this field every passing day, and this is inevitable.

Even though the success and popularity of the use of social media are related to the last five years, the first social media began to emerge in the late 1990s when the Internet began to expand on a large scale everywhere (Boyd & Ellison, 2007). The first social networks to emerge were Sixdegrees ('97) and LiveJournal ('99), both created with the purpose of storing profiles and facilitate contact between users and their friends. In subsequent years, dozens of other social media followed, which brought many innovative features, up to the emergence of more consolidated social media, from 2003 to 2007, which remain to this day, like MySpace, Orkut, YouTube, LinkedIn, Facebook, Twitter and Buzz.

With the popularization of the Internet and social media growing every day, companies have turned their attention to this new mean of communication to strengthen ties with customers and potential customers. However, people have gained more freedom to talk, discuss and give opinions about a particular product or brand. According to Ramalho (2010), social media gave a voice to millions of people to express their opinions and experiences to a global audience at no cost or close to it. For this reason among others, a proper planning is necessary to companies wishing to enter this new way of communication.

Almost every day we witness the creation of a new communication tool. There are countless social media in Brazil and all over the world with very different goals. Below, we describe some of these different types of social media categories, according to the purpose and the resources available, along with examples.

Social Networks

Social networks are social networking sites that allow users to set up and maintain connections with each other, share information and media, and mobilize social and political causes (Diani & McAdam, 2003). Social networks are the most commonly found kind of social media on the Internet; these sites have a large number of users, reaching about hundreds of millions. According to Ibope NetRatings, an important Brazilian research institute, more than 80% of Brazilian Internet users have profiles on social networks, something around 50 million users. Thus, social networks allow to people interact with each other, sharing ideas and experiences.

The main purpose of these communication tools is to allow socializing among friends, col-

leagues and others. It is possible to notice that there is a multitude of social networks with many different purposes and goals, however, most of them work similarly, offering basically the same features as creating a profile, sharing information, photos, videos and still posts on what one is thinking or doing at any given time. These days, Facebook, Orkut, MySpace and LinkedIn are some examples of popular social networks in the world.

Facebook is, currently, the largest social network worldwide. Created by two students from Harvard University in 2004, initially was just a networking site for students of the university itself. Due to the enormous success and popularity, it is now open for high school students, professionals within corporate networks, and later to all interested parties. It is a social network geared for leisure which is growing exponentially. In Brazil, Facebook surpassed Orkut in December 2011, outpacing social networks, with 36.1 million visitors, an increase of 192% over the previous year.

Orkut, created in 2004 by a Google employee, is a relationship social network that aims to provide recreation for its users, so that they form new friendships and participate in communities related to different topics. Users have a profile where they personal information, photos and videos are made available and where you can leave messages, the main way of communication in the network. In addition, you can interact with friends through virtual applications.

MySpace has the same spirit of other networks allowing people to create their profiles and connect to others with common interests. However, its main difference to what existed then is that much of its users are musical groups. It is a social network focused on sharing and music reviews, established in 2003.

LinkedIn is a social network with professional character, launched in 2003, characterized as the largest professional network on the Internet in the world, present in more than 200 countries and having over 100 million users. It is a network focused on the professional, whose main objective is to enable its users to interact with people who are or were part of his/her academic and/or professional life and may testify in his favor.

Forums and Blogs

Personal diaries or blogs, as they are better known, are a type of social media whose functionality allows users to post articles on a web site through a structure of easy and rapid updating, being possible to be managed even from mobile devices like cell phones, smart phones and tablets. In general, articles are organized by publication date, keeping track of everything that was posted for subsequent consultation. It is also possible, in most blogs, that readers can add their own comments on any post of the author, contributing to discussions on the subject in focus and promoting interaction between the author and his followers. Among the most prominent blog services today are Blogger, WordPress, Blogspot and Blog.com.

Another type of social media with similar characteristics, even older than blogs, is discussion forums. Used for a specific public, usually gathered around a particular area of knowledge, the forums are intended for more technical discussions and require a little more rigor in content posted, since it is usually necessary to make an endorsement before posting no comment. Moreover, there is the figure of a moderator, who filters the content posted by members, avoiding harm and inappropriate content to topics under discussion.

Microblogging

Microblogging is a special kind of blog where posts are composed of short sentences, whose main objective is to allow the user to be able to share his/her status with his/her followers through fragments of text. It is a very dynamic communication tool that allows users to express their feelings and report facts and events extremely quickly through instant messages and which can be seen immediately by a large number of people.

The main tool in this category nowadays is Twitter, which allows users to post and view messages from other users, called tweets, with a maximum of 140 characters. The idea of Twitter was founded in 2006 and the initial purpose was a system for communication between co-workers and the company itself that developed it, but soon gained prominence in the world, expanding on a large scale. Pownce, Jaiku and Tumblr are other examples of microblogging tools.

Instant Communication Tools

Instant communication tools initially were designed only for the exchange of information through text. However, its users soon incorporated a mechanism to include feelings in their messages, through the use of certain sequences of characters to display emotions and moods, with which came the so-called emoticons (or smileys). Subsequently, these tools included features that allow file sharing among its users, mainly to support the transmission of images. More recently, with the increased bandwidth communication with the speech features (VoIP) and real-time image has been made viable, thus overcoming the traditional forms of communications such as telephones or cell phones, because of the low cost of calls.

Examples of instant communication tools: ICQ, MSN, Skype and GTalk. ICQ and MSN were the first two instant messaging services to emerge in the late '90s. Over time, the ICQ has been losing ground to other competitors, such as AIM (AOL Instant Messaging), MSN Messenger and Yahoo!, among others. MSN, in particular, has become a widely used communication tool to be integrated into the Microsoft Windows operating system. Skype, on its turn, which uses features of VoIP–Voice over IP, provides a more stable communication, being, then, preferred for voice conversations and GTalk, instant communication tool developed by Google, allows users to chat directly with their GMail contacts while reading your e-mails.

Currently, Windows Live Messenger replaces the former MSN and has the largest number of users in the segment of instant communication tools. Both Windows Live Messenger and Skype, as well as GTalk, support text messaging, voice and video, they enable file sharing.

Collaborative Work Tools

The principle of the Web 2.0, or social web, is that the content shared on the network is collaboratively produced, and can be continually modified and enhanced by its own users, using a set of collaborative work tools that make up the so-called Web 2.0 (Kaplan & Haenlein, 2010). Tools for collaborative work, also known as collaborative software, computer-supported cooperative work, or simply, groupware, are computer-based systems that help groups of people involved in common tasks (or goals) and that provide interface to a shared work environment.

The major representatives of this category are wiki tools and Content Management Systems (CMS). Wiki tools are an open source collaborative technology that enables users to access, browse, and edit hypertext pages in a real-time context, allowing them collaboratively to create, edit and organize content from a website (Leuf & Cunningham, 2001). Usually, this kind of social media gathers people with common interests who share their knowledge. The main icon in this segment is Wikipedia, a virtual encyclopedia created and maintained entirely by its users.

The Content Management Systems allow you to manage a Website, creating and updating content without the need for knowledge about web programming. This technology, similarly to the previous one, allows editing, organizing and managing content from a website in a collaborative way. The tools Drupal, Joomla and WordPress are the most popular content management systems. Both wiki tools and content management systems encourage collaborative work, developed at a distance (Kling, 2007).

Tools for Photo and Video Sharing

It can be said that photo-sharing sites have been the major inspiration for the appearances of social media. Ramalho (2010) regards the photo-sharing sites as one of the oldest forms of social networks. However, authors such as Strauss and Frost (2011) disagree with this point of view and describe these sites as a kind of social media in the category of multimedia sharing, an application arising from the facilities provided by the emergence of social media. Anyway, the rise of Facebook, the largest social network today, was brought about from a photo sharing application for college students (Kirkpatrick, 2011).

Most of these sites work similarly to social networks require registration and provide a space for the user to store their photos and videos, which might be shared with other users. Sites like Flickr and Picasa are examples of tools for photo sharing, better known as digital photo albums. Flickr, with more than 10 million active groups, allows its users to create photo albums to store and interact with about 60 million photographers. It was launched in 2004, by Ludicorp, in order to facilitate the photo sharing, and soon became popular and was sold to Yahoo in 2005.

Picasa, as well as Flickr, enables photo sharing, whose main function is to organize the collection of digital pictures. Created by the Picasa, and acquired in July 2004 by Google. Since then, this North-American company began offering the program for free at their website.

The video-sharing sites have become a major attraction of the Internet. YouTube, Vimeo,

Metacafe, among others, are examples of video-sharing websites. Among these, YouTube is the most accessed in the world, allowing its users to upload and share videos in digital format.

Developed in February 2005 by Chad Hurley and Steve Chen, YouTube has come up with a view to facilitating video sharing, due to the inconvenience, existent at the time, of sharing videos via email. Today, it has become one of the most popular websites in this category.

BUSINESS AND SOCIAL MEDIA

Digital Marketing

The twenty-first century marketing requires integration of new communication channels in an environment for multichannel relationships (e-mail, SMS, RSS, microblogging, social networks, etc.) which can be used for the provision of products and services, customer loyalty campaigns, contests and promotions, in order to optimize resources and better target messages through appropriate channels.

Reedy et al. (2003) defines this new requirement for digital marketing as all online or electronic activities that facilitate production and marketing of products and services to meet the needs and desires of the consumer and complements this definition stating that the technological or electronic tools are resources used by electronic marketing to implement the marketing guidelines.

Digital marketing has the same goals of traditional marketing: meeting the needs and desires of consumers. However, digital marketing has a much greater reliance on technological resources in order to accomplish its goals, since these goals are closely related to the use of these resources (Las Casas, 2009). Market research depends on the preparation, collection and analysis of information that circulates via digital networks, as well as on the production and presentation of results to the administrative levels of the company depends

heavily on the use of data analysis computational tools. Moreover the digital marketing is essential in (i) collecting consumer opinions in order to guide the development of new products; (ii) in the development and deployment of strategies and tactics to persuade customers, such as events and promotions; and (iii) in some cases, in the online gift distribution and product and services samples, such as in the case of products and services offered in digital media.

According to Kotler (2009), the information revolution and the advent of cyberspace have substantially changed the environment of modern marketing. Merino (2006) compares the traditional marketing to digital marketing and claims that the latter can be considered an evolution of traditional marketing, offering benefits that traditional media cannot offer, such as immediate interactivity with the consumer, thus enhancing the effect of advertising, when it is well designed and produced. Other benefits include reduced advertising costs, the fast and easy access to information about products and/or services and greater flexibility in respect of the company with suppliers and customers, to identify gaps and make decisions more efficiently. The author also emphasizes the strengthening of groups of individuals and opinion multipliers.

The Internet is changing business environments with the automation of inter-organizational processes. And, through it, it is possible to establish individual relationships with customers like never before (Brown, 2001). The interactive nature of the Internet provides increased customer engagement, once that it enables personally controlled marketing, where individual customers control the nature and extent of their contact with the web sites they visit (Lovelock & Wirtz, 2010).

For many managers, advertisers and marketers, the Internet is just another channel of communication between company and consumer. They often plan the dissemination campaigns through the Internet the same way you do when using a television or print media. However, Weber (2007) argues that, contrary to what has been propagated in recent years, the Internet is not a marketing channel, but a means to support multiple channels. In fact, the Internet has become a powerful umbrella that supports a lot of channels and customer relationships with society in general. Some strategies in traditional and digital marketing are presented in Figure 1.

One major problem of digital marketing is that many companies still do not have the exact perception of what they intend to use the Internet. Having a site with beautiful appearance does not guarantee the company the field of new technologies with the ability that is required. It is necessary to draw a well-defined marketing strategy that includes goals and objectives desired by the campaign. To help solve this problem, so the company can improve the level of knowledge and perception on the Internet, Côrtes & Rosochansky (2001) cite a few basic questions for the design of the insertion of business on the Internet:

- The executive and administrative staffs use the Internet regularly.
- What the company seeks to use the Internet (to sell products and services, vehicle information, institutional promotion, provide technical support).
- The company has a well-defined chart pattern that can guide the preparation of printed materials and publicity.

- What budget is available for the Internet project.

The Internet, as a channel for marketing, has unique features that no other marketing channel has, as well as others that are shared with other marketing channels, which include the following (Sheth et al., 2002):

- Capacity of inexpensively storing huge amount of information in different virtual locations.
- Availability of powerful and economical ways to search, organize and disseminate information.
- Interactivity and ability to provide information on request.
- Ability to provide perceptual experiences that are far superior to a printed catalog, even though not as complete as a personal inspection.
- Ability to work as a vehicle for transactions.
- Capability to serve as a means of physical distribution for some goods and services (music, video, software, etc.).
- Relatively low costs of entry and property for sellers.

To Karsaklian (2001), the Internet provides the relationship between the company and its target purchasing public, being the electronic commerce

Figure 1. Some marketing strategies in traditional and digital marketing

is the means by which the customers are seduced through innovative marketing actions, which is the embodiment of the cybermarketing. The author also suggests some things to be considered, to integrate the Internet in marketing strategy:

- To use the internet for marketing, competitive analysis is the first use.
- To establish the layout of your site, it is necessary to know the presence of its competitors on the web.
- Use economic intelligence to obtain accurate, rapid and inexpensive information.
- Even free information, analysis and interpretation can be costly, once that it requires competent professionals.
- Hiring of specialized economic intelligence should be considered, if the company does not have internal competence.
- Knowing what information to seek will help to save time before starting to use the internet.
- Make benchmarking of information obtained on the website.
- Do not confuse information cost with the value of information, because free information can provide significant gains.
- By using specialized public relations services for creating daily clipping, and looking for a company specialized in its field.
- By not creating its web site, without elaborating a master plan, which contains:
  - Its target public (e.g., businesses, consumers, etc.).
  - The visual identity that will be used (consistent with other media).
  - What is the difference that the website will bring in relation to other media? What is the value to the company?
  - Not making the website an extra copy of other media presentation of the company.

- Not forgetting that the Internet does not replace a marketing strategy, but must be integrated to it.

Social Media in Business

Social media have been regarded as a business strategy for companies and may be used in different ways, for instance, for advertising campaigns, establishing a channel of relationship with customers, generate sales and even as a virtual customer service center, among others. However, the use of such media is not as simple as following a recipe cookbook (Ramalho, 2010). It is not enough to create profiles on Twitter and Facebook, create your own blog or open a YouTube channel. It requires, first of all, planning and organization. However, it is noticeable that most companies are not attentive to it, thereby running the risk of achieving no positive results in the future.

Some companies are using social media simply because of its faddish character, without any strategic planning. In most cases, they are unaware of the benefits and risks of using these channels and do not know exactly how to interact in that environment, such as being able to point out who their target audience is and where they are located, and knowing how to evaluate whether an action was positive or negative. This happens due to a lack of knowledge and criteria for evaluating the results.

The use of any marketing strategy requires planning and in the case of social media it is not different. The lack of criteria for evaluating the results can make a certain action impracticable, or even, bring financial loss to the company. To use these means of communication in order to obtain good results for the company, it is necessary, no doubt, to establish a strategic planning (Sousa & Azevedo, 2010). Ramalho (2010) points out that doing so is mandatory to clearly define the necessary information which will be the basis for such planning. It is important to identify the target public, as well as their behavior and interest, so that actions may be properly applied. It is also necessary to clearly explicit the goals aimed for (i.e., to be certain on which goals are expected to be reached).

Some researchers argue that monitoring is the first step of planning that must be followed. At this stage, it is possible to identify what people are talking about a brand or product, who the opinion formers and influencers are and what the social media in which the company appears the most are. It is also possible to learn a little more competing businesses and how a given company is positioned in the market since the monitoring will provide an analysis of the market and how the company is publically seen (Cipriani, 2011; Ramalho, 2010). After monitoring, it is possible to perform actions that will benefit the company, such as direct actions in a particular social media in which the brand or product appears the most, correcting or attempting to reduce problems related to consumer dissatisfaction, directing marketing campaigns towards a particular group of consumers, among other actions.

In short, monitoring is the starting and essential point for companies wishing to join social media, since it supports making decisions about what actions to take in them. Once the company has established its presence in social media, monitoring helps identify adjustments that may be needed in marketing strategies and also new factors arising in the relationship between company and consumer, which is useful as a starting point to further action.

It is important to note that there are some pitfalls in the use of social media, as well as it still occurs with latest technologies, whose use is not fully consolidated yet. In fact, social media offer numerous advantages in the management of the relationship between business and consumers, but many companies still make some basic mistakes when using these communication tools. Although these errors may seem simple, they can transform these channels of communication in a dangerous

tool that can tarnish the image and reputation. A survey conducted by WebMint, a Brazilian company specialized in digital communication, identified a number of common mistakes which companies make in their use of social media strategies, and some which are described as follows (Moreira, 2011).

One of the most common errors is the lack of (or failures in) communication with consumers, which includes everything from listening to critical acclaim and praises they have, to the dialogue that the company has with them, or in other words, the interaction between company and consumer. These errors can cause significant losses for the company, for example, damage the reputation of the brand or its products on the market due to feedback of customers. In addition, the company may miss an excellent opportunity to change based on comments and criticisms that come from their customers. Thus, communication with the customer is extremely important for companies that have joined or think about joining social networks in their business strategy.

An important point that often companies do not pay attention to is what people are talking positively about the company, brand or product. Most of them are so preoccupied with monitoring only the negative side (i.e., identifying bad reviews) that they forget to pay special attention those consumers who spend their time talking positively about their brand or about their products. Learning from mistakes is as important as learning from successes, although the latter usually has a much lower cost.

Another common mistake is the way many companies precipitously react to a given situation, such a claim or a complaint posted on social media. In fact, it is very important to act quickly, but the company may need some time to further investigate the problem and identify its causes. Taking precipitated actions, in order to try to hide the problem, may worsen further. In this case, the company needs to express itself publicly through social media and maintain dialogue with the customer until the problem is finally solved. Hence the needs to create a healthy environment for dialogue through social media, where it is possible this interaction between customer and company. It is important to remember that the media partners are a two-way communication channel: more important than speaking is listening and responding to questions that customers have to ask.

In some cases, the company takes cognizance of the problem only when it has already reached enormous proportions, making its solution more difficult and, in most cases, bringing damages to the image of the company. It is therefore essential that there may be continuous monitoring, so that the post is identified as soon as possible and the company may engage in finding a solution to the problem.

The amount of information sent to consumers is an important point to be considered. Overflowing the e-mail inbox of the clients or their timeline on social media with institutional information or self-promotion of the company, or even with promotions and product offerings on which consumers are seldom interested in, are mistakes commonly made not only by startups, but even by companies that already have some experience on the Internet (Kreutz, 2011). On the other hand, the quality of published material is also very important and should be carefully reviewed to avoid spelling and grammatical mistakes, which usually cause a negative impression about the company (Almeida & Silva, 2011). It is worth remembering that the contents posted on the Internet spreads rapidly and, in a short period of time, millions of people can have access to information and can mass comment and spread the content posted.

One last mistake is the position the company assumes regarding its competition (Moreira, 2011). Criticizing or defaming competition is not a good strategy to promote a business; on the contrary, it can often cause a bad impression about the defamatory party and help in spreading the defamed company. On the other hand, monitor-

ing competition, following up the actions being performed is a great business strategy because it helps the company to evaluate the key mistakes that its competitors are making and examine market trends from their successes.

As previously described, using social media in business strategy requires, above all, strategic planning. Divulgating a brand or company in these media is not effective if advantage is not taken of them. Moreover, with the large number of widespread social media and ease of access to them, it becomes impossible not to have the name of a company or brand circulating in social media. Even if companies are not interested in divulgating their names or brand, consumers do it, whether by posting on the network good experiences–which is great for businesses–or, in many cases, sharing cases of dissatisfaction with a product or brand.

This current divulgation of companies on social media is beyond the administrative or managerial control. Even if a company does not wish to be exposed in the media, if there are reasons for this exposure, its clients will do it. This demonstrates the need for companies to establish presence in social media, and interaction with customers is one of the most important ways of doing so (Mignone, 2010). Thus, due to its popularity and democratic characteristics, where everyone has powers of action and expression, social media emerge as one of the main channels of communication and iteration between companies, customers, suppliers and employees. If used properly in business strategy, social media can yield good results and, under no circumstances, should be overlooked by companies aimed at growth and market expansion.

Customer Relationship Management

Customer Relationship Management (CRM) can be defined as a business strategy based on a technology platform whose goal is to conduct satisfactorily the relationship between companies and their customers. For Greenberg (2001), the CRM provides the basis for integration with the enterprise system of consumers, in order to increase the interactivity between consumers and businesses, so that it can maintain a profitable long-term relationship with its customers and thus satisfy both parties.

The strongest feature of CRM is undoubtedly the use of a set of technological resources that enable the practice of relationship marketing, in order to add value to the relationship and practice new ways of communication as a means of obtaining a sustainable competitive advantage (Bretzke, 2000). However, CRM is not only composed of technology, although technology is primarily responsible for providing this interesting approach. CRM involves business strategies and vision of business and, if not addressed in this way, it will only be a system of sales, marketing or records of consumers.

The use of CRM can add value to a product or service, for example, allowing customization of an item or its production in a flexible way, but this requires detailed knowledge about customers, their needs, expectations and desires. Kotler (2009) emphasizes that the CRM covers the management of information about each customer and all contacts with him, in order to maximize their loyalty. Deeply understanding customers means understanding their behavior to their needs, so that it can help satisfy them. By adopting the use of CRM in a company, it is also necessary to adopt the concepts of marketing and direct its actions to clients, achieving success in business (Sheth et al., 2002).

The origin of CRM dates from the records of early farmers who sold their surplus, thus becoming one of the first indicators of selling process focused on the customers. In the 1980s, with the emergence of the concept of Database Marketing, companies began using databases to find the following information: *who* buys, *what* they buy, *how much* and *how regularly* they buy. In the 1990s, companies improved their CRM in order to customize their services to customers and encourage customer loyalty. Thus, the CRM

started being used to increase sales and improve customer service.

In the early years of this century, software companies began to create more advanced solutions that allowed using information in a dynamic way for the different areas of a company. This sort of software continuously updates databases, allowing better understanding needs and behavior of the customers. The Internet was a benefit to the development of databases for information about customers. The increased fluidity of CRM programs has created a more flexible relationship involving sales, customer service and marketing, allowing the development of new strategies for a more cooperative work among the different areas through shared information. Currently, CRM software solutions are used more often by companies that rely heavily on two distinct aspects: customer service or technology. CRM can also have other terms complementary to itself, according to its focus and it may also have other complementary terms connected to it:

- Electronic Customer Relationship Management (eCRM)
- Mobile Customer Relationship Management (mCRM)
- Enterprise Relationship Management (ERM)
- Partner Relationship Management (PRM)
- Supplier Relationship Management (SRM)
- Collaborative Customer Relationship Management (cCRM)

Currently, the relationship marketing involves a two-way communication with the individuals involved (1:1) and, through social media on the Internet, companies can understand the individual needs of each customer or partner (Strauss & Frost, 2011).

Relationship marketing has three pillars (Figure 2), which support the relationship of customers with products and services of a company. The CRM is the first, with a focus on customer acquisition,

Figure 2. Pillars of the customer relationship

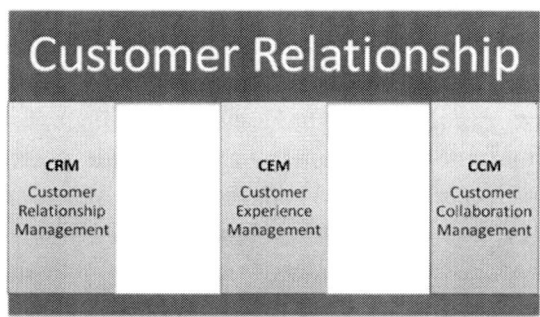

transaction, service, retention and building long term customer relationships. The basis of CRM is data, information, suggestions and knowledge about customers. The second pillar is the customer experience management (CEM), which represents the methodology, discipline and/or process comprehensively used to manage the exposure of multichannel to a customer, interaction and transaction with a company, product, brand or service (Strauss & Frost, 2011). The last pillar is the client collaboration management (CCM), also called CRM 2.0 or social CRM. The CCM is controlled by customers, in spite of being monitored and directed by the company, wherever possible, which grew from the growth of social media.

According to Strauss and Frost (2011), the CCM is a very new concept, whose definite term to be used is uncertain (CCM, collaborative CRM, Social CRM or CRM 2.0). To Forrester Research, Social CRM increases the social network to working as a new channel within the current processes and investments on CRM.

FAILURE AND SUCCESS IN USING SOCIAL MEDIA

The area of advertising is full of cases of success and failure in marketing campaigns. Experts agree that recurring success formulas of earlier marketing campaigns is not sufficient to ensure the success of new campaigns, which must be specifically developed for each product or service, taking into account the particularities of each target market alvo (Peter & Olson, 2009; Kotler & Keller, 2011). Nevertheless, analyzing previous successes and failures helps in understanding new marketing strategies, also favoring the identification of errors in positioning in the market, as well as the misuse of certain media and communication channels. Below some successful cases of using social media in the relationship between business and consumers are illustrated.

The web radio Last FM (www.last.fm) is a successful example that unites an online radio to the concept of social networks. The site keeps a record of songs that the user selects to hear, which allows the company to enhance its programming from the knowledge acquired from each user (Zenone, 2007). Users can create a profile and from the songs selected, the radio suggests other music based on their musical taste. In this case, the company's CRM is tightly integrated to the social network, acting decisively on the choice of the programming broadcast by this web radio.

A similar strategy is used by the site Musicovery (www.musicovery.com), which allows users to build a schedule based on their mood. The site has a bidimensional plane formed by two mutually perpendicular axes. The horizontal axis ranges from dark to positive and the vertical axis ranges from calm to energetic. By positioning the cursor within a region in the bidimensional plane, users choose a selection of songs based on their mood. However, user interaction goes beyond this choice in a 2D plane, since playlists are built considering artists of the country where the user is located, favorite genres and decades, and positive/negative signals ("I like"/"I do not like") that the user can select the songs that are suggested.

Using social media in product development in a collaborative way is a relatively new idea, which has been, however, gaining ground with several companies. Based on the concept of customization as a way to meet the specific needs of consumers, companies are offering new web-based forms of interaction that allow customers to tailor products exactly to your requirements or your local market. Recently, Fiat launched the Fiat Mio (www.fiatmio.cc), a fully developed model from consumer suggestions and ideas that have worked collaboratively on a project without copyright under Creative Commons license, allowing the creation and distribution of free contents.

Another successful example in product development in a collaborative way is the American company uFlavor (www.uflavor.com), which provides a software/hardware platform that enables its customers to create and sell new soft drink flavors that can be developed from the combination of several ingredients, available smart vending machines that produce dynamically new flavors on demand. Consumers can still produce custom labels for their drink and be paid according to the success of product development, since it will receive a percentage (US$ 0.18) per bottle of their product which is sold.

The power of rapid dissemination of information in social media can also contribute negatively to the image of a company, especially when the company failed in its relationship with consumers. Two recent cases have been highlighted in the Brazilian press, due to the impact and effect that they had on social media and, subsequently, in traditional media. Both cases involved failures of products that were not resolved in a timely manner by their respective manufacturers and hence, generated dissatisfaction and revolt of its customers and other consumers in social media. Both cases are reported below and, although the names of persons and companies involved have been omitted in this work, more information about these cases can be found in the references cited.

In Brazil, one of the first cases causing great negative impact on social media involved a company in the field of home appliances, a consumer purchased a mis-operating. After 90 days without getting a solution to the problem, after repeated repair attempts by technical assistance and after several contacts with the consumer service of the company, not having success, the consumer posted a YouTube video describing his dissatisfaction, which he appeared beside the refrigerator, placed strategically in the garden in front of his house. Simultaneously, he created a Twitter profile which started describing the daily progress of negotiations with the company. After hundreds of accesses to the video posted on YouTube and the company name hitting the Worldwide Twitter Trending Topics, the company moved swiftly to resolve the problem, thereby circumventing the situation (Alasse, 2011).

A second case which had negative influence on social media occurred involving Brazilian companies with a car manufacturer, but in this case the company took a little longer to act in the solution of the problem and, consequently, the damage to its image was much larger (Alasse, 2011). A consumer purchased a vehicle of this brand in the end of 2010 and, after a few days, diagnosed that the engine of the vehicle was flawed. Several times the consumer returned to the dealership taking the vehicle for repairs, but the problem was never solved. Even taking the case to court, the process persisting for several months without reaching a solution and the warranty period, which lasted two years, had expired.

Outraged after nearly four years of legal fights, the consumer decided to appeal to social media; she posted a video on YouTube exposing her problem and created a website where she presented details on the case. The response of the company was a lawsuit to remove the site from the air, which in a few months received millions of hits and messages of support. The campaign gained other social media like Twitter and Facebook, and forced the company to retreat and make a deal with the consumer. According to marketing experts, the position of the company in denying the fact and trying to court "shut up the mouth" of the consumer, ended up working as negative publicity for the company (Alasse, 2011; Furtado, 2011).

FUTURE RESEARCH DIRECTIONS

Innovation is the keyword in the maintenance of lasting relationships between companies and consumers, requiring the company to reinvent itself every day to keep the interest of their clients. In the same way that static and non-interesting websites do not appeal to consumers and therefore are increasingly out of favor; marketing campaigns focused only on the placement of advertising are becoming less effective, because besides not contributing to taking companies nearer to consumers, they cannot sustain their interest for long.

Therefore, so that companies may always be innovating, it is necessary to introduce mechanisms to continually reassess the market in order to understand the changes that are occurring as well as discover new consumer trends. These mechanisms include algorithms and techniques to carefully analyze the data that is obtained through these new channels of relationship between businesses and consumers in order to extract really useful–but not always obvious–information.

The concept of semantic web requires the integration of various inter-related content available in different formats and geographically distributed through the web. It also assumes the inclusion of meanings to such content, in order to enable their automatic classification and cataloging by smart algorithms (Herman, 2009). Applications of Web 2.0 and 3.0 seek to increasingly make use of these resources to enable greater integration between businesses and consumers (Kazienko et al., 2012). It is possible, for example, to obtain information about the user profile on social networks while they browse through the website of the company in order to provide it with personalized offers. Obviously, there are several matters about security, anonymity and privacy they must and should be discussed.

Opinion mining and sentiment analysis are recent lines of research related to Natural Language Processing, which aims to identify, through computational algorithms, feelings and opinions that users provide through the web and social media, towards any entity, event or attribute of interest, which may be a product, service, company, place, person, among others (Liu, 2010; Plaza & Albornoz, 2012). The main objective is to allow users to obtain a survey about the opinion of people on a particular topic, in order to measure popularity and influence, without the need to closely monitor every posting.

The Internet offers fast and free access to a considerable amount of information and, therefore, it became the most important source for details about products and services. However, in most cases, there are thousands of pages of content about a particular product/service and the users are often confused by huge amount of complementary and often contradictory information available. Recommender systems are processes and applications focused on web 2.0, performed by ordinary users and based on their personal experience, that describe their level of appreciation about any entity of interest, such as products, services, events, people, etc. (Gorgônio et al., 2012). These tools integrate data from various companies, arranged in different formats, providing a platform navigation to access the information available.

CONCLUSION

Social media differ from traditional media, particularly as interaction is concerned. Unlike other media, where you can not choose which advertising materials will be served along with the desired content, the Internet offers interactivity, allowing consumers to select exactly which companies or advertisements will appear in their timeline or even no advertising, if so desires. Unlike a magazine, where it is not possible to separate information from publicity material, unwanted emails can be deleted or have their permanently blocked senders.

On the other hand, the costs of using social media are much lower than traditional media, especially when trying to reach a large volume of consumers, which attracts the attention of advertisers and marketers for their use. Thus, by virtue of its popularity, ease of use and low cost of placement, the misuse of media in promotion of products and services has contributed significantly to reducing the efficiency of promotional campaigns in social media. Companies that have used these channels are so exaggerated in many cases, contributing negatively in the relationship with their customers.

This fact has required special attention from companies, in terms of quality, usefulness and frequency of the material that is transmitted through these channels of communication. As the goal of the company is to maintain a lasting relationship with their customers, this relationship must be strongly based on providing useful and interesting content, constantly re-evaluated, in order to be adapted to the specific profile of each user and having satisfactory amount without letting consumers forget the brand, nor annoying them with too much content. Gradually, companies are beginning to realize that it is more important to focus on providing information that helps their customers during the purchase decision than the placement of advertisements and publicity.

It is precisely this point that the conscious use of technology resources becomes increasingly necessary. Currently, the use of computational tools for data analysis and tracking of digital content (e-clipping) is essential for successful customer relationship management, especially considering the large volume of data flowing in social media (the big data phenomenon). Therefore, it is not difficult to see that some cases of successful use of social media in order to intensify the relationship between companies and customers are based on the use of new collaboration technologies available in the communication tools of web 2.0 and web 3.0, as described in the previous section.

Recent examples of successful marketing campaigns have sought to increasingly involve consumers in decision-making of enterprises and production of digital content to be conveyed in marketing campaigns. After all, there is no one better than the very consumers to say what type of product and/or service they want and how it must be advertised. Such actions, in fact, contribute to improving the relationship between companies and consumers.

REFERENCES

Alasse, L. (2011). *Como Brastemp, Renault, Arezzo e Twix reverteram a crise nas redes sociais. Mundo do Marketing*, August 17. Retrieved July 10, 2012, from http://mundodomarketing.com. br/ reportagens/digital/20148/como-brastemp-renault-arezzo-e-twix-reverteram-a-crise-nas-redes-sociais.html

Almeida, C., & Silva; L. (2011). Comunicação Corporativa nas Mídias Sociais: o Twitter como ferramenta de relacionamento entre organizações e seus públicos. *Pós em revista, 3*(4), 1-18.

Bacon, J. (2012). *The art of community: Building the new age of participation*. Sebastopol, CA: O'Reilly Media.

Barefoot, D., & Szabo, J. (2009). *Friends with benefits: A social media marketing handbook*. San Francisco, CA: No Starch Press.

Boyd, D., & Ellison, N. (2007). Social network sites: Definition, history, and scholarship. *Journal of Computer-Mediated Communication, 13*(1). doi:10.1111/j.1083-6101.2007.00393.x.

Bretzke, M. (2000). *Marketing de relacionamento e competição em tempo real com CRM (Customer Relatioship Management)*. São Paulo, Brazil: Atlas.

Brown, S. A. (2001). *CRM – Customer Relationship Management: Uma ferramenta estratégica para o mundo do e-business*. São Paulo, Brazil: Makron Books.

Cipriani, F. (2011). *Estratégia em Mídias Sociais: como romper o paradoxo das redes sociais e tornar a concorrência irrelevante*. São Paulo, Brazil: Elsevier.

Côrtes, P. L., & Rosochansky, M. (2001). *Web Marketing: Estabelecendo vantagens competitivas na Internet*. São Paulo, Brazil: Érica.

Costa, R. (2005). On a new community concept: Social networks, personal communities, collective intelligence. *Interface: Comunicacao, Saude, Educacao, 9*(17), 235–243. doi:10.1590/S1414-32832005000200003.

Diani, M., & McAdam, D. (2003). *Social movements and networks: Relational approaches to collective action*. New York: Oxford University Press. doi:10.1093/0199251789.001.0001.

Furtado, B. (2011). Acordo Meu Carro Falha & Renault. *Mundo do Marketing*, March 23. Retrieved July 10, 2012, from http://mundodomarketing.com.br/blogs/consumo-e-inovacao/ 18068/acordo-meu-carro-falha-renault.html

Gorgônio, F. L., Araújo Neto, J. P., & Silva, T. M. (2012). A framework for designing recommender system for consumers using distributed data clustering. In Colomo-Palacios, R. et al. (Eds.), *Customer relationship management and the social semantic web: Enabling cliens conexus* (pp. 231–252). Hershey, PA: IGI Global.

Greco, D., & White, B. (2009). Alphabet soup: How CRM, ERP, Web 2.0 & Sales 2.0 is creating a superior sales experience: A case study. In IS-ECON (Ed.), *The Proceedings of the Information System Education Conference 2009* (vol. 26, pp. 1-9). Washington, DC.

Greenberg, P. (2001). *CRM – Customer Relationship Management na velocidade da luz: conquista e lealdade de clientes em tempo real na Internet*. Rio de Janeiro, Brazil: Campus.

Haythornthwaite, C. (2005). Social networks and internet connectivity effects. *Information Communication and Society, 8*(2), 125–147. doi:10.1080/13691180500146185.

Herman, I. (2009). *W3C semantic web frequently asked questions*. Retrieved July 8, 2012, from http://www.w3.org/RDF/FAQ

Kaplan, A., & Haenlein, M. (2010). Users of the world, unite! The challenges and opportunities of Social Media. *Business Horizons, 53*(1), 59–68. doi:10.1016/j.bushor.2009.09.003.

Karsaklian, E. (2001). *Cybermarketing*. São Paulo, Brazil: Atlas.

Kazienko, P., Doskocz, P., & Kajdanowicz, T. (2012). Social network analysis in marketing. In Colomo-Palacios, R. et al. (Eds.), *Customer relationship management and the social semantic web: Enabling cliens conexus* (pp. 231–252). Hershey, PA: IGI Global.

Kirkpatrick, D. (2011). *The Facebook effect: The inside story of the company that is connecting the world*. New York: Simon & Schuster.

Kling, R. (2007). What is social informatics and why does it matter? *The Information Society, 23*(4), 205–220. doi:10.1080/01972240701441556.

Kotler, P. (2009). *Marketing para o século XXI: Como criar, conquistar e dominar o mercado*. São Paulo, Brazil: Ediouro.

Kotler, P., & Keller, K. (2011). *Marketing management*. Upper Saddle River, NJ: Prentice Hall.

Kreutz, R. (2011). *O uso corporativo das mídias sociais*. Unpublished dissertation. University of Brasília, Brasília, DF, Brazil.

Las Casas, A. L. (2009). *Marketing: Conceitos, exercícios e casos*. São Paulo, Brazil: Atlas.

Leuf, B., & Cunningham, W. (2001). *The Wiki way: Collaboration and sharing on the internet*. Addison-Wesley Professional.

Liu, B. (2010). Sentiment analysis: A multi-faceted problem. *IEEE Intelligent Systems*, 25(3), 76–80.

Lovelock, C., & Wirtz, J. (2010). *Services marketing*. Upper Saddle River, NJ: Prentice Hall.

Merino, D. (2006) *Web Marketing*, November 16. Retrieved May 18, 2012, from http://www.administradores.com.br/informe-se/informativo/web-marketing/8322/

Mignone, B. C. (2010). *A contribuição das redes sociais para o marketing business-to-business no mercado industrial de pet shops*. Unpublished dissertation, Feevale University, Novo Hamburgo, RS, Brazil.

Moreira, D. (2011). *8 erros que as empresas cometem nas redes*. Retrieved May 4, 2012, from http://info.abril.com.br/noticias/mercado/erros-que-empresas-cometem-nas-redes-sociais-23082011-26.shl

Owyang, J., Bernoff, J., Pflaum, C., & Bowen, E. (2009). *The future of the social web: A social computing report*. Technical Report. Retrieved June 18, 2012, from http://www.forrester.com/The+Future+Of+The+Social+Web/fulltext/-/E-RES46970?docid=46970

Peter, J. P., & Olson, J. C. (2009). *Consumer behavior & marketing strategy* (9th ed.). New York: McGraw-Hill/Irwin.

Plaza, L., & Albornoz, J. C. (2012). Sentiment analysis in business intelligence: A survey. In Colomo-Palacios, R. et al. (Eds.), *Customer relationship management and the social semantic web: Enabling cliens conexus* (pp. 231–252). Hershey, PA: IGI Global.

Ramalho, J. A. (2010). *Mídias sociais na prática*. São Paulo, Brazil: Elsevier.

Reedy, J., Schullo, S., & Zimmerman, K. (2003). *Electronic marketing: Integrating electronic resources into the marketing process*. Mason, OH: South-Western.

Sheth, J. N., Eshghi, A., & Krishnan, B. C. (2002). *Marketing na Internet*. Porto Alegre, Brazil: Bookman.

Sousa, L. M. M., & Azevedo, L. E. (2010). *O uso de mídias sociais nas empresas: Adequação para cultura, identidade e públicos*. Paper presented at the IX Congresso de Ciências da Comunicação na Região Norte. Rio Branco, Brazil.

Strauss, J., & Frost, R. (2011). *E-Marketing* (6th ed.). São Paulo, Brazil: Pearson Prentice Hall.

Telles, A. (2010). *A revolução das mídias sociais*. São Paulo, Brazil: Editora M. Books.

Torres, C. (2009). *A bíblia do marketing digital: Tudo o que você queria saber sobre marketing e publicidade na internet e não tinha a quem perguntar*. São Paulo, Brazil: Novatec Editora.

Weber, L. (2007). *Marketing to the social web: How digital customer communities build your business*. New York: Wiley Publishing.

Zenone, L. C. (2007). *CRM – Customer Relationship Management: Gestão do relacionamento com o cliente e a competitividade empresarial*. São Paulo, Brazil: Novatec Editora.

KEY TERMS AND DEFINITIONS

Creative Commons License: A license based on the current copyright laws, which allows users to share their creations with other users, and allows the use of music, movies, images, and online texts that are marked with a Creative Commons license.

Customer Relationship Management (CRM): A business strategy based on a technological platform whose goal is to conduct satisfactorily the relationship between companies and their customers.

Collaborative Customer Relationship Management (cCRM): A CRM which integrates customers, processes, strategies and positioning of the company, thus serving customers and retaining them.

Electronic Customer Relationship Management (eCRM): A web-based CRM view.

Enterprise Relationship Management (ERM): A CRM used to identify organizational relationships.

Mobile Customer Relationship Management (mCRM): A CRM view combined with mobile technologies.

Partner Relationship Management (PRM): A CRM designed to support channel of partners and other intermediaries between the company and its ultimate consumer.

Supplier Relationship Management (SRM): A CRM that objectives the management of relationships with suppliers.

Chapter 13
Using Social Network Data to Identify Key Influencers for Social CRM Activities

Goetz Greve
HSBA Hamburg School of Business Administration, Germany

ABSTRACT

Social network data can be used to identify key influencers within a company's customer database. Key influencers are consumers that are equipped with a large and strong network of connected neighbors. Within such a strong network, marketing messages can be passed on easily via the key influencers. The purpose of the chapter is to elaborate on the social effects of customer networks and the possibility to use data from these networks for Social CRM. First, the foundations of social contagion in networks and the relationship between social effects and Social CRM performance measures are explained. Second, possible ways of data acquisition and data integration are discussed and an overview of analytical software solutions is given. Fourth, the implementation process and its challenges are elaborated. The chapter closes with an outline of further research directions.

INTRODUCTION

Social CRM can be defined as "a philosophy and a business strategy, supported by a technology platform, business rules, processes and social characteristics, designed to engage the customer in a collaborative conversation in order to provide mutually beneficial value in a trusted and transparent business environment. It's the company's response to the customer's ownership of the conversation" (Greenberg, 2010, p. 34). However,

with the rise of Web 2.0 and social media Social CRM is closely refered to customer management with the help of social networking sites. Social networking sites are applications that enable users to connect by creating personal information profiles, inviting friends and colleagues to have access to those profiles, and sending e-mails and instant messages between each other (Kaplan & Haenlein, 2009).

The diffusion of social networking sites stresses the importance of word-of-mouth in marketing

DOI: 10.4018/978-1-4666-4026-9.ch013

as interaction and collaboration are key features of social networks (e.g., Facebook, and LinkedIn), and online communities (e.g., Wikipedia, YouTube, and Flickr). Social networking sites provide constant connectivity among consumers (Jansen, Zhang, & Sobel, 2009) and marketers are focusing on leveraging these social interactions among customers to achieve benefits for their customer relationships. In today's connected world, online content is an integral part of a customer, and sharing online content can have a big impact on sales and the development of customer relationships (Chevalier & Mayzlin, 2006; Godes & Mayzlin, 2009). For companies it is of fundamental importance to make customers share their opinions among others. Thus, seeding strategies for initiating word-of-mouth are gaining importance. Seeding to key influencers with a strong network may be the winning approach because these people are more likely to pass the word to others (Hinz, Skiera, Barrot, & Becker, 2011). Furthermore, firms should take the social networks of their customers into account when trying to predict and manage customer churn (Nitzan & Libai, 2011). Thus, for Social CRM it is of fundamental importance to combine existing customer data and data from social networks. Hence, the main objectives of the chapter are first, to discuss fundamentals of word-of-mouth marketing. Second, for facilitating Social CRM it focuses on the customer characteristics that effect virality and third, it shows a possibility for companies to enrich their data with social data from social networking sites to optimize Social CRM activities.

BACKGROUND

Social networks have been studied fairly extensively over two decades in the general context of analyzing interactions between people, and determining the important structural patterns in such interactions. In recent years research has focussed on online social networks. Online social networks have rapidly grown in popularity, because they are no longer constrained by the geographical limitations of a conventional social network in which interactions are mainly bound to face-to-face meetings or personal friendships. In addition, social networks are extremely rich, in that they contain a huge amount of content such as text, images or video for further analysis. Generally, social networking sites are just online equivalents of offline social networks. A social network is defined as a network of interactions or relationships, where the nodes consist of actors, and the edges consist of the relationships or interactions between these actors.

Managing relationships in social networks means managing customer interactions initiated by word-of-mouth (WOM) within a social media channel. Thus, a central aspect of Social CRM is word-of-mouth marketing. Word-of-mouth marketing is the volitional influencing of consumer-to-consumer communications by marketing instruments (Kozinets, de Valck, Wojnicki, & Wilner, 2010). The diffusion of social media channels on the Internet with its reach and transparency is empowering CRM managers who are interested in managing WOM through targeted one-to-one seeding or viral marketing campaigns, with the internet allowing detailed measurement and management of Social CRM activities. Godes and Mayzlin (2009) distinguish between endogenous WOM and exogenous WOM. The former is characterized by conversations that occur naturally among consumers as a function of their experiences with the product. In contrast, the latter refers to WOM created as the result of the firm's actions. Consumers in social media channels can be regarded as active coproducers of firm-initiated WOM.

WOM in an online context can be defined as "a statement made by potential, actual, or former customers about a product or company, which is made available to a multitude of people and institutions via the Internet" (Hennig-Thurau, Gwinner,

Walsh, & Gremle, 2004, p. 39). Thus, WOM communications are co-produced in consumer networks. Before the diffusion of social media on the internet, WOM has been modeled as a conversation between one consumer and another without direct prompting, influence, or measurement by marketers (Arndt, 1967). Most recent, marketers directly influence the consumer or opinion leader through targeted one-to-one seeding and viral marketing campaigns. In a network model structure (e.g., social networking sites), WOM messages do not flow unidirectionally, but rather are exchanged bidirectionally among members of the social network (see Figure 1).

For managing Social CRM activities in social networks it should be considered, that:

1. The content of WOM affects the virality of a social CRM campaign,
2. The conversation characteristics affect the virality of a Social CRM campaign,
3. The customer characteristics affect the virality of a Social CRM campaign.

Content Characteristics Affect Virality

People share information for different reasons (e.g. for self-enhancement purposes or altruistic reasons) (Wojnicki & Godes, 2008), or for emotional aspects (Heath, Bell, & Sternberg, 2001). Emotionally related content may be particularly viral (Berger & Milkman, 2012) whereas non-emotional content may only gradually influence WOM activity of consumers.

Conversation Characteristics Affect the Virality of a Social CRM Campaign

Conversations in social networks (e.g., Facebook or Twitter) are usually discontinuous in nature. Consumers post comments but do not expect an immediate response right away. And if a consumer decides to respond, it could happen hours or even days later as breaks in conversations are not regarded as lack of interest in these conversations (Berger & Iyengar, 2011). Thus, in online conversations normally people think through what they say. Thus, a threshold for discussion can be

Figure 1. Network coproduction model (Kozinets et al., 2010)

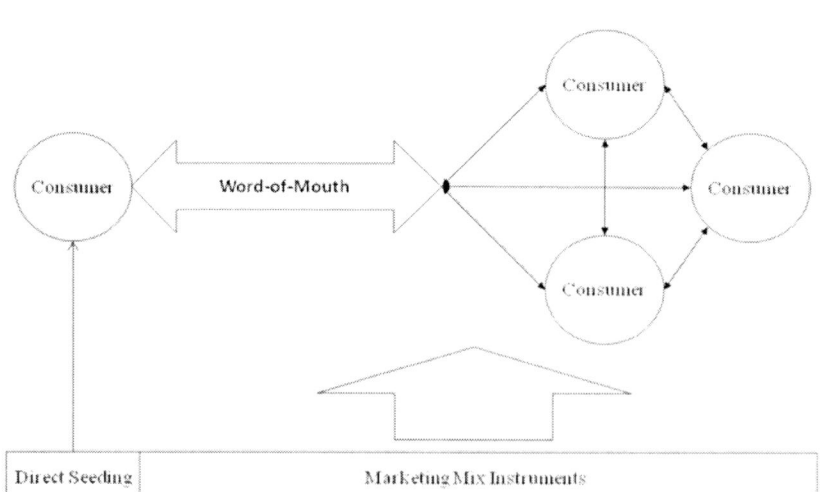

expected. People do not share everything they discover, yet it should be regarded as interesting for others.

In contrary, continuous conversations, (e.g., face-to-face communications), the threshold for discussion is much lower. People normally dislike if the conversation partner is not responding quickly to statements. Periods of quietness are regarded as uncomfortable situations in continuous conversations. To conclude, in online conversations, interesting brands, products or customer-related issues (e.g., service issues), should receive more WOM than less interesting counterparts.

Customer Characteristics Affect Virality

WOM processes, however, require an underlying social network's "infrastructure" to unfold their potential for innovation diffusion. Different mechanisms of social effects shape the WOM behavior of consumers. Research suggests three major mechanisms: tie strength, homophily, and degree of connectivity.

Tie Strength

All WOM communication occurs within a social relationship that may be categorized according to the closeness of the relationship between consumers, represented by the construct tie strength. Tie strength is "a multidimensional construct that represents the strength of the dyadic interpersonal relationships in the context of social networks" (Money, Gilly, & Graham, 1998, p. 79) and includes closeness, intimacy, support, and association (Frenzen & Davis, 1990).

Granovetter (1973) distinguishes between "strong ties" and "weak ties" for understanding interpersonal communication flows. Weak ties form bridges to otherwise isolated strong-tie networks. Thus, information spreaded via a weak tie results in a greater increase in the number of people informed (Goldenberg, Libai, & Muller,

2001) and people may be more affected by people with whom they have closer relationships (Brown & Reingen, 1987).

Tie strength may indicate the intensity of a social relationship (Van den Bulte & Wuyts, 2007). Research suggests that tie strength affects information flows. Consumers with a strong tie relationship tend to exchange more and more frequently information, compared to consumers in a weak tie relationship (Brown & Reingen, 1987). From a social CRM perspective, it is of particular interest that tie strength influences referral behavior among social contacts.

Homophily

Homophily explains group composition in terms of the similarity of members' characteristics: the extent to which pairs of individuals are similar in terms of certain attributes, such as age, gender, education, or lifestyle (Rogers, 1983)."The measure of homophily reflects the level of similarity between two people who take part in a social tie, that is, how alike they are with respect to their personal attributes" (Nitzan & Libai, 2011, p. 26). Customers are more likely to trust people whose preferences they share, and people are likely to feel more comfortable sharing experiences with people who are similar to them (Feick & Higie, 1992). Thus, the stronger the social tie between two consumers is, the more similar they tend to be (McPherson & Smith-Lovin, 1987; Granovetter, 1973). Tie strength, therefore, increases with homophily.

Degree of Connectivity

Degree centrality represents the degree of connectivity of a person in the network (Monge & Contractor, 2003). It measures the number of other consumers directly related to one consumer. Highly connected consumers are considered to likely influence others consumers' behavior (Van den Bulte & Wuyts, 2007) and vice versa. Conventional wisdom is that the best seeds for facilitating WOM are consumers with high degrees of social connectivity (i.e., social hubs) because they have access to and can reach more people than others (Stephen & Lehmann, 2012). This logic is supported by prior research showing that diffusion processes speed up once higher-connectivity consumers transmit WOM (Goldenberg, Han, Lehmann, & Hong 2009) and that, for social CRM, hub seeding often outperforms alternatives in field experiments (Hinz et al. 2011), simulations (Libai, Muller, & Peres, 2012), and analytical models (Zubcsek & Sarvary, 2011).

SOCIAL EFFECTS ON CRM PERFORMANCE METRICS

Social effects by influencers are unquestioned. Many researchers (Trusov, Bucklin, & Pauwels, 2009; Nitzan & Libai, 2011) have proved that social contagion can influence CRM performance measures (i.e., acquisition and retention).

Social Effects on Customer Acquisition

Targeting opinion leaders and strongly connected members of a social network ensures rapid diffusion (Iyengar, Van den Bulte, & Valente, 2011) through WOM referrals that have a strong impact on new customer acquisition. The elasticity for WOM in social networking sites is "approximately 20 times higher than that for marketing events and 30 times that of traditional media appearances" (Trusov et al., 2009, p. 91).

This aspect seems to be eminently attractive, as often WOM campaigns are relatively inexpensive: Customer's social networks take care of spreading the marketing message instead of expensive media exposure needs to be purchased. Stephen and Lehmann (2012) empirically showed that incentivizing consumers to spread the word to highly-connected friends result in a higher speed

of information diffusion. Hinz et al. (2011) found that seeding to well-connected people is the most successful approach as these people are more likely to take part in WOM, thus highlighting the importance of gathering social network data. Thus, using social network data may enable marketers to accurately target key influencers to make their marketing activities effective. Nevertheless, using social networks for CRM requires a data integration approach that combines customer data and social network data as well as new modeling techniques to forecast how a social CRM activity will develop over time and how many responses will be received (Van der Lans, van Bruggen, Eliashberg, & Wierenga, 2010, p. 362).

Social Effects on Customer Retention

In social networks, a defecting customer may have a direct effect on its connected neighbors, thus, mere exposure to defecting customers has a relatively strong effect on the defection decision of its neighbors. Nitzan & Libai's (2011) results indicate that customers connected to a defecting customer show an increase of 80% in the defection probability. The level of social influence on retention declines exponentially over time, and the likelihood of customer churn is affected by tie strength and homophily with defecting neighbors and by these neighbors' average number of connections. On the one hand, highly connected customers are more affected. On the other hand, loyal customers are less affected by defections that take place in their social networks as social interaction between consumers can increase future purchase intention and willingness to pay a price premium (Srinivasan, Anderson, & Ponnavolu, 2002).

Therefore, when determining how much a firm should spend to retain a customer, the customer's social network should be taken into account (Trusov, Bodapati, & Bucklin, 2010). Thus, the addition of network related information to the commonly used geographic, demographic, and prior purchase data might substantially improve analysis

INTEGRATION OF SOCIAL NETWORK DATA

Social network data can be described as "big data" (Dijcks, 2012). Big data refers to datasets whose size is beyond the ability of typical database software tools to capture, store, analyze, and disseminate. The volume of social network data could be extremely large, as millions of users constantly create content by communicating and interacting with their peers and public audiences through internet-based social media.

Because of their unique features, social network data represents a huge challenge to the analytic techniques used in traditional research. Generally, standard software for traditional research cannot analyze some forms of social network data (e.g., pictures or videos). Generally, social network data is characterized as unstructured data. Unstructured data refers to data that does not exist in a database. It can be textual or non-textual (e.g., audio, videos or images). Unlike structured data (e.g., transactional customer data) which tells what customers did, unstructured data provides insights into why users of social networks did something, what they will do next, and what issues they might have. Thus, whereas traditional research (e.g., surveys or experiments) test hypotheses and validate theories, social media data analysis needs to follow a data-driven approach. Instead of testing hypotheses or validating theories based on the data generated by selected participants under the conditions specified by researchers, the goal of social network data analysis is to detect trends or patterns from massive data, to analyze the causal relationships underpinning the trends or patterns, and to predict future trends or patterns based on the causal relationships.

Data Acquisition and Integration

Acquiring data from a social network site (e.g., Facebook, LinkedIn or Twitter), requires an exploration of the network population with the goal of collecting information about the network links between users, uploaded content, sentiment, comments, or ratings. Table 1 provides an overview of commonly used Social CRM metrics.

Three main techniques to acquire data from social networks can be outlined. First, network traffic analysis (Gill, Arlitt, Li, & Mahanti, 2007; Nazir, Raza, & Chuah, 2009); second, ad-hoc applications (Nazir et al., 2009); and third, user graph sampling (Mislove, Marcon, Gummadi, Druschel, & Battacharjee, 2007).

Network Traffic Analysis

Network traffic analysis is a technique that captures request-response pairs of user interactions within a social network. Analyzing this information it is possible to conclude which users are visiting other user pages. However, these procedures can present legal issues regarding data privacy. Several countries impose restrictions on network traffic analysis for protecting the privacy of their citizens. Thus, collection of network traffic can be carried out only in private contexts and only for a limited period of time.

Ad-Hoc Applications

Ad-hoc applications are third party applications that exploit a set of application programming interfaces (API), such as the Facebook Developer Platform to provide games or services to the users. The API allows software, with the user's password-protected permission, to construct a listing of the user's friends, and the friends' friends. First, the API typically allows to access information about the registered user profiles. Second, analyzing the log file on the application server offers the

Table 1. Commonly used social CRM metrics

Metric	Description
Conversation buzz	The amount of discussion around certain topics, generally determined by the number of responses to blog posts or online discussions. A widely read news site may post a story, but if there are no comments and no readers discussing the topic, then it shows little consumer interest.
Conversation value	The revenue contribution of a conversation about a particular product or brand. Proposed by Chat Threads, this metric comes from understanding how conversations spread through different channels and the incremental value each conversation adds to the brand's bottom line.
Conversation volume	The number of social media entities (blog posts, forum discussions, tweets, etc.) discussing a topic. Volume is a stronger metric when measured over time - marketers use conversation volume to set baselines for future campaigns.
Demographic metrics	The collection of metrics making up the background details of online consumers. Listening platforms can collect data on consumer location, gender, and age. Marketers use demographic data to determine whether their campaigns reach targeted consumers.
Level of influence	The authority of an online consumer, measured by his or her overall reach online. A consumer with a highly read blog and thousands of Twitter followers is assigned a high influence score, while a commenter on a small forum has low influence.
Message reach	The number of eventual impressions of an online discussion. Measured by the number of different sources covering a topic and each source's potential page views. Many discussions start small, but once picked up by a larger source, will reach a large number of consumers.
Sentiment type	The positive or negative attitudes consumers express, scored positive, negative, or neutral. Although many online brand mentions are neutral, containing no sentiment, listening platforms track adjectives around keywords to determine consumers' tonality about a topic.
Share of voice	The ratio of discussion volume between multiple brands — often represented as a percentage pie chart. Many marketers track their brands against competitors' to determine which company has a larger share of voice.
Topic frequency	The most common themes for consumer discussion around a brand. Marketers use topic frequency data to collect insight into how consumers view their brands and how they discuss them online.
Virality	The amount and speed at which a discussion spreads, measured by the number of different entries around the same topic within a certain time period. Around a highly viral event, such as the Motrin Moms saga, hundreds of bloggers write posts in the following days.

Band and Petouhoff, 2010

possibility to extract longitudinal information about the user's behaviour. The advantage of ad-hoc applications is that it is not affected by legal issues. Nevertheless, social networks must offer the possibility for the integration of such applications. Another disadvantage is that the popularity of the application determines the size of the dataset. Thus, unappealing applications limit the possibility to gain valuable insights into the population of a social network. Last, designing attractive applications for a target user group within a social network can be costly and time-consuming.

User Graph Sampling

User-graph sampling can be evaluated as the most prominent solution for acquiring data in social networks. It exploits openly available information about users and its network by crawling the social graph of a user. Crawling is an iterative process that starts from a set of randomly selected initial users and proceed by discovering new users at every step. The result is a distinct user graph of its social network and the corresponding user information.

Crawling can be applied using different methods (e.g., breadth-search-first, depth-first-search, or random walk). Crawling can be a very time consuming approach as social network structures of Facebook or LinkedIn can be very complex. Often, crawler can only reach a small proportion of the overall network structure. Crawling an entire user graph may require months. Thus, crawling cannot guarantee for obtaining a continuously updated knowledge about the overall network. Moreover, often the data collection process is further delayed by countermeasures of user-graph crawling such as IP banning or limiting the maximum number of returning results.

Given the limited access to social network data, managers' abilities to integrate social network data into an existing CRM system depends on the extent to which new technologies will enable the collection of more data on the social behavior of customers. One possibility might be to enrich customer data through social networking sites. To integrate social network data into firm's CRM database, information about key influencers in social networks is needed. Several vendors are offering solutions and provide distinct indices to rank key influencers/opinion leaders of social networks. All approaches have in common that they aggregate different indicators of opinion leader behavior (e.g., degree of connectivity, tie strengths,

impact, and activity). Thus, these commercially available solutions incorporate substantial parts of the academic conceptualization. Table 2 provides an overview of vendors of Social CRM metrics.

Using the application's results in a Social CRM customer data and social network data can be matched; for example, matching key influencers of social network sites (see Figure 2 as an example) and customer data. The matched data can then be used for data mining to extract customers of high influence and potential that then can be targeted with Social CRM activities, e.g. one-to-one seeding. Results should be monitored closely.

Data Integration Process

Integrating data of different sources and providing users with a unified view of these data is one of the central issues in IT management. Merging social network data and customer data can take place at several levels in database architecture. One of the most commonly deployed architectures is based on data warehousing. The data warehouse system extracts, transforms, and loads data from both sources into a single, compatible database.

Table 2. Vendors of social CRM metrics

Influencer Metrics	Scores Profiles Based On	Website
Facebook		
Booshaka	Posts, comments, likes, quality of participation, activity	www.booshaka.com
Twitter		
TwitterScore	Number of friends and followers, tweet frequency	www.twitterscore.info
Twittalyzer	Follower, mentions, retweet frequency, tweet frequency	www.twitalyzer.com
Tweetrank	Tweets, follower, followees, retweets, replies, mentions, shared links	www.tweetrank.com
Tweetreach	Reach, exposure, impression	www.tweatreach.com
Multiple Site Metrics		
Peerindex	activity, authority, audience	www.peerindex.com
Klout	True reach, amplification, network impact	www.klout.com
Sirank	Activity, true reach, engagement	www.sirank.de
Proliphiq	engagement, credibility, audience	www.proliphiq.com

Figure 2. Exemplary vendor application (http://www.crowdfactory.com/social-crm-database/)

One central problem is that integrating databases of vendors leads to outdated data in the warehouse.

State-of-the-art data integration applies a unified query-interface to access real time data over a virtual database (see Figure 3). As a result of that, information can be retrieved directly from vendor databases without combining customer and social network data obtained from vendors.

Incorporating social data into your CRM can be managed following a seven-step process:

1. Extract customer data.
2. Extract social network data (e.g. from crawling or a vendor).
3. Match customer data with social data.
4. Load it into a Social CRM data warehouse.
5. Apply data mining and OLAP techniques to refine data.
6. Use results for seeding / CRM activities.
7. Monitor success.

Data Analysis: Analytical Software Solutions

A key aspect of many social networks is that they are rich in data and provide opportunities from the perspective of knowledge excerption and

Figure 3. Social CRM data warehouse process integration

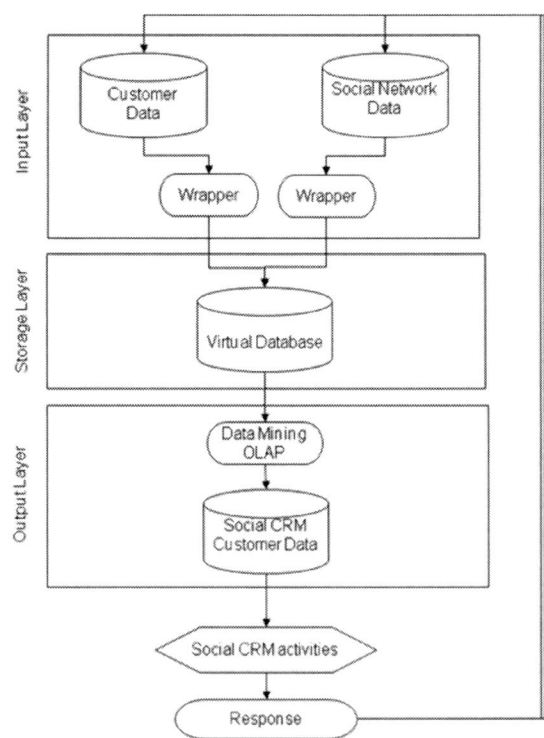

data mining. There are two primary kinds of data which are often analyzed in the context of social networks (Aggarwal, 2011).

Linkage-Based and Structural Analysis

In linkage-based and structural analysis, the connections of the network are analyzed in order to determine important nodes, communities and relationships of the network. Such analysis provides a good overview of the evolution behavior of the underlying network.

Adding Content-Based Analysis

Many social networks such as Facebook, LinkedIn and Youtube contain a huge amount of content which can be leveraged in order to improve the quality of the analysis. For example, a social networking site such as Facebook contains an impressive amount of text and image information linked to personal user profiles. Software solutions often combine content-based analysis with linkage-based analysis to provide insightful results.

As with any new disruptive technology, the social business solution landscape faces a dynamic, confusing, and converging market. The following section tends to give an overview over the most popular analytical software solutions for analyzing social network data. All software applications are mainly based on content-based analysis.

Alterian SM2

Alterian SM2 tracks mentions on blogs and forums as well as on social networks like Facebook or microblogs like Twitter. Alterian SM2 monitors the daily volume, demographics, location, tone and emotion of conversations regarding a brand and aggregates results into positive and negative categories for quick analysis by social media employees. The pricing is based on the volume of results and ranges from US$500 per month to US$15,000 per month. A trial plan allows for five keyword or phrase searches and a total of 1,000 results. Alterian also provides additional custom solutions. References are AstraZeneca, Deutsche Bank, Harley Davidson, Pfizer, T-Mobile, and Vodafone. Alterian is an independent company.

Attensity360

Attensity360 operates on four key principles: listen, analyze, relate, and act. Attensity360 will help monitor important topics, key influencers and the reach of the company's brand. Attensity Analyze applies content-based analytics to unstructured text to extract meaning and uncover trends. Attensity Respond helps automate the routing of inbound social media mentions into user-defined queues. Pricing is US$3.99 per month for one license. Discounts for longer subscriptions are available. Attensity also offers 15-day free trials. References are Whirlpool, Vodafone, Versatel, T-Mobile, Oracle, and Wiley. Attensity is an independent company.

Collective Intellect

Collective Intellect has evolved into a top-tier player in the marketplace of social media intelligence gathering. Using a combination of self-serve client dashboards and human analysis, Collective Intellect offers a substantial monitoring and measurement tool suited to mid-size to large companies with its Social CRM Insights platform. It applies spam management techniques and text analysis to clean data sets, delivering customers rich intelligence. Pricing starts at US$300 per month and scales based on specific client needs. References are CBS, Dole, General Mills, MillerCoors, NBC Universal, Paramount, Pepsi, Siemens, Unilever, Verizon Wireless, Viacom, and Wal-Mart. Collective Intellect is owned by Oracle.

Lithium

Lithium monitors search-specific mentions and sentiment in social media channels and exports them into easy-to-read graphs and numbers. Lithium aggregates information from a variety of platforms, including blog posts and comments, Twitter, Facebook, and Flickr. Lithium assesses emotions surrounding the company's brand pre-, mid-, and post campaign. References are Barnes & Noble, Best Buy, BT, Coca Cola, Disney Online, FICO, Focus Features, Motorola, Netflix, and Stubhub. Lithium is an independent vendor and bought ScoutLabs in May 2010.

My BuzzMetrics

My BuzzMetrics is a fully customizable dashboard allowing Social CRM managers to easily monitor, analyze word-of-mouth on social networking sites. Accessible via a Web interface, My BuzzMetrics provides real-time analysis and segmentation capabilities, at-a-glance metrics and a range of delivery options. My BuzzMetrics captures and analyzes content and messages from more than 150 million blogs, user groups and social networking sites worldwide. Three analysis modules allow for quick searches across discussions, building out comprehensive reports and for creating alerts. Content coverage includes: A wide range of consumer-generated media (CGM) sources: blogs, user groups, social networks and boards. References are Disney, Honda, Mitsubishi Motors, Procter & Gamble, Western Union, and 3M. Owner: nm incite (Nielsen / McKinsey).

Radian 6

Radian 6 works with brands to help them listen more intelligently to consumer buzz, competitors and key influencers by offering detailed, real-time insights. Beyond the monitoring dashboard, which tracks mentions on more than 100 million social media sites, Radian 6 offers an engagement console that allows companies to coordinate the internal responses to external activity by immediately updating blog, Twitter, and Facebook accounts. Radian6 uses a monthly subscription based pricing model with the monthly fee varying depending on the number of topics monitored each month.

References are Adobe, AAA, Cirque du Soleil, H&R Block, March of Dimes, Microsoft, Pepsi, Red Cross, Southwest Airlines. Radian 6 is owned by salesforce.com.

Spiral16

Spiral16 takes an in-depth look at who is saying what about a brand and compares results with those of top competitors. The goal is to help you monitor the effectiveness of your social media strategy, understand the sentiment behind conversations online and mine large amounts of data. It uses impressive 3D displays and a standard dashboard. Cost: Pricing starts at US$500 for five queries or Internet searches, though there is no solid pricing model and Spiral16 will work with companies to tailor plans that fit their budget. Online demo available. Refercnes are Cadbury, Lee, and Toyota. Spiral6 is an independent vendor.

Spredfast

Spredfast is an enterprise social media management system that allows an organization to manage, monitor, and measure its voices across multiple social media channels. Spredfast also offers a white label option for agencies. Pricing starts at US$250 per month for businesses. References are AOL, IBM, Nokia, and Sierra Club. Spredfast is an independent vendor.

SOCIAL CRM IMPLEMENTATION

Implementing Social CRM is a tremendous effort. Taken into account that lately companies have become increasingly displeased with CRM implementations, as the majority of them are falling short of the expectations that precede them (Rigby, Reichheld, & Schefter, 2002; Zablah, Bellenger, & Johnston, 2004; Dickie & Trailer, 2006) and are therefore considered failures. Empirical results in the field of CRM performance research reveals that

that it is not sufficient to merely implement CRM activities of an technological nature and hope for direct effects CRM performance measures such as acquisition and retention (Becker, Greve, & Albers, 2009). Social CRM implementation effort must take into consideration two important factors: First, the buy-in of people within the organization. Motivated, well-trained Social CRM personnel do in fact affect performance if managerial support for Social CRM exists and organisational structures are aligned. Second, performance of technological social CRM solutions such as analytical tools and databases is moderated by its users' support (Jayachandran et al., 2005). Third, social CRM implementation efforts need support from both the management and employee levels; they cannot merely be "bought off the shelf."

This shows that implementing social CRM involves not only technology and/or processes but also people. In sum, it can be concluded that successful CRM implementations require processes, people, operations, and marketing capabilities that are cross-functionally integrated and enabled through the use of information, technology, and applications (Payne & Frow, 2005). Successful social CRM projects are dependent on support within companies and hence need to involve employees and management extensively throughout the implementation process.

FUTURE RESEARCH DIRECTIONS

From a vendor perspective social network data analytics are already well developed. Nevertheless, companies must find a way to combine customer and vendor databases. This aspect raises two fundamental issues: First, data interfaces for exchanging information need to be aligned. Second, data privacy regarding customer data and data obtained from social networks need to be taken into account. Social networks keep track of all interactions used on their sites and save them for later use. The Federal Trade Commission of the United States has released a report postulating that companies engaged on the Internet will need to increase their protection for online consumers. Online consumers often unknowingly opt in on making their information public, though the FTC is urging Internet companies to make privacy notes simpler and easier for the public to understand, therefore increasing their option to opt out (American Civil Liberties Union, 2010). One central issue is that most social network sites unintentionally provide third party advertising and tracking sites with personal user information. This fact raises the issue of private information inadvertently being sent to third party sites via referrer strings or cookies (Krishnamurthy & Wills, 2009; Krishnamurthy, Naryshkin, & Wills, 2011) for integration with customer data.

From a scientific point of view, the following research issues are prevalent: First, it is difficult, if not impossible, for a firm to know comprehensively when and how users interact with one another through other digital media. Many users maintain profiles on different social network sites. Park and Fader (2004) note the immanent limitations of social CRM activities built on behavioral data collected on a single social network site when users' activities go beyond it. Padmanabhan, Zheng, and Kimbrough (2001) also warn of possibly misleading conclusions from models that are limited to such data. Of course, offline interactions of users will still be relevant and, commonly, not available to analysts or managers. Second, social networks are inherently dynamic entities; new users join, existing members stop participating or even exit. Dynamically, new links emerge as new relationships are built, and existing links can become obsolete as the members stop interacting with one other (Aggarwal, 2011). This leads to changes in the structure of the social network as a whole and of the communities in it and thus, the information used for facilitating social CRM. Finally, identifying key influencers does not necessarily mean identifying exactly those users that are likely to be to highly responsive to marketing actions conducted by the company. Until now this means that key influencers that respond to social CRM activities can only be identified through straight forward field experiments.

CONCLUSION

Social network sites offer the possibility to obtain social network data of customers to enrich the information basis. However, most of the links in a network are rather characterized as weak as these relationships do not significantly influence behavior. Thus, "identifying the "strong" links (i.e., the links corresponding to friends who affect a given user's behavior)" (Trusov et al., 2010) is of fundamental importance. Identifying key influencers within a company's customer database can lead to substantial improvements in facilitating CRM. With then refined information one-to-one seeding activities can be facilitated to optimize customer acquisition and retention. This may be realized at significantly lower cost compared to traditional marketing channels. However, identifying key influencers is a difficult problem for two reasons. First, the number of links between users of a social network is rather large. Second, the company wants to identify key influencers fairly quickly so they can be used for Social CRM activities. Both issues raise the demand for IT solutions to acquire, integrate and analyze social network data. Often, methods (e.g., user-graph crawling) lack the speed to identify key influencers in a rather short period of time. An alternative could be the use of commercially available software solutions that focus on an index approaches. All approaches have in common that they aggregate different indicators of opinion leader behavior (e.g., degree of connectivity, tie strengths, impact, and activity). Thus, these commercially available solutions incorporate substantial parts of the academic conceptualization. Once social network data is available, companies could apply analytical software solutions to plan, execute and control their CRM activities.

Analyzing social network data can give visibility into millions of conversations taking place across social networks, every day. Social network data provides a new type of actionable data about customers, members, fans, partners, and prospects. Fans can be identified and rewarded and their influence leveraged. At-risk and former customers can be tracked, nurtured, and enticed back into the fold. Social CRM provides data to help you understand market trends and customer needs, resulting in more effective marketing messaging. But on its own, this approach does not offer a clear path to strengthening customer relationships, improving service or optimizing operations. With the right people, processes and tools in place, Social CRM closes the gap between gathering social network data and strengthening customer relationships; and between gathering interaction data and strengthening the organization.

REFERENCES

Aggarwal, C. C. (2011). An intoduction to social network data analytics. In Aggarwal, C. C. (Ed.), *Social Network Data Analytics* (pp. 1–15). New York: Springer. doi:10.1007/978-1-4419-8462-3_1.

American Civil Liberties Union. (2010). *Commerce department releases important report urging comprehensive privacy protections*. Retrieved July 2012, from http://www.aclu.org/technology-and-liberty/commerce-department-releases-important-report-urging-comprehensive-privacy-pr

Arndt, J. (1967). Role of product-related conversations in the diffusion of a new product. *JMR, Journal of Marketing Research*, 4(August), 291–295. doi:10.2307/3149462.

Band, W., & Petouhoff, N. L. (2010). *Topic overview: Social CRM goes mainstream*. Cambridge, MA: Forrester Research Inc..

Becker, J. U., Greve, G., & Albers, S. (2009). The impact of technological and organizational implementation of CRM on customer acquisition, maintenance, and retention. *International Journal of Research in Marketing*, 26(3), 207–215. doi:10.1016/j.ijresmar.2009.03.006.

Berger, J., & Iyengar, R. (2011). How interests shapes word-of-mouth over different channels. *Marketing Science Institute Working Paper Series*, Report No. 11-110.

Berger, J., & Milkman, K. L. (2012). What makes online content viral? *JMR, Journal of Marketing Research*, 49(April), 192–205. doi:10.1509/jmr.10.0353.

Brown, J. J., & Reingen, P. H. (1987). Social ties and word-of-mouth referral behavior. *The Journal of Consumer Research*, 14(December), 350–362. doi:10.1086/209118.

Chevalier, J. A., & Mayzlin, D. (2006). The effect of word-of-mouth on sales: Online book reviews. *JMR, Journal of Marketing Research*, 43(August), 345–354. doi:10.1509/jmkr.43.3.345.

Dickie, J., & Trailer, B. (2006). *2006 sales performance optimization – Survey results and analysis*. Boulder, CO: CSO Insights.

Dijcks, J.-P. (2012). Oracle: Big data for the enterprise. *Oracle Whitepaper*. Retrieved October 13, 2001, from http://www.oracle.com/us/products/database/big-data-for-enterprise-519135.pdf

Feick, L., & Higie, R. A. (1992). The effects of preference heterogeneity and source characteristics on ad processing and judgments about endorsers. *Journal of Advertising*, 21(2), 9–23.

Frenzen, J. K., & Davis, H. L. (1990). Purchasing behavior in embedded markets. *The Journal of Consumer Research*, 17(1), 1–12. doi:10.1086/208532.

Gill, P., Arlitt, M., Li, Z., & Mahanti, A. (2007). YouTube traffic characterization: A view from the edge. In *Proceedings of Internet Measurement Conference*. San Diego, CA: ACM.

Godes, D., & Mayzlin, D. (2009). Firm-created word-of-mouth communication: Evidence from a field test. *Marketing Science*, 28(4), 721–739. doi:10.1287/mksc.1080.0444.

Goldenberg, J., Han, S., Lehmann, D. R., & Hong, W. J. (2009). The role of hubs in the adoption process. *Journal of Marketing*, 73(2), 1–13. doi:10.1509/jmkg.73.2.1.

Goldenberg, J., Libai, B., & Muller, E. (2001). Talk of the network: A complex systems look at the underlying process of word-of-mouth. *Marketing Letters*, 12(3), 211–223. doi:10.1023/A:1011122126881.

Granovetter, M. S. (1973). The strength of weak ties. *American Journal of Sociology*, 78, 1360–1380. doi:10.1086/225469.

Greenberg, P. (2010). *CRM at the speed of light: Social CRM strategies, tools, and techniques for engaging your customers* (4th ed.). New York: McGraw Hill.

Heath, C., Bell, C., & Sternberg, E. (2001). Emotional selection in memes: The case of urban legends. *Journal of Personality and Social Psychology*, 81(6), 1028–1041. doi:10.1037/0022-3514.81.6.1028 PMID:11761305.

Hennig-Thurau, T., Gwinner, K. P., Walsh, G., & Gremle, D. D. (2004). Electronic word-of-mouth via consumer-opinion platforms: What motivates consumers to articulate themselves on the internet? *Journal of Interactive Marketing*, 18(1), 38–52. doi:10.1002/dir.10073.

Hinz, O., Skiera, B., Barrot, C., & Becker, J. U. (2011). Seeding strategies for viral marketing: An empirical comparison. *Journal of Marketing*, 75(November), 55–71. doi:10.1509/jm.10.0088.

Iyengar, R., Van den Bulte, C., & Valente, T. (2011). Opinion leadership and social contagion in new product diffusion. *Marketing Science, 30,* 195–212. doi:10.1287/mksc.1100.0566.

Jansen, B. J., Zhang, M., & Sobel, K. (2009). Twitter power: tweets as electronic word-of-mouth. *Journal of the American Society for Information Science and Technology, 60*(11), 2169–2188. doi:10.1002/asi.21149.

Jayachandran, S., Sharma, S., Kaufman, P., & Raman, P. (2005). The role of relational information processes and technology use in customer relationship management. *Journal of Marketing, 69*(4), 177–192. doi:10.1509/jmkg.2005.69.4.177.

Kaplan, A. M., & Haenlein, M. (2009). Users of the world, unite! The challenges and opportunities of social media. *Business Horizons, 53*(1), 59–68. doi:10.1016/j.bushor.2009.09.003.

Kozinets, R. V., de Valck, K., Wojnicki, A. C., & Wilner, S. J. S. (2010). Networked narratives: Understanding word-of-mouth marketing in online communities. *Journal of Marketing, 74*(2), 71–89. doi:10.1509/jmkg.74.2.71.

Krishnamurthy, B., Naryshkin, K., & Wills, C. (2011). Privacy leakage vs. protection measures: the growing disconnect. *Web 2.0 Security and Privacy Workshop.* Retrieved May 12, 2012, from http://www.research.att.com/~bala/papers/w2sp11.pdf

Krishnamurthy, K., & Wills, C. (2009). On the leakage of personally identifiable information via online social networks. In *Proceedings of ACM SIGCOMM Workshop on Online Social Networks.* Retrieved from http://www.research.att.com/~bala/papers/wosn09.pdf

Libai, B., Muller, E., & Peres, R. (2012). *Sources of social value in word-of-mouth programs.* Working paper. Hebrew University of Jerusalem, Israel.

McPherson, J. M., & Smith-Lovin, L. (1987). Homophily in voluntary organizations: Status, distance and the composition of face-to-face groups. *American Sociological Review, 52,* 370–379. doi:10.2307/2095356.

Mislove, A., Marcon, M., Gummadi, K. P., Druschel, P., & Bhattacharjee, B. (2007). Measurement and analysis of online social networks. In *Proceedings of the 7th ACM SIGCOMM Conference on Internet Measurement.* Vouliagmeni, Greece: ACM.

Money, R. B., Gilly, M. C., & Graham, J. L. (1998). Explorations of national culture and word-of-mouth referral behavior in the purchase of industrial services in the United States and Japan. *Journal of Marketing, 62*(November), 76–87. doi:10.2307/1252288.

Monge, P. R., & Contractor, N. S. (2003). *Theories of communication networks.* New York: Oxford University Press.

Nazir, A., Raza, S., & Chuah, C.-N. (2008). Unveiling Facebook. A measurement study of social network based applications. In *Proceedings of the 9th ACM SIGCOMM Conference on Internet Measurement.* Chicago, IL.

Nitzan, I., & Libai, B. (2011). Social effects on customer retention. *Journal of Marketing, 75*(November), 24–38.

Padmanabhan, B., Zheng, Z., & Kimbrough, S. O. (2001). Personalization from incomplete data: What you don't know can hurt. In *Proceedings of the 7th ACM SIGKDD International Conference on Knowledge Discovery and Data Mining* (pp. 154-164). New York: ACM.

Park, Y.-H., & Fader, P. S. (2004). Modeling browsing behavior at multiple websites. *Marketing Science, 23*(3), 280–303. doi:10.1287/mksc.1040.0050.

Payne, A., & Frow, P. (2005). A strategic framework for customer relationship management. *Journal of Marketing*, *69*(4), 167–176. doi:10.1509/jmkg.2005.69.4.167.

Rigby, D. K., Reichheld, F. F., & Schefter, P. (2002). Avoid the four perils of CRM. *Harvard Business Review*, *80*(2), 101–109. PMID:11894676.

Rogers, E. M. (1983). *Diffusion of innovations.* New York: Free Press.

Srinivasan, S. S., Anderson, R., & Ponnavolu, K. (2002). Customer loyalty in e-commerce: An exploration of its antecedents and consequences. *Journal of Retailing*, *78*(1), 41–50. doi:10.1016/S0022-4359(01)00065-3.

Stephen, A. T., & Lehmann, D. R. (2012). *Using incentives to encourage word-of-mouth transmissions that lead to fast information diffusion.* Columbia Business School Research Paper No. 12/36.

Trusov, M., Bodapati, A. V., & Bucklin, R. E. (2010). Determining influential users in internet social networks. *JMR, Journal of Marketing Research*, *47*(August), 643–658. doi:10.1509/jmkr.47.4.643.

Trusov, M., Bucklin, R. E., & Pauwels, K. H. (2009). Effects of word-of-mouth versus traditional marketing: Findings from an internet social networking site. *Journal of Marketing*, *73*(5), 90–102. doi:10.1509/jmkg.73.5.90.

Van den Bulte, C., & Wuyts, S. (2007). *Social networks and marketing.* Cambridge, MA: Marketing Science Institute.

Van der Lans, R., van Bruggen, G., Eliashberg, J., & Wierenga, B. (2010). A viral branching model for predicting the spread of electronic word-of-mouth. *Marketing Science*, *29*(2), 348–365. doi:10.1287/mksc.1090.0520.

Wojnicki, A. C., & Godes, D. (2008). *Word of mouth as self enhancement.* HBS Marketing Research Paper No. 06-01.

Zablah, A. R., Bellenger, D. N., & Johnston, W. J. (2004). An evaluation of divergent perspectives on customer relationship management: Towards a common understanding of an emerging phenomenon. *Industrial Marketing Management*, *33*(6), 475–489. doi:10.1016/j.indmarman.2004.01.006.

Zubcsek, P. P., & Sarvary, M. (2011). Advertising to a social network. *Quantitative Marketing and Economics*, *9*(1), 71–107. doi:10.1007/s11129-010-9093-9.

ADDITIONAL READING

Barbier, G., & Liu, H. (2011). Data mining in social media. In Aggarwal, C. C. (Ed.), *Social network data analytics* (pp. 327–351). New York: Springer. doi:10.1007/978-1-4419-8462-3_12.

Cormode, G., & Krishnamurthy, B. (2008). Key differences between Web 1.0 and Web 2.0. Retrieved August 11, 2012. from http://www.research.att.com/export/sites/att_labs/people/Cormode_Graham/library/publications/CormodeKrishnamurthy08.pdf

Fuhrt, B. (2011). *Handbook of social network technologies and applications.* New York: Springer.

Hoi, S. C. H., Luo, J., Boll, S., Xu, D., Jin, R., & King, I. (2011). *Social media modeling and computing.* London: Springer. doi:10.1007/978-0-85729-436-4.

Jaokar, A. V., Jacobs, B., & Moore, A. (2009). *Social media marketing: How data analytics helps to monetize the user base in telecoms, social networks, media and advertising in a converged ecosystem.* London: Future Text.

Kaushik, A. (2010). *Web analytics 2.0. The art of online accountability & science of customer centricity.* Indianapolis, IL: Wiley.

Lo, B. (2008). *Social media analytics in business intelligence applications.* Cambridge, MA: MIT.

Lovett, J. (2000). *Social media metrics secrets.* Indianapolis, IL: Wiley.

Metz, A. (2012). *The social customer. How brands can use Social CRM to acquire, monetize, and retain fans, friends, and followers.* New York: McGraw Hill.

Parthasarathy, S., Ruan, Y., & Satuluri, V. (2011). Community discovery in social networks: Applications, methods and emerging trends. In Aggarwal, C. C. (Ed.), *Social Network Data Analytics* (pp. 79–114). New York: Springer. doi:10.1007/978-1-4419-8462-3_4.

Roebuck, K. (2011). *Social CRM: High-impact strategies - What you need to know: Definitions, adoptions, impact, benefits, maturity, vendors.* Newstead, Australia: Emereo Pty Limited.

Roebuck, K. (2011). *Social analytics: High-impact emerging technology - What you need to know: Definitions, adoptions, impact, benefits, maturity, vendors.* Newstead, Australia: Emereo Pty Limited.

Sponder, M. (2012). *Social media analytics. Effective tools for building, interpreting, and using metrics.* New York: McGraw Hill.

Stern, J. (2010). *Social media metrics. How to measure and optimize your marketing investment.* Hoboken, NJ: Wiley.

KEY TERMS AND DEFINITIONS

Data Integration: Ability to include additional data into an existing system.

Degree of Connectivity: Represents the connectivity of a person in the network.

Homophily: Extent to which pairs of individuals are similar in terms of certain attributes, such as age, gender, education, or lifestyle.

Network Coproduction Model: Approach where consumers are regarded as active coproducers of value and meaning, whose word-of-mouth use of marketing communications can be idiosyncratic, creative, and even resistant.

Social CRM: Business strategy designed to engage customers in a collaborative conversation in order to provide mutually beneficial value for the company and the customers.

Social Effects: Influence of social interaction on e.g. customer acquisition and retention.

Social Network: Online service, platform, or site that focuses on facilitating the building of social relations among people.

Tie Strength: Multidimensional construct that represents the strength of the dyadic interpersonal relationships in the context of social networks and includes closeness, intimacy, support, and association.

Virality: Social, cultural, emotional and affective contagions that spread through networks.

Word-of-Mouth: Statement made by potential, actual, or former customers about a product or company, which is made available to a multitude of people and institutions via the Internet.

Chapter 14
Best Practices for Social CRM

Fabiana Lorenzi
Lutheran University of Brazil (ULBRA), Brazil

Stanley Loh
Lutheran University of Brazil (ULBRA), Brazil & Faculty of Technology Senac, Brazil

ABSTRACT

This chapter presents a study of integration of traditional CRM systems with new social networking technologies available on the Web, such as Twitter, blogs, and communities, showing a set of the best practices on the use of these technologies to improve business relationships with customers. The authors present a set of best practices with guidance on how social networking technologies can help companies squeeze and improve the relationship with their customers.

INTRODUCTION

The growing use of social networks by people and the recent need of companies to keep in touch with customers make social networks an efficient means for relationship and trust. A survey conducted by Amcham has detected that companies recognize social media as an important channel for business and that they plan to expand their investments in the next year (Furtado, 2012).

Information technologies provide an adequate support for these actions, allowing companies to store more information about their customers and about a greater number of people. Some companies already use social networks for contacts with customers and for generating promotions. Actions on social networks enable companies to

be closer to the people, allowing them to collect wishes and complaints, as to offer better products and services in a way that is more natural than advertisements.

However, as these technologies are very recent, there are no studies about the best practices for companies on social networks. Traditional CRM systems only use traditional communication channels such as the telephone, physical presence in shops or malls, and multimedia totems. The Internet is only utilized to supply customers with product catalogs, e-mail, or "contact us", where the answers to the customers are not quick enough or accurate or even do not occur.

Such considerations suggest a gap: the lack of guidelines and tips for companies on how they can engage in relationships with customers

DOI: 10.4018/978-1-4666-4026-9.ch014

via social networks and on how to expand their traditional CRM systems to the Web, in two-way touch-points. In order to fill this gap, this chapter presents a compendium of the best practices identified through case studies. Studies on new social networking technologies available on the Web were conducted as well as the verification of how these networks are being used by people and companies. The sources of such case studies include periodicals, scientific and traditional Websites, and surveys.

As a result of these studies, the chapter has identified social technologies that can be used to support CRM systems and how they can be used by companies. Also included in this study is a discussion about personalization (recommendation) of services and products to support CRM systems. Finally, a set of best practices for using these new technologies indicates how social networking technologies can help companies squeeze and improve the relationship with their customers.

BACKGROUND

Relationship marketing refers to the attraction, development and retention of customer relationships. Therefore, the main idea is to develop and manage unique relationships with individual customers. For authors like Payne and Holt (2001), Relationship Marketing represents a paradigm shift in terms of orientation and marketing approach.

Customer Relationship Management (CRM) is considered by Srivastava, Shervani, and Fahey (1999) as one of three business processes that create value for the customer. The other two are the management of product development and supply chain management. The CRM is responsible for the consumer identification process, creation of knowledge about the consumer, the construction of a relationship with him/her, and the adequacy of consumer perceptions about the company and its products. CRM is used to describe the process of deployment and management of relationship marketing.

Gummesson (1998) says that, despite that the relationship between a company and a consumer may be commercial, it requires a long-term vision, mutual respect, win-win strategy, and the adoption of the consumer as a partner and co-producer of value--not just a receiver of goods or services. In relationship marketing, the consumer is first recognized as an individual, then as a member of a community or a group of affinity, and finally as an anonymous member of a segment.

Peppers, Rogers, and Dorf (1999) presented four essential steps to implement a program of relationship marketing in the company: consumer identification, differentiation between them, interaction with them, and customization of products or services in such a way to meet individual needs of each consumer. These steps have a particular complexity, but also lead to an increasing level of benefits to the company. These steps are explained in detail:

1. **Identification:** It is critical to know the customers individually, with as many details as possible and to be able to recognize them at all points of contact, through all kinds of messages, across all product lines, in all places, and in all divisions. In this step, the idea is that the company is able to locate and contact directly at least a reasonable portion of their more valuable consumers. It is important that the company learn about its consumers individually, not only their names, addresses and phone numbers, but also, their habits, preferences, attitudes, and other relevant characteristics.

2. **Differentiation:** Consumer differentiation implies that they are different in two broad directions: different value to the company (some have very high value, others, not so much) and different needs of company's products and services. Differentiation

enables the company to focus its efforts in order to acquire greater advantage with more valuable consumers. Companies have to know which consumers will never buy the company's product, and stop to invest resources and efforts to convince them. This implies an establishment of some kind of stratification criteria, profitability model, or customer value measure.

3. **Interaction:** Cost efficiency and effectiveness in interacting with consumers are very important to the success of a relationship marketing program. Cost efficiency can be obtained through interactions by more automated channels and are less expensive to the company. Effectiveness depends on how each consumer interaction happens, generating relevant information about consumer needs and values.

4. **Customization:** Personalization of relationships improves customer service. To encourage customers to maintain a learning relationship, the company has to adapt itself to needs expressed by each customer. What relationship marketing really means is simply to treat different customers differently, so that the relationship is meaningful to customers as individuals.

CRM and Information Technology (IT)

Gonçalves and Gonçalves (1997) point out that ancient owners of commercial establishments practiced, in their own way, Relationship Marketing by learning about customers needs and desires in order to offer customized products. Currently, however, it is impossible to know all customers from a large organization without the use of information technology (IT). According to these authors, "information technology appear as trainers of a different Marketing, in which new ways of customer communication arise."

The IT may help CRM systems in different ways:

1. Through the storage of customer information (identification, relationship history, profile of interests, preferences and habits).
2. Through tools for analyzing customers and making differentiation.
3. Through tools for generating recommendations, appropriate to the profile of each customer.
4. By generating new channels for relationship.

About this last item, IT has provided new communication channels and touch-points between companies and customers. D'Antonio (2010) states that the number of companies that are adhering to mobile devices is increasing each year. This happens because customers expect to do business anywhere and anytime, through their mobile devices. In this sense, Pedron and Saccol (2009) propose the use blogs, social networks and RSS to leverage new businesses. Neves (2010) recalls the Gartner Group forecast: "until 2016, social technologies will be integrated with most business applications."

Recommender Systems

Personalization is one of the main characteristics of a CRM system, and under certain points-of-view, making personalized offers is the final goal of a CRM. This task filters options to be presented to customers, reducing the information overload problem. Recommender systems were created to deal with this task and their main goal is to personalize the results presented to customers, helping people in the decision-making process in different environments and especially when too many options are available (Resnick et al., 1994).

In e-commerce, recommender systems are able to recommend products to customers according to their preferences. Recommendations are also necessary in organizational environments, especially when people search information or other people (example.g., experts). In these cases, recommender systems can make the difference between solving a problem correctly and quickly or facing serious consequences and high costs.

To be able to generate recommendations for the customers, it is necessary to collect information about the customers' behavior, set up their profiles and then select the options more attractive according to their profiles, recommending relevant items to them. We can say that the recommendation of items that meet the desires and preferences of customers is related to customer loyalty. According to Reichheld (1993), in a market where competitors are just a click away, creating a relationship of fidelity is an essential business strategy.

Profiling techniques are becoming more complex and creative. Demographic data like age, gender, and profession, and data about preferences and interests such as preferred film genres, hobbies, leisure activities, and music tastes are traditional attributes to represent the user. However, recent works have demonstrated that analyzing people who are similar to themselves (a kind of similarity) influences the choices of decision-makers (Bonhard et al., 2006).

Collaborative filtering (or social information filtering) is a recommendation approach that analyzes similarities among people. There are two kinds of collaborative filtering techniques: item-item and user-user. Item-item based techniques identify correlations between items in order to define new items to be recommended to users; recommended items are those similar to items associated to the user. User-user based techniques evaluate the similarity between users to find users with similar tastes or needs; in this case, items that will be recommended to a test user are those associated to similar users.

In the second case, two approaches may be used. In the memory-based one, a similarity between users is evaluated by identifying items with common ratings in historical data from two users. In the model-based approach, items associated to users are employed to define a model for each user; after that, the similarity between users is evaluated by similarity between their models (Wang et al., 2006).

Different attributes can be used to represent users' interest or characteristics in order to evaluate similarity between users in a user-user recommendation approach. For example, Stoilova et al. (2005) propose evaluating the similarity between users by their bookmarks. Bookmark files are employed as a source of knowledge about what is important to people. Bookmarks have implicit and explicit knowledge as URLs, titles, hierarchical structure, browser, platform and time (date of inclusion or access). Although Web pages listed in the bookmarks can be used to represent the user's profile (as a memory-based approach), the cited work uses the tree/hierarchy of themes for evaluating similarity between users (represented by their bookmarks). One of its main advantages is to minimize the sparsity limitation due to the small number of common items.

Collaborative filtering techniques and systems suffer from the "cold start" or "startup" problem: this happens when there are few ratings for a item or made by an user; the latter case is also called the "new user problem" (Adomavicius & Tuzhilin, 2005). There are some works that try to solve this problem. Rashid et al. (2002) and Sampaio et al. (2006), for example, evaluate techniques to select only a few items for the user to rate at the beginning; these few items are then used to find similar users. These approaches minimize the burden on the user for rating a sufficient number of good items. Schickel and Faltings (2006) use inference over the structure of an ontology to obtain possible preferences of a user. Using few ratings of the user over a few classes, the system can infer the ratings of this user on non-rated classes or concepts in the ontology. Zeng et al. (2003) transform user-item relations in user-class relations to minimize the sparsity problem with new users. Since the number of classes is far less than the number of items, the density of rated items increases greatly.

A recent technique to evaluate similarity between users is to examine their social relations or networks. Spertus et al. (2005) compare six distinct measures of similarity for recommending online communities to members of the Orkut social network. All of these measures of community similarity involve the overlap between two communities (i.e., the number of common users). Although this is an item-item approach, the cited work suggests evaluating similarity between users (user-user approach) through common community memberships or by the distance between users in the friendship graph.

Social CRM

The use of social technologies for business relationship with their customers generated a new term: social CRM (Chess Media Group, 2010). The idea is to complement a customer's profile by capturing information in social media and to interact with the customer using the same ways by how customers interact with other people and not by rules imposed by the company, through communication channels and traditional touch points, such as phone and stores. The social CRM use technologies such as blogs, microblogs (e.g., Twitter), social networks (e.g., Facebook and Orkut) and social media (e.g., Youtube) to interact with customers (current or potential).

Greenberg (2009) reports some possible causes for the raising of social CRM. One of them is the technological development: the raising of multiple technologies and the easy access to them by whatever person. Nowadays people can publish whatever kind of information in the Web, at low cost and easily, while other people can find this information in a quick and easy way. This phenomenon is one of the bases for the growing use of social media and thus an emerging strategy for social CRM.

Furtado (2012) presents some tendencies to social CRM. The traditional retail has used e-commerce as an additional sales channel, without realizing the true benefit in brand positioning and relationships with customers. With the change of the shopping experience, there are examples of companies like Apple, Amazon, Google, Zappos, and Best Buy that differ on social networks because they were "intimate" of consumer, authentic, agile and collaborative:

1. **Customer Service:** While retailers are worried about the store, shoppers are looking for convenience and solving its problems. Customer service is crucial to the success or failure of a brand in the social network. And all the customer service must be integrated, regardless of the means of communication, to enable companies to anticipate solutions, customizing products or services;

2. **Facebook and Google+:** With 36 million users in 2011, Brazil, for example, became the 4th largest country on Facebook. The growth was also seen in relation to the engagement and the number of monthly visits. ComScore research shows that Google+ has 4.3 million users. Google has announced the function "Search plus Your World," which includes information published by Google+'s contacts in the results of the search. Meanwhile, Facebook announced the "Open Graph," which enables application developers to customize the actions of users, how to "see" and "play";

3. **Social Commerce:** In 2011, features implemented by Facebook allowed the entry of numerous retailers with the purpose of connecting to your customers. Despite the F-commerce (Facebook) being a reality in Brazil, most of the shops are small and still do not show significant results. The reason

is that people haven't gotten used to "buying" in the network and still not secure with putting personal data there.

4. **Mobile Commerce (M-Commerce):** The projection for 2015 is that Brazil will arrive in 4th position comparing to the world in e-commerce sales. Increasingly the Brazilians use social networks and mobile devices (mobile) to exchange information and make purchases. According to Mobile Search Entertainment Forum (MEF), about 80 of the Brazilians have already used the phone in any stage of the purchase process.

5. Other networks such as Linkedin, Youtube, Vimeo, Flickr, Twitpic, and blogs are already being used by brands that want to innovate and to relate to their audience. These companies will certainly win the consumer. Without forgetting the Twitter, that they will launch a new layout and "pages" for brands (already in the testing phase in the U.S.). All networks will continue to be monitored, a task that will become increasingly automated and crucial to the growth and influence of social networks–beyond crisis management

The report of Band and Petouhoff (2010) proposes seven steps for social CRM success:

1. **Initiate social CRM experiments immediately:** The idea is to have some practical experience, renewing ideas "on the fly."

2. **Benchmark customer and prospect social readiness:** The idea is to make an initial survey of customers looking at their behavior in social media and then to make a plan to align with these profiles.

3. **Define your social customer objectives:** The idea is to make strategies to achieve people and objectives and after that to define the technology to be used.

4. **Assess your social CRM capabilities:** The idea is to define a focus using the organization capabilities.

5. **Understand the social CRM solutions landscape:** The idea is to integrate traditional solutions for CRM with new social technologies.

6. **Map out your social CRM capabilities-building plan:** "A social CRM plan should be tightly linked to business goals, focused on customer benefits, clearly identify the processes and constituencies that will be affected, and specify the associated information and capabilities required."

7. **Define your CRM metrics for success:** The fundamental premise to success is the right definition of metrics, using traditional ones (like e-mail marketing) and the novelties (like sentiment analysis).

Besides that, Greenberg (2009) also points out the entrance of Generation Y into the workforce as another cause for the raising of social CRM. People from Generation Y use the Internet in their own cell phone (94%), as primary source of news (34%), and communicate through instant messaging (76%), logged 24/7 (15%), Facebook (75% of college students), blogs (44% reading, 28% as author). "These social customers didn't have to rely on corporate literature." They use Internet and friends opinion (through technology) to evaluate potential purchases and "for deeper knowledge about their common interests - work or play."

Band and Petouhoff (2010) also proposes some metrics for social CRM: conversation buzz, conversation value, conversation volume, demographic metrics, level of influence, message reach, sentiment type, share of voice, topic frequency, and virality. These measures may help companies to evaluate their Social CRM systems and to understand where the failures are.

Customer Profiles in Social Media

Social CRM systems have to collect information about customers in social media and networks. There are three ways to collect information:

1. **Explicit Elicitation:** Happens when users spontaneously offer information about him/herself or when he/she answers questions asked by the organization; for example, forms on the Internet where users can sign in to sites for services or information.

2. **Implicit Elicitation:** The acquisition of information by observation; for example, in a supermarket, a check-out employee can observe the gender and age of the customer in order to associate to a specific basket; Underhill (1999) discusses the use and benefits of observation techniques for understanding customers´ behavior; using recorded video or false customers, Underhill team collects until 200 attributes about people in retail shops; these data are later analyzed using statistical techniques (example.g., data mining) in order to identify shopping patterns and to advise companies.

3. **Elicitation by Inference:** When deduction rules are utilized to generate new information; for example, a supermarket may associate the attribute "having freezer" to customers that buy frozen food.

In these three ways, information technology has an essential role. First, automated systems make easier the elicitation of data through electronic surveys on the Internet, surveys in public locations using mobile devices, among others. Second, electronic spreadsheets and databases help companies in storing and organizing collected data. Furthermore, data mining and business intelligence techniques and software tools are useful to analyze data and to find statistical patterns. Third, systems embedded with artificial intelligence techniques utilize inference rules to raise great volumes of new data without human intervention. Derivation rules, heuristic rules, decision trees, genetic algorithms, artificial neural networks, and so on, are used broadly in automated systems.

Information Quality and Privacy in Social Media

One problem that social CRM systems may face is the quality of information collected from social media. The first discomfort is with incomplete information. Surveys have to set which attributes are mandatory and which ones are optional. By other side, long surveys are boring and may lead users to give up from the process. The other problem is that when using the explicit paradigm, users may lie or give misleading information. Organizations have to define processes to validate collected information.

Collecting information by analyzing profiles available on the Internet is a good way to free customers from boring surveys and to collect true data. To do that, a special kind of software (called crawlers or spiders) has to be developed to get access into Websites. When Websites publish information without the need for authentication, crawlers may collect information by analyzing html codes of web pages. However, some data are available only inside private areas in Websites. In this case, crawlers have to get permission by using a login and password. In social networks, users may set what information will be publicly available and what information will be considered private. In the second case, even when the system has a login/password to get into the social network, not all information can be accessed. There are functionalities in social networks on the Internet to allow users to define whether private information may be seen only by direct connections ("friends") or also by users indirectly connected to these first degree connections ("friends of friends"). Social CRM systems have to face these challenges in order to gather information about customers from social media.

Besides that, in some cases, it is necessary to usetext analysis techniques for collecting information about customers, because information available on the Internet and social media is not standardized or formatted for computational analysis. For example, for identifying that a certain user likes shopping, software systems have to analyze posts of that user in Twitter or Facebook and semantically understand that sentiment in the words. The use of domain ontologies and natural language processing techniques are helpful to capture data from texts.

An alternative way to collect information about customers is to use Web mining techniques, that is, by observing his/her actions in an electronic system or Website. The Web pages seen by users, the items selected, the sequence of clicks (clickstream), the actions in the browser, the buttons selected and products acquired are different ways to understand the preference or interest of the user. However, some customers may consider this kind of elicitation a way of privacy invasion. Systems that utilize this kind of technique have to explicitly inform users about this kind of actions in a privacy policy or in a contract with terms of usage.

BEST PRACTICES IN SOCIAL CRM

Following, we present a set of the best practices for using this new technology. The set of best practices are composed by hints that may indicate how social networking technologies can help companies to squeeze and improve the relationship with their customers. These practices were identified through case studies and surveys. Studies on new social networking technologies available on the Web were conducted as well as the verification of how these technologies are being used by people and companies. The source of such case studies also includes periodicals, and scientific and traditional Websites. Surveys were carried out to listening companies and employees about the different ways they utilize social technologies to make relationships with customers. The goal was to understand what is going right and what the mistakes are.

Companies are complementing demographic data about their customers looking for information in user profiles inside social networks like Facebook and Twitter. Starting with the name of the customer, it is possible to find people in social media. However, this task is usually made by hand. Automatic systems have difficulty getting into social networks, since it is necessary to be logged in to accomplish searches and to see profiles. Only a few users let their data publicly available. Even search engines do not attain permission to analyze private profiles.

The other practice is to analyze what customers are publishing in blogs and social media. There are software tools that retrieve these posts and analyze the sentiment present in the texts. There are sentiment models (like ontologies) that help identifying different kinds of sentiments as, for example, positive and negative, emotions (OCC model) and humor states (POMS model). The goal is not only to understand what customers are saying, but more importantly to demonstrate respect to their feelings, establishing trust between the parts.

Posts in social media also help to predict general behavior of customers or markets. After the identification of sentiments or humors, it is possible to extract a correlation between the quantity of posts in each category and numerical series like Dow Jones index and product sales.

Some companies are allowing users to log in to their sites using accounts from social networks. This is useful for companies to identify a user/customer and then to access information about users available in social networks to complement traditional cadastres.

Usually information available in social networks includes structured data like name, sex, city, country, age, among others. However, there is non-structured information (images, photos, videos and text messages). Texts can be analyzed using text mining, sentiment analysis, or opinion mining software. Regarding images, there is no current technology with the capacity to analyze content and understand semantics. Google Images are trying to develop such technology. The functionality of finding similar images may help by searching similar images inside a defined category. Images can be classified using tags (as in Tagsonomies and Folksonomies).

In some social networks, it is possible to collect private information about customers. To do that, companies have to create a profile in the social network and to be connected to that particular customer. Few users made private information available publicly to non-connected users. So, having a profile, companies may get closer to their customers. Besides that, the company profile demonstrates the personification of the company, remembering customers, characteristics, sentiments, goals, politics, and that customers may interact with the company as if it was a person.

One way to collect information about customers is to verify which communities they belong to inside social media. Usually the name (title) of the community or group identifies the subject or areas of interest.

Besides information about customers, companies try to obtain information about people related to customers, including friends or any kind of social relation. Information collected with related people complements the cadastre of customers, since there is a premise that users linked in social networks have similar tastes and behaviors.

For collecting related people, companies can launch a promotion offering rewards for users to reTweet, forward, or pass messages to their friends. This is a low cost way to get new customers and to promote products or services. Besides that, recommendations from friends are more reliable.

In the context of social media, companies have the interest of finding the most influential people. Two indicators are: the number of "friends" (contacts or related people) and the number of messages re-passed on or replied. Companies want to establish ways to conquer these opinion leaders and thus to get their support to achieve other people.

Social networks boost collaboration among people, including companies X companies and companies X customers. New products and improvements may be developed by this way, new services emerge from collaboration, gathering more people and establishing new communication channels. The crowd sourcing technique utilizes collaboration without charges for companies. People are rewarded by other means than financial return and results are better even than made by experts (Wisdom of Crowds). The relations established by social networks may outlast relations made by buy-sell tasks and marketing promotions and they are made on more solid bases.

Companies must be proactive when concerning relationship with customers in social media. The suggestion is that companies should not wait for customers complaining, but should then start the communication. Campaign with videos can be an option for dealing with known problems. Humor can be a way to return back to company unsatisfied customers and a way to explain how drawbacks are being addressed. Communities in social networks are a good way to gather customers for communication and to know who the customers are and what they are thinking about different subjects. In this kind of sentiment analysis, companies can observe what customers say about subjects that are not directly related to company market, as for example thoughts about economy, family, money, jobs, marriage and personal feelings about youngness, adolescence and aging. In conclusion, answering claims is the second step in the relationship.

The final hint is that business should not be restricted to one social media or network. Although there are some channels that gather the majority of the users in the web, in some sense, this works like a kind of fashion and users may migrate from one to another in few mouths. Besides that, technology changes so fast that new media arises every day and get thousands of followers in a quick time. Companies must be aware of new media and new channels. Unfortunately, these actions involve money and effort. Companies must think like investment and not cost. This is like advertisement and traditional marketing campaigns in TV, radio and newspapers. When calculating the payback of these actions, companies will be surprised. Recent researches have demonstrated that information that flows inside social networks has more power than traditional marketing. This occurs because the source is who is really using products and services and not who is selling them. People are more compelled to accept recommendation from their pairs (friends, team mates, professional colleges).

FUTURE DIRECTIONS

The final objective of a social CRM system is to sell or to raise income. Social media and networks have particular ways to support companies that want to advertise or to sell. Advertisement is the most traditional way. Inside videos and Web pages, companies can offer their products and services. But recently a new approach arose: the social commerce. Recently social networks started a system with shopping facilities. Their users can buy and companies can sell. The critics are skeptics and visualize that this kind of commerce will not take off. However, this is an alternative to companies completing the CRM cycle.

Another trend is a change in the consumer behavior. Researchers have discovered that people want to produce content and not only to consume, generating what is called "prosumer" (producer + consumer). People do not want to assist passively what is happening in the world. Since the fall of the Berlin Wall and the birth of ecology, people are more active and wishing to be a source of changes (and not only an audience). User-generated content is part of social media (without them, Youtube and Facebook would not exist). Companies have to support this wish not only in public media but also on their Websites. A food company, for example, may allow customers to publish their recipes. Electronic companies may allow customers to comment about different ways to use products. Even computer manufacturers

have sites where their own customers can answer questions and doubts of other customers. How companies deal with negative comments is still a creativity task. But even this kind of information has to be published uncensored. Because, to be honest, customers want companies to also be honest.

CONCLUSION

This chapter presented a study in the social CRM area where we studied how companies are using social networking technologies to increase their traditional CRM systems. Studies were carried out on new social networking technologies available on the Web, such as Twitter, blogs, and communities and how they are being used by people and companies. These studies have identified the types of social networking technologies that can be used to support CRM systems and how they can be used by companies. Also, types of personalization (recommendation) of services and products to support the CRM systems were discussed.

The final result of this work is a compendium of the best practices identified in case studies. These best practices indicate how social networking technologies can help companies to squeeze and improve the relationship with their customers. The best practices presented in this chapter can be used in different ways, as following in short:

1. For companies and institutions interested in increasing their traditional CRM systems, to improve the relationship with customers.
2. For companies and people interested in accelerating relationships with other persons or customers through technologies available on the Internet.
3. For communication departments, marketing, and public relations, which could generate relationship strategies and build the company image on the Internet based on tips experienced by other companies.

4. By teachers in graduate and undergraduate disciplines related to the theme of CRM or digital marketing, since the set of best practices are real cases and successful strategies for current use of social networks to CRM.

REFERENCES

Adomavicius, G., & Tuzhilin, A. (2005). Toward the next generation of recommender systems: A survey of the state-of-the-art and possible extensions. *IEEE Transactions on Knowledge and Data Engineering*, *17*(6), 734–749. doi:10.1109/TKDE.2005.99.

Band, W., & Petouhoff, N. L. (2010). *Social CRM goes mainstream*. Cambridge, MA: Forrester Research.

Bonhard, P., Harries, C., McCarthy, J., & Sasse, M. A. (2006). Accounting for taste: Using profile similarity to improve recommender systems. In *Proceedings of the SIGCHI Conference on Human Factors in Computing Systems* (pp. 1057-1066). Montreal, Canada: ACM.

Chess Media Group. (2010). *Guide to understanding social CRM*.

D'Antonio, M. (2010). Navigating on the wave of mobile (in Portuguese). *Peppers and Rogers*. Retrieved from http://www.1to1.com.br/view.aspx?docId=34345

Furtado, B. (2012). *Social Media: Trends to 2012*. Retrieved from http://www.baguete.com.br/artigos/1102/bianca-furtado/16/04/2012/social-media-tendencias-para-2012

Gonçalves Filho, C., & Gonçalves, C. A. (1997). Relationship marketing and information technologies: Analyzes in financial institutions. In *Encontro Anual Da Associação Nacional De Programas De Pós-Graduação Em Administração*, 21., 1997, Rio das Pedras. Anais. Rio das Pedras: ANPAD, 1997. 1 CD-ROM.

Greenberg, P. (2009). *Social CRM Comes of Age*. Retrieved from http://www.oracle.com/us/products/applications/crmondemand/036062.pdf

Gummesson, E. (1998). Implementation requires a relationship marketing paradigm. *Journal of the Academy of Marketing Science*, *26*(3), 242–249. doi:10.1177/0092070398263006.

Neves, G. (2010). *Gartner: 10 strategic technologies for 2011*. Retrieved from http://www.baguete.com.br/noticias/negocios-e-gestao/22/10/2010/gartner-10-tecnologias-estrategicas-para-2011

Payne, A., & Holt, S. (2001). Diagnosing customer value: Integrating the value process and relationship marketing. *British Journal of Management*, *12*, 159–182. doi:10.1111/1467-8551.00192.

Pedron, C. D., & Saccol, A. Z. (2009). What lies behind the concept of customer relationship management? Discussing the essence of CRM through a phenomenological approach. *BAR. Braz. Adm. Rev.*, *6*(1), 34–49.

Peppers, D., Rogers, M., & Dorf, B. (1999). Is your company ready for one-to-one Marketing? *Harvard Business Review*, *77*(1), 151–160. PMID:10345390.

Rashid, A., Albert, I., Cosley, D., Lam, S., McNee, S., & Konstan, J. … Riedl, J. (2002). Getting to know you: Learning new user preferences in recommender systems. In *Proceedings of the International Conference on Intelligent User Interface* (pp. 127-134). San Francisco, CCA: ACM.

Reichheld, F. (1993). Loyalty-Based Management. *Harvard Business School Review*, *2*, 64–73. PMID:10124634.

Resnick, P., Iacovou, N., Suchak, M., Bergstrom, P., & Riedl, J. (1994). GroupLens: An Open Architecture for Collaborative Filtering of NetNews. In *Proceedings of the 1994 Computer Supported Cooperative Work* (pp. 175-186). Chapel Hill, NC: ACM.

Sampaio, I., Ramalho, G., Corruble, V., & Prudêncio, R. (2006). Acquiring the preferences of new users in recommender systems: the role of item controversy. In *Proceedings of the Workshop on Recommender Systems* (in conjunction with the 17th European Conference on Artificial Intelligence - ECAI 2006) (pp. 107-110). Riva del Garda, Italy: ACM.

Schickel, V., & Faltings, B. (2006). Using ontological a-priori score to infer user's preferences. In *Proceedings of the Workshop on Recommender Systems* (in conjunction with the 17th European Conference on Artificial Intelligence - ECAI 2006) (pp. 102-106). Riva del Garda, Italy: ACM.

Spertus, E., Sahami, M., & Buyukkokten, O. (2005). Evaluating similarity measures: a large-scale study in the orkut social network. In *Proceedings of the eleventh ACM SIGKDD International Conference on Knowledge Discovery and Data Mining KDD '05* (pp. 678-684). Chicago, IL: ACM

Srivastava, R. K., Shervani, T. A., & Fahey, L. (1999). Marketing, business processes and shareholder value: An organizationally embedded view of marketing activities and the discipline of Marketing. *Journal of Marketing, 63*, 168–179. doi:10.2307/1252110.

Stoilova, L., Holloway, T., Markines, B., Maguitman, A. G., & Menczer, F. (2005). GiveALink: Mining a semantic network of bookmarks for Web search and recommendation. In *Proceedings of the 3rd International Workshop on Link discovery LinkKDD* (pp. 66-73). New York: ACM.

Underhill, P. (1999). *Why we buy: The science of shopping*. New York: Obat Inc..

Wang, J., De Vries, A. P., & Reinders, M. J. T. (2006). Unifying user-based and item-based collaborative filtering approaches by similarity fusion. In *Proceedings of the 29th annual International ACM SIGIR Conference on Research and Development in Information Retrieval SIGIR '06* (pp. 501-508). Seattle, WA: ACM.

Zeng, C., Xing, C. X., & Zhou, L. Z. (2003). Similarity measure and instance selection for collaborative filtering. In *Proceedings of the 12th International Conference on World Wide Web* (pp. 652-658). New York: ACM.

ADDITIONAL READING

Gonçalves, C. A., & Gonçalves, F. C. (1995). Information technology and marketing: How to obtain customers and market. *Revista de Administração de Empresas, São Paulo, 35*(4), 21–32.

KEY TERMS AND DEFINITIONS

Customer Relationship Management (CRM): Methods and tools used by organizations to improve the relationship with their customers.

Recommender System: Can make personalized offers to customers individually.

Social CRM: Customer relationship management through social media and networks. It means the use of CRM jointly with social media/networks to complement customer´s data or to extend marketing campaigns.

Social Media: Electronic means where people can maintain relationships with each other.

Social Network: Electronic communication tools where virtual relationships are created and maintained.

Section 6
Organizations and Social Technologies

Chapter 15
E-Business Planning in Morphing Organizations:
Maturity Models of Business Transformation

Sharon A. Cox
Birmingham City University, UK

ABSTRACT

E-business has changed the external face of many organizations widening and extending access to products and services. This has required large scale changes to be made to business processes to accommodate new ways of working. Social media technologies have introduced a new wave of change through organizational trading networks. Further business transformation is needed to embrace the opportunities and challenges of social media technologies. This chapter presents a framework to help morphing organizations plan the business transformation needed to embed social media technologies within their e-business service provision. Business and technological maturity models are analysed and a set of maturity measures for e-business is proposed. The business transformation needed to embed e-business technology in organizational systems is discussed in two UK manufacturers. Dimensions of business transformation and critical success factors for adopting social media technologies are proposed from these cases.

INTRODUCTION

Organizations engaging in e-business have learnt that conducting business electronically requires more than the introduction of appropriate information technology (IT). The introduction of e-business technologies into organizations has been the initial trigger for a series of changes from which few areas of the business have escaped unchanged. The traditional barriers of trading hours, location and service delivery channels which previously constrained organizational activity have been broken down by IT. Beneath the surface level changes to systems providing the

DOI: 10.4018/978-1-4666-4026-9.ch015

interface between customer and partner organizations in the supply chain, a series of adjustments to business processes and working practices have been needed, changing the form of organizations. Social media technology provides organizations with opportunities for more direct engagement with customers and consumers, suppliers and trading partners. It has triggered further changes to organizations to take advantage of opportunities and to respond to new challenges. However, amid the seemingly constant waves of change, the organization must seek to preserve its identity within its morphing form. Morphing organizations need to learn from the transformations initiated by e-business engagement and develop plans to manage the further transformations needed to embrace continuing technological developments, in areas such as social media technologies. This chapter explores the problem of how to identify the business transformation needed to effectively incorporate social media technologies in organizations.

A number of models proposed to map the impact of introducing new IT into organizations are explored in this chapter to explore business transformation. Traditional maturity models such as Nolan's stages of growth model (Nolan, 1973) are compared with more recent models which focus on the impact of e-business technology in organizations. The suitability of existing maturity models to represent the introduction of social network technology in organizations is then considered. From this examination of maturity models, a set of maturity measures is proposed to help organizations assess their current status of business transformation and plan the changes needed to further embed social media technologies into the business.

Previously, action research with a major UK manufacturer (Case A) led to the formulation of a framework to assist organizations in preparing and implementing an e-business strategy. Action research is a research approach which addresses a practical situation in a client organization, whilst simultaneously increasing knowledge in a theoretical domain. A cyclical process is applied in which action in the real-world and existing theoretical knowledge are reflected upon. The process seeks to understand and address practical problems in the organization through the application of existing theoretical knowledge and the generation of new knowledge in the domain. The framework for developing an e-business strategy, which evolved through action research, is analysed as to how far it supports the proposed set of maturity measures. A second case study is then outlined (Case B) in which the framework is applied with a different UK manufacturer operating in a similar supply chain. The aim of this case is to assess the effectiveness of the framework to assist in formulating strategies for business transformation to embed social media technologies in organizations. Dimensions of business transformation are defined which provide a structure within which to assess the degree of business process transformation needed to embrace social media technologies. The chapter concludes by presenting critical success factors, gained from experience in the two organizations, to inform the planning of social media technologies in morphing organizations, aligned with organizational strategies.

BACKGROUND

A morphing organisation is defined as one which continually changes its external face whilst retaining its own identity (Cox, 2013). The face of an organization provides the image that it wishes to convey to its external environment, reflecting its core values. It also provides the main means of communication between the organization and its environment. Beneath the face lies the network of interacting components which are continually adjusting in response to internal and external triggers in order to achieve the organization's objectives. The morphing organization gradually changes its external image whilst retaining its identity in response to adjustments in the relationships between its internal components (Cox, 2013). Leavitt (1965) proposed that organizational systems comprise the interaction between the components: task, structure, technology and people. Waterman Jr. et al. (1980) adopted a wider view of the organizational context and proposed that organizational effectiveness emerges from the dynamic interactions between the organization's structure, strategy, systems (including formal and informal procedures), style (of management and culture), skills (i.e., capabilities), the staff resource (including morale, attitude, behaviour, training and appraisal) and subordinate goals (later renamed shared values (Peters & Waterman Jr., 1989) representing the values underlying the mission of the organization). This became known as the McKinsey 7-S framework©. Socio-technical analysis focuses on the transformation that emerges within morphing organizations from interaction between the components in these two models and the processes of meaning construction, within communities of practice, mediated by information technology.

E-business and social media technology change the interface between the organization and its external partners. Changing the interface affects the elements in the 7-S framework, initiating business transformation throughout the organization. The following section outlines a number of maturity models which have been developed to explore the stages of IT led transformation within morphing organizations. This provides a basis towards understanding the impact of social media technologies on organizations.

Maturity Models

Maturity models have been established in the IS/IT domain to represent the business transformation initiated by technology in organizations. Models such as those by Greiner (1972) and Nolan (1979) represent the progress and management of IT in organizations (Wilson, 2000). Nolan's maturity model (1973) outlines an organization's transition between four stages of technological maturity driven by growth in the number and complexity of computer applications, growth in specialization of technical staff, and growth in formalization of organizational control of technological systems. Two further stages were incorporated into this model representing growth in the integration of technical systems and data prior to reaching maturity (Nolan, 1979). The model focuses on the technological function; in contrast, the Capability Maturity Model (Software Engineering Institute and Carnegie Mellon University, 1995) focuses on the quality of business processes through structure and optimization of efficiency and effectiveness (Wettstein & Kueng, 2002). In both models, maturity of business transformation is reflected in increasing levels of standardization and policy control.

Historically, the introduction and development of IS/IT in organizations represented in these models has been internally focused. Lockamy III and McCormack (2004) suggest that as processes mature, they move from being internally focused to externally focused. E-business and social media focus IT externally, reaching out into the trading network and demanding changes to the internal organizational processes (Cox et al., 2001).

Wilson (2000) identifies a four phase maturity model which represents the sequential transformation of an organization's engagement in e-business. In phase one, organizations start exploring the potential of e-business with the introduction of a non-interactive web page. Following Nolan's (1973) model, the number and complexity of e-business applications increase as the organization starts to support on-line ordering (phase two of Wilson's model) and provide an on-line catalogue (phase three of Wilson's model). The final level of maturity in Wilson's (2000) model is achieved when back office processes are available on-line. In contrast, back office automation is an early phase of development in Nolan's model (1973). E-business represents an inversion of traditional maturity models which progress from back office to front office applications of IT; e-business applications move from front office, customer-focused applications, to the back office (Cox, et al., 2006). This backwards movement through the organizational processes reflects three levels of transformation. Firstly, after initial stand-alone pilot projects to explore the potential of e-business in organizations, e-business becomes accepted into the organization's structure and strategy. Secondly, it is recognized that data and process integration are needed for e-business systems to operate effectively, embedding e-business into the systems and work practices within the organization Thirdly, as e-business technology becomes taken for granted in organizations, it seeks to replicate the benefits achieved externally with its internal-facing systems. During these stages of transformation organizations morph through changes to their strategy and structure, integration of systems, and finally to changes to their internal systems.

Croom (2005) proposes a five phase maturity model of the evolution of e-business in the supply chain which adopts this outside-in approach. In phase one, e-business is used to achieve sales growth by integrating sales and payment processes. In phase two, strategic account management is achieved through relationship management processes. Integration of operations occurs in phase three as process planning and control systems are integrated (e.g., resource planning systems). In phase four, procurement is improved with supply-based management processes and in phase five, supply chain integration is achieved using e-business technology to support logistics processes (e.g., e-fulfillment). Each phase in Croom's model (2005) focuses on further integration of e-business processes transforming the organization's experience and expectations as e-business matures. This model again first starts with an external focus of e-business systems. The applications become more complex, requiring further backward integration into existing processes. E-business is then used

to transform the way in which the organization conducts business internally and is finally extended outward again at the opposite end of the organization's value chain, prompting the start of a new maturity cycle.

Lockamy III and McCormack (2004) propose a supply chain maturity model based on the Capability Maturity Model comprising the following levels:

1. **Ad hoc:** The supply chain processes are unstructured.
2. **Defined:** The processes are documented.
3. **Integrated:** Organizations start to cooperate, illustrated by forecasting and performance monitoring, resulting in reduced costs.
4. **Extended:** Inter-organizational collaboration includes the transfer of processes between organizations and the development of a trusting, customer-focused culture.

This model emphasizes the strengthening of communication between trading partners within the supply chain as e-business processes become more mature. Electronic communication offers increased opportunity for dialogue and increased frequency of contact between trading partners, enhancing both forward and backward facing business processes in the chain (Gammelgaard & Ritter, 2005). For example, e-business systems can improve collaborative relationships with customers by distributing product information, tracking order status and attaining customer feedback, in addition to enhancing the flow of information to support marketing initiatives (Bhatt & Emdad, 2001). A series of transformations are needed in the organization before effective communication can be achieved as e-business matures.

Feeny et al. (1996) define the relative maturity of IT as being the extent to which the:

- Technology is stable with a low rate of change.

- Application is well understood.
- Organization has prior experience of the technology and the application.

When maturity is low, Feeny et al. (1996) recommend a high level of end-user involvement; as the technology matures, the emphasis moves to the IS/IT function to formalize standards and procedures.

E-business technology has become well established and has been used to enhance established business processes in the supply chain. It is therefore proposed that assessments of e-business maturity need to consider two dimensions, the:

- Degree to which e-business processes have become standardized and embedded in organizations (i.e., business transformation has taken place).
- Extent to which e-business strengthens communication between organizations in the supply chain.

The following measures of e-business process maturity are proposed:

Measure A: Number of external relationships supported by e-business processes.
Measure B: Range of communications that are supported by e-business.
Measure C: Strategic significance of e-business in the organization.
Measure D: Synchronicity of the communication supported by e-business processes.
Measure E: Formalization of business processes to act upon the communication received through e-business technologies.
Measure F: Integration of processes to act upon the communication received.

Social media technologies offer organizations the opportunity to develop more personal and meaningful communications within the supply chain, raising collaboration to a higher level. Par-

sons (1983) recognized that information technology held the potential to enable organizations to develop a greater understanding of their customer needs. This is being realized with social media technologies.

Social Media Technology

Social network sites have become internationally established as a dominant media of communication. For example, in 2009 the U.S. government asked the social networking site Twitter to delay scheduled maintenance. The maintenance would have meant that the service would be unavailable for a short time and it was considered to be inappropriate to withdraw an essential means of communication for citizens in Iran following disrupted elections (Pleming, 2009). Lee et al. (2006) define social media as people being connected through meaningful relationships. It is the active engagement in these relationships which is critical to the successful use of social media in organizations. Social networking is not a technological fad, it is a cultural phenomenon though the take up from business is slower than consumer adoption (Information Age, 2011). Social media encompasses three elements: content, community and Web 2.0 technology (Ahlqvist et al., 2010).

Grippa (2009) compares a range of media (including face-to-face, e-mail and video conferencing) in terms of: the synchronicity of the communication; the reach, communicating to a number of people simultaneously; richness of the communication; channel, whether voice and/ or text could be supported and storage, the ability to retain the communication. Grippa (2009) suggests that reach and richness are key factors which need to be considered in order to increase the effectiveness of communication.

Social media technology provides organizations with the means to extend their reach with multimedia rich content. It provides a means of disintermediation in the supply chain, allowing manufacturers direct access to the consumers of their products and services. However, social media should not be seen as another channel to distribute existing information (Hall, 2010). Social media has changed the role of individuals from being just consumers of information to taking a prominent active role in content creation (Bateman et al., 2011). This requires organizations to develop strategies for engaging with consumers in this forum (Kietzmann et al., 2011).

Social media provides a means of enabling conversations within the marketplace to help build relationships (Booth & Matic, 2011). The use of social media to build relationships with consumers is discussed in Case B. Direct and indirect connections within the social network of interactions quickly result in a vast international communication network. Booth and Matic (2011) propose an influencer index which uses a range of variables (including frequency of posting, visitors per month, inbound and outbound links) to assess the value of a blogger's influence in a market place. The power of relationships in social networks should not be neglected as negative issues can soon 'snowball' as they spread through the social network. It is therefore critical that organizations respond to any issues promptly.

Davies (2010) suggests that the key to using social media in the supply chain starts with identifying areas where social media can be used to gather information to improve performance or influence customers. For example, a YouTube contest enables organizations to gather information about demographics and public perceptions of their product quickly with limited investment (Davies, 2010). However, it should be noted that typical measures of return on investment are not suitable for assessing social media as it is not about saving money, but about different ways of working (Information Age, 2011). Romero (2011) explains that measures of return in social media need to include direct measures such as number of engagements and intermediate returns relating to branding.

Social media has two main roles in organizations: firstly, to support marketing and customer relationship management by providing a forum for customer queries and complaints; secondly, to support internal communication and collaboration (Information Age, 2011). These roles relate to both externally focused and internally focused business processes.

Ashcroft (2010) suggests that social media can offer benefits to the supply chain in the following areas:

- People engagement, listening, learning and improving through development of communities.
- Extended supply chain management, integrating views and improving the visibility of data, activities to enable insights to be identified, discovering synergies and accelerating cycles.
- Risk identification achieved through early warning and monitoring systems providing an integrated view of information from multiple sources enabling transactional data to be understood in context.
- Functional integration, breaking down barriers to communication between departments and organizations to create a shared focus on the end result.

These benefits can also be regarded as forming stages of maturity in the deployment of social media. In the initial phase, individual pilot systems are established with an external focus. As an organization's use of social media technology becomes established, social media systems and technology become integrated within existing systems in the organization. In the later stages, social media technology becomes embedded into the organization, supporting internal communication. Organizations need to develop a strategy to align the introduction of social media with their strategic objectives and to understand the business transformation needed to support the communication technology.

The following section briefly outlines a framework, which was developed through action research with a major UK manufacturer of soft drinks (Case A), to support the formulation of e-business strategies. The framework is then revisited to assess its suitability for developing strategies for social media technologies.

FRAMEWORK TO SUPPORT E-BUSINESS PLANNING

Cox et al. (2001) proposed a framework which comprises three phases for developing an e-business strategy. The framework incorporates a number of tools for assessing the maturity of e-business processes in an organization and enables new opportunities for extending the reach and integration of e-business processes to be planned. The application of the framework in a UK manufacturer (Case A) is briefly demonstrated in the following sections.

Phase 1: Explore Trading Relationships (Case A)

The main purpose of the first phase in the framework is to enable an organization to identify potential trading relationships which can be initiated or enhanced with e-business technology. Van Hooft and Stegwee (2001) recommend that Porter's five forces model (Porter, 1980) should be used to formulate an e-business vision. Cox et al. (2001) emphasize that in addition to identifying existing parties in the organization's trading environment, consideration should also be given to actors who have previously had a relationship with the organization, and to those who could potentially have a relationship with the organization in the future. For example, consumers of substitute products could be considered as a potential group of actors with whom the organization could seek to initiate a relationship. A grid is used to summarize the organization's trading network. The grid provides a list of questions to help organizations to identify key actors in their network. Examples of some of the questions included in the grid are shown in Figure 1. Analysis of the completed grid assists organizations in reviewing their position in the supply chain and helps to identify potential strategic relationships.

Figure 1. Grid for analysing extended trading network

Actors	**Previous**	**Current**	**Competitor**	**Substitute**	**Potential**
Consumer				*Who consumes substitute products?*	
Customer	*Who no longer buys from us and why?*	*Who are the main groups buying our products?* *[major supermarket chains]*			*Who might start buying our products?*
Supplier		*Who supplies our key raw materials?* *[syrup producer X]*	*Who supplies our competitors?*		

The current use of e-business technology in the organization is mapped to the grid. For example, Figure 1 shows that Manufacturer A currently uses e-business technology to support communication with its main customers and one of its main suppliers. There is therefore potential to increase the breadth of whom relationships that are supported by e-business technologies. The grid represents the organization's maturity in terms of the number of external relationships currently supported by e-business processes (Measure A).

Phase 2: Position Activity and Generate Strategic Initiatives (Case A)

The aim of phase two is to help organizations to identify specific opportunities to use e-business to improve or initiate relationships with one or more parties. It focuses on aligning the deployment of e-business technology with the organization's strategic objectives.

Enslow and Smith (1998) highlight three segments of supply chain management activities with increasing potential for competitive advantage. These are: market differentiation (e.g., promotions, product design), process enhancement (e.g., ordering, product catalogues, inventory levels) and channel reinvention for structural advantage (e.g., disintermediation and reintermediation of phases in the supply chain). The use of e-business technology can be mapped against specific objectives of the organization to provide the business case for investment in e-business. Figure 2 is used to align e-business initiatives with trading parties against business objectives. It focuses on *who* the trading relationships is with, *what* the objective of the trading relationship is and *how* e-business is supporting, or could support, the trading relationship. Both current and potential e-business initiatives are included in the grid to demonstrate the current maturity of e-business processes in relation to supporting business objectives. For example, Figure 2 shows that Manufacturer A is currently using e-business to support automated ordering with major customers which supports the manufacturer's objective to reduce transaction costs.

The grid maps the maturity of e-business in the organization in terms of the number of trading relationships supported (Measure A), the range of communication activities supported (Measure B) and the strategic significance of the e-business activities to the organization (Measure C). It also assists organizations to identify further opportunities for extending the number and type of e-business activities to align with its strategic objectives. For example, it prompted Manufacturer A to consider how it might use e-business to gain a structural advantage in the supply chain.

A third model was then created to analye the complexity of the communication being supported by the e-business activity (Measure D). The model differentiates between: one-way communication (i.e., sending information via static web site or receiving orders via electronic data interchange);

Figure 2. Position strategic activity in trading relationships against business objectives

Strategy (WHY)	Business Objective (WHAT)	E-business Activity (HOW)	Trading Party (WHO)
Market Differentiation			
Process Enhancement	Reduce transaction costs.	Automated ordering.	Major customers.
Structural Advantage			

two-way communication exchange (i.e., sending and receiving information via on-line forms) and two-way interaction (i.e., interactive negotiation via collaborative systems). This reflects Wilson's (2000) maturity model of e-business. The model (Figure 3) was extended to incorporate the four levels of inter-organization relationships identified by Ward et al. (1996): Transaction Processing (where information is transmitted for processing; Enquiry or Information Exchange (allowing external partners to access data); Transaction Driven Interaction Systems (supporting on-line transactions) and Interactive Processing Systems (where information is updated simultaneously on customer's and supplier's systems). The complexity and dependency of the relationship increases at each of these four levels as greater access is permitted to internal computer systems. Transaction interaction and interactive processing (levels three and four) relate to those proposed by Lockamy III and McCormack's (2004) model of e-business maturity. Organizations co-operate at level three and then start to transfer ownership and responsibility for processing at level four (for example, updating a customer's inventory when a delivery is completed).

Figure 3 provides examples of Manufacturer A's engagement in a range of e-business activities, of differing levels of complexity, with its customers. For example, Figure 2 shows that the manufacturer uses on-line ordering with its customers to support the business objective to enhance it processes. This is mapped to the model in Figure 3 to show that on-line ordering relates to level three, transaction processing in Ward et al. (1996) model. Separate models are created for each trading party identified in Figure 2. The completed collection of models shows the maturity of e-business in the organization, measured by the range and complexity of e-business activities with each trading partner. As the complexity of the trading relationship increases, greater formalization of processes is needed (Measure E). The deeper the e-business processes need to be embedded into the organization, the greater the transformation is needed in the organization to integrate the e-business processes (Measure F).

Figure 3. Aligning e-business activity with business objectives

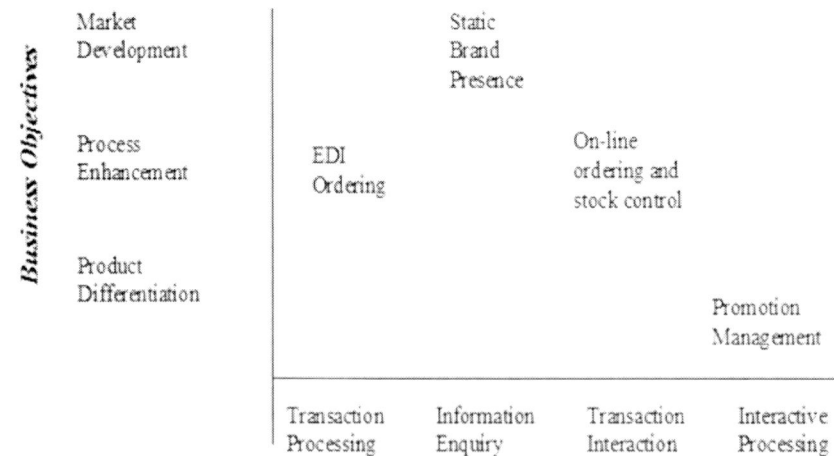

Complexity of Interaction with CUSTOMER

(Source: Cox et al., 2001)

Phase 3: Manage Internal Change (Case A)

The success of e-business initiatives is dependent upon the integration of e-business processes into the organization to meet the expectations of customers (Cox et al., 2001). Phase three of the framework explores the areas of transformation needed to effectively embed e-business processes into the organization. E-business processes establish a means of communication between the organization and other parties in its trading environment. Initial e-business projects were viewed as separate systems acting at the interface between, for example, the outbound logistics of one organization and the inbound logistics of their customer. This relates to stage one of Lockamy III and McCormack's (2004) model and phases one and two of Ward et al. (1996). These systems were considered to be additional periphery systems of communication and often the extensive transformation outlined in the McKinsey 7-S framework© needed to underpin the communication was neglected. However, all the activities in the organization's value chain need to be assessed in terms of how they will be affected by the implementation of the strategic decisions in phase two.

When defining a new business model initiated by technological change, Pateli and Giaglis (2005) suggest that the transformation is modelled within seven categories. The categories broadly examine collaboration from three perspectives: strategic view of the rationale for collaboration (business objectives, core competencies, market scope, critical success factors); integration view of what is being integrated and the emergent value (relationship model, value exchange) and the community view of how the collaboration operates in practice (involving actors, roles and responsibilities). The strategic view is partly addressed in phase two of the framework where e-business initiatives are aligned with, and influence, the organization's strategy. The following sections consider the areas of transformation needed in the integration view and the community view.

Implementing e-business systems in the manufacturing organization involved extensive changes to the business. Figure 4 shows the introduction of

Figure 4. Scope of e-business transformation

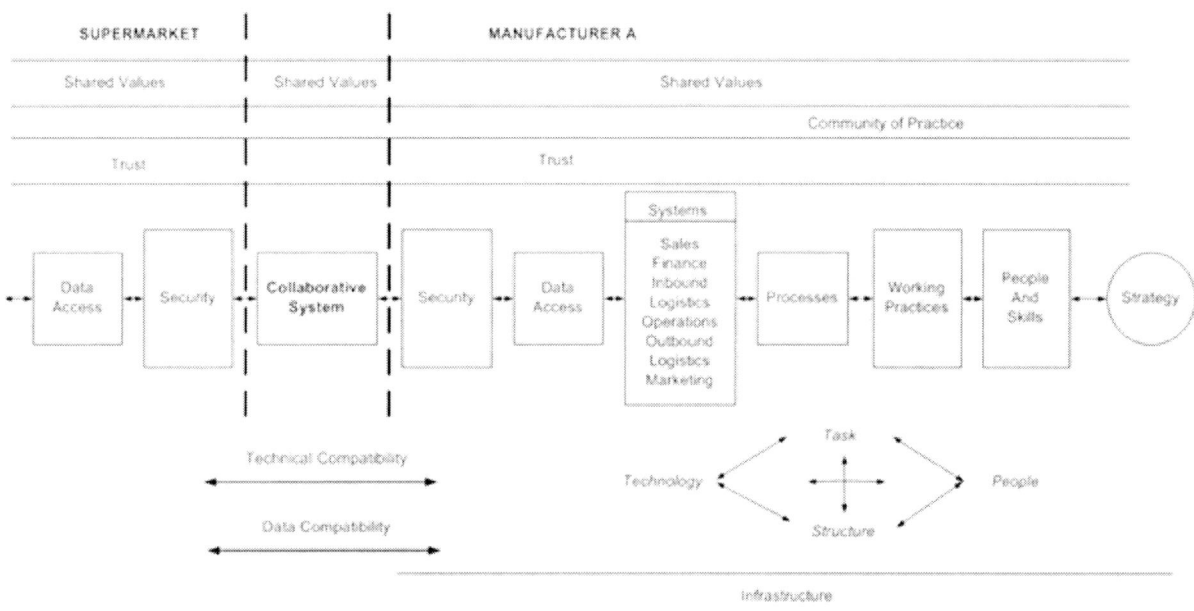

a collaborative system, owned by a supermarket, which provided the interface between Manufacturer A and a major UK supermarket. The collaborative system impacted the following areas in both organizations (Cox et al., 2006): structure, security, data, processes, systems, people, working practices and trust (shown in Figure 4). Both Manufacturer A and the supermarket had to change their policies on data access and security. Physical security of additional equipment was also a concern in a similar case involving an SME (Cox et al., 2006). The impact of the collaborative system was not restricted to one point of access in one system; the data and processes which the collaborative system needed to access encompassed the majority of systems in the organization. The collaborative system provided the interface to, for example, order processing systems, production systems, delivery systems and finance systems. Enabling this access required technical and process integration issues to be addressed.

Data required by the e-business systems was accessed from a range of internal systems including sales systems, finance systems, production planning systems, distribution systems and warehouse systems in both organizations. This raised issues relating to technological and data compatibility. The data needed to be understood and trusted by the people using it. A significant issue hindering effective communication was differences in data definitions. Changes also had to be made to a range of systems to act upon the data received.

The introduction of the collaborative system required working practices to change to incorporate the system. For example, face-to-face negotiation between the two organizations was replaced with on-line negotiation which required different skills to be developed. The introduction of the e-business system changed the way in which each organization worked and how the two organizations worked together. This resulted in the formation of a new shared community to develop on-line within the

context of the collaborative system (Cox & Perkins, 2008). E-business technology changed the tasks involved in the supply chain, affecting the people, skills and processes needed to support and act upon the information exchanged. The maturity of the e-business systems were assessed by the degree to which they became embedded into the organization's policy, processes and practice of people in both organizations (Measure F).

REVIEW OF THE FRAMEWORK FOR SOCIAL MEDIA TECHNOLOGIES

The framework outlined in the previous section was developed over 10 years ago. Since then, the environment within which organizations operate has been subject to extensive changes triggered by developments in technology, the natural environment, the economy and society. For example, Ahlqvist et al. (2010) identify the following developments in society which have supported the growth of social media technologies:

- Increasing role of transparency in society.
- Increasing role of ubiquitous participatory communication.
- Empowerment of citizens.
- Duality of personalization/fragmentation versus mass effects/integration.
- New relations of physical and virtual worlds.

The framework was therefore revisited with a different UK manufacturer (Case B) operating in a similar marketplace, providing a popular brand of grocery products to the major supermarket chains. The aim of the case was to assess whether the framework outlined in the previous section was still valid as a means of e-business planning in light of the growth of social media technology and the changing context described by Ahlqvist et al. (2010). The following sections outline the second application of the framework used by Manufacturer B in developing a plan to extend its current use of e-business technology to include social media technologies.

Phase 1: Explore Trading Relationships (Case B)

The grid introduced in Figure 1 was used to assess Manufacturer B's maturity in terms of the number of external relationships currently supported by e-business processes (Measure A). The manufacturer used e-business technology to initiate, develop and sustain relationships with all its current and previous customers, some of the customers of its competitors, all its current suppliers and all of its potential suppliers. An opportunity was identified to introduce pilot projects to assess the most effective ways of using technology to interact with consumers for maximum reach and impact. The grid also prompted the manufacturer to consider further opportunities to extend relationships with its suppliers using social media technology (Measure A).

Phase 2: Position Activity and Generate Strategic Initiatives (Case B)

The grid in Figure 2 was used to map the maturity of e-business in Manufacturer B in terms of the number of trading relationships supported (Measure A), the range of communication activities supported (Measures B) and the strategic significance of the e-business activities to the organization (Measure C). Booth and Matic (2011) emphasize that the use of social media needs to be linked to strategic objectives; the proposed grid provides the means to support this alignment. Figure 5 shows the application of the grid in Case B. The use of the micro blogging site Twitter was proposed as a means to add value to the relationship between Manufacturer B and its main suppliers by providing more timely information about, for example, delays of materials in transit. The manufacturer's product design team also proposed using a blog to gain reactions from consumers about potential product designs and to foster loyalty with consumers through establishing adjunct communities. Manufacturer B recognized the growing power of the 'network neighbour' and sought to take advantage of this through short message service (SMS) and mobile viral marketing. Mobile viral marketing is a means of distributing marketing

Figure 5. Examples of use of social media technology

Factors (WHY)	Business Objective (WHAT)	E-business Activity (HOW)	Trading Party (WHO)
Market Differentiation	Product promotion.	Viral marketing.	Consumers
	Relationship development	Social network sites.	
	Concept design.	Blogs.	
Process Enhancement	Order tracking.	Twitter.	Suppliers.
	Reduce transactions costs relating to employer expenses.	SMS.	Employees.

content which relies on consumers to transmit the content to others in their social network (Palka et al., 2009).

The grid also revealed a further use of e-business technology. Whilst previously the implementation of e-business technology was largely deployed for communicating with external partners, Manufacturer B sought to use the same principles and technology to communicate internally, enhancing relationships with employees. Many back office processes were already supported on-line, the highest level of maturity in Wilson's (2000) maturity model. Manufacturer B wanted to explore the use of Short Message Service (SMS) to improve the processing of employee travel expenses. The use of social networking technologies internally in organizations has been found to offer potential improvements in employee engagement and productivity (Ou et al., 2010). The grid helped Manufacturer B to plan new activities using social media technologies, aligned with its business objectives.

In Case A, the complexity of the communication in e-business initiatives had been assessed by the nature of the interaction and strength of the integration between the inter-organizational systems (Measure D). As social media is a two way interaction (Williams, 2010) the relevance of assessing communication complexity was therefore revisited. Communication complexity was found to still be relevant in social media. It can be used to distinguish between what Adams (2009) refers to as the difference between connection and interaction in social networks. Although a person may have established many connections in their social network, they regularly interact with less than half of those connections (Adams, 2009). Adams (2009) defines three levels of social relationship and suggests that different forms of social media technology are needed to support the interaction in the relationship. At the lowest level are temporary ties. These are often established to satisfy a need for information, complete a task or share an ongoing interest. The ties are then often broken when

the information need has been satisfied. Adams (2009) suggests that technology could be used to support communication with temporary ties who occupy the same physical space at different times. For example, provide recommendations to enable organizations to benefit from the 'network neighbour' principle.

Weak ties form the second level (Adams, 2009); these are loose connections, such as friends of friends. The connections may be based on, for example, shared interests but are less trusted than stronger direct connections. This means that technology needs to consider how to develop communication with these links in the social network without compromising privacy (Adams, 2009). Strong ties are the most trusted reflecting strong relationships they have been established through other forms of communication (e.g., face-to-face contact). Social network technology can provide additional opportunities to strengthen the relationship rather than replacing existing methods.

The distinction between the connection among strong ties and the interaction among weak ties relates to the distinction between *forging* links and *tempering* links in the supply chain proposed by Dingley and Perkins (1999). Forging links refers to the establishment of co-operative partnerships between trading partners; tempering strengthens the relationship making it more difficult to breakdown. The concept of the strength of the e-business relationship is therefore still valid within the context of social media technologies. The strength or fragility of the communication link established between the manufacturer and its partners, whether major supermarkets or individual consumers, is dependent on trust. Trust differentiates partnerships from traditional relationships (Handy, 1995).

ASDA, a major UK supermarket owned by Wal-Mart, used social media to develop trust with its customers and changed how its customers responded to a potentially problematic situation (Swabey, 2009). ASDA announced a book promotion but customers were left disappointed when stocks of the book ran out. The book buyer at ASDA used her blog to explain that a limited number of copies were bought to be sold at the discounted price and because demand was so high, the remaining stock was also sold at the discounted price too. The openness of the situation and the action that had been taken to try to address the situation appeased customers, promoting greater trust. In contrast, lack of engagement with social media can weaken trust; this is shown in the following example.

The impact of the growing power of social media needs to be considered by all organizations. One of Manufacturer B's suppliers produces part of the packaging used by the manufacturer in their products. The supplier reported that they considered themselves to be too small to concern themselves with social media. Looking forward in the supply chain, they dealt with their customers directly and maintained good communication through a combination of face-to-face, email and telephone communication. Looking backward in the supply chain the Managing Director commented "Keeping your ear to the ground is a basic part of doing business… using networks of contacts to find out the latest gossip on your suppliers and competitors existed long before gadgets made it fashionable." They were therefore shocked to be contacted by a local news reporter inviting them to comment on remarks made about their product on Facebook. Organizations need to monitor comments and have a response plan in place (Williams, 2010) to deal promptly with such situations.

Both Manufacturer A and Manufacturer B had previously been forced to develop e-business processes in response to pressures imposed by their customers. The major supermarket chains initiated the use of collaborative systems to support activities such as ordering and promotion management. Manufacturer B recognized the need to become proactive in using social media by establishing and maintaining a presence on social networking sites rather than been forced to continually react to situations. The need for formalizing processes

to support social networking was therefore identified (Measure E).

Although technology has changed, the models in phase two of the framework still provide a valid means of mapping maturity of e-business in terms of the range of and complexity of e-business activities with each trading partner (Measures B, C, D). For trading partners, whether an organization or a member of the public, the fundamental question raised by Ward et al. (1996) remains, "How far do we want to tie ourselves into other parts of the chain?"

Phase 3: Manage Internal Change (Case B)

The third part of the framework aims to help organizations to identify and plan the changes needed within the organization. This section discusses the extent to which the model in Figure 4 helped Manufacturer B to plan the changes needed to implement social media technologies to improve relationships with its consumers through social networking sites.

In Case A, the transformation for Manufacturer A was driven by the need for the organization to refocus all communication, information exchange, information transaction and information processing with each major customer through the customer's proprietary collaborative system. This required transaction processing to take place between the manufacturer's systems and the collaborative system (which provided the interface to the customer's systems). In Case B, the use of social media systems to communicate with consumers was initially considered to be simpler and less intrusive in terms of the organizational transformation needed to support the proposal.

A range of analytical tools are available to assist organizations in monitoring data about consumer perceptions reported on social networking sites. However, processes need to be in place to act on the information when it has been identified

E-Business Planning in Morphing Organizations

(Measures E and F). The following components of the organization affected by change in Case A were used as a means to plan the potential organizational transformation needed in Case B.

- **Security:** In Case A, the interface to the external collaborative system provided a means for the supermarket to access some of the manufacturer's data. This required a range of security issues to be addressed to enable the supermarket to gain access to the data. Security restrictions were then also reviewed in the manufacturer's internal systems that would need to provide some access to the collaborative system. In Case B, the manufacturer planned to use existing social network systems. It was initially considered that this required relatively minor changes to existing security as direct technical integration with existing systems would not be required. Manufacturer B only considered security from a technical perspective; it did not consider the non-technical risks to information security. However, the greatest security risk in social networking arises from employees maliciously or accidentally releasing unauthorized information (Cox, 2013).
- **Data Access:** Three forms of data access were identified. Firstly, staff in manufacturer B would need to be able to access data in existing social media sites about the organization. Secondly, staff would need to access data within the manufacturer's existing systems in order to respond to comments, queries and complaints raised by consumers on social media sites. Thirdly, the manufacturer wanted to be able to access internal data to prepare content to be posted on social media sites proactively, promoting its products, as well as reactively in response to consumers.
- **Systems:** Staff would need to be able to access data held within Manufacturer B's ex-

isting systems to investigate issues raised by consumers. It was considered that this need could be met by using the existing reporting systems in the customer services function. The creation of new content to be posted on-line is considered to be an extension of the existing services provided by the marketing function.
- **Processes:** New processes were defined within the marketing and customer services function to support the three forms of data access identified.
- **Working Practices:** Implementation of the new processes in the marketing and customer services function required new working practices to be developed to monitor, respond to and create social media content.
- **People and Skills:** In Case A, it was recognized that different skills are required in tasks such as negotiating on-line as opposed to negotiating face-to-face. Manufacturer B therefore advertised for staff with experience in social media content. The manufacturer also planned a training programme for existing staff in marketing which focused on the communication issues of creating on-line content.
- **Strategy:** The implementation of systems to incorporate the use of social media in the organization was aligned with the strategic objectives relating to product promotion.

The use of social media in Manufacturer B was considered to be a means of enhancing the existing marketing and customer service functions. However, Manufacturer B found that existing customer service processes lacked the flexibility to respond quickly to issues arising through social media. Martin (1999) recognized that the on-line consumer has a different profile to traditional consumers in that they are better informed and more demanding. The social networker is even more demanding in terms of speed and quality of response to postings. This imposes greater pressure on organizations and employees. After complaints, manufacturer B formed 'first response teams' to become quickly mobilized to respond to issues raised through social media. This required new systems to be put in place internally to enable quick access to information and people in order to respond to queries and complaints (shown in Figure 6).

In both cases, maturity of e-business was considered to have been achieved when pilot project teams were disbanded and e-business was established as 'business as usual' in the organization. Over time, it is therefore anticipated that the first response teams will become embedded within the customer service function. The different working practices needed to support social media technology will become standardized and form the normal practice of customer services and marketing. Manufacturer B's use of e-business has evolved through a number of stages using e-business technologies in backward facing, forward facing and internal facing processes. E-

business technology has been used to improve: service provision to customers; efficiency in the supply chain and service provision to employees.

Social media technology starts a new cycle of technological maturity. It started as an outward facing pilot project. The internal business transformation needed to underpin its use was then identified and is being actioned. From the application of the framework, Manufacturer B has developed the following plans for the use of social media technology. It plans to:

- Increase the number of external relationships supported by social media, particularly in relation so consumers and suppliers (Measure A).
- Increase the range of social media it uses (Measure B) and increase the reach, personalization and engagement with, for example, consumers to strengthen connections and develop trusting relationships (Measure D).

Figure 6. Transformation for social media

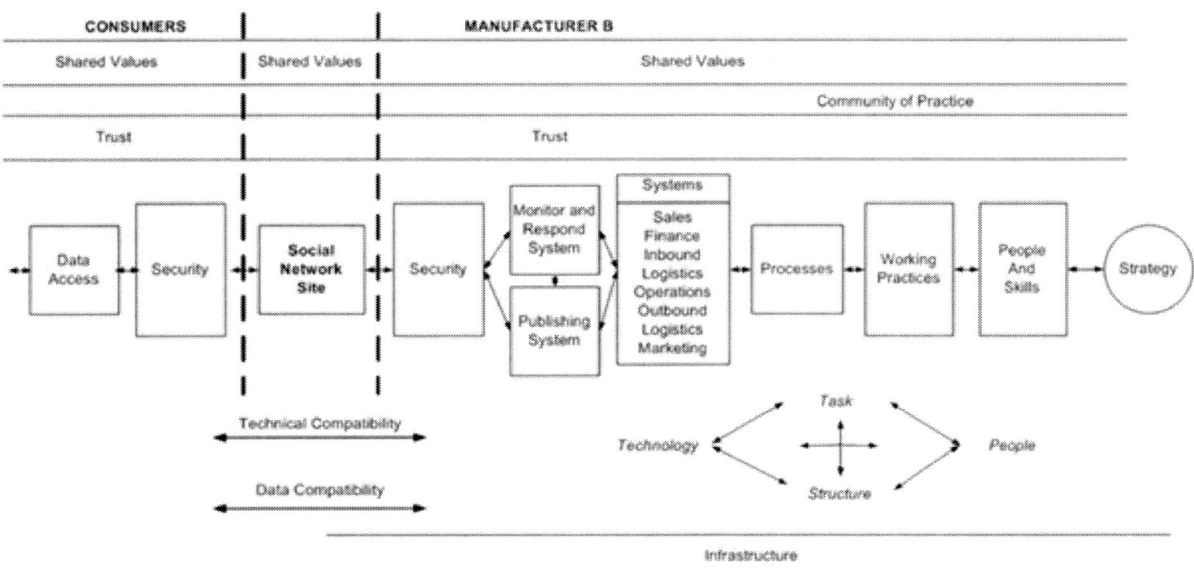

- Align the social media with its strategic objectives in relation to product promotion, concept design and order tracking (Measure C).
- Formalize business processes to ensure that the data collected through social media informs decision making (Measure E).
- Integrate social media into the business to become established as 'business as usual' (Measure F).

The following section discusses the components of business transformation that have been identified in Case A and B (Figures 4 and 6) and recommends a model for planning business transformation.

RECOMMENDATIONS FROM THE CASES

The following checklist of areas to consider when implementing an e-business system is recommended from the analysis of the organizational transformation that occurred in Case A (Figure 4):

- Security
- Infrastructure
- Data
- Processes
- Systems
- Working Practices
- Skills
- People
- Trust
- Shared Values
- Strategy

This checklist was used by Manufacturer B to prompt discussion of areas that may be affected by the introduction of the social media technology. Figure 7 shows that changing the *strategy* to develop closer relationships with consumers through the use of social networking triggered

the following planned series of transformations in the organization.

- Changing the strategy triggered changes to business systems; the customer service system and the marketing system.
- Changes to systems triggered changes to business processes. The customer service system introduced two new processes to monitor and respond to consumer views reported in social networking sites. The marketing system introduced a new process to publish corporate information on social networking sites.
- Changes to the business processes triggered relatively minor technological changes to facilitate access to social media sites.
- Changes to business processes triggered changes to the working practices in the customer service and marketing functions.
- Changes to the working practices in publishing marketing material triggered changes in the skills required in marketing. Media training was introduced to provide the new skills required.
- Changing working practices and the skills required impacted upon the staff involved in the marketing and customer service functions.
- Changes to the business processes also triggered changes to the data required to perform the new processes. For example the customer services function needed access to a range of information to effectively respond to queries received.

In practice, the following additional issues arose which initiated further transformations (shown by the dotted lines in Figure 7):

- **Security of Data:** Staff released unauthorized data in response to consumer queries. Changes to the data required in the new processes raised security issues relating

Figure 7. Planned business transformation for social media technology

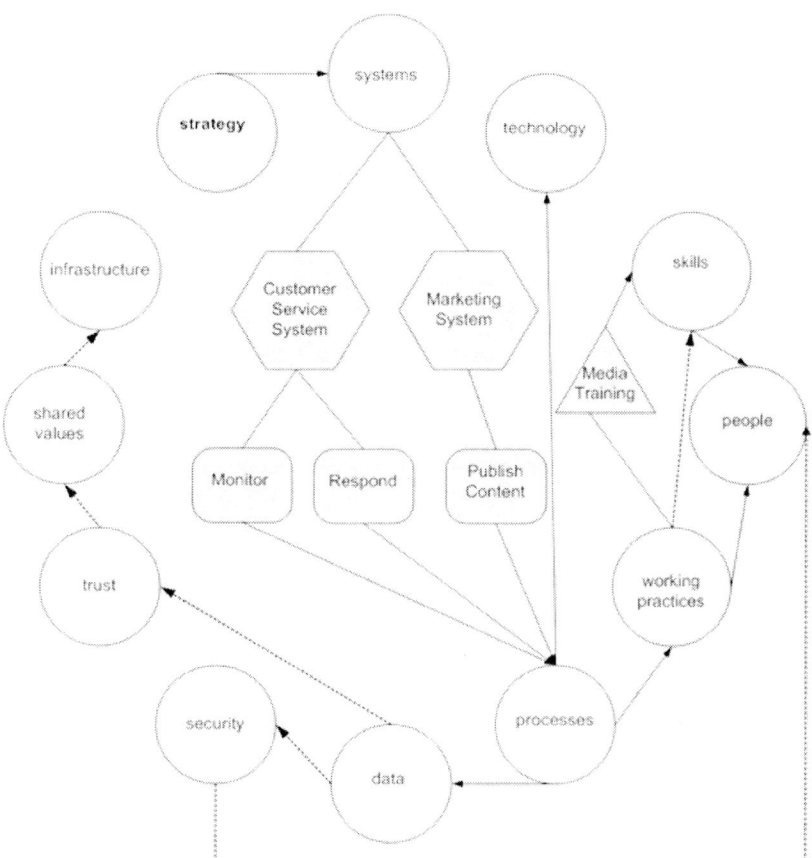

to the unauthorized disclosure of information. The security issues triggered the need for further staff training. Bateman et al. (2011) refer to self-disclosure in social media from the perspective of individuals which has three main parameters: amount, depth and duration. Further work is needed to investigate these parameters from an organizational perspective.

- **Inadequate Response to Queries:** Customer service staff lacked the skills to effectively communicate in social media communities and additional training needs were identified. Changes to working practices triggered changes in the skills required by all the new processes and the initial media training was therefore insufficient.

- **Lack of Trust:** The data provided by the customer service function on social networking sites was intended to increase trust with consumers. However, the difference in values between consumers and customer service staff meant that consumers did not trust the information provided to them. The customer service staff was not aware of the different level of expectations of the social media community. This required changes to be made in the shared values needed within the communication process between the manufacturer and its consumers.

- **Response Times:** The values embedded in the working practices in the customer services function and the overall organizational infrastructure did not match the values expected by consumers in relation to acceptable response times to queries raised. The infrastructure hindered ability to access the information needed in different systems to provide immediate response to queries. This was addressed by the formation of the 'first response team.'

These omissions arose due to the lack of specific analysis of the connections between the transformation components indicated by the bold dotted lines in Figure 7. Detailed analysis is needed of the relationships between all the transformation components in order to fully appreciate the business transformation needed to support technological change. In addition, security was only considered from a technical standpoint. A broader view of the concept of security needed to be taken incorporating technical security, physical security and information security.

Strategic Planning Framework for Business Transformation

The three phase framework used in Case 1 was originally developed to support the formulation of e-business strategies, based on the experience of developing collaborative e-business systems in the supply chain. Case 2 has shown that the framework is transferable and can support the development of strategies for introducing social media technology into organizations. The framework is therefore recommended to assist in planning business transformation.

The framework has three main strengths. Firstly, a key strength of the framework is that it helps organizations to reflect on their current use of technology to support a broad spectrum of relationships within their supply chain and value chain. A number of maturity measures are embedded within the framework. These enable organizations to consider their current status of maturity with the technology and identify factors

to consider in order to increase their use of the technology. Secondly, the framework encourages organizations to align plans to implement new technologies with their business strategy, providing a clear direction and rationale for the investment. Thirdly, phase three of the framework explores the business transformation needed to implement technology. A checklist of organizational components is proposed which provides a starting point for organizations to consider the depth of business transformation needed to embed the technology into the organization. This list is based on the work of Leavitt (1965) and Waterman Jr. et al. (1980), and the experience gained in Case A. In Case B, limitations of this checklist were identified, for example, the concept of security was considered too narrowly and risk factors were not sufficiently identified. In addition, the components in this list were mainly considered independently, adopting a systematic, reductionist perspective. In listing the components to prompt areas of discussion, the importance of the interaction between the components and the properties emerging from the interaction was lost. The issues arising in Case B related to insufficient understanding of the potential impact of the new processes on people, working practices, trust and skills. These components were explicitly considered by Manufacturer B, however, they were not considered in sufficient depth within a systemic context. A distinction is therefore proposed between the components of business transformation and the dimensions of business transformation.

Dimensions of Business Transformation

The list of transformation components provides a structure within which to explore the scope and limits of business transformation but the interaction between the components should not be neglected. The following dimensions of business transformation are proposed to support analysis of the interactions between components:

- **Infrastructure:** Including technical, organizational and social structures. This considers the interactions between systems, people, the formal and informal organizational structure as well as the technical infrastructure.
- **Trust:** Incorporating both trust within the organization and trust in the relationship between the organization and the individuals or organizations with whom it is communicating. This considers trust emerging from the interactions between people (both internal and external to the organization), the formal and informal structures, processes and working practices.
- **Community of Practice:** Emerging within and between organizations. This considers the resulting interaction people, skills, working practices and shared values.
- **Value Chain:** Value arising in activities within and between organizations from interactions between systems, processes, data and people.

These dimensions are shown horizontally in Figure 4. People are included in each dimension, emphasizing their importance in business transformation, and recognizing that the needs of people outside of the organization also need to be considered. For example, in Case B problems arose due to the different expectations of social media community and the customer service staff. The transformation dimensions incorporate the interactions between different components and emphasize the properties emerging from the interactions.

Critical Success Factors

The following critical success factors are recommended for planning the introduction of social media technology in organizations.

- Align the use of social media technology with the organizational strategy. The grid shown in Figures 2 and 5 can be used to directly link social media to organizational objectives, justifying investment.
- Introduce business processes to respond to and manage the information and knowledge generated by active engagement arising from the introduction of new technologies. Social media provides the opportunity to easily gather a range of information about consumer perceptions of the organization. However, this information will have no value to the organization unless there are clear processes into which this information is input.
- Identify the impact on business processes at an early stage. Case A and B both demonstrated that the introduction of e-business and social media technology in the organizations initiated wide scale transformation. A checklist has been provided to assist organizations in identifying areas which may be impacted by social media. The application of the checklist is shown in Figure 7 which demonstrates the impact of social media in Case B.
- Understand the different profiles of social media users and their levels of expectations. The profile of the e-consumer differs from the traditional consumer. Users of social media have high expectations relating to speed of response and depth of disclosure. These needs must be understood in order to effectively engage in social networks.
- Assess staff training needs in relation to the technical skills, communication skills and working practices required in social media communities. Case B showed that different skills are needed as working practices change. Training needs analysis is required

when implementing changes to organizational practice.

- Consider the organizational transformation required from a social-technical perspective. The introduction of social media impacts the business processes, working practices and the skills required. Plans are needed to manage the change in these areas which are initiated by changes in technology.
- Develop a response plan to address issues swiftly arising in social media sites. Case B found that its existing business processes and functional boundaries hindered its ability to resolve issues raised by consumers through social media. Action plans were developed through the introduction of first response teams in order to fully address issues quickly.
- Establish proactive processes to maximize control of both positive and negative situations. In addition to reacting to social media, new business processes are needed to proactively seize control of social media content relating to the organization. This develops a foundation of trust with consumers which can then help to mitigate potential adverse consequences when things go wrong.

FUTURE RESEARCH DIRECTIONS

Feeny et al. (1996) proposed that when the maturity of technology is low, the IT function should work closely with end users to explore how the technology can add value to the organization. Although the technology which underpins social media is well established, it's potential to change the way organizations and individuals communicate is not yet fully understood. Organizations therefore need to work closely with customers and consumers to learn how social media technologies can be used to enhance communication. The power of social media and its impact on the dynamics of trading relationships needs further research. For example, in case A, the introduction of the collaborative system between the manufacturer and its main customer changed not only the means of communication, it also changed the balance of power in the supply chain relationship. The needs and expectations of users of social media need to be understood; for example, technology requires a personal, rather than an anonymous, face of organizations to be presented in social networks.

A framework has been recommended that provides tools to help organizations to:

- Align the introduction of communication technology with strategic objectives.
- Identify the degree of business transformation needed to embed communication technology in the organization.

The framework has been used in a number of manufacturing and retail organizations. Further work is needed to verify its transferability to other domains.

Organizations are complex social entities and the series of transformations triggered by the introduction of new technology requires further investigation. As technological advancement continues, the need to understand how to quickly complete the transformation needed to use the technology becomes increasingly important. Components of an organization affected by IT-led change have been identified and chains of transformation paths between components have been identified in the cases presented. Further work is being undertaken to understand and measure the dynamic transformations that take place in morphing organizations.

CONCLUSION

Maturity models proposed to map the use of IT in organizations, demonstrate that the introduction of technology requires business processes and practices to change. E-business technologies invert traditional models of IT maturity where technology was first introduced to support existing back office processes. In contrast, e-business technology was first introduced to support front office processes; back office processes then had to be changed to support the Internet transactions. As organizations' use of e-business technology matured, the technology was adopted to improve efficiency and effectiveness of internally focused systems. This inversion highlights the progression from IT, as a means of information transmission, to information and communication technology, as a means of communication within in e-business. Social media technologies introduce a further phase of business transformation. Technological maturity models are therefore cyclical. Maturity models plot the sequential development of technology in organizations and each new technology initiates the start of another cycle of technological maturity and business transformation.

A framework has been recommended which enables the planning of social media technologies to be directly aligned with organizational objectives and ensures that the potential impact on business processes is identified at an early stage. A number of transformation components have been proposed to prompt organizations to consider the changes needed in the business to support the introduction of social media. Although this list provided a useful starting point to consider business transformation in Case B, the need for a systemic analysis of business transformation was identified. A number of dimensions of business transformation have therefore been proposed to support a richer analysis of business transforma-

tion. Work is currently being undertaken to develop measures for each of these dimensions.

Critical success factors for implementing social media technology have been proposed from the two cases of e-business planning and implementation discussed in this chapter. In both cases, issues arose in the implementation of e-business strategies due to insufficient understanding of the business transformation needed. Although the organizations systematically considered a range of transformation components, insufficient consideration was given to the inter-relationships between components and the properties which emerge through a series of complex interactions. It is these interactions which form the continual adjustments taking place in morphing organizations. People form the core of all communication processes and the importance of considering the role of people, both internal and external to the organization, in business transformation is emphasized. In 1998, Boddy et al. concluded that culture and behavioural change remain the challenge of e-collaboration systems. This chapter demonstrates that these still remain the major challenges facing organizations introducing social media technologies. The maturity of e-business and social media systems in organizations is assessed by the degree to which they became embedded into the organization's policy, processes and practice. A cycle of business transformation is complete when adjustments to the organization's form have been completed, such that people within the organization accept the technology as forming 'business as usual'.

REFERENCES

Adams, P. (2009). Designing for social interaction. *Boxes and Arrows*. Retrieved February 24, 2011, from http://boxesandarrows.com/view/designing-for-social

Ahlqvist, T., Bäck, A., Heinonen, S., & Halonen, M. (2010). Road-mapping the societal transformation potential of social media. *Foresight: The Journal of Future Studies. Strategic Thinking and Policy, 12*(5), 3–26. doi:10.1108/14636681011075687.

Ashcroft, J. (2010). Social media in the supply chain. *Presentation to the Supply Chain Management Summit.* Retrieved February 24, 2011, from http://summits.aberdeen.com/1/Day1-%20 Jeff%20Ashcroft.pdf

Bateman, P. J., Pike, J. C., & Butler, B. S. (2011). To disclose or not: Publicness in social networking sites. *Information Technology & People, 24*(1), 78–100. doi:10.1108/09593841111109431.

Bhatt, G. D., & Emdad, A. F. (2001). An analysis of the virtual supply chain in electronic commerce. *Logistics Information Management, 14*(1/2), 78–84. doi:10.1108/09576050110362465.

Boddy, D., Cahill, C., Charles, M., Fraser-Kraus, H., & Macbeth, D. K. (1998). Success and failure in implementing supply chain partnering: An empirical study. *European Journal of Purchasing and Supply Management, 4*(2/3), 143–151. doi:10.1016/S0969-7012(97)00026-9.

Booth, N., & Matic, J. A. (2011). Mapping and leveraging influencers in social media to shape corporate brand perceptions. *Corporate Communications: An International Journal, 16*(3), 184–191. doi:10.1108/13563281111156853.

Cox, S., Perkins, J., & Green, P. (2001) A positioning framework for developing an e-business strategy. In *Proceedings of the Eighth European Conference on Information Technology Evaluation,* Oxford, UK: Oriel College.

Cox, S. A. (2013). *Managing information in morphing organizations.* Basingstoke, UK: Palgrave Macmillan.

Cox, S. A., Krasniewicz, J. A., Perkins, J. S., & Cox, J. A. (2006). Modelling the organizational transformation associated with implementing e-business collaborative systems in the supply chain. In *Proceedings of the British Academy of Management Conference (BAM2006) in Association with the University of Ulster and Queen's University,* Belfast, Northern Ireland: BAM.

Cox, S. A., & Perkins, J. S. (2008). Factors for effective e-collaboration in the supply chain. In Kock, N. (Ed.), *Encyclopaedia of E-Collaboration* (pp. 279–285). Hershey, PA: IGI Global.

Croom, S. R. (2005). The impact of e-business on supply chain management: An empirical study of key developments. *International Journal of Operations & Production Management, 25*(1), 55–73. doi:10.1108/01443570510572240.

Davis, M. (2010, October 4). *Social media to improve supply chain?* [Web log comment]. Retrieved from http://blogs.gartner.com/matthew-davis/2010/10/04/social-media-to-improve-supply-chain/ (February 24, 2011).

Dingley, S., & Perkins, J. (1999). Tempering links in the supply chain with collaborative systems. In *Proceedings of the 9th Annual Conference of Business Information Technology: Generative Futures* (document 51). Manchester, UK: Manchester Metropolitan University.

Enslow, B., & Smith, C. (1998). Developing internet-enabled supply chain strategies. *GartnerGroup Strategic Analysis Report, (R-05-9476).*

Feeny, D. F., Earl, M. J., & Edwards, B. (1996). Organizational arrangement for IS: Roles of users and specialists. In Earl, M. J. (Ed.), *Information Management: The Organizational Dimension* (pp. 231–246). Oxford, UK: Oxford University Press.

Gammelgaard, J., & Ritter, T. (2005). The knowledge retrieval matrix: Codification and personalisation as separate strategies. *Journal of Knowledge Management*, 9(4), 133–143. doi:10.1108/13673270510610387.

Greiner, L. E. (1972). Evolution and revolutions as organizations grow. *Harvard Business Review*, (July-August): 37–46.

Grippa, F. (2009). A social network scorecard to monitor knowledge flows across communication media. *Knowledge Management Research and Practice*, 7(4), 317–328. doi:10.1057/kmrp.2009.24.

Hall, H. (2010). Relationship and role transformations in social media environments. *The Electronic Library*, 29(4), 421–428. doi:10.1108/02640471111156704.

Handy, C. (1995). Trust and the virtual organization. *Harvard Business Review*, (May): 40–49.

Information Age (2011). Network Effects. *Information Age*, January, 20-21.

Kietzmann, J. H., Hermkens, K., McCarthy, I. P., & Silverstre, B. S. (2011). Social media? Get serious! Understanding the functional building blocks of social media. *Business Horizons*, 54(3), 181–288. doi:10.1016/j.bushor.2011.01.005.

Leavitt, H. J. (1965). Applying organizational change in industry: Structural, technological, and humanistic approaches. In March, J. G. (Ed.), *Handbook of Organizations*. Chicago, IL: Rand McNally.

Lee, B.-R., Yu, W.-B., Maguluru, N., & Nichols, M. (2006). Enhancing business networks using social network based virtual communities. *Industrial Management & Data Systems*, 106(1), 121–138. doi:10.1108/02635570610641022.

Lockamy, A. III, & McCormack, K. (2004). The development of a supply chain management process maturity model using the concepts of business process orientation. *Supply Chain Management*, 9(3/4), 272–278.

Martin, C. (1999). *Net future*. New York: McGraw-Hill.

Nolan, R. L. (1973). Managing the computer resource: A stage hypothesis. *Communications of the ACM*, 16(7), 399–405. doi:10.1145/362280.362284.

Nolan, R. L. (1979). Managing the crises in data processing. *Harvard Business Review*, (March-April): 115–126.

Ou, C. X. J., Davison, R. M., Zhong, X., & Liang, U. (2010). Empowering employees through instant messaging. *Information Technology & People*, 23(2), 193–211. doi:10.1108/09593841011052165.

Palka, W., Pousttchi, K., & Wiedemann, G. (2009). Mobile word-of-mouth – A grounded theory of mobile viral marketing. *Journal of Information Technology*, 24(2), 172–185. doi:10.1057/jit.2008.37.

Parsons, G. L. (1983). Information technology: A new competitive weapon. *Sloan Management Review*, 25(1), 3–14.

Pateli, A. G., & Giaglis, G. M. (2005). Technology innovation-induced business model change: A contingency approach. *Journal of Organizational Change Management*, 18(2), 167–183. doi:10.1108/09534810510589589.

Peters, T. J., & Waterman, R. H. Jr. (1989). *In search of excellence: Lessons from America's best run organizations*. New York: Harper Collins.

Pleming, S. (2009). U.S. State Department speaks to Twitter over Iran. Retrieved February 24, 2011, from http://www.reuters.com/article/2009/06/16/us-iran-election-twitter-usa-idUSWBT01137420090616

Porter, M. E. (1980). *Competitive advantage*. New York: Free Press.

Romero, N. L. (2011). ROI. Measuring the social media return on investment in a library. *The Bottom Line: Managing Library Finances, 24*(2), 145–151. doi:10.1108/08880451111169223.

Software Engineering Institute and Carnegie Mellon University. (1995). *The capability maturity model: Guidelines for improving the software process (SEI)*. Canada: Addison Wesley.

Swabey, P. (2009). Asda launches transparency strategy. *Information Age*. Retrieved February 24, 2011, from http://www.information-age.com/channels/information-management/it-case-studies/1101887/asda-launches-transparency-strategy.thtml

Van Hooft, F. P. C., & Stegwee, R. A. (2001). E-business strategy: How to benefit from a hype. *Logistics Information Management, 14*(1/2), 44–53. doi:10.1108/09576050110360223.

Ward, J., Griffiths, P., & Whitmore, P. (1996). *Strategic planning for information systems* (2nd ed.). Chichester, UK: Wiley.

Waterman, R. H. Jr, Peters, T. J., & Phillips, J. R. (1980). Structure is not organization. *Business Horizons, 23*(3), 14–26. doi:10.1016/0007-6813(80)90027-0.

Wettstein, T., & Kueng, P. (2002). A maturity model for performance measurement systems. In Brebbia, C., & Pascola, P. (Eds.), *Management. Information Systems* (pp. 113–122). Southampton, UK: WIT Press.

Williams, J. (2010). What's in store for social media? *Computer Weekly*, 7-13.

Wilson, D. W. (2000). Maturity models and information systems: From S-curves to e-commerce. In *Proceedings of the Fifth Conference of the UK Academy of Information Systems* (pp. 628-633). Cardiff, Wales: UKAIS.

ADDITIONAL READING

Agarwal, A., & Shankar, R. (2003). On-line trust building in e-enabled supply chain. *Supply Chain Management: An International Journal, 8*(4), 324–334. doi:10.1108/13598540310490080.

Aspara, J., Lamberg, J. H., Laukia, A., & Tikkanen, H. (2011). Strategic management of business model transformation: Lessons from Nokia. *Management Decision, 49*(4), 622–647. doi:10.1108/00251741111126521.

Baird, C. H., & Parasnis, G. (2011). From social media to social customer relationship management. *Strategy and Leadership, 39*(5), 30–37. doi:10.1108/10878571111161507.

Barratt, M. (2004). Understanding the meaning of collaboration in the supply chain. *Supply Chain Management: An International Journal, 9*(1), 30–42. doi:10.1108/13598540410517566.

Berg, E., Mörtberg, C., & Jansson, M. (2005). Emphasizing technology: Socio-technical implications. *Information Technology & People, 18*(4), 343–358. doi:10.1108/09593840510633310.

Bititci, U. S. (2007). An executive's guide to business transformation. *Viewpoint, 8*(3), 203–213.

Bryson, J. (2006). *Managing information services: A transformational approach*. Aldershot, UK: Ashgate.

Burnes, B., & Dale, B. (Eds.), *Working in partnership: Best practice in customer-supplier relations*. Aldershot, UK: Gower.

Cheuk, B. (2007). Social networking analysis: Its application to facilitate knowledge transfer. *Business Information Review, 24*(3), 170–177. doi:10.1177/0266382107081612.

Cox, S. (2009). Assessing the impact of mobile technologies on work-life balance. In Torres-Coronas, T., & Arias-Oliva, M. (Eds.), *Encyclopedia of Human Resources Information Systems: Challenges in e-HRM* (pp. 63–69). Hershey, PA: IGI Global.

Cruz, D., & Fill, C. (2008). Evaluating viral marketing: Isolating the key criteria. *Marketing Intelligence & Planning*, *26*(7), 743–758. doi:10.1108/02634500810916690.

Dixon, S. E. A., Meyer, K. E., & Day, M. (2010). Stages of organizational transformation economies: A dynamic approach. *Journal of Management Studies*, *47*(3), 416–436. doi:10.1111/j.1467-6486.2009.00856.x.

Earl, M. J. (Ed.), *Information management: The organizational dimension*. Oxford, UK: Oxford University Press.

Engeström, Y. (2001). Expansive learning at work: Toward an activity theoretical reconceptualisation. *Journal of Education and Work*, *14*(1), 133–156.

Galbraith, J. R. (1995). *Designing organizations*. San Francisco, CA: Jossey-Bass.

Golden, M. (2011). *Social media strategies for professionals and their firms: The guide to establishing credibility and accelerating relationships*. Chichester, UK: John Wiley & Sons.

Hanna, N. K. (2010). *Enabling enterprise transformation: Business and grassroots innovation for the knowledge economy (innovation, technology, and knowledge management)*. New York: Springer Press. doi:10.1007/978-1-4419-1508-5.

Herring, S. C., Scheidt, L. A., Wright, E., & Bonus, S. (2005). Weblogs as a bridging genre. *Information Technology & People*, *18*(2), 142–171. doi:10.1108/09593840510601513.

La Rotta, A. P., & Herrera, L. C. (2011). Integral business transformation: A global case study. *Industrial and Commercial Training*, *43*(2), 75–78. doi:10.1108/00197851111108890.

Lovett, J. (2011). *Social media metric secrets*. Chichester, UK: John Wiley & Sons.

Nadler, D. A., Gerstein, M. C., & Shaw, R. B. et al. (Eds.). (1992). *Organizational architecture: Designs for changing organizations*. San Francisco, CA: Jossey-Bass.

Nahapiet, J., Gratton, L., & Rocha, H. O. (2005). Knowledge and relationships: When cooperation is the norm. *European Management Review*, *2*, 3–14. doi:10.1057/palgrave.emr.1500023.

Prasopoulou, E., Pouloudi, A., & Panteli, N. (2006). Enacting new temporal boundaries: The role of mobile phones. *European Journal of Information Systems*, *15*(3), 277–284. doi:10.1057/palgrave.ejis.3000617.

Schein, E. H. (2004). *Organizational culture and leadership*. San Francisco, CA: Wiley.

Senior, B. (2002). *Organisational change (2nd ed.)*. Harlow, UK: Pearson Publishing.

Shu, W., & Chuang, Y.-H. (2011). The perceived benefits of six-degree-separation social networks. *Internet Research*, *21*(1), 26–45. doi:10.1108/10662241111104866.

Simatupang, T. M., & Sridharan, R. (2005). The collaboration index: A measure for supply chain collaboration. *International Journal of Physical Distribution & Logistics Management*, *35*(1), 44–62. doi:10.1108/09600030510577421.

Wenger, W. (1999). *Communities of practice: Learning, meaning and identity*. Cambridge, UK: Cambridge University Press.

KEY TERMS AND DEFINITIONS

Business Transformation: The series of changes to the formal and informal structures, processes and practices in the organization to change how it operates and interfaces with its environment.

Disintermediation: Bypassing a level in the supply chain.

E-Business Strategy: A statement outlining the planned role of e-business technology in an organization, aligned with the objectives of the organization. Strategies differ in scope and may include a plan of the business transformation needed to facilitate the implementation of the technology.

E-Business: The use of communication technology to facilitate and support business transactions and collaboration between partners in the supply chain.

Maturity Model: An abstraction of the stages of business transformation initiated by the introduction of information communication technology in organizations.

Morphing Organization: A social entity that changes the way in which it interfaces with its external environment.

Reintermediation: Increasing the importance of a level within the supply chain.

Shared Values: A set of informal measures, tacitly accepted by a group of people, which reflect the cultural beliefs of the group (e.g., honesty, integrity and responsibility).

Social Media Technologies: The use of information communication technologies to facilitate direct and meaningful interaction between individuals.

Supply Chain: The sequential transactions that take place between organizations and the processes involved in mobilizing resources to produce a product or service and deliver it to its final consumer.

Working Practices: The actions taken by individuals in an organization which may not be explicitly documented but are needed to perform a task.

Chapter 16
The New Age E-Enterprise:
Internet-Based Collaboration, Innovation, and Co-Creation

Vandana Ahuja
Jaypee Institute of Information Technology, India

ABSTRACT

Globalization and the resultant transition to virtual work are changing the dynamics of critical business relationships today. The organizational fabric is undergoing a transformation. The new knowledge economy, coupled with the modern customer based relationship approach has transformed the shape of business, catalyzed further by the internet revolution. Shrinking distance barriers and the emergence of new ways of building and delivering products and services online, is enabling the rapid globalization of markets. This chapter traces how the new knowledge economy, along with the modern customer based relationship approach, impacts the organizational fabric. The collaborative Web along with the e-enterprise, has brought into vogue the use of emergent social software platforms within companies, or between companies and their partners or customers. This, along with organizational willingness to take risks, has created new opportunities for companies in the domain of innovation, Internet based collaboration and co-creation.

INTRODUCTION

The chapter discusses concepts pertaining to the new knowledge economy, approaches how organizations function and studies the modern customer based relationship approaches being followed in organizations. It further details the tools of the collaborative web-viz., corporate blogs, online communities, business and social networks, wikis and micromedia-Twitter in the context of the e-enterprise and proceeds to discuss how Procter and Gamble, a modern day enterprise, uses these new approaches on innovation, harnessing consumers, e-commerce, and brand-customer centricity through four case studies.

DOI: 10.4018/978-1-4666-4026-9.ch016

BACKGROUND

The New Knowledge Economy

Signifying volatility with extremely fast change, explosive upsurges and sudden downturns, the new knowledge economy is characterized by market changes that are fast and unpredictable. The lifecycle of products and technologies is short and innovation and entrepreneurship are the buzzwords. Competition has adopted a global face and differentiation is the name of the marketing game. The pace of business is appreciably faster with ever-rising customer expectations. Change management is the focus area and business development approach has become opportunity driven with dynamic strategies. Knowledge has become the source of strategic planning for the creation of a value proposition for consumers. Market sensing is a core business process and organizations which are able to manage, analyze and combine knowledge faster for product innovation and improvement in line with customer expectations are succeeding in the competitive scenario. The connected millennium lays tremendous importance on the concepts of market opportunity analysis and global marketing.

Innovation processes are continuous and appropriate human capital is fast becoming a scarce resource. Distinctive capabilities coupled with institutional excellence now spell sources of competitive advantage. Organizations are transforming from hierarchical, bureaucratic, functional, pyramid structures to interconnected subsystems, characterized by flexibility, employee empowerment, and flat or networked structures. People, knowledge and capabilities are the key organizational assets.

The Organization

Ad hoc workgroups and communities are constantly forming and operating in diverse locations over widespread geographic areas, countries and companies. Geographic proximity is no longer essential for people working together, courtesy the advances made in the field of information and communication technology. People are engaged in project-based work with an ever changing and increasing circle of colleagues, customers and partners, many of whom they have never met. Employee attrition is frequently ushering in new work partners, leading to an intrinsic need for better documentation which can enable projects to withstand the change in project participants and maintain continuity. Optimum teaming of world class competencies is the order of the day. Work is now no longer limited to the office;-it can take place in the electronic network. The ability to access vast information resources within a matter of minutes and to communicate across huge distances at ever lower costs while maintaining quality levels along with dramatic changes in competition, technology, and workforce values are causing organizations to search for new and more human ways of increasing productivity and competitiveness. Newer systems support collaboration and employee interaction. Examples of successful projects of this type include worldwide product launches involving training, presentations and project planning that eliminate the need to bring employees from multiple locations to a single site, with substantial savings in travel and associated costs and time.

The Modern Customer-Based Relationship Approach

Marketing is shifting from making and maximizing profit from individual transactions to building mutually beneficial relationships with consumers and other parties. Relationship marketing focuses on customer satisfaction and retention as organizations move from product based campaign marketing to a customer based relationship approach. Economies have become customer driven. Companies are going global, reaching out to customers located afar as e-commerce and online buying facilitate consumer purchase thus diminishing locational restrictions. Increasing competition between organizations is leading to the implementation of relationship strategies and multi-channel relationship programs, as consumer retention becomes a vital imperative for organizational sustenance. Further, vast opportunities are available to consumers who are well informed and further analyze competing products and make intelligent choices. In view of the increased need for the organization to communicate with its consumers, the internet provides an excellent low cost solution for better connectivity between the organization and its partners.

MAIN FOCUS OF THE CHAPTER

The Collaborative Web and the Enterprise

The collaborative version of the internet, termed Web 2.0, as coined by Tim O'Reilly in 2005, has altered the manner in which information is published, consumed and utilized on the internet resulting in a paradigm shift in the way interactions take place within the organizational workspace as well as between the organization and the external customers. Web 2.0 is a collection of open-source, interactive and user-controlled online applications expanding the experiences, knowledge and market power of the users as participants in business and social processes.

Personal websites have been replaced by blogs, content management systems by wikis, directories by tagging, encyclopedias by Wikipedia and participation is the new keyword connecting organizations, employees, customers, suppliers, partners and any other intermediaries. Differential patterns of combining data, content, services through collaboration and increased access to information by consumers has opened up new dimensions for organizations to interact with the various players involved in the business.

Content creation by consumers facilitating the flow of ideas and knowledge has given corporations access to huge volumes of data which can be leveraged for decision making. Commonly and collectively called Web 2.0 tools, these new content-sharing sites, discussion and collaborative webspaces, and application design patterns or mashups, are transforming the consumer Web. They also represent a significant opportunity for organizations to build new social and web-based collaboration, productivity, and business systems, and to improve cost and revenue returns (Platt, 2007).

Corporate blogs, online communities, social networks, wikis, micromedia and folksonomies are some Web 2.0 concepts being used by businesses in the field of marketing, brand promotion and customer relationship management. Web 2.0 also appears to have a substantial effect on consumer behaviour and has contributed to an unprecedented customer empowerment. The consequences are far reaching, affecting not only the area of technology development but also the domains of business strategy and marketing owing to changing consumer attitudes, new customer needs, emerging new value perceptions and the change of consumer search tactics and buying behaviour. Of significance is the emergence of the collaborative web as an influencer in consumer buying behavior. Several organizations are using collaborative product-development tools, such as initiating discussions in blogs to test ideas, involving customers in the use of collaborative design tools, or testing how well products sell in virtual worlds. It is interesting to study the applications of Web 2.0 features in the domain of customer relationship management by improving interactivity and soliciting greater consumer engagement and further integrating the same for Campaign management with other CRM functionalities. This along with the above stated applications to marketing and consumer behavior will be discussed in subsequent chapters.

Web 2.0 activities and other collaborative entities are illustrated in Figure 1.

Figure 1. Collaborative entities and activities of Web 2.0

Corporate Blogging

The dictionary meaning of a blog is a frequent, chronological publication of personal thoughts and links. Millions of people use blogs as personal diaries on the internet and they are emerging as collaborative spaces that can be put to multiple uses and have emerged as the latest mode of computer mediated communication (Herring, 1993). As these become repositories for cumulative information, blogging is shaping into a useful organizational tool for brand propagation and interaction with consumers. Corporations have effectively launched corporate blogs with objectives ranging from catering to exploratory consumer browsing, aiding a consumer's quest for information, helping consumers gain access to organizational promotional campaigns to responding to controversies regarding organization or brand or product. While this creates consumer involvement with this organizational endeavor, it eventually achieves consumer engagement for the organization as the consumer commences participation-a perfect tool for connecting a well defined brand strategy to online presence enhancement.

An effective blog fosters community and conversation (Gill, 2004), drives traffic to the product website, and serves as a medium for interaction with consumers thereby shaping consumer perception, eliciting responses, and through a two way thought exchange process, aids in fostering a connection with the consumers. Further, consumer feedback can be leveraged for organizational consumption for innovation and product improvement, while serving as a market sensing tool for gauging consumer expectations. Blogs have a comparative advantage of speedy publication-they have a first mover advantage in socially constructing interpretive frames for current events (Drezner & Farell, 2004). Blogs are no longer a subculture of the Internet; they have become a mainstream information resource. They further provide a tremendous opportunity for forward-thinking companies and management to have a significant positive impact on their public perception (Sifry, 2004). People who read organizational blogs perceive an organization's relational maintenance strategies as higher than those who read traditional Web content only, thereby making a blog a useful tool for creating and maintaining value laden relationships with current and potential customers (Kelleher & Miller, 2006). Launching a corporate brand blog is representative of an organizational desire to share information and engage in conversation. This is especially true when the blog allows visitors to post their own comments. The informality of communication helps companies build trust (Dwyer, 2007), converse with people and even manage public perception by posting suitable responses. The ability of a blog to induce consumer participation by making consumers comment on the posts hosted by the organization creates a dialogue and helps the organization achieve consumer engagement. While the ability of a blog to achieve higher volumes of engagement in terms of volume of comments is significant, of greater importance is the knowledge capital created through exchange with consumers which can be mined to extract explicit information which can be leveraged by the organization as a decision support system for consumer segmentation and strategy formulation.

Online Communities

An online community or a virtual community represents a group of people that primarily or initially communicates or interacts via the internet. The dawn of the information age found groups communicating electronically rather than face to face. A computer-mediated community (CMC) uses social software to regulate the activities of the participants. These are places where people gather to share knowledge, build recognition and tap opportunities. Initially sensed to be resource pools for value addition, where people ventured to fulfill their need for self-actualization, participation in online communities and forums started as a medium for exchange of ideas and information, and now organizations have started using these communities for marketing through consumer evangelism and support. A web based communication model utilizes the features of the network for B2C as well as peer to peer communication. Consumers join these forums because of the multifaceted opportunities they provide to members. Not only do they provide information on products and services and latest promotional

schemes, they are also triggers for innovation. As like minded people converge together, these are new cliques where organizations can use opinion leaders for evangelism, while harnessing consumer generated content for product improvement and co-creation. Corporations like Dell have introduced 'Ideastorm' as a virtual interaction centre for consumers who participate in the development and enhancement of Dell's products and services by sharing their ideas online. Enabling interactive electronic dialogue with user communities is one way of getting closer to the customers.

Business and Social Networks

Networking on business and social networks-groups of individuals and organizations has emerged successful in modern marketing. The high volume of individual presence across these networks makes them viable marketing tools. While increased consumer interaction results in higher levels of trust, these are also being used extensively by salespeople for generation of leads to drive demand.

The focus is hence on the VCP model (Visibility, Credibility, Profitability) of Relationship Marketing (Misner, 2008):

1. **Visibility:** The success of all networking is based on the ability of people to remember an individual/organization or product/service associated with the same. As network connections grow much faster than the number of participants, the growth of a communications network strongly enhances its value.

2. **Managing Relationships:** Evolving simple acquaintances into credible relationships is the essential thought. Real networks have a high local clustering which can be utilized to build relationships.

3. **Collaborating:** Joining together for achieving business goals, by making best use of opportunities, because of high level of participation by network members, which

speeds up with the involvement of certain network hub members.

4. Many brands have successfully used social networks like Facebook and Myspace. By involving the audience on the networks, supporting community goals, allowing self expression of members, providing greater access to information, referrals and integrating the campaigns on these networks along with the other organizational channels, companies have been able to build substantial brand recognition and adoption. The relationship capital has huge potential to create better opportunity pipelines and acts as a catalyst in creating business relationships. A network's value grows quickly as participants join. As per Metcalfe's law, the value of a network is the summation of the individual values in the network and the community value of a network grows at a much faster rate than the individual values. Hence, as the network grows, the added links accelerate the growth of the community value. Each new user benefits from joining the network and contributes a new value laden connection to all the existing members of the network. Organizations can capture the values of large networks which can be leveraged for marketing and customer relationship management, in both the B2B and B2C domains. Business networks are useful where people can try and locate prospective clients, and further by posting messages regarding products and services on available networks, generating enquiries automatically.

Wikis

A wiki is a collection of Web pages designed to enable individuals to contribute or modify content, using a simplified markup language. Wikis are often used to create and power collaborative and community websites. The most prominent Wiki application is the "Wikipedia" on which every Internet user can become the knowledge provider of its content. In such architecture, both peers and experts are equally welcomed and valued to participate in the knowledge refinement process. Wikis are used in business as effective knowledge management systems. Wikis enable site visitors to add their own content and build up, in an additive fashion, on the content created by others. They hence create a common platform for people in the targeted and specified community to not merely participate in the communications but also be the content and knowledge providers of the group. The properties of a wiki platform make it easy to track activities such as the viewing, reading, adding, and editing of content, changes to content over time, the most active contributors, as well as the opportunity to recruit specific users for more focused research projects. When done right, wikis can drive key metrics that online marketers labor to achieve including increased page views, a higher level of consumer engagement, and higher rates of user contributions. Wikis can also be used for gathering market intelligence-by analyzing the content added by consumers which can provide insight into possible future trends or competitor offerings. They can also aid in market research where researchers enter the discussion and conduct focused surveys or discrete experiments. Wikis offer companies the opportunity to encourage user generated content. User-generated content can serve multiple purposes as a market intelligence tool, a competitive intelligence tool, as forums for advertising, and as a platform for consumer interaction.

MicroMedia: Twitter

A form of text-based "MicroMedia" (Owyang, 2007), Twitter is really much like blogging, but on a miniature scale. The character limit of 140 calls for simplification of messages. A tool with social network features, Twitter is a next-generation instant-messaging tool; where users can blast messages to their network, send private messages, or search. When users publish messages, those are often called "tweets." Twitter was founded by Jack Dorsey, Biz Stone, and Evan Williams, and began as a research and development project inside San Francisco podcasting company Odeo in March, 2006 (Glaser, 2007). Twitter helps extend the reach for those individuals or companies that already have a blogging strategy in place, and want to further work on strengthening the consumer relationships through increased interaction with the consumer. It can be used by retailers for promotional campaigns and building a buzz and is of special use to companies launching new products or product variants, where it can also be used as part of an organizational branding strategy. Twitter's usability for developing and engaging a community can be leveraged as a tool for market sensing and understanding consumer sentiment.

Folksonomies

With the increased informational and exchange needs, there has been an emergence of new communication models producing incredible amounts of distributed information that knowledge workers need to link, aggregate, and organize in order to extract knowledge. Folksonomies attempt to provide a solution to this issue by introducing an innovative distributed approach based on social classification (Quintarelli, 2005). The huge volume of content available online today, has resulted in the evolution of more relevant aggregation and concept matching tools, by addressing web-specific classification issues, specifically with reference to the vast volumes of content created by consumers on the web.

Folksonomy (also known as collaborative tagging, social classification, social indexing, and social tagging) is the practice and method of collaboratively creating and managing tags to annotate and categorize content. *Folksonomy* describes the bottom-up classification systems that emerge from social tagging (Smith, 2008). In contrast to traditional subject indexing, metadata is

generated not only by experts but also by creators and consumers of the content. Usually, freely chosen keywords are used instead of a controlled vocabulary (Voss, 2007). Folksonomy (from folk + taxonomy) is a user-generated taxonomy.

As companies formulate strategies for using the collaborative web for consumer targeting, a better segmentation of the consumer can be achieved by studying the customers' level of social networking participation, or 'Social Technographics', before developing any social strategies (Forrester, 2008). 'Social Technographics' is a term coined by Forrester Research, and is based on a range of six user participation levels: inactive, spectator, joiner, collector, critic, and creator. For marketers, understanding the level of participation of consumers in the segment they propose to promote their products will enable them to fine-tune their use of the various social marketing tools, and engage with consumers within their comfort level. This 'participation ladder' can be used to identify which social strategies to deploy first–and also how to encourage users to climb up from being spectators to becoming more engaged (Lee, 2008).

The Collaborative Web and the E-Enterprise

Enterprise 2.0 is the use of emergent social software platforms within companies, or between companies and their partners or customers (McAfee, 2006). This use of Web 2.0 within the enterprise to improve efficiency and productivity finds applications where shared knowledge work becomes the intellectual capital for the company and a smooth flow of communication through the 'connected' enterprise takes place.

Similarly, these tools have widespread application with respect to their application to the organization consumer interface-in improving organization-consumer relationships, increasing brand value, improving the productivity of marketing and enhancing consumer perceived value about the organization.

Harnessing Collaborative Intelligence

Collaborative intelligence as the collaborative ability of an entity or a group. To succeed, companies need to innovate faster, collaborate better, and operate more efficiently than ever before. To do so, they need to depend on close collaborative relationships with strategic partners, the ability to exchange prudent information rapidly, and to act on that information in real-time, across end-to-end business processes. The key to unlocking this performance potential is to tap into the power of communities that drive business success. Relationships matter, particularly for the knowledge-intensive activities that make organizations unique (IBM, 2007). Given the increasingly dispersed, project-based work environments that are characteristic of companies today, it is important to help people become better connected-with one another and with the information and applications they need. In building on a theme of collaborative intelligence, the following list of features may be considered as the objectives of knowledge content development via Web 2.0 (Lee & Lan, 2007).

1. **Contribution:** Every internet user has the opportunity to freely provide their knowledge content to the relevant subject domains.
2. **Sharing:** Knowledge content is freely available to others. Secured mechanisms may be enforced to enable the knowledge sharing amongst legitimate members within specific communities.
3. **Collaboration:** Knowledge content is created and maintained collaboratively by knowledge providers. Internet users participating in creation of content can have conversations as a kind of social interaction.
4. **Dynamic:** Knowledge content is updated constantly to reflect the changing environment and situation.

5. **Reliance:** Knowledge contribution should be based on trust between knowledge providers and domain experts.

Enterprises with large employee, partner, and customer bases have long known the value of the knowledge living in employees' heads and in the databases and unstructured documents found across the organization. Attempts to collect this information into knowledge management systems have been made in the past, with varying degrees of success. Web 2.0 technologies such as blogs, wikis, and enterprise search for people and data are providing a new platform for collaborating on complex and creative tasks in the organizational domains. Technological advances are simplifying online collaboration and communication. These advances are increasing productivity by helping people to more easily capture, share and reuse work practices (such as project workflows) and link them to the widest possible range of supporting services (for example, instant messaging, Web conferencing and tools for team collaboration). Interactivity interfaced with technology enhances the knowledge base of the community which includes organizational employees, customers and partners; hence the content generated by the community can be harnessed for the collaborative intelligence it offers. Further, the preservation of these intangible assets can form a source of competitive advantage for a firm. This is slightly complex as they differ from normal assets in a crucial way-most of the firm's intangible assets are locked up in the brains of the employees, who can come and go. Be it the Microsoft Developer Network which hosts a series of employee blogs to share tips on software, programming tips and solutions to programming issues or the GE research blogs, or the Sun Microsystems employee blogs, the volume of company specific knowledge available on these online webspaces is huge. Sun Microsystems CEO Jonathan Schwartz uses his blog for product announcements and discussion of new knowledge issues as part of his bid to interact with the community. The transparency of the channels is breathtaking- for instance, a common Sun consumer can gain access to a Sun whitepaper on 'multiplatform virtualization' by merely logging onto the online blog community! Accumulation of company specific information has also made these online webspaces virtual repositories to be tapped whenever required. The volume of knowledge that can be retrieved regarding a person's work in an organization post his departure, through his contributions to his blogs etc. makes these viable organizational endeavors.

Organizations are waking up to the need of extending business processes beyond corporate firewalls which implies inclusion of people outside the company as readily as they do people inside the firm. IBM has taken the lead in applying the consumer-based, social networking concept to cross-organizational business networks. With IBM networking services, organizations can securely and easily tap into collective knowledge by enabling formation of fluid communities of interest. Enterprise Collaboration Platforms offer to employees what social networks offer to consumers- ease of use, speed and ubiquity combined with a high level of security, availability, quality of service, and reliability that enterprises require. To cite an example, *The Greater IBM Connection* is a business social network designed to connect current and former IBMers and to enable them to connect, communicate and collaborate in a variety of new ways, by interacting via a virtual environment. Greater IBM seeks to contribute to advancing societal innovations by creating an *innovation network* that can orchestrate collaborative work, the sharing of insights, and facilitate community-based, productive projects for social and business innovation.

These technologies have the potential to usher in a new era by making practices and outputs of organizational workers visible by knitting together the enterprise and facilitating knowledge work in

new ways. Content sharing owing to high degrees of centralization and commonality not only facilitate knowledge capture, but also better levels of productivity due to greater accessibility. Mining the inputs of the consumers, with respect to the content they generate on corporate blogs, branded online communities and other organizational networks, serves as an excellent market sensing tool. The consumer ideas and thoughts can be leveraged by organizations to achieve greater customer centricity through product improvements and co-creation. Some examples (O'Reilly, 2005):

- Amazon sells the same products as competitors such as Barnes & Noble, and they receive the same product descriptions, cover images, and editorial content from their vendors. But Amazon has used its user engagement to gain a competitive edge. The high volumes of user reviews, and invitations for consumers to participate in varied ways results in enhanced user activity which can produce better search results.

- EBay's competitive advantage comes almost entirely from the critical mass of buyers and sellers, which makes any new entrant offering similar services significantly less attractive. EBay grows organically in response to user activity, and the company's role is as an enabler for creation of an environment facilitating the collective activity of all involved entities.

Case Study: Procter and Gamble

Web 2.0 and Open Innovation

The world's largest consumer packaged goods giant, Procter & Gamble (P&G), operated one of the most widely admired and successful research and development operations in corporate history. But their closed innovation model was not up to the task of driving the corporate growth needed to sustain an enterprise of P&G's size. So in 2000, under the leadership of the then newly-appointed CEO, A. G. Lafley, they began looking for a better global innovation model. Lafley's stated objective was the radical idea that half of the company's new products would be acquired from outside the company (Lindegaard, 2009). In the words of Larry Huston, Vice President, Innovation and Knowledge, P&G, Cincinnati, and Nabil Sakkab, Senior Vice President for Corporate R&D at P&G in Cincinnati (Huston & Sakkab, 2006):

We discovered that important innovation was increasingly being done at small and midsize entrepreneurial companies. Even individuals were eager to license and sell their intellectual property. University and government labs had become more interested in forming industry partnerships, and they were hungry for ways to monetize their research. The Internet had opened up access to talent markets throughout the world. And a few forward-looking companies like IBM and Eli Lilly were beginning to experiment with the new concept of open innovation, leveraging one another's (even competitors') innovation assets—products, intellectual property, and people.

What set them off towards an open innovation model was the discovery that there were 200 researchers and scientists just as good or even better outside P&G for each of their own 7,500 researchers and scientists. That appeared a humongous volume of talent the company could tap into. It does this through an open innovation program called Connect & Develop that reaches out to independent researchers, suppliers and other industrial companies to solve problems it cannot solve by itself.

The company has also adopted the use of Web 2.0 tools--an example of the resulting model is the *Vocalpoint* program. *Engaging users is among the many secrets that underlie successful innovation. The newest innovation in innovation is the use of rich media and online interactivity to involve broad audiences in the process* (Read, 2008).

The technology that underlies Web 2.0 enables full bi-directional conversations online, putting users into the creation seat for the bulk of new internet content. From the perspective of firms creating new products and services, this can open innovation to a community of millions of possible innovators, people who may be more likely to adopt the resulting offering as they had a hand in developing it. This suggests that Web 2.0 might offer firms both more leverage on the enormous global corporate expenditure on innovation and increase the likelihood of innovation adoption at the same time. Adaptation of this concept enables consumers to voice their thoughts and then subsequently participate in new product ideas, executions of which represent win-win situations for both organizations and consumers.

Harnessing Consumers

P&G has a Vocalpoint program for mothers, a Tremor program for adolescents and a Living It program for lead-customers. All three programs use different ways to harness customers as sources of ideas and to test new products before they hit the market (Hill, 2009). Vocalpoint leverages the community for propagation of word of mouth and innovation and strikes a careful balance using no-frills packaging that is clearly branded to establish credibility. P&G's role as a trusted broker, protecting the consumer while offering an instant WOM network to clients, has proven successful. These programs give P&G a peep into the everyday lives and thought processes of their customers. The brief, concise nature of these ventures demonstrate a level of simplicity and honesty, Vocalpoint's FAQ is straightforward in stating it expects members to participate in the programs, share opinions and feedback and spread the word about the products to friends. This also gives members a feeling of exclusivity when they get access to items before other consumers and can help improve them before they hit the shelves. This enhances interest in a product and ensures a second wave of buzz once it is fully launched. The right environment where people can contribute, interact and engage, enables creation by the community by offering a high return on investment when considered at a cost per individual interaction perspective. It is interesting to see that even with the enormous resources of one of the biggest companies in the world at their disposal; P&G recognizes that it cannot do all its innovation in-house. Its further acceptance of the fact that it needs to understand customer needs much better than it did in the past to drive successful innovation in the future may well be the key to a successful and brighter future for the business giant.

Electronic Commerce

Electronic commerce is rapidly changing the way people do business all over the world. In the business-to-consumer segment, sales through the web have been increasing dramatically over the last few years. Customers, not only those from well developed countries but also those from developing countries, are getting used to the new shopping channel (Cheung et al., 2003). An organization's key to survival in the new information age revolution is in its ability to successfully integrate and adapt its management practices with new information technologies offered by the internet (Cudmore et al., 2011). Procter & Gamble has teamed up with PFSweb to launch PGeStore.com representing several popular brands such as Tide, Pampers and Gillette. Rather than build and operate its own web store, Procter & Gamble chose an outsourcing arrangement with an established e-commerce service provider so it can concentrate on how online shoppers interact with its hundreds of brands.

The digital paradigm plays two very significant roles in marketing-influencing consumer behavior and harnessing consumer intelligence. While it is vital for an organization to evaluate consumer intentions and provide consumers the necessary information they are looking for, equally impor-

tant is the need for collecting consumer data by studying the consumer behavioral patterns on the internet and subsequently nurturing long term relationships with consumers. This is where P&G is attempting to position its new online venture.

Procter & Gamble in the past has participated in several smaller e-commerce initiatives. To maintain control of their brand and deal with the consolidating ranks of retailers, competing private-label brands and shrinking store space, they will be doing much more selling online. The Internet has a substantial impact on consumer behavior and has contributed to the emergence of an era of consumer empowerment. The consequences are far reaching, affecting not only the area of technology development but also the domains of business strategy and marketing. Online consumers have noticed that these applications offer new and previously unknown possibilities and empowerment not only in the form of information sourcing, but also as forums of dialogue and confrontation of producers and vendors with their social, ethical and commercial responsibilities. The shift in consumer needs is reflected in the growing demand of online services, particularly in the e-commerce domain, where consumers can not only interact with marketers but also access peer communities (Constantinides & Fountain, 2008).

Brand Customer Centricity

As part of our research, we developed a Brand Customer Centricity Calculator (BCCC). Building customer centricity in a brand is one alternative available to organizations in the wake of the rising vulnerabilities of brands and branding in the face of rising consumer empowerment. It creates new opportunities for brand-customer dialogue, knowledge creation, and, critically, provides a new context in which the interests of a corporation and those of its customers can be more closely aligned. Customer centric brands represent one effective means for firms to achieve better alignment of their brands with the customers. To become a successful customer centric brand, however, the brand management function must first acknowledge the effective and efficient determinants of emotional connection and consumer brand knowledge in a brand for the consumers.

Studies have revealed that Procter & Gamble's Product Brand *Tide* depicted a 'medium' level of Brand Customer-Centricity. The BCCC was used to calculate a brand customer centricity score, which was a weighted sum of the performance of the brand across the functions of *Building an emotional connection with the consumer, ability of the brand to cater to a particular consumer lifestyle and image, consumer perception, consumer brand knowledge, Trust, responsibility towards the customer.*

Tide was found to have scope of improvement in its ability to build an emotional connection with its consumers and demonstrate higher levels of Consumer Brand knowledge.

CONCLUSION AND RECOMMENDATIONS

There are four trends reshaping the world of business–technological advances and the speed with which new technologies are created and copied, the loss of geographic advantage resulting from globalisation, the shake-up of traditionally stable industries as a result of deregulation and the rising power of the consumer and their ability to get what they want, when they want it, from whomever they want. This has made companies realise the significance of the 4 levers of Customer Value Management – Retention, Efficiency (understanding cost to serve), Acquisition and Penetration (cross-sell and up-sell). Further, with the internet having built an open network where information can flow freely, innovation, entrepreneurship and democracy are fast thriving over the world.

The buzzword of globalisation holds no meaning without the concept of what is being termed

as 'Digitization.' The internet today provides a research resource for buyers, sellers and learners. While elevating and extending strong, existing brands, it is cost-effective for customer self-service and ongoing business. It allows unprecedented one to one communication and dynamic personalisation during an online session. The internet opens the market to new groups of customers and customizes powerful extranets to the company and individuals. It offers unlimited real estate on the web, so prospects can dig deeper and marketers can present items that wouldn't be cost effective in print, thereby allowing for profitable strategic business alliances and affiliations by offering unique ways to present information and increase sales and profits. This has widespread applications for branding, CRM, consumer engagement and internet marketing.

REFERENCES

Cheung, C. M. K., Zhu, L., Kwong, T., Chan, G. W. W., & Limayem, M. (2003). Online consumer behavior: A review and agenda for future research. In *Proceedings of 16ᵗʰ Bled eCommerce Conference eTransaction* (pp. 194-218).

Constantinides, E., & Fountain, S. (2008). Web 2.0: Conceptual foundations and marketing issues. *Journal of Direct. Data and Digital Marketing Practice*, *9*, 231–244. doi:10.1057/palgrave. dddmp.4350098.

Cudmore, A. B., Bobrowski, E. P., & Kiguradze, T. (2011). Encouraging consumer searching behavior on healthcare web sites. *Journal of Consumer Marketing*, *28*(4), 290–299. doi:10.1108/07363761111143187.

Drezner, D. W., & Farell, H. (2004). *The power and politics of blogs*. Paper presented at the 2004 American Political Science Association. Chicago, IL.

Dwyer, P. (2007). *Building trust with corporate blogs.* Paper presented at the International Conference on Weblogs and Social Media. Boulder, CO.

Forrester Social Technographics Profile tool. (2008). *Forrester Research.* Retrieved from http://www.forrester.com/Groundswell/profile_tool.html

Gill, K. E. (2004). How can we measure the influence of the blogosphere? In *Proceedings of the WWW2004 Conference.* New York: ACM. Retrieved from http://citeseerx.ist.psu.edu/viewdoc/download?doi=10.1.1.124.2509&rep=rep1&type=pdf

Glaser, M. (2007). Twitter founders thrive on micro-blogging constraints. *Public Broadcasting Service (PBS).* Retrieved from http://www.pbs.org/mediashift/2007/05/twitter-founders-thrive-on-micro-blogging-constraints137.html

Herring, S. C. (1993). Gender and democracy in computer-mediated communication. *Electronic Journal of Communication, 3*(2).

Hill, G. (2009). How customers drive innovation at P&G. *Customerthink Research Library.* Retrieved from http://www.customerthink.com

Huston, L., & Sakkab, N. (2006). Connect and develop: Inside Procter & Gamble's new model for innovation. *Harvard Business Review, 84*(3), 58–66.

IBM. (2007). Innovative collaboration to advance your business. Tapping the collaborative intelligence of your business network. Retrieved from http://www-304.ibm.com/jct03004c/businesscenter/

Kelleher, T., & Miller, B. M. (2006). Organizational blogs and the human voice: Relational strategies and relational outcomes. *Journal of Computer-Mediated Communication, 11*(2). Retrieved from http://jcmc.indiana.edu/vol11/issue2/kelleher.html doi:10.1111/j.1083-6101.2006.00019.x.

Lee, C. (2008). *Social Technographics Report.* Forrester Research.

Lee, M. R., & Lan, Y. C. (2007). From Web 2.0 to conversational knowledge management: Towards collaborative intelligence. *Journal of Entrepreneurship Research, 2*(2), 47–62.

Lindegaard, S. (2009). *P&G: How open innovation is done.* Retrieved from http://stefanlindegaard.com/2009/04/14/pg-how-open-innovation-is-done

McAfee, A. P. (2006). Enterprise 2.0: The dawn of emergent collaboration. *MIT Sloan Review, 47*(3), 21–28.

Misner, I. (2008). The VCP process of relationship marketing. Masters of sales. *Academy Online Research.* Retrieved from http://bni-india.com/the-vcp-process-of-relationship-marketing/

O'Reilly, T. (2005). What is Web 2.0. Retrieved from http://www.oreillynet.com/pub/a/oreilly/tim/news/2005/09/30/what-is-web-20.html-page=2

Owyang, J. (2007). Trendwatch - MicroMedia provides bite-sized voice and video to micro audiences. *Web Strategy.* Retrieved from http://www.web-strategist.com/

Platt, M. (2007). *Web 2.0 in the Enterprise. The Architecture Journal. Microsoft Developer Network.* MSDN Architecture Centre.

Quintarelli, E. (2005). Folksonomies: Power to the people. In *Proceedings of the ISKO Italy-UniMIB Meeting.* Milan, Italy: ISKO.

Read, S. (2008). *What is the next big innovation in innovation.* Laussane, Switzerland: IMD.

Sifry, D. (2004). *Sifry's Alerts: October 2004 State of the Blogosphere.* Retrieved from http://www.sifry.com/alerts/archives/000387.html

Smith, G. (2008). *Tagging: People-powered metadata for the social web.* Berkeley, CA: New Riders.

Voss, J. (2007). Tagging, folksonomy & Co-Renaissance of manual indexing. In *Proceedings of the International Symposium of Information Science* (234–254).

ADDITIONAL READING

Sinha, N., Ahuja, V., & Medury, Y. (2011). A brand customer centricity calculator - An empirical approach to customer centric branding. *International Journal of Marketing and Management Research*, 2(11), 125–144.

KEY TERMS AND DEFINITIONS

Business Innovation: Modernisation or improvements in processes, methodologies, products, services or technology which result in the growth and profitability of an organisation.

Co-Creation: A marketing strategy which enables customers to share, combine and renew each other's resources and capabilities to create value through new forms of interaction, service and learning mechanisms.

Collaborative Intelligence: The sum total of the intelligence level of a set of people working in collaboration, often used for mutual benefit and growth.

Customer Based Relationship Approach: Customer driven economies overseeing the implementation of relationship strategies and multi-channel relationship programs, with emphasis on consumer retention for organizational sustenance.

Emerging Technologies: All new technological tools which improve efficiency and productivity in organizations and find application in enhancing organizational communication and collaboration.

Knowledge Economy: The new economic structure where knowledge has become the source of strategic planning for the creation of a value proposition for consumers.

Chapter 17
Negotiation by Software Agents in Electronic Business:
An Example of Hybrid Negotiation

Nosheen Riaz
Government College University, Pakistan

Moez Rehman
Government College University, Pakistan

ABSTRACT

Electronic negotiation is one of many applications that software agents can perform to facilitate electronic business. Negotiations between software agents and humans (hybrid negotiation), can make electronic business efficient and intelligent. It can save time, effort and other valueable resources by replacing the human in electronic business activities and many other domains. However, to enable hybrid negotiation, a software agent needs clear machine interpretable semantics to understand and generate natural language content. Although it is not simple to make natural language content understandable by software agents as a whole, it can be achieved in different domains--in this case electronic business. For this purpose, an example of hybrid negotiation is presented, in which a software agent and a human agent negotiate for a business contract. Problems involved in this negotiation process are partially resolved through ontologies (the main Semantic Web technology), NSS (negotiation support system) and hand written rules.

INTRODUCTION

Electronic business performs using the Web as a platform. The ubiquity of the Web has made its evolution fast that we need new business models and technologies for electronic business to perform efficiently. The current Web is challenge for businesses to attract new customers while retaining existing customers as well as for consumers to search optimal solutions within time. The Semantic Web is a promising solution for challenges to the current Web (Berners-Lee, Lassila, & Hendler, 2001). Software agents (operating on Semantic Web) are valuable support to meet the changing demands of electronic business. The Semantic Web and software agents together can become

DOI: 10.4018/978-1-4666-4026-9.ch017

supporting business entities to boost electronic business performance. However, the Semantic Web is facing criticism of being an overestimation, as AI (Artificial Intelligence) has faced for a long time. This huge ambitious aim has a slow progress due to a "chicken and egg problem." Markups are required before developers start building smart applications; applications are required before it is worth the hard work of doing markup (Pell, 2007). By providing intelligent applications in electronic business, the Semantic Web and software agent will cash benefit to attract the research communities that will involve the Semantic Web and its technologies to other applications. The whole process will gradually evolve the current Web (web of documents) to the Semantic Web (web of data).

Objectives of the chapter include describing the significance of the Semantic Web and software agents for electronic business, discussion on the negotiation process by software agents in electronic business, and an elaboration of hybrid negotiation through an example. In the end, we discuss in detail the issues and their solutions in enabling hybrid negotiation.

BACKGROUND

The Web has rapidly progressed since its start. The Internet System Consortium advertised nearly 100 million hosts on DNS in January 2000. In January 2012, the amount has increased to 1 billion, and each host maintains from tens to millions of webpages (www.isc.org). Human limited ability is a resistance to search the information of interest from this massive collection. The thousands of webpages come as result against a search query. Because main search tools for today's web such as Yahoo and Google are Keyword-based (Antoniou & Harmelen, 2008). Many problems occur with keyword based searches including "high recall, low precision", "low or no recall," among

others. Moreover, results are single webpages, in the case when information is spread over various documents and a separate query is needed to access each document. A human user cannot screen all the webpages to choose a page containing the required content. Machines can be involved for a solution; obviously, machines can process millions of pages within seconds. But the question is, how do machines behave like they understand Web content (Chou, 2007)? Most of today's Web content is only appropriate for human utilization (Antoniou & Harmelen, 2008). An alternative approach is to represent the Web content in a form that is machine-processable and to use intelligent techniques (e.g., intelligent agents) to take advantage of these representations. This plan of revolutionizing the Web is the Semantic Web initiative (Antoniou & Harmelen, 2008).

The real worth of the Semantic Web is that it is machine interpretable and uses intelligent tools and software agents to assist humans. The Semantic Web will explore the collaboration of humans through software agents and automated Web services (Chou, 2007). Antoniou and Harmelen (2008) provide an outlook for how software agents in the Semantic Web will support humans in the future. In this vision, a person, Michael, who had a minor car accident, wants to take physical therapy sessions. Michael assigns his Semantic Web agent to find out a few suitable opportunities. The agent gets him an appointment for a therapist, maintained by Michael's health insurance company, and is near his office and not disturbing his busy schedule. In another case study, Berners-Lee, Lassila, and Hendler (2001) gave an illusion that a brother "Pete" and sister "Luce," manage a doctor's appointment for their mother. They get the appointment organized by their software agents according to the given preferences, suitable time, and nearest path. Their agents manage it by cooperating with each other and communicating with the doctor's agent. A vision yet, but going to meet now, as agents have started providing services in different domains. Software agents in the future will be very different from their current incarnation, and will be empowered with human-like intelligence (Chou, 2007).

The Semantic Web and Electronic Business

The World Wide Web has provided a new way of communication and business conduction (Antoniou & Harmelen, 2008). Traditional businesses are benefiting from the current Web as a commercial medium. Consumers have access to greater amounts of dynamic information to support queries for decision-making. The interactive nature of the Web and the hypertext environment are motivation for a customer to start and maintain meaningful and customized searches. Electronic business can also gather market intelligence and monitor consumer choices through customers' revealed preferences in purchasing behavior on the Web (Hoffman, Novak, & Chatterjee, 2000). The electronic market is vast, so there is more competition and better quality, and it also leads to an additional advantage of low cost for online shoppers. Moreover, with the realization of the Semantic Web, the electronic business processes will become more efficient. Lytras and Garcia (2008) deliver real-life cases of electronic business and electronic commerce that avail the benefits of Semantic Web technologies. Enterprise software vendors like IBM, Oracle, SAS and Microsoft have started to add semantic search as a feature, as have the Web search engines like Google, Microsoft's Bing, and Yahoo (Horwitt, 2011). With the development of Semantic Web research, applications of its technologies are getting more important to the professional and academic communities (Singh, Iyer, & Salam, 2005). The semantic electronic business founds upon three active streams of research where the Semantic Web technologies including ontologies and intelligent agents are among first research stream of electronic business. The Semantic Web

technologies provide organizations the means to design collaborative and integrative, inter- and intra-organizational business processes (Singh, Iyer, & Salam, 2005). Feigenbaum et al. (2007) provide a latest overview of businesses, companies and projects where the Semantic Web is in action. They provide a list of many companies, consumers and vendors that use the Semantic Web to enhance business-to-business interactions. EBay (online bidding system for selling and buying a variety of products) is the best example of such an electronic business platform. To buy a vehicle, not just say, "Find me the Toyota Priuses for sale." Instead, "find me only used, red Priuses for sale, for less than $14,000, by people who are within 80 miles of my house, and make them an offer." Grand visions rarely progress exactly as planned but the Semantic Web is indeed emerging and is making online information.

Electronic Business and Intelligent Agents

The agent technology is one of the most interesting technologies to support the electronic business activities successfully (Negri, Poggi, Turci, & Tomaiuolo, 2006). Amazon is a virtual business platform that has become more assisting and reliable by using the agent technology. It delivers customized information to the online shopper. Real shoppers at physical/traditional bookstores are limited to what is on the shelf-space. Reviews and comments simply do not exist while perusing a shelf of books. Amazon uses "dubbed Eyes and Ears," intelligent software agents who retain the history about the customer's liking and preferences while buying. These agents then provide suggestions to customers in their next visit to Amazon and update them about the importance or shopping trends for new articles or books (Peter, 1998). Opportunities for using intelligent agents in electronic business are enormous (Papazoglou, 2001). They may facilitate a variety of relevant functions such as advertising, matchmaking and brokering (Klusch, 2005). They can perform real-time pricing and auctioning, involving different parties in a supply-chain network. Suppliers can present their products on the Web and collect real-time price bids from multiple customers. Intelligent software agents can carry out work on behalf of human knowledge workers, on both the supplier and customer's behalf. Agents can even suggest the best price to their online shoppers to gain higher profit (Hertweck, Rakes, & Rees, 2010). A latest survey (Kowalczyk, 2010) shows existing research and development efforts involve mobile and intelligent agents for advanced e-commerce solutions. The survey points out many e-commerce systems that use intelligent software agents for shopping comparisons, auction bidding and contract negotiation. A natural language search agent (shopping boot) can even interestingly solve many online shopping problems. According to another survey (Horrigan, 2008), 58% of internet users get frustrated and hostile by other resistances while doing online shopping. Agents can cope with all these problems and can be the best assistance for electronic business sellers and customers. The software agents can replace humans in many stages of electronic business. The six common stages extracted from the models try to capture the *consumer buying behavior* (Maes, Guttman, & Moukas, 1999). These stages are: (i) need identification, (ii) product brokering, (iii) merchant brokering, (iv) negotiation, (v) purchase and delivery, and (vi) product service and evaluation. Agent technology can be applied in many of these stages to work on a human's behalf. We discuss here the agent technology in the *negotiation* stage.

Intelligent Agents and Electronic Negotiation

Negotiations that use electronic media are called electronic negotiations. Electronic negotiation is one of the significant tasks that intelligent agents can perform in electronic business. Electronic

negotiations promise higher levels of process efficiency and effectiveness, most importantly a higher quality and faster emergence of agreements (Bichler, Kersten, & Strecker, 2003). Maes, Guttman, and Moukas (1999) describe six common stages extracted from the models that try to capture the customer buying behavior. Negotiation is among one of six stages where agents can either alternate or support humans. The agent can help the negotiators by searching and providing information about the markets such as latest prices and deals, analysis of user preferences, assisting the negotiator in defining suitable negotiation strategy, profiling an opponent by maintaining background information, and coordinating and setting negotiation issues (Braun, et al., 2006). They can participate in high-level (task-oriented) dialogues using interaction protocols in conjunction with built in organizational knowledge (Papazoglou, 2001). With the popularity of electronic business, the importance of automated negotiations has increased. For example, when a virtual shopping mall receives product orders from a customer then it is needed to make the delivery orders automatically without human interference, so a proposal is generated and announced to multiple delivery companies. Then, the mall and delivery companies negotiate over the price and quality (for example, delivery date) of a specific delivery service. Thus, there is a need for agent-mediated electronic commerce, and intelligent agents are required to assist in the negotiation process (Huang, Liang, Lai, & Lin, 2010; Lau, 2007). A case study (Berners-Lee, Lassila, & Hendler, 2001) of a brother "Pete" and sister "Luce" shows a reflection of future agents. They manage a doctor's appointment for their mother, organized by their software agents according to their preferences (suitable time, nearest path, insurance policy, etc.). The agents manage it by cooperating with each other and communicating with the doctor's agent. A vision yet, but going to meet now, as agents have started providing services in different domains (e.g., buyer and shopper agents). Humans will relay on intelligent software agents in the near future to search and interact with Web resources over the World Wide Web (Chou, 2007).

Electronic Negotiation Process

The electronic negotiation process has a negotiation arena, agenda, decision-making rules and protocol as ingredients (Bichler, Kersten, & Strecker, 2003). *Outcome* is a conclusion reached through a negotiation process. It helps to take decision. It can be a compromise or a disagreement. Negotiation arena provides a ground on which negotiating parties make mutual discussions and convey their interests and options (offers, counter offers) to one another. *Agenda* contains actual concerns (possibly contradictory) to settle down. It provides the complete structure of the negotiation. That structure or framework includes all negotiable issues, arrangement of these issues and their presentation either sequentially or simultaneously. Every individual negotiation may have a different agenda. *Decision-making rules* are used to determine, analyze and select decision alternatives and concessions. Mutual decision-making rules are set to come on an agreed upon bunch of choices or options that resolve conflict. For example, in the problem (discussed in the next section) an agent has decision power if values are within the range set by a human master. However, a human takes the final decision himself if the values go beyond the range. *A negotiation protocol* includes all rules that define the negotiation arena, agenda, permissible decision-making and communication activities of the negotiators. In conservative face-to-face negotiations, communication is flexible but un-structured. Communication in electronic negotiations needs to be structured in order to make the communication processes efficient and effective (Schoop, Jertila, & List, 2003). We can distinguish different levels of negotiation structure depending on the protocol (Bichler, Kersten, & Strecker, 2003).

- Unstructured negotiations do not follow any protocol, allowing for exchanges that do not conform to any rules (e.g., face-to-face negotiations). These may also be referred to as unsupported negotiations, as typical scenarios in this case are being physically co-located and no information system is involved. A human manages the process and decisions completely.

- Semi-structured negotiations follow certain rules but the protocol is not fully defined. Therefore, the participants have some agility in their decision making and information exchange activities. Negotiations supported by NSS (Negotiation support System) are an example of semi-structured negotiations. This leads to the scenario where people control the negotiation process and decisions but rules are fixed up to some extent. Negotiation is semi-automated in this case (e.g., involving some information system or agent). Hybrid negotiation is an example of semi-structured negotiations.

- Structured negotiations follow a set of rules, which fully defines the parties' decision-making and allowable activities (e.g., auctions). Agent to agent communication is a typical example of structured negotiation. Here all the rules, protocols and specifications are defined and followed strictly from both sides. Exchange of offers, counter offers, concessions are all done by the agents, based on the pre settled rules.

Every negotiation process has some features or characteristics depending upon the environment (Lin & Kraus, 2010).

- **Number of negotiators or the parties participating in the negotiation process:** Negotiation parties can be two (bilateral negotiations) or more (multilateral negotiations).

- **Single- or multi-attribute issue:** A negotiation may be single issues (simplest form) or multi issue (complex). A negotiation consists of multi-attribute issues if the parties have to negotiate on an agreement that involves several attributes for each issue.

- **Set of objectives or issues to be resolved:** The negotiation environment also consists of a set of objectives and issues to be resolved. Issues can be of various types that include discrete enumerated value sets, integer-value sets, and real-value sets.

- **Cooperative or non-cooperative negotiators:** The negotiation environment can consist of non-cooperative negotiators or cooperative negotiators. Generally, cooperative agents seek to capitalize on mutual joint utilities while non-cooperative agents make an effort to increase their own utilities regardless of the other sides' utilities.

- **Domain specific or independent:** The negotiation domain covers the negotiation goals and issues, also assigns differ-

ent values to each. Thus, an agent may be designed to adapt a given domain or it may domain independent.

Negotiation by agents comes under following two states:

1. Agent to agent negotiation.
2. Agent to human negotiation (hybrid negotiation).

Figure 1 presents three scenarios. The first scenario is when two persons or group of persons (parties) negotiate or consult something, they need some common ground. The one basic element of this common ground is shared thinking or concepts. Otherwise, confusions and misunderstanding may lead to an unsuccessful result. When the first human agent wants to communicate to a second human agent in Figure 1, they manually maintain their shared concepts (based on common knowledge). Humans communicate via natural language. Communication bases upon pre-settled

Figure 1. A framework representing communication between human agent and intelligent software agents

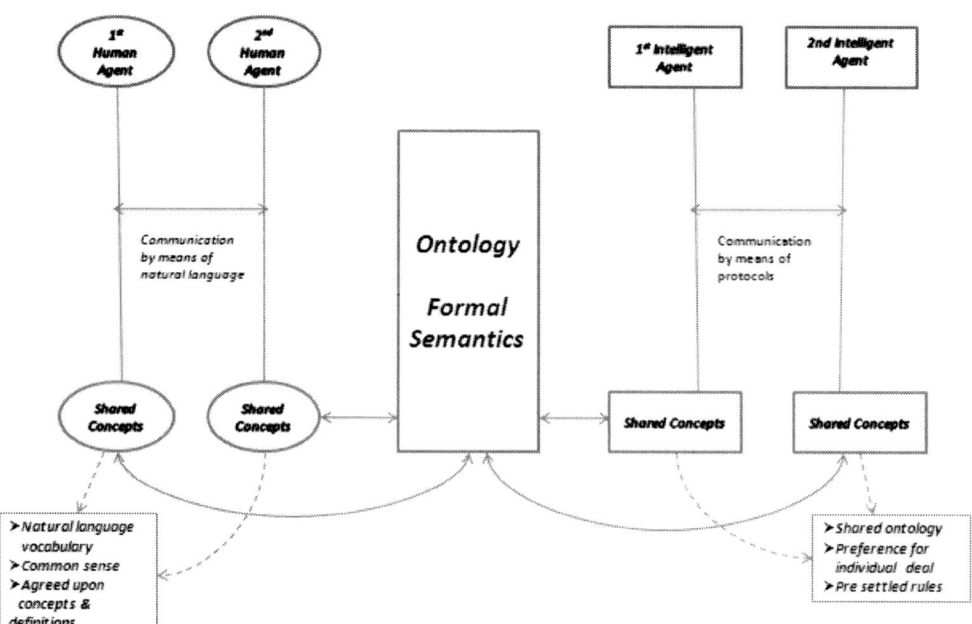

thinking about different concepts. These concepts are learned from different past experiences and common sense. Common sense is another factor involved in human negotiations. Common sense is similar to obvious thinking obtained from either experience or unconsciousness. Common sense involves concepts or terms upon which people in common agree and during negotiation that things do not need to specify explicitly. This is good for unstructured communication but often we need structured communication. In structured communications, an underlying structure such as database structure may be different on both sides. Therefore, a middle standard is required such that both the human negotiators agree on that standard. Ontology can be involved for such structured negotiations between human agents.

The second scenario is when two intelligent agents negotiate. Every term needs to be defined completely when we are concerned with software agents. Communication between agents is achieved via protocols. Protocols completely define tolerable offers, threshold for acceptance of the offers, timing of all the events and behavior during the negotiation. "Shared ontology" is the main component of shared concepts or common ground in the case of agent-to-agent communication. Terms and requisites have to be defined explicitly for a particular field because agents have no common sense and previous knowledge. This refers to the concept of ontology. Both the negotiating parties (software agents) agree on some ontology. Ontology with formal semantics is a standard ontology for domains (in this case electronic business) in Figure 1. A standard ontology will cover the whole market. All the communications between buyers and sellers (either humans or software agents) can involve this ontology for structured negotiation. Such a standard ontology can preserve the annotations for Semantic Web. Every negotiation scenario may involve separate rules (company's own constraints), preferences (regarding separate deal) and vocabulary (specifically for negotiate able item). Software

agents maintain rules and preferences for individual negotiations. Moreover, shared ontology gives vocabulary for every separate negotiation scenario.

Third is hybrid negotiation, a form of electronic negotiation in which a human agent negotiates with a software agent. Hybrid negotiation involves shared concepts and elements from both of previous scenarios, human-to-human and agent-to-agent communication. Both above scenarios have sufficient work done on and under progress. A relatively new discussion is to explore terms and conditions, when a human needs to communicate with software agent during electronic negotiation. That refers to hybrid negotiation. Hybrid negotiation bases upon natural language processing, ontology, formal semantics and grammatical rules.

PROBLEM SCENARIO

The problem is to conduct hybrid negotiation in a business domain. It hits contractual agreements between companies (either business to business or business to customer). Three entities are involved in the negotiation process. It is like a meeting on a three-corner table, shown in Figure 2. First, a human agent (master of intelligent agent) is on one side of table. Second, a human agent and an intelligent agent (counter part of first human) are on the other two sides of the table. Let it be a business to customer deal. The first human (master) and intelligent agent (slave) are from the business side. In the beginning, human negotiators start negotiation, and at this level an agenda is set. They exchange negotiation concerns, and negotiate able items or issues (specific for every negotiation scenario). Later on, the agent (from business side) takes control of negotiation and bargaining. Further negotiation continues between the agent (business) and second human (customer). The agent acts according to its human master's will and preferences. The human has assigned it a fix range (minimum and maximum acceptance

Figure 2. Representation of problem scenario

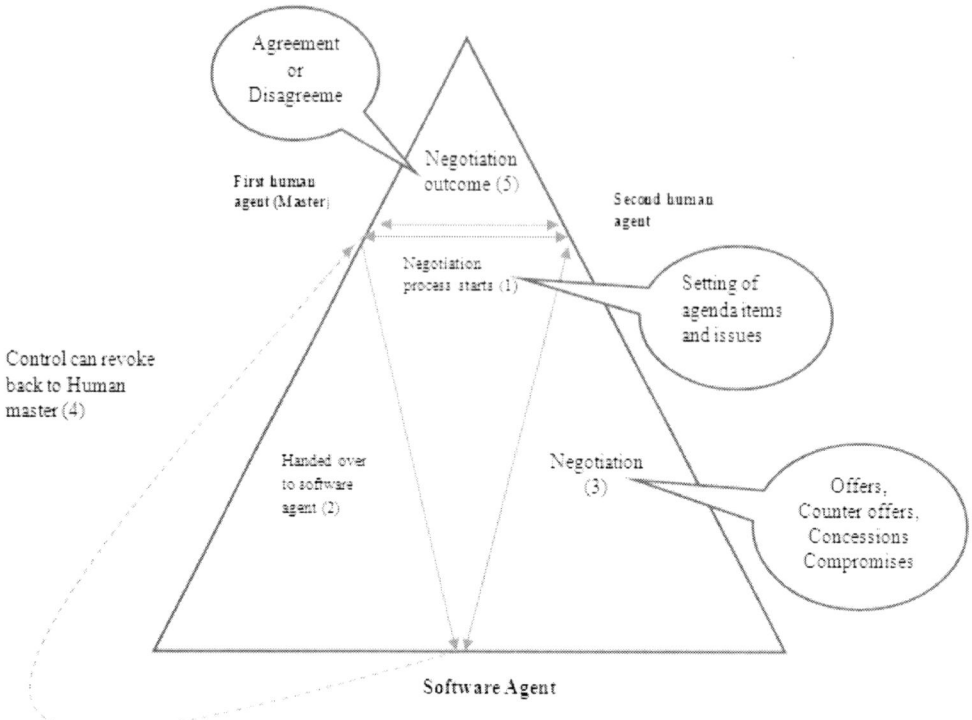

value for the business deal). For example, the range is from US$100 to US$200. The agent has to sell an item for a minimum of US$100. The agent tries to sell at a maximum by sending offers and generating counter offers. The negotiation will end successfully if, for example, the human finally sends an offer or accepts a counter offer (by intelligent agent) for US$150 and this offer is declared as the final value. The intelligent agent will accept it (as it is within the range) and report to the human master. Conversely, there may be other another case. The second human (customer) continuously rejects the counter offers and sends a final offer for even less than US$100 (e.g., US$80). This value is out of the intelligent agent's acceptance range. Now the intelligent agent will give control back to the human and show the last offer. The human (master) will finally decide; either he has to accept (compromised agreement) or reject (disagreement); this is the final negotiation outcome. However, the human master can

revoke back negotiation control from the software agent at any time during negotiations and after that, both human agents are able to carry on a conversation. Because this is hybrid negotiation (agent-to-human), we cannot handle it using the technique adopted in agent-to-agent or human-to-human communication.

Based on this problem scenario, we have implemented our work on the data obtained from an actual inter-human negotiation experiment. Natural language negotiation content that is used in the following sections is taken from the actual experiment conducted between human counter-parts using the newer version of the Negotiation Support System (NSS) Negoisst (Schoop, Jertila, & List, 2003). In this experiment simulation of human-agent negotiation has performed. German car manufacturer company Hurm AG and a Chinese manufacturer Yu Tech negotiate for joint venture to produce engines in China. Representatives of both the companies negotiate over a number of issues to reach a final agreement. The human representative of one of these companies can be replaced with a software agent that is able to conduct the negotiation in the same way to reach the final agreement. Salient features of this negotiation environment are following.

This is a bilateral negotiation held between representatives of two companies: Hurm AG and Yu Tech. Moreover, it is a multi-attribute issue; the agent has to negotiate on multiple issues; for example, "share of ownership", "directors in board," and "payment of workers," among others. These issues are of various types including discrete enumerated value sets, integer-value sets, and real-value sets. For example, "directors in board" may vary between 1-5 members (integer values), payment of common workers by either "Hurm AG" or "Yu Tech" or "half-half" (enumerated value set). This is a joint venture so negotiators are cooperative and both negotiators try to reach on a mutually agreed upon result that will favor the interest of both the companies. Our software agent is a domain specific (business domain) agent; it specifically accomplishes the objectives of electronic business negotiation.

Shung Li is a representative of Chinese company Yu Tech and Tom Smith is a representative of German company Hurm AG. They start negotiations on the issues of joint venture but after some time, Tom Smith delegates the process of negotiation to his counterpart software agent. Both human negotiators were communicating using natural language, so it's the same environment for the software agent. The software agent also receives a negotiation message written in natural language. To make the negotiation message understandable by the software agent, a solution has been provided through NLP (Natural Language Processing, a field of AI that works specifically with natural language). However, the human-agent communication also needs some common ground on which both the human and agent share vocabulary and concepts. The Semantic Web has a technology by the name of "ontology," which

promises to give such a strong base on which agent can possess knowledge and vocabulary enough to communicate with the world. Therefore, the solution of the problem has provided on the base of ontology and NLP with a special focus on Natural Language Understanding (NLU) and Information Extraction (IE).

The goal is to transform the unstructured negotiation message (written in natural language) into a structured message (machine processable), after passing different levels of language processing shown in Figure 3. In the beginning, preprocessing steps (tokenization and sentence splitting) have performed on the unstructured message that is taken as input. After that, lexical analysis has performed. At this level, humans, as well as NLP systems, interpret the meaning of the individual words. Several types of processing contribute to word-level understanding, the first of these being an assignment of a single part-of-speech tag to each word (Liddy, 2001). After assigning parts of speech tags, syntactical analysis has performed. This level focuses on analyzing the words in a sentence so as to uncover the grammatical structure of the sentence. Identification of nouns (persons, organizations, places), and the number of occurrences of the same noun in different ways at various places in the text has been achieved at this level. Now the message is in semi-structured form. Ontology has involved for annotation of this semi-structured message to convert it into a fully structured form. Initially, semantic analysis has been done, where semantic processing determines the possible meanings of a sentence by focusing on the interactions among word-level meanings in the sentence. This level of processing can include the semantic disambiguation of words with multiple senses in an analogous way. For example, amongst other meanings, "file" as a noun can mean either a folder for storing papers, or a tool to shape one's fingernails, or a line of individuals in a queue. The purpose of semantic analysis in our work is to recognize issues or agenda of negotiation. Therefore, software agent picks the issues and

Figure 3. Solution for hybrid negotiation

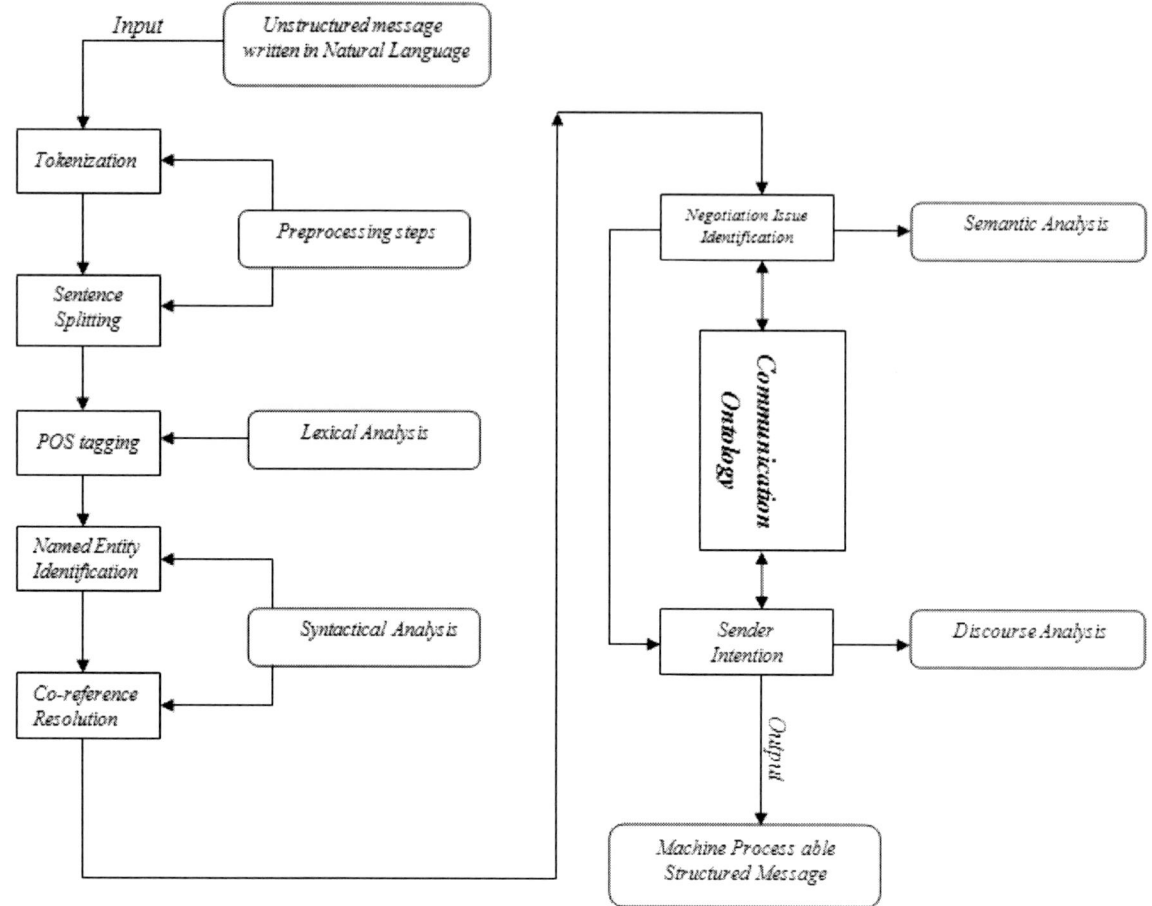

values (against these issues) in the negotiation message and generates a counter offer on the base of these offered values for a response to sender.

At the last level, discourse analysis is performed. Discourse/text structure recognition finds out the purpose of sentences in the text that leads to extraction of meaningful representation of the text. We have used discourse analysis to understand the intention of the sender by categorizing the negotiation message into predefined classes defined in ontology. After applying the systematic processing of different levels of NLP, a structured message is finally achieved. As the structured message is machine interpretable a software agent can respond to the sender of the offer retaining

its own preferences. Therefore, the process of hybrid negotiation continues. We have used GATE framework and a graphical development environment, which enables users to develop and deploy language engineering components and resources in a robust fashion (Cunningham, Maynard, Bontcheva, & Tablan, 2002). GATE is open source software that asserts to be capable of solving almost all text-processing problems. GATE contains numerous plug-ins and resources for NLP tasks, especially for information extraction. Information extraction is a focus of the research work that is to extract information from negotiation content and make meaningful for the software agent.

Challenges and Problems

Language heterogeneity is major issue to achieve hybrid negotiation; on the base of this issue, we have encountered the following challenges for implementation of hybrid negotiation.

- **Structure vs. Flexibility:** Hybrid negotiation is not fully structured. A human uses natural language for communication so in response, it needs valuable and reasonable dialogues.
- **Ambiguity:** Although domain is specific (business domain) and terms have *defined* meaning, ambiguity still exists as the level of interpretation is different (machine vs. human) on both sides.
- **Implicit Meaning:** Terms have defined explicitly in a business domain and both sides share common understanding. However, many things having implicit meaning on either side can create uncertainty.
- **Contextual Meaning:** Humans can easily understand and continue negotiation while considering context of conversation, but this is difficult for agents. They can interpret and even show rational behavior better than humans show. However, to do the things using common sense may be a problem for them.
- **Strategy of Intelligent Agent:** A human can easily con the intelligent agent if he learns the intelligent agent's behavior or strategy and can get most of the negotiation deal. Therefore, security may also be an issue.

The first issue is to choose structure vs. flexibility. We need to provide flexibility (to support the human) in hybrid negotiation to preserve dynamic and vibrant changes. A structured approach (to support the software agent) is needed on the other hand in complex electronic negotiation. It is necessary for instantly recognizable and clear conciliation to reach a successful agreement. Flexibility can be supported up to a reasonable extent. Conversely, too much flexibility may arise many chatty problems, as possibly expected ambiguity of utterances may reveal the intentions of the negotiator. Therefore, in hybrid negotiation, a common middle ground is required. NSS (Negotiation support system) provides this middle ground. A small introduction of two NSSs can clear flexibility vs. rigidly structured. NSS can be chosen according to the problem scenario and the negotiator's preference.

The negotiation support system "inspire" focuses on structured negotiations and implements negotiations for only pre-defined problem scenarios. Every negotiation item is specified with all possible alternate values. Negotiators exchange documents (representing new counter-offers) that consists only of pre-defined negotiation items. Furthermore, each message has a text field that can fill with comments, questions and explanations by negotiators (Schoop & Jertila, 2004).

The negotiation support system "Negoisst" facilitates for flexible negotiation by allowing the exchange of semi structured messages. It provides a facility to write messages in natural language to retain flexibility. Structured ontologies define common background to avoid communication problems and to enable formal reasoning about the communicative content (Schoop & Jertila, 2004). See Figure 4.

The second and third issues are "ambiguity" and "implicit meaning of terms." Ontology can be helpful in resolving the problem of ambiguity and implicit meaning on either side of negotiation. "Ontology is a formal, explicit specification of a shared conceptualization. A 'conceptualization' refers to an abstract model of some phenomenon in the world by having identified the relevant concepts of that phenomenon. 'Explicit' means that the type of concepts used and the constraints on their use are explicitly defined. 'Formal' refers to the fact that the ontology should be machine readable, which excludes natural language.

Figure 4. Negoisst message window shows structured (on top right by the name of "agenda"), semi structured content (bottom left) and meta data (message detail on top left) (Schoop M., The Negoisst System Tutorial, 2008)

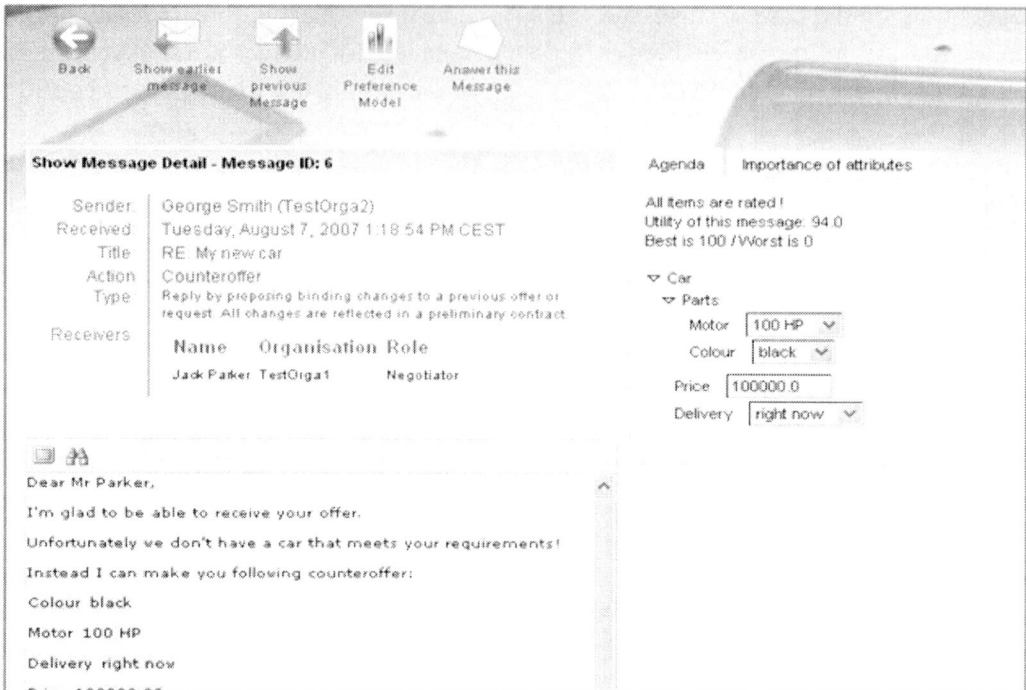

'Shared' reflects that ontology captures consensual knowledge i.e., it is not private to some individual but accepted by a group" (Staab & Studer, 2009). Ontology makes the terms and provisions semantically meaningful and understandable for software agents. Negotiations consist of a large number of communicative acts that are exchanged during negotiation (Schoop & Jertila, 2004). Prime need is that the negotiations parameters find a common background to interact efficiently. Shared understanding provides vocabulary to the human and software agent to carry on negotiations. Confusion may be involved without ontology and can detract the conciliation because the agent and human may misunderstand a term. Ontology ensures the agents are referring to exactly the same good. It is easy to specify a compact disc but to distinguish an automobile, or a food product, or a delivery schedule may be a relatively complex task. Many give-and-take

negotiations, attributes such as delivery time, delivery quantity, batch quality and financing terms are up for debate. In addition, to evaluate the tradeoffs and implications of all these variables is crucial for the software agent (Beam & Segev, 1997).

Ontology provides inter common lay to both negotiators. Schoop and Jertila (2004) give concepts of ontology to support the negotiation process as a whole. The application ontology describes the possible workflow of the negotiation. It specifies the negotiation protocol by describing the conditions for interaction between the negotiators and the permitted sequences. The contract ontology is the initial ontology that contains a set of general concepts that can be used for each contract negotiation. This ontology is the base for each ontology refinement. The contract ontology contains concepts such as contract partner, client, supplier, service, good, delivery, payment, among others. That represents the main structure of each business contract. The domain ontology is branch specific. It contains specialized concepts related to a defined business domain. The user ontology is a collection of user-specific concepts that have been defined in several negotiations. Ontology is extendable with concepts and relations. Thus, the user ontology contains all concepts that one user requires, including those defined or refined during the ontology negotiation process. Ontology can be extended if during negotiation a term or definition is not present in the negotiation ontology. The negotiator that faces the problem offers this change in ontology to make it more enriching. The negotiator on the other side can accept or reject this change. The whole process is called ontology refinement or negotiation over ontology. Ontology-based negotiation approaches enable efficient, complex and unambiguous exchanges that result in business contracts (Schoop & Jertila, 2004).

The fourth issue is processing of natural language content and context. Processing of natural language text is a significant problem in hybrid negotiation. The level of understanding is different on both sides. The software agent can only perform this negotiation when:

- It will be able to understand natural language conversation (in relevant domain);
- It can generate a reasonable reply based on the understanding of human offer or message (dialogues, arguments, counter offers).

The negotiation process can be divided into three phases in Table 1 (Kersten & Noronha, 1999). Focusing on the negotiation phase from the above three phases, structured negotiation can be handled using ontology and predefined rules. Only specific words (offers, counter offers, sender, receiver, timing, delivery, etc.) and values are used in structured negotiation. These words have defined and fixed meanings in the domain.

Table 1. Three phases of negotiation process

Pre-Negotiation	Negotiation	Post-Settlement
Negotiation problem Issues and option rating Preference verification Utility construction	Offer Construction Offer Submission Message composition and submission Counter offer analysis Revision of ratings Update utility Negotiation history	Assess Compromise Efficiency analysis Joint improvement Negotiation review

However, unstructured and semi structured negotiations need processing of both content and context of natural language.

Therefore, to make a natural language negotiation message understandable for a software agent, we need:

- Processing of content (syntactic processing).
- Processing of context (semantic processing).

The software agent can process natural language content only if it is in structured form. On the other hand, negotiation content is unstructured and does not contain semantics (Rehman & Riaz, 2011). Therefore, it requires machine interpretable semantics (structured form) to process natural language text by software agent. These machine interpretable semantics can be attached using NLP. NLP techniques such as information extraction, disambiguation, term recognition, and others, give meaning to unstructured text (Rehman & Riaz, 2011).

HUMAN-AGENT COMMUNICATION

Following is a step by step discussion to syntactically process natural language content. Because the underlying problem is hybrid business negotiation, the content of a negotiation message (taken by the scenario discussed above) sent by human to software agent has processed here.

Tokenization

Tokenization or word segmentation is breaking up the given text into small units called tokens. These units may be different types (upper or lower case) of words, numbers and punctuation marks. It is a basic linguistic analysis step. Tokenization is a mature field of linguistic processing. It is a preprocessing step for further analysis. It is performed on the base of word boundaries. Boundaries can be recognized from the ending point of one world to the starting point of the next adjacent word. The simple looking task is not always simple because the word boundaries are not always easily distinguishable. Challenges to tokenization depend upon language. For example, English, Urdu, and French use spaces between words, so each word is identifiable separately. However, many other languages such as Chinese, Arabic, and Thai do not use any space to separate the words. Therefore, to distinguish word boundaries and make tokens is relatively difficult for these languages.

Figure 5 is a screenshot of "Tokenization" of a negotiation message sent to a software agent by a human. The top right corner of the figure shows the annotation set "Token"; the left side shows a tokenized message and the table at the bottom represents features of tokenized words. For example, the highlighted word "Dear" has kind "word," length is "four" and it is "Upperinitial."

Sentence Splitting

Sentence splitting is to divide a paragraph or chunk of text into its small components (sentences), such that each component conveys meaning. Sentence splitting is a substantial step to develop most of the NLP systems. Generally, sentence splitting is performed on the base of full stop, because in many languages full stop represents the end of a sentence. However, in some cases it may be complex. Its complexity depends upon language used and nature of the text (domain to which it belongs). For example, in English (which mostly use full stop to end the sentences), a full stop does not always show a sentence ending. Many abbreviated words include full stop such as "Mr." and "Mrs." among others. Similarly, text from specific domains can also frequently use dots (full stop) such as abbreviations used in biomedical and

Figure 5. Tokenization

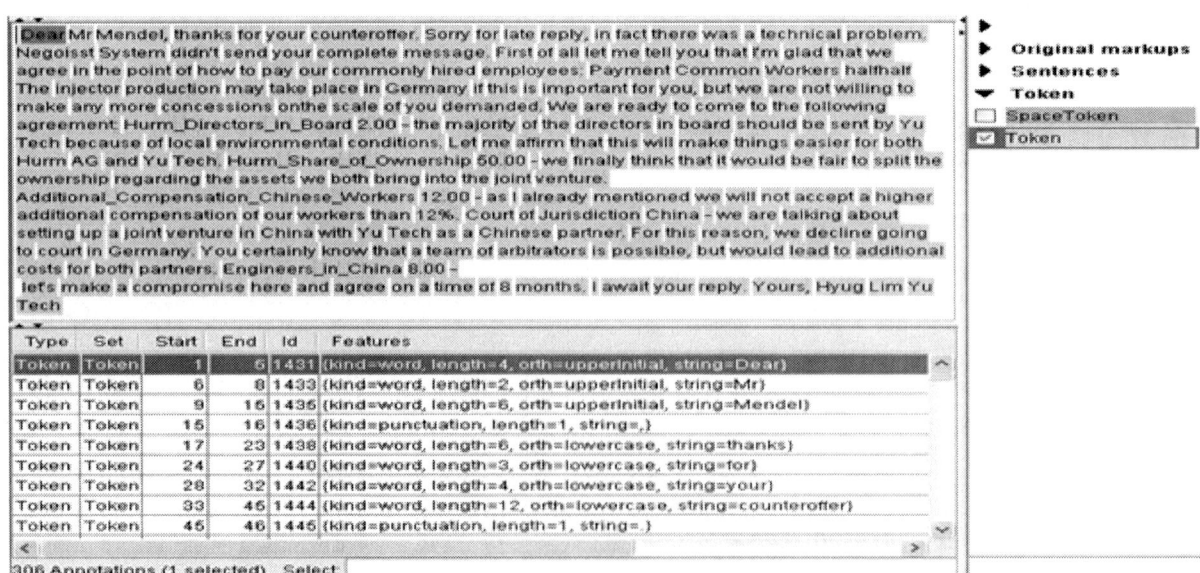

other life sciences. Figure 6 shows a screenshot of sentence splitting of a previously tokenized negotiation message.

POS Tagging

Parts of speech tagging (POS tagging), also called grammatical tagging or word categorization is the process of tagging the words in a text by attaching parts of speech recognition, based on both its definition, as well as its context (i.e., relationship with adjacent and related words in a phrase, sentence, or paragraph). Table 2 shows an example.

Besides the example discussed above, POS tagging may be uncertain and complex because with some words more than one, parts of speech can be attached at different times, and some parts of speech are composite and tacit. Because natu-ral language is highly ambiguous and rich, words and the way of their use can often make POS tagging confusing. For example:

The bandage was wound around the wound.

Here first "wound" is a verb, whereas, second "wound" is a noun object. Therefore, to categorize the words correctly, both syntactic and semantic analysis is required. Figure 7 shows the result of POS tagging performed on a negotiation message.

In Figure 7, POS has represented under the annotation set "message POS". For example, a highlighted token "Mendel" has assigned, "NNP" as POS tag. NNP represents a proper noun, as Mendel is a person's name, so it falls under the category of proper noun.

Figure 6. Sentence splitting

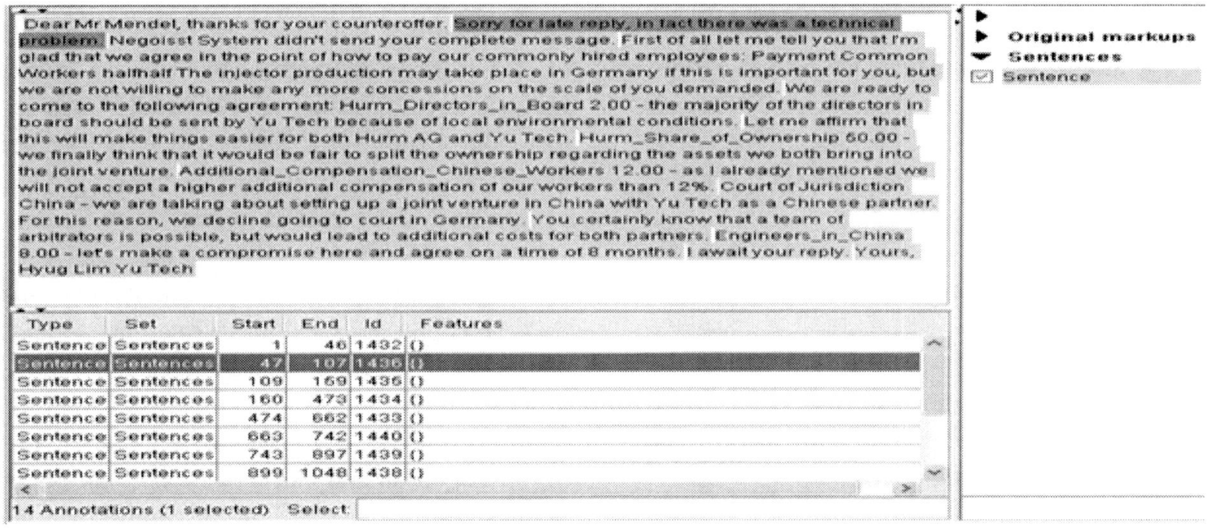

Table 2. Asian foods are delicious but acidic.

Parts of Speech Tagging				
Asian Foods	*are*	*delicious*	*but*	*acidic*
Noun Subject	Helping verb	Adjective	Conjunction	Adjective

Figure 7. POS tagging

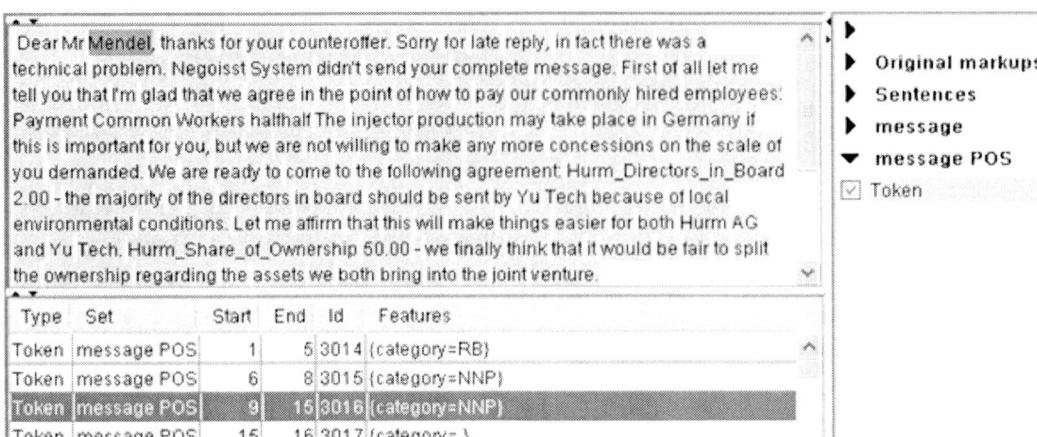

Named Entity Recognition

Named entity recognition (NER), also known as entity identification and entity extraction, is a sub task of Information Extraction. It searches for the atomic named entities in text and assigns them to predefined categories, such as the names of persons, organizations, locations, expressions of times, quantities, financial values, percentages, and others. For example:

Danial lives in Lahore. He works there in National Bank.

Here an NER system can recognize nouns "Danial" as a person, "Lahore" as a location, and "National Bank" as an organization. Or:

Ali bought got admission in Govt. College University in 2009.

Again here, an NER system will recognize noun entities and identify "Ali" as a person,

"Govt. College" as an organization and "2009" as an expression of time.

Named Entity Recognition is almost 20 years old filed that was observed when Sixth Message Understanding Conference (MUC-6) was trying the Information Extraction (IE) tasks to extract the structured information of company activities from the unstructured text such as newspaper articles (Grishman, 1996). In defining the task, people observed that it is crucial to be familiar with information units like names, including person, organization and location names, and numeric expressions including time, date, money, and percent expressions. Identifying mentions of these entities in text was known as one of the vital sub-tasks of IE and was called "Named Entity Recognition and Classification" (Nadeau & Sekine, 2007). Figure 8 shows a screenshot of the negotiation message that has been processed by the NER system. All the tokens of type "person," "location" and "organization" has been tagged. The table at bottom of the figure shows features of each tagged entity.

Figure 8. Named entity recognition

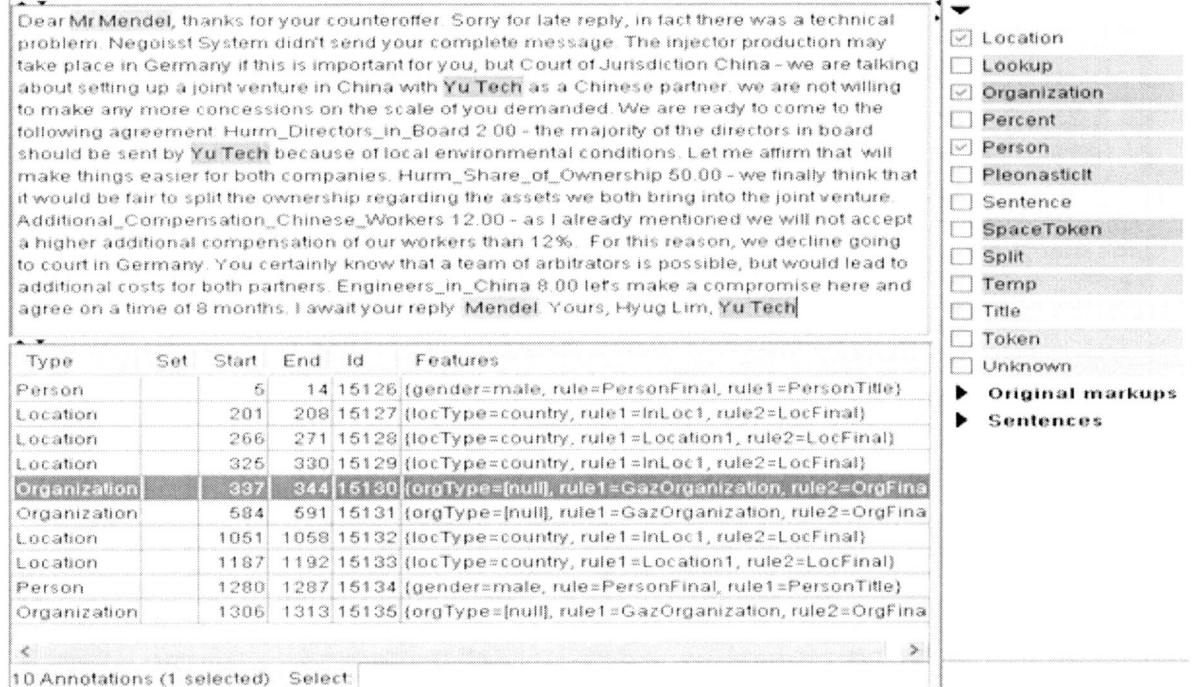

Co-Reference Resolution

It is the process of determining, whether two expressions in natural language refers to the same entity in the world (Soon, Ng, & Lim, 2001). Noun entities (person, location, organization, etc.) tagged in the NER system may ambiguously appear in text at various places. The problem of identifying, whether different entity mentions are pointing the same concept (or they have same referent) is resolved by co-reference resolution. It is an important task in natural language processing systems. For example, in the previous example, "Danial lives in Lahore. He works there in National Bank." "Danial" and "Lahore" both are referring to the same person, so they are co referent.

However, this is a typical case. In this sentence, the noun was introduced before its use so it illustrates a clear reference. There may be other ambiguous cases, for example; "Danial said he would take insurance policy." The most likely perception is "Danial" and "he" are referring to

the same person, "he" could instead refer to someone else (may be someone introduced earlier in a dialog). Co-reference resolving algorithms first seek for the nearest foregoing word which is best fit to the referring expression. For example, "he" might attach to a preceding expression such as "the man" or "Danial" but not to "Mary" (female). The co-reference resolution task is challenging, requiring a human or automated reader to identify "mentions" and link them to an underlying set of referents. Human readers use syntactic and semantic cues to identify and disambiguate the referring phrases. A successful automated system must replicate this behavior by linking mentions that refer to the same underlying entity (Huang, Liang, Lai, & Lin, 2010). Identifying relations between named entities can provide tracking of noun elements and ontological information; that will further lead to scenario building. Therefore, the co-reference resolution becomes the basis for the further semantic processing. Figure 9 shows a co-reference resolution of a preprocessed mes-

Figure 9. Co-reference resolution

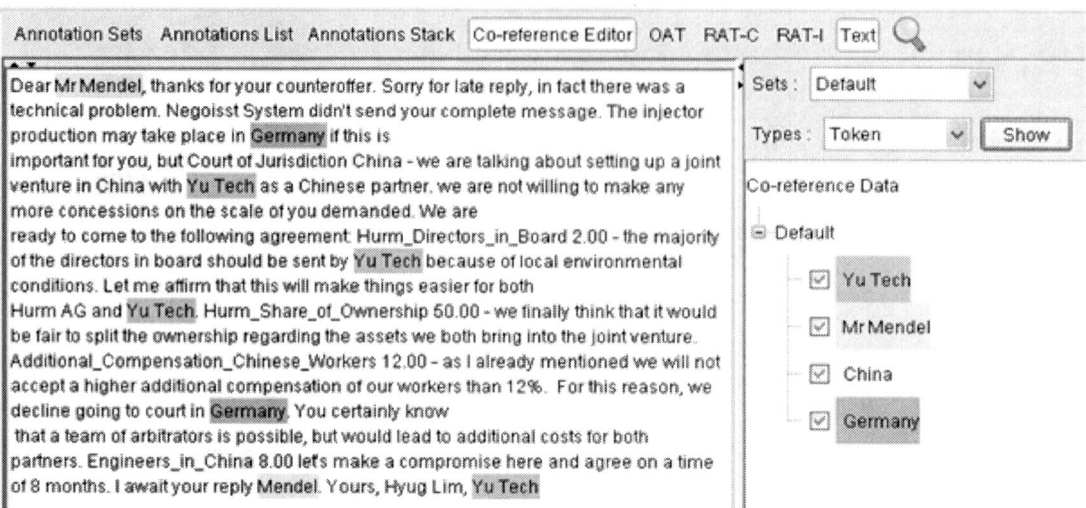

sage. The co-reference module has gathered all the entities of the same type under one tag set.

To process negotiation context (or understand a sender's intention), a message can be analyzed by dividing it into nine content categories (Auer-Srnka & Koeszegi, 2007). These categories are helpful for negotiating agents to identify and recognize different terms and their context used in negotiation content. These categories describe communicative behavior, actions, expectations and expressions through communication units. Negotiation content is supposed to be a set or collection of communication units. A communication unit or unit of analysis may be verb-object sequence, an entire sentence, one world, or even just one sign that conveys one single thought of the negotiator. Following are the main categories.

- **Substantive Communication Units:** Represent primary negotiation behavior such as offers and counteroffers, concessions, logrolling, agreement, rejection, etc.
- **Task-Oriented Communication Units:** Assist for problem solving such as requesting or providing information.

- **Persuasive Communication Units:** Hold up the negotiation attitude of the negotiator such as convincing arguments.
- **Tactical Communication Units:** Control the expectations and actions of the opponent. These include threats, commitments, excuses, promises, etc.
- **Affective Communication Units:** Express feelings about the content, the opponent or the bargaining situation. They show positive or negative emotions, apology or regret, etc.
- **Private Communication Units:** Take account of speech acts that do not talk directly about the negotiation task itself.
- **Procedural Communication Units:** The statements about the negotiation process, such as "I will reach at 10:00 am at Friday morning."
- **Formality Communication Protocol:** The polite formal wording such as greeting and welcome statements at the start and end of the negotiation message.
- **Text-Specific Communication Units:** Mostly associated with written electronic

communication. For example, these units include text-specific elements like fillers "anyhow", or text structuring elements like "p.s." or "e.g."

Attaching a category tag with each sentence of message text can help software agent to understand hidden intention of human so that it can behave accordingly.

The fifth issue is negotiation strategy. The software agent will suffer considerable disadvantage if the corresponding agent becomes familiar with its negotiation strategy (Beam & Segev, 1997). For example, if the human agent (suppose buyer) knows the intelligent agent's strategy, that is threshold frequency for accepting the number of offers and generating counter offers. It can start from minimum value and increase very slightly until a frequency value is met. The agent has to accept the offers according to strategy after the frequency threshold is met. The intelligent agent will suffer a significant loss in this case. Similarly is the other case; let's suppose the seller is a human agent and the buyer is an intelligent agent. The seller can strictly make the buyer "a take or leave" offer if he learns the buyer's willingness to pay and can extract the buyer's entire surplus (Varian, 1995). But we have allocated final control to the human, so he/she can get the best advantages of agent assistance but the corresponding human agent can't con the intelligent agent by knowing about strategy.

FUTURE RESEARCH DIRECTIONS

Future research involves integration of the processing steps discussed in the fourth issue (processing of natural language content and context). It also involves practical implementation of "communication ontology" on hybrid negotiation. Especially, it will deal with:

- Communication ontology covering above discussed scenario of electronic business.
- Categorization of message content by nine content categories (discussed above) through ontology.
- Recognition of negotiation issues from message content.

Therefore, software agents might be able to communicate with human using high-level language (natural language). Moreover, unstructured negotiations might possible between human and agents. Electronic business may achieve more reliability after having this research complete successfully.

CONCLUSION

The rapidly changing environment of electronic business needs new reliable assistance to continue its way to success because notions and terms have changed. The market has changed into a "digital market." Products are more likely called "customized products." "Web 2.0" has a step forward to "Web 3.0" or "Semantic Web." Moreover, a computer is now no more for the use of back end activities (e.g., storage and retrieval of files and data). Now it's used for direct, lively, one-to-one interaction with the customer. Therefore, the first thing is, the key to success is "agility." The second thing is "ubiquitous Web" has changed the requirements and outputs. Now the customer's needs are not limited to manually go and buy from the stores and markets. There is also the need to maintain a live interactive behavior (regarding comments, questions, customer requirements, etc.) with customers. In short, success in the e-commerce is "to show more communicative and interactive behavior," "agility" and "get updated about customer interest." Therefore, to meet these continuously changing electronic business requirements, intelligent software agents are the most promising solution. Hybrid negotiation provides a view of how they can perform electronic business activities. More research effort in this perspective may push the electronic business to a new horizon.

REFERENCES

Antoniou, G., & Harmelen, F. V. (2008). *A semantic web primer* (2nd ed.). Cambridge, MA: MIT press.

Auer-Srnka, K. J., & Koeszegi, S. (2007). From Words to Numbers: How to Transform Qualitative Data into Meaningful Quantitative Results. *Journal of Schmalenbach Business Review*, *59*, 29–57.

Beam, C., & Segev, A. (1997). Automated Negotiations: A Survey of the State of the Art. *Journal of Wirtschafts-informatik*, *39*(3), 263–268.

Berners-Lee, T., Hendler, J., & Lassila, O. (2001). The Semantic Web. *Scientific American*, *284*(5), 34–43. doi:10.1038/scientificamerican0501-34

Bichler, M., Kersten, G., & Strecker, S. (2003). Towards a structured design of electronic negotiations. *Journal of Group Decision And Negotiation*, *12*(4), 311–335. doi:10.1023/A:1024867820235

Braun, P., Brzostowski, J., Kersten, G., Kim, J., Kowalczyk, R., & Strecker, S. (2006). Electronic negotiation Systems and Software Agents: Methods, Models, and Applications. In *Intelligent Decision-making Support Systems* (pp. 271–300). London: Springer. doi:10.1007/1-84628-231-4_15

Chou, C. L. (2007). From World Wide Web to Semantic Web. In Li, E., & Du, T. (Eds.), *Advances in Electronic Business* (*Vol. 2*, pp. 1–30). Hershey, PA: Idea Group Publishing.

Cunningham, H., Maynard, D., Bontcheva, K., & Tablan, V. (2002). GATE: A Framework and Graphical Development Environment for Robust NLP Tools and Applications. In *Proceedings of the 40th Anniversary Meeting of the Association for Computational Linguistics* (pp. 349-373.). Philadelphia, PA.

Feigenbaum, L., Herman, I., Hongsermeier, T., Neumann, E., & Stephens, S. (2007). The Semantic Web in Action. *Scientific American Magazine*, *297*, 64–71. doi:10.1038/scientificamerican1207-90

Grishman, R. (1996). Message Understanding Conference-6: A brief history. *In Proceedings of the 16th Conference on Computational Linguistics* (pp. 466-471). Stroudsburg, PA: Association for Computational Linguistics Press.

Hertweck, B. M., Rakes, T. R., & Rees, L. P. (2010). Using an Intelligent agent to classify competitor behavior and develop an effective E-market counterstrategy. *Expert Systems with Applications: An International Journal*, *37*(12), 8841–8849. doi:10.1016/j.eswa.2010.06.013

Hoffman, D. L., Novak, T. P., & Chatterjee, P. (2000). Commercial Scenarios for the Web: Opportunities and Challenges. *Journal of Computer-Mediated Communication*, *1*(3), 107–136.

Horrigan, J. (2008). *Online Shopping*. Washington, DC: Pew Internet & American Life Project Report.

Horwitt, E. (2011). *The semantic Web gets down to business*. Retrieved October 30, 2011, from http://www.computerworld.com/s/article/9209118/The_semantic_Web_gets_down_to_business

Huang, C., Liang, W., Lai, Y., & Lin, Y. (2010). The agent-based negotiation process for B2C e-commerce. *Expert Systems with Applications*, *37*(1), 348–359. doi:10.1016/j.eswa.2009.05.065

Kersten, G. E., & Noronha, S. J. (1999). WWW-based negotiation support: Design, implementation, and use. *Decision Support Systems*, *25*(2), 135–154. doi:10.1016/S0167-9236(99)00012-3

Klusch, M. (2005). Agent-Mediated Trading: Intelligent Agents and Electronic business. In Hayzelden, A. L., & Bourne, R. A. (Eds.), *Agent Technology for Communication Infrastructures* (pp. 59–76). Chichester, UK: John Wiley & Sons.

Kowalczyk, R. U. (2010). Integrating Mobile and Intelligent Agents in Advanced E-commerce: A Survey. In J. Carbonell, J. Siekmann, R. Kowalczyk, J. Müller, H. Tianfield., & R. Unland (Eds.), *Lecture Notes In Computer Science LNCS 2592*. Berlin: Springer.

Lau, R. Y. (2007). Towards a web services and intelligent agents-based negotiation system for B2B eCommerce. *Journal of Electronic Commerce Research and Applications*, *6*(3), 260–273. doi:10.1016/j.elerap.2006.06.007

Liddy, E. D. (2001). Natural Language Processing. In *Encyclopedia of Library and Information Science* (2nd ed.). New York: Marcel Decker, Inc.

Lin, R., & Kraus, S. (2010). Can automated agents proficiently negotiate with each other? *Communications of the ACM*, *53*(1), 78–88. doi:10.1145/1629175.1629199

Lytras, M., & Garcia, R. (2008). Semantic Web applications: A framework for industry and business exploitation. *International Journal of Knowledge and Learning*, *4*(1), 93–108. doi:10.1504/IJKL.2008.019739

Maes, P., Guttman, R., & Moukas, A. (1999). Agents that Buy and Sell. *Communications of the ACM*, *42*(3), 81–92. doi:10.1145/295685.295716

Nadeau, D., & Sekine, S. (2007). A survey of named entity recognition and classification. *Journal of Lingvisticae Investigationes*, *30*(1), 3–26. doi:10.1075/li.30.1.03nad

Negri, A., Poggi, A., Turci, P., & Tomaiuolo, M. (2006). Agents for electronic business applications. In *Proceedings of the 5th International Joint Conference on Autonomous Agents and Multiagent Systems* (pp. 907 - 914). New York: ACM.

Papazoglou, M. P. (2001). Agent-oriented technology in support of electronic business. *Communications of the ACM*, *44*(4), 71–77. doi:10.1145/367211.367268

Pell, B. (2007). *POWERSET - Natural Language and the Semantic Web*. Presented at 6th International Semantic Web Conference. Busan, South Korea. Retrieved January 10, 2011, from http://videolectures.net/iswc07_pell_nlpsw/

Peter, F. (1998). *A CEO's Guide to eCommerce Using Object-Oriented Intelligent Agent*. Retrieved December 29, 2011, from http://home1.gte.net/pfingar/eba.htm

Rehman, M., & Riaz, N. (2011). A Preliminary Framework For Human-Agent Communication. In *Proceedings of the 2011 International Conference on Information and Communication Technologies* (pp. 95-100). Karachi, Pakistan: IBA Karachi.

Schoop, M. (2008). *The Negoisst System Tutorial*. Retrieved March 22, 2012, from http://negoisst.wi1.uni-hohenheim.de/Negoisst2/faces/documents/Tutorial.pdf

Schoop, M., & Jertila, A. (2004). Electronic Commerce in the Semantic Web Era. In M. Bichler, C. Holtmann, S. Kirn, J.P. Müller., & C. Weinhardt (Eds.), *Coordination and Agent Technology in Value Networks*. Essen, Germany: Multikonferenz Wirtschaftsinformatik.

Schoop, M., Jertila, A., & List, T. (2003). Negoisst: A Negotiation Support System for Electronic Business-to-Business Negotiations in E-Commerce. *Data & Knowledge Engineering*, 371–401. doi:10.1016/S0169-023X(03)00065-X

Singh, R., Iyer, L. S., Salam, A., & Editors, G. (2005). The Semantic Electronic business Vision. *Communications of the ACM, 48*(4), 38–42. doi:10.1145/1101779.1101806

Soon, W. M., Ng, H. T., & Lim, D. C. (2001). A Machine Learning Approach to Coreference Resolution of Noun Phrases. *Computational Linguistics - Special Issue on Computational Anaphora Resolution, 27*(4), 521-544.

Staab, S., & Studer, R. (Eds.). (2009). *Handbook on Ontologies* (2nd ed.). New York: Springer. doi:10.1007/978-3-540-92673-3

Varian, H. R. (1995). Economic mechanism design for computerized agents. In *Proceedings of the 1st Conference on USENIX Workshop on Electronic Commerce* (pp. 13-21). Berkeley, CA: USENIX Association Berkeley.

ADDITIONAL READING

Benyoucef, M., Alg, H., & Keller, R. (2001). An Infrastructure for Rule-Driven Negotiating Software agents. *Proceedings of the 12th International Workshop on Database and Expert Systems Applications*, Munich, Germany: Institute of Electrical and Electronics Engineers.

Berners-Lee, J. H. (2010). From the Semantic web to social machines: A research challenge for AI on the World Wide Web. *Artificial Intelligence, 174*(2), 156–161. doi:10.1016/j.artint.2009.11.010

Berners-Lee, T. H. (2001). Publishing on the semantic web. *Nature*, 1023–1025. doi:10.1038/35074206

Bizer, C., Heath, T., & Berners-Lee, T. (2009). Linked Data - The Story So Far. *International Journal on Semantic Web and Information Systems, 5*(3), 1–22. doi:10.4018/jswis.2009081901

Chen, E., Kersten, G., & Vahidov, R. (2005). Agent-supported negotiations in the e-marketplace. *International Journal of Electronic Business, 3*(1), 28–49. doi:10.1504/IJEB.2005.006387

Hendler, J. (2001). Agents and the Semantic web. *IEEE Intelligent Systems, 16*(2), 30–37. doi:10.1109/5254.920597

Hepp, M., Leymann, M., Domingue, J., & Wahler, A. (2005). Semantic business process management: A vision towards using semantic web services for business process management. *IEEE International Conference on electronic business engineering*, Beijing, China: IEEE.

Huang, P., & Sycara, K. (2002). Computational Model for Online Agent Negotiation. In *Proceedings of 35th Annual Hawaii International Conference on System Sciences Vol 1*. Washington, DC: IEEE.

Kim, H., Kim, W., & Lee, M. (2009). Semantic web Constraint Language and its application to an intelligent shopping agent. *Decision Support Systems, 46*(4), 882–894. doi:10.1016/j.dss.2008.12.004

Krishna, V., & Ramesh, V. C. (1998). Intelligent agents for Negotiations in Market Games. *IEEE Transactions On Power Systems PWRS, 13*(3), 1103–1108. doi:10.1109/59.709106

Li, E., & Du, T. C. (2007). *Advances in Electronic Business* (Vol. 2, pp. 1–344). Hershey, PA: IGI Global.

Li, E., & Yuan, S. (2008). *Agent Systems in Electronic Business*. Hershey, PA: IGI Global.

Li, E. Y., & Du, T. C. (2005). Collaborative Commerce. In Li, E., & Du, T. (Eds.), *Advances in Electronic Business* (Vol. 1, pp. 1–18). Hershey, PA: Idea Group Publishing.

Liang, W.-Y. (2011). The Assessment of Intelligent agent in the B2C. In *Proceedings of International MulitiConference of Engineers and Computer Scientists* (pp. 69–72). Hong Kong: IMECS.

Lin, R. J., & Chou, S. T. (2008). Agent based matching of demands and supplies in business transaction formation. In Li, E., & Yuan, S. (Eds.), *Agent Systems in Electronic Business*. Hershey, PA: IGI Global.

Luo, X. M. (2011). KEMNAD: A Knowledge Engineering Methodology for Negotiating Agent Development. *Computational Intelligence, 28*(1), 1–47.

Michael, S., & Christof, W. (2003). The Montreal Taxonomy for Electronic Negotiations. *Group Decision and Negotiation, 12*(2), 143–164. doi:10.1023/A:1023072922126

Rahwan, I., Kowalczyk, R., & Pham, H. (2002). Intelligent agents for automated one-to-many e-commerce negotiation. In *Proceedings of the 25th Australasian Conference on Computer Science* (pp. 197-204). Darlinghurst, Australia: Australian Computer Society, Inc.

Robert, K., Lai, & Lin, M. (2004). Modeling Agent Negotiation Via Fuzzy Constraints in Electronic business. *Computational Intelligence, 20*(4), 624–642. doi:10.1111/j.0824-7935.2004.00257.x

Schoop, M., & Quix, C. (2001). DOC.COM: A framework for effective negotiation support in electronic marketplaces. *Electronic Business Systems, 37*(2), 153–170.

Shadbolt, N., Berners-Lee, T., & Hall, W. (2006). The Semantic web Revisited. *Intelligent Systems, IEEE, 21*(3), 96–101. doi:10.1109/MIS.2006.62

Sheila, A., & McIlraith, T. C. (2001). Semantic web Services. *IEEE Intelligent Systems And Their Applications, 16*(2), 46–53. doi:10.1109/5254.920599

Weigand, H., Schoop, M., Moor, A., & Dignum, F. (2003). B2B Negotiation Support: The Need for a Communication Perspective. *Group Decision and Negotiation, 12*(1), 3–29. doi:10.1023/A:1022294708789

Yen, H. L. (2008). Understanding the Gap between Website Value and Consumer Shopping Orientation: An Application of Task-Technology Fit Theory to Online shopping Values. In *Proceedings of the 8th International Conference on Electronic Business*. Big Island, Hawaii.

Zhang, S., Ye, S., Makedon, F., & Ford, J. (2004). A hybrid negotiation strategy mechanism in an automated negotiation system. In *Proceedings of the 5th ACM conference on Electronic commerce* New York: ACM.

KEY TERMS AND DEFINITIONS

Electronic Negotiation: Uses the electronic technologies such as computer, internet, information systems, etc. It may human-to-human, agent-to-agent or hybrid.

Formal Meaning: Conveyed through annotations or ontology, which is process able and understandable by machines (software agents).

Human Master: Intelligent agent is not fully autonomous; a human master or principal governs it. It acts according to instructions and preferences of that human master.

Hybrid Negotiation: Negotiation occurring between human and intelligent software agent.

Negotiation Content: Dialogues and offers exchanged between a human and an intelligent agent.

Shared Concepts: Shared elements which become the basis for an equal level of thinking and interpretation.

Structured Negotiation: Generally, structured negotiation only uses formally defined terms either in ontology or in agenda.

350

Chapter 18
The Transformative Effect of Social Media:
Revolutionizing Business Models of Mass Production to Individual Production by the Masses

Anna Farmery
University of Bradford, UK

ABSTRACT

Over the last decade, digital technology in general and social media in particular, has changed the way people interact and communicate. Current day marketers have embraced the technological tools to socialise with the customer but those tools are now spreading across e-business and breaking down the traditional business walls. It is argued in this chapter that social media is now transforming into a wider ``social business' concept with marketing being just one element of the potential social relationship between business and consumer. Using the emergence of 3D printing as an example, this chapter highlight how the consumer is not only gaining the power of voice, but also the power of production. It discusses the potential effects on future commercial revenue streams and what business needs to do today to protect their economic value and business model of tomorrow. It argues that this transformative technology should not be seen as a threat to business but an opportunity to create a revolutionary social business model with the customer.

INTRODUCTION

When the forerunner of the Internet was born, the goal was protection, securing information from military attack through the distribution of data across many computers. When Tim Berners-Lee developed the World Wide Web he replaced this goal of protecting data packets with a web of information, so that 'any person could share information with anyone else, anywhere' (Berners-Lee, 2010). There was no major risk to the business value creation model rather an opportunity for the creation of a further channel to market.

DOI: 10.4018/978-1-4666-4026-9.ch018

However, the emergence of social media technology over the last decade has established a new closer relationship between business and customers. Although Beer and Burrows (2007) talk of changing relations between production and consumption of Internet content, these are in relation to the marketing strategies of companies, not the value creation model itself. In effect in creating digital interfaces, it has created the opportunity of 'mass communication at an individual level', termed the power of the voice (Levine et al., 2000).

This chapter will argue that the next technological evolution has an even greater potential to destroy the wall between the consumer and business. The epochs of business models have already come through the Iron Age, the Renaissance, the Industrial Revolutions, the computer age, and now there is potentially one of social business.

Social media has created digital interfaces, strengthened not just by accessibility but also through conversations. However these added social elements have centered on communication and collaborative tools, creating a socialization of the business relationship, which can be defined as the first step on the way to a truly social business model. This transformation to a social relationship has brought risks, but the risks have been more cultural rather than legal or ethical; the risks have not challenged the very foundations of the traditional business model, but rather the architectural style of doing business. This next social business transformation could shake the very foundations of the traditional business model itself, however for those who recognize the move from social marketing to social business early, then the next stage could be the biggest opportunity of all.

There are many technological advances that could be used as a way of illustrating the move to a social business model. 3D printing has been chosen, as it is an existing and proven technology, which is now capable of socializing the business process to an even greater level. It is a technology which may be less researched or understood but could it could be the most revolutionary of all. It will be used as an example of how the customer will need to be incorporated into a 'social business model' because the very essence of traditional value creation is under threat. The challenge for business is not how to prevent it from happening, but how to make value creation work over the next decade.

The aim of this chapter is to start a discussion on how to evolve to this social business model. It will provide insights into what is creating this change and how business can embrace this new social model; one that creates opportunities for both the individual and the businesses. In summary, using the example of 3D printing as a technology that enables social production, the goal of this chapter will be to highlight:

- The challenge to future revenue streams through social production.
- Discuss what businesses need to think about today, to protect their value of tomorrow, including how this technology can be used internally to reduce outsourcing processes.
- Highlight ways of creating a social business model with the customer being part of the financial model
- How to learn from how social media has transformed the marketing and customer service process and apply to this new transformative technology.
- Highlight legal changes required to balance the relationship between sharing of intellectual property for societal benefits whilst maintaining corporate ownership and financial benefit for the reinvestment in future ideas for the good of society.

BACKGROUND TO THE NEW SOCIAL BUSINESS REVOLUTION

Wherever life is, it never retreats. (Kelly, 2005)

The words of Kevin Kelly at his TedTalk in 2005; words used to illustrate that as much as we may want to delay the advancement in technology, life has an inert evolutionary power, a power that over the last few years has seen the merging of our digital and physical lives. Evolutionary steps, which had seemed impossible in the last decade, are transforming our lives, both individually and corporately. Business may want to stop the socializing of their business model, but the power that the consumer is developing may render this as impossible. The business model will need to change and in some ways has already taken the first steps to this evolution.

Over the last decade the Web 2.0 (O'Reilly, 2005) has provided a voice to each citizen and reduced the world from a few disparate continents to a global village of many potential consumers. For business it has meant creating channels for accessibility and then recently conversational relationships with consumers. For business, one could argue this has been a positive move and bringing an extension of their markets and the emergence of the e-business model. It has increased the possible revenue opportunities and it has helped reduce the fixed overhead burden, reducing the need for large advertising spends. The benefits have been great with only more cultural downsides. The move from financial to time investment in attracting their customer, the move from local or national to global competitors and also the move from mass production to individualization, they have all brought complexity to the business model, but not challenged the essence of the 20th Century business model.

The complexity has focused upon the customer relationship management process, which has become a complex mix of social and transactional (socio–transactional process) elements. Influence has been replaced by persuasion. Control replaced with collaboration. Purchasing processes replaced with real-time buying. This intricacy has brought a closer relationship to the consumer market but the consumer remains officially outside the business model, only occasionally invited to share ideas or collaborate on projects from a marketing angle. In essence the first step achieved by Web 2.0 has brought two key communication concepts, which will provide the core stimulus to the future of social production: transparency and speed. The world has a voice; a complaint to friends about service now not only spreads in your local social sphere but also reverberates across the world. Fake claims, incorrect information, bad service can no longer be swept under the carpet or hidden in the annual report, the brand has a window into its soul, and that window is called social media.

A brands reputation is now held to account. Promises made must be delivered and if not, then the transparency and speed of the web will likely inflict financial harm. However, transparency and speed has also created an opportunity for business. If this is embraced then it can make the brand more human and indeed humans will accept mistakes when made by a sincere and authentic humanized brand. Business can use this transparency and speed to transform the way their brand is perceived and connecting on a more personal level, differentiating their brand through the development of a brand personality in order to create shareholder value.

Culture is an integral part of the traditional business model. Culture is the oil in the business engine, it is the driver of how the company operates, and is seen by many as the defining factor on how the company succeeds (Buckingham, 2008). Culture used to be judged by the employees; now that culture is spreading to the consumer, but with the advent of the social production processes, this will extend the idea of culture through the factory gates and directly into the consumer's home. This creates the need to embrace the consumer as part of the business model, no longer a recipient of value but a co-creator of that value. In essence the business model has already had to reflect a greater transparency, flexibility and personality. However, the creation of added value and the generation of profit have remained relatively static with only pricing models augmented through for instance the 'freemium' model (Wilson, 2006).

In this chapter, 3D printing will be used to illustrate how this cultural aspect is spreading outside the business walls. How the business model will now be inclusive of the consumer and when 3D printing allows the printing out of scanned objects, it transforms the concept of mass production for individual consumption to individual production consumed by the masses (Levine et al., 2000). In removing this barrier to production for the masses, business will now need to find a new model of value creation or risk extinction. It is this barrier removal, which means that the social aspect is spreading from communication to production, from marketing to manufacturing. In the same way that social media changed how business communicated, there is a corresponding need for a major intellectual shift in the traditional, well established business concepts of value creation, cost reduction and revenue streams. The prospect of social production could affect the whole business process from ideation to profit generation.

In such economically and technologically turbulent times where nothing is predictable except change itself, how do e-businesses ensure they do not become the corporate dinosaurs of the past century? How do e-businesses change with the times whilst protecting their return on investment? This chapter is the start of that ongoing discussion because as with any new and emerging technologies, the opportunities and threats arising are initially unclear as 3D printing can potentially provide previously inconceivable possibilities.

If an individual can scan a photo and produce a replica object; if an individual has the ability to design and print in any material; if an individual has the ability to 'produce' an idea themselves, 'copy' an idea in the market, or 'purchase' items

not through the established digital businesses process but through their own production capacity, what are the implications for business? Ostensibly it would appear that customers no longer pay for the value-added provided by business production. So how does the business create revenue streams? How do we articulate the transformative leap in conceptual understanding of how e-business models will be affected by 3D printing? There are big questions that need to be discussed in the business world to try and initiate a new way of socializing profit.

The challenge facing business leaders will be to incorporate the security of intellectual property whilst maintaining the social freedom to produce at an individual level. The challenge must be to transform the traditional business model of rewarding the inventor or creator of the idea while embracing the societal shift to social business models. The long established business processes of production and marketing will have limited value. The customer perceptions of value will ultimately shift to the idea itself, rewarding the process of innovation, research, and development, whilst adding the social dimension of the individual consumer production concept.

The new e-business model will need to recognise that the production in itself will not create the value in the product. It will not safeguard the future production of copies made from scanning and 3D printing and it will not necessarily provide future revenue streams as the return on initial investment. Thus the potential solution will be to radically reengineer the value creation model of the future to incorporate the shifting perceptions of value in a world increasingly dominated by social media technology, which is empowering consumers. Just as social media has transformed marketing, then 3D printing will transform both the operational, research and development parts of the business. The value added may no longer be in the idea creation and the production to market cycle but in 'socializing' the profit.

Four Stimuli for Future Social Business Models

There are four societal catalysts, which are further powering the need for a new social business model. These catalysts have been created through the development of technology and now that technology is enabling the consumer to dictate the future direction of business models.

Firstly, social media has undoubtedly created a power shift away from the companies to their consumer (Lovari & Parisi, 2011) It is interesting to note that the impact on society has not been in terms of the content produced, but the medium being used as the message (McLuhan, 1964). In relation to this chapter, this is a pertinent point as the production of content is not as relevant as the effect of the medium used - desktop home production units as a way of replacing factory production.

Secondly, the effect of globalization combined with the power of search brings greater availability, and with that the desire for individualization (Scott, 2011). As people have gained access to a greater array of products, the need for more personalized products has been stimulated. People previously gained that personalization from the locality of accessible products, now mass production creates the necessity for standardized products to keep costs down but human beings now desire individualized products at the same price. For instance one can see people using covers for Kindles as a way of personalizing a mass-produced product.

Thirdly, the banking crisis has encouraged people to be more self-reliant. It has dented trust in capitalism as a model for the future (Haque, 2011) and as technology matures, more applications to benefit society are emerging to further democratize business (Dentchev, 2005).

Finally, mass production at the individual level is now entering the consumer price range creating a trillion dollar business opportunity (Business Insider, 2011)

Traditional business models create profit through adding value; the turning of a concept into production or combining inputs to create the output. The premium is the brand or the intellectual property of the business. This output is supplied to the customer. The customer exchanges money for the right to own or use something that they could either have not created themselves through lack of productive means or through lack of money to fund the production.

In short the transactional exchange has been one of financial value. However it is argued that these four stimuli are changing that exchange model.

Social media has augmented that transactional exchange (O'Reilly & Battelle, 2010). As well as a financial value exchange, there is an exchange of values. Values are based on the social aspect of the brand personality and promise (Bhargava, 2008)

The next stage is moving from a financial value with social values to one of 'value', 'values', and 'valuables.' Once the customer has control of printing out whatever they want, objects are not transactions, they are personal creations, and the social business is now possible (Benkler, 2011).

3D Printing: Advent of Social Production

The next section will summarize why and how additive manufacturing will start to challenge the manufacturing base of the business model and how it has the capacity to add a social element to production, forcing a social business model.

Since the 1970s there has been the manufacturing capability of producing prototypes from a blueprint. The 3D printing technology has been called additive manufacturing, because instead of taking a block of material and trimming until the object is created, this process involves the layering of raw material into the object itself. It is in simple terms vertical rather than horizontal printing.

3D printing has primarily only been used for prototypes because significant investment has been required; investment, which could mean over US$200,000. However, the cost of investment is starting to fall with the cost of printers entering the consumer price range. This ability to buy for under £1,000 creates the possibility of the ultimate niche, a market of one.

Accompanied with this price reduction has been an expansion of materials capable of additive manufacturing. Materials as varied as human tissue to chocolate, from metals to bone structures can all be used in the additive manufacturing process. This powerful combination of lower prices and increased versatility is at the heart of the social production revolution (The Economist, 2011).

It is important to note that the additive process has far reaching benefits for manufacturing internally as well as for home production by the consumers themselves. For instance

- It allows for designs of nano-sized objects and technology to be reproduced.
- It also creates less waste in the production process, as there is no cutting away of material, only layering. This decreases wastage and reduces the cost of production.
- It allows for the creation of objects that have moving, internal mechanisms. Therefore again, reducing the cost of production through reduced or totally eliminated, assembly.
- It removes the need for costly tooling, which needs large production runs, in order to recoup the investment.
- It increases the possibility of mass individualization. There is no significant issue in printing out different versions of the same object—maybe jewelry with different names, or personalized prosthetic limbs for patients.
- It means as the cost of printing machines comes down, the ability to produce becomes accessible to any individual.

Historically the process is used in conjunction with a computer aided design program, however the technology is there now to scan an object and recreate it in physical form. This further reduces the barrier to the wider public. Critically, it increases the possibility of mass individualization meaning that production becomes accessible to any individual.

In short, production, replication, and sharing of physical objects are becoming a reality, causing 2012 to be declared the year of 3D printing (Hart, 2012) and the transformation from the era of mass production to mass production by individuals is underway. Unlike social media technologies, the prospect of social production could affect the whole business process from ideation to profit generation. Indeed, "We at the dawn of the age of sharing where even if you try and sell things the world is going to share it anyway" (Pettis, 2012). When 3D printing can offer society the ability to print out kidneys (Atala, 2011), personalized chocolates, or even spare parts for white goods, then as Malone and Lipson (2007) contend, the 'Factory in your kitchen' is now emerging. Although this creates opportunities for small businesses, it creates risk for the established business model of value creation. If an individual can scan a photo and produce a replica object; if an individual has the ability to design and print in any material; if an individual has the ability to 'produce' an idea themselves, 'copy' an idea in the market, or 'purchase' items through their own production capacity, what can business offer in the way of value?

This technology has followed a similar path to other disruptive technology such as the computer. First there is the breakthrough--a mainframe computer; then as the advancements are made, the technology reduces both in size and price leading, for example, to the desktop being borne. The need to differentiate and apply in different parts of a consumer's life means the laptop, smartphone, and iPad all follow at a relatively quick rate.

The emergence of desktop 3D printers creates an urgent requirement to transfigure the business model to incorporate the security of their intellectual property, whilst maintaining the social freedom to produce at an individual level. Society benefits from the research and development but this is only conducted with the premise of intellectual property rights that reward the business for sharing with the public. Research by Schacht (2000) shows that up to half of the U.S. economic growth is attributed to technological innovation; if you put at risk the revenue gained through the ability to copy and share, then you potentially put at risk the society's continued evolution.

This transfiguration needs three areas of society to recognize this revolution. It needs business to accept that the consumer is no longer dependent on you to create products. It requires government to amend the ethical and legal frameworks to protect society and it needs the academic community to research the definition of the social business model and how the transmogrification can be completed without risking the value creation model, which benefits society.

How to Add the Social Element to 3D Printing

Social is defined as 'needing companionship and therefore best suited to living in communities' (Oxford Dictionary, 2012). At one of my recent seminars of 24 people, people were asked for how they perceived the word social; the replies included: fun, informal, friends, sharing, networking, and friendly. Social is about people; the ability for a community to share, the ability for people to be distinct but to belong and the ability to emote in some way. Therefore in talking about the social aspect to 3D printing it is necessary to see how the social element crystallizes.

In a world in which people are often separated from their family members, imagine the power of being able to print out the family chair you remember from home. Today, 'things' are relatively cheap and because of that can be ephemeral, but 3D printing is a manufacturing capability, which can time shift objects when people miss them; when people regret losing them as individuals can scan a photo and print it out, memories are given life. The individual has gained the power to share not only their opinions and their words but also tangible items, bringing the ability to share real world memories with anyone, anywhere in the world. The social element means that production is more than the creation of objects and more the creation of shared memories and experiences. The joy of creating together and seeing that item produced on a desktop 3D printer enhances the socializing aspect of Web 2.0. 3D desktops can be perceived as socializing the manufacturing process. The question is whether business will invite customers in to socialize, or whether customers will feel through this technology and free of the restrictions businesses often place on them, they feel ready to produce their own objects without business involved.

Social media has through the advent of such digital sharing capabilities of RSS, social networking and micro blogging, helped bring a social element the web but the need to work with a third party can often slow the productive process as the idea still has to be passed over to the third party, for the creation element. Manufacturing indeed is in many ways one of the last bastions of traditional business models. For instance marketing can converse with the customer; research can be conducted online, new designs chosen through the input from the customer and sales made through word of mouth recommendations. The social element to life on the web is not a new behavior but synchronization with how people relate and work in everyday life. Of course many people enjoy solitude but collaboration can also be an important part of production. Collaboration could be across continents, across expertise or even between family members on a memento for a special occasion. Recently our family purchased a photo book that we all contributed to for an 80th celebration. The excitement was tangible waiting for it to arrive, only to find that it had been lost in transit. For all the hard work the gift was almost ruined by the third party.

Imagine if the gift can be worked on together online, imagine if the gift can be personalized to exactly what is required and then printed out there and then. The web will be the enabler to the creation but the final manufacture will potentially lie in the hands of the individuals. This means that sharing is enhanced from words and images to physical objects; it means that the third party is no longer necessity only a potential choice for the consumer.

3D printing allows the individual to take greater control. They don't have to wait for Amazon to deliver a spare part of a replacement object; they can just print out there and then. It is technology that reduces waiting times, feeds into the immediacy need for the modern consumer. It also has a major environmental benefit for the modern consumer because it improves the environmental footprint of modern consumerism by a reduction in traffic costs, wastage, and packaging.

Most notably for the customer it brings simplicity to the process, simplicity from conception from idea to reality and from creation to sharing. A technology based on simplifying a consumers life, is one that becomes commercial; think of the web itself, the dishwasher, the DVD player. This reality may seem futuristic, yet the technology has been working for thirty years; it seems futuristic yet the power of the web means that when a concept becomes wildly known about, it commercializes itself through the sharing capacity of the web. The irony of technology is that it is makes the theoretical impossibilities, possible in reality.

The power of the web cannot be underestimated. It was Larry Page who said that he wanted Google to be the 'ultimate search engine...something as smart as people - or smarter' (Carr, 2008). The goal of creating artificial intelligence is real and as companies such as Google make the web smarter, then people will want even more from the web; not just data but things as well.

There is a naturally inherent social aspect to a web of things that is not about virtual reality or augmenting reality but giving virtual, tangible 'things' a real life. The ironic part of this social evolution is that business is providing the consumer with the ways of bypassing their own business models and are slower to perceive the inherent risk, which the consumer themselves are embracing. People were born to share but business finds the art of sharing more difficult despite being composed of people themselves.

The solutions are happening quicker because of the social element of the web. People are socializing with blogs, networks, micro-blogs etc. and sharing knowledge, information and connections. Connections in the past have been data driven and the web runs through the linkages of that data. However, with the emergence of social networking and the concept of the semantic web, the connections are becoming more specific to 'things" and furthermore it is the person that gives the strength of the connection. 3D printing is not stand-alone technology as previously thought when the barrier was cost and usage; it is becoming an enabler of the sharing of real life.

The 3D printing revolution can only strengthen the connection between individuals, as they cannot only pass the ideas but also the physical objects between themselves. That transfer is done through bits of data not through packaging an item, posting an item, and then being in to receive the item. The 3D printer will make the real world transportable, as the Internet made the conversation possible between global businesses and friends. This concept of the 3D printer being the vehicle for physical objects to move across the web is creating a new semantic concept; a concept of real world linkages through digital data transfer. The semantic web is seen as a linking of things, the 3D printer could be the bridge to a linking of physical items as well as physical data.

It is a strange fact that as much as our networks broaden, as much as we want to be part of a social community on the web, from Facebook to Twitter and from mommy bloggers to forums, we also want to be individuals. We want access to Nike trainers but give our little touch of colour to personalize this mass-produced item. We want access to every record in iTunes to create our own personal album. We want access to millions of hours of video and yet want to create a channel that is specific for our interests. As much as consumers want to belong, they want to be different from the crowd. As much as business wants to benchmark success, they want to differentiate their offering. The world is a dichotomy of contradictions. 3D printing plays into this dichotomy between mass and personal. It brings manufacturing from generic to personal. It takes the barriers to making one of every item ever sold cost effective. It gives the opportunity for Nike to print 60 million different pairs of shoes for the UK population. Individuals are happy that they are seen to be wearing Nike and yet at the same time, stand out from the generic crowd. Significantly the concept of individualization could also be an opportunity from which a new business model could emerge. Social marketing strategist, Hugh Macleod talks about the emphasis on creating a social object (MacLeod, 2009), a social object so that social media can then be used to get people talking about you, a social object is in essence something that has a gossip factor built into it.

A business that develops a social business model that embraces new technology in a social way will be creating a social object. Indeed the social business model may be based on the crowd developing the model themselves. It is here where the social business model starts to take shape. In the past the only limited editions, which although not mass were still substantial in number, could provide some degree of exclusivity. The opportunity for sharing of physical objects seems an obvious next step but presently there are two main blocks to this happening and in a sense create today's business opportunities.

Firstly, the most cost effective way of inputting the blueprint is through computer-aided design. That is a specialized skill and why companies such as Shapeways and Sculpteo are acting as the intermediary between consumer and personal object. However this is only a short-term opportunity, already packages are entering the market, which are starting to build simple user interfaces to computer-aided design.

Secondly, the printers presently only print one material. This is not necessarily an issue for individual items but means that if you buy a printer that uses titanium as the additive material, all your objects will have to be made from titanium. Firms therefore are providing a small range of materials from which the consumer can choose and of course, presently niche markets are being established in specialized areas ranging as far from human tissue to chocolate.

Both of these will be overcome in the short to medium term but does provide a gap for the business world to transform from a traditional transactional business model to a new social platform that co-create value with the consumer.

How to Move from Traditional to Social Business Model

This leads us into a discussion about how a new social business model can be built, putting the customer inside the process rather than outside the business walls, incorporating social into manufacturing as marketing embraced social media. At the same time developing a profit stream the funding of research and ideas, and the maintenance of the economy.

There are three key ways that the move to a social business model could happen. Firstly, the businesses themselves could become a social production unit. Thereby becoming a nexus hub for the consumer and competing for their business rather than a selling machine to that consumer base. Business could achieve this by using 3D printing internally to reduce the lead-time from concept to manufacture, the reduction in cost base, the reduction in stockholding and therefore release of cash into the business and of course true individualization for individual consumers. Business themselves can deliver it through conversational marketing (Scott, 2011) relationships, stifling the desire for the consumer to do it for themselves. Business will need to think of themselves as a nexus rather than transactional hub. The Internet is moving from data to an "internet of things" (Ashton, 2009) all linked globally (Kelly, 2005). Filters and gateways are required to be able to find this collection of things, this and business can provide added value; a part which is no longer manufactured could be provided through a blueprint. There is no real cost to the business, but incremental revenue is earned and value created for the consumer. The customer has already been empowered to talk about ideas, to share thoughts and to receive customer service around the clock. (Castells, 2009) The customer is enjoying that power and with the prospect of more, is not frightened anymore to possess that power. The technology becomes an enabler of differentiation, much as social media became the differentiator for brands.

Secondly, the socialization of the production process could affect the business model in three key areas; transferring the production from business to home, the risk of lost royalty and licensing income and the need to bring the consumer from outside to inside the business model. In this sense, manufacturing is outsourced but not to another country, to the consumer's home. The technology in this case becomes potentially the enabler to a social business model. The web allows collaboration of ideas and designs. However, at the moment the consumer has restricted ability to give physical life to the outcome of that collaboration. The output still has to be performed by an intermediary, through a 'manufacturer'. Collaboration can occur at the front end of the

product lifecycle but not at the end. 3D printing is starting to offer that bridge to social production, extending the socialization of the business model. People can share objects, people can create together, and people can produce a generic object with their own individual twist. People can share blueprints and then tweak the final version. People can create objects together, for instance the family album has historically been about audio and visual items on the web. But what if you can scan old furniture, jewelry, and heirlooms? Imagine the emotional value to scanning the necklace that a father gave your mother on their engagement. Imagine being able to print that out 25 years later for the daughter's 'old' wedding item. The physical object has time travelled, the physical object is more than a 'thing'; it is a tangible memory. In a sense that sounds sentimental, sounds too emotive for the discussion on how business models are transforming. However, it is this inherent emotion, this structural simplicity of time shifting objects, this fundamental ability to control that creates the value for the customer (Banks, 2011)

Thirdly, how can the concept be absorbed ahead of 3D home printers becoming commonplace? The emergence of 3D printing either within the home or offered as a service through companies such as Shapeways and Sculpteo, is attempting to create value through the marketplace for this technology. The business model becomes a cooperative or agent supplying the access or skills partnering with customers rather than selling to them. With home production a possibility, the concept of outsourcing to the consumer becomes a potential reality. The consumer will love the timeliness of delivery; they will love the sense of control. The business will enjoy the reduction in delivery costs, stock holdings and reduction in capital investment. In a sense both sides win in the short term.

Social Profit Models of Value Creation

For individuals, society, and business it is important to find a model that finds revenue and value added to sustain business. There are different solutions which appear possible and are at the heart of the my ongoing research:

- The future may be in an increase in cooperative style businesses, which allow for exchange and collaboration. The business is not an identity but a community nexus for crowd sourced outputs.
- The future may lie through subscriptions to expertise. Instead of royalties on goods sold, it may be royalties for the latest idea blueprints.
- The future may require business to remain one step ahead in technological terms. Thereby creating the reason why consumers will need them.
- The future may be in consumers using businesses to buy mass raw materials and expertise.
- The future may be giving away the printer for free, if they lock into your brand.

Social production may mean consumers renting their machines to others for specific material requirements or using the web as the meeting room for translating ideas into workable objects. It may also be the ability to sell and share personal items, personalized with your own personal brand or grouping together people for expertise, purchasing and swapping of value.

It is hard not to envisage a royalty system; however it may be contained within a monthly fee paid for the use of the printer. It may mean a move from productive capacity to creative capacity. It may mean that scanning could become the revenue generator by being limited to industrial use. This will invariably lead to the requirement for the employment contract to change. Employees may well pay the 'business' for the social space to share ideas.

Current Opportunities for Social Business

In discussing the effect of 3D printing on the current business model, it is important to recognize current opportunities which business could and should be exploiting, either now or in the near future. These benefits are not about evolving a new business model they are about reducing cost or removing overheads from current practices.

The benefits to the consumer previously mentioned are as pertinent to a business as to an individual. All the benefits are capable of improving your cost base and returning manufacturing in house for greater control over the product cycle. By embracing this new technology early it may be that the full effect on the business model can be alleviated. If the business provides the benefits to the consumer then the consumer may delay or suspend any thought of production at home. The important aspect from the business model angle is to manage this latest technological innovation – manage being defined as exploiting it before consumers, to transition to the new social business model.

As Thomas Friedman (2005) says, the 'world is flat.' The geographical boundaries have been replaced with an Internet, which acts as a shop window to the world. For business, this means that their competition has gone from local to global, giving increased choice to the modern customer. Interestingly, it has also meant a much more informed customer and therefore one who knows exactly what they want.

With both increased customer choice and knowledge comes price competition and the pressure to develop a differentiated offering becomes key to protecting the price premium. Differentiation has historically increased the traditional cost base, but with additive manufacturing this is about to change and in that change lies an opportunity to differentiate your business model from the competition without adding to your cost base.

As stated, global competition means maintaining a low cost base through developing a lean manufacturing strategy. Over the last decade, that has meant often outsourcing parts of the supply chain and for Western companies to look towards the east for the reduced cost of labor. Additive manufacturing or 3D printing as it is more usually known offers a solution to this cost dilemma. Interestingly Western governments are under pressure to bring home manufacturing from the Far East; this may be a way of fulfilling that aim. 3D printing allows for much shorter runs and the possibility of manufacturing totally individualized products at no extra cost. It also provides a means of same day tooling and same day delivery. Businesses can now achieve shorter lead times, reduced packaging, less air miles, and most of all mass customization. The modern business needs to have trust and respect as core values. Trust is imperative in a social business model. Trust inside the organization has always been part of successful companies but that now must stretch beyond the walls of the organization. 3D printing offers companies an opportunity to increase trust in their brand.

In the annual Edelman Trust Barometer Survey 2012 across 25 countries, four attributes were identified globally for business to create trust.

- Recognise that operational factors responsible for current trust won't build future trust, societal and engagement behaviors will.
- Shape the public discourse.
- Practice radical transparency.
- Exercise principle–based leadership, not rules-based performance.

Trust is now a core element to creating a strong business model and the emergence of social media has created the need for a more social model to create that trust. People have greater trust in a recommendation made by a friend; people do not trust advertising in the same way as they did in the previous century. The more you get people talking, the more you deliver what you're promised, the more visible you become to the World Wide Web.

The technology itself is both a catalyst for social interaction and now with the advent of new technology such as 3D printing it can become the social object itself. It can help companies move from the social conversation which is already becoming a given, to a social contract between 'marketplace friends' who want to create together, thereby creating that currency of trust. Consumers and providers are now on the same side, working together for each other rather than a two way transactional relationship.

The customer in the past has benefited from the mass production through lower price, with the compromise that it is not designed specifically for them. It is generic in nature even if some personalization through inscription or color for example may be available. The more differentiated your offering can be, the more productive capacity you can fill, the cheaper you can produce the goods and therefore in theory the more return on investment for the shareholders is made; a model that has worked well over the centuries. This subtle move from transaction of value to ultimately a creation of valuables looks almost semantic in nature. However, just as marketing had to adapt to the social web, operations will need to start adapting to this additive manufacturing process. The process needs to be embraced internally for differentiation and cost reduction but externally to embrace a social approach to production.

Over the last half a century, the manufacturing landscape has had to evolve within the business walls. This evolution however has been through choice to remain competitive and survive, but the ultimate decision whether to go just in time, outsource or kaizen has not been forced upon them by the customer but an internal decision. If external forces have been present it has been from competitors not the individual consumer.

The risk is that if businesses don't take up this opportunity of mass customization, then the consumer will; maybe not tomorrow but in the coming years. Desktop 3D printing is already available which means mass social production is an emerging opportunity. If businesses remain tied to the existing model of making and selling their own ideas, then the business will become redundant to the consumer market by losing their trust. Their desire for the ultimate customization at home, production to their own specification and on their own timescales, destroys the underlying necessity for mass production models.

It may be that the corporate business model will disappear over time. This sounds absurd, yet what would prevent individuals being self-employed? It may be that we need to evolve the market from being corporate led to cooperative led, a return to the future. It is interesting that in terms of social media, which is also a return to the future for marketing. In centuries past and the absence of television and publication advertising, people relied on word of mouth. Social media just returned the personal recommendation into a modern day tool that could spread further than your village. This may be true with social business. The return to the future is individuals working together, rather than for corporate bodies. At a time when people are so connected and yet live relatively lonely existences, this may improve societal well-being as well as individual choice.

The World Wide Web has changed the business world from a top down structure to a social model. Business needs to see 3D printing as the further catalyst of social business. In itself it is an amazing technology, but taken with the wider web it is the final jigsaw piece the consumer needed not to be tied to a business. Of course there will be elements that cannot be replicated but if the item is physical than the chances are, it will be under threat from outsourcing. Only this time the outsourcing is not a different continent, it is the

very consumer who pays your wages. Business has been slow in many ways to embrace the social media aspects of the web. Indeed after ten years there are people who still see it as a passing fad. However, this first step on socializing business is a training ground for the social business of the future. It is almost testing the capability through one channel – sales and marketing – to ready the business for full socialization. The approach for social media can be the approach taken with 3D printing. Social media works best when you listen first, then participate, then create your own conversations. The more you fight opening up the channels of communication, the more you antagonize the marketplace and make yourself open for attack. 3D printing offers the chance to get ahead of the competition. Learn about the capabilities, try out the technology and then start creating a future revenue stream. The excitement of this area is only just beginning, so the business that is brave enough to work with consumers on creating the future will be best placed to succeed over the next decade.

People argue that because the technology is not quite cheap enough, because it is limited at the moment to one substrate per machine, that people haven't started buying the machines that the time for assessing is not now. However, past history shows that delaying the embrace of technological advancement is not good for market value. Indeed that stronger argument would be that any technology that helps you to differentiate yourself in the marketplace is worth embracing, staying ahead of the curve is more vital than ever in this constantly changing world. The reason that the thinking needs to start is that business is at the core of society. It makes money, to employ people, to research new technology, to create wealth in the region. If business is undermined then what happens to the fabric of society? Consumers may enjoy the flexibility and control over what they can make, however if this creates unemployment and a reduction in social evolution, is that a price worth paying?

Legal and Ethical Barriers to the Social Business Model

The future revenue streams in a sense depend on the ethical and legal frameworks thereby requiring government and regulating authorities to update for this social production model. The ethical and legal frameworks are engrained in our society, and to a certain extent business relies on their protection for future revenue streams. The latest patent trolls and patent purchasing by technology companies, illustrates the revenue generating capacity of intellectual property.

However, the birth of the Web has pushed at the boundaries of intellectual property law (Daugherty, Li & Biocca, 2008). Digital file sharing has allowed piracy to flourish and the erosion of royalty income. Digital rights management has been an attempt to prevent abuse, but the barriers were usually shattered with little difficulty. Digital data can be shared, copied, transferred and the legal frameworks are struggling to cope with the extension of technology. The ethical sense of doing the right thing by the consumer is often the biggest barrier to abuse. The one aspect of digital data that helps with the tracking of illegal sharing is that usually the digital footprint can be tracked and tracked to an individual computer. The problem will be even worse with the ability to create physical objects (Bradshaw, Bowyer & Haufe, 2010). This chapter cannot go into depth on the potential legal issues for copyright, design rights, trademarks, and patents. However, a brief review of current legal implications is necessary.

In terms of registered designs there are two risks to revenue for a company. It has long been the case that spare parts are only protected if novel and can be seen by the user in ordinary usage. That means that many items are not protected because they cannot be seen, especially when it comes to washing machines and electronic items. This means that any consumer will be able to print from a blueprint or scan, a relevant spare part. No mark up on the consumable, and if expert enough to fit themselves then all revenue lost from the company. Even when the design has been registered the revenue will be lost, if the consumer is only using it for personal use. The repairs and maintenance industry will need a new business model. This may be in the sale of blueprints, being the Amazon of all spare parts or by charging a monthly subscription fee for access to the information. The fate of unregistered designs will lie in the specific details of each case, however the risk of lost income remains real. Indeed for design rights if the reproduction is for personal use then protection is lost.

Patent infringement is similar in that private use will normally be acceptable. However, the sharing of the blueprint may cause infringement. The problem would be globally policing each household with a 3D printer to ensure no patent infringement. The music industry attempted to control through Digital Rights Management but the fact that a printer could make different classes of items protected and not protected would make this unfeasible. Indeed the printed out version will never be an exact copy, therefore the system of protection would not work.

In terms of copyright similar issues arise. Once again the exposure for firms is tangible, with little or no protection for copies for personal use. People could copy and print out, without presently being subject to the law. This means that just as digital transfer caused a shift in how the music industry made money, the business world will need to re-think their creative or research and development investments (Perry, 2012). Crowdsourcing and open source challenge the very essence of the legislation; 3D printing may destroy the framework all together.

In summary protection of ideas must be found (Oppenheim, 1951), however as Benjamin (1936) stated mechanical reproduction has never been and will never be stopped. It is therefore about creating ethical and legal structures which allow for the move to mass production at the individual level whilst rewarding the creators.

SUMMARY OF BUSINESS MODEL RECOMMENDATIONS

The requirement is that business accepts the potential threat to their business model. Ignoring the threat of a technology that is already in action, that is already allowing crafts to be designed at home, then printed and sold through a third party site like Shapeways, would be dangerous and demands a risk management strategy.

An understanding of the technology is required in four ways for business to embrace this new social technology as an opportunity.

Firstly, business needs to investigate whether 3D manufacturing can be used in the short term, internally to reduce cost or increase flexibility. In the short term it could lead to a reduction in delivery costs, tooling, fixed overhead in procurement and of course wastage. This could release cost to spend on revenue generating ideas including the social business model.

Secondly, business needs to review the market opportunity from ultimate flexibility and simple mass individualization. Personalization is already starting to be incorporated into manufacture but as consumers engage more with social media and become more comfortable with corporate interaction, then individualization will become a requirement for all businesses.

This is true from small jewelry makers through to house builders. The first structures have been "printed out" in the USA. Imagine the flexibility this gives to construction companies. This includes market research into what people are looking for but also market research with the laboratories developing this technology to see the impossibilities that are being made possible.

This will require a shift in intellectual thinking in the business world, a shift to seeing the market as a conglomerate of individual requirements rather than mass marketing.

Thirdly, business needs to start brainstorming now how they can evolve their revenue model.

The technology is disruptive; it needs disruptive thinking to change the business model. Social business will mean different things to different industrial sectors; each business will need to define what it will mean for their value creation model. A new set of skill sets may well need identifying for the next decade, leaders and employees with collaborative and people centric mindsets. The emergence of the next generation of managers who have been part of the creative social media revolution will be key to understanding the next generation of customers.

Finally business needs to lead the call for ethical and legal reviews of the societal frameworks. Intellectual property has long acted as the gatekeeper to copying or stealing ideas from others, but the law needs now to reflect the ongoing shift in technology. Personal use has been a relevant term over the last century but would become irrelevant if the scanning of objects for family and personal use is possible. The consumer is unlikely to buy two chairs when they can buy one and scan it and presently that would be allowable. The loss of revenue to business would affect society in the long term with risk overtaking reward for return on investment.

Previous epochs show that technological revolutions can be disruptive and can damage existing profit creation, but they also show that businesses find a way of embracing the changes to create new models. The crucial lesson to learn from these previous epochs is that change will happen and the earlier businesses embrace them, the likelier they survive and indeed thrive in the commercial world.

FURTHER RESEARCH

Research in the past has concentrated on the emergence of social media and how social entrepreneurship can benefit society. There is little research which brings together social media, the business model and the legal and ethical impact of all of this change. Presently my work is focused on the emergence of this new social business model and hopefully will provide useful insights of a general nature. However there are three areas within my research which needs more detailed work presently.

Research is now required on how value creation is possible when the consumer is inside the manufacturing process rather than outside. Research is also required on the legal and ethical frameworks and how you protect the creators of ideas from a new social world of sharing and even replicating without rewarding. This is an area, which I am presently researching and hoping to bring a more in depth analysis over the next year. Research is also required on the additive manufacturing process and to what extent will this replace the industrial manufacturing process. A review of what is possible and how that will affect the world. For instance the ability to print out organs could mean an average longer life for citizens but how will governments need to react this further ageing of the population. Research is also now required on the potential effects of production by the masses rather than mass production. It is important to balance the customization benefits with the loss of future commercial revenue streams and to understand what needs to be addressed today, to protect the business model of tomorrow.

CONCLUSION

3D printing may seem futuristic, but the technology is thirty years old, which means that it is well, established as a means of production. Presently business retains the sole right of use, through the barriers of computer-aided design and indeed the financial investment required. This is changing and cannot be ignored by business leaders.

Business has been challenged over the last decade to open their doors and invite the customer into their existing processes by social media. However this has been merely a communication shift that has been more cultural than structural. Business is now on the verge of being transformed, with the customer not just an invited guest but as a potentially fully paid up part of the business. Once the ability to manufacture is created at home, then the question for leaders to answer is how to create value in the future.

The transformation needs to put the customer at the heart of the model. It needs to be the nexus of rather than seller to the marketplace. Business needs to rethink the added value model. It is not necessarily taking raw materials, manufacturing and delivering. The added value may come in supporting the customer, in developing new ideas for the customer to use, in developing niche expertise that the customer cannot possibly attain. The transformation needs to start with business embracing the technology before the customer. The technology is there to provide ultimate personalization on a mass scale. Of course in the long run, the customer will be able to achieve this, but until that time why not use the technology to create social value? This allows a business to build a social model of working together, to build a trust element to the social relationship so that over the long term the relationship stays strong. It may even reduce the desire of the customer to invest in home production.

This chapter cannot provide concrete answers to this very complex issue but it can create discussion for the future so that the boundaries are highlighted and leaders recognize that business is on the edge of transformation. The only certainty offered is that 'business as usual' today will not be 'business as usual' tomorrow. It is the start of a new business model but most importantly it remains ours to define.

REFERENCES

Ashton, K. (2009). That 'Internet of Things' Thing. *RFID Journal*. Retrieved May 20, 2012 from http://www.rfidjournal.com/article/view/4986

Atala, A. (2011). Printing a human kidney blog. *Ted Talks*. Retrieved April 14, 2012 from http://ted.com/.../printing-a-human-kidney-anthony-atala-on-ted-com/

Banks, R. (2011). *The future of looking back*. Redmond, WA: Microsoft Press.

Beer, D., & Burrows, R. (2007). Sociology and, of and in Web 2.0: Some initial considerations. *Sociological Research Online*, *12*(5), 17. doi:10.5153/sro.1560.

Benjamin, W. (1936). *The Work of Art in the Age of Mechanical Reproduction*. Retrieved April 14, 2012, from http://www.marxists.org/reference/subject/philosophy/works/ge/benjamin.htm

Benkler, Y. (2011). *The penguin and the leviathan*. New York: Crown Business.

Berners-Lee, T. (2010). Long Live the Web: A Call for Continued Open Standards and Neutrality Scientific American November 2010. Retrieved on June 18, 2012 from http://www.scientificamerican.com/article.cfm?id=long-live-the-web

Bhargava, R. (2008). *Personality not included*. New York: McGraw-Hill.

Bradshaw, S., Bowyer, A., & Haufe, P. (2010). The intellectual property implications of low cost 3d printing. *ScriptEd*, *7*(1), 5–31.

Buckingham, I. (2008). *Brand engagement*. Basingstoke: Palgrave-Macmillam.

Business Insider. (2011). The next trillion dollar industry: 3D Printing Retrieved. Retrieved May 16, 2012, from: www.businessinsider.com/3d-printing-2011-2?op=1

Carr, N. (2008). Is Google making us stupid? *Yearbook of the National Society for the Study of Education*, *107*(2), 89–94. doi:10.1111/j.1744-7984.2008.00172.x.

Castells, M. (2009). *Communication power*. New York: Oxford University Press.

Daugherty, T., Li, H., & Biocca, F. (2008). Consumer learning and the effects of virtual experience. *Psychology and Marketing*, *25*(7), 568–586. doi:10.1002/mar.20225.

Dentchev, N. A. (2005). *Integrating Corporate social responsibility in business models. 05/284*. Working paper. Ghent University, Belgium.

Edelman (2012). *Edelman Trust Barometer Survey*. Retrieved April 24, 2012, from http://trust.edelman.com/trust-download/global- results/

Friedman, T. L. (2005). *The world is flat*. New York: Farrar, Straus & Giroux.

Haque, U. (2011). *The new capitalist manifesto*. Boston: Harvard Business Publishing.

Hart, B. (2012). Will 3D Printing Change the World? *Forbes*. Retrieved May 14, 2012, from http://www.forbes.com/sites/gcaptain/2012/03/06/will-3d-printing-change-the-world/

Kelly, K. (2005). How technology evolves. *Ted Talks*. Retrieved March 13, 2012, from http://blog.ted.com/2009/08/18/how_technology/

Levine, F., Locke, C., Searls, D., & Weinberger, D. (2000). *The cluetrain manifesto*. New York: Basic Books.

Lovari, A., & Parisi, L. (2011). Public administrations and citizens 2.0: Exploring digital public communication strategies and civic interaction within Italian municipality pages on Facebook. In Comunello, F. (Ed.), *Networked sociability and individualism: Technology for personal relationships*. Hershey, PA: IGI Global. doi:10.4018/978-1-61350-338-6.ch012.

MacLeod, H. (2009). Social Objects are the Future of Marketing. *Gaping Void*. Retrieved June 17, 2012, from http://gapingvoid.com/so/

Malone, E., & Lipson, H. (2007). The factory in your kitchen. In *Proceedings of World Conference on Mass Customization and Personalization*. Cambridge, MA: MIT Press.

McLuhan, M. (1964). *Understanding media: The extensions of man* (1st ed.). New York: McGraw Hill.

O'Reilly, T. (2005). What is Web 2.0? Design patterns and business models for the next generation of software. Retrieved May 19, 2012, from: http://oreilly.com/web2/archive/what-is-web-20.html

O'Reilly, T., & Battelle, J. (2010). Web Squared: Web 2.0 Five Years On. *Web 2.0 Summit*. Retrieved May 17, 2012 from http://assets.en.oreilly.com/1/event/28/web2009_websquared-whitepaper.pdf

Oppenheim, S. C. (1951). A new approach to evaluation of the American patent system. *Journal of the Patent and Trademark Office Society, 33*(8), 555–568.

Oxford Dictionary. (2012). *Oxford Dictionary*. New York: Oxford University Press.

Perry, J. (2012). All future roads lead to problems with intellectual property. Retrieved May 3, 2012, from: http://declineofscarcity.com/?cat=43

Pettis, B. (2012). 3D Printer makers' rival visions of the future. *BBC*. Retrieved June 18, 2012, from www.bbc.co.uk/news/technology-16503443

Schacht, W. H. (2000). The national council for science and environment, industrial competitiveness and technological advancement. Brief for US Congress, September, Washington, D.C.

Scott, D. M. (2011). *New rules of marketing and PR* (3rd ed.). New York: Wiley.

The Economist. (2011). The Shape of Things to Come. Retrieved May 17, 2012, from http://www.economist.com/node/21541382

Wilson, F. (2006). *My favourite business models*. Retrieved March 2, 2012, from http://www.avc.com/a_vc/2009/07/freemium-and-freeconomics.html

ADDITIONAL READING

Alpern, P. (2011). *Rapid Manufacturing Breaks Down Old Production Constraints*. Retrieved June 20, 2012, from http://www.industryweek.com/articles/rapid_manufacturing_breaks_down_old_production_constraints_23641.aspx?ShowAll=1

Bell, C., & Patterson, J. (2011). *Wired and dangerous*. San Francisco, CA: Berrett-Koehler.

BIS. (2012). *The Hargreaves Review of Intellectual Property: Where next? First Report of Session 2012–13* Retrieved June 30, 2012, from http://www.publications.parliament.uk/pa/cm201213/cmselect/cmbis/367/36702.htm

Bloy, D., & Hadwin, S. (2011). *Law and the media*. London: Thompson Reuters.

Didier, A., Rajon, F. J., Bova, R., Bhasin, R., & Friedman, W. (2006). An investigation of the potential of rapid prototyping technology for image-guided surgery. *Journal of Applied Clinical Medical Physics, 7*(4), 239–247.

Fanning, P. (2012). *Designing in 3D: How 3D printing is changing the way product design and development are taking place*. Retrieved June 15, 2012, from http://www.eurekamagazine.co.uk/article/40995/Designing-in-3D-How-3D-printing-is-changing-the-way-product-design-and-development-are-taking-place.aspx

Flaherty, J. (2012). *10 Amazing Thing The 3D Printers Can Do Now*. Retrieved June 3, 2012, from http://www.wired.com/design/2012/04/10-things-3d-printers-can-do-now/?pid=164

Gerzema, J., & Leber, J. (2008). *The brand bubble*. San Francisco, CA: Jossey Bass.

Girdwood, A. (2011). *3D printing - A new copyright challenge? A retail revolution?* Retrieved February 3, 2012, from http://blog.arhg.net/2011/06/3d-printing-new-copyright-challenge.html

Hargreaves, I. (2011). *Digital Opportunity*. Retrieved June 2, 2012, from http://www.parliament.uk/business/committees/committees-a-z/commons-select/business-innovation-and-kills/Publications/

Hart, B. (2012). Will 3D Printing Change The World? Retrieved June 15, 2012, from http://www.forbes.com/sites/gcaptain/2012/03/06/will-3d-printing-change-the-world/

Heath, N. (2012). *The 3D Printer that's heading for your home*. Retrieved July 8, 2012, from http://www.techrepublic.com/blog/european-technology/reprap-the-3d-printer-thats-heading-for-your-home/229

Howie, P. (2011). *The evolution of revolutions*. New York: Prometheus Books.

Korvascus, J. (2012). The Future of Organ Replacement. Retrieved May 24, 2012, from http://bigthink.com/humanizing-technology/the-future-of-organ-replacement?utm_source=feedburner&utm_medium=feed&utm_campaign=Feed%3A+big think%2Fmain+%28Big+Think+Main%29&utm_content=Google+Reader

Lee, B. (2012). *Hidden wealth of customers*. Boston, MA: Harvard Business Press.

Medina, S. (2012). *The Man Behind the World's Largest 3D Printer*. Retrieved May 15, 2012, from http://www.architizer.com/en_us/blog/dyn/39077/the-man-behind-the-worlds-largest-3d-printer/

Neil, S. (2011). Community-Orientated Manufacturers: Crowdsourcing & Micro-Factories. *Manufacturing Executive*. Retrieved May 16, 2012, from http://www.manufacturing-executive.com/community/leadership_dialogues/game-changing_technologies/blog/2011/11/01/community-oriented-manufacturers

Novella, S. (2012). *3D Printing*. Retrieved June 15, 2012, from http://theness.com/neurologicablog/index.php/3d-printing/?utm_source=twitterfeed&utm_medium=twitter

Pine, J. B. (2011). *Infinite possibility*. San Francisco, CA: Berrett-Koehler.

Pine, J. B., & Gilmore, J. H. (2011). *The experience economy*. New York: Routledge.

Rappaport, A. (2011). *Saving capitalism from short termism*. New York: McGraw Hill.

Summit, S. (2010). *Future of 3D Printing*. Retrieved May 24, 2012, from http://www.youtube.com/ watch?v=6lJ8vId4HF8&feature=related

Tamarjan, D. (2012). *9 Benefits of 3D Printing*. Retrieved February 3, 2012, from http://augmentedtomorrow.com/9-benefits-3d-printing/

Tapscott, D. (1996). *The digital economy*. New York: McGraw Hill.

Tate, P. (2011). *Additive Manufacturing – Boom Time for 3D Printing*. Retrieved March 23, 2012, from http://www.manufacturing-executive.com/message/2679#2679

KEY TERMS AND DEFINITIONS

3D Printing: A manufacturing technique which builds an object; vertical printing.

Additive Manufacturing: Manufacturing which adds substrates to make objects rather than cutting material away.

Business Model: The process by which a company creates, delivers, and captures value.

Intellectual Property: A term covering trademarks, copyright, design rights and patents which allow people to own the property they create.

Social Business: A business which removes the walls between themselves and the marketplace.

Social Marketing: The use of social media to engage customers.

Social Media: Electronic information which allows people to share, collaborate and publish to the web.

Compilation of References

Adams, P. (2009). Designing for social interaction. *Boxes and Arrows*. Retrieved February 24, 2011, from http://boxesandarrows.com/view/designing-for-social

Adams, R. (2011). MySpace cuts 47% of workforce. *The Wall Street Journal*. Retrieved May 20, 2011, from http://online.wsj.com/article/SB10001424052748703791904576075892399066126.html

Adomavicius, G., & Tuzhilin, A. (2005). Toward the next generation of recommender systems: A survey of the state-of-the-art and possible extensions. *IEEE Transactions on Knowledge and Data Engineering*, *17*(6), 734–749. doi:10.1109/TKDE.2005.99.

Aggarwal, C. C. (2011). An intoduction to social network data analytics. In Aggarwal, C. C. (Ed.), *Social Network Data Analytics* (pp. 1–15). New York: Springer. doi:10.1007/978-1-4419-8462-3_1.

Ahlqvist, T., Bäck, A., Heinonen, S., & Halonen, M. (2010). Road-mapping the societal transformation potential of social media. *Foresight: The Journal of Future Studies. Strategic Thinking and Policy*, *12*(5), 3–26. doi:10.1108/14636681011075687.

Ahn, T. R., Ryu, S., & Han, I. (2007). The impact of Web quality and playfulness on user acceptance of online retailing. *Information & Management*, *44*(3), 263–275. doi:10.1016/j.im.2006.12.008.

Ajzen, I. (2006). *Constructing a TpB questionnaire: Conceptual and methodological considerations*: Retrieved from http://www.people.umass.edu/aizen/tpb.html

Ajzen, I. (1991). The theory of planned behavior. *Organizational Behavior and Human Decision Processes*, *50*(2), 179–211. doi:10.1016/0749-5978(91)90020-T.

Ajzen, I., & Fishbein, M. (1980). *Understanding Attitude and Predicting Social Behavior*. NJ: Prentice-Hall.

Akar, E. (2009). Web 2.0'la Değişen Pazarlama ve Yeni Kuralları. *Pazarlama ve İletişim Kültürü Dergisi. Bahar*, *02*, 50–55.

Akar, E. (2010). *Sosyal Medya Pazarlaması*. Ankara, Turkey: Efil Yayınevi.

Alasse, L. (2011). *Como Brastemp, Renault, Arezzo e Twix reverteram a crise nas redes sociais. Mundo do Marketing*, August 17. Retrieved July 10, 2012, from http://mundodomarketing.com.br/ reportagens/digital/20148/como-brastemp-renault-arezzo-e-twix-reverteram-a-crise-nas-redes-sociais.html

Alford, J. R., & Hibbing, J. R. (2007). Personal, interpersonal, and political temperaments. *ANNALS of the American Academy of Political and Social Sciences*, *614*, 696–212. doi:10.1177/0002716207305621.

Allred, C. R., Smith, S. M., & Swinyard, W. R. (2006). E-shopping lovers and fearful conservatives: A market segmentation analysis. *International Journal of Retail & Distribution Management*, *34*(4/5), 308–333. doi:10.1108/09590550610660251.

Almeida, C., & Silva; L. (2011). Comunicação Corporativa nas Mídias Sociais: o Twitter como ferramenta de relacionamento entre organizações e seus públicos. *Pós em revista*, *3*(4), 1-18.

Altman, I., & Taylor, D. A. (1973). *Social penetration: The development of interpersonal relationships*. Oxford, UK: Holt, Rinehart & Winston.

Amazon.com. (2012). *This is your brain on 80s*. Retrieved April 4, 2012, from http://www.amazon.com/Brain-Drugs-Bacon-Poster-Print/dp/B000R2LTTW

American Civil Liberties Union. (2010). *Commerce department releases important report urging comprehensive privacy protections.* Retrieved July 2012, from http://www.aclu.org/technology-and-liberty/commerce-department-releases-important-report-urging-comprehensive-privacy-pr

Amichai-Hamburger, Y. (2002). Internet and personality. *Computers in Human Behavior, 18*(1), 1–10. doi:10.1016/S0747-5632(01)00034-6.

Amichai-Hamburger, Y. (2007). Personality, individual differences and internet use. In Joinson, A. N., McKenna, K. Y. A., Postmes, T., & Reips, U. (Eds.), *The Oxford Handbook of Internet Psychology* (pp. 187–204). Oxford, UK: Oxford University Press.

Amichai-Hamburger, Y., & Ben-Artzi, E. (2003). Loneliness and Internet use. *Computers in Human Behavior, 19*(1), 71–80. doi:10.1016/S0747-5632(02)00014-6.

Amichai-Hamburger, Y., & Vinitzky, G. (2010). Social network use and personality. *Computers in Human Behavior, 26*(6), 1289–1295. doi:10.1016/j.chb.2010.03.018.

Amichai-Hamburger, Y., Wainapel, G., & Fox, S. (2002). "On the Internet no one knows I'm an introvert": Extraversion, neuroticism, and Internet interaction. *Cyberpsychology & Behavior, 5*(2), 125–128. doi:10.1089/109493102753770507 PMID:12025878.

Anderson, P. (2007). What is Web 2.0? Ideas, technologies and implications for education. *JISC Technology and Standards Watch*, February, 1-64. Retrieved December 15, 2010, from http://www.educause.edu/ir/library/pdf/ERM0621.pdf

Anderson, J. C., & Gerbing, D. W. (1988). Structural Equation modeling in Practice: A Review and Recommended two-step Approach. *Psychological Bulletin, 13*(3), 411–423. doi:10.1037/0033-2909.103.3.411.

Anderson, M. R. (2009). Beyond membership: A sense of community and political behavior. *Political Behavior, 31*(4), 603–627. doi:10.1007/s11109-009-9089-x.

Antoniou, G., & Harmelen, F. V. (2008). *A semantic web primer* (2nd ed.). Cambridge, MA: MIT press.

Arakji, R. Y. & Lang, K. R. (2008). "Avatar business value analysis: A method for the evaluation of business value creation in virtual commerce. *Journal of Electronic Commerce Research, 9*(3)3, 207-218.

Armstrong, M., & Wright, J. (2004). *Demand Estimation for Italian Newspapers: The Impact of Weekly Supplements.* Working Paper.

Armstrong, M. (2002). The theory of access pricing and interconnection. In Cave, M. et al. (Eds.), *Handbook of Telecommunications Economics* (*Vol. 1*, pp. 297–381). Amsterdam, The Netherlands: Elsevier.

Arndt, J. (1967). Role of product-related conversations in the diffusion of a new product. *JMR, Journal of Marketing Research, 4*(August), 291–295. doi:10.2307/3149462.

Arrington, M. (2011). Amazingly, Myspace's decline is accelerating. *TechCrunch.* Retrieved August 10, 2011, from http://techcrunch.com/2011/03/23/amazingly-myspaces-decline-is-accelerating/

Arroyo, N. (2007). ¿Web 2.0? ¿web social? ¿qué es eso? [Web 2.0?, Social Web? What it is?]. *Educación y biblioteca, 161*, 69-74.

Artesia (2008). *Introduction to Virtual Worlds.* Retrieved January 15, 2011, from http://www.scribd.com/doc/5570819/Introduction-to-virtual-worlds

Ashcroft, J. (2010). Social media in the supply chain. *Presentation to the Supply Chain Management Summit.* Retrieved February 24, 2011, from http://summits.aberdeen.com/1/Day1-%20Jeff%20Ashcroft.pdf

Ashton, K. (2009). That 'Internet of Things' Thing. *RFID Journal.* Retrieved May 20, 2012 from http://www.rfidjournal.com/article/view/4986

Atala, A. (2011). Printing a human kidney blog. *Ted Talks.* Retrieved April 14, 2012 from http://ted.com/.../printing-a-human-kidney-anthony-atala-on-ted-com/

Atkinson, N. L., Saperstein, S. L., & Pleis, J. (2009). Using the Internet for health-related activities: Findings from a national probability sample. *Journal of Medical Internet Research, 11*(1), e4. doi:10.2196/jmir.1035 PMID:19275980.

Aubert-Gamet, V., & Cova, B. (1997, April). *Exit, voice, loyalty and twist: consumer research in search of the subject.* Paper presented at the European Institute for Advanced Studies in Management Workshop on Interpretive Consumer Research, Oxford, England.

Auer-Srnka, K. J., & Koeszegi, S. (2007). From Words to Numbers: How to Transform Qualitative Data into Meaningful Quantitative Results. *Journal of Schmalenbach Business Review, 59,* 29–57.

Austin, C. G., Zinkhan, G. M., & Song, J. H. (2007). Peer-to-peer media opportunities. In Tellis, G. J., & Ambler, T. (Eds.), *The SAGE Handbook of Advertising* (pp. 349–365). London: Sage Publications Ltd. doi:10.4135/9781848607897.n22.

Bachmann, I., Correa, T., & Gil de Zúñiga, H. (in press). Profiling online political content creators: Advancing the paths to democracy. *International Journal of E-Politics.*

Bacon, J. (2012). *The art of community: Building the new age of participation.* Sebastopol, CA: O'Reilly Media.

Bagozzi, R. P., & Dholakia, U. M. (2002). Intentional social action in virtual communities. *Journal of Interactive Marketing, 16*(2), 2–21. doi:10.1002/dir.10006.

Bagozzi, R. P., & Dholakia, U. M. (2006). Antecedents and purchase consequences of customer participation in small group brand communities. *International Journal of Research in Marketing, 23*(1), 45–61. doi:10.1016/j.ijresmar.2006.01.005.

Baker, R. K., & White, K. M. (2011). In Their Own Words: Why Teenagers Don't Use Social Networking Sites. Cyberpsychology, Behavior, and Social Networking, 14(6), 395-398.

Balasubramanian, S. K. (1994). Beyond advertising and publicity: Hybrid messages and public policy issues. *Journal of Advertising, 23*(4), 29–46.

Bandura, A. (1977). Self-efficacy: Toward a unifying theory of behavioral change. *Psychological Review, 84*(2), 191–215. doi:10.1037/0033-295X.84.2.191 PMID:847061.

Bandura, A. (1982). Self-efficacy mechanism in human agency. *The American Psychologist, 37*(2), 122–147. doi:10.1037/0003-066X.37.2.122.

Bandura, A. (1986). *Social Foundations of Thought and Action.* Englewood Cliffs, NJ: Prentice-Hall.

Bandura, A. (Ed.). (1995). *Self-efficacy in Changing Societies.* Cambridge, MA: Cambridge University Press. doi:10.1017/CBO9780511527692.

Band, W., & Petouhoff, N. L. (2010). *Social CRM goes mainstream.* Cambridge, MA: Forrester Research.

Band, W., & Petouhoff, N. L. (2010). *Topic overview: Social CRM goes mainstream.* Cambridge, MA: Forrester Research Inc..

Banks, R. (2011). *The future of looking back.* Redmond, WA: Microsoft Press.

Bansal, H. S., & Voyer, P. A. (2000). Word-of-mouth processes within a services purchase decision context. *Journal of Service Research, 3*(2), 166–177. doi:10.1177/109467050032005.

Barefoot, D., & Szabo, J. (2009). *Friends with benefits: A social media marketing handbook.* San Francisco, CA: No Starch Press.

Bargh, J. A., McKenna, K. Y. A., & Fitzsimons, G. M. (2002). Can you see the real me? Activation and expression of the "true self" on the Internet. *The Journal of Social Issues, 58*(1), 33–48. doi:10.1111/1540-4560.00247.

Barker, V. (2009). Older adolescents' motivations for social network site use: The influence of gender, group identity, and collective self-esteem. *CyberPyschology and Behavior, 12,* 209–213. doi:10.1089/cpb.2008.0228 PMID:19250021.

Barnes, S. J., & Böhringer, M. (2009). Continuance Usage Intention in Microblogging services: The Case of Twitter. In *Proceedings of the 17th European Conference on Information Systems (ECIS).* Verona, Italy: ECIS. Retrieved July 18, 2010, from http://www.ecis2009.it/papers/ecis2009-0164.pdf

Bateman, P. J., Pike, J. C., & Butler, B. S. (2011). To disclose or not: Publicness in social networking sites. *Information Technology & People, 24*(1), 78–100. doi:10.1108/09593841111109431.

Baxter, W. F. (1983). Bank interchange of transactional paper: Legal and economic perspectives. *The Journal of Law & Economics, 26,* 541–588. doi:10.1086/467049.

Beam, C., & Segev, A. (1997). Automated Negotiations: A Survey of the State of the Art. *Journal of Wirtschafts-informatik, 39*(3), 263–268.

Beatty, S. E., & Ferrell, M. E. (1998). Impulse buying: Modeling its precursors. *Journal of Retailing, 74*(2), 169–191. doi:10.1016/S0022-4359(99)80092-X.

Beaumont, C. (2008). Tweet, tweet, here comes Twitter. *The Telegraph.* Retrieved February 11, 2012, from http://www.telegraph.co.uk/technology/3357007/Tweet-tweet-here-comes-Twitter.html

Becker, J. U., Greve, G., & Albers, S. (2009). The impact of technological and organizational implementation of CRM on customer acquisition, maintenance, and retention. *International Journal of Research in Marketing, 26*(3), 207–215. doi:10.1016/j.ijresmar.2009.03.006.

Beck, L., & Ajzen, I. (1991). Predicting dishonest actions using the theory of planned behavior. *Journal of Research in Personality, 25*(3), 285–301. doi:10.1016/0092-6566(91)90021-H.

Beer, D., & Burrows, R. (2007). Sociology and, of and in Web 2.0: Some initial considerations. *Sociological Research Online, 12*(5), 17. doi:10.5153/sro.1560.

Benbasat, I., & Barki, H. (2007). Quo Vadis TAM? *Journal of the Association for Information Systems, 8*(4), 211–218.

Beniger, J. (1988). 'The personalization of mass media and the growth of pseudo-community. *Communication Research, 14*(3), 352–371. doi:10.1177/009365087014003005.

Benjamin, W. (1936). *The Work of Art in the Age of Mechanical Reproduction.* Retrieved April 14, 2012, from http://www.marxists.org/reference/subject/philosophy/works/ge/benjamin.htm

Benkler, Y. (2011). *The penguin and the leviathan.* New York: Crown Business.

Bennett, W. L., & Iyengar, S. (2008). A new era of minimal effects? The changing foundations of political communication. *The Journal of Communication, 58*(4), 707–731. doi:10.1111/j.1460-2466.2008.00410.x.

Bentler, P. M. (1990). Comparative fit indexes in structural models. *Psychological Bulletin, 107*(2), 238–246. doi:10.1037/0033-2909.107.2.238 PMID:2320703.

Berger, J., & Iyengar, R. (2011). How interests shapes word-of-mouth over different channels. *Marketing Science Institute Working Paper Series,* Report No. 11-110.

Berger, C. R. (2009). Interpersonal communication. In Tacks, D. W., & Salwen, M. B. (Eds.), *An integrated approach to communication theory and research* (pp. 260–279). Mahwah, NJ: Lawrence Erlbaum Associates.

Berger, J., & Milkman, K. L. (2012). What makes online content viral? *JMR, Journal of Marketing Research, 49*(April), 192–205. doi:10.1509/jmr.10.0353.

Berners-Lee, T. (2010). Long Live the Web: A Call for Continued Open Standards and Neutrality Scientific American November 2010. Retrieved on June 18, 2012 from http://www.scientificamerican.com/article.cfm?id=long-live-the-web

Berners-Lee, T., Hendler, J., & Lassila, O. (2001). The Semantic Web. *Scientific American, 284*(5), 34–43. doi:10.1038/scientificamerican0501-34 PMID:11396337.

Bernoff, J., & Li, C. (2008). Harnessing the Power of the Oh-So-Social Web. *MIT Sloan Management Review, 49*(3), 36-42. Retrieved January 15, 2012, from http://www.inforesearching.com/downloads/oh-so-social-web.pdf

Berscheid, E., & Walster, E. H. (1978). *Interpersonal attraction.* Reading, MA: Addison-Wesley.

Bhargava, R. (2008). *Personality not included.* New York: McGraw-Hill.

Bhatt, G. D., & Emdad, A. F. (2001). An analysis of the virtual supply chain in electronic commerce. *Logistics Information Management, 14*(1/2), 78–84. doi:10.1108/09576050110362465.

Bichler, M., Kersten, G., & Strecker, S. (2003). Towards a structured design of electronic negotiations. *Journal of Group Decision And Negotiation, 12*(4), 311–335. doi:10.1023/A:1024867820235.

Bickart, B., & Schindler, R. M. (2001). Internet forums as influential sources of consumer information. *Journal of Interactive Marketing, 15*(3), 31–40. doi:10.1002/dir.1014.

Biever, C. (2006). Web 2.0 is all about the feel-good factor. *New Scientist, 192*(December), 30. doi:10.1016/S0262-4079(06)61451-6.

Birdsall, W. F. (2007). Web 2.0 as a social movement. *Webology, 4*(2). Retrieves January 18, 2011, from http://www.webology.ir/2007/v4n2/a40.html

Bishop, J. (2007). Increasing participation in online communities: A framework for human–computer interaction. *Computers in Human Behavior, 23*(4), 1881–1893. doi:10.1016/j.chb.2005.11.004.

Biswas, A., & Krishnan, R. (2004). The Internet's impact on marketing. *Journal of Business Research, 57*(7), 681–684. doi:10.1016/S0148-2963(02)00346-6.

Blood, R. (2002). *The weblog handbook: Practical advice on creating and maintaining your blog*. Cambridge, MA: Perseus Publishing.

Blumler, J., & Katz, E. (1974). *The uses of mass communication research: Current perspectives on gratifications research*. Beverly Hills, CA: Sage Publications.

Boddy, D., Cahill, C., Charles, M., Fraser-Kraus, H., & Macbeth, D. K. (1998). Success and failure in implementing supply chain partnering: An empirical study. *European Journal of Purchasing and Supply Management, 4*(2/3), 143–151. doi:10.1016/S0969-7012(97)00026-9.

Bolger, N., Davis, A., & Rafaeli, E. (2003). Diary methods: Capturing life as it is lived. *Annual Review of Psychology, 54*(1), 579–616. doi:10.1146/annurev.psych.54.101601.145030 PMID:12499517.

Boll, S. (2007). MultiTube—Where Web 2.0 and Multimedia Could Meet. *IEEE MultiMedia, 14*(1), 9–13. doi:10.1109/MMUL.2007.17.

Bolton, R. N. (1998). A dynamic model of the duration of the customer's relationship with a continuous service provider: The role of satisfaction. *Marketing Science, 17*(1), 45–65. doi:10.1287/mksc.17.1.45.

Bonhard, P., Harries, C., McCarthy, J., & Sasse, M. A. (2006). Accounting for taste: Using profile similarity to improve recommender systems. In *Proceedings of the SIGCHI Conference on Human Factors in Computing Systems* (pp. 1057-1066). Montreal, Canada: ACM.

Booth, N., & Matic, J. A. (2011). Mapping and leveraging influencers in social media to shape corporate brand perceptions. *Corporate Communications: An International Journal, 16*(3), 184–191. doi:10.1108/13563281111156853.

Borges, B. (2009). *Marketing 2.0 Bridging the Gap between Seller and Buyer through Social Media Marketing*. Tucson, AZ: Wheatmark.

Bornstein, D. (2011). Mothers-to-be are getting the message. *New York Times*. Retrieved February 7, 2011, from http://opinionator.blogs.nytimes.com/2011/02/07/pregnant-mothers-are-getting-the-message

Bouchard, Y. J. J. (1997). The genetics of personality. In Blum, K., & Noble, E. P. (Eds.), *Handbook of Psychiatric Genetics* (pp. 273–296). Boca Raton, FL: CRC Press.

Boulos, M. N. K., & Wheeler, S. (2007). The emerging Web 2.0 social software: An enabling suite of sociable technologies in health and health care education. *Health Information and Libraries Journal, 24*, 2–23. doi:10.1111/j.1471-1842.2007.00701.x PMID:17331140.

Boush, D. M., Friestad, M., & Rose, G. M. (1994). Adolescent skepticism toward TV advertising and knowledge of advertiser tactics. *The Journal of Consumer Research, 21*(1), 165–175. doi:10.1086/209390.

Boyd, D. M., & Ellison, N. B. (2007). Social network sites: Definition, history, and scholarship. *Journal of Computer-Mediated Communication, 13*(1), 210–230. doi:10.1111/j.1083-6101.2007.00393.x.

Boyd, D., & Ellison, N. (2007). Social network sites: Definition, history, and scholarship. *Journal of Computer-Mediated Communication, 13*(1). doi:10.1111/j.1083-6101.2007.00393.x.

Bradshaw, S., Bowyer, A., & Haufe, P. (2010). The intellectual property implications of low cost 3d printing. *ScriptEd, 7*(1), 5–31.

Braun, P., Brzostowski, J., Kersten, G., Kim, J., Kowalczyk, R., & Strecker, S. et al. (2006). Electronic negotiation Systems and Software Agents: Methods, Models, and Applications. In *Intelligent Decision-making Support Systems* (pp. 271–300). London: Springer. doi:10.1007/1-84628-231-4_15.

Bray, D. A., & Konsynski, B. R. (2007). Virtual Worlds: Opportunities for Multi-Disciplinary Research. Draft Version: Final Version to appear in The Data Base for Advances in Information Systems, *SIGMIS Database. Special Issue on Virtual Worlds, 38*(4), 17–25.

Brehm, J. W. (1966). *A Theory of Psychological Reactance*. New York: Academic Press.

Breslin, J., & Decker, S. (2007). The Future of Social Networks on the Internet The Need for Semantics. *IEEE Internet Computing*, (November-December): 86–90. doi:10.1109/MIC.2007.138.

Bretzke, M. (2000). *Marketing de relacionamento e competição em tempo real com CRM (Customer Relatioship Management)*. São Paulo, Brazil: Atlas.

Bronfenbrenner, U. (1979). *The Ecology of Human Development: Experiments by Nature and Design*. Cambridge, MA: Harvard University Press.

Brown, S. (2011). Social networks will receive 11% of online ad spending in 2011. *WealthVest Marketing*. Retrieved August 20, 2011, from http://www.wealthvest.com/blog/2011/01/20/statistics-social-networks-will-recieve-11-of-online-ad-spending-in-2011/

Brown, J. D., & Bobkowski, P. S. (2011). Older and newer media: Patterns of use and effects on adolescents' health and well-being. *Journal of Research on Adolescence*, *21*(1), 95–113. doi:10.1111/j.1532-7795.2010.00717.x.

Brown, J. J., & Reingen, P. H. (1987). Social ties and word-of-mouth referral behavior. *The Journal of Consumer Research*, *14*(December), 350–362. doi:10.1086/209118.

Brown, M. R., Pope, N., & Voges, K. E. (2003). Buying or browsing? An exploration of shopping orientations and online purchase intentions. *European Journal of Marketing*, *37*(11/12), 1666–1684. doi:10.1108/03090560310495401.

Brown, S. A. (2001). *CRM – Customer Relationship Management: Uma ferramenta estratégica para o mundo do e-business*. São Paulo, Brazil: Makron Books.

Brunet, P. M., & Schmidt, L. A. (2007). Is shyness context specific? Relation between shyness and online self-disclosure with and without a live webcam in young adults. *Journal of Research in Personality*, *41*(4), 938–945. doi:10.1016/j.jrp.2006.09.001.

Bruns, A., & Bahnisch, M. (2009). Social Media: Tools for User-Generated Content Social Drivers behind Growing Consumer Participation in User-Led Content Generation. *State of the Art*. Retrieved May 18, 2011, from http://www.smartservicescrc.com.au/PDF/Social_Media_State_of_the%20Art_March2009.pdf

Bryant, J., & Davies, L. (2006). Selective exposure processes. In Bryant, J., & Vorderer, P. (Eds.), *Psychology of Entertainment* (pp. 19–33). Mahwah, NJ: Lawrence Erlbaum Associates.

Bryant, J., & Zillmann, D. (1984). 'Using television to alleviate boredom and stress: Selective exposure as a function of induced excitational states. *Journal of Broadcasting*, *28*(1), 1–20. doi:10.1080/08838158409386511.

Bryant, S. C. (2008). A Strategic Framework for Integrating Web 2.0 into the Marketing Mix. In Deans, P. C. (Ed.), *Social Software and Web 2.0 Technology Trends* (pp. 29–43). New York: Information Science Reference. doi:10.4018/978-1-60566-122-3.ch003.

Buckingham, I. (2008). *Brand engagement*. Basingstoke: Palgrave-Macmillam.

Bughin, J. (2007). How companies can make the most of user-generated content. Retrieved from http://www.mckinseyquarterly.com/article_abstract_visitor.aspx?ar=2041&12=16&13=16

Burrows, P., & Galante, J. (2008). Yelp: Advertise or else? Bloomberg Businessweek, March 15, 2010, p. 27.

Business Insider. (2011). The next trillion dollar industry: 3D Printing Retrieved. Retrieved May 16, 2012, from: www.businessinsider.com/3d-printing-2011-2?op=1

Bustillo, M., & Zimmerman, A. (2009, April 23). Paid to pitch: Product reviews by bloggers draw scrutiny. *The Wall Street Journal*, p. B9.

Byrne, D. E. (1971). *The attraction paradigm*. New York, NY: Academic Press.

Byrne, D., & Nelson, D. (1965). Attraction as a linear function of proportion of positive reinforcements. *Journal of Personality and Social Psychology*, *1*(6), 659. doi:10.1037/h0022073 PMID:14300244.

Calder, B. J., Phillips, L. W., & Tybout, A. M. (1981). Designing research for application. *The Journal of Consumer Research*, *8*(September), 197–207. doi:10.1086/208856.

Campbell, M. C., & Kirmani, A. (2000). Consumers' use of persuasion knowledge: The effects of accessibility and cognitive capacity on perceptions of an influence agent. *The Journal of Consumer Research*, *27*(1), 69–83. doi:10.1086/314309.

Carney, D. R., Jost, J. T., Gosling, S. D., & Potter, J. (2008). The secret lives of liberals and conservatives: Personality profiles, interaction styles, and the things they leave behind. *Political Psychology, 29*(6), 807–840. doi:10.1111/j.1467-9221.2008.00668.x.

Carr, N. (2008). Is Google making us stupid? *Yearbook of the National Society for the Study of Education, 107*(2), 89–94. doi:10.1111/j.1744-7984.2008.00172.x.

Castells, M. (2009). *Communication power*. New York: Oxford University Press.

Centers for Disease Control and Prevention. (2012). *Are you pregnant or a new mom?* Retrieved April 2, 2012, from http://www.cdc.gov/Features/Text4Baby

Chai, S., & Kim, M. (2010). What makes bloggers share knowledge? An investigation on the role of trust. *International Journal of Information Management, 30*(5), 408–415. doi:10.1016/j.ijinfomgt.2010.02.005.

Chakrovorti, S., & Roson, R. (2004). Platform competition in two-sided markets: The case of payment networks. *Federal Reserve Bank of Chicago Emerging Payments Occasional Paper Series*.

Chan, A. (2006). Social interaction design case study: MySpace'. Retrieved from http://www.gravity7.com/G7_SID_case_myspace_v2.pdf

Chen, L. S.-L. (2008). Subjective well-being: Evidence from the different personality traits of online game teenager players. *Cyberpsychology & Behavior, 11*(5), 579–581. doi:10.1089/cpb.2007.0192 PMID:18771394.

Chen, Y. F. (2008). *A Study for the Effect of the experience Characteristics of the Web 2.0 based Video Blog on the User's Intention. Unpublished Master's theses.* Taiwan: Chung Yuan Christian University.

Chess Media Group. (2010). *Guide to understanding social CRM*.

Cheung, C. M. K., Zhu, L., Kwong, T., Chan, G. W. W., & Limayem, M. (2003). Online consumer behavior: A review and agenda for future research. In *Proceedings of 16th Bled eCommerce Conference eTransaction* (pp. 194-218).

Cheung, C. M. K., & Lee, M. K. O. (2008). The structure of Web-based information systems satisfaction: Testing of competing models. *Journal of the American Society for Information Science and Technology, 59*(10), 1617–1630. doi:10.1002/asi.20881.

Chevalier, J. A., & Mayzlin, D. (2006). The effect of word-of-mouth on sales: Online book reviews. *JMR, Journal of Marketing Research, 43*(August), 345–354. doi:10.1509/jmkr.43.3.345.

Chin, W. W., Marcolin, B. L., & Newsted, P. R. (2003). A partial least squares latent variable modeling approach for measuring interaction effects: Results form a Monte Carlo simulation study and an electronic-mail emotion adoption study. *Information Systems Research, 14*(2), 189–217. doi:10.1287/isre.14.2.189.16018.

Cho, H., & Salmon, C. (2007). Unintended effects of health communication campaigns. *The Journal of Communication, 57*(2), 293–317. doi:10.1111/j.1460-2466.2007.00344.x.

Choi, J., Watt, J., Dekkers, A., & Park, S. (2004). *Motives of Internet uses: Crosscultural perspective - the US, the Netherlands, and S. Korea.* Paper presented at annual meeting of the International Communication Association. New Orleans, LA.

Chou, C. L. (2007). From World Wide Web to Semantic Web. In Li, E., & Du, T. (Eds.), *Advances in Electronic Business* (Vol. 2, pp. 1–30). Hershey, PA: Idea Group Publishing.

Chou, W. S., Hunt, Y. M., Beckjord, E. B., Moser, R. P., & Hesse, B. W. (2009). Social media use in the United States: Implications for health communication. *Journal of Medical Internet Research, 11*(4), e48. doi:10.2196/jmir.1249 PMID:19945947.

Chung, D., & Kim, S. (2007). *Blog use among cancer patients and their companions: Uses, gratifications, and predictors of outcomes.* Paper presented at annual meeting of the International Communication Association. San Francisco, CA.

Cialdini, R. B. (2003). Crafting normative messages to protect the environment. *Current Directions in Psychological Science, 12*(4), 105–109. doi:10.1111/1467-8721.01242.

Cialdini, R. B., Reno, R. R., & Kallgren, C. A. (1990). A focus theory of normative conduct: Recycling the concept of norms to reduce littering in public places. *Journal of Personality and Social Psychology*, *58*(6), 1015–1026. doi:10.1037/0022-3514.58.6.1015.

Cipriani, F. (2011). *Estratégia em Mídias Sociais: como romper o paradoxo das redes sociais e tornar a concorrência irrelevante.* São Paulo, Brazil: Elsevier.

Clay, E. G., Snyder, M., Ridge, R., Copeland, J., Stukas, A., Haugen, J., & Miene, P. (1998). Understanding and assessing the motivations of volunteers: A functional approach. *Journal of Personality and Social Psychology*, *74*(6), 1516–1530. doi:10.1037/0022-3514.74.6.1516 PMID:9654757.

Clemons, E. (2009). The complex problem of monetizing virtual electronic social networks. *Decision Support Systems*, *48*, 46–56. doi:10.1016/j.dss.2009.05.003.

Cobb, C. J., & Hoyer, W. D. (1986). Planned versus impulse purchase behavior. *Journal of Retailing*, *62*(4), 384–409.

Cobo, C., & Pardo, H. (2007). *Planeta web 2.0. Inteligencia colectiva o medios fast food [Web 2.0 planet. Collective intelligence or fast food media].* Barcelona / México DF: Grup de Recerca d'Interaccions Digitals, Universitat de Vic. Flacso México.

Cole, J. (2000). *Surveying the Digital Future.* Los Angeles: UCLA Center for Communication Policy.

Collins, N. L., & Miller, L. C. (1994). Self-disclosure and liking: A meta-analytic review. *Psychological Bulletin*, *116*(3), 457–475. doi:10.1037/0033-2909.116.3.457 PMID:7809308.

Constant, D., Sproull, L., & Kiesler, S. (1996). The kindness of strangers: The usefulness of electronic weak ties for technical advice. *Organization Science*, *7*(2), 119–135. doi:10.1287/orsc.7.2.119.

Constantinides, E. (2004). Influencing the online consumer's behavior: The Web experience. *Internet Research*, *14*(2), 111–126. doi:10.1108/10662240410530835.

Constantinides, E., & Fountain, S. (2008). Web 2.0: Conceptual foundations and marketing Issues. *Journal of Direct. Data and Digital Marketing Practice*, *9*(3), 231–244. doi:10.1057/palgrave.dddmp.4350098.

Constantinides, E., Lorenzo, C., & Gómez, M. A. (2008). Social Media: A New Frontier for Retailers? *European Retail Research*, *22*(1), 1–28.

Correa, T. (2010). The participation divide among "online experts": Experience, skills, and psychological factors as predictors of college students' web content creation. *Journal of Computer-Mediated Communication*, *16*(1), 71–92. doi:10.1111/j.1083-6101.2010.01532.x.

Correa, T., Hinsley, A. W., & de Zuniga, H. G. (2010). Who interacts on the Web?: The intersection of users' personality and social media use. *Computers in Human Behavior*, *26*, 247–253. doi:10.1016/j.chb.2009.09.003.

Correa, T., & Jeong, S.-H. (2011). Race and online content creation: Why minorities are actively participating in the Web. *Information Communication and Society*, *14*(5), 638–659. doi:10.1080/1369118X.2010.514355.

Correa, T., Willard Hinsley, A., & Gil de Zúñiga, H. (2010). Who interacts on the Web?: The intersection between users' personality and social media use. *Computers in Human Behavior*, *26*(2), 247–253. doi:10.1016/j.chb.2009.09.003.

Côrtes, P. L., & Rosochansky, M. (2001). *Web Marketing: Estabelecendo vantagens competitivas na Internet.* São Paulo, Brazil: Érica.

Costa, R. (2005). On a new community concept: Social networks, personal communities, collective intelligence. *Interface: Comunicacao, Saude, Educacao*, *9*(17), 235–243. doi:10.1590/S1414-32832005000200003.

Courtois, C., Mechant, P., De Marez, L., & Verleye, G. (2009). Gratifications and Seeding Behavior of Online Adolescents. *Journal of Computer-Mediated Communication*, *15*, 109–137. doi:10.1111/j.1083-6101.2009.01496.x.

Cox, S. A., Krasniewicz, J. A., Perkins, J. S., & Cox, J. A. (2006). Modelling the organizational transformation associated with implementing e-business collaborative systems in the supply chain. In *Proceedings of the British Academy of Management Conference (BAM2006) in Association with the University of Ulster and Queen's University,* Belfast, Northern Ireland: BAM.

Cox, S., Perkins, J., & Green, P. (2001) A positioning framework for developing an e-business strategy. In *Proceedings of the Eighth European Conference on Information Technology Evaluation*, Oxford, UK: Oriel College.

Cox, E. P. I. (1980). The optimal number of response alternatives for a scale: A review. *JMR, Journal of Marketing Research*, *17*(4), 407–422. doi:10.2307/3150495.

Cox, S. A. (2012). *Managing information in morphing organizations*. Basingstoke, UK: Palgrave Macmillan.

Cox, S. A., & Perkins, J. S. (2008). Factors for effective e-collaboration in the supply chain. In Kock, N. (Ed.), *Encyclopaedia of E-Collaboration* (pp. 279–285). Hershey, PA: IGI Global.

Coyle, K. (2007). The Library Catalog in a 2.0 World. *Journal of Academic Librarianship*, *33*(2), 289–291. doi:10.1016/j.acalib.2007.02.003.

Cozby, P. C. (1973). Self-disclosure: A literature review. *Psychological Bulletin*, *79*(2), 73. doi:10.1037/h0033950 PMID:4567729.

Craig, E. (2007). Changing paradigms: Managed learning environments and Web 2.0. *Campus-Wide Information Systems*, *24*(3), 151–161. doi:10.1108/10650740710762185.

Cronin, J. J. (2009). Upgrading to Web 2.0: An Experiential Project to Build a Marketing Wiki. *Journal of Marketing Education*, *31*(1), 66–75. doi:10.1177/0273475308329250.

Croom, S. R. (2005). The impact of e-business on supply chain management: An empirical study of key developments. *International Journal of Operations & Production Management*, *25*(1), 55–73. doi:10.1108/01443570510572240.

Cudmore, A. B., Bobrowski, E. P., & Kiguradze, T. (2011). Encouraging consumer searching behavior on healthcare web sites. *Journal of Consumer Marketing*, *28*(4), 290–299. doi:10.1108/07363761111143187.

Cunningham, H., Maynard, D., Bontcheva, K., & Tablan, V. (2002). GATE: A Framework and Graphical Development Environment for Robust NLP Tools and Applications. In *Proceedings of the 40th Anniversary Meeting of the Association for Computational Linguistics* (pp. 349-373.). Philadelphia, PA.

Cymfony. (2006). Making the case for a social media strategy. Retrieved October 8, 2010, from http://www.nedma.com/pdfs/making%20the%20case%20for%20social%20media%202007.pdf

D'Antonio, M. (2010). Navigating on the wave of mobile (in Portuguese). *Peppers and Rogers*. Retrieved from http://www.1to1.com.br/view.aspx?docId=34345

Dacko, S. G. (2008). *Advanced Dictionary of Marketing: Putting Theory to Use*. Oxford, UK: Oxford University Press.

D'Angelo, J. M. (2010). *Spa Business Strategies: A Plan for Success* (2nd ed.). Milady.

Darke, P. R., & Ritchie, R. J. B. (2007). The defensive consumer: Advertising deception, defensive processing, and distrust. *JMR, Journal of Marketing Research*, *44*(1), 114–127. doi:10.1509/jmkr.44.1.114.

Daugherty, T., Eastin, M. S., & Bright, L. (2008). Exploring consumer motivations for creating user-generated content. *Journal of Interactive Advertising*, *8*(2), 16–25.

Daugherty, T., Eastin, M. S., & Bright, L. (2008). Exploring consumer motivations for creating user-generated content. *Journal of Interactive Advertising*, *8*, 16–25.

Daugherty, T., Li, H., & Biocca, F. (2008). Consumer learning and the effects of virtual experience. *Psychology and Marketing*, *25*(7), 568–586. doi:10.1002/mar.20225.

Davis, M. (2010, October 4). *Social media to improve supply chain?* [Web log comment]. Retrieved from http://blogs.gartner.com/matthew-davis/2010/10/04/social-media-to-improve-supply-chain/ (February 24, 2011).

Davis, F. D. (1989). Perceived usefulness, perceived ease of use and user acceptance of Information Technology. *Management Information Systems Quarterly*, *13*(3), 319–340. doi:10.2307/249008.

Davis, F. D., Bagozzi, R. P., & Warshaw, P. R. (1989). User acceptance of computer technology: A comparison of two theoretical models. *Management Science*, *35*(8), 982–1003. doi:10.1287/mnsc.35.8.982.

Davis, F. D., Bagozzi, R. P., & Warshaw, P. R. (1992). Extrinsic and intrinsic motivation to use computers in the workplace. *Journal of Applied Social Psychology*, *22*(14), 1111–1132. doi:10.1111/j.1559-1816.1992.tb00945.x.

de Valck, K., van Bruggen, G., & Wierenga, B. (2009). Virtual communities: A marketing perspective. *Decision Support Systems, 47*, 185–203. doi:10.1016/j.dss.2009.02.008.

DeBono, A., Shmueli, D., & Muraven, M. (2011). Rude and inappropriate: The role of self-control in following social norms. *Personality and Social Psychology Bulletin, 37*(1), 136–146. doi:10.1177/0146167210391478 PMID:21177879.

DeFelice, A. (2006). A new Marketing Medium. *CRM Magazine, 10*(1), 32–35.

Deighton, J., & Grayson, K. (1995). Marketing and seduction: Building exchange relationships by managing social consensus. *The Journal of Consumer Research, 36*(1), 660–676. doi:10.1086/209426.

Deighton, J., & Kornfeld, L. (2009). Interactivity's unanticipated consequences for marketers and Marketing. *Journal of Interactive Marketing, 23*, 4–10. doi:10.1016/j.intmar.2008.10.001.

Deighton, J., Romer, D., & McQueen, J. (1989). Using drama to persuade. *The Journal of Consumer Research, 16*(3), 335–343. doi:10.1086/209219.

Delia, J. G., & O'Keefe, B. J. (1979). Constructivism: The development of communication in children. In Wartella, E. (Ed.), *Children communicating: Media and development of thought, speech, understanding* (pp. 157–185). Beverly Hills, CA: Sage.

Dellarocas, C. (2003). The digitization of word of mouth: Promises and challenges of online feedback mechanisms. *Management Science, 49*(10), 1407–1424. doi:10.1287/mnsc.49.10.1407.17308.

DeLone, W. H., & McLean, E. R. (1992). Information systems success: The quest for the dependent variable. *Information Systems Research, 3*(1), 60–95. doi:10.1287/isre.3.1.60.

DeLone, W. H., & McLean, E. R. (2003). The DeLone and McLean Model of Information System success: A ten-year update. *Journal of Management Information Systems, 19*(4), 9–30.

Dentchev, N. A. (2005). *Integrating Corporate social responsibility in business models. 05/284.* Working paper. Ghent University, Belgium.

Derlega, V. J., & Berg, J. H. (1987). *Self-disclosure: Theory, research, and therapy.* Newbury Park, CA: Sage.

Derlega, V. J., & Grzelak, J. (1979). Appropriateness of self-disclosure. In Chelune, G. J. (Ed.), *Self-disclosure: Origins, Patterns, and Implications of Openness in Interpersonal Relationships* (pp. 151–176). San Francisco, CA: Jossey-Bass.

Deshpande, A., & Jadad, A. (2006). Web 2.0: Could it help move the health system into the 21st century? *Journal of Men's Health & Gender, 3*(4), 332–336. doi:10.1016/j.jmhg.2006.09.004.

Dhar, R., & Wertenbroch, K. (2000). Consumer choice between hedonic and utilitarian goods. *JMR, Journal of Marketing Research, 37*(1), 60–71. doi:10.1509/jmkr.37.1.60.18718.

Diani, M., & McAdam, D. (2003). *Social movements and networks: Relational approaches to collective action.* New York: Oxford University Press. doi:10.1093/0199251789.001.0001.

Dickerson, M. D., & Gentry, J. W. (1983). Characteristics of Adopters and Non-Adopters of Home Computers. *The Journal of Consumer Research, 10*(September), 225–235. doi:10.1086/208961.

Dickie, J., & Trailer, B. (2006). *2006 sales performance optimization – Survey results and analysis.* Boulder, CO: CSO Insights.

Diener, E., Emmons, R., Larsen, R., & Griffin, S. (1985). The satisfaction with life scale. *Journal of Personality Assessment, 49*(1), 71–75. doi:10.1207/s15327752jpa4901_13 PMID:16367493.

Dijcks, J.-P. (2012). Oracle: Big data for the enterprise. *Oracle Whitepaper.* Retrieved October 13, 2001, from http://www.oracle.com/us/products/database/big-data-for-enterprise-519135.pdf

Dillon, W. R., & Kumar, A. (1994). Latent Structure and Other Mixture Models in Marketing: An Integrative Survey and Overview. In Bagozzi, R. P. (Ed.), *Advanced Methods of Marketing Research* (pp. 259–351). Cambridge, MA: Blackwell Business.

Dingley, S., & Perkins, J. (1999). Tempering links in the supply chain with collaborative systems. In *Proceedings of the 9th Annual Conference of Business Information Technology: Generative Futures* (document 51). Manchester, UK: Manchester Metropolitan University.

Dittmar, H., & Drury, J. (2000). Self-image – is it in the bag? A qualitative comparison between "ordinary" and "excessive" consumers. *Journal of Economic Psychology*, *21*(2), 109–142. doi:10.1016/S0167-4870(99)00039-2.

Dorbe, C., Dragomir, A., & Preda, G. (2009). Consumer Innovativeness: A Marketing Approach. *Journal of Management & Marketing*, *4*(2), 19–34.

Drezner, D. W., & Farell, H. (2004). *The power and politics of blogs*. Paper presented at the 2004 American Political Science Association. Chicago, IL.

Drury, G. (2008). Social media: Should marketers engage and how can it be done effectively? *Journal of Direct. Data and Digital Marketing Practice*, *9*(3), 274–277. doi:10.1057/palgrave.dddmp.4350096.

Duck, S. (1991). *Understanding relationships*. New York: The Guilford Press.

Duck, S., Rutt, D. J., Hoy, M., & Strejc, H. H. (1991). Some evident truths about conversations in everyday relationships all communications are not created equal. *Human Communication Research*, *18*(2), 228–267. doi:10.1111/j.1468-2958.1991.tb00545.x.

Du, H., & Wagner, C. (2006). Weblog success: Exploring the role of Technology. *International Journal of Human-Computer Studies*, *64*, 789–798. doi:10.1016/j.ijhcs.2006.04.002.

Dwyer, P. (2007). *Building trust with corporate blogs*. Paper presented at the International Conference on Weblogs and Social Media. Boulder, CO.

Dwyer, P. (2007). Measuring the Value of Electronic word of Mouth and Its Impact in Consumer Communities. *Journal of Interactive Marketing*, *21*(2), 63–79. doi:10.1002/dir.20078.

Ebersbach, A., Glaser, M., Heigl, R., & Warta, A. (2008). *Wiki Web Collaboration (2nded.)*. Berlin, Germany: Springer Verlag.

Edelman (2012). *Edelman Trust Barometer Survey*. Retrieved April 24, 2012, from http://trust.edelman.com/trust-download/global- results/

Ehrenberg, A., Juckes, S., White, K. M., & Walsh, S. P. (2008). Personality and self-esteem as predictors of young people's technology use. *Cyberpsychology & Behavior*, *11*(6), 739–741. doi:10.1089/cpb.2008.0030 PMID:18991531.

Ellison, N. B., Steinfield, C., & Lampe, C. (2007). The benefits of Facebook "friends": Social capital and college students' use of online social network sites. *Journal of Computer-Mediated Communication*, *12*(4), 1143–1168. doi:10.1111/j.1083-6101.2007.00367.x.

eMarketer (2010). *Social network ad spending to approach $1.7 billion this year*. Retrieved May 10, 2011, from http://www.mcvaynewmedia.com/social-network-ad-spending-to-approach-17-billion-this-year/

Enslow, B,., & Smith, C. (1998). Developing internet-enabled supply chain strategies. *GartnerGroup Strategic Analysis Report, (R-05-9476)*.

Escalas, J. E. (2004). Imagine yourself in the product: Mental simulation, narrative transportation, and persuasion. *Journal of Advertising*, *33*(2), 37–48. doi:10.1080/00913367.2004.10639163.

E-tailing Group. (2009). *The E-tailing group/Power Reviews 1st annual community and social media survey*. Retrieved August 1, 2011, from http://www.e-tailing.com/content/?p=120

eUKhost.com. (2008). *What does YouTube Videos Mean To Internet Marketers?* Retrieved January 15, 2011, from http://blog.eukhost.com/webhosting/what-does-youtube-mean-to-internet-marketers/

Farquhar, L., & Meeds, R. (2007). Types of fantasy sports users and their motivations. *Journal of Computer-Mediated Communication*, *12*, 1208–1228. doi:10.1111/j.1083-6101.2007.00370.x.

Feeny, D. F., Earl, M. J., & Edwards, B. (1996). Organizational arrangement for IS: Roles of users and specialists. In Earl, M. J. (Ed.), *Information Management: The Organizational Dimension* (pp. 231–246). Oxford, UK: Oxford University Press.

380

Fehr, B. (2000). The life cycle of friendship. In Hendrick, C., & Hendrick, S. S. (Eds.), *Close relationships: A sourcebook* (pp. 71–82). Thousand Oaks, CA: Sage. doi:10.4135/9781452220437.n6.

Feick, L., & Higie, R. A. (1992). The effects of preference heterogeneity and source characteristics on ad processing and judgments about endorsers. *Journal of Advertising, 21*(2), 9–23.

Feigenbaum, L., Herman, I., Hongsermeier, T., Neumann, E., & Stephens, S. (2007). The Semantic Web in Action. *Scientific American Magazine, 297*, 64–71. doi:10.1038/scientificamerican1207-90 PMID:18237102.

Fishbein, M., & Ajzen, I. (1975). *Belief, attitude, intentions and behavior: An introduction to theory and research.* Boston, MA: Addison-Wesley.

Fletcher, G. J. O., & Kerr, P. S. G. (2010). Through the eyes of love: Reality and illusion in intimate relationships. *Psychological Bulletin, 136*(4), 627–658. doi:10.1037/a0019792 PMID:20565171.

Flickr Blog. (2011, August 4). *6,000,000,000.* Retrieved February 25, 2012, from http://blog.flickr.net/en/2011/08/04/6000000000/

Flynn, L. R., & Goldsmith, R. (1993). A validation of the Goldsmith and Hofacker innovativeness scale. *Educational and Psychological Measurement, 53*(4), 1105–1116. doi:10.1177/0013164493053004023.

Ford, G. T., Smith, D. B., & Swasy, J. L. (1990). Consumer skepticism of advertising claims: Testing hypotheses from economics of information. *The Journal of Consumer Research, 16*(4), 433–441. doi:10.1086/209228.

Fornell, C. R., & Bookstein, F. L. (1982). Two structural equation model: LISREL and PLS Applied to Consumer Exit-Voice Theory. *JMR, Journal of Marketing Research, 19*(4), 440–452. doi:10.2307/3151718.

Fornell, C., & Larcker, D. F. (1981). Structural equation models with unobservable variables and measurement error: Algebra and statistics. *JMR, Journal of Marketing Research, 18*(3), 382–388. doi:10.2307/3150980.

Forrester Research. (2008). Trends 2008: European eCommerce and Online Retail. Retrieved September 23, 2010, from http://www.forrester.com/Trends+2008+European+eCommerce+And+Online+Retail/fulltext/-/E-RES44528

Forrester Social Technographics Profile tool. (2008). *Forrester Research.* Retrieved from http://www.forrester.com/Groundswell/profile_tool.html

Fox, S. (2009). e-Riches 2.0: Next-Generation Marketing Strategies for Making Millions Online. New York: Amacom.

Frenzen, J. K., & Davis, H. L. (1990). Purchasing behavior in embedded markets. *The Journal of Consumer Research, 17*(1), 1–12. doi:10.1086/208532.

Friedman, T. L. (2005). *The world is flat.* New York: Farrar, Straus & Giroux.

Friestad, M., & Wright, P. (1994). The persuasion knowledge model: How people cope with persuasion attempts. *The Journal of Consumer Research, 21*(1), 1–31. doi:10.1086/209380.

FTC. (2009). Guides concerning the use of endorsements and testimonials in advertising. Retrieved August 1, 2011 from http://www.ftc.gov/os/2009/10/091005 revisedendorsementguides.pdf

Funk, T. (2011). *Social Media Playbook for Business: Reaching Your Online Community with Twitter, Facebook, LinkedIn, and More.* Santa Barbara, CA: Praeger.

Furtado, B. (2011). Acordo Meu Carro Falha & Renault. *Mundo do Marketing*, March 23. Retrieved July 10, 2012, from http://mundodomarketing.com.br/blogs/consumo-e-inovacao/ 18068/acordo-meu-carro-falha-renault.html

Furtado, B. (2012). *Social Media: Trends to 2012.* Retrieved from http://www.baguete.com.br/artigos/1102/bianca-furtado/16/04/2012/social-media-tendencias-para-2012

Gabszewicz, J. J., & Wauthy, X. Y. (2004). *Two-sided markets and price competition with multi-homing, Mimeo CORE.* Louvain-la-Neuve University.

Galegher, J., Sproull, L., & Kiesler, S. (1998). Legitimacy, authority, and community in electronic support groups. *Written Communication, 15*(4), 493–530. doi:10.1177/0741088398015004003.

Gammelgaard, J., & Ritter, T. (2005). The knowledge retrieval matrix: Codification and personalisation as separate strategies. *Journal of Knowledge Management, 9*(4), 133–143. doi:10.1108/13673270510610387.

Gangadharbatla, H. (2008). Facebook me: Collective self-esteem, need to belong, and Internet self-efficacy as predictors of the iGeneration's attitudes toward social networking sites. *Journal of Interactive Advertising, 8,* 5–15.

Gangadharbatla, H. (2009). Exploring Gen Y's motivations to join social networking sites. *Media Asia, 36,* 240–248.

Gangadharbatla, H. (2009). Individual Differences in Social Networking Site Adoption. In Romm-Livermore, C., & Setzekorn, K. (Eds.), *Social Networking Communities and E-Dating Services: Concepts and Implications* (pp. 1–17). Hershey, PA: IGI Global. doi:10.4018/978-1-60566-984-7.ch101.

Gangadharbatla, H. (2012). Social media and advertising theory. In Rodgers, S., & Thorson, E. (Eds.), *Advertising Theory* (pp. 402–416). New York: Routledge.

Gartner Inc. (2008). *Gartner says 90 per cent of corporate virtual world projects fail within 18 months.* Retrieved from http://www.gartner.com/it/page.jsp?id=670507

Gefen, D., Karahanna, E., & Straub, D. W. (2003). Trust and TAM in online shopping: An integrated model. *Management Information Systems Quarterly, 27*(1), 51–90.

Gerber, A. S., Huber, G. A., Doherty, D., & Dowling, C. M. (2011). Big Five personality traits in the political arena. *Annual Review of Political Science, 14,* 265–281. doi:10.1146/annurev-polisci-051010-111659.

Gerber, A. S., Huber, G. A., Doherty, D., Dowling, C. M., & Ha, S. E. (2010). Personality and political attitudes: Relationships across issue domains and political contexts. *The American Political Science Review, 104,* 111–133. doi:10.1017/S0003055410000031.

Giffin, K. (1967). The contribution of studies of source credibility to a theory of interpersonal trust in the communication process. *Psychological Bulletin, 68*(2), 104–120. doi:10.1037/h0024833 PMID:6065581.

Gil de Zúñiga, H., & Valenzuela, S. (2011). The mediating path to a stronger citizenship: Online and offline networks, weak ties and civic engagement. *Communication Research, 38*(3), 397–421. doi:10.1177/0093650210384984.

Gill, K. E. (2004). How can we measure the influence of the blogosphere? In *Proceedings of the WWW2004 Conference.* New York: ACM. Retrieved from http://citeseerx.ist.psu.edu/viewdoc/download?doi=10.1.1.124.2509&rep=rep1&type=pdf

Gill, P., Arlitt, M., Li, Z., & Mahanti, A. (2007). YouTube traffic characterization: A view from the edge. In *Proceedings of Internet Measurement Conference.* San Diego, CA: ACM.

Gillin, P. (2007). *The new influencers: A marketer's guide to the new social media.* Sanger, CA: Quill Driver.

Gillin, P. (2009). *Secrets of Social Media Marketing.* Fresno, CA: Quill Driver Books.

Ginossar, T. (2005). *Exploring participation in cancer-related virtual communities.* Paper presented at annual meeting of the International Communication Association. New York.

Glaser, M. (2007). Twitter founders thrive on micro-blogging constraints. *Public Broadcasting Service (PBS).* Retrieved from http://www.pbs.org/mediashift/2007/05/twitter-founders-thrive-on-micro-blogging-constraints137.html

Global Footprint Network. (2012). *Personal footprint.* Retrieved April 2, 2012, from http://www.footprintnetwork.org/en/index.php/GFN/page/personal_footprint

Godes, D., & Mayzlin, D. (2009). Firm-created word-of-mouth communication: Evidence from a field test. *Marketing Science, 28*(4), 721–739. doi:10.1287/mksc.1080.0444.

Goffman, E. (1959). *The Presentation of Self in Everyday Life.* New York: Doubleday.

Goldberg, L. R. (1990). An alternative "description of personality": The Big-Five Factor Structure. *Journal of Personality and Social Psychology, 59*(6), 1216–1229. doi:10.1037/0022-3514.59.6.1216 PMID:2283588.

Goldenberg, J., Han, S., Lehmann, D. R., & Hong, J. W. (2009). The role of hubs in the adoption process. *Journal of Marketing, 72*(March), 1–12. doi:10.1509/jmkg.73.2.1.

Goldenberg, J., Libai, B., & Muller, E. (2001). Talk of the network: A complex systems look at the underlying process of word-of-mouth. *Marketing Letters*, *12*(3), 211–223. doi:10.1023/A:1011122126881.

Goldsmith, R. E., & Hofacker, C. F. (1991). Measuriing Consumer Innovativeness. *Journal of the Academy of Marketing Science*, *19*, 209–221. doi:10.1007/BF02726497.

Goldsmith, R., & Flynn, L. R. (1992). Identifying innovators in consumer product markets. *European Journal of Marketing*, *26*(2), 42–55. doi:10.1108/03090569210022498.

Gonçalves Filho, C., & Gonçalves, C. A. (1997). Relationship marketing and information technologies: Analyzes in financial institutions. In Encontro Anual Da Associação Nacional De Programas De Pós-Graduação Em Administração, 21., 1997, Rio das Pedras. Anais. Rio das Pedras: ANPAD, 1997. 1 CD-ROM.

Goodhue, D. L., & Thompson, R. L. (1995). Task-technology fit and individual performance. *Management Information Systems Quarterly*, *19*(2), 213–236. doi:10.2307/249689.

Google. (2011). Introducing the Google+ project: Real-life sharing, rethought for the web. *Google Blog*. Retrieved Aug 15, 2011, from http://googleblog.blogspot.com/2011/06/introducing-google-project-real-life.html

Gorgônio, F. L., Araújo Neto, J. P., & Silva, T. M. (2012). A framework for designing recommender system for consumers using distributed data clustering. In Colomo-Palacios, R. et al. (Eds.), *Customer relationship management and the social semantic web: Enabling cliens conexus* (pp. 231–252). Hershey, PA: IGI Global.

Gosling, S. D., Augustine, A. A., Vazire, S., Holtzman, N., & Gaddis, S. (2011). Manifestations of personality on online social networks: Self-reported Facebook-related behaviors and observable profile information. *Cyberpsychology, Behavior, and Social Networking*, *14*(9), 483–488. doi:10.1089/cyber.2010.0087 PMID:21254929.

Gosling, S. D., Rentfrow, P. J., & Swann, W. B. J. (2003). A very brief measure of the big five personality domains. *Journal of Research in Personality*, *37*(6), 504–528. doi:10.1016/S0092-6566(03)00046-1.

Grabber, D. A. (1993). *Mass Media and American Politics* (4th ed.). Washington, DC: Congressional Quarterly.

Graham, P. (2005). *Web 2.0*. Retrieved October 11, 2006, from http://www.paulgraham.com/web20.html

Grandon, E., & Pearson, J. (2003). Strategic Value and Adoption of Electronic Commerce: An Empirical Study of Chilean Small and Medium Businesses. *Journal of Global Information Technology Management*, *6*(3), 22–43.

Granovetter, M. S. (1973). The strength of weak ties. *American Journal of Sociology*, *78*(6), 1360–1380. doi:10.1086/225469.

Granovetter, M. S. (1973). The strength of weak ties. *American Journal of Sociology*, *78*, 1360–1380. doi:10.1086/225469.

Grappone, J., & Couzin, G. (2008). *Search Engine Optimization: An Hour A Day* (2nd ed.). Hoboken, NJ: Wiley Publishing.

Greco, D., & White, B. (2009). Alphabet soup: How CRM, ERP, Web 2.0 & Sales 2.0 is creating a superior sales experience: A case study. In ISECON (Ed.), *The Proceedings of the Information System Education Conference 2009* (vol. 26, pp. 1-9). Washington, DC.

Greenberg, P. (2009). *Social CRM Comes of Age*. Retrieved from http://www.oracle.com/us/products/applications/crmondemand/036062.pdf

Greenberg, P. (2001). *CRM – Customer Relationship Management na velocidade da luz: conquista e lealdade de clientes em tempo real na Internet*. Rio de Janeiro, Brazil: Campus.

Greenberg, P. (2010). *CRM at the speed of light: Social CRM strategies, tools, and techniques for engaging your customers* (4th ed.). New York: McGraw Hill.

Green, M. C., & Brock, T. C. (2000). The role of transportation in the persuasiveness of public narratives. *Journal of Personality and Social Psychology*, *79*(5), 701. doi:10.1037/0022-3514.79.5.701 PMID:11079236.

Greiner, L. E. (1972). Evolution and revolutions as organizations grow. *Harvard Business Review*, (July-August): 37–46.

Grewal, D., Iyer, G. R., & Levy, M. (2004). Internet retailing: Enablers, limiters and market consequences. *Journal of Business Research*, *57*(7), 703–713. doi:10.1016/S0148-2963(02)00348-X.

Grippa, F. (2009). A social network scorecard to monitor knowledge flows across communication media. *Knowledge Management Research and Practice, 7*(4), 317–328. doi:10.1057/kmrp.2009.24.

Grishman, R. (1996). Message Understanding Conference-6: A brief history. In *Proceedings of the 16th Conference on Computational Linguistics* (pp. 466-471). Stroudsburg, PA: Association for Computational Linguistics Press.

Guadagno, R. E., Okdie, B. M., & Eno, C. A. (2008). Who blogs? Personality predictors of blogging. *Computers in Human Behavior, 24*, 1993–2004. doi:10.1016/j.chb.2007.09.001.

Gummesson, E. (1998). Implementation requires a relationship marketing paradigm. *Journal of the Academy of Marketing Science, 26*(3), 242–249. doi:10.1177/0092070398263006.

Guttman, N., & Salmon, C. T. (2004). Guilt, fear, stigma and knowledge gaps: Ethical issues in public health communication interventions. *Bioethics, 18*(6), 531–553. doi:10.1111/j.1467-8519.2004.00415.x PMID:15580723.

Haenlein, M., & Kaplan, A. M. (2009). Flagship brand stores within virtual worlds: The impact of virtual store exposure on real life band attitudes and purchase intent. *Recherche et Applications en Marketing, 24*(3), 57–80. doi:10.1177/076737010902400304.

Hair, J. F. Jr, Anderson, R. E., Tatham, R. L., & Black, W. C. (2000). *Multivariate data analysis with reading.* New York: MacMillan.

Hall, H. (2011). Relationship and role transformations in social media environments. *The Electronic Library, 29*(4), 421–428. doi:10.1108/02640471111156704.

Halligan, B., & Shah, D. (2010). *Inbound Marketing.* Hoboken, NJ: Wiley Publishing.

Hamburger, Y. A., & Ben-Artzi, E. (2000). The relationship between extraversion and neuroticism and the different uses of the Internet. *Computers in Human Behavior, 16*(4), 441–449. doi:10.1016/S0747-5632(00)00017-0.

Hampton, K. N., Sessions Goulet, L., Rainie, L., & Purcell, K. (2011). *Social networking sites and our lives.* Washingston, D.C.: Pew Internet & American Life Project.

Handy, C. (1995). Trust and the virtual organization. *Harvard Business Review,* (May): 40–49.

Haque, U. (2011). *The new capitalist manifesto.* Boston: Harvard Business Publishing.

Hardey, M. (2008). Public health and Web 2.0. *The Journal of the Royal Society for the Promotion of Health, 128*(4), 181–189. doi:10.1177/1466424008092228 PMID:18678114.

Harding, S., Phillips, D., & Fogarty, M. P. (1986). *Contrasting values in Western Europe: Unity, diversity and change.* London: Macmillan.

Hargittai, E., & Walejko, G. (2008). The participation divide: Content creation and sharing in the digital age. *Information Communication and Society, 11*(2), 239–256. doi:10.1080/13691180801946150.

Harris, L., & Rae, A. (2011). Building a personal brand through social networking. *The Journal of Business Strategy, 32*(5), 14–21. doi:10.1108/02756661111165435.

Hart, B. (2012). Will 3D Printing Change the World? *Forbes.* Retrieved May 14, 2012, from http://www.forbes.com/sites/gcaptain/2012/03/06/will-3d-printing-change-the-world/

Hausman, A. (2000). A multi-method investigation of consumer motivations in impulse buying behavior. *Journal of Consumer Marketing, 17*(5), 403–426. doi:10.1108/07363760010341045.

Hayes, G., & Papworth, L. (2008). *The future of social media entertainment.* Paper presented at the Screen Producers Association of Australia Fringe. Sydney, Australia.

Haythornthwaite, C. (2005). Social networks and internet connectivity effects. *Information Communication and Society, 8*(2), 125–147. doi:10.1080/13691180500146185.

Heath, C., Bell, C., & Sternberg, E. (2001). Emotional selection in memes: The case of urban legends. *Journal of Personality and Social Psychology, 81*(6), 1028–1041. doi:10.1037/0022-3514.81.6.1028 PMID:11761305.

Heinonen, K. (2009). The Influence of Customer Activity on e-Service Value-in-use. *International Journal of Electronic Business, 7*(2), 190–214. doi:10.1504/IJEB.2009.024627.

Heinonen, K., & Strandvik, T. (2009). Monitoring value-in-use of e-service. *Journal of Service Management, 20*(1), 33–51. doi:10.1108/09564230910936841.

Hennig-Thurau, T., Gwinner, K. P., Walsh, G., & Gremle, D. D. (2004). Electronic word-of-mouth via consumer-opinion platforms: What motivates consumers to articulate themselves on the internet? *Journal of Interactive Marketing, 18*(1), 38–52. doi:10.1002/dir.10073.

Herman, I. (2009). *W3C semantic web frequently asked questions.* Retrieved July 8, 2012, from http://www.w3.org/RDF/FAQ

Herring, S. C. (1993). Gender and democracy in computer-mediated communication. *Electronic Journal of Communication, 3*(2).

Herring, S. C., Scheidt, L. A., Wright, E., & Bonus, S. (2005). Weblogs as a bridging genre. *Information Technology & People, 18*(2), 142–171. doi:10.1108/09593840510601513.

Hertweck, B. M., Rakes, T. R., & Rees, L. P. (2010). Using an Intelligent agent to classify competitor behavior and develop an effective E-market counterstrategy. *Expert Systems with Applications: An International Journal, 37*(12), 8841–8849. doi:10.1016/j.eswa.2010.06.013.

Heyman, J., & Ariely, D. (2004). Effort for payment: A tale of two markets. *Psychological Science, 15*(11), 787–793. doi:10.1111/j.0956-7976.2004.00757.x PMID:15482452.

Hill, G. (2009). How customers drive innovation at P&G. *Customerthink Research Library.* Retrieved from http://www.customerthink.com

Hinz, O., Skiera, B., Barrot, C., & Becker, J. U. (2011). Seeding strategies for viral marketing: An empirical comparison. *Journal of Marketing, 75*(November), 55–71. doi:10.1509/jm.10.0088.

Hirschman, E. C. (1980). Innnovativeness, Novelty Seeking and Consumer Creativity. *The Journal of Consumer Research, 7*, 283–295. doi:10.1086/208816.

Hoffman, D. L. (2012). Internet indispensability, online social capital, and consumer well-being. In Mick, D. G., Pettigrew, S., Pechmann, C., & Ozanne, J. L. (Eds.), *Transformative Consumer Research for Personal and Collective Well-being* (pp. 193–204). New York: Routledge.

Hoffman, D. L., & Novak, T. P. (1996). Marketing in hypermedia computer-mediated environments: Conceptual foundations. *Journal of Marketing, 60*(3), 50–68. doi:10.2307/1251841.

Hoffman, D. L., Novak, T. P., & Chatterjee, P. (2000). Commercial Scenarios for the Web: Opportunities and Challenges. *Journal of Computer-Mediated Communication, 1*(3), 107–136.

Hogarth, R. M., & Einhorn, H. J. (1992). Order effects in belief updating: The belief-adjustment model. *Cognitive Psychology, 24*(1), 1–55. doi:10.1016/0010-0285(92)90002-J.

Holbrook, M. B., & Hirschman, E. C. (1982). The experiential aspects of consumption: Consumer fantasies, feelings, and fun. *The Journal of Consumer Research, 9*(2), 132–140. doi:10.1086/208906.

Holmes, J. H., & Letts, J. D. (1977). Product sampling and word of mouth. *Journal of Advertising Research, 17*(5), 35–40.

Holzwarth, M., Janiszewski, C., & Neumann, M. M. (2006). The influence of avatars on online consumer shopping behavior. *Journal of Marketing, 70*(4), 19–36. doi:10.1509/jmkg.70.4.19.

Honan, E. (2008). Web site allows anonymous warnings of STD infections. Retrieved February 14, 2008, from http://www.reuters.com/article/2008/02/14/us-syphilis-website-idUSN1419876020080214

Horowitz, D., & Goldsmith, R. E. (2006). Measuring motivations for online opinion seeking. *Journal of Interactive Advertising, 6*(2).

Horrigan, J. (2008). Online Shopping. Washington, DC: Pew Internet & American Life Project Report.

Horwitt, E. (2011). *The semantic Web gets down to business.* Retrieved October 30, 2011, from http://www.computerworld.com/s/article/9209118/The_semantic_Web_gets_down_to_business

Houston, M.J., & Rothschild, M.L. (1978). Conceptual and methodological perspectives on involvement. *Research Frontiers in Marketing: Dialogues and Directions,* 184-187.

Hovland, C. I., Janis, I. L., & Kelly, H. H. (1953). *Communication and Persuasion: Psychological Studies of Opinion Change.* New Haven, CT: Yale University Press.

Hrubes, D., Ajzen, I., & Daigle, J. (2001). Predicting hunting intentions and behavior: An application of the theory of planned behavior. *Leisure Sciences, 23*(3), 165–178. doi:10.1080/014904001316896855.

http://www.text4baby.org/index.php/about/partners

Huang, C., Liang, W., Lai, Y., & Lin, Y. (2010). The agent-based negotiation process for B2C e-commerce. *Expert Systems with Applications, 37*(1), 348–359. doi:10.1016/j.eswa.2009.05.065.

Huffaker, D. A., & Calvert, S. L. (2005). Gender, identity, and language use in teenage blogs. *Journal of Computer-Mediated Communication, 10,* 30–56.

Hughes, D. J., Rowe, M., Batey, M., & Lee, A. (2012). A tale of two sites: Twitter vs. Facebook and the personality predictors of social media usage. *Computers in Human Behavior, 28*(2), 561–569. doi:10.1016/j.chb.2011.11.001.

Hu, L.-T., & Bentler, P. M. (1999). Cutoff criteria for fit indexes in covariance structure analysis: Conventional criteria versus new alternatives. *Structural Equation Modeling, 6*(1), 1–55. doi:10.1080/10705519909540118.

Hulbert, J. M. (2008). *Defining Relevancy: Managing the New Academic Library.* Oxford, UK: Harcourt Education.

Huston, L., & Sakkab, N. (2006). Connect and develop: Inside Procter & Gamble's new model for innovation. *Harvard Business Review, 84*(3), 58–66.

Hwang, H. (2005). *Predictors of instant messaging: Gratifications sought, gratifications obtained, and social presence.* Paper presented at annual meeting of the International Communication Association. New York.

IBM. (2007). Innovative collaboration to advance your business. Tapping the collaborative intelligence of your business network. Retrieved from http://www-304.ibm.com/jct03004c/businesscenter/

Igbaria, M., & Tan, M. (1997). The consequences of the information technology acceptance on subsequent individual performance. *Information & Management, 32*(3), 113–121. doi:10.1016/S0378-7206(97)00006-2.

Information Age (2011). Network Effects. *Information Age,* January, 20-21.

Institute for Information Industry. (2006). *Applications for Web2.0 innovations cases.* Taipei, Taiwan. Institute for Information Industry. ISBN/ISSN: 9789575813475.

It Gets Better Project. (2012). *It Gets Better Project | Give hope to LGBT youth.* Retrieved April 2, 2012, from http://www.itgetsbetter.org/

It Gets Better Project. (2012). *It Gets Better Project: Dan and Terry.* Retrieved September 18, 2012, from http://www.itgetsbetter.org/#7IcVyvg2Qlo

It Gets Better Project. (2012). *What is the It Gets Better Project?* Retrieved September 18, 2012, from http://www.itgetsbetter.org/pages/about-it-gets-better-project/

Iyengar, R., Van den Bulte, C., & Valente, T. (2011). Opinion leadership and social contagion in new product diffusion. *Marketing Science, 30,* 195–212. doi:10.1287/mksc.1100.0566.

Jain, A., & Ganesh, J. (2007). *Harnessing the Power of Web 2.0 in Online Retail. Part II: An Implementation Roadmap for Retailers.* Retrieved June 1, 2010, from http://www.infosys.com/offerings/industries/retail/white-papers/documents/harnessing-power-2.pdf

Jansen, B. J., Zhang, M., & Sobel, K. (2009). Twitter power: tweets as electronic word-of-mouth. *Journal of the American Society for Information Science and Technology, 60*(11), 2169–2188. doi:10.1002/asi.21149.

Jansen, B. J., Zhang, M., Sobel, K., & Chowdury, A. (2009). Twitter Power: Tweets as Electronic Word of Mouth. *Journal of the American Society for Information Science and Technology, 60*(11), 2169–2188. doi:10.1002/asi.21149.

Jayachandran, S., Sharma, S., Kaufman, P., & Raman, P. (2005). The role of relational information processes and technology use in customer relationship management. *Journal of Marketing, 69*(4), 177–192. doi:10.1509/jmkg.2005.69.4.177.

Jebb, S. A., Ahern, A. L., Olson, A. D., Aston, L. M., Holzapfel, C., Stoll, J., & Caterson, I. D. (2011). Primary care referral to a commercial provider for weight loss treatment versus standard care: A randomised controlled trial. *Lancet*, *378*(9801), 1485–1492. doi:10.1016/S0140-6736(11)61344-5 PMID:21906798.

Jennings, M. K., & Zeitner, V. (2003). Internet use and civic engagement: A longitudinal analysis. *Public Opinion Quarterly*, *67*(3), 311–334. doi:10.1086/376947.

John, O. P., Robins, L. W., & Pervin, L. A. (2008). *Handbook of personality: Theory and research*. New York: Guilford.

John, O. P., & Srivastava, S. (1999). The Big Five trait taxonomy: History, measurement, and theoretical perspectives. In Pervin, L. A., & John, O. P. (Eds.), *Handbook of personality: Theory and research* (2nd ed., pp. 102–138). New York: Guilford.

Johnson, B. (2010). Turmoil at Myspace blamed on News Corporation. *The Guardian*. Retrieved May 21, 2011, from http://www.guardian.co.uk/technology/2010/feb/14/myspace-news-corporation-owen-van-natta.

Jones, S., & Fox, S. (2009). Generations online in 2009. Pew Internet and American Life Project. Retrieved March 19, 2009, from http://www.pewinternet.org/Reports/2009/Generations-Online-in-2009.aspx

Jones, K. (2011). Effect of social media intervention on chlamydia incidence when compared with no formalized Internet instruction. *Western Journal of Nursing Research*, *33*(8), 1114–1115. doi:10.1177/0193945911413677.

Jones, Q., Ravid, G., & Rafaeli, S. (2004). Information overload and the message dynamics of online interaction spaces. *Information Systems Research*, *15*(2), 194–210. doi:10.1287/isre.1040.0023.

Jöreskog, K. G., & Goldberger, A. S. (1975). Estimation of a model with multiple indicators and multiple causes of a single latent variable. *Journal of the American Statistical Association*, *70*(351), 631–639. doi:10.2307/2285946.

Jourard, S. M. (1971). *Self-disclosure: An experimental analysis of the transparent self*. New York: Wiley-Interscience.

Joyce, E., & Kraut, R. E. (2006). Predicting Continued Participation in Newsgroups. *Journal of Computer-Mediated Communication*, *11*(3), 723–747. doi:10.1111/j.1083-6101.2006.00033.x.

Kalmus, V., Pruulmann-Vengerfeldt, P., Runnel, P., & Siibak, A. (2009). Mapping the terrain of generation C: Places and practices of online content creation among Estonian teenagers. *Journal of Computer-Mediated Communication*, *14*(4), 1257–1282. doi:10.1111/j.1083-6101.2009.01489.x.

Kang, H., Hahn, M., Fortin, D. R., Hyun, Y. J., & Eom, Y. (2006). Effects of perceived behavioral control on the consumer usage intention of e-coupons. *Psychology and Marketing*, *23*(10), 841–864. doi:10.1002/mar.20136.

Kao, C., Wu, Y., & Tsai, C. (2011). Elementary school teachers' motivation toward web-based professional development, and the relationship with Internet self-efficacy and belief about web-based learning. *Teaching and Teacher Education*, *27*, 406–415. doi:10.1016/j.tate.2010.09.010.

Kao, N.-Y. (2007). *Uses and Gratifications Theory On Web 2.0 Application-A Case of Online Video Sharing Websites. Unpublished master theses*. Taiwan: National Taiwan University of Science and Technology.

Kaplan, A. M. (2009), Virtual worlds and business schools: The case of INSEAD. In C. Wankel, J. Kingsley, Higher education in virtual worlds: Teaching and learning in second life. Bingley, UK: Emerald Group Publishing.

Kaplan, A. M. & Haenlein, M. (2009). Consumer use and business potential of virtual worlds: The case of Second Life. The International Journal on Media Management, 11(¾), 93-101.

Kaplan, A. M. (2010). User participation within virtual worlds. In Fogliatto, F. S., & Da Silveira, G. J. C. (Eds.), *Mass customization – Engineering and managing global operations* (pp. 333–351). Springer.

Kaplan, A. M. (2011). Social media between the real and the virtual: How Facebook, YouTube & Co. can become an extension of the real life of their users - And sometimes even more. *Prospective Stratégique*, *38*(March), 8–13.

Kaplan, A. M. (2012). If you love something, let it go mobile: Mobile marketing and mobile social media 4x4. *Business Horizons*, 55.

Kaplan, A. M., & Haenlein, M. (2006). Toward a parsimonious definition of traditional and electronic mass customization. *Journal of Product Innovation Management*, *23*(2), 168–182. doi:10.1111/j.1540-5885.2006.00190.x.

Kaplan, A. M., & Haenlein, M. (2009). Users of the world, unite! The challenges and opportunities of social media. *Business Horizons*, *53*(1), 59–68. doi:10.1016/j.bushor.2009.09.003.

Kaplan, A. M., & Haenlein, M. (2009). Consumers, companies and virtual social worlds: A qualitative analysis of Second Life. *Advances in Consumer Research. Association for Consumer Research (U. S.)*, *36*(1), 873–874.

Kaplan, A. M., & Haenlein, M. (2009). The fairyland of Second Life: About virtual social worlds and how to use them. *Business Horizons*, *52*(6), 563–572. doi:10.1016/j.bushor.2009.07.002.

Kaplan, A. M., & Haenlein, M. (2010). Users of the world, unite! The challenges and opportunities of Social Media. *Business Horizons*, *53*(1), 59–68. doi:10.1016/j.bushor.2009.09.003.

Kaplan, A. M., & Haenlein, M. (2010). From Real to Virtual and Back Again: The Use and Potential of Virtual Social Worlds within the IT Industry. In Papadopoulou, P., Kanellis, P., & Martakos, D. (Eds.), *Social Computing Theory And Practice: Interdisciplinary Approaches* (pp. 285–300). Hershey, PA: IGI Global. doi:10.4018/978-1-61692-904-6.ch014.

Kaplan, A. M., & Haenlein, M. (2011). The early bird catches the news: Nine things you should know about micro-blogging. *Business Horizons*, *54*, 105–113. doi:10.1016/j.bushor.2010.09.004.

Kaplan, A. M., & Haenlein, M. (2011). Two hearts in 3/4 time: How to waltz the Social Media – Viral Marketing dance. *Business Horizons*, *54*(3), 253–263. doi:10.1016/j.bushor.2011.01.006.

Kaplan, A. M., & Haenlein, M. (2012). The Britney Spears universe: Social media and viral marketing at its best. *Business Horizons*, *55*.

Kargaonkar, P. K., & Wolin, L. D. (1999). A multivariate analysis of web usage. *Journal of Advertising Research*, *39*, 53–68.

Karger, D., & Quan, D. (2005). What would it mean to blog on the semantic web? *Web Semantics: Science. Services and Agents on the World Wide Web*, *3*(2/3), 147–157. doi:10.1016/j.websem.2005.06.002.

Karsaklian, E. (2001). *Cybermarketing*. São Paulo, Brazil: Atlas.

Katona, Z., Zubcsek, P., & Sarvary, M. (2011). Network effects and Personal Influences. *Marketing Science*, *30*(1), 42–60.

Katz, E., Blumler, J., & Gurevitch, M. (1974). Utilization of mass communication by the individual. In J. Blumler., & E. Katz (Eds.), The Uses of Mass Communications: Current Perspectives on Gratifications Research. Beverly Hills, CA: Sage.

Katz, D. (1960). The functional approach to the study of attitudes. *Public Opinion Quarterly*, *24*, 27–46. doi:10.1086/266945.

Katz, E., Blumler, J., & Gurevitch, M. (1973). Uses and gratifications research. *Public Opinion Quarterly*, *37*, 509–523. doi:10.1086/268109.

Katz, E., Blumler, J., & Gurevitch, M. (1974). Utilization of mass communication by the individual. In Blumler, J. G., & Katz, E. (Eds.), *The uses of mass communications: Current perspectives on gratifications research*. Beverly Hills, CA: Sage Publications.

Katz, E., Gurevitch, M., & Haas, H. (1973). On the use of the mass media for important things. *American Sociological Review*, *38*(April), 164–181. doi:10.2307/2094393.

Katz, E., & Lazarsfeld, P. F. (1955). *Personal influence: The part played by people in the flow of mass communications*. New York: Free Press.

Kaye, B. (2005). It's a blog, blog, blog world: Users and uses of weblogs. *Atlantic Journal of Communication*, *13*, 73–95. doi:10.1207/s15456889ajc1302_2.

Kazienko, P., Doskocz, P., & Kajdanowicz, T. (2012). Social network analysis in marketing. In Colomo-Palacios, R. et al. (Eds.), *Customer relationship management and the social semantic web: Enabling cliens conexus* (pp. 231–252). Hershey, PA: IGI Global.

Kelleher, T., & Miller, B. M. (2006). Organizational blogs and the human voice: Relational strategies and relational outcomes. *Journal of Computer-Mediated Communication, 11*(2). Retrieved from http://jcmc.indiana.edu/vol11/issue2/kelleher.html doi:10.1111/j.1083-6101.2006.00019.x.

Kelly, K. (2005). How technology evolves. *Ted Talks.* Retrieved March 13, 2012, from http://blog.ted.com/2009/08/18/how_technology/

Kelly, T. S., & Rhind, A. (2007). Marketing in Second Life and Other Virtual Worlds. *Media Contacts-Havas Digital,* October. Retrieved January 15, 2011, from http://www.mediacontacts.com/images/common/mc-insight/mc_insight_outubro.pdf

Kerbel, M. R., & Bloom, J. D. (2005). Blog for America and civic involvement. *The Harvard International Journal of Press/Politics, 10*(4), 3–27. doi:10.1177/1081180X05281395.

Kersten, G. E., & Noronha, S. J. (1999). WWW-based negotiation support: Design, implementation, and use. *Decision Support Systems, 25*(2), 135–154. doi:10.1016/S0167-9236(99)00012-3.

Kidd, J. (2011). Enacting engagement online: Framing social media use for the museum. *Information Technology & People, 24*(1), 64–77. doi:10.1108/09593841111109422.

Kietzmann, J. H., Hermkens, K., McCarthy, I. P., & Silverstre, B. S. (2011). Social media? Get serious! Understanding the functional building blocks of social media. *Business Horizons, 54*(3), 181–288. doi:10.1016/j.bushor.2011.01.005.

Kim, P. (2007, October 16). Microblogging For Marketers. *Forrester.* Retrieved July 18, 2010, from http://captivatingconnections.typepad.com/captivating_connections/files/051104355000.pdf

Kim, J., & Bae, Z. (2008). The role of online brand community in New Product Development. *International Journal of Innovation Management, 12*(3), 357–376. doi:10.1142/S1363919608002011.

Kirchler, E. (1988). Diary reports on daily economic decisions of happy versus unhappy couples. *Journal of Economic Psychology, 9*(3), 327–357. doi:10.1016/0167-4870(88)90039-6.

Kirkpatrick, D. (2011). *The Facebook effect: The inside story of the company that is connecting the world.* New York: Simon & Schuster.

Kling, R. (2007). What is social informatics and why does it matter? *The Information Society, 23*(4), 205–220. doi:10.1080/01972240701441556.

Klusch, M. (2005). Agent-Mediated Trading: Intelligent Agents and Electronic business. In Hayzelden, A. L., & Bourne, R. A. (Eds.), *Agent Technology for Communication Infrastructures* (pp. 59–76). Chichester, UK: John Wiley & Sons.

Kock, N. (2008). E-Collaboration and E-Commerce In Virtual Worlds: The Potential of Second Life and World of Warcraft. *International Journal of e-Collaboration, 4*(3), 1–13. doi:10.4018/jec.2008070101.

Ko, H., Cho, C.-H., & Roberts, M. S. (2005). Internet uses and gratifications: A structural equation model of interactive advertising. *Journal of Advertising, 34*(2), 57–70. doi:10.1080/00913367.2005.10639191.

Kolbitsch, J., & Mauer, H. (2007). *The growing importance of e-communities on the Web.*

Kollat, D. T., & Willett, R. P. (1967). Customer impulse purchasing behavior. *JMR, Journal of Marketing Research, 4*(1), 21–31. doi:10.2307/3150160.

Kollock, P. (1999). The economics of online cooperation: Gifts and public goods in cyberspace. In Smith, M., & Kollock, P. (Eds.), *Communities in Cyberspace* (pp. 220–242). London: Routledge.

Korgaonkar, P., & Wolin, L. (1999). 'A multivariate analysis of web usage. *Journal of Advertising Research, 39*(2), 53–68.

Kotler, P., & Keller, K. L. (2006). Marketing Management (12th ed.) Ed. Upper Saddle River, NJ: Prentice Hall.

Kotler, P. (2009). *Marketing para o século XXI: Como criar, conquistar e dominar o mercado.* São Paulo, Brazil: Ediouro.

Kotler, P., & Keller, K. (2011). *Marketing management.* Upper Saddle River, NJ: Prentice Hall.

Koufaris, M. (2002). Applying the Technology Acceptance Model and Flow Theory to Online Consumer Behavior. *Information Systems Research, 13*(2), 205–223. doi:10.1287/isre.13.2.205.83.

Kowalczyk, R. U. (2010). Integrating Mobile and Intelligent Agents in Advanced E-commerce: A Survey. In J. Carbonell, J. Siekmann, R. Kowalczyk, J. Müller, H. Tianfield., & R. Unland (Eds.), Lecture Notes In Computer Science LNCS 2592. Berlin: Springer.

Kozinets, R. V. (2002). The field behind the screen: Using netnography for marketing research in online communities. *JMR, Journal of Marketing Research, 39*(1), 61–72. doi:10.1509/jmkr.39.1.61.18935.

Kozinets, R. V., Belz, F. M., & McDonagh, P. (2012). Social media for social change: A transformative consumer research perspective. In Mick, D. G., Pettigrew, S., Pechmann, C., & Ozanne, J. L. (Eds.), *Transformative Consumer Research for Personal and Collective Well-being* (pp. 205–223). New York: Routledge.

Kozinets, R. V., de Valck, K., Wojnicki, A. C., & Wilner, S. J. S. (2010). Networked narratives: Understanding word-of-mouth marketing in online communities. *Journal of Marketing, 74*(2), 71–89. doi:10.1509/jmkg.74.2.71.

Krämer, K. (2006). Web 2.0 for the Enterprise. *YMC*. Retrieved January 15, 2011, from www.ymc.ch/content/download/487693/3301925/file/web20_for_the_enterprise_2008.pdf

Kreutz, R. (2011). *O uso corporativo das mídias sociais*. Unpublished dissertation. University of Brasília, Brasília, DF, Brazil.

Krishnamurthy, B., Naryshkin, K., & Wills, C. (2011). Privacy leakage vs. protection measures: the growing disconnect. *Web 2.0 Security and Privacy Workshop*. Retrieved May 12, 2012, from http://www.research.att.com/~bala/papers/w2sp11.pdf

Krishnamurthy, K., & Wills, C. (2009). On the leakage of personally identifiable information via online social networks. In *Proceedings of ACM SIGCOMM Workshop on Online Social Networks*. Retrieved from http://www.research.att.com/~bala/papers/wosn09.pdf

Krishnamurthy, S., & Dou, W. (2008). Advertising with User-Generated Content: A Framework and Research Agenda. *Journal of Interactive Advertising, 8*(2), 1–7.

Kuk, G., & Yeung, F. T. (2002). Interactivity in e-Commerce. *Quarterly Journal of Electronic Commerce, 3*(3), 223–234.

Kyung-Hyan, Y., & Gretzel, U. (2011). Influence of personality on travel-related consumer-generated media creation. *Computers in Human Behavior, 27*(2), 609–621. doi:10.1016/j.chb.2010.05.002.

Laing, R. D., Phillipson, H., & Lee, A. R. (1966). *Interpersonal Perception: A Theory and a Method of Research*. New York: Springer.

Lakhani, K. R., & von Hippel, E. (2003). How open source software works: Free user-to-user assistance. *Research Policy, 32*(6), 923–943. doi:10.1016/S0048-7333(02)00095-1.

Lampe, C., Ellison, N., & Steinfeld, C. (2006). A face(book) in the crowd: Social searching vs. social browsing. In *Proceedings of the 2006 20th anniversary conference on computer-supported cooperative work (CSCW 2006)* (pp. 167–170). New York: ACM Press.

Lanchester, J. (2006). *A bigger bang*. Retrieved from www.guardian.co.uk/weekend/story/0,1937496,00.html

LaRose, R., & Eastin, M. S. (2002). *A social cognitive explanation of Internet uses and gratifications: Toward a new theory of media attendance*. Paper presented at annual meeting of the International Communication Association. Seoul, Korea.

Las Casas, A. L. (2009). *Marketing: Conceitos, exercícios e casos*. São Paulo, Brazil: Atlas.

Lau, R. Y. (2007). Towards a web services and intelligent agents-based negotiation system for B2B eCommerce. *Journal of Electronic Commerce Research and Applications, 6*(3), 260–273. doi:10.1016/j.elerap.2006.06.007.

Leavitt, H. J. (1965). Applying organizational change in industry: Structural, technological, and humanistic approaches. In March, J. G. (Ed.), *Handbook of Organizations*. Chicago, IL: Rand McNally.

LeCompte, M. D. (2000). Analyzing qualitative data. *Theory into Practice*, *39*(3), 146–154. doi:10.1207/s15430421tip3903_5.

Lee, J. (2005). Very big ad shows why we still call Carlton a beer. *The Sydney Morning Herald*, Business, July 29, p. 28.

Lee, S. (2004). *The uses and gratifications approach in the Internet age*. Paper presented at annual meeting of the International Communication Association. New Orleans, LA.

Lee, B.-R., Yu, W.-B., Maguluru, N., & Nichols, M. (2006). Enhancing business networks using social network based virtual communities. *Industrial Management & Data Systems*, *106*(1), 121–138. doi:10.1108/02635570610641022.

Lee, C. (2008). *Social Technographics Report*. Forrester Research.

Lee, K., & Shavitt, S. (2009). Can McDonald's food ever be considered healthful? Metacognitive experiences affect the perceived understanding of a brand. *JMR, Journal of Marketing Research*, *46*(2), 222–233. doi:10.1509/jmkr.46.2.222.

Lee, M. R., & Lan, Y. C. (2007). From Web 2.0 to conversational knowledge management: Towards collaborative intelligence. *Journal of Entrepreneurship Research*, *2*(2), 47–62.

Lees, N. (2005). Big ad hits one millionth viewer. *AdNews*. Retrieved June 30, 2007, from http://www.AdNews.com.au

Lee, Y. W., Strong, D. M., Kahn, B. K., & Wang, R. Y. (2002). AIMQ: A methodology for information quality assessment. *Information & Management*, *42*(2), 133–146. doi:10.1016/S0378-7206(02)00043-5.

Lehtimäki, T., Salo, J., Hiltula, H., & Lankinen, M. (2009). Harnessing Web 2.0 for Business to Business Marketing - Literature Review and an Empirical Perspective from Finland. Working paper, Faculty of Economics and Business Administration, University of Oulu, Finland.

Lemmens, J. S., & Bushman, B. J. (2006). The appeal of violent video games to lower educated aggressive adolescent boys from two countries. *Cyberpsychology & Behavior*, *9*(5), 638–641. doi:10.1089/cpb.2006.9.638 PMID:17034335.

Lenhart, A. (2009). *Adults and social network Web sites*. Retrieved March 19, 2009, from http://www.pewinternet.org/Reports/2009/Adults-and-Social-Network-Websites.aspx

Lenhart, A., & Fox, S. (2006). Bloggers: A portrait of the internet's new story tellers. *Pew Internet and American Life Project*. Retrieved on August 4, 2009, from www.pewinternet.org

Lenhart, A., Horrigan, J., & Farrows, D. (2004). *Content creation online*. Retrieved March 19, 2009, from http://www.pewinternet.org/Reports/2004/Content-Creation-Online.aspx.

Lenhart, A., Madden, M., Macgill, A. R., & Smith, A. (2007). *Teens and social media*. Retrieved March 19, 2009, from http://www.pewinternet.org/Reports/2007/Teens-and-Social-Media.aspx

Leuf, B., & Cunningham, W. (2001). *The Wiki way: Collaboration and sharing on the internet*. Addison-Wesley Professional.

Leung, L. (2009). User-generated content on the Internet: An examination of gratifications, civic engagement and psychological empowerment. *New Media & Society*, *11*, 1327–1347. doi:10.1177/1461444809341264.

Levine, D., McCright, J., Dobkin, L., Woodruff, A., & Klausner, J. (2008). SexInfo: A sexual health text messaging service for San Francisco youth. *American Journal of Public Health*, *98*(3), 393–395. doi:10.2105/AJPH.2007.110767 PMID:18235068.

Levine, F., Locke, C., Searls, D., & Weinberger, D. (2000). *The cluetrain manifesto*. New York: Basic Books.

Li, D. (2007). *Why do you blog: A uses-and-gratifications inquiry into bloggers' motivations*. Paper presented at annual meeting of the International Communication Association. San Francisco, CA.

Li, Y.-M., & Li, T.-Y. (2011). Deriving Marketing Intelligence over Microblogs. In *Proceedings of the 44th Hawaii International Conference on System Sciences*. Koloa, HI: IEEE. Retrieved February 13, 2012, from http://www.lancs.ac.uk/ug/wilkina4/__files/Deriving%20Marketing%20Intelligence%20over%20Microblogs.pdf

Libai, B., Muller, E., & Peres, R. (2012). *Sources of social value in word-of-mouth programs*. Working paper. Hebrew University of Jerusalem, Israel.

Liddy, E. D. (2001). Natural Language Processing. In *Encyclopedia of Library and Information Science* (2nd ed.). New York: Marcel Decker, Inc..

Liedtke, M. (2011). LinkedIn market value now $9 billion. *The Sun News*. Retrieved August 10, 2011, from http://www.thesunnews.com/2011/05/20/2169130/linkedin-market-value-now-9-billion.html

Lim, H., & Dubinsky, A. J. (2005). The theory of planned behavior in e-Commerce: Making a case for interdependencies between salient beliefs. *Psychology and Marketing*, *22*(10), 833–855. doi:10.1002/mar.20086.

Lincoln, S. R. (2009). *Mastering Web 2.0, Transform your business using key website and social media tools*. London: Kogan Page.

Lindegaard, S. (2009). *P&G: How open innovation is done*. Retrieved from http://stefanlindegaard.com/2009/04/14/pg-how-open-innovation-is-done

Lin, K. (2001). *An Exploratory Study for Commercial Application of Virtual Community. Unpublished Master's theses*. Taiwan: Soochow University.

Linkenbach, J. W. (2006). *How to Use Social Norms Marketing to Prevent Driving After Drinking: A MOST Of US® Toolkit. MOST of Us® Institute*. MT: Bozeman.

Linkenbach, J., & Otto, J. (2009). *The Positive Community Norms Overview*. Bozeman, MT: The Montana Institute.

Lin, R., & Kraus, S. (2010). Can automated agents proficiently negotiate with each other? *Communications of the ACM*, *53*(1), 78–88. doi:10.1145/1629175.1629199.

Little, B. R. (1972). Psychological man as scientist, humanist and specialist. *Journal of Experimental Research in Personality*, *6*(2), 95–118.

Liu, B. (2010). Sentiment analysis: A multi-faceted problem. *IEEE Intelligent Systems*, *25*(3), 76–80.

Liu, C., & Arnett, K. P. (2000). Exploring the factors associated with Web site success in the context of electronic commerce. *Information & Management*, *38*(1), 23–34. doi:10.1016/S0378-7206(00)00049-5.

Livingstone, S., & Helsper, E. (2007). Gradations in digital inclusion: Children, young people and the digital divide. *New Media & Society*, *9*(4), 671–696. doi:10.1177/1461444807080335.

Lockamy, A. III, & McCormack, K. (2004). The development of a supply chain management process maturity model using the concepts of business process orientation. *Supply Chain Management*, *9*(3/4), 272–278.

Lofgren, E. T., & Fefferman, N. H. (2007). The untapped potential of virtual game worlds to shed light on real world epidemics. *The Lancet Infectious Diseases*, *7*(9), 625–629. doi:10.1016/S1473-3099(07)70212-8 PMID:17714675.

Lovari, A., & Parisi, L. (2011). Public administrations and citizens 2.0: Exploring digital public communication strategies and civic interaction within Italian municipality pages on Facebook. In Comunello, F. (Ed.), *Networked sociability and individualism: Technology for personal relationships*. Hershey, PA: IGI Global. doi:10.4018/978-1-61350-338-6.ch012.

Lovelock, C., & Wirtz, J. (2010). *Services marketing*. Upper Saddle River, NJ: Prentice Hall.

Lytras, M., & Garcia, R. (2008). Semantic Web applications: A framework for industry and business exploitation. *International Journal of Knowledge and Learning*, *4*(1), 93–108. doi:10.1504/IJKL.2008.019739.

MacKenzie, S. B., & Spreng, R. A. (1992). How does motivation moderate the impact of central and peripheral processing on brand attitudes and intentions? *The Journal of Consumer Research*, *18*(4), 519–529. doi:10.1086/209278.

MacLeod, H. (2009). Social Objects are the Future of Marketing. *Gaping Void*. Retrieved June 17, 2012, from http://gapingvoid.com/so/

Mader, S. (2008). *Wikipatterns*. Indianapolis, IN: Wiley Publishing.

Mäenpää, K. (2006). Clustering the consumers on the basis of their perceptions of the Internet banking. *Internet Research*, *16*(3), 304–322. doi:10.1108/10662240610673718.

Maes, P., Guttman, R., & Moukas, A. (1999). Agents that Buy and Sell. *Communications of the ACM*, *42*(3), 81–92. doi:10.1145/295685.295716.

Mahar, S. M., & Mahar, J. (2009). *The Unofficial Guide to Building Your Business in the Second Life Virtual World.* New York: Amacom.

Malone, E., & Lipson, H. (2007). The factory in your kitchen. In *Proceedings of World Conference on Mass Customization and Personalization.* Cambridge, MA: MIT Press.

Mangold, G. W., & Faulds, D. J. (2009). Social media: The new hybrid element in the promotions mix. *Business Horizons*, *54*, 209–217.

Marketing Charts. (2008). *Study: Web 2.0 Awesome for Integrating Brand and Direct Marketing.* Retrieved May 15, 2011, from http://www.marketingcharts.com/direct/study-web-20-awesome-for-integrating-brand-and-direct-marketing-4429/

Marsden, P. V., & Campbell, K. E. (1984). Measuring tie strength. *Social Forces*, *63*(2), 482–501.

Martin, C. (1999). *Net future.* New York: McGraw-Hill.

Martinex, E., Yolanda, P., & Carlos, F. (1998). The Acceptance and Diffusion of New Consumer Durables: Difference between First and Last Adopter. *Journal of Consumer Marketing*, *15*(4), 323–342. doi:10.1108/07363769810225975.

Mathwick, C., Wiertz, C., & de Ruyter, K. (2008). Social capital production in a virtual P3 community. *The Journal of Consumer Research*, *34*(6), 832–849. doi:10.1086/523291.

Mauri, M., Cipresso, P., Balgera, A., Villamira, M., & Riva, G. (2011). Why is Facebook so successful? Psychophysiological measures describe a core flow state while using Facebook. *Cyberpsychology, Behavior, and Social Networking*, *14*(12), 723–731. doi:10.1089/cyber.2010.0377 PMID:21879884.

McAfee, A. P. (2006). Enterprise 2.0: The dawn of emergent collaboration. *MIT Sloan Review*, *47*(3), 21–28.

McCrae, R. R., & Costa, P. T. (1997). Personality trait structure as a human universal. *The American Psychologist*, *52*(5), 509–516. doi:10.1037/0003-066X.52.5.509 PMID:9145021.

McKenna, K. Y. A., & Bargh, J. A. (2000). Plan 9 from cyberspace: The implications of the Internet for personality and social psychology. *Personality and Social Psychology Review*, *4*(1), 57–75. doi:10.1207/S15327957PSPR0401_6.

McKenna, K., & Bargh, J. (1999). Causes and consequences of social interaction on the Internet: A conceptual framework. *Media Psychology*, *1*(3), 249–269. doi:10.1207/s1532785xmep0103_4.

McKenna, K., & Bargh, J. (2000). 'Plan 9 from cyberspace: The implications of the Internet for personality and social psychology. *Personality and Social Psychology Review*, *4*(1), 57–75. doi:10.1207/S15327957PSPR0401_6.

McKenna, K., Green, A., & Gleason, M. (2002). Relationship formation on the Internet: What's the big attraction? *The Journal of Social Issues*, *58*(1), 9–31. doi:10.1111/1540-4560.00246.

McKinsey. (2007). How companies are marketing online. *The McKinsey Quarterly*, September. Retrieved October 15, 2010, from www.mckinseyquarterly.com/Marketing/Digital_Marketing

McLuhan, M. (1964). *Understanding media: The extensions of man* (1st ed.). New York: McGraw Hill.

McPherson, J. M., & Smith-Lovin, L. (1987). Homophily in voluntary organizations: Status, distance and the composition of face-to-face groups. *American Sociological Review*, *52*, 370–379. doi:10.2307/2095356.

McQuail, D. (1983). Mass Communication Theory (1st ed.). London: Sage.

McQuail, D. (1987). *Mass communication theory: An introduction.* Thousand Oaks, CA: Sage.

McQuail, D. (2000). *McQuail's Mass Communication Theory* (4th ed.). London: Sage.

Mennecke, B. E., McNeill, D., Ganis, M., Roche, E. M., Bray, D. A., Konsynski, B., et al. (2008). Second Life and Other Virtual Worlds: A Roadmap for Research. *Communications of the Association for Information Systems (CAIS)*, *Article 20, 22*, 371-388. Retrieved January 15, 2011, from http://www.bus.iastate.edu/mennecke/CAIS-Vol22-Article20.pdf

Merino, D. (2006) *Web Marketing*, November 16. Retrieved May 18, 2012, from http://www. administradores. com.br/informe-se/informativo/web-marketing/8322/

Messinger, P. R., Stroulia, E., Lyons, K., Bone, M., Niu, R. H., Smirnov, K., & Perelgut, S. (2009). Virtual worlds -past, present, and future: New directions in social computing. *Decision Support Systems*, *47*(3), 204–228. doi:10.1016/j.dss.2009.02.014.

Metts, S. (1997). Face and facework: Implications for the study of personal relationships. In Duck, S. (Ed.), *Handbook of personal relationships* (pp. 373–390). Hillsdale, NJ: Lawrence Erlbaum Associates.

Mezirow, J. (1995). Transformation theory of adult learning. In Welton, M. R. (Ed.), *Defense of the Life-world* (pp. 39–70). Albany, NY: State University of New York Press.

Mezirow, J. (1998). On critical reflection. *Adult Education Quarterly*, *48*(3), 185–191. doi:10.1177/074171369804800305.

Mezirow, J. (2000). Learning to think like an adult: Core concepts of transformation theory. In Mezirow, J. et al. (Eds.), *Learning as Transformation* (pp. 3–34). San Francisco, CA: Jossey-Bass.

Mezirow, J. (2003). Transformative learning as discourse. *Journal of Transformative Education*, *1*(1), 58–63. doi:10.1177/1541344603252172.

Mick, D. G. (2006). Presidential address: Meaning and mattering through transformative consumer research. *Advances in Consumer Research. Association for Consumer Research (U. S.)*, *33*, 1–4.

Midgley, D. F., & Dowling, G. R. (1993). A longitudinal study of product form innovation: The interaction between predispositions and social messages. *The Journal of Consumer Research*, *19*, 611–625. doi:10.1086/209326.

Midgley, E. D., & Grahame, R. D. (1978). Innovativeness: The Concept and Its Measurement. *The Journal of Consumer Research*, *4*(March), 229–242. doi:10.1086/208701.

Mignone, B. C. (2010). *A contribuição das redes sociais para o marketing business-to-business no mercado industrial de pet shops*. Unpublished dissertation, Feevale University, Novo Hamburgo, RS, Brazil.

Miles, M.B. & Huberman, M. (1994). *Qualitative data analysis: An expanded sourcebook.*

Miller, C. H., Burgoon, M., Grandpre, J. R., & Alvaro, E. M. (2006). Identifying principal risk factors for the initiation of adolescent smoking behaviors: The significance of psychological reactance. *Health Communication*, *19*(3), 241–252. doi:10.1207/s15327027hc1903_6 PMID:16719727.

Miller, M. (2011). *YouTube for Business* (2nd ed.). Upper Saddle River, NJ: Que Publishing.

Mills, J., & Bogenschneider, K. (2001). Can communities assess support for preventing adolescent alcohol and other drug use? Reliability and validity of a community assessment inventory. *Family Relations*, *50*(4), 355–375. doi:10.1111/j.1741-3729.2001.00355.x.

Mislove, A., Marcon, M., Gummadi, K. P., Druschel, P., & Bhattacharjee, B. (2007). Measurement and analysis of online social networks. In *Proceedings of the 7th ACM SIGCOMM Conference on Internet Measurement*. Vouliagmeni, Greece: ACM.

Misner, I. (2008). The VCP process of relationship marketing. Masters of sales. *Academy Online Research*. Retrieved from http://bni-india.com/the-vcp-process-of-relationship-marketing/

Mittal, V., Kumar, P., & Tsiros, M. (1999). Attribute-level performance, satisfaction and behavioral intentions over time: A consumption-system approach. *Journal of Marketing*, *63*(2), 88–101. doi:10.2307/1251947.

Momtaz, N. J., Aghaie, A., & Alizadeh, S. (2011). Identifying opinion leaders for marketing by analyzing online social networks. *International Journal of Virtual Communities and Social Networking*, *3*(1), 43–59. doi:10.4018/jvcsn.2011010105.

Mondak, J. J., & Halperin, K. (2008). A framework for the study of personality and political behaviour. *British Journal of Political Science*, *38*(2), 335–362. doi:10.1017/S0007123408000173.

Mondak, J. J., Hibbing, M. V., Canache, D., Selgson, M. A., & Anderson, M. R. (2010). Personality and civic engagement: An integrative framework for the study of trait effects on political behavior. *The American Political Science Review*, *104*, 85–110. doi:10.1017/S0003055409990359.

Money, R. B., Gilly, M. C., & Graham, J. L. (1998). Explorations of national culture and word-of-mouth referral behavior in the purchase of industrial services in the United States and Japan. *Journal of Marketing, 62*(November), 76–87. doi:10.2307/1252288.

Monge, P. R., & Contractor, N. S. (2003). *Theories of communication networks.* New York: Oxford University Press.

Mook, D. G. (1996). *Motivation* (2nd ed.). New York: Norton.

Moon, J.-W., & Kim, Y.-G. (2001). Extending the TAM for a World-Wide-Web context. *Information and Management, 38*(4), 217.230.

Moreira, D. (2011). *8 erros que as empresas cometem nas redes.* Retrieved May 4, 2012, from http://info.abril.com.br/noticias/mercado/erros-que-empresas-cometem-nas-redes-sociais-23082011-26.shl

Morry, M. M. (2005). Relationship satisfaction as a predictor of similarity ratings: A test of the attraction-similarity hypothesis. *Journal of Social and Personal Relationships, 22*(4), 561–584. doi:10.1177/0265407505054524.

MOST of Us. (2010). *The Positive Community Norms Workbook.* Bozeman, MT: The Montana Institute.

MOST of Us. (2012). *What is Social Norms Marketing?* Retrieved May 16, 2012, from http://www.mostofus.org/about-us/what-is-social-norms-marketing/

MOST of Us. (2012). *What is the Positive Community Norms Model?* Retrieved September 18, 2012, from http://www.mostofus.org/about-us/what-is-the-positive-community-

Multisilta, J. (2009). A service science perspective on the design of social media activities. *International Journal of Web Engineering and Technology, 5*(3), 327–342. doi:10.1504/IJWET.2009.031013.

Muñiz, A. C., & Schau, H. J. (2011). How to inspire value-laden collaborative consumer-generated content. *Business Horizons, 54*, 209–217. doi:10.1016/j.bushor.2011.01.002.

Murray, S. L., Holmes, J. G., & Griffin, D. W. (1996). The self-fulfilling nature of positive illusions in romantic relationships: Love is not blind, but prescient. *Journal of Personality and Social Psychology, 71*(6), 1155–1180. doi:10.1037/0022-3514.71.6.1155 PMID:8979384.

Muthén, L. K., & Muthén, B. O. (1998-2007). *Mplus User's Guide* (5th ed.). Los Angeles, CA: Muthen & Muthen.

Nadeau, D., & Sekine, S. (2007). A survey of named entity recognition and classification. *Journal of Lingvisticae Investigationes, 30*(1), 3–26. doi:10.1075/li.30.1.03nad.

Nambisan, P., & Watt, J. (2004). *The impact of online community participation: Insights from the uses and gratifications' perspective.* Paper presented at annual meeting of the International Communication Association. New Orleans, LA.

Nardi, B. A., Schiano, D. J., Gumbrecht, M., & Swartz, L. (2004). Why we blog. *Communications of the ACM, 47*(12), 41–46. doi:10.1145/1035134.1035163.

National Healthy Mothers. Healthy Babies Coalition. (2012). You're pregnant! *National Healthy Mothers, Healthy Babies Coalition.* Retrieved April 2, 2012, from http://www.hmhb.org/pregnant.html

Nazir, A., Raza, S., & Chuah, C.-N. (2008). Unveiling Facebook. A measurement study of social network based applications. In *Proceedings of the 9th ACM SIGCOMM Conference on Internet Measurement.* Chicago, IL.

Needleman, M. (2007). Web 2.0/Lib 2.0—What Is It? (If It's Anything at All). *Serials Review, 33*(3), 202–203. doi:10.1016/j.serrev.2007.05.001.

Negri, A., Poggi, A., Turci, P., & Tomaiuolo, M. (2006). Agents for electronic business applications. In *Proceedings of the 5th International Joint Conference on Autonomous Agents and Multiagent Systems* (pp. 907 - 914). New York: ACM.

Neves, G. (2010). *Gartner: 10 strategic technologies for 2011.* Retrieved from http://www.baguete.com.br/noticias/negocios-e-gestao/22/10/2010/gartner-10-tecnologias-estrategicas-para-2011

Nielson. (2010). Social networks/blogs now account for one in every four and a half minutes online. *Nielsen Wire.* Retrieved June 10, 2011, from http://blog.nielsen.com/nielsenwire/online_mobile/social-media-accounts-for-22-percent-of-time-online/

Nitzan, I., & Libai, B. (2011). Social effects on customer retention. *Journal of Marketing, 75*(November), 24–38.

Nocke, V., Peitz, M., & Stahl, C. (2004). *Platform Ownership in Two-Sided Markets.* Mimeo.

Nolan, R. L. (1973). Managing the computer resource: A stage hypothesis. *Communications of the ACM, 16*(7), 399–405. doi:10.1145/362280.362284.

Nolan, R. L. (1979). Managing the crises in data processing. *Harvard Business Review*, (March-April): 115–126.

O'Reilly, T. (2005). What is Web 2.0? Design patterns and business models for the next generation of software. Retrieved May 19, 2012, from: http://oreilly.com/web2/archive/what-is-web-20.html

O'Reilly, T., & Battelle, J. (2010). Web Squared: Web 2.0 Five Years On. *Web 2.0 Summit.* Retrieved May 17, 2012 from http://assets.en.oreilly.com/1/event/28/web2009_websquared-whitepaper.pdf

OECD. (2007). *Participative web and user-created content: Web 2.0, wikis, and social networking.* Paris, France: Organisation for Economic Co-operation and Development.

Oliver, P. E., & Marwell, G. (2001). Whatever happened to critical mass theory? A retrospective and assessment. *Sociological Theory, 19*(3), 292–311. doi:10.1111/0735-2751.00142.

Oppenheim, S. C. (1951). A new approach to evaluation of the American patent system. *Journal of the Patent and Trademark Office Society, 33*(8), 555–568.

O'Reilly, T. (2006). *Web 2.0 Principles and Best Practices.* Retrieved May 29, 2009, from http://oreilly.com/catalog/web2report/chapter/web20_report_excerpt.pdf

Orwin, R. G., Francisco, L., & Bernichon, T. (2001). *Effectiveness of Women's Substance Abuse Treatment Programs: A Meta-analysis,* (NEDS Contract No. 270–97–7016), Substance Abuse and Mental Health Services Administration (SAMHSA), Center for Substance Abuse Treatment, Arlington, VA.

Ostlund, L. E. (1974). Perceived Innovation Attributes as Predictors of Innovativeness. *The Journal of Consumer Research, 1*(September), 23–29. doi:10.1086/208587.

Ou, C. X. J., Davison, R. M., Zhong, X., & Liang, U. (2010). Empowering employees through instant messaging. *Information Technology & People, 23*(2), 193–211. doi:10.1108/09593841011052165.

Owyang, J. (2007). Trendwatch - MicroMedia provides bite-sized voice and video to micro audiences. *Web Strategy.* Retrieved from http://www.web-strategist.com/

Owyang, J., Bernoff, J., Pflaum, C., & Bowen, E. (2009). *The future of the social web: A social computing report.* Technical Report. Retrieved June 18, 2012, from http://www.forrester.com/The+Future+Of+The+Social+Web/fulltext/-/E-RES46970?docid=46970

Oxford Dictionary. (2012). *Oxford Dictionary.* New York: Oxford University Press.

Padmanabhan, B., Zheng, Z., & Kimbrough, S. O. (2001). Personalization from incomplete data: What you don't know can hurt. In *Proceedings of the 7th ACM SIGKDD International Conference on Knowledge Discovery and Data Mining* (pp. 154-164). New York: ACM.

Pagani, M., Hofacker, C. F., & Goldsmith, R. E. (2011). The influence of personality on active and passive use of social networking sites. *Psychology and Marketing, 28*(5), 441–456. doi:10.1002/mar.20395.

Palka, W., Pousttchi, K., & Wiedemann, G. (2009). Mobile word-of-mouth – A grounded theory of mobile viral marketing. *Journal of Information Technology, 24*(2), 172–185. doi:10.1057/jit.2008.37.

Palmgreen, P., Wenner, L. A., & Rosengren, K. E. (1985). Uses and gratifications research: The past ten years. In Rosengren, K. E., Wenner, L. A., & Palmgreen, P. C. (Eds.), *Uses and gratifications research: Current perspectives.* Beverly Hills, CA: Sage Publications.

Pal, S. K., & Kapur, V. (2010). Blog Marketing Strategies for Mature and Emerging Markets. *International Journal of Innovation. Management and Technology, 1*(4), 411–418.

Papacharissi, Z., & Rubin, A. M. (2000). Predictors of Internet use. *Journal of Broadcasting & Electronic Media, 44*, 175–196. doi:10.1207/s15506878jobem4402_2.

Papazoglou, M. P. (2001). Agent-oriented technology in support of electronic business. *Communications of the ACM, 44*(4), 71–77. doi:10.1145/367211.367268.

Parasuraman, A., Zeithaml, V. A., & Berry, L. L. (1988). SERVQUAL: A Multiple-Item Scale for Measuring Consumer Perceptions of Service Quality. *Journal of Retailing, 64*(1), 12–40.

Parise, S., & Guinan, P. J. (2008). Marketing using Web 2.0. In *Proceedings of the 41st Annual Hawaii International Conference on System Sciences*. Waikoloa, HI: IEEE.

Parise, S., & Guinan, P. J. (2008). Marketing Using Web 2.0. In *Proceedings of the 41st Hawaii International Conference on System Sciences*. Waikoloa, HI: IEEE.

Park, N., Kee, K. F., & Valenzuela, S. (2009). Being Immersed in Social Networking Environment: Facebook Groups, Uses and Gratifications, and Social Outcomes. *Cyberpsychology & Behavior, 12*(6), 729–733. doi:10.1089/cpb.2009.0003 PMID:19619037.

Park, Y.-H., & Fader, P. S. (2004). Modeling browsing behavior at multiple websites. *Marketing Science, 23*(3), 280–303. doi:10.1287/mksc.1040.0050.

Parsons, G. L. (1983). Information technology: A new competitive weapon. *Sloan Management Review, 25*(1), 3–14.

Pateli, A. G., & Giaglis, G. M. (2005). Technology innovation-induced business model change: A contingency approach. *Journal of Organizational Change Management, 18*(2), 167–183. doi:10.1108/09534810510589589.

Payne, A., & Frow, P. (2005). A strategic framework for customer relationship management. *Journal of Marketing, 69*(4), 167–176. doi:10.1509/jmkg.2005.69.4.167.

Payne, A., & Holt, S. (2001). Diagnosing customer value: Integrating the value process and relationship marketing. *British Journal of Management, 12*, 159–182. doi:10.1111/1467-8551.00192.

Pedron, C. D., & Saccol, A. Z. (2009). What lies behind the concept of customer relationship management? Discussing the essence of CRM through a phenomenological approach. *BAR. Braz. Adm. Rev., 6*(1), 34–49.

Pell, B. (2007). *POWERSET - Natural Language and the Semantic Web*. Presented at 6th International Semantic Web Conference. Busan, South Korea. Retrieved January 10, 2011, from http://videolectures.net/iswc07_pell_nlpsw/

Peppers, D., Rogers, M., & Dorf, B. (1999). Is your company ready for one-to-one Marketing? *Harvard Business Review, 77*(1), 151–160. PMID:10345390.

Perkins, H. W. (Ed.). (2003). *The Social Norms Approach to Preventing School and College Age Substance Abuse: A Handbook For Educators, Counselors, and Clinicians*. San Francisco, CA: Jossey-Bass.

Perkins, H. W., & Berkowitz, A. D. (1986). Perceiving the community norms of alcohol use among students: some research implications for campus alcohol education programming. *Substance Use & Misuse, 21*(9-10), 961–976. doi:10.3109/10826088609077249 PMID:3793315.

Perry, J. (2012). All future roads lead to problems with intellectual property. Retrieved May 3, 2012, from: http://declineofscarcity.com/?cat=43

Peter, F. (1998). *A CEO's Guide to eCommerce Using Object-Oriented Intelligent Agent*. Retrieved December 29, 2011, from http://home1.gte.net/pfingar/eba.htm

Peter, J. P., & Olson, J. C. (2009). *Consumer behavior & marketing strategy* (9th ed.). New York: McGraw-Hill/Irwin.

Peter, J., Valkenburg, P. M., & Schouten, A. P. (2007). Precursors of adolescents' use of visual and audio devices during online communication. *Computers in Human Behavior, 23*(5), 2473–2487. doi:10.1016/j.chb.2006.04.002.

Peters, T. J., & Waterman, R. H. Jr. (1989). *In search of excellence: Lessons from America's best run organizations*. New York: Harper Collins.

Petrassi, J. (2008). Web 2.0 – Potential Impact On Business. *CSC Global Business Solutions, CSC Papers*. Retrieved January 15, 2011, from http://assets1.csc.com/lef/downloads/Web_Potential.pdf

Petter, S., & McLean, E. R. (2009). A meta-analytic assessment of the DeLone and McLean IS success model: An examination of IS success at the individual level. *Information & Management, 46*(3), 159–166. doi:10.1016/j.im.2008.12.006.

Pettis, B. (2012). 3D Printer makers' rival visions of the future. *BBC*. Retrieved June 18, 2012, from www.bbc.co.uk/news/technology-16503443

Petty, R. D., & Andrews, J. C. (2008). Covert marketing unmasked: A legal and regulatory guide for practices that mask marketing messages. *Journal of Public Policy & Marketing, 27*(1), 7–18. doi:10.1509/jppm.27.1.7.

Petty, R. E., & Cacioppo, J. T. (1986). *Communication and persuasion: Central and peripheral routes to attitude change*. New York: Springer-Verlag.

Piller, F., & Walcher, D. (2006). Toolkits for idea competitions: a novel method to integrate users in new product development. *R & D Management*, *36*(3), 307–318. doi:10.1111/j.1467-9310.2006.00432.x.

Planned Parenthood Federation of America. (2012). Retrieved April 2, 2012, from http://www.ppfa.org

Platt, M. (2007). *Web 2.0 in the Enterprise. The Architecture Journal. Microsoft Developer Network.* MSDN Architecture Centre.

Plaza, L., & Albornoz, J. C. (2012). Sentiment analysis in business intelligence: A survey. In Colomo-Palacios, R. et al. (Eds.), *Customer relationship management and the social semantic web: Enabling cliens conexus* (pp. 231–252). Hershey, PA: IGI Global.

Pleming, S. (2009). U.S. State Department speaks to Twitter over Iran. Retrieved February 24, 2011, from http://www.reuters.com/article/2009/06/16/us-iran-election-twitter-usa-idUSWBT01137420090616

Ploderer, B., Howard, S., & Thomas, P. (2008). Being Online, Living Offline: The Influence of Social Ties over the Appropriation of Social Network Sites. In *Proceedings of CSCW 2008*. Retrieved January 15, 2011, from http://disweb.dis.unimelb.edu.au/student/rhd/berndp/research/CSCW2008Ploderer.pdf

Plummer, J. T. (1981). Life style patterns and commercial bank credit card usage. *Journal of Marketing*, *35*(April), 35–41.

Podsakoff, P. M., MacKenzie, S. B., Lee, J.-Y., & Podsakoff, N. P. (2003). Common method bias in behavioral research: A critical review of the literature and recommended remedies. *The Journal of Applied Psychology*, *88*(5), 879–903. doi:10.1037/0021-9010.88.5.879 PMID:14516251.

Porter, M. E. (1980). *Competitive advantage*. New York: Free Press.

Postman, J. (2009). *SocialCorp: Social Media Goes Corporate*. Upper Saddle River, NJ: New Riders.

PR. *Week*. (2010). *Social Media Survey: The Social Connection.* Retrieved May 18, 2011, from http://www.mslworldwide.com/library/SocialMediaSurvey.pdf

Prat-Sala, M., & Redford, P. (2010). The interplay between motivation, self-efficacy, and approaches to studying. *The British Journal of Psychology*, *80*, 283–305. PMID:20021729.

Preece, J., Nonnecke, B., & Andrews, D. (2004). The top 5 reasons for lurking: Improving community experiences for everyone. *Computers in Human Behavior*, *20*(2), 201–223. doi:10.1016/j.chb.2003.10.015.

Price, L. L., & Arnould, E. J. (1999). Commercial friendships: Service provider-client relationships in context. *Journal of Marketing*, *63*(4), 38–56. doi:10.2307/1251973.

Processor (2008). Social Networking Sites Pose New Opportunities. General Information. *Processor, 30*(48). Retrieved January 15, 2011, from http://s3.amazonaws.com/lyro-production/bf161e8907f9a079e0270230df68d594%2FSocial-Networking-Sites-Pose-New-Opportunities.pdf

Project. Retrieved September 18, 2012, from http://www.thetrevorproject.org

Qiu, G., & Papatla, P. (2008). An empirical analysis of inter-acquisition time of free online content. *Journal of Interactive Marketing*, *22*(2), 19–27. doi:10.1002/dir.20111.

Quan-Haase, A. (2007). College students' local and distance communication: Blending online and offline media. *Information Communication and Society*, *10*(5), 671–693. doi:10.1080/13691180701658020.

Quercia, D., Kosinski, M., Stillwell, D., & Crowcroft, J. (2011). *Our Twitter profiles, our selves: Predicting personality with Twitter*. Paper presented at the 3rd IEEE Conference on Social Computing (SocialCom). Boston, MA.

Quercia, D., Lambiotte, R., Kosinski, M., Stillwell, D., & Crowcroft, J. (in press). The personality of popular Facebook users. *Proceedings of the Association of Computing Machinery Conference on Computer Supported Cooperative Work 2012*.

Quiggin, J. (2006). Blogs, wikis and creative innovation. *International Journal of Cultural Studies*, *9*(4), 481–496. doi:10.1177/1367877906069897.

Quintarelli, E. (2005). Folksonomies: Power to the people. In *Proceedings of the ISKO Italy-UniMIB Meeting*. Milan, Italy: ISKO.

Raacke, J., & Bonds-Raacke, J. (2008). MySpace and Facebook: Applying the uses and gratifications theory to exploring friend-networking sites. *Cyberpsychology & Behavior, 11*(2), 169–174. doi:10.1089/cpb.2007.0056 PMID:18422409.

Rai, A., Lang, S. S., & Welker, R. B. (2002). Assessing the validity of IS success models: An empirical test and theoretical analysis. *Information Systems Research, 13*(1), 50–69. doi:10.1287/isre.13.1.50.96.

Ramalho, J. A. (2010). *Mídias sociais na prática*. São Paulo, Brazil: Elsevier.

Ramirez, J., Dimmick, J., Feaster, J., & Shu-Fang, L. (2008). Revisiting interpersonal media competition: The gratification niches of instant messaging, e-mail, and the telephone. *Communication Research, 35*, 529–547. doi:10.1177/0093650208315979.

Rashid, A., Albert, I., Cosley, D., Lam, S., McNee, S., & Konstan, J. ... Riedl, J. (2002). Getting to know you: Learning new user preferences in recommender systems. In *Proceedings of the International Conference on Intelligent User Interface* (pp. 127-134). San Francisco, CCA: ACM.

Read, S. (2008). *What is the next big innovation in innovation*. Laussane, Switzerland: IMD.

Red Bridge Marketing. (2008). *Social Network Marketing: The Basics*. Retrieved January 15, 2011, from http://www.redbridgemarketing.com/social_networking_the_basics.pdf

Reedy, J., Schullo, S., & Zimmerman, K. (2003). *Electronic marketing: Integrating electronic resources into the marketing process*. Mason, OH: South-Western.

Regus Report. (2010). A global survey of business social networking. Retrieved February 1, 2010, from https://www.regus.presscentre.com/imagelibrary/downloadMedia.ashx?MediaDetailsID=463

Rehman, M., & Riaz, N. (2011). A Preliminary Framework For Human-Agent Communication. In *Proceedings of the 2011 International Conference on Information and Communication Technologies* (pp. 95-100). Karachi, Pakistan: IBA Karachi.

Reichheld, F. (1993). Loyalty-Based Management. *Harvard Business School Review, 2*, 64–73. PMID:10124634.

Reid, E. (1995). Virtual worlds: Culture and imagination. In Jones, S. G. (Ed.), *CyberSociety: Computer-mediated communication and community* (pp. 164–183). Thousand Oaks, CA: Sage.

Reissman, C., Aron, A., & Bergen, M. R. (1993). Shared activities and marital satisfaction: Causal direction and self-expansion versus boredom. *Journal of Social and Personal Relationships, 10*(2), 243–254. doi:10.1177/026540759301000205.

Resnick, P., Iacovou, N., Suchak, M., Bergstrom, P., & Riedl, J. (1994). GroupLens: An Open Architecture for Collaborative Filtering of NetNews. In *Proceedings of the 1994 Computer Supported Cooperative Work* (pp. 175-186). Chapel Hill, NC: ACM.

Rha, J.-Y., Widdows, R., Hooker, N. H., & Montalto, C. P. (2002). E-consumerism as a tool for empowerment. *Journal of Consumer Education, 19*(20), 61–69.

Rheingold, H. (2005). Mobile Phones, Ritual Interaction and Social Capital. *The Feature*. Retrieved February 15, 2010, from http://www.thefeaturearchives.com/topic/Culture/Mobile_Phones__ Ritual_Interaction_and_Social_Capital.html

Rhodes, S. D. (2004). Hookups or health promotion? An exploratory study of a chat room-based HIV prevention intervention for men who have sex with men. *AIDS Education and Prevention, 16*(4), 315–327. doi:10.1521/aeap.16.4.315.40399 PMID:15342334.

Rhodus, T., Buchem, V. V., & Witney, B. (2007). Web 2.0: Building Online Communities Using Social Networking Technologies. *The Buckeye*. Retrieved January 15, 2011, from http://webgarden.osu.edu/buckeye2007.pdf

Ricci, F., & Werthner, H. (2006). Introduction to the special issue: Recommender systems. *International Journal of Electronic Commerce, 11*(2), 5–9. doi:10.2753/JEC1086-4415110200.

Richmond, V. P. (1995). Amount of communication in marital dyads as a function of dyad and individual marital satisfaction. *Communication Research Reports, 12*(2), 152–159. doi:10.1080/08824099509362051.

Riegner, C. (2007). Word of Mouth on the Web: The Impact of Web 2.0 on Consumer Purchase Decisions. *Journal of Advertising Research*, *47*(4), 436–447. doi:10.2501/S0021849907070456.

Rigby, D. K., Reichheld, F. F., & Schefter, P. (2002). Avoid the four perils of CRM. *Harvard Business Review*, *80*(2), 101–109. PMID:11894676.

Robertson, T. S. (1971). *Innovative Behavior and Communication*. New York: Holt, Rinehart and Winston Publishing.

Robertson, T. S., & Gatignon, H. (1991). How innovators thwart new entrants into their market. *Strategy and Leadership*, *19*(5), 4–11. doi:10.1108/eb054333.

Roberts, R. R. (2008). *Walk Like a Giant, Sell Like a Madman*. Hoboken, NJ: WileyPublishing.

Rochet, J-C, & Tirole, J. (1999). *Cooperation among competitors: The economics of credit card associations*. C.E.P.R. Discussion Papers, No. 2101.

Rochet, J.-C., & Tirole, J. (2003). Platform competition in two-sided markets. *Journal of the European Economic Association*, *1*(4), 990–1029. doi:10.1162/154247603322493212.

Rogers, E. M. (2005). Diffusion of Innovations (4th ed.). New York: The Free PressRheingold, H. (1993). The Virtual Community: Homesteading on the Electronic Frontier. Reading, MA: Addison-Wesley.

Rogers, E. M. (1983). *Diffusion of innovations*. New York: Free Press.

Rogers, E. M. (2002). Diffusion of preventive innovations. *Addictive Behaviors*, *27*(6), 989–993. doi:10.1016/S0306-4603(02)00300-3 PMID:12369480.

Rogers, E. M., & Allbritton, M. M. (1995). Interactive communication technologies in business organizations. *Journal of Business Communication*, *32*(2), 175–195. doi:10.1177/002194369503200206.

Rogers, E. S., Chamberlin, J., Ellison, M. L., & Crean, T. (1997). A consumer-constructed scale to measure empowerment among users of mental health services. *Psychiatric Services (Washington, D.C.)*, *48*(8), 1041–1047. PMID:9255837.

Rojas, H., & Puig-i-Abril, E. (2009). Mobilizers mobilized: Information, expression, mobilization and participation in the digital age. *Journal of Computer-Mediated Communication*, *14*(4), 902–927. doi:10.1111/j.1083-6101.2009.01475.x.

Romero, N. L. (2011). ROI. Measuring the social media return on investment in a library. *The Bottom Line: Managing Library Finances*, *24*(2), 145–151. doi:10.1108/08880451111169223.

Rook, D. W. (1987). The buying impulse. *The Journal of Consumer Research*, *14*(2), 189–199. doi:10.1086/209105.

Rook, D. W., & Fisher, R. J. (1995). Normative influences on impulsive buying behavior. *The Journal of Consumer Research*, *22*(3), 305–313. doi:10.1086/209452.

Rose, S. M. (1985). Same-and cross-sex friendships and the psychology of homosociality. *Sex Roles*, *12*(1), 63–74. doi:10.1007/BF00288037.

Ross, C., Orr, E. S., Sisic, M., Arseneault, J. M., Simmering, M. G., & Orr, R. R. (2009). Personality and motivations associated with Facebook use. *Computers in Human Behavior*, *25*(2), 578–586. doi:10.1016/j.chb.2008.12.024.

Rotherham-Borus, M. J., & Duan, N. (2003). Next generation of preventive interventions. *Journal of the American Academy of Child and Adolescent Psychiatry*, *42*(5), 518–526. doi:10.1097/01.CHI.0000046836.90931.E9 PMID:12707555.

Rotschild, C. (2011). Social media use in sports and entertainment venues. *International Journal of Event and Festival Management*, *2*(2), 139–150. doi:10.1108/17582951111136568.

Rowan, D. (2009). The suits come to Second Life. *Times (London, England)*.

Rubin, A. M. (1984). Ritualized and instrumental television viewing. *The Journal of Communication*, *34*, 67–81. doi:10.1111/j.1460-2466.1984.tb02174.x.

Rubin, D. C. (1997). *Memory in oral traditions: The cognitive psychology of epic, ballads, and counting-out rhymes*. New York: Oxford University Press.

Rufer-bach, K. (2009). *The Second Life Grid The Official Guide to Communication, Collaboration, and Community Engagement.* Indianapolis, IN: Wiley Publishing.

Ryan, R. M., & Deci, E. L. (2000). Self-determination theory and the facilitation of intrinsic motivation, social development, and well-being. *The American Psychologist, 55,* 68–78. doi:10.1037/0003-066X.55.1.68 PMID:11392867.

Sadoski, M., Goetz, E. T., & Rodriguez, M. (2000). Engaging texts: Effects of concreteness on comprehensibility, interest, and recall in four text types. *Journal of Educational Psychology, 92*(1), 85–95. doi:10.1037/0022-0663.92.1.85.

Safko, L., & Brake, D. K. (2009). *The Social Media Bible.* Hoboken, NJ: Wiley Publishing.

Sampaio, I., Ramalho, G., Corruble, V., & Prudêncio, R. (2006). Acquiring the preferences of new users in recommender systems: the role of item controversy. In *Proceedings of the Workshop on Recommender Systems* (in conjunction with the 17th European Conference on Artificial Intelligence - ECAI 2006) (pp. 107-110). Riva del Garda, Italy: ACM.

Schacht, W. H. (2000). The national council for science and environment, industrial competitiveness and technological advancement. Brief for US Congress, September, Washington, D.C.

Schau, H. J., & Gilly, M. C. (2003). We are what we post? The presentation of self in personal websites. *The Journal of Consumer Research, 30*(4), 384–404.

Schickel, V., & Faltings, B. (2006). Using ontological a-priori score to infer user's preferences. In *Proceedings of the Workshop on Recommender Systems* (in conjunction with the 17th European Conference on Artificial Intelligence - ECAI 2006) (pp. 102-106). Riva del Garda, Italy: ACM.

Schifter, D. E., & Ajzen, I. (1985). Intention, perceived control, and weight loss: An application of the theory of planned behavior. *Journal of Personality and Social Psychology, 49*(3), 843–851. doi:10.1037/0022-3514.49.3.843 PMID:4045706.

Schimmack, U., Shigehiro, O., Furr, R. M., & Funder, D. C. (2008). Personality and life satisfaction: A facet-level analysis. *Personality and Social Psychology Bulletin, 30*(8), 1065–1075. PMID:15257789.

Schlosser, A. E. (2003). Experiencing products in the virtual world: The role of goal and imagery in influencing attitudes versus purchase intentions. *The Journal of Consumer Research, 30*(2), 184–198. doi:10.1086/376807.

Schlosser, A. E. (2005). Posting versus lurking: Communicating in a multiple audience context. *The Journal of Consumer Research, 32*(2), 260–265. doi:10.1086/432235.

Schlosser, A. E. (2006). Learning through virtual product experience: The role of imagery on true versus false memories. *The Journal of Consumer Research, 33*(3), 377–383. doi:10.1086/508522.

Schmugar, C. (2008). The Future of Social Networking Sites. *McAfee Security Journal,* Fall, 28-30.

Schoop, M. (2008). *The Negoisst System Tutorial.* Retrieved March 22, 2012, from http://negoisst.wi1.uni-hohenheim.de/Negoisst2/faces/documents/Tutorial.pdf

Schoop, M., & Jertila, A. (2004). Electronic Commerce in the Semantic Web Era. In M. Bichler, C. Holtmann, S. Kirn, J.P. Müller., & C. Weinhardt (Eds.), Coordination and Agent Technology in Value Networks. Essen, Germany: Multikonferenz Wirtschaftsinformatik.

Schoop, M., Jertila, A., & List, T. (2003). Negoisst: A Negotiation Support System for Electronic Business-to-Business Negotiations in E-Commerce. *Data & Knowledge Engineering,* 371–401. doi:10.1016/S0169-023X(03)00065-X.

Schramm, W. (1954). *The process and effects of mass communication.* Urbana, IL: University of Illinois Press.

Schroeder, R., Huxor, A., & Smith, A. (2001). Active-worlds: Geography and social interaction in virtual reality. *Futures, 33*(7), 569–587. doi:10.1016/S0016-3287(01)00002-7.

Scott, D. M. (2007). *The New Rules of Marketing and PR: How to Use News Releases, Blogs, Podcasting, Viral Marketing and Online Media to Reach Buyers Directly.* Hoboken, NJ: Wiley Publishing.

Scott, D. M. (2011). *New rules of marketing and PR* (3rd ed.). New York: Wiley.

Seda, C. (2007). *How to Win Sales & Influence Spiders: Boosting Your Business & Buzz on the Web (Voices That Matter)* (1st ed.). Berkeley, CA: New Riders Press.

Seddon, P. B., & Kiew, M. Y. (1994). A partial test and development of DeLone and McLean's model of IS success. In J.I. DeGross, S.L. Huff, & M.C. Munro (Eds.), *Proceedings of the International Conference on Information Systems* (pp. 99-110). Atlanta, GA: Association for Information Systems.

Semertzidis, T., Daras, P., & Ballesteros, I. L. (2010). Social Networks Overview: Current Trends and Research Challenges. *European Commission, Information Society and Media*. Retrieved February 25, 2012, from http://cordis.europa.eu/fp7/ict/netmedia/docs/publications/social-networks.pdf

Sen, S., & Bhattacharya, C. B. (2001). Does doing good always lead to doing better? Consumer reactions to corporate social responsibility. *JMR, Journal of Marketing Research*, *38*(2), 225–243. doi:10.1509/jmkr.38.2.225.18838.

Serbmongkolchai, V., & Chen, X. (2008). *v-Business model in virtual world Second Life case study*. Master's Thesis, Lund University, Sweden. Retrieved January 15, 2011, from http://biblioteket.ehl.lu.se/olle/papers/0003119.pdf

Shah, D., Cho, J., Eveland, W. P. J., & Kwak, N. (2005). Information and expression in a digital age: Modeling internet effects on civic participation. *Communication Research*, *32*(5), 531–565. doi:10.1177/0093650205279209.

Shang, R.-A., Chen, Y.-C., & Liao, H.-J. (2006). The value of participation in virtual consumer communities on brand loyalty. *Internet Research*, *16*(4), 398–418. doi:10.1108/10662240610690025.

Shao, G. (2009). Understanding the Appeal of User-Generated Media: A Uses and Gratification Perspective. *Internet Research*, *19*(1), 7–25. doi:10.1108/10662240910927795.

Shapiro, E. G. (1980). Is seeking help from a friend like seeking help from a stranger? *Social Psychology Quarterly*, *43*(2), 259–263. doi:10.2307/3033629.

Sharma, A., & Sheth, J. N. (2004). Web-based marketing: The coming revolution in marketing thought and strategy. *Journal of Business Research*, *57*(7), 696–702. doi:10.1016/S0148-2963(02)00350-8.

Shen, J., & Eder, L. B. (2009). Exploring intentions to use virtual worlds for business. *Journal of Electronic Commerce Research*, *10*(2), 94–103.

Sheppard, B. H., Hartwick, J., & Warshaw, P. R. (1988). The theory of reasoned action: A meta-analysis of past research with recommendations for modifications and future research. *The Journal of Consumer Research*, *15*(3), 325–343. doi:10.1086/209170.

Sheth, J. N., Eshghi, A., & Krishnan, B. C. (2002). *Marketing na Internet*. Porto Alegre, Brazil: Bookman.

Shiu, E., Hair, J., Bush, R., & Ortinau, D. (2009). *Marketing Research*. McGraw-Hill Higher Education.

Sifry, D. (2004). *Sifry's Alerts: October 2004 State of the Blogosphere*. Retrieved from http://www.sifry.com/alerts/archives/000387.html

Simon, G. K. (1996). *In sheep's clothing: Understanding and dealing with manipulative people*. Little Rock, AR: A. J. Christopher & Co..

Singhal, A., & Rogers, E. M. (1999). *Entertainment-education: A Communication Strategy for Social Change*. Mahwah, NJ: Lawrence Erlbaum.

Singh, R., Iyer, L. S., Salam, A., & Editors, G. (2005). The Semantic Electronic business Vision. *Communications of the ACM*, *48*(4), 38–42. doi:10.1145/1101779.1101806.

Singh, T., Veron-Jackson, L., & Cullinane, J. (2008). Blogging: A new play in your marketing game plan. *Business Horizons*, *51*, 281–292. doi:10.1016/j.bushor.2008.02.002.

Smith, G. (2008). *Tagging People-Powered Metadata for the Social Web*. Berkeley, CA: New Riders.

Smith, M. B. (1973). Political attitudes. In Knutson, J. (Ed.), *Handbook of Political Psychology*. San Francisco, CA: Jossey-Bass.

Software Engineering Institute and Carnegie Mellon University. (1995). *The capability maturity model: Guidelines for improving the software process (SEI)*. Canada: Addison Wesley.

Solis, B. (2010). *Engage!: The Complete Guide for Brands and Businesses to Build, Cultivate, and Measure Success in the New Web*. Hoboken, NJ: Wiley.

Soon, W. M., Ng, H. T., & Lim, D. C. (2001). A Machine Learning Approach to Coreference Resolution of Noun Phrases. *Computational Linguistics - Special Issue on Computational Anaphora Resolution, 27*(4), 521-544.

Sorice, C. (2006). It's official(sih): Myspace is the biggest site on the Internet. *TechCrunch.* Retrieved May 15, 2011, from http://techcrunch.com/2006/12/12/its-officialish-myspace-is-biggest-site-on-internet/

Sousa, L. M. M., & Azevedo, L. E. (2010). *O uso de mídias sociais nas empresas: Adequação para cultura, identidade e públicos.* Paper presented at the IX Congresso de Ciências da Comunicação na Região Norte. Rio Branco, Brazil.

Spertus, E., Sahami, M., & Buyukkokten, O. (2005). Evaluating similarity measures: a large-scale study in the orkut social network. In *Proceedings of the eleventh ACM SIGKDD International Conference on Knowledge Discovery and Data Mining KDD '05* (pp. 678-684). Chicago, IL: ACM

Spiggle, S. (1994). Analysis and interpretation of qualitative data in consumer research. *The Journal of Consumer Research, 21*(3), 491–503. doi:10.1086/209413.

Srinivasan, S. S., Anderson, R., & Ponnavolu, K. (2002). Customer loyalty in e-commerce: An exploration of its antecedents and consequences. *Journal of Retailing, 78*(1), 41–50. doi:10.1016/S0022-4359(01)00065-3.

Srivastava, R. K., Shervani, T. A., & Fahey, L. (1999). Marketing, business processes and shareholder value: An organizationally embedded view of marketing activities and the discipline of Marketing. *Journal of Marketing, 63*, 168–179. doi:10.2307/1252110.

Staab, S., & Studer, R. (Eds.). (2009). *Handbook on Ontologies* (2nd ed.). New York: Springer. doi:10.1007/978-3-540-92673-3.

Stafford, L., Kline, S. L., & Rankin, C. T. (2004). Married individuals, cohabiters, and cohabiters who marry: A longitudinal study of relational and individual well-being. *Journal of Social and Personal Relationships, 21*(2), 231–248. doi:10.1177/0265407504041385.

Stafford, T. F., Stafford, M., & Schkade, L. L. (2004). Determining Uses and Gratifications for the Internet. *Decision Sciences, 35*(2), 259–288. doi:10.1111/j.00117315.2004.02524.x.

Steenkamp, Jan-Benedict, E.M., Frenkel ter H., & Michael, W. (1999). A Cross-National Investigation into the Individual and National Cultural Antecedents of Consumer Innovativeness. *Journal of Marketing, 63*(April), 55–69. doi:10.2307/1251945.

Steinfield, C., Ellison, N. B., & Lampe, C. (2008). Social capital, self-esteem, and use of online social network sites: A longitudinal analysis. *Journal of Applied Developmental Psychology, 29*(6), 434–445. doi:10.1016/j.appdev.2008.07.002.

Stelzner, A. M. (2011). 2011 Social Media Marketing Industry Report. *Social Media Examiner*, April. Retrieved May 18, 2011, from http://www.socialmediaexaminer.com/SocialMediaMarketingReport2011.pdf

Stephen, A. T., & Lehmann, D. R. (2012). *Using incentives to encourage word-of-mouth transmissions that lead to fast information diffusion.* Columbia Business School Research Paper No. 12/36.

Stern, H. (1962). The significance of impulse buying today. *Journal of Marketing, 26*(2), 59–62. doi:10.2307/1248439.

Stoilova, L., Holloway, T., Markines, B., Maguitman, A. G., & Menczer, F. (2005). GiveALink: Mining a semantic network of bookmarks for Web search and recommendation. In *Proceedings of the 3rd International Workshop on Link discovery LinkKDD* (pp. 66-73). New York: ACM.

Stoll, C. (1995). *Silicon Snake Oil: Second Thoughts on the Information Highway.* New York: Doubleday.

Strauss, A., & Corbin, J. (1998). *Basics of Qualitative Research: Techniques and Procedures for Developing Grounded Theory* (2nd ed.). Thousand Oaks, CA: Sage.

Strauss, J., & Frost, R. (2011). *E-Marketing* (6th ed.). São Paulo, Brazil: Pearson Prentice Hall.

Subrahmanyam, K., Reich, S. M., Waechter, N., & Espinoza, G. (2008). Online and offline social networks: Use of social networking sites by emerging adults. *Journal of Applied Developmental Psychology, 29*, 420–433. doi:10.1016/j.appdev.2008.07.003.

Summers, J. O. (1971). 'Generalized Change Agents and Innovativeness. *JMR, Journal of Marketing Research, 8*(August), 313–316. doi:10.2307/3149568.

Swabey, P. (2009). Asda launches transparency strategy. *Information Age*. Retrieved February 24, 2011, from http://www.information-age.com/channels/information-management/it-case-studies/1101887/asda-launches-transparency-strategy.thtml

Swaine, M. (2007). Web 2.0 and the engineering of trust. *Dr. Dobb's Journal*, *32*(1), 16–18.

Swann, W. B. (1983). Self-verification: Bringing social reality into harmony with the self. In Suls, J., & Greenwald, A. G. (Eds.), *Social Psychological Perspectives on the Self*. Hillsdale, NJ: Erlbaum.

Sweetser, K., & Kaid, L. (2008). Stealth soapboxes: Political information efficacy, cynicism and uses of celebrity weblogs among readers. *New Media & Society*, *10*, 67–91. doi:10.1177/1461444807085322.

Swisher, P. S. (2007). The managed web: A look at the impact of Web 2.0 on media asset management for the enterprise. *Journal of Digital Asset Management*, *3*, 32–42. doi:10.1057/palgrave.dam.3650061.

Tajfel, H. (1981). *Human groups and social categories*. Cambridge, MA: Cambridge University Press.

Tajfel, H., & Turner, J. C. (1979). An integrative theory of intergroup conflict. In Austin, W. G., & Worchel, S. (Eds.), *The Social Psychology of Intergroup Relations* (pp. 33–47). Monterey, CA: Brooks/Cole.

Tan, M., & Teo, T. (2000). Factors influencing the adoption of Internet banking. *Journal of the Association for Information Systems*, *1*(5), 1–44.

Tashakkori, A., & Teddlie, C. (1998). *Mixed Methodology: Combining Qualitative and Quantitative Approaches*. Thousand Oaks, CA: Sage Publications.

Taylor, D., Lewin, J., & Strutton, D. (2011). Friends, fans, and followers: Do ads work on social networks? How gender and age shape receptivity. *Journal of Advertising Research*, *51*, 258–275. doi:10.2501/JAR-51-1-258-275.

Taylor, S., & Todd, P. (1995). Decomposition and crossover effects in the theory of planned behavior: A study of consumer adoption intentions. *International Journal of Research in Marketing*, *12*(2), 137–155. doi:10.1016/0167-8116(94)00019-K.

Taylor, S., & Todd, P. A. (1995). Assessing IT Usage: The role of prior experience. *Management Information Systems Quarterly*, *19*(4), 561–570. doi:10.2307/249633.

Teece, D. J. (2010). Business Models, Business Strategy and Innovation. *Long Range Planning*, *43*, 172–194. doi:10.1016/j.lrp.2009.07.003.

Telles, A. (2010). *A revolução das mídias sociais*. São Paulo, Brazil: Editora M. Books.

text4baby. (2012). *text4baby –FAQ*. Retrieved May 15, 2012, from http://www.text4baby.org/index.php/about/faq

text4baby. (2012). *text4baby – Get Involved*. Retrieved May 15, 2012, from http://www.text4baby.org/index.php/get-involved-pg

text4baby. (2012). *text4baby – Legacy Camera Program*. Retrieved May 15, 2012, from http://www.text4baby.org/index.php/get-involved-pg/2-uncategorised/165

text4baby. (2012). *News – text4baby*. Retrieved March 19, 2011, from http://www.text4baby.org/news/t4b_comprehensive_platform.html

Thackeray, R., Neiger, B. L., Hanson, C. L., & McKenzie, J. F. (2008). Enhancing Promotional Strategies Within Social Marketing Programs: Use of Web 2.0 Social Media. *Health Promotion Practice*, *9*(4), 338–343. doi:10.1177/1524839908325335 PMID:18936268.

The Economist. (2011). The Shape of Things to Come. Retrieved May 17, 2012, from http://www.economist.com/node/21541382

The Gilbane Report. (2005). Blogs & Wikis: Technologies For Enterprise Applications? *12*(10). Retrieved January 15, 2011, from http://gilbane.com/artpdf/GR12.10.pdf

The Nielsen Company. (2009). *Nielsen Global Online Consumer Survey: Trust, Value, and Engagement in Advertising*. Retrieved on August 1, 2009, from www.nielsen.comShao, G. (2009). Understanding the appeal of user-generated media: A uses and gratification perspective. *Internet Research, 19*(1), 7-25.

The Trevor Project. (2012). *Preventing Suicide Amond LGBTQ Youth | The Trevor*

The We Got Your Back Project. (2012). Retrieved May 15, 2012, from http://wegotyourbackproject.wordpress.com

The Wireless Foundation. (2012). *CTIA The Wireless Foundation*. Retrieved May 15, 2012, from http://wirelessfoundation.org/Home.aspx

Thelwall, M. (2008). No place for news in social network web sites? *Online Information Review, 32*(6), 726–744. doi:10.1108/14684520810923908.

Torres, C. (2009). *A bíblia do marketing digital: Tudo o que você queria saber sobre marketing e publicidade na internet e não tinha a quem perguntar*. São Paulo, Brazil: Novatec Editora.

Trammell, K. (2005). *Looking at the pieces to understand the whole: An analysis of blog posts, comments, and trackbacks*. Paper presented at annual meeting of the International Communication Association. New York.

Trammell, K., Tarkowski, A., Hofmokl, J., & Sapp, A. (2006). Rzeczpospolita blogów [Republic of Blog]: Examining Polish bloggers through content analysis. *Journal of Computer-Mediated Communication, 11*, 702–722. doi:10.1111/j.1083-6101.2006.00032.x.

Tredinnick, L. (2006). Web 2.0 and Business: A pointer to the intranets of the future? *Business Information Review, 23*(4), 228–234. doi:10.1177/0266382106072239.

Trepte, S. (2005). Daily talk as self-actualisation: An empirical study on participation in daily talk shows. *Media Psychology, 7*(2), 165–189. doi:10.1207/S1532785XMEP0702_3.

Trusov, M., Bodapati, A. V., & Bucklin, R. E. (2010). Determining influential users in internet social networks. *JMR, Journal of Marketing Research, 47*(August), 643–658. doi:10.1509/jmkr.47.4.643.

Trusov, M., Bucklin, R. E., & Pauwels, K. H. (2009). Effects of word-of-mouth versus traditional marketing: Findings from an internet social networking site. *Journal of Marketing, 73*(5), 90–102. doi:10.1509/jmkg.73.5.90.

Turkle, S. (2011). *Alone Together: Why We Expect More From Technology and Less From Each Other*. New York: Basic Books.

Tustin, N. (2010). The role of patient satisfaction in online health information seeking. *Journal of Health Communication, 15*, 3–17. doi:10.1080/10810730903465491 PMID:20390974.

Twitter. (2011). *About*. Retrieved August 15, 2011, from http://twitter.com/abou

Underhill, P. (1999). *Why we buy: The science of shopping*. New York: Obat Inc..

Urban, G. (2005). *Don't Just Relate - Advocate!: A Blueprint for Profit in the Era of Customer Power*. Wharton School Publishing.

Utz, S. (2010). Show me your friends and I will tell you what type of person you are: How one's profile, number of friends, and type of friends influence impression formation on social network sites. *Journal of Computer-Mediated Communication, 15*, 314–335. doi:10.1111/j.1083-6101.2010.01522.x.

Valenzuela, S., Park, N., & Kee, K. F. (2009). Is there social capital in a social network site?: Facebook use and college students' life satisfaction, trust and participation. *Journal of Computer-Mediated Communication, 14*(4), 875–901. doi:10.1111/j.1083-6101.2009.01474.x.

Van den Bulte, C., & Wuyts, S. (2007). *Social networks and marketing*. Cambridge, MA: Marketing Science Institute.

Van der Lans, R., van Bruggen, G., Eliashberg, J., & Wierenga, B. (2010). A viral branching model for predicting the spread of electronic word-of-mouth. *Marketing Science, 29*(2), 348–365. doi:10.1287/mksc.1090.0520.

van der Merwe, R., & van Heerden, G. (2009). Finding and utilizing opinion leaders: Social networks and the power of relationships. *South African Journal of Business Management, 40*(3), 65–76.

Van Gestel, S., & Van Broeckhoven, C. (2003). Genetics of personality: Are we making progress? *Molecular Psychiatry, 8*, 840–852. doi:10.1038/sj.mp.4001367 PMID:14515135.

Van Grove, J. (2010). How CEOs will use social media in the future. *Gist*. Retrieved May 30, 2011, from http://mashable.com/2010/08/30/ceo-social-media-future/

Van Hooft, F. P. C., & Stegwee, R. A. (2001). E-business strategy: How to benefit from a hype. *Logistics Information Management, 14*(1/2), 44–53. doi:10.1108/09576050110360223.

Vangelisti, A. L., & Banski, M. A. (1993). Couples' debriefing conversations: The impact of gender, occupation, and demographic characteristics. *Family Relations, 42*(2), 149–157. doi:10.2307/585448.

VanLear, C., Sheehan, M., Withers, L., & Walker, R. (2005). AA online: The enactment of supportive computer mediated communication. *Western Journal of Communication, 69*(1), 5–26. doi:10.1080/10570310500033941.

Varadarajan, R., & Yadav, M. (2002). Marketing Strategy and the Internet: An Organizing Framework. *Journal of the Academy of Marketing Science, 30*(4), 296–312. doi:10.1177/009207002236907.

Varian, H. R. (1995). Economic mechanism design for computerized agents. In *Proceedings of the 1st Conference on USENIX Workshop on Electronic Commerce* (pp. 13-21). Berkeley, CA: USENIX Association Berkeley.

Vaughan, C. (2011). San Diego researchers first to report positive impact of Text4Baby program. Retrieved March 4, 2012, from http://www.text4baby.org/index.php/news/180-sdpressrelease

Vavreck, L. (2007). The exaggerated effects of advertising on turnout: The dangers of self-reports. *Quarterly Journal of Political Science, 2*(4), 325–343. doi:10.1561/100.00006005.

Veith, L. (2011). Insightful incentives. *Marketing News, 45*(14), 8–8.

Venkatesh, V., & Bala, H. (2008). Technology Acceptance Model 3 and a Research Agenda on Interventions. *Decision Sciences, 39*(2), 273–315. doi:10.1111/j.1540-5915.2008.00192.x.

Vermunt, J. K., & Magidson, J. (2002). Latent class cluster analysis. In Hagenaars, J., & McCutcheon, A. (Eds.), *Applied Latent Class Models* (pp. 89–106). New York: Cambridge University Press. doi:10.1017/CBO9780511499531.004.

Vermunt, J. K., & Magidson, J. (2005). *Latent GOLD 4.0 User's Guide*. Washington, DC: IEEE.

Vickery, G., & Wunsch-Vincent, S. (2007). *Participative web and user-created content: Web 2.0 Wikis and social networking*. Paris, France: OECD.

Visser, P. S., & Mirabile, R. R. (2004). Attitudes in the social context: The impact of social network composition on individual-level attitude strength. *Journal of Personality and Social Psychology, 87*(6), 779–795. doi:10.1037/0022-3514.87.6.779 PMID:15598106.

Vohs, K. D., & Faber, R. J. (2007). Spent resources: Self-regulatory resource availability affects impulse buying. *The Journal of Consumer Research, 33*(4), 537–547. doi:10.1086/510228.

Voss, J. (2007). Tagging, folksonomy & Co-Renaissance of manual indexing. In *Proceedings of the International Symposium of Information Science* (234–254).

Walther, J. (1997). Group and interpersonal effects in international computer-mediated communication. *Human Communication Research, 23*(3), 342–369. doi:10.1111/j.1468-2958.1997.tb00400.x.

Wang, J., De Vries, A. P., & Reinders, M. J. T. (2006). Unifying user-based and item-based collaborative filtering approaches by similarity fusion. In *Proceedings of the 29th annual International ACM SIGIR Conference on Research and Development in Information Retrieval SIGIR '06* (pp. 501-508). Seattle, WA: ACM.

Wang, Y., & Fesenmaier, D. R. (2003). Assessing Motivation of Contribution in Online Communities: An Empirical Investigation of an Online Travel Community. *Electronic Markets, 13*(1), 33–45. doi:10.1080/1019678 032000052934.

Wang, Y.-S. (2008). Assessing e-commerce systems success: A respecification and validation of the DeLone and McLean model of IS success. *Information Systems Journal, 18*(5), 529–557. doi:10.1111/j.1365-2575.2007.00268.x.

Ward, J., Griffiths, P., & Whitmore, P. (1996). *Strategic planning for information systems* (2nd ed.). Chichester, UK: Wiley.

Warr, W. A. (2008). Social software: fun and games, or business tools? *Journal of Information Science, 34*(4), 591–604. doi:10.1177/0165551508092259.

Waterman, R. H. Jr, Peters, T. J., & Phillips, J. R. (1980). Structure is not organization. *Business Horizons, 23*(3), 14–26. doi:10.1016/0007-6813(80)90027-0.

Watkins, K. E., & Marsick, V. J. (1999). Sculpting the learning community: New forms of working and organizing. *National Association of Secondary School Principals Bulletin, 83*(604), 78–88.

Watson, D., Clark, L. A., & Tellegen, A. (1988). Development and validation of brief measures of positive and negative affect: The PANAS scales. *Journal of Personality and Social Psychology, 54*(6), 1063–1070. doi:10.1037/0022-3514.54.6.1063 PMID:3397865.

Weber, L. (2007). *Marketing to the social web: How digital customer communities build your business.* New York: Wiley Publishing.

Wei, C. (2004). Formation of norms in a blog community. In L. Gurak, S. Antonijevic, L. Johnson, C. Ratliff, & J. Reyman (Eds.), *Into the blogosphere: Rhetoric, community, and the culture of weblogs.* Retrieved May 15, 2011, from http://blog.lib.umn.edu/blogosphere/formation_of_norms.html

Wei, L., & Williams, M.-A. (2007). Strategies For Business In Virtual Worlds: Case Studies In Second Life. Retrieved January 15, 2011, from http://www.pacis-net.org/file/2008/PACIS2008_Camera-Ready_Paper_198.pdf

Weide, K., & Dangson, C. (2008). *U.S. consumer online attitudes survey results, part III: Social networking.* Framingham, MA: Internet Data Corporation.

Wei, F. (2009). Birthdays then and now: Applying uses and gratifications theory to analyze the media progression cycle. *Communication Teacher, 23*, 23–27. doi:10.1080/17404620802592940.

Weight Watchers. (2012). *The Four Pillars: Supportive Atmosphere.* Retrieved September 18, 2012, from http://www.weightwatchers.com/util/art/index_art.aspx?tabnum=4&art_id

Weight Watchers. (2012). *Weightwatchers.com: Science Center.* Retrieved September 18, 2012, from http://www.weightwatchers.com/health/sciencecenter/index.aspx

Weight Watchers. (2012). *Weightwatchers.com: Monthly Pass.* Retrieved September 18, 2012, from http://www.weightwatchers.com/monthlypass/index.aspx

Weimann, G. (1991). The influentials: back to the concept of opinion leaders? *Public Opinion Quarterly, 55*(2), 267–279. doi:10.1086/269257.

Weiss, L., & Lowenthal, M. F. (1975). Life-course perspectives on friendship. In Lowenthal, M. F., Thurnher, M., & Chiriboga, D. (Eds.), *Four stages of life: A comparative study of women and men facing transitions* (pp. 48–61). San Francisco, CA: Jossey-Bass.

Wellman, B., Quan-Haase, A., Boase, J., Chen, W., Hampton, K., Isla de Diaz, I., et al. (2003). The social affordances of the Internet for networked individualism. *Journal of Computer-Mediated Communication, 8*(3). Retrieved January 10, 2009, from http://jcmc.indiana.edu/vol8/issue3/wellman.html

Werner, H. (1957). The concept of development from a comparative and organismic point of view. In Harris, D. (Ed.), *The Concept of Development.* Minneapolis, MN: University of Minnesota Press.

Wettstein, T., & Kueng, P. (2002). A maturity model for performance measurement systems. In Brebbia, C., & Pascola, P. (Eds.), *Management. Information Systems* (pp. 113–122). Southampton, UK: WIT Press.

Weun, S., Jones, M. A., & Beatty, S. E. (1998). Development and validation of the impulse buying tendency scale. *Psychological Reports, 82*(4), 1123–1133. PMID:9709520.

Wibbels, A. (2006). *Blog Wild A Guide For Small Business Blogging.* New York: Penguin Group Inc..

Williams, D. A. (2011). U.S. social network usage: 2011 demographic and behavioral trends. Retrieved August 1, 2011, from http://www.emarketer.com/docs/eMarketer_US_Social_Network_Usage-2011_Demographic_and_Behavioral_Trends.pdf

Williams, J. (2010). What's in store for social media? *Computer Weekly,* 7-13.

Williams, A. P., & Tedesco, J. C. (2006). *The Internet election: Perspectives on the Web in campaign 2004.* New York: Rowman & Littlefield.

Wilson, D. W. (2000). Maturity models and information systems: From S-curves to e-commerce. In *Proceedings of the Fifth Conference of the UK Academy of Information Systems (pp.* 628-633). Cardiff, Wales: UKAIS.

Wilson, F. (2006). *My favourite business models.* Retrieved March 2, 2012, from http://www.avc.com/a_vc/2009/07/freemium-and-freeconomics.html

Wind, J., & Mahajan, V. (2001). The Challenge of Digital Marketing. In Wind, J., & Mahajan, V. (Eds.), *Digital Marketing: Global Strategies from the world's leading experts* (pp. 3–25). New York: Wiley Publishing.

Winster, S. G., & Swamynathan, S. (2010). Blog Trust Model for Blog Readers. In *Proceedings of International Conference on Recent Trends in Information Telecommunication and Computing* (pp. 314-317). Kerala, India: ACEEE.

Witte, K., Meyer, G., & Martell, D. (2001). *Effective Health Risk Messages: A Step-by-step Guide*. Thousand Oaks, CA: Sage Publications.

Wixom, B. H., & Todd, P. A. (2005). A Theoretical Integration of User Satisfaction and Technology Acceptance. *Information Systems Research*, *16*(1), 85–102. doi:10.1287/isre.1050.0042.

Wofford, J. C., & Goodwin, V. L. (1990). Effects of feedback on cognitive processing and choice of decision style. *The Journal of Applied Psychology*, *75*(6), 603–612. doi:10.1037/0021-9010.75.6.603.

Wojnicki, A. C., & Godes, D. (2008). *Word of mouth as self enhancement*. HBS Marketing Research Paper No. 06-01.

Wolburg, J. M. (2006). College students' responses to antismoking messages: Denial, defiance, and other boomerang effects. *The Journal of Consumer Affairs*, *40*(2), 294–323. doi:10.1111/j.1745-6606.2006.00059.x.

Womack, B. (2010). Facebook advertisers boost spending 10-fold, COO says. *Bloomberg Businessweek*. Retrieved May 10, 2011, from http://www.businessweek.com/news/2010-08-04/facebook-advertisers-boost-spending-10-fold-coo-says.html

Wood, S. L., & Swait, J. Psychological indicators of innovation adoption: cross-classification based need for cognition and need for change. *Journal of Consumer Psychology*, *12*(1), 1–13. doi:10.1207/S15327663JCP1201_01.

Wright, J. (2006). *Blog Marketing*. New York: McGraw-Hill.

Xu, L., & Chen, H. M. (2006). The new development of pricing theory of bank cards. *China Industrial Economics*, *6*, 22–29.

Yakel, E. (2006). Inviting the user into the virtual archives. *OCLC Systems & Services*, *22*(3), 159–163. doi:10.1108/10650750610686207.

Yazdanifard, R., Obeidy, W. K., Yusoff, W. F. W., & Babaei, H. R. (2011). Social Networks and Microblogging: The Emerging Marketing Trends & Tools of the Twenty-first Century. In *Proceedings of International Conference on Computer Communication and Management*. Singapore:IACSIT Press, Singapore.

Yoo, K.-H., & Gretzel, U. (2011). Influence of personality on travel-related consumer-generated media creation. *Computers in Human Behavior*, *27*(2), 609–621. doi:10.1016/j.chb.2010.05.002.

YouTube. (2012). *Statistics*. Retrieved June 30, 2012, from http://www.youtube.com/t/press_ statistics?hl=en Zviran, M., Glezer, C., & Avni, I. (2006). User satisfaction from commercial web sites: The effect of design and use. *Information and Management*, *43*(2), 157-178.

Zablah, A. R., Bellenger, D. N., & Johnston, W. J. (2004). An evaluation of divergent perspectives on customer relationship management: Towards a common understanding of an emerging phenomenon. *Industrial Marketing Management*, *33*(6), 475–489. doi:10.1016/j.indmarman.2004.01.006.

Zaichkowsky, J. L. (1985). Measuring the involvement construct. *The Journal of Consumer Research*, *12*(3), 341–352. doi:10.1086/208520.

Zanker, M., Ricci, F. F., Jannach, D., & Terveen, L. (2010). Measuring the impact of personalization and recommendation on user behavior. *International Journal of Human-Computer Studies*, *68*, 469–471. doi:10.1016/j.ijhcs.2010.04.002.

Zarrella, D. (2010). *The Social Media Marketing Book*. Sebastopol, Canada: O'Reilly Media, Inc..

Zeng, C., Xing, C. X., & Zhou, L. Z. (2003). Similarity measure and instance selection for collaborative filtering. In *Proceedings of the 12th International Conference on World Wide Web* (pp. 652-658). New York: ACM.

Zenone, L. C. (2007). *CRM – Customer Relationship Management: Gestão do relacionamento com o cliente e a competitividade empresarial*. São Paulo, Brazil: Novatec Editora.

Zhang, J., Qu, Y., Cody, J., & Wu, Y. (2010). A Case Study of Micro-blogging in the Enterprise: Use, Value, and Related Issues. Retrieved July 18, 2010, from http://networkcrowds.files.wordpress.com/2010/03/pap1633-zhang.pdf

Zhao, D., & Rosson, M. B. (2009). How and Why People Twitter: The Role that Microblogging Plays in Informal Communication at Work. In *Proceedings of GROUP 2009*. Sanibel Island, FL: ACM. Retrieved February 11, 2012, from http://www.personal.psu.edu/duz108/blogs/publications/group09%20microblogging.pdf

Zillmann, D. (1988). Mood management: Using entertainment to full advantage. In Donohew, L., Sypher, H., & Higgins, E. (Eds.), *Communication, Social Cognition and Affect*. Hillsdale, NJ: Lawrence Erlbaum Associates.

Zillmann, D., & Bryant, J. (Eds.). (1985). *Selective Exposure to Communication*. Hillsdale, NJ: Lawrence Erlbaum Associates.

Zimmerman, J., & Sahlin, D. (2010). *Social Media Marketing All-In-One For Dummies*. Indianapolis, IN: Wiley Publishing. doi:10.1002/9781118257661.

Zubcsek, P. P., & Sarvary, M. (2011). Advertising to a social network. *Quantitative Marketing and Economics*, 9(1), 71–107. doi:10.1007/s11129-010-9093-9.

Zubcsek, P., & Sarvary, M. (2011). Advertising to a social network. *Quantitative Marketing and Economics*, 19, 71–107. doi:10.1007/s11129-010-9093-9.

Zwaan, R. A., & Radvansky, G. A. (1998). Situation models in language comprehension and memory. *Psychological Bulletin*, 123(2), 162–185. doi:10.1037/0033-2909.123.2.162 PMID:9522683.

Zywica, J., & Danowski, J. (2008). The faces of Facebookers: Investigating social enhancement and social compensation hypotheses. *Journal of Computer-Mediated Communication*, 14(1), 1–34. doi:10.1111/j.1083-6101.2008.01429.x.

About the Contributors

Eldon Y. Li (eli@nccu.edu.tw) is the University Chair Professor of Management Information Systems at National Chengchi University in Taiwan. He is also professor emeritus of MIS in the College of Business at California Polytechnic State University, USA. He was a professor and Dean of the College of Informatics at Yuan Ze University in Taiwan, as well as a professor and the coordinator of the MIS Program at Cal Poly, and also a professor and Founding Director of the Graduate Institute of Information Management at National Chung Cheng University in Chia-Yi, Taiwan. He holds a PhD (1982) from Texas Tech University. His current research interests are in service science, entrepreneurship and technology management, electronic business, research methods, and information systems management. He is the editor-in-chief of several international journals.

Stanley Loh (sloh@terra.com.br) is a professor at the Lutheran University of Brazil and in the SENAC Faculty of Technology. He has a PhD in Computer Science (2001), a Master's degree in Computer Science (1991) and a Bachelor's degree in Computer Science (1988). He also works as consultant in IT companies (Invenio, InText Mining, and ADS Digital). His interests include recommendation systems, text mining, Web search, business intelligence, competitive intelligence, and knowledge management.

Cain Evans (cain.evans@bcu.ac.uk) is the Academic and Research Leader for Computer Science and Information Systems. He completed a Computer Science degree at Bristol University, UK, focusing on client/server systems and Internet technologies. After graduating he worked at EDS in various roles, including Systems Development and IT Project Management. He has lived and travelled widely in the Far East, teaching MIS and IT at undergraduate and postgraduate levels. He returned to the UK to read for a PhD at Birmingham University. His current research interests are service engineering, electronic business, intelligent systems, e-health informatics and decision support systems. He has published in a number of journals, books, and conferences, and is a reviewer for a number of journals and conferences in computer science and e-commerce.

Fabiana Lorenzi (fabilorenzi@gmail.com) has a PhD in Computer Science from the Federal University of Rio Grande do Sul (UFRGS), Brazil, and is a professor at the Lutheran University of Brazil. She works as a consultant at Invenio Softare Inteligente and her interests include recommendation systems, case-based reasoning, and multi-agent systems.

* * *

Vandana Ahuja (vandana.ahuja@jiit.ac.in) is an assistant professor at Jaypee Institute of Information Technology (JIIT), India, where she teaches Internet Marketing and E-Commerce and Customer Relationship Management. She has earlier worked with JILIT--the IT division of the Jaypee Group, which she joined after having worked as a Business Manager with the software giant NIIT and Elbee Express. She has research interests in the domain of contribution of the collaborative Web to diverse areas of marketing and CRM.

Erkan Akar (akar@aku.edu.tr) is an Associate Professor of Marketing, and is currently lecturing on internet marketing, e-commerce and new marketing approaches in the Department of Production Management and Marketing at the University of Afyon Kocatepe, Turkey. His research interests focus on social media and the Internet. He is the author of *Blogla Pazarlama* (Tiem Yayıncılık, 2006) and *Sosyal Medya Pazarlaması* (Efil Yayınevi, 2. Baskı, 2011). His two books are about social media. His article has drawn attention which was published by the *Journal of Internet Commerce* in 2011, namely "An Examination of the Factors Influencing Consumers' Attitudes Toward Social Media Marketing." He was the Vice Manager of the Institute of Social Sciences between 2007 and 2010 at the University of Afyon Kocatepe, Turkey.

María-del-Carmen Alarcón-del-Amo (mcarmenalarcon@gmail.com) received a degree in Business Administration and European PhD in Business Strategic and Marketing from the University of Castilla-La Mancha, Spain. Her main research line is focused on the analysis of online consumer behaviour in the context of social networking sites, electronic commerce, and Web 2.0. Her work has been presented in national and international conferences, and has been published in several journals, such as *Cyberpsychology, Behavior and Social Networking*, *Social Behavior and Personality*, *Journal of Research in Interactive Marketing*, and *International Journal of Internet Marketing and Advertising*. She is a member of the editorial board of the Internet Research. Due to her research work, she has received several awards: CajaMurcia research award, Junior AEDEMO (Spanish Association of Market Research, Marketing and Opinion) Award, and Second QUANDO Young Research Award for the Doctoral Dissertation.

Caroline Graham Austin (caroline.austin@montana.edu) is a marketing professor at Montana State University, where she teaches Freshman Seminars, Principles of Marketing, and Consumer Behavior. Her research centers on consumer perceptions of market initiatives, brand strategy, peer-to-peer communication, and the impact of social networks on consumer decision-making. She has worked as a consultant and research partner with such diverse groups as the National Park Service, the Montana Brewer's Association, and the Greater Gallatin Watershed Council. Dr. Austin received her PhD in Marketing in 2008 from The University of Georgia, USA. She has an M.A. in American studies from the University of Notre Dame, USA, and a B.A. in History from Mercer University, USA.

Ingrid Bachmann (ibachman@uc.cl), PhD, is an assistant professor in the Faculty of Communications at the Pontificia Universidad Católica de Chile. A former reporter and blogger, her research interests include gender, political communication, and the public sphere, with emphasis in cross-national comparisons and electoral politics. She also focuses on the role of the news media in the definition of identities and meanings in public discourse. Her recent research has been published in the *International Journal of Communication, Journalism Studies, Journalism & Mass Communication Quarterly, Howard Journal of Communication*, and others, and includes works examining activists' use of social networking sites, media coverage of female politicians, dissenting voices on the Iraq War in news dialogue, and how minority youth use media for political purposes.

Barbara A. Bickart (bickart@bu.edu) is Associate Professor of Marketing at Boston University School of Management. Her research focuses on how situational factors influence consumers' judgment and decision-making processes. She has examined these issues as they relate to retail displays, the design of consumer surveys, and salesperson and online word-of-mouth communication.

Frederic A. Brunel (brunel@bu.edu) is Associate Professor of Marketing at Boston University School of Management. His research interests include consumers' perceptions of product design and visual aesthetics, consumer relationships, and socio-cultural, gender, and personality issues in marketing.

Shu-Hsun Chang (98356504@nccu.edu.tw) is a PhD candidate in the Department of Management Information Systems at the National Chengchi University, Taiwan. He received his B.S. from Yuan Ze University, Taiwan, and his M.S. from the National Chengchi University, both in Management Information Systems. His research interest lies in social networking, virtual community, technology acceptance, user behaviors, and business analytics.

Efthymios Constantinides (e.constantinides@utwente.nl) received a degree in Economics in Athens and followed postgraduate studies in Economics of European Integration in Amsterdam. He received his PhD in Marketing in Virtual Environments. After a corporate career of 10 years, he worked for 10 years as Senior Lecturer Marketing for the International Agricultural College Larenstein, The Netherlands, and since 2001 has worked as Assistant Professor E-Commerce in the School of Management and Governance at the University of Twente, The Netherlands. His research interests include consumer behaviour and marketing strategy in virtual environments, particularly on utilizing the social Web environment as a source of market intelligence and as an active marketing instrument.

Teresa Correa (teresa.correa@udp.cl), Ph.D (University of Texas at Austin), is assistant professor in the School of Journalism, Diego Portales University, Chile. Her areas of research are new technologies, digital media access, and media sociology. Specifically, she is interested in digital media access and the social, cultural, and psychological factors that affect the usage of information and communication technologies. Her research has been published or is forthcoming in *Journal of Computer-Mediated Communication, Journal of Broadcasting and Electronic Media, Computers in Human Behavior, Information, Communication, & Society, Journalism & Mass Communication Quarterly, Journalism: Theory Practice and Criticism, International Communication Gazette,* and *Newspaper Research Journal*, among others.

Sharon Cox (Sharon.cox@bcu.ac.uk) is a Professor of Information Systems and the Associate Head of School with responsibility for research for the School of Computing, Telecommunications and Networks at Birmingham City University, UK. She has over 20 years of experience as an information systems researcher and practitioner. Professor Cox has worked with companies in the manufacturing industry such as IMI Computing, Jaguar Cars, and Britvic Soft Drinks. She attained her PhD at Aston University and developed a framework for aligning IS/IT with the strategic information needs of an organization. She has contributed to a number of funded projects and is currently collaborating on a European funded project relating to the management of information in smart cities. Her research has been published in international conferences and journals, in addition to contributing chapters to a number of books in the areas of e-business and knowledge management. Her current research interests focus on the contextual analysis of information and IS, with particular emphasis on organizational transformation.

Anna Farmery (anna@theengagingbrand.com) A.C.A, LLB (Hons), has a First-Class Honours degree in Law and is presently researching a PhD in the School of Management at the University of Bradford, UK, on the Social Business Model of the Future, looking at how law and business need to develop to allow for value creation with the customer part of the process. She was qualified as a Chartered Accountant with KPMG before joining the printing industry as a financial controller and was later promoted to managing director. She continued in the industry, working for FMCG companies for 20 years latterly as a Group HR/finance director for a major worldwide brand before establishing her own company--The Engaging Brand. She now is a regular speaker and renowned coach on social media and developing the social business of the future. She also produces The Engaging Brand podcast--nominated five years running for the Best Business Podcast. The podcast show interviews a wide range of people looking at social business and interviews the leading thought leaders on social media, branding, and leadership.

Harshavardhan Gangadharbatla (harsha@uoregon.edu) is an assistant professor in the School of Journalism and Communication at the University of Oregon, USA. His research focuses on new and emerging media, social and economic effects of advertising, and environmental communication. His publications have appeared in (or are forthcoming in) the *Journal of Current Issues and Research in Advertising*, *Creativity Research Journal*, *International Journal of Advertising*, the *Journal of Interactive Advertising*, *Journal of Computer-Mediated Communication*, and various other conferences.

Ronald E. Goldsmith (rgoldsmith@cob.fsu.edu) is the Richard M. Baker Professor of Marketing at Florida State University. Dr. Goldsmith received his PhD in European History from Michigan State University, USA, in 1979 and his PhD in Marketing from the University of Alabama, USA, in 1983. He has taught marketing at Florida State University since 1981 and has published over 150 journal articles and edited three books in marketing and consumer behavior. His major research areas are diffusion of innovations, personality in consumer behavior, and the marketing of information products. His interest in online consumer behavior, especially its social aspects, motivated this book chapter.

Flavius da Luz e Gorgônio (flavius@ufrnet.br) is an associate professor at the Department of Exact and Applied Sciences of the Federal University of Rio Grande do Norte, Brazil, where he acts as a researcher and leader at the Laboratory of Computational Intelligence Applied to Business. His research interests include applied research in information systems, artificial intelligence, data mining, and social networks. He received his PhD in Electrical Engineering and Computer Science (2009) from the Federal University of Rio Grande do Norte. He also holds a Master's degree (1999) and a Graduate degree (1995) from the Federal University of Campina Grande, Brazil. Previously, he worked as a professor for several years in other educational institutions in Brazil.

Goetz Greve (goetz.greve@hsba.de) has been a professor and head of Department Marketing and Sales at HSBA Hamburg School of Business Administration, Germany, since 2007, and serves as a visiting professor to the School of Business, Economics and Social Sciences at the University of Hamburg, Germany. He holds a diploma and PhD of Business Administration from Christian-Albrechts-University at Kiel, Germany. In his research, Professor Greve focuses on the areas of customer relationship management, sales management, and online marketing. In particular, he explores the fundamental drivers of CRM performance. His research findings have been published in international and German journals such as *International Journal of Research in Marketing* and *Marketing Review St. Gallen*. Prof. Greve published three books in the field of CRM, customer management, and online targeting. He is on the editorial board of the *International Journal of Marketing Studies* and serves as an ad-hoc reviewer for other journals, such as *European Journal of Marketing* and *Journal of Marketing Theory and Practice*. Before returning to academia, Goetz Greve worked as a strategy consultant for Accenture and OC&C Strategy Consultants from 2001 to 2007. He conducted marketing strategy and CRM implementation management projects for numerous clients, particularly in financial services, consumer, and media industries.

Michael Haenleinn (haenlein@escpeurope.eu) is a Professor of Marketing at the Business School ESCP Europe and Editor-in-Chief of the *European Management Journal* (EMJ). His research interests and expertise deal with the subjects of customer relationship management (CRM), marketing research, and social media. In particular, he works on the best methods to manage unprofitable customers and divest undesirable client relationships. More recently, his research analyzes the relationship between social networks and customer profitability and specifically the concept of consumption assortativity and its implications for customer relationship management (CRM) practices. Furthermore, he is an expert in quantitative marketing research, particularly structural equation modeling, and has co-authored several articles in the area of social media. Professor Haenlein has published extensively in journals such as the *Journal of Marketing, International Journal of Research in Marketing, Marketing Letters, European Management Journal*, and *Business Horizons*. Furthermore, he is a member of the editorial boards of the *Journal of Marketing, Journal of Marketing Research, International Journal of Research in Marketing, Recherche et Applications en Marketing*, and *Business Horizons*. As a consultant, he has worked with a large number of international companies in a variety of industry sectors such as telecommunications, financial services, technology, and private equity. He holds a PhD from the WHU, Otto Beisheim School of Management, Germany.

Kristina Heinonen (Kristina.heinonen@hanken.fi) is the Hanken Foundation Assistant Professor (tenure) in the Department of Marketing at Hanken School of Economics, Finland. She is also the Director of the Centre for Relationship Marketing and Service Management (CERS), a knowledge and research centre associated with the Department of Marketing at Hanken. Heinonen's research interests concern service value, social media, dynamics of customer relationships, and marketing communication. Her work has been published in several academic journals and books, including *Journal of Service Management, Management Decision, European Business Review, Managing Service Quality, International Journal of Mobile Communications, International Journal of Electronic Business*, and *International Journal of Internet Marketing and Advertising*.

Amber Hinsley (ahinsley@slu.edu) is an assistant professor in the Department of Communication at Saint Louis University, USA. Her research focuses on issues in media management, as well as the use of new media/social media by journalists and the public. In addition to several book chapters, her research has been published in journals including *Journalism, Newspaper Research Journal*, and *Computers in Human Behavior*. She is co-editor of the book *The Future of News: An Agenda of Perspectives*. She is an officer in the Media Management and Economics Division of the Association for Education in Journalism & Mass Communication. Prior to entering academia, she was a reporter and city editor for community sections of the Los Angeles Times.

Tobias Hopp (hopp@uoregon.edu) is a PhD student in the School of Journalism and Communication at the University of Oregon, USA. His research interests lie at the intersection of communication and technology. He has a presented at various conferences such as ICA and NCA.

Andreas Kaplan (mail@andreaskaplan.eu) is Professor of Marketing at ESCP Europe where he currently serves as the Director of Brand and Communication Europe. Previously, he acted as head of the Marketing Department. Before joining ESCP Europe, Andreas started his career as Marketing Professor at the ESSEC Business School and Sciences, France. Professor Kaplan did his Habilitation (French post-doctoral qualification for PhD supervisor) at the University of Paris 1 Pantheon-Sorbonne and his PhD at the University of Cologne in cooperation with HEC School of Management, France. He holds a Master of Public Administration (MPA) from the Ecole Nationale d'Administration (ENA; French National School of Public Administration), an M.S. from ESCP Europe, and a B.S. from the University of Munich. Additionally, Andreas was a visiting PhD at INSEAD and participated in the International Teachers Programme (ITP) in the Kellogg School of Management at Northwestern University, USA.

Mete Karayel (mkarayel@aku.edu.tr) is an Assistant Professor of Business Administration. He earned his PhD in Business Administration at the University of Suleyman Demirel, Turkey. His doctoral thesis' title is "Past, Present and Future of Corporate Governance in Turkey: A Corporate Governance Rating Study On Istanbul Stock Exchange 100 Companies." He had been in the Mihaylo College of Business and Economics at California State University Fullerton, USA, as a visiting scholar for nine months in 2011. Currently he is lecturing on organizational change management, human resources management, and management and organization courses in the Department of (English) Business Administration at the University of Afyon Kocatepe, Turkey. His research interests focus on social media marketing, Internet marketing, corporate governance, corporate social responsibility, corporate ethics, and organizational change management.

Sarah N. Keller (skeller@msubillings.edu), PhD, has developed a service learning curriculum that has been well attended by students and enthusiastically received by the community at Montana State University Billings, USA. The curriculum allows her to apply professional experiences from overseas entertainment education and health communication campaigns with Population Communication International, USAID, and Family Health International. Her students have produced diverse social marketing campaigns over the past eight years to promote issues such as HIV testing, physical activity and nutrition, and the awareness of domestic violence. Each campaign has been supported by external grants and in-kind services from area broadcast and media professionals. Dr. Keller's ongoing research agenda centers on examining the use of mass media to promote health behavior and attitude change on a variety of public health topics.

Soyean (Julia) Kim (sokim@bu.edu) is a PhD candidate at Boston University School of Management, USA and will be joining Kyung Hee University, Korea. Kim's research focuses on providing insights into social media strategies. Specifically, she examines how online communicators reveal themselves in their messages and how such self-disclosures are perceived and processed by their audiences in different types of relationships.

Jeff Linkenbach (jwl@coe.montana.edu), EdD, is a Senior Research Scientist and Director for the Center for Health & Safety Culture at Montana State University, USA. In this role, he also leads the National MOST Of Us® Project for Positive Community Norms. Dr. Linkenbach is known for founding The Science of the Positive and the National Conference on the Social Norms Model. Jeff has a Doctorate in Adult and Community Education and a Master's degree in Counseling with over 25 years of experience focusing on transformation and change strategies.

Carlota Lorenzo-Romero (Carlota.Lorenzo@uclm.es) received a degree in Business Administration and PhD in Business Administration from the University of Castilla-La Mancha, Spain. She is an assistant professor at the University of Castilla-La Mancha. Her main research line is focused on electronic commerce, social Web environments, store atmosphere, e-merchandising, consumer behaviour, marketing research, experimental designs, and quantitative analysis. She has participated in several international and national conferences and she has published some papers in international and national journals such as *Cyberpsychology*, *Behavior and Social Networking Sites*, *Social Behavior and Personality*, *Internet Research*, *International Journal of Internet Marketing and Advertising*, *International Retail and Marketing Review*, and several international and national book chapters. She is a member of the editorial board of the Internet Research.

Selena Xiaojing Lu (selenalu@sjtu.edu.cn) is a PhD candidate in Economics at Shanghai Jiao Tong University, China. Her specialty is two-sided markets, which she studies from a variety of perspectives, including the econometric, social, and psychological. She spent the academic year 2011-2012 studying at Florida State University, USA, with Dr. Ronald Goldsmith, during which she completed several projects related to her major focus of study. On her return to China she will complete her PhD and teach at a comprehensive university in her country while continuing to research the important phenomenon of two-sided markets in China and around the world.

Jay Otto (jayotto3@gmail.com) is a Research Scientist and Managing Director for the Center for Health and Safety Culture at Montana State University. Otto holds a Master's degree and works for the Center assisting with research design, research projects, and data analysis. His areas of interest are in substance abuse prevention, comprehensive community development, and child wellness. His research interests involve applying the Positive Community Norms approach to impact community systems to improve health and wellness. He lives on a small farm in rural West Virginia with his wife, Lynette, two dogs, three horses, and a cat.

Margherita Pagani (Margherita.pagani@unibocconi.it) is Associate Professor of Marketing at Bucconi University, Italy. She earned her Bachelor's degree in Business Administration from Bocconi University and earned advanced degrees from the Massachusetts Institute of Technology. She has taught marketing at Bucconi University since 2006. She has been a visiting scientist at the MIT Sloan School of Management (2008) and a visiting scholar at the same institution (2003). She has published over 17 articles in international journals and has made presentations at a variety of international conferences. Most of her research is in the field of electronic commerce, where she specializes in strategic issues.

Seema Pai (seemapai@bu.edu) is Assistant Professor of Marketing at Boston University School of Management, USA. Her research interests include buzz marketing, online word-of-mouth, econometric models of consumer behavior, and formation, as well as maintenance of corporate reputation.

Moez ur Rehman (moez.rehman.gcu@gmail.com) has been an assistant professor in the Computer Science Department at Government College University at Lahore, Pakistan, since 2009. While studying for his Computer Science M.S. at International Islamic University, Pakistan, he joined Netsol Technologies Pakistan as a software engineer in 1998. At Netsol he worked on several software projects that include projects on leasing, logistics, and accounting. In 2002 he joined the Chair of Computer Science 5 (Information Systems & Databases) at Aachen University, Germany, as a research assistant and worked on intelligent agents to assist human negotiators in electronic negotiations. This research was part of the SEWASIE project funded by the European Commission. He moved to Chair of Information Systems I at the University of Hohenheim, Germany, in 2004, where he received a PhD (2008). His PhD work was on the integration of negotiation support and automated negotiation models to enable human-agent negotiations. The research mainly focused on a comparison of decision making and communication components of two models. Currently, Dr. Rehman teaches software engineering, software quality assurance, and Semantic Web at undergraduate and graduate levels, and is working on the implementation of components for the Hybrid Negotiation System to enable hybrid (Human-Agent) negotiation.

Nosheen Riaz (nosheen.riaz@yahoo.com) received a Master's degree in Information Technology from the Computer Science Department at the University of Punjab at Gujranwala Campus, Pakistan, in 2008, and an M.S. in Computer Science from the Computer Science Department at Government College University, Pakistan, in 2012. Her main area of research is to study the usefulness of Semantic Web technology (Ontologies) to enhance Natural Language Processing semantically. In her M.S. thesis, she has focused on communication between a human and a software agent in hybrid electronic negotiation using the GATE framework and Ontologies. She is determined to resolve Natural Language Negotiations by Software Agent for E-business and Semantic Web. Her research interests are HCI (Human Computer Interaction) and software engineering.

Kim Sheehan (ksheehan@uoregon.edu) is currently Professor of Advertising at the University of Oregon and Director of the Master's Program in Strategic Communication. Before she joined academe, she worked for more than a dozen years at ad agencies in Chicago, Boston, and St. Louis. She holds a Bachelor's degree in Radio-TV-Film from Northwestern University, USA, the MBA from Boston University, USA, and the PhD from the University of Tennessee, USA. Her research involves culture and new technology, and she has published extensively about privacy and the Internet, and about direct-to-consumer prescription drug advertising. She currently serves as Associate Editor of the *Journal of Advertising* and on the editorial boards of several other publications.

Eric Shiu (e.c.shiu@bham.ac.uk) achieved an M.A. with Distinction at Lancaster University, UK. Afterwards, he underwent a doctoral research training programme through which he was awarded an M.S. by Research degree, and then accomplished a Doctorate at the University of Edinburgh, UK Prior to joining the University of Birmingham Business School, UK, Eric taught at the University of Edinburgh. He has received a Certificate of Award after a successful completion of the International Teachers Programme organised by the International Schools of Business Management. Eric has accumulated more than 10 years of research experience across academic, governmental, and industry domains, which earned him a number of research excellence awards. Additionally, an adapted paper of his PhD research has assisted him in receiving the first prize research award from the UK Online User Group. More recently, he has won the best research paper award from the European Applied Business Research Conference in Athens, Greece. To date, he has published more than 30 research papers. Eric has also been recently awarded a grant from the European Science Foundation, allowing him to carry out research collaboration with like-minded academics at continental European universities. He has also successfully completed a high-tech product research consultancy project funded by Advantage West Midlands.

Gilson Gomes da Silva (admgilsong@gmail.com) is currently working as substitute professor in the Department of Exact and Applied Sciences of Federal University of Rio Grande do Norte, Brazil. His research interests include administration, information technology, information systems, and IT governance. He graduated in Business Administration (2004), and he has an Educational Specialist degree with emphasis in Management of Information Technology (2010) and holds a Master's degree in Business Administration from Federal University of Rio Grande do Norte (2009). He has been working as a professor in several educational institutions for undergraduate and postgraduate degrees in the areas of: business, engineering, health sciences, and humanities in Rio Grande do Norte, Brazil.

Huliane Medeiros da Silva (hulianeufrn@gmail.com) is an Information Systems undergraduate student, currently attending the eighth semester in Federal University of Rio Grande do Norte, Brazil. She works as technical support at Centro de Ensino Superior do Seridó and she is also a researcher at the Laboratory of Computational Intelligence Applied to Business. Her interest areas include artificial intelligence, data mining, education, and social networking.

Homero Gil de Zúñiga (hgz@austin.utexas.edu) has a PhD, in Politics at the European University of Madrid (2006) and a PhD in Mass Communication at the University of Wisconsin at Madison, USA (2008), and is an associate professor at the University of Texas at Austin, USA, where he heads the CJCR: Community, Journalism and Communication Research unit within the School of Journalism. In 2010 he was appointed Nieman Journalism Lab Research Fellow at Harvard University. His research focuses on all forms of new technologies and digital media and their effects on society. In particular, he investigates the influence of Internet use in people's daily lives as well as the effect of such use on the overall democratic process. He has published over 30 articles and book chapters in a diverse number of peer-reviewed journals illustrating his research framework, including *Journal of Communication, Journal of Information Technology & Politics, Communication Research, International Journal of Public Opinion Research, New Media & Society, Journalism: Theory, Practice & Criticism, Mass Communication & Society, Computers in Human Behavior, Human Communication Research, Journalism & Mass Communication Quarterly*, and *Journal of Computer Mediated Communication*, among others.

Index